Wonders

Mc
Graw
Hill

Also Available from McGraw Hill

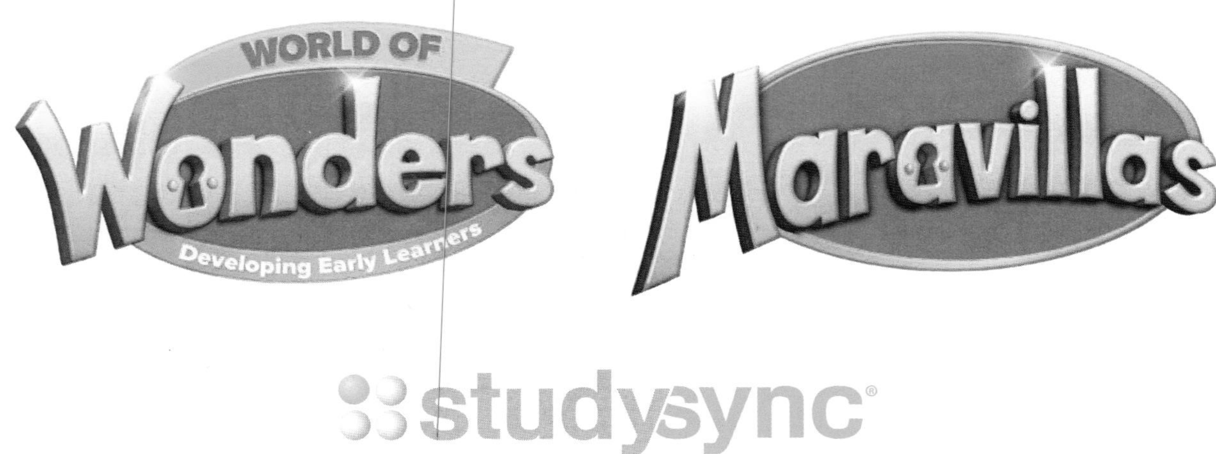

TIME for KiDS

mheducation.com/prek-12

Send all inquiries to:
McGraw Hill
1325 Avenue of the Americas.
New York, NY 10019

ISBN: 978-1-26570386-8
MHID: 1-26-570386-8

Printed in the United States of America

3 4 5 6 7 8 9 LMN 26 25 24 23 22 B

Wonders

Welcome to *Wonders*

Designed to support teachers and empower students.

You want all your students to build knowledge while fostering exploration of our world through literacy. Literacy is the key to understanding – across time, across borders, across cultures – and will help students realize the role they play in the world they are creating.

The result: an evidence-based K–5 ELA program, aligned with standards and based on the Science of Reading, that empowers students to take an active role in learning and exploration. Your students will enjoy unparalleled opportunities for student-friendly self-assessments and self-expression through reading, writing, and speaking. By experiencing diverse perspectives and sharing their own, students will expand their learning. Best-in-class differentiation ensures that all your students have opportunities to become strong readers, writers, and critical thinkers.

We're excited for you to get to know *Wonders* and honored to join you and your students on your pathways to success!

Authors and Consultants

With unmatched expertise in English Language Arts, supporting English language learners, intervention, and more, the *Wonders* team of authors is composed of scholars, researchers, and teachers from across the country. From managing ELA research centers, to creating evidence-based classroom practices for teachers, this highly qualified team of professionals is fully invested in improving student and district outcomes.

Authors

Dr. Douglas Fisher
Close Reading and Writing,
Writing to Sources,
Text Complexity

Dr. Diane August
English Language Learners,
Dual Language

Kathy Bumgardner
Instructional Best Practices,
Multi-Sensory Teaching,
Student Engagement

Dr. Vicki Gibson
Small Group Instruction,
Social Emotional Learning,
Foundational Skills

Dr. Josefina V. Tinajero
English Language Learners,
Dual Language

Dr. Timothy Shanahan
Text Complexity,
Reading and Writing,
Oral Reading Fluency,
Close Reading,
Disciplinary Literacy

Dr. Donald Bear
Word Study, Vocabulary,
Foundational Skills

Dr. Jana Echevarria
English Language Learners,
Oral Language Development

Dr. Jan Hasbrouck
Oral Reading Fluency,
Foundational Skills,
Response to Intervention

"My hope for our students is that their teacher can help every student become a skillful reader and writer." - Dr. Jan Hasbrouck

Consultants

Dr. Doris Walker-Dalhouse
Multicultural Literature

Dr. David J. Francis
Assessment, English Language Learners Research

Jay McTighe
Understanding by Design

Dr. Tracy Spinrad
Social Emotional Learning

Dinah Zike
Professional Development, Multi-Sensory Teaching

"My hope for our students including English Learners, is that they will receive outstanding English language arts and reading instruction to allow them to reach their full academic potential and excel in school and in life." - Dr. Josefina V. Tinajero

Developing **Student Ownership** of Learning

Reflect on What You Know	Monitor Learning	Choose Learning Resources	Reflect on Progress	Set Learning Goals

The instructional routines in *Wonders* guide students to understand the importance of taking ownership of their own learning. The **Reading/Writing Companion** Welcome pages introduce students to routines they will be using throughout the year.

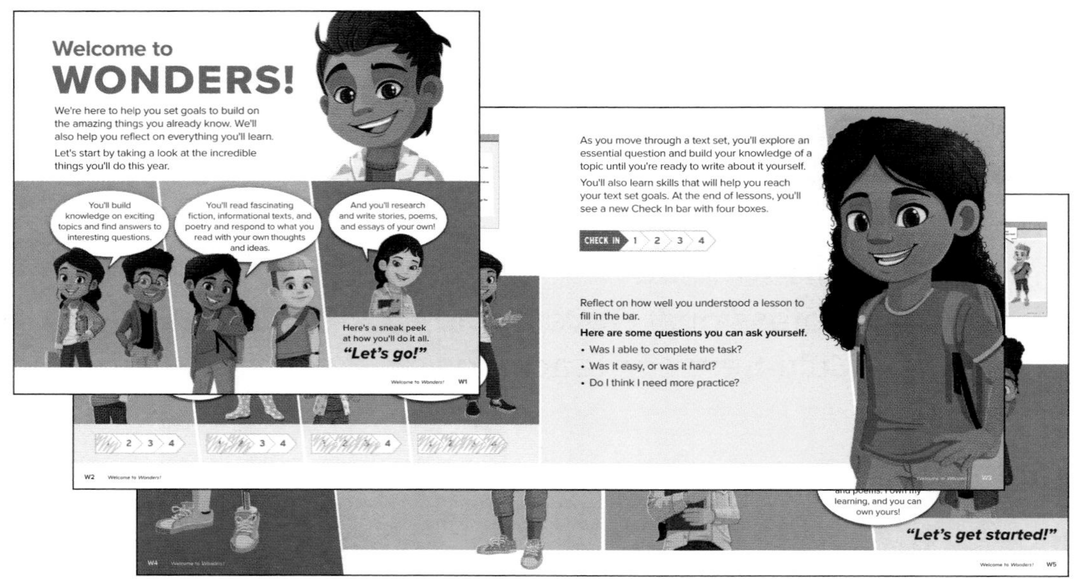

AUTHOR INSIGHT

Learning how to identify what they are learning, talk about what they know, figure out what they need more help with, and figure out next steps are all important aspects of taking ownership of learning that students develop in *Wonders*.

- Dr. Douglas Fisher

Reflect on What You Know

Text Set Goals

Students are introduced to three overarching goals for each text set. Students first evaluate what they know before instruction begins.

Reading and Writing

Students evaluate what they know about reading in a particular genre and writing in response to texts using text evidence.

Build Knowledge Goals

Each text set is focused on building knowledge through investigation of an Essential Question. After an introduction to the Essential Question, students self-evaluate how much they already know about the topic.

Extended Writing Goals

Students also think about their ability to write in a particular genre before instruction begins.

Courtesy of Douglas Fisher

Monitor Learning

Lesson Learning Goals

The journey through a text set and extended writing is made up of a sequence of lessons. The learning goals of these lessons build toward achieving the overarching goals. At the start of each lesson, a targeted learning goal, presented as a "We Can" statement, is introduced to students.

The learning goals are shared with students and parents so that they can track their learning as they work through the lessons.

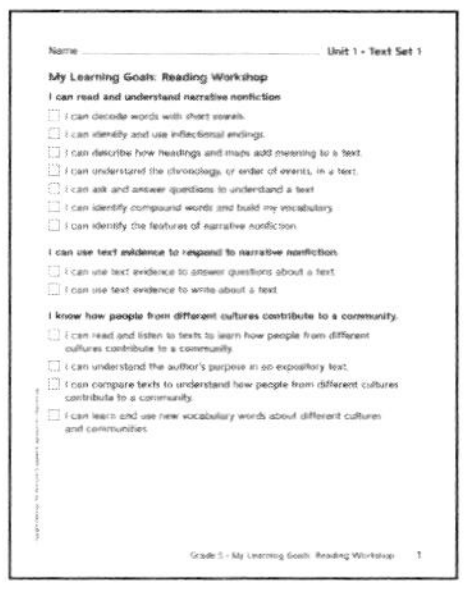

Check-In Routine

At the end of each lesson, students are asked to self-assess how well they understood the lesson learning goal.

At the end of the lesson, students conference with a partner. They review the lesson learning goal "We Can" statement.

Review

CHECK-IN ROUTINE

Review the lesson learning goal.
Reflect on the activity.
Self-Assess by

- filling in the bars in the Reading/Writing Companion
- holding up 1, 2, 3, or 4 fingers

Share with your teacher.

Reflect

Students take turns self-reflecting on how well they understood the learning goal.

TEACHING TIP

As students develop their ability to reflect on their work, provide sentence frames to support them.

Ask yourself:
Can I ______?
Respond:
I can almost ______.
I am having trouble______.
I need to work on ______.

Self Assess

Students hold up 1, 2, 3 or 4 fingers to self-assess how well they understood the learning goal. When appropriate, they will fill in the bars in the Reading/Writing Companion as well. At the start of the year, review the ratings with students emphasizing that we all learn differently and at a different pace. It is okay to score a 1 or 2. Understanding what they do not know will help students figure out what to do next.

TEACHING TIP

1 I did not understand the learning goal.
2 I understood some things about the learning goal. I need more explanation.
3 I understood how to do the lesson, but I need more practice.
4 I understood the learning goal really well. I think I can teach someone how to do it.

Share

Students share their self-assessments with you by holding up their fingers and sharing the filled-in bars. This lets you know how students think they are doing.

TEACHING TIP

Valuing students' self-assessments is important to enabling students to take ownership of their learning. As students progress throughout the year, they become more adept at self-assessing what they know and what help they need moving forward.

Developing **Student Ownership** of Learning

Reflect on What You Know	Monitor Learning	Choose Learning Resources	Reflect on Progress	Set Learning Goals

Choose Learning Resources

Student-Teacher Conferencing

As students evaluate what they understand, the next step is to think about whether they need more teaching or more practice. The **Reading/Writing Companion** can serve as a powerful conferencing tool. Reviewing their filled-in bars while conferring with each student provides you the opportunity to guide students into identifying what they should do next to improve their understanding.

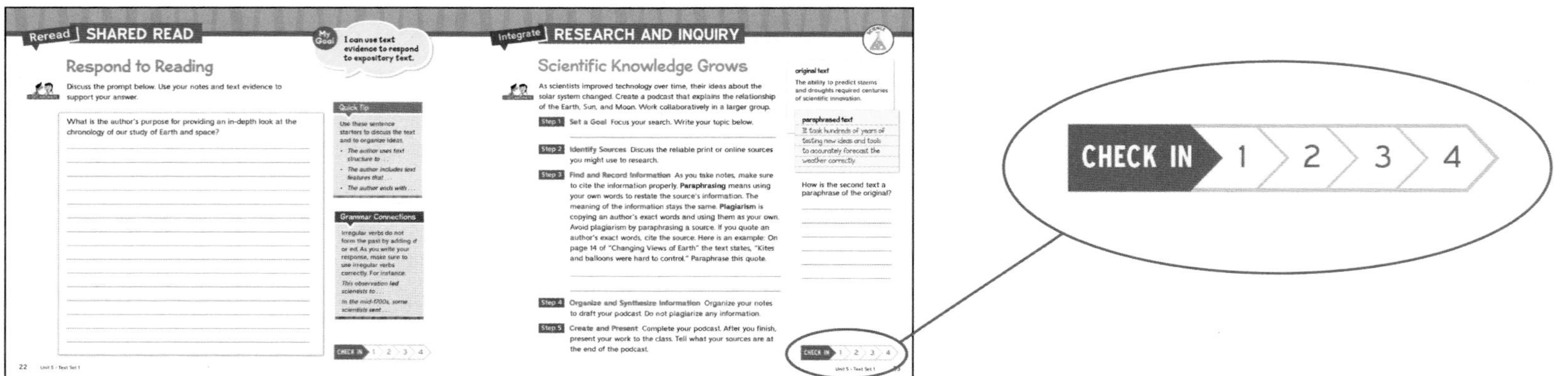

Small Group Teacher-Led Instruction

You and the student may decide that they need more teaching. Student Check-Ins and your observations at the end of each lesson provide timely data that informs the focus for teacher-led small group instruction. Teachers can choose from the small group differentiated lessons provided.

Small Group Independent/Collaborative Work

While meeting with small groups, other students can practice the skills and concepts they have determined they need practice with.

My Independent Work lists options for collaborative and independent practice. Based on student input and your informal observations, you identify "Must Do" activities to be completed. Students then choose activities focused on areas of need and interests they have identified—promoting student choice and voice.

Name ______ Unit 1 • Text Set 1

My Independent Work

	Reading	Phonics/Word Study	Writing
Center Activity Cards	Card: Activity:	Card: Activity:	Card: Activity:
Digital Activities my.mheducation.com	Activity:	Activity:	Activity:
Practice Pages	Content Area Reading:	Practice:	Practice:
Independent Choices	Independent Reading:	Activity:	Self-Selected Writing:

Grade 5 • My Independent Work 1

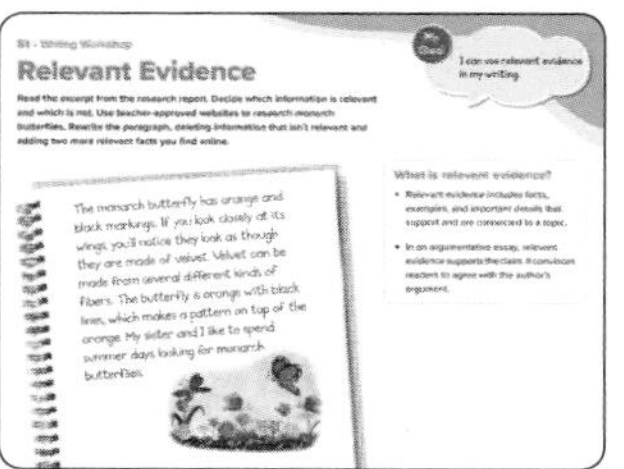

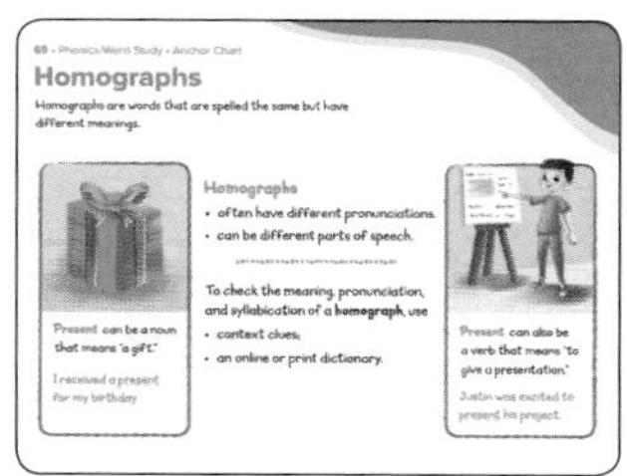

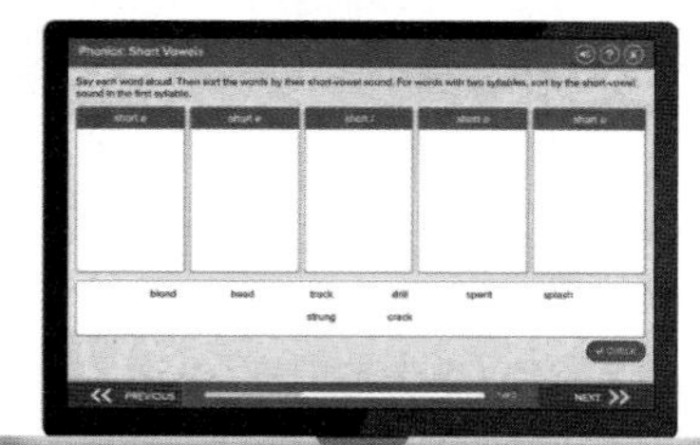

Reflect on Progress

After completing the lessons in the text set and extended writing, students reflect on their overall progress, taking notes to share with their peers and at teacher conferences. The focus of the conversations is on progress made and figuring out next steps to continued progress.

TEACHING TIP

As students discuss their progress, ask them to reflect on the following:

- In what areas did you feel that you made a lot of progress?
- What are some examples?
- What areas do you still need to work on?
- What things can you do to make more progress in these areas?

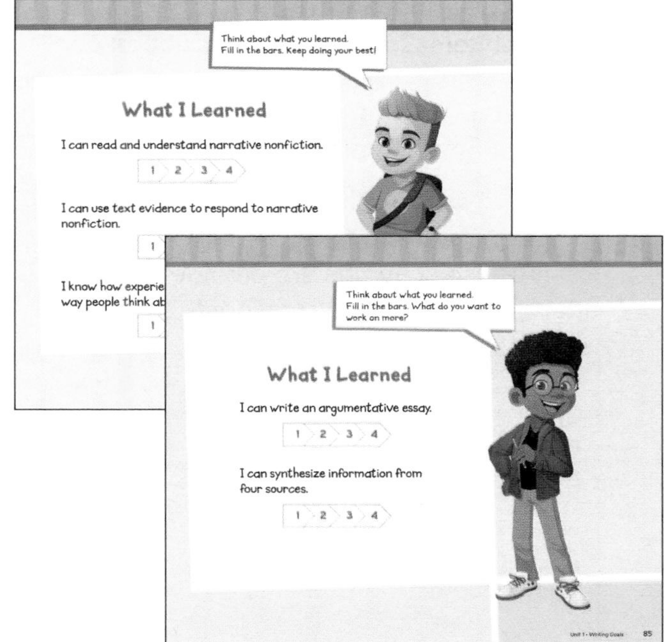

Set Learning Goals

At the end of the unit, students continue to reflect on their learning. They are also asked to set their own learning goals as they move into the next unit of instruction.

See additional guidance online for supporting students in evaluating work, working toward meeting learning goals, and reflecting on progress.

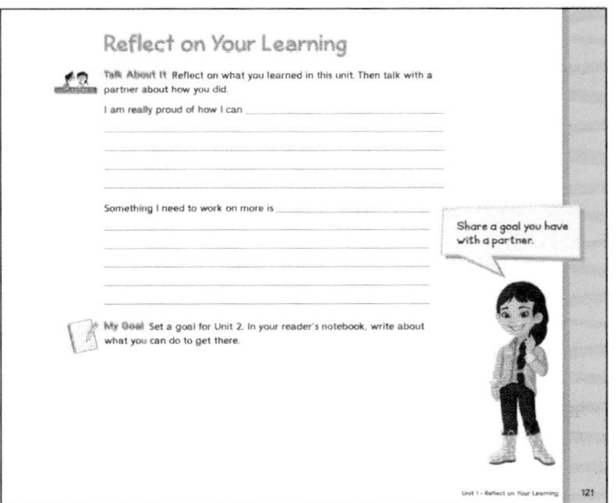

Equity and **Access**

Differentiated Resources

Every student deserves high-quality instruction. *Wonders* provides high-quality, rigorous instruction that supports access to grade-level content and ELA Skills through equitable, differentiated instruction and resources.

Scaffolded Instruction

Gradual Release Model of Instruction Explicit skills lessons start with teacher explanation and modeling, then move to guided and collaborative practice, then culminate with independent practice with the Your Turn activities.

Access Complex Text The complex features of texts students are asked to read are highlighted. Point-of-use scaffolds are provided to help students to attend to those complex aspects of the text.

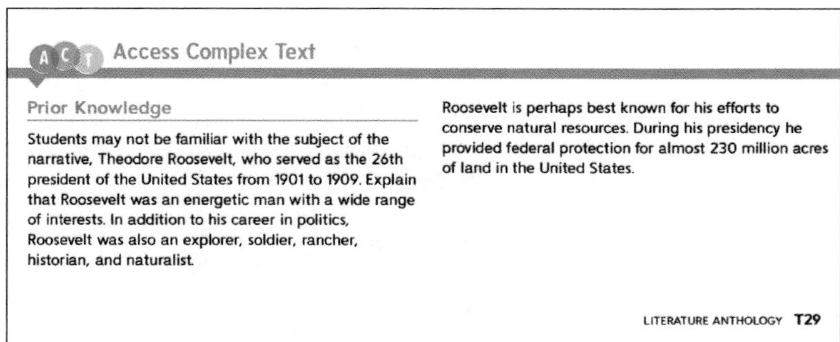

Access Complex Text

Prior Knowledge

Students may not be familiar with the subject of the narrative, Theodore Roosevelt, who served as the 26th president of the United States from 1901 to 1909. Explain that Roosevelt was an energetic man with a wide range of interests. In addition to his career in politics, Roosevelt was also an explorer, soldier, rancher, historian, and naturalist.

Roosevelt is perhaps best known for his efforts to conserve natural resources. During his presidency he provided federal protection for almost 230 million acres of land in the United States.

LITERATURE ANTHOLOGY **T29**

Data Informed Instruction *Wonders* offers frequent opportunities for informal and formative assessment. The student Check-Ins and teacher Check for Success features provide daily input allowing adjustments for instruction and student practice. The Data Dashboard collects data from online games and activities and the Progress Monitoring assessments.

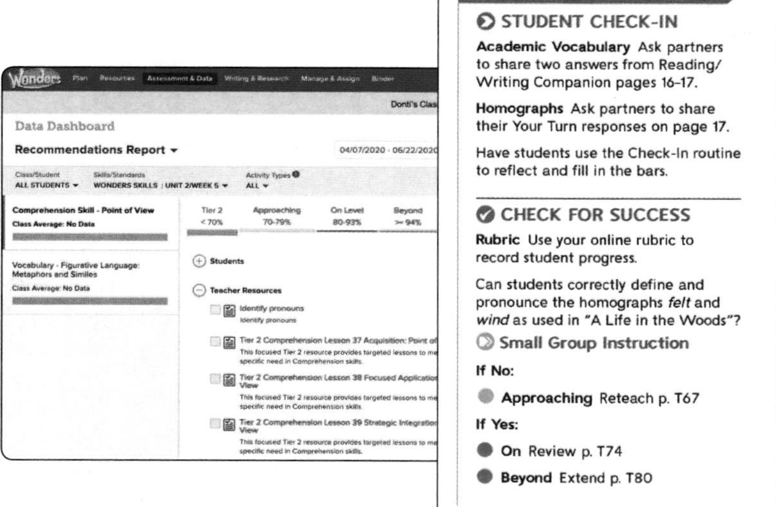

FORMATIVE ASSESSMENT

STUDENT CHECK-IN

Academic Vocabulary Ask partners to share two answers from Reading/Writing Companion pages 16–17.

Homographs Ask partners to share their Your Turn responses on page 17.

Have students use the Check-In routine to reflect and fill in the bars.

CHECK FOR SUCCESS

Rubric Use your online rubric to record student progress.

Can students correctly define and pronounce the homographs *felt* and *wind* as used in "A Life in the Woods"?

Small Group Instruction

If No:

Approaching Reteach p. T67

If Yes:

On Review p. T74

Beyond Extend p. T80

Differentiated Small Group Time

Teacher-Led Instruction Key skills and concepts are supported with explicit differentiated lessons. The Differentiated Genre Passages and Leveled Readers provide a variety of differentiated texts. Literature Small group lessons guide teachers in scaffolding support so all students have access to the same text.

TIER 2 **Tier 2** instruction is incorporated into the Approaching level lessons. Additional Tier 2 instruction is available online.

GIFTED and TALENTED **Gifted and Talented** activities are also provided for those students who are ready to extend their learning.

Independent/Collaborative Work

A range of choices for practice and extension are provided to support the key skills and concepts taught. Students use this time to work on their independent reading and writing. Resources include the Center Activity Cards, online games, Practice Book, and Content Area Reading blackline masters.

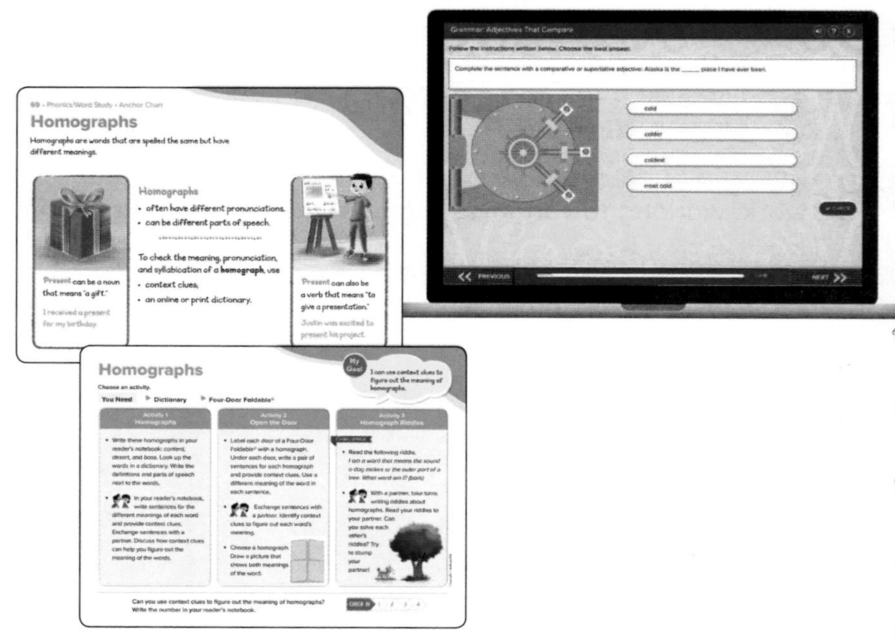

English Language Learners

Access to Grade Level Lessons

English Language Proficiency Levels Targeted support addressing the different English Language Proficiency Levels allows all students to participate.

Spotlight on Language Point-of-use support that highlights English phrases and vocabulary that may be particularly difficult for English Language Learners.

> **English Language Learners**
>
> Use the following scaffolds with **Guided Practice**. For small group support, see the **ELL Teacher's Guide**.
>
> **Beginning**
> Review primary and secondary sources with students. Reread the third sentence in "Cabin Life" with students. Have students point to quotations marks. Remind them that quotation marks show that a person wrote or said this. Ask: *What did Thoreau write?* "I have a great deal of company in my house." *Is this quote from a primary source?* (yes)
>
> **Intermediate**
> Review primary and secondary sources with students. Have students reread the first three sentences of "Cabin Life" and point to the quotation marks. Ask: *What do the quotation marks show?* They show that a person wrote or said this. *Who wrote* "I have a great deal of company in my house"? (Thoreau) Help partners discuss if this quote is from a primary or secondary source using: The words "he wrote" tells me this quote is from a primary source.
>
> **Advanced/Advanced High**
> Have partners take turns reading "Cabin Life" on page 4. Have them identify the quote and tell if it's a primary source. Ask questions to guide them: *Who wrote or said this? How do you know? Why is the primary source unique?*

Multilingual Resources

Home Language Support The following features are available in Spanish, Haitian-Creole, Portuguese, Vietnamese, French, Arabic, Chinese, Russian, Tagalog, and Urdu:

- Summaries of the Shared Read and Anchor Texts.
- School–to-Home Letters that help families support students in their learning goals.
- Multilingual Glossary of key content words with definitions from grade-level texts.
- Spanish and Haitian-Creole Leveled Readers available online.

Strategic Support

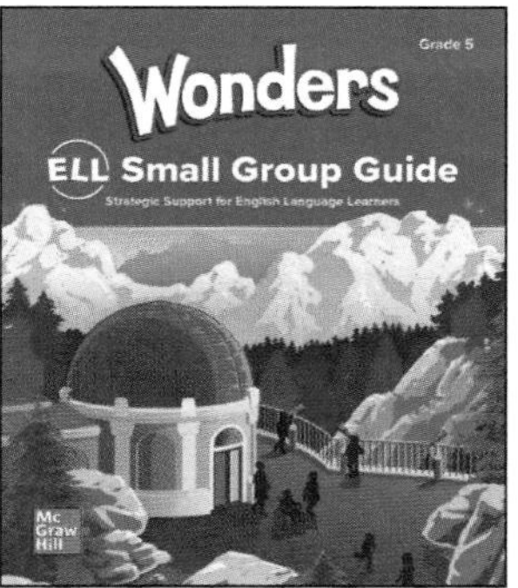

A separate resource is available for small group instruction focused specifically on English Language Learners. The lessons are carefully designed to support the language development, grade level skills, and content. The instruction and resources are differentiated to address all levels of English Language Proficiency and carefully align with the instruction in Reading and Writing.

Additional Resources for Differentiation

Newcomer Kit Instructional cards and practice focused on access to basic, high-utility vocabulary.

Language Development Kit Differentiated instruction and practice for key English grammar concepts.

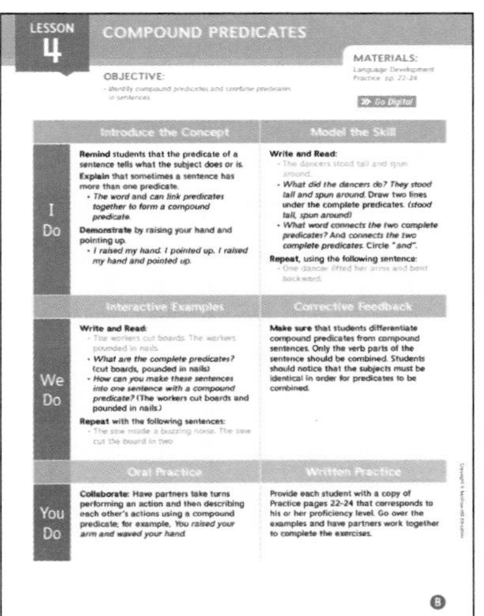

LESSON 4 COMPOUND PREDICATES

OBJECTIVE:
- Identify compound predicates and combine predicates in sentences.

MATERIALS:
Language Development Practice pp. 22-24

Go Digital

	Introduce the Concept	Model the Skill
I Do	**Remind** students that the predicate of a sentence tells what the subject does or is. **Explain** that sometimes a sentence has more than one predicate. • *The word and can link predicates together to form a compound predicate.* **Demonstrate** by raising your hand and pointing up. • *I raised my hand. I pointed up. I raised my hand and pointed up.*	**Write and Read:** • The dancers stood tall and spun around. • *What did the dancers do? They stood tall and spun around.* Draw two lines under the complete predicates. *(stood tall, spun around)* • *What word connects the two complete predicates? And connects the two complete predicates.* Circle "*and*". **Repeat**, using the following sentence: • One dancer lifted her arms and bent backward.
	Interactive Examples	**Corrective Feedback**
We Do	**Write and Read:** • The workers cut boards. The workers pounded in nails. • *What are the complete predicates?* (cut boards, pounded in nails) • *How can you make these sentences into one sentence with a compound predicate?* (The workers cut boards and pounded in nails.) **Repeat** with the following sentences: • The saw made a buzzing noise. The saw cut the board in two.	**Make sure** that students differentiate compound predicates from compound sentences. Only the verb parts of the sentence should be combined. Students should notice that the subjects must be identical in order for predicates to be combined.
	Oral Practice	**Written Practice**
You Do	**Collaborate:** Have partners take turns performing an action and then describing each other's actions using a compound predicate; for example, *You raised your arm and waved your hand.*	Provide each student with a copy of Practice pages 22-24 that corresponds to his or her proficiency level. Go over the examples and have partners work together to complete the exercises.

Collection of Diverse Literature

The literature in *Wonders* provides a diverse representation of various individuals and cultures. The texts give students the opportunity to see themselves and others within and outside of their communities. As students read, listen to, discuss, and write about texts, they are able to make real-life connections to themselves and the world around them.

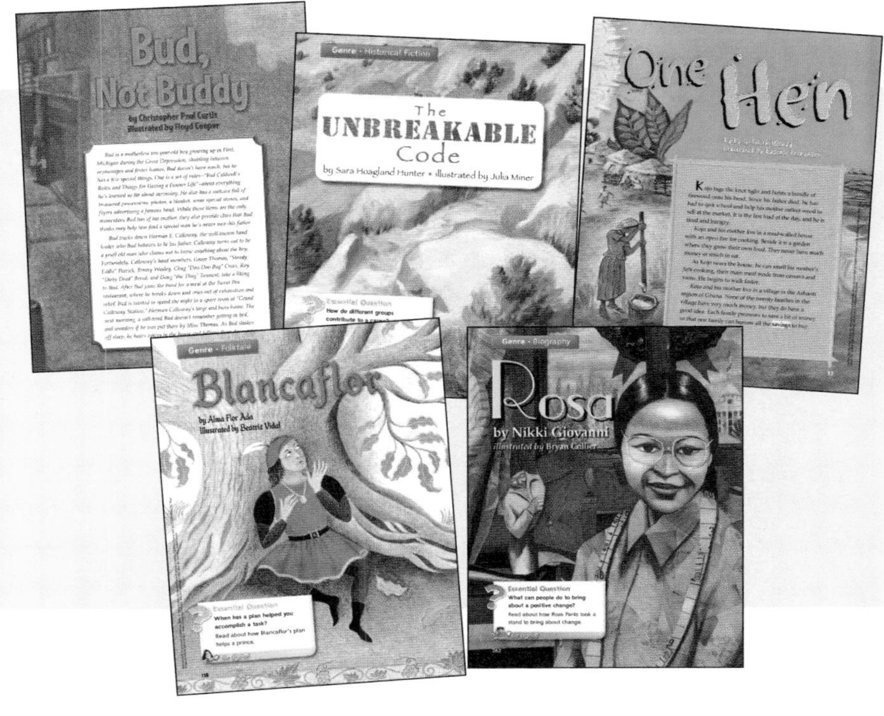

Culturally Responsive Teaching

Drawing from the research, there are a number of factors that support classroom equity and enable the underpinnings of culturally responsive teaching: high academic expectations for all students; a socially and emotionally positive classroom; a safe school climate; authentic and rigorous tasks; inclusive, relevant, and meaningful content; open and accepting communication; drawing from students' strengths, knowledge, culture, and competence; critically and socially aware inquiry practices; strong teaching; and school staff professional support and learning about equity and inclusion (Aronson & Laughter, 2016; Gay, 2010; Krasnoff, 2016; Ladson-Billings, 2006; Morrison, Robbins, & Rose, 2008; NYSED, 2019; Saphier, 2017; Snyder, Trowery & McGrath, 2019; Waddell, 2014). It is important to note the emphasis on developing classrooms and instructional practices that support all students, rather than focusing solely on who the students are and what they bring to school.

Through the high-quality content and research-based best practices of the instructional routines embedded in the program, the *Wonders* curriculum supports all important aspects of culturally responsive teaching.

The Learning Community: providing avenues for the development of a classroom community grounded in collaboration, risk-taking, responsibility, perseverance, and communication. This allows all learners to find a pathway to deep learning and academic success.

Wonders promotes classroom practices that best support meaningful learning and collaboration among peers. Valuing students' voices on what they think about the world around them and what they know allows teachers to build on students' funds of knowledge and adapt instruction and application opportunities. Starting in Kindergarten and progressing through the grades, students develop their ability to engage in focused academic discussions, assisting each other in deep understanding of the texts they read and building knowledge on various topics.

Authentic and Rigorous Learning Tasks: providing multiple methods to learn new material, challenging content for all levels of learners, opportunities to discuss, grapple with, and critique ideas, and space to personally connect to the content. This allows all learners to develop enthusiasm and dedication in their academic endeavors.

In *Wonders*, many of the texts center on relevant issues, examples, and real-world problems, along with prompts and questions that encourage students to engage and think critically about how they would address a similar problem or issue. The Essential Question for each text set introduces the topic that will be explored, culminating in a Show Your Knowledge activity. This allows students to synthesize information they learned analyzing all the texts. Extended writing tasks allow additional opportunities for flexible connections, elaboration of student thinking, and original expression.

Differentiation Opportunities: providing instructional pathways to meet the individual needs of all learners, which creates a more equitable learning experience.

In *Wonders*, clarity around differentiation of instruction, flexibility, adaptability, and choice are some of the key guiding principles on which the resources have been built. In addition to providing a range of differentiated leveled texts, *Wonders* is designed to ensure all students have access to rich, authentic grade-level informational and literary texts. A variety of print and digital resources are provided as options for differentiating practice opportunities.

FatCamera/Getty Images

Evidence of Learning: providing continuous opportunities to gather information about each learner's academic progress through a variety of assessment methods. This allows for timely feedback to learners and supports differentiation for meeting the needs of all learners.

In *Wonders*, students' self-evaluation of their own learning and progress over time is integral to student success. Student Check-In Routines assist students in documenting how well they understand leaning goals and encourage them to reflect on what may have been difficult to understand. Resources such as the Learning Goals Blackline Masters and features in the Reading/Writing Companion assist students in monitoring their progress. Teachers use the results of the Student Check-Ins and their informal observations of students with the Check for Success features in the Teacher's Edition to inform decisions about small group differentiated instruction. A range of innovative tools equip the teacher for assessment-informed instructional decision making, and ensure students are equipped to fully participate in responsive, engaging instruction. This Data Dashboard uses student results from assessments and activities to provide instructional recommendations tailored to the individual needs.

Relevant, Respectful, and Meaningful Content: providing content that represents the lives and experiences of a range of individuals who belong to different racial, ethnic, religious, age, gender, linguistic, socio-economic, and ability groups in equitable, positive, and non-stereotypical ways. This allows all learners to see themselves reflected in the content they are learning.

In *Wonders*, resources have been created and curated to promote literacy and deepen understanding for every student. A commitment to multicultural education and our nation's diverse population is evident in the literature selections and themes found throughout every grade. *Wonders* depicts people from various ethnic backgrounds in all types of environments, avoiding stereotypes. Students of all backgrounds will be able to relate to the texts. The authors of the texts in *Wonders* are also diverse and represent a rich range of backgrounds and cultures, which they bring to their writing.

Shutterstock

Supporting Family Communication: providing open communication avenues for families by developing regular and varied interactions about program content. This provides opportunities for all families to be involved in the academic progress of their learner.

In *Wonders*, the School to Home tab on the ConnectEd Student Workspace provides information to families about what students are learning. The letters introduce the Essential Questions that the students will be investigating in each text set, as well as the key skills and skills. Activities that families can complete with students at home are provided. Access to texts that students are reading is also available through the Student Workspace. Home-to-school letters and audio summaries of student texts are available in multiple languages, including English, Spanish, Haitian-Creole, Portuguese, Vietnamese, French, Arabic, Chinese (Cantonese and Mandarin), Russian, Tagalog, and Urdu.

Professional Learning: providing instructional guidance for administrators and teachers that supports enacting culturally responsive and sustaining pedagogical practices and focuses on asset-based approaches, bias surfacing, cultural awareness, and connections to learner communities, cultures, and resources.

In *Wonders*, a comprehensive set of resources assists administrators and teachers in a successful implementation of the program to ensure teacher and student success. Information embedded in the Teacher's Edition, and targeted components such as the Instructional Routines Handbook, as well as online Professional Learning Videos and resources, provide a wide range of support. Resources focused on helping teachers reflect on their understanding of the different cultures of their students, as well as assisting teachers in facilitating meaningful conversations about texts, are also provided.

Teaching the **Whole Child**

Your students are learning so much more than reading from you. They're learning how to learn, how to master new content areas, and how to handle themselves in and out of the classroom. Research shows that this leads to increased academic success. *Wonders* resources have been developed to support you in teaching the whole child, for success this year and throughout your students' lives.

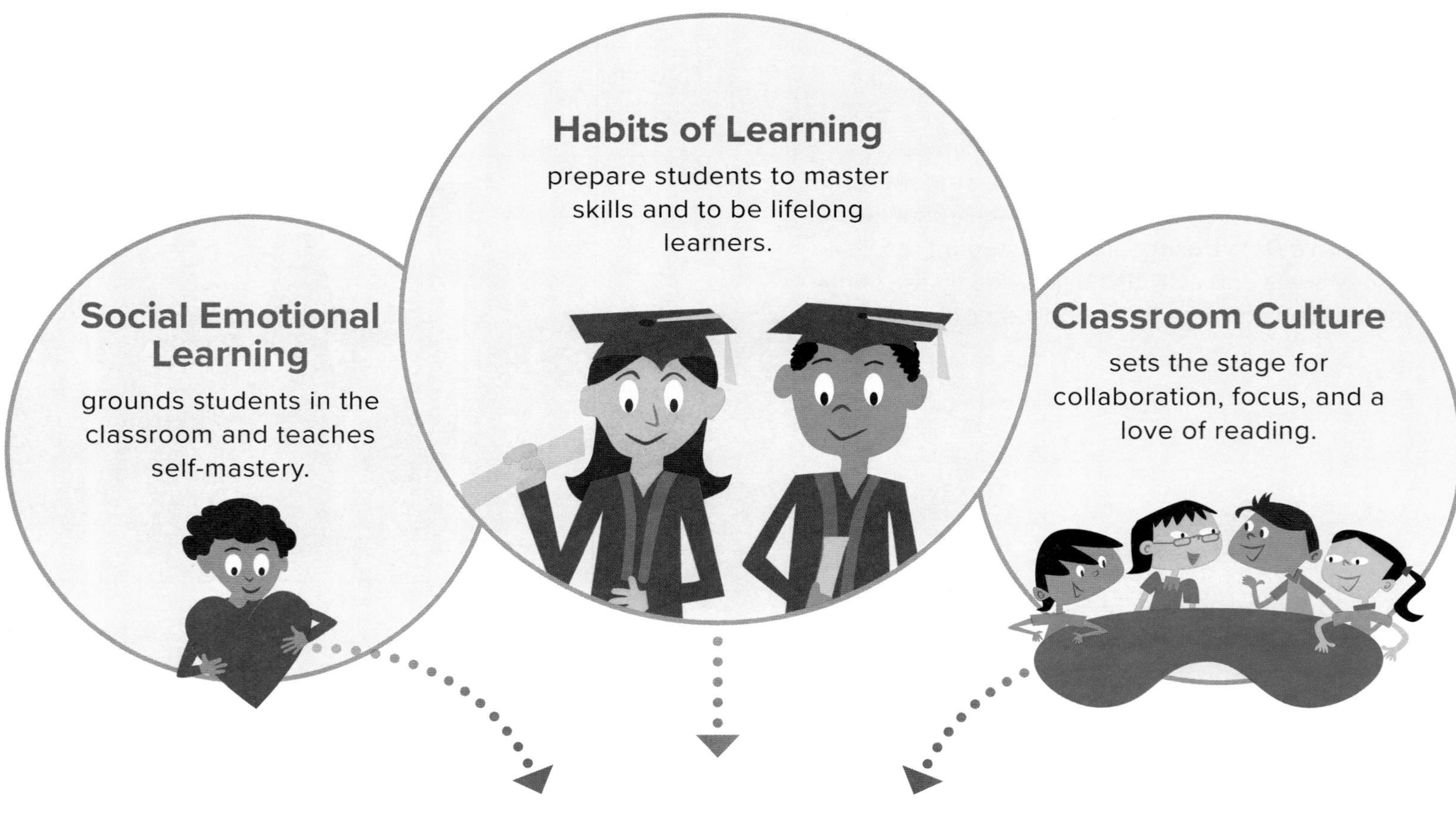

Habits of Learning
prepare students to master skills and to be lifelong learners.
Social Emotional Learning
grounds students in the classroom and teaches self-mastery.
Classroom Culture
sets the stage for collaboration, focus, and a love of reading.

DEVELOPING CRITICAL THINKERS

- Mastery of reading, writing, speaking, and listening
- Knowledge that spans content areas
- College and career readiness
- Strong results this year and beyond

Habits of Learning

I am part of a community of learners.

- ☐ I listen actively to others to learn new ideas.
- ☐ I build upon others' ideas in a conversation.
- ☐ I work with others to understand my learning goals.
- ☐ I stay on topic during discussion.
- ☐ I use words that will make my ideas clear.
- ☐ I share what I know.
- ☐ I gather information to support my thinking.

I use a variety of strategies when I read.

- ☐ I make predictions.
- ☐ I take notes.
- ☐ I think about how a text is organized.
- ☐ I visualize what I'm reading.
- ☐ I think about the author's purpose.

I think critically about what I read.

- ☐ I ask questions.
- ☐ I look for text evidence.
- ☐ I make inferences based on evidence.
- ☐ I connect new ideas to what I already know.

I write to communicate.

- ☐ I think about what I read as models for my writing.
- ☐ I talk with my peers to help make my writing better.
- ☐ I use rubrics to analyze my own writing.
- ☐ I use different tools when I write and present.

I believe I can succeed.

- ☐ I try different ways to learn things that are difficult for me.
- ☐ I ask for help when I need it.
- ☐ I challenge myself to do better.
- ☐ I work to complete my tasks.
- ☐ I read independently.

I am a problem solver.

- ☐ I analyze the problem.
- ☐ I try different ways.

Classroom Culture

We respect and value each other's experiences.

- ☐ We value what each of us brings from home.
- ☐ We work together to understand each other's perspectives.
- ☐ We work with our peers in pairs and in small groups.
- ☐ We use new academic vocabulary we learn when we speak and write.
- ☐ We share our work and learn from others.

We promote student ownership of learning.

- ☐ We understand what our learning goals are.
- ☐ We evaluate how well we understand each learning goal.
- ☐ We find different ways to learn what is difficult.

We learn through modeling and practice.

- ☐ We practice together to make sure we understand.
- ☐ We access many different resources to get information.
- ☐ We use many different tools when we share what we learn.

We foster a love of reading.

- ☐ We create inviting places to sit and read.
- ☐ We read for enjoyment.
- ☐ We read to understand ourselves and our world.

We build knowledge.

- ☐ We investigate what we want to know more about.
- ☐ We read many different types of texts to gain information.
- ☐ We build on what we know.

We inspire confident writers.

- ☐ We analyze the connection between reading and writing.
- ☐ We understand the purpose and audience for our writing.
- ☐ We revise our writing to make it stronger.

Social Emotional Learning

Social emotional learning is one of the most important factors in predicting school success. *Wonders* supports students in social emotional development in the following areas so that they can successfully engage in the instructional routines.

Relationships and Prosocial Behaviors

Engages in and maintains positive relationships and interactions with familiar adults and other students.

Social Problem Solving

Uses basic problem solving skills to resolve conflicts with other students.

Rules and Routines

Follows classroom rules and routines with increasing independence.

Working Memory

Maintains and manipulates distinct pieces of information over short periods of time.

Focus Attention

Maintains focus and sustains attention with minimal teacher supports.

Self Awareness

Recognizes self as a unique individual as well as belonging to a family, community, or other groups; expresses confidence in own skills and perspectives.

Creativity

Expresses creativity in thinking and communication.

Initiative

Demonstrates initiative and independence.

Task Persistence

Sets reasonable goals and persists to complete the task.

Logic and Reasoning

Thinks critically to effectively solve a problem or make a decision.

Planning and Problem Solving

Uses planning and problem solving strategies to achieve goals.

Flexible Thinking

Demonstrates flexibility in thinking and behavior to resolve conflicts with other students.

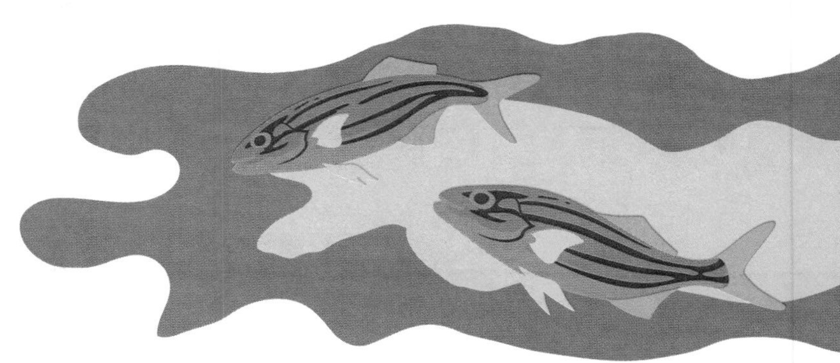

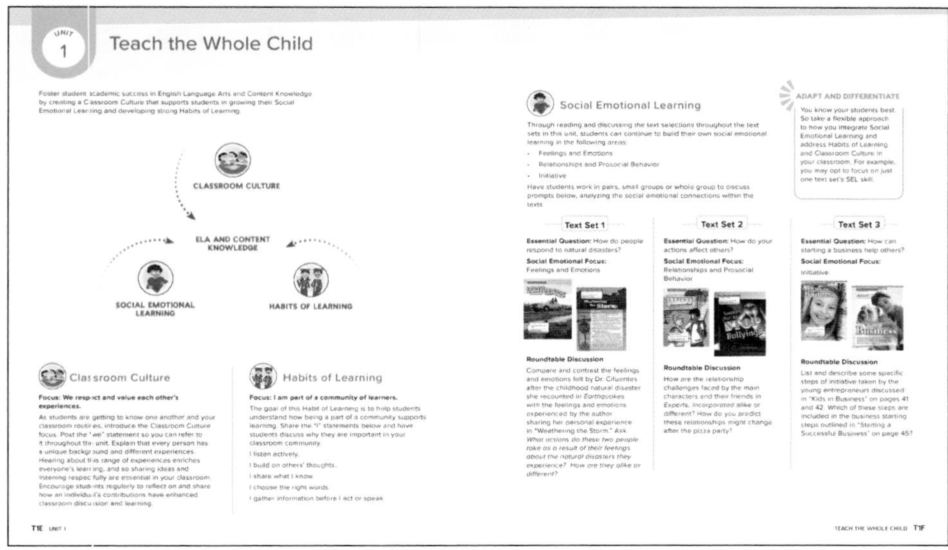

UNIT 1 Teach the Whole Child

Foster student academic success in English Language Arts and Content Knowledge by creating a Classroom Culture that supports students in growing their Social Emotional Learning and developing strong Habits of Learning.

Classroom Culture

Focus: We respect and value each other's experiences.

As students are getting to know one another and your classroom routines, introduce the Classroom Culture focus. Post the "we" statement so you can refer to it throughout the unit. Explain that every person has a unique background and different experiences. Hearing about this range of experiences enriches everyone's learning, and so sharing ideas and listening respectfully are essential in your classroom. Encourage students regularly to reflect on and share how an individual's contributions have enhanced classroom discussion and learning.

Habits of Learning

Focus: I am part of a community of learners.

The goal of this Habit of Learning is to help students understand how being a part of a community supports learning. Share the "I" statements below and have students discuss why they are important in your classroom community.

I listen actively.

I build on others' thoughts.

I share what I know.

I choose the right words.

I gather information before I act or speak.

T1E UNIT 1

Social Emotional Learning

Through reading and discussing the text selections throughout the text sets in this unit, students can continue to build their own social emotional learning in the following areas:

- Feelings and Emotions
- Relationships and Prosocial Behavior
- Initiative

Have students work in pairs, small groups or whole group to discuss prompts below, analyzing the social emotional connections within the texts.

ADAPT AND DIFFERENTIATE

You know your students best. So take a flexible approach to how you integrate Social Emotional Learning and address Habits of Learning and Classroom Culture in your classroom. For example, you may opt to focus on just one text set's SEL skill.

Text Set 1

Essential Question: How do people respond to natural disasters?

Social Emotional Focus: Feelings and Emotions

Roundtable Discussion

Compare and contrast the feelings and emotions felt by Dr. Cifuentes after the childhood natural disaster she recounted in *Earthquakes* with the feelings and emotions experienced by the author sharing her personal experience in "Weathering the Storm." Ask: *What actions do these two people take as a result of their feelings about the natural disasters they experience? How are they alike or different?*

Text Set 2

Essential Question: How do your actions affect others?

Social Emotional Focus: Relationships and Prosocial Behavior

Roundtable Discussion

How are the relationship challenges faced by the main characters and their friends in *Experts, Incorporated* alike or different? How do you predict these relationships might change after the pizza party?

Text Set 3

Essential Question: How can starting a business help others?

Social Emotional Focus: Initiative

Roundtable Discussion

List and describe some specific steps of initiative taken by the young entrepreneurs discussed in "Kids in Business" on pages 41 and 42. Which of these steps are included in the business starting steps outlined in "Starting a Successful Business" on page 45?

TEACH THE WHOLE CHILD T1F

For each text set in a unit, a social emotional focus is identified and discussed in the context of the texts students read.

Weekly School-to-Home Communication

Weekly school-to-home family communication letters, ready to send in multiple languages, encourage parents to log on and share resources with their children, including listening to audio summaries of all main selections so they can ask questions. This deepens the connection between community and classroom, supporting social emotional development. This helps ensure that each and every child comes to school engaged, motivated, and eager to learn!

- English
- Spanish
- Chinese
- French
- Portuguese
- Tagalog
- Vietnamese
- Urdu
- Arabic
- Haitian-Creole
- Russian

E-books include audio summaries in the same languages.

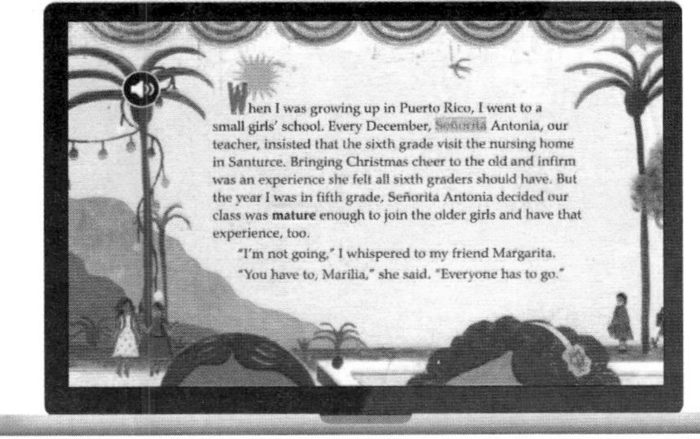

Wonders and the Science of Reading

Dr. Timothy Shanahan

Wonders supports the delivery of high-quality literacy instruction aligned to the science of reading. It provides a comprehensive, integrated plan for meeting the needs of all students. Carefully monitoring advances in literacy research, the program is developed to ensure that lessons focus on teaching the right content at the right time. The right content refers to teaching sufficient amounts of the content that has been proven to deliver learning advantages to students. The right time refers to a carefully structured scope and sequence within a grade and across grades. This ensures that teaching is presented in the most effective and efficient manner, with sound guidance to better support diverse learners.

Foundational Skills

English is an alphabetic language; developing readers must learn to translate letters and spelling patterns to sounds and pronunciations, and to read text accurately, automatically, and with proper expression. When students learn to manage these foundational skills with a minimum of conscious attention, they will have the cognitive resources available to comprehend what they read.

Research shows that the explicit teaching of phonemic awareness, phonics, and text reading fluency are the most successful ways to succeed in foundational skills. *Wonders* presents a sequence of research-aligned learning activities in its grade-level placements, sequences of instruction, and instructional guidance across the following areas:

- Phonemic Awareness
- Phonics/Decoding
- Text Reading Fluency

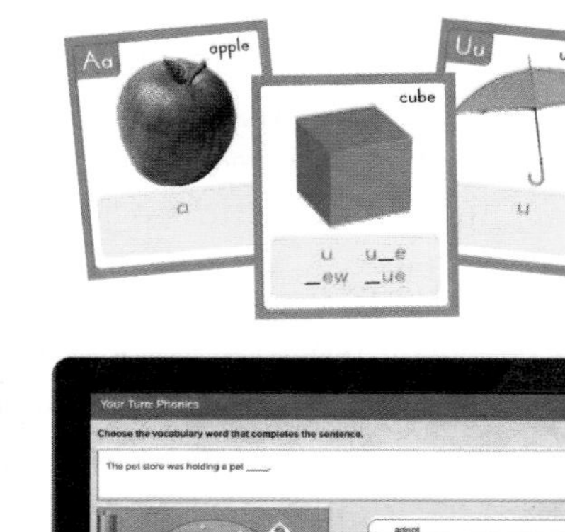

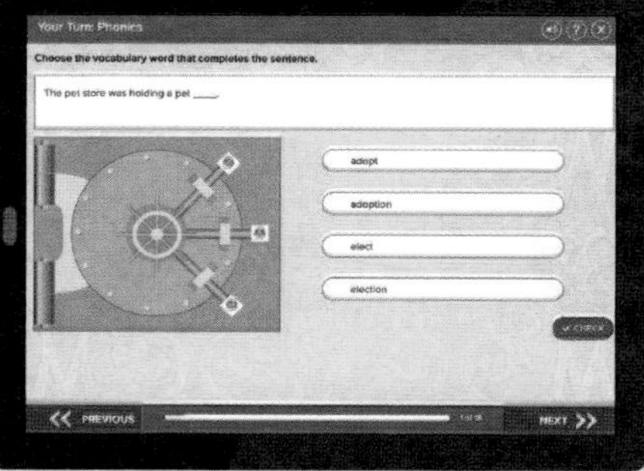

Courtesy of Tim Shanahan

Reading Comprehension

Reading comprehension requires that students extract and construct meaning from text. To comprehend, students must learn to apply the prior knowledge they bring to the text to the information expressed through written language in the text. To accomplish this successfully, readers must do three things. They must:

- expand their knowledge through the reading of high-quality informative texts;
- learn to negotiate increasingly sophisticated and complex written language;
- develop the cognitive abilities to manage and monitor these processes.

Wonders provides lessons built around a high-quality collection of complex literary and informational texts, focused on both the natural and social worlds. Teachers using *Wonders* will find explicit, research-based lessons in vocabulary and other language skills, guidance for high-level, high-quality discussions, and well-designed lessons aimed at building the executive processes that can shift reading comprehension into high gear, including:

- Building Knowledge/Using Knowledge
- Vocabulary and other aspects of written language
- Text complexity
- Executive processes and comprehension strategies

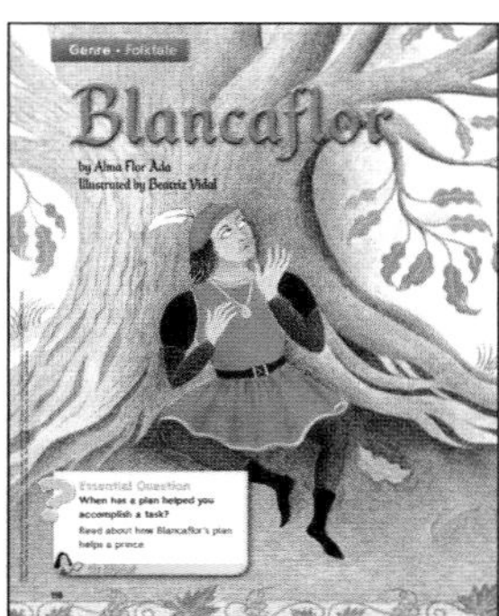

Writing

In the 21st century, it is not enough to be able to read, understand, and learn from the writing of others. Being able to communicate one's own ideas logically and effectively is necessary, too. As with reading, writing includes foundational skills (like spelling and handwriting), as well as higher-order abilities (composition and communication) and the executive processes required to manage the accomplishment of successful writing. Research shows that reading and writing strengthen one another. Focusing writing instruction in the following areas will help students improve their reading:

- Writing foundations
- Quality writing for multiple purposes
- The writing processes
- Writing to enhance reading

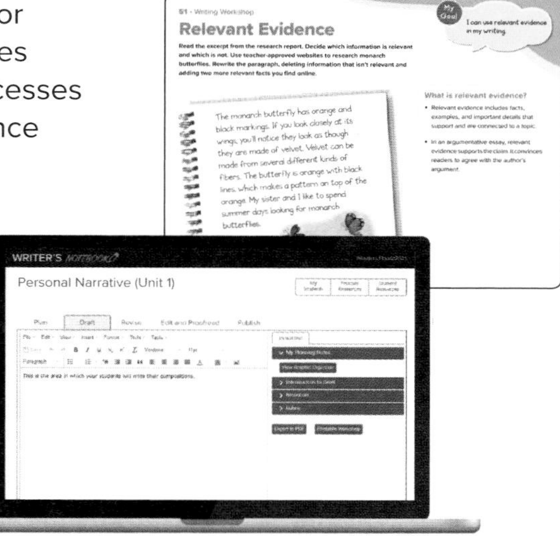

Quality of Instruction

The science of reading is dependent upon the sciences of teaching and learning, as well as on reading research. Reading research has identified specific best practices for teaching particular aspects of literacy. However, research has also revealed other important features of quality instruction that have implications for all learners and that may better support certain student populations. *Wonders* lessons reflect these quality issues in teaching:

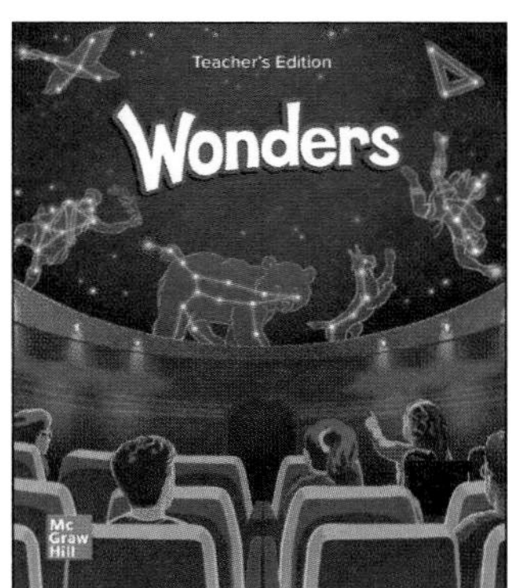

- Lessons with explicit and appropriate purposes
- High-challenge levels
- Appropriate opportunities for review
- Quality discussions promoted by high DOK-level questions
- Ongoing monitoring of learning
- Supports for English language learners
- Connections to social emotional learning

Build Critical Readers, Writers, Communicators, and Thinkers

LISTENING

SPEAKING

READING

Build Knowledge Through a Text Set

- **Investigate** an Essential Question.
- **Read** a variety of texts.
- **Closely read** texts for deeper meaning.
- **Respond** to texts using text evidence.
- **Conduct** research.
- **Share** your knowledge.
- **Inspire** action.

WRITING

Communicate Effectively Through Writing

- **Analyze** mentor texts and student models.
- **Understand** purpose and audience.
- **Plan** writing, using sources as needed.
- **Conference** with peers and teachers.
- **Evaluate** work against a rubric.
- **Improve** writing continuously.
- **Share** your writing.

SMALL GROUP

EXTEND CONNECT ASSESS

COLLABORATING

Instruction Aligned to the **Science of Reading**

Reading

Explicit instruction supports students in building knowledge.

- Foundational Reading Skills
  - Phonics/Word Analysis
  - Fluency
- Reading Literature
- Reading Informational Texts
- Comparing Texts
- Vocabulary
- Researching

Writing

Skills-based minilessons support students in developing their writing.

- Writing
  - Narrative
  - Argumentative
  - Expository
- Handwriting
- Speaking and Listening
- Conventions
- Creating and Collaborating

Differentiation

Differentiate resources, instruction, and level of scaffolds.

Small Group Teacher-Led Instruction

- Choose from small group skills lesson options to target instruction to meet students' needs.
- Read texts with scaffolded support.

Independent/Collaborative Work

- Students transfer knowledge of skills to independent reading and practice.
- Students transfer skills to their writing.

Extend, Connect, and Assess

At the end of the unit, students transfer and apply knowledge gained to new contexts.

Demonstrate Understanding

- Extend knowledge through online reading and Reader's Theater.
- Connect ELA skills to content area reading with science and social studies texts.
- Assess learning with program assessments.

Grade 5

Resources

The resources in *Wonders* support skills mastery, differentiated instruction, and the transfer and application of knowledge to new contexts. Teachers will find ways to enhance student learning and ownership through multimodal supports, a strong focus on foundational skills, opportunities to build knowledge, and fostering of expression through writing. All of your *Wonders*-created print resources are available digitally to support a variety of learning environments. The resources shown represent the key instructional elements of your *Wonders* classroom and are a portion of the supports available to you and your students. Login to your **Teacher Workspace** to explore multimedia resources, professional learning, and thousands of resources to meet your students where they are.

Component	Differentiate	Extend, Connect, Assess	Available Digitally
Teacher's Edition	●	●	●
Reading/Writing Companion		●	●
Literature Anthology		●	●
Classroom Library	●		
Classroom Library Lessons	●		●

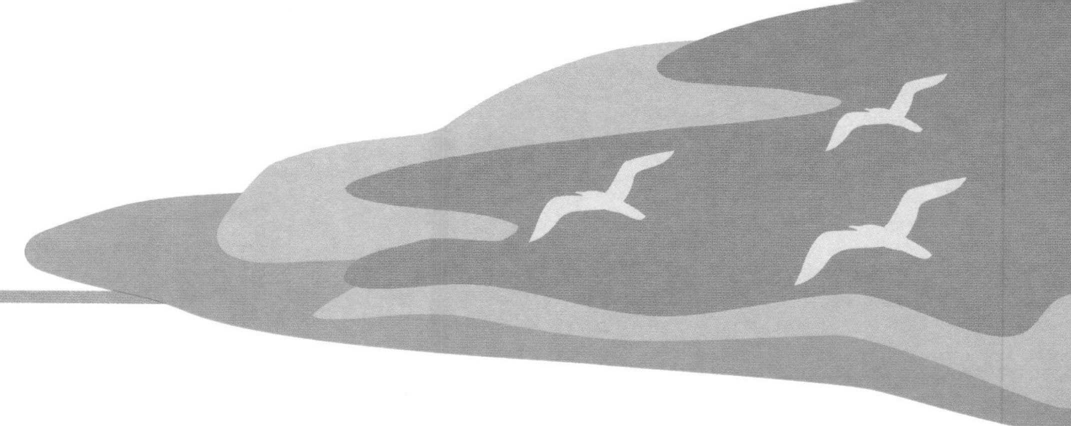

Component	Differentiate	Extend, Connect, Assess	Available Digitally
Leveled Readers & Lesson Cards	●	●	●
Center Activity Cards	●	●	●
ELL Small Group Guide	●		●
Data Dashboard	●	●	●
Progress Monitoring Assessment		●	●
Unit Assessment		●	●
Benchmark Assessments		●	●
Practice Book Blackline Masters		●	●
Inquiry Space		●	●
Online Writer's Notebook		●	●
Foundational Skills Resources: multimodal manipulatives, cards, activities, and games to build key skills	●	●	●
Skills-Based Online Games	●	●	●
Differentiated Genre Passages	●	●	●
Content Area Reading Blackline Masters		●	●

Professional Learning
Every Step of the Way

Get Started Using *Wonders*. Every day of instruction is based on evidence-based classroom best practices, which are embedded into the daily routines to strengthen your teaching and enhance students' learning. Throughout *Wonders*, you'll find support for employing these new routines and making the most of your literacy block.

Use this checklist to access support resources to help you get started with *Wonders* during the first weeks of school. Then refer to this list during the year for ongoing implementation support and to get the most from *Wonders*.

Beginning the Year

We encourage you to review these resources before the first day of school and then use them to support your first weeks of instruction.

In Your Teacher's Edition: Support pages for planning and teaching are embedded throughout your Teacher's Edition to support your big-picture understanding and help you teach effectively.

- ☐ **Start Smart:** In Unit 1 of your Teacher's Edition, Start Smart provides an overview of the instructional lessons and routines within *Wonders* by providing an explanation of the Unit 1 Text Set 1 Teacher's Edition lessons and select other lessons.
- ☐ **Text Set Support:** Each text set is accompanied by an introduction that supports your understanding of the content and simplifies instructional planning. These pages include a daily planner, differentiated learning support, guidance for developing student ownership and building knowledge, and more.
- ☐ **Progress Monitoring and Assessment:** Use data to track progress toward mastery of skills-based content, lesson objectives, and student goals.
  The **My Goals Routine** supports continuous self-monitoring and student feedback.

Online Resources: The digital Teacher Dashboard is your access point for key resources to get you up and running with *Wonders*. From the Teacher Dashboard, select *Resources > Professional Development > Overview*

- ☐ ***Wonders* Basics Module:** Set up your classroom, get to know your materials, learn about the structure of *Wonders*, and receive support for placement testing and grouping students for small group learning.
  ▶ Select *Learn to Use Wonders*
- ☐ **Placement and Diagnostic Assessment:** Access assessments, testing instructions, and placement charts that can be used at the beginning of the year to assess and place students in small groups.
  ▶ Select *Assessment & Data*

Ongoing Support

Your online **Teacher Workspace** also includes a wide range of additional resources. Use them throughout the year for ongoing support and professional learning. From the Teacher Dashboard, select *Resources > Professional Development*

- ☐ **Instructional Routines Handbook:** Reference this handbook throughout the year for support implementing the *Wonders* evidence-based routines and understanding the research behind them, and for guidance on what student success looks like.
  - ▶ Select *Overview > Instructional Routines*
- ☐ **Small Group Differentiated Learning Guide:** Use the first few weeks of small group time to teach and model routines and establish small group rules and procedures.
  - ▶ Select *Overview > Instructional Routines > Managing Small Groups: A How-to Guide PDF*
- ☐ **Suggested Lesson Plans and Pacing Guides:** Adjust your instruction to your literacy block and meet the needs of your classroom with flexible lesson plans and pacing.
  - ▶ Select *Overview > Instructional Routines*
- ☐ **Classroom Videos:** Watch *Wonders* teachers model classroom lessons in reading, writing, collaboration, and teaching English language learners.
  - ▶ Select *Classroom Videos*
- ☐ **Small Group Classroom Videos:** Watch *Wonders* teachers model small group instruction and share tips and strategies for effective differentiated lessons.
  - ▶ Select *Classroom Videos > Small Group Instruction*
- ☐ **Author & Coach Videos:** Watch Dr. Douglas Fisher, Dr. Timothy Shanahan, and other *Wonders* authors as they provide short explanations of best practices and classroom coaching. Also provided are videos from Dr. Sheldon Eakins, founder of the Leading Equity Center, that focus on important aspects of educational equity and cultural responsive teaching.
  - ▶ Select *Author & Coach Videos*
- ☐ **Assessment Handbook:** Review your assessment options and find support for managing multiple assessments, interpreting their results, and using data to inform your instructional planning.
  - ▶ Select *Overview > Assessment & Data*
- ☐ **Assessment & Data Guides:** Review your assessment resources and get to know your reporting tools.
  - ▶ Select *Overview > Assessment & Data*
- ☐ **Digital Help:** Access video tutorials and printable PDFs to support planning, assessment, writing and research, assignments, and connecting school to home.
  - ▶ Select *Digital Help*

Explore the Professional Development section in your Teacher Workspace for more videos, resources, and printable guides. Select *Resources > Professional Development*

Notes

UNIT 5

Contents

UNIT 5

Unit Overview

English Language Arts is not a discrete set of skills. Skills work together to help students analyze the meaningful texts. In *Wonders*, skills are not taught in isolation. Rather they are purposefully combined to support student learning of texts they read.

Reading

Text Set 1	Text Set 2	Text Set 3
Essential Question: How can scientific knowledge change over time?	**Essential Question:** How do shared experiences help people adapt to change?	**Essential Question:** How do natural events and human activities affect the environment?
Phonics and Word Analysis Suffixes; Homophones **Fluency** Expression; Accuracy and Phrasing **Reading Informational Text** ✓ Text Features: Diagrams ✓ Central Idea and Relevant Details Summarize **Reading Literature** ✓ Figurative Language: Imagery **Compare Texts** Compare and contrast information **Vocabulary** Academic Vocabulary ✓ Greek Roots Thesaurus **Researching** Scientific Knowledge Grows	**Phonics and Word Analysis** Prefixes; Suffixes *-less* and *-ness* **Fluency** Accuracy and Rate **Reading Literature** ✓ Plot: Characterization ✓ Plot: Conflict Summarize **Reading Informational Text** ✓ Text Structure: Compare and Contrast **Compare Texts** Compare and contrast information **Vocabulary** Academic Vocabulary ✓ Idioms ✓ Puns **Researching** Supporting One Another	**Phonics and Word Analysis** Suffix *-ion* **Fluency** Accuracy and Rate **Reading Informational Text** ✓ Text Features: Charts and Headings ✓ Author's Perspective ✓ Figurative Language: Puns Summarize **Compare Texts** Compare and contrast information **Vocabulary** Academic Vocabulary ✓ Root Words **Researching** Environmental Changes

Writing

Extended Writing 1		Extended Writing 2
Writing Handwriting ✓ Research Report Improving Writing: Writing Process **Speaking and Listening** Oral Presentation	**Conventions** ✓ Grammar: Clauses; Complex Sentences; Adjectives; Adjectives That Compare Spelling: Suffixes, Homophones, Prefixes, Suffixes *-less*, *-ness* **Creating and Collaborating** Writer's Notebook	**Writing** Handwriting ✓ Personal Narrative Improving Writing: Writing Process **Speaking and Listening** Oral Presentation

Key

✓ Tested in *Wonders* Assessments

Extend, Connect, and Assess

Extend previously taught skills and connect to new content.

Extend

Reading Informational Text
Reading Digitally

Central Idea and Relevant Details

Conduct Research

Fluency
Reader's Theater

Phrasing and Rate

Connect

Connect to Science

Forces That Cause Objects to Move; Force and Changes in Motion of Objects

Connect to Social Studies

Use of Primary and Secondary Sources to Understand History; Use of Maps to Identify Physical Features of the United States

Assess

✓ Unit Assessment Test

Fluency Assessment

Conventions

✓ Grammar: Comparing with *Good* and *Bad*

Spelling: Words with Suffix *-ion*

Creating and Collaborating

Writer's Notebook

Key Skills Trace

Reading Literature

Plot

Introduce: Unit 1 Text Set 2

Review: Unit 2 Text Set 2; Unit 3 Text Set 1; Unit 5 Text Set 2; Unit 6 Text Set 1

Assess: Unit 1, Unit 2, Unit 3, Unit 5, Unit 6

Literal and Figurative Language

Introduce: Unit 3 Text Set 2

Review: Unit 3 Text Set 3; Unit 5 Text Set 1

Assess: Unit 3, Unit 5

Reading Informational Text

Central Idea and Relevant Details

Introduce: Unit 3 Text Set 2

Review: Unit 5 Text Set 1

Assess: Unit 3, Unit 5

Text Features

Introduce: Unit 1 Text Set 3

Review: Unit 2 Text Set 1; Unit 4 Text Set 1; Unit 5 Text Set 1, Text Set 3; Unit 6 Text Set 1, Text Set 2

Assess: Unit 1, Unit 2, Unit 4, Unit 5, Unit 6

Text Structure

Introduce: Unit 1 Text Set 1

Review: Unit 1 Text Set 2; Unit 2 Text Set 1, Text Set 2; Unit 3 Text Set 2, Text Set 3; Unit 4 Text Set 1; Unit 5 Text Set 2; Unit 6 Text Set 2

Assess: Unit 1, Unit 2, Unit 3, Unit 4, Unit 5, Unit 6

Author's Perspective and Purpose

Introduce: Unit 1 Text Set 1

Review: Unit 1 Text Set 3; Unit 3 Text Set 1; Unit 4 Text Set 1; Unit 5 Text Set 3

Assess: Unit 1, Unit 3, Unit 4, Unit 5

Vocabulary

Greek and Latin Roots

Introduce: Unit 2 Text Set 2

Review: Unit 3 Text Set 2; Unit 5 Text Set 1, Text Set 3

Assess: Unit 2, Unit 3, Unit 5

Idioms, Adages, and Proverbs

Introduce: Unit 3 Text Set 1

Review: Unit 4 Text Set 2; Unit 5 Text Set 2

Assess: Unit 3, Unit 4, Unit 5

Root Words

Introduce: Unit 2 Text Set 2

Review: Unit 5 Text Set 3

Assess: Unit 2, Unit 5

Grammar

Clauses and Adjectives

Introduce: Unit 5

Review: Grammar Handbook and Extended Writing: Unit 6

Assess: Unit 5

Extended Writing

Unit 1: Argumentative Writing/Write to Sources

Unit 2: Expository Writing/Write to Sources

Unit 3: Argumentative Writing/Write to Sources

Unit 4: Expository Writing/Write to Sources

Unit 5: Expository Writing, Personal Narrative

Unit 6: Fictional Narrative, Poem

Independent Reading

Self-Selected Reading Options

Classroom Library Titles

Students can choose from the following titles to read and further investigate text set Essential Questions.

Online Lessons Available

A Black Hole Is NOT a Hole
Carolyn Cinami DeCristofano
Expository Text
Lexile 900L

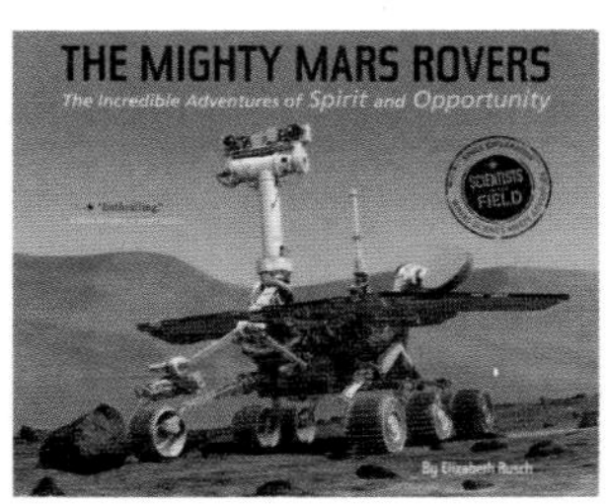

The Mighty Mars Rovers: The Incredible Adventures of Spirit and Opportunity
Elizabeth Rusch
Expository Text
Lexile 950L

SeeSaw Girl
Linda Sue Park
Historical Fiction
Lexile 810L

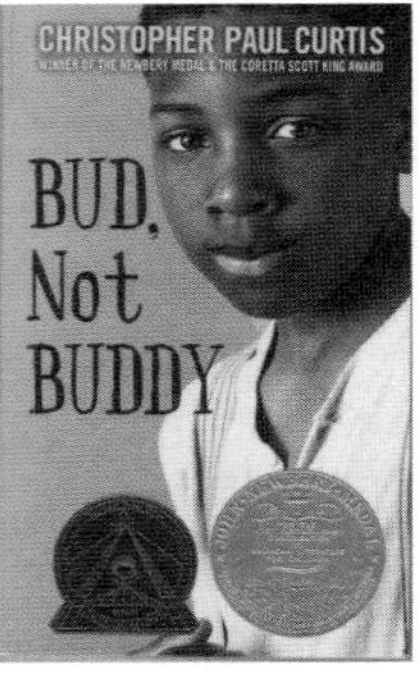

Bud, Not Buddy
Christopher Paul Curtis
Historical Fiction
Lexile 950L

More Leveled Readers to Explore

Search the **Online Leveled Reader Library** and choose texts to provide students with additional texts at various levels to apply skills or read about various topics.

Unit Bibliography

Have students self-select independent reading texts related to the text set Essential Question. Titles in the same genre as the Anchor Text as well as titles in different genres are provided. See the online bibliography for more titles.

Text Set 1

Compare Texts

Horowitz, Anthony. *Stormbreaker*. Penguin, 2006. Fiction **Lexile** 670L

Hoberman, Mary Ann. *The Tree That Time Built: A Celebration of Nature, Science, and Imagination*. Sourcebooks Jabberwocky, 2009. Poetry **Lexile** NP

More Expository Texts

Than, Ker. *Black Holes*. Scholastic, 2010. **Lexile** 940L

Graham, Ian. *What Do You Know About the Solar System?* Raintree, 2011. **Lexile** 970L

Text Set 2

Compare Texts

Creech, Sharon. *Ruby Holler*. HarperCollins, 2003. Realistic Fiction **Lexile** 660L

Blumberg, Rhoda. *Shipwrecked! The True Adventures of a Japanese Boy.* HarperCollins, 2003. Narrative Nonfiction **Lexile** 1020L

More Historical Fiction

Whelan, Gloria. *The Locked Garden.* HarperCollins, 2009. **Lexile** 850L

Curtis, Christopher Paul. *The Mighty Miss Malone*. Wendy Lamb Books, 2012. **Lexile** 750L

Text Set 3

Compare Texts

Landau, Elaine. *Oil Spill!: Disaster in the Gulf of Mexico*. Lerner Publishing Group, 2011. Expository Text **Lexile** 780L

Orr, Tamra B. *Pondering Pollution*. Cherry Lake Publishing, 2014. Narrative Nonfiction **Lexile** 840L

More Argumentative Texts

Cherry, Lynne. *The Great Kapok Tree: A Tale of the Amazon Rain Forest*. First Voyager Books, 2000. **Lexile** 590L

Jenkins, Martin. *Can We Save the Tiger?* Candlewick, 2011. **Lexile** 970L

Teach the Whole Child

Foster student academic success in English Language Arts and Content Knowledge by creating a Classroom Culture that supports students in growing their Social Emotional Learning and developing strong Habits of Learning.

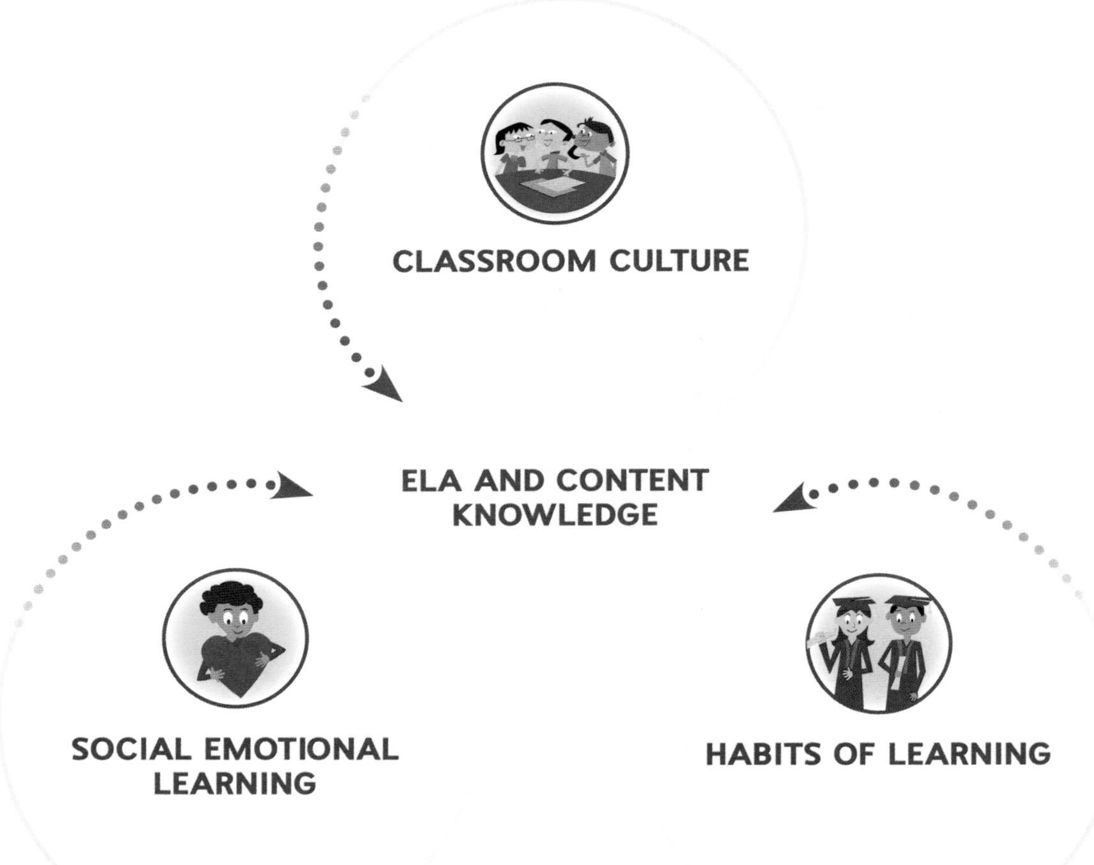

Classroom Culture

Focus: We build knowledge.

Explain to students that building knowledge is highly valued in your classroom. Remind students that many of your classroom routines, such as close reading, thinking about essential questions, and doing research and inquiry projects, are important ways of building knowledge. Read and discuss the statements below. Encourage students to share specific examples of how each statement is supported in your classroom.

We investigate what we want to know more about.

We read many different types of texts.

Habits of Learning

Focus: I think critically about what I am reading.

The goal of this Habit of Learning is to help students understand that they should think critically about everything they read, both in school and out. Share the "I" statements below and have students discuss how they help them become careful and critical readers.

I ask questions.

I look for text evidence.

I make inferences based on evidence.

I look for connections across the different things I learn and know.

Social Emotional Learning

Through reading and discussing the text selections throughout the text sets in this unit, students can continue to build their own social emotional learning in the following areas:

- Logic and Reasoning
- Relationships and Prosocial Behavior
- Curiosity

Have students work in pairs, small groups, or whole group to discuss prompts below, analyzing the social emotional connections within the texts.

ADAPT AND DIFFERENTIATE

You know your students best. So take a flexible approach to how you integrate Social Emotional Learning and address Habits of Learning and Classroom Culture in your classroom. For example, you may opt to focus on just one text set's SEL skill.

Text Set 1

Essential Question: How can scientific knowledge change over time?

Social Emotional Focus: Logic and Reasoning

Roundtable Discussion

As with many expository texts, in *When Is a Planet Not a Planet?* the author uses cause and effect as a text structure. Ask: *What are some specific examples of this structure, and how do these examples help readers ask and answer questions as they read?*

Text Set 2

Essential Question: How do shared experiences help people adapt to change?

Social Emotional Focus: Relationships and Prosocial Behavior

Roundtable Discussion

Compare and contrast some ways shared experiences and relationships help characters in *Bud, Not Buddy* adapt to challenge and change.

Text Set 3

Essential Question: How do natural events and human activities affect the environment?

Social Emotional Focus: Curiosity

Roundtable Discussion

In *The Case of the Missing Bees,* the authors address opposing perspectives about the current situation with bee populations. What are some specific ways the authors support their positions?

Notes

READING Build Knowledge Through Text Sets

Text Set 1

Essential Question: How can scientific knowledge change over time?

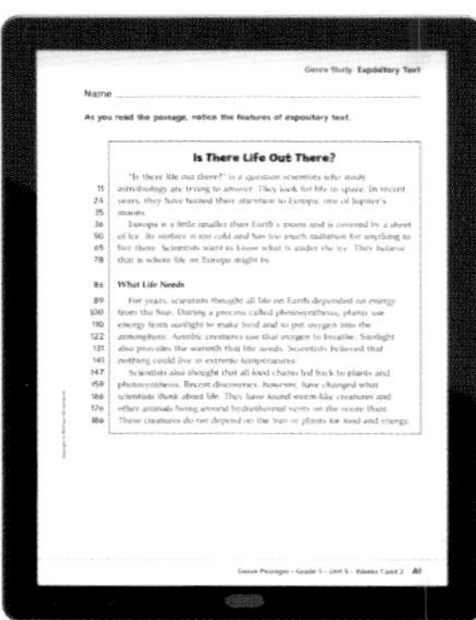

Text Set 2

Essential Question: How do shared experiences help people adapt to change?

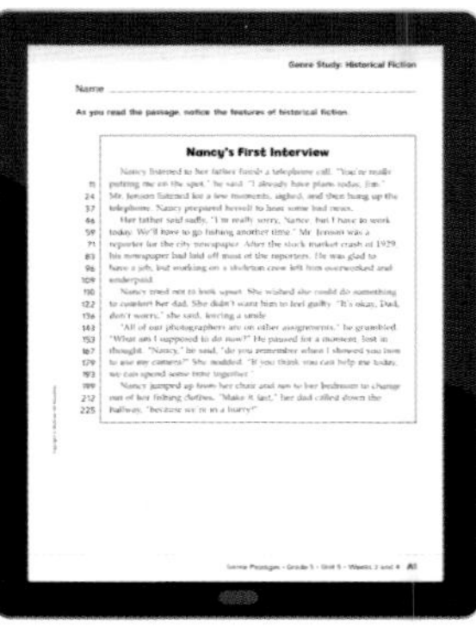

Text Set 3

Essential Question: How do natural events and human activities affect the environment?

Classroom Library Books

Student Outcomes

✓ Tested in *Wonders* Assessments

FOUNDATIONAL SKILLS

Phonics and Word Analysis

- Use knowledge of suffixes to decode words
- Use knowledge of homophones to decode words

Fluency

- Read grade-level texts with accuracy, appropriate rate, expression, and automaticity

READING

Reading Informational Text

✓ Explain how text features contribute to the understanding of a text.
✓ Explain how relevant, or key, details in a text support the central, or main, idea(s), implied or explicit
- Read and comprehend texts in the grades 4-5 text complexity band
- Summarize a text to enhance comprehension
- Write in response to texts

Compare Texts

✓ Compare and contrast how authors present information on the same topic or theme

COMMUNICATION

Writing

Writing Process

- Write an expository text researching a topic, using multiple sources, relevant evidence, and elaboration
- With guidance and support from peers and adults, develop and strengthen writing as needed by planning, revising, and editing

Speaking and Listening

- Report on a topic or text or present an opinion, sequencing ideas; speak clearly at an understandable pace

Conventions

Grammar

✓ Identify independent and dependent clauses
✓ Identify complex sentences
✓ Use commas correctly with clauses
- Use appositives correctly

Spelling

- Spell words with suffixes
- Spell homophones

Researching

- Conduct short research projects that build knowledge through investigation of different aspects of the topic

Creating and Collaborating

- Add audio recordings and visual displays to presentations when apppropriate
- With some guidance and support from adults, use technology to produce and publish writing

VOCABULARY

Academic Vocabulary

- Acquire and use grade-appropriate academic vocabulary

Vocabulary Strategy

✓ Use context to determine the meaning of multiple-meaning words

CONTENT AREA LEARNING

Earth in Space and Time

- Distinguish among objects in the Solar System, including the Sun, Earth, planets, moons, asteroids, and comets, and discuss their interactions. **Science**

Scientists and the History of Science

- Connect grade-level-appropriate science concepts with the history of science, science careers, and contributions of scientists. **Science**

ELL Scaffolded supports for English Language Learners are embedded throughout the lessons, enabling students to communicate information, ideas, and concepts in English Language Arts and for social and instructional purposes within the school setting.

See the **ELL Small Group Guide** for additional support of the skills for the text set.

FORMATIVE ASSESSMENT

For assessment throughout the text set, use students' self-assessments and your observations.

Use the Data Dashboard to filter class, group, or individual student data to guide group placement decisions. It provides recommendations to enhance learning for gifted and talented students and offers extra support for students needing remediation.

Develop Student Ownership

To build student ownership, students need to know what they are learning and why they are learning it, and to determine how well they understood it.

Students Discuss Their Goals

READING

TEXT SET GOALS

- I can read and understand expository text.
- I can use text evidence to respond to expository text.
- I know how scientific knowledge changes over time.

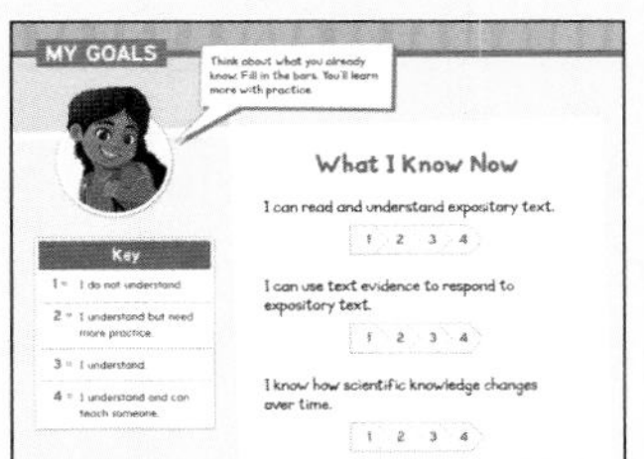

Have students think about what they know and fill in the bars on **Reading/Writing Companion** page 10.

WRITING

EXTENDED WRITING GOALS

Extended Writing 1:

- I can write a research report.
- I can write a personal narrative.

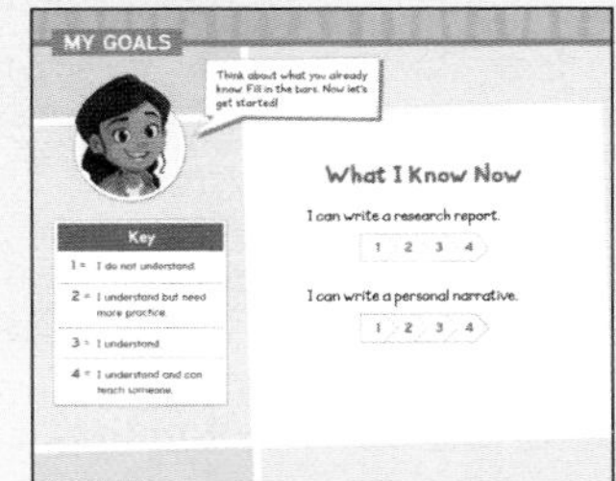

Have students think about what they know and fill in the bars on **Reading/Writing Companion** page 84.

Students Monitor Their Learning

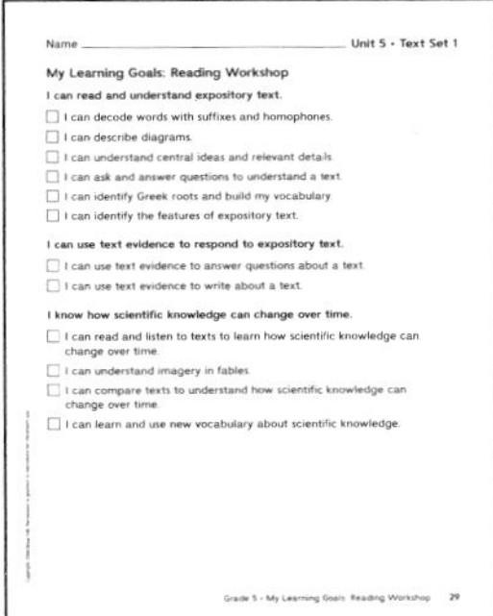

Name ______________________ Unit 5 • Text Set 1

My Learning Goals: Reading Workshop

I can read and understand expository text.

- ☐ I can decode words with suffixes and homophones.
- ☐ I can describe diagrams.
- ☐ I can understand central ideas and relevant details.
- ☐ I can ask and answer questions to understand a text.
- ☐ I can identify Greek roots and build my vocabulary.
- ☐ I can identify the features of expository text.

I can use text evidence to respond to expository text.

- ☐ I can use text evidence to answer questions about a text.
- ☐ I can use text evidence to write about a text.

I know how scientific knowledge can change over time.

- ☐ I can read and listen to texts to learn how scientific knowledge can change over time.
- ☐ I can understand imagery in fables.
- ☐ I can compare texts to understand how scientific knowledge can change over time.
- ☐ I can learn and use new vocabulary about scientific knowledge.

Grade 5 • My Learning Goals: Reading Workshop 29

LEARNING GOALS

Specific learning goals identified in every lesson make clear what students will be learning and why. These smaller goals provide stepping stones to help students reach their Text Set and Extended Writing Goals.

CHECK-IN ROUTINE

The Check-In Routine at the close of each lesson guides students to self-reflect on how well they understood each learning goal.

Review the lesson learning goal.
Reflect on the activity.
Self-Assess by

- filling in the bars in the **Reading/Writing Companion**
- holding up 1, 2, 3, or 4 fingers

Share with your teacher.

Students Reflect on Their Progress

READING

TEXT SET GOALS

After completing the Show Your Knowledge task for the text set, students reflect on their understanding of the Text Set Goals by filling in the bars on **Reading/Writing Companion** page 11.

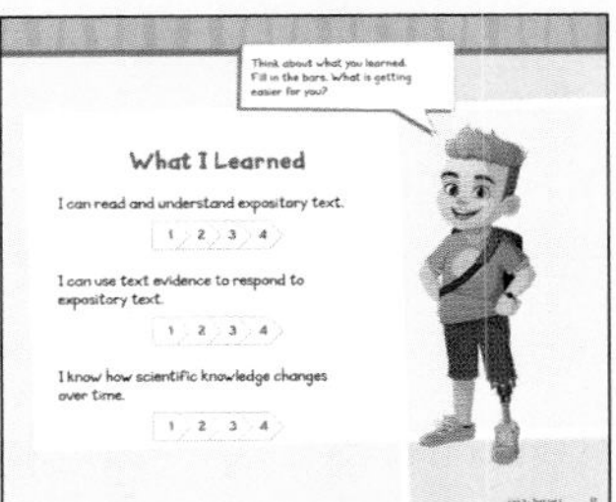

WRITING

EXTENDED WRITING GOALS

After completing their extended writing projects, students reflect on their understanding of the Extended Writing Goals by filling in the bars on **Reading/Writing Companion** page 85.

Build Knowledge

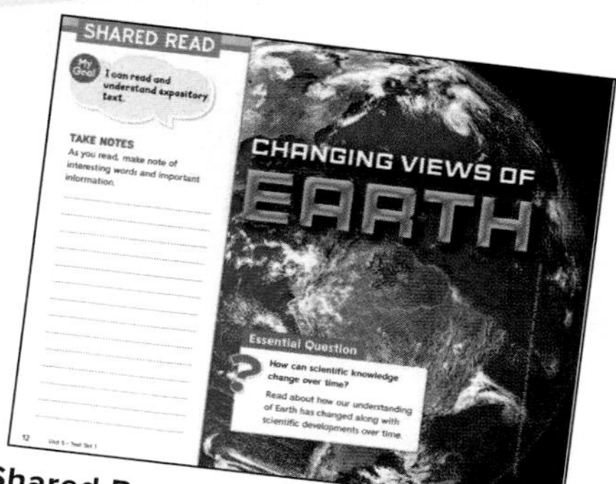

Shared Read
Reading/Writing Companion p. 12

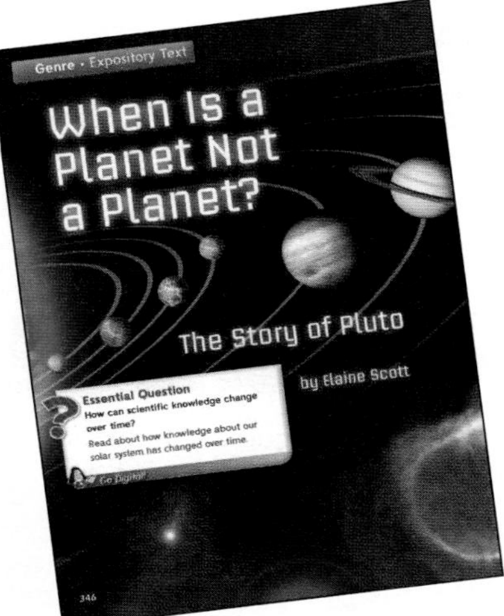

Anchor Text
Literature Anthology p. 346

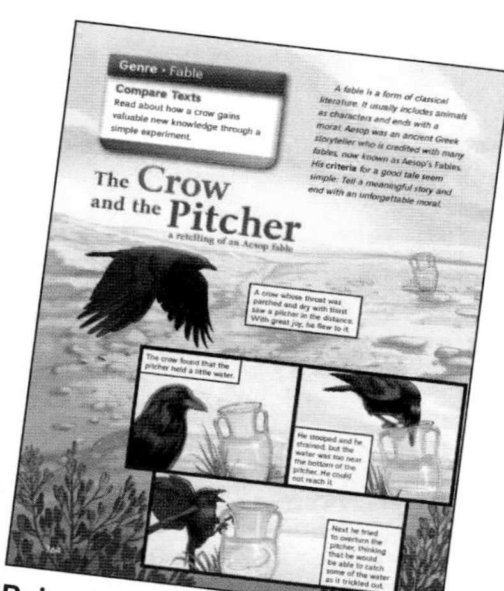

Paired Selection
Literature Anthology p. 364

Essential Question

How can scientific knowledge change over time? 

Video Scientific knowledge has improved over time. Microscopes and telescopes can now reveal the complexities of caterpillar feet and the sun in action.

Study Sync Blast Satellites have changed since Russia launched *Sputnik I* in 1957. Today satellites beam TV and telephone signals to different locations. Satellites have strengthened the economy and improved life on Earth.

Interactive Read Aloud People used to believe that the Sun revolved around the Earth. But as technology progressed, we learned that the Sun is the center of our solar system.

Shared Read Scientists used kites and balloons in the 1700s to gain knowledge of the Earth. In the 1900s, they used airplanes and radio technology. By the late 20th century, they used satellites and astronauts to gather increasingly complex information about Earth and space.

Anchor Text Science changes as new information is revealed. Discoveries about Pluto challenged our old ideas about the solar system and our definition of a planet.

Paired Selection An old fable has a fresh message: In a life-threatening situation, you must invent if you want to survive.

Make Connections A painting of a comet in 1858 helps to inspire people to learn and understand more about the night sky.

Differentiated Sources

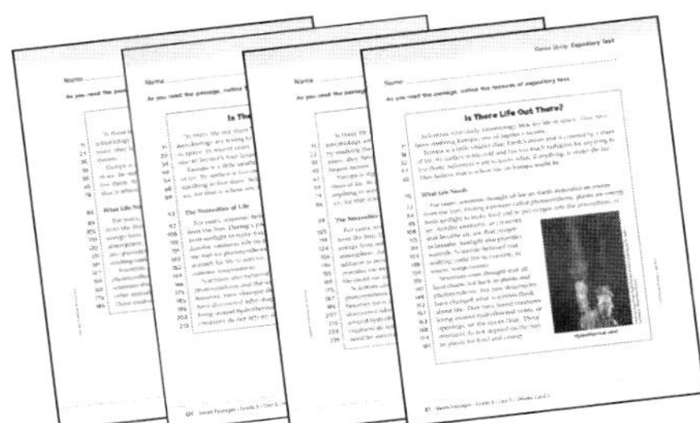

Leveled Readers

For centuries, astronomers have studied Mars. Telescopes, space probes, landers, and rovers have improved over time, allowing them to see more details and revise their conclusions about the red planet.

Differentiated Genre Passages

Scientists used to think that food supplies of living things depended on plants and photosynthesis. They later found that living things near hydrothermal vents did not need plants or sunlight for food.

Build Knowledge Routine

After reading each text, ask students to document what facts and details they learned to help answer the Essential Question of the text set.

Talk About the source.

Write About the source.

Add to the Class Anchor Chart.

- Add to your Vocabulary List.

Show Your Knowledge

Write a Report

Have students show how they built knowledge across the text set by writing a report. Have them start by thinking about the Essential Question: *How can scientific knowledge change over time?* Students will write a report about the importance of conducting experiments or improving technology even when something has been proven.

Social Emotional Learning

Logic and Reasoning

Anchor Text: Students must have strong reasoning skills to be able to think critically and make decisions. Ask: *What caused astronomers to question how to define a planet?* Have students list the reasons found in the text that Pluto is no longer considered a planet.

Paired Selection: Students can work to develop their own problem-solving processes. Ask: *How did thinking about the problem logically help the crow?*

Roundtable Discussion: Guide students in comparing and contrasting how logic and reasoning apply to *When Is a Planet Not a Planet?* and "The Crow and the Pitcher." Ask: *How do logic and reasoning affect the way we solve problems and explain the world around us?*

Explore the Texts

Essential Question: How can scientific knowledge change over time?

ACT — Access Complex Text (ACT) boxes throughout the text set provide scaffolded instruction for seven different elements that may make a text complex.

Teacher's Edition	Reading/Writing Companion	Literature Anthology	
	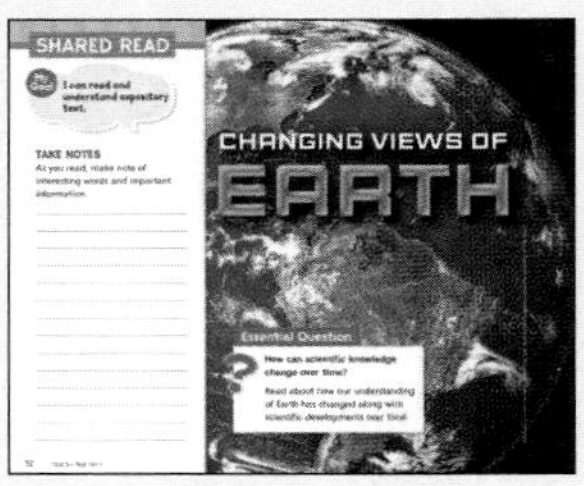		
"The Sun: Our Star" Interactive Read Aloud p. T7 Expository Text	**"Changing Views of Earth"** Shared Read pp. 12–15 Expository Text	***When Is a Planet Not a Planet?*** Anchor Text pp. 346–361 Expository Text	**"The Crow and the Pitcher"** Paired Selection pp. 364–365 Fable
Qualitative			
Meaning/Purpose Moderate Complexity **Structure** Moderate Complexity **Language** Moderate Complexity **Knowledge Demands** Moderate Complexity	**Meaning/Purpose** Moderate Complexity **Structure** Moderate Complexity **Language** Moderate Complexity **Knowledge Demands** Moderate Complexity	**Meaning/Purpose** Moderate Complexity **Structure** Moderate Complexity **Language** Moderate Complexity **Knowledge Demands** Moderate Complexity	**Meaning/Purpose** Moderate Complexity **Structure** Moderate Complexity **Language** Low Complexity **Knowledge Demands** High Complexity
Quantitative			
Lexile 900L	**Lexile** 910L	**Lexile** 980L	**Lexile** 640L
Reader and Task Considerations			
Reader Students would benefit with background knowledge about evolving ideas about the Sun, from ancient civilizations to today.	**Reader** Students will benefit from background on how scientific advances over time have helped meteorologists predict weather.	**Reader** Language and structure will be most challenging. Explain that authors sometimes omit subjects; discuss constructions and complex sentences.	**Reader** Students will not need background knowledge to understand the story.

Task The questions for the read aloud are supported by teacher modeling. The tasks provide a variety of ways for students to begin to build knowledge and vocabulary about the text set topic. The questions and tasks provided for the other texts are at various levels of complexity, ensuring that all students can interact with the text in meaningful ways.

Additional Texts

Classroom Library

The Black Hole Is NOT a Hole
Genre: Expository
Lexile: 900L

The Mighty Mars Rover
Genre: Expository
Lexile: 950L

See **Classroom Library Lessons**

Content Area Reading BLMs

Additional online texts related to grade-level Science, Social Studies, and Arts content

Leveled Readers

(A) ***Mars***	(O) ***Mars***	(B) ***Mars***	(ELL) ***Mars***
Qualitative			
Meaning/Purpose Low Complexity	**Meaning/Purpose** Low Complexity	**Meaning/Purpose** Low Complexity	**Meaning/Purpose** Low Complexity
Structure Moderate Complexity	**Structure** Moderate Complexity	**Structure** Moderate Complexity	**Structure** Moderate Complexity
Language Low Complexity	**Language** Moderate Complexity	**Language** Moderate Complexity	**Language** Low Complexity
Knowledge Demands Moderate Complexity	**Knowledge Demands Moderate Complexity**	**Knowledge Demands Moderate Complexity**	**Knowledge Demands Moderate Complexity**
Quantitative			
Lexile 700L	**Lexile** 900L	**Lexile** 970L	**Lexile** 700L
Reader and Task Considerations			
Reader Students should have some background knowledge of the solar system.	**Reader** Students should have some background knowledge of the solar system.	**Reader** Students should have some background knowledge of the solar system.	**Reader** Students should have some background knowledge of the solar system.

Task The questions and tasks provided for the Leveled Readers are at various levels of complexity, ensuring that all students can interact with the text in meaningful ways.

Differentiated Genre Passages

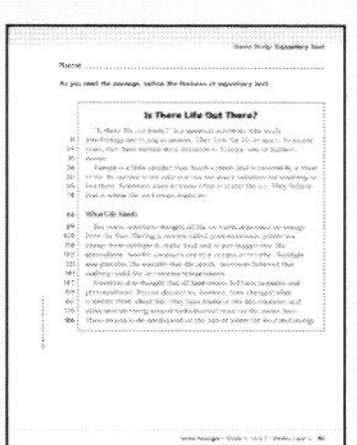
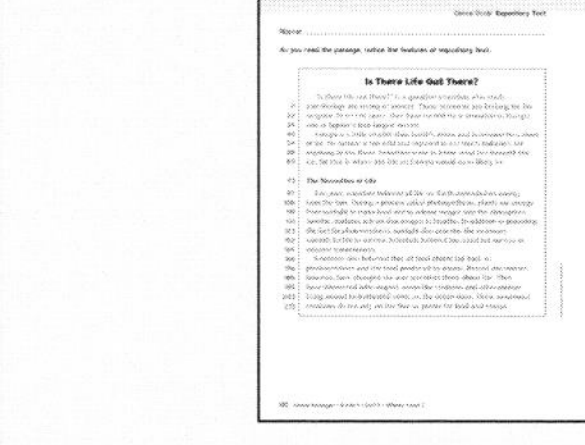
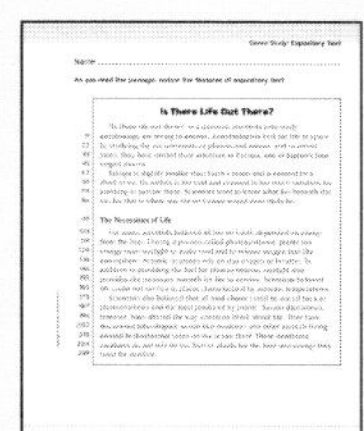
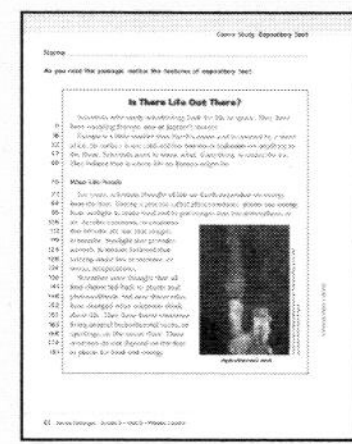

(A) "Is There Life Out There?"	(O) "Is There Life Out There?"	(B) "Is There Life Out There?"	(ELL) "Is There Life Out There?"
Qualitative			
Meaning/Purpose Moderate Complexity	**Meaning/Purpose** Moderate Complexity	**Meaning/Purpose** Moderate Complexity	**Meaning/Purpose** Moderate Complexity
Structure Moderate Complexity	**Structure** Moderate Complexity	**Structure** Moderate Complexity	**Structure** Moderate Complexity
Language Low Complexity	**Language** Low Complexity	**Language** Moderate Complexity	**Language** Low Complexity
Knowledge Demands Moderate Complexity	**Knowledge Demands** Moderate Complexity	**Knowledge Demands** High Complexity	**Knowledge Demands** Low Complexity
Quantitative			
Lexile 790L	**Lexile** 910L	**Lexile** 990L	**Lexile** 850L
Reader and Task Considerations			
Reader Students should have some background knowledge of the necessities to support human life on a planet.	**Reader** Students should have some background knowledge of the necessities to support human life on a planet.	**Reader** Students should have some background knowledge of the necessities to support human life on a planet.	**Reader** Students should have some background knowledge of the necessities to support human life on a planet.

Task The questions and tasks provided for the Differentiated Genre Passages are at various levels of complexity, ensuring that all students can interact with the text in meaningful ways.

Week 1 Planner

Customize your own lesson plans at **my.mheducation.com**

READING LESSON GOALS

- **I can read and understand expository text.**
- **I can use text evidence to respond to expository text.**
- **I know how scientific knowledge changes over time.**

SMALL GROUP OPTIONS The designated lessons can be taught in small groups. To determine how to differentiate instruction for small groups, use Formative Assessment and Data Dashboard.

Reading

Lesson 1	Lesson 2
Introduce the Concept, T4–T5 Build Knowledge **Listening Comprehension, T6–T7** "The Sun: Our Star" **Shared Read, T8–T11** Read "Changing Views of Earth" Quick Write: Summarize **Vocabulary, T12–T13** Academic Vocabulary Greek Roots **Expand Vocabulary, T56**	**Shared Read, T8–T11** Reread "Changing Views of Earth" **Minilessons, T14–T21** Ask and Answer Questions Text Features: Diagrams Central Idea and Relevant Details Craft and Structure **Respond to Reading, T22–T23** **Phonics, T24–T25** Suffixes **Fluency, T25** Expression **Research and Inquiry, T26–T27** **Expand Vocabulary, T56**

WRITING LESSON GOALS

I can write a research report.

Writing

Lesson 1	Lesson 2
Extended Writing 1: Research Report	
Writing Lesson Bank: Craft Minilessons, T260–T263	
Teacher and Peer Conferences	
Grammar Lesson Bank, T266 Clauses Talk About It **Spelling Lesson Bank, T276** Suffixes	**Grammar Lesson Bank, T266** Clauses Talk About It **Spelling Lesson Bank, T276** Suffixes

SMALL GROUP

Teacher-Led Instruction

Differentiated Reading

Leveled Readers
- *Mars,* T58–T59
- *Mars,* T68–T69
- *Mars,* T74–T75

Differentiated Skills Practice

Approaching Level
Phonics/Decoding, T62
- Decode Words with Suffixes (Tier 2)
- Practice Words with Suffixes

Vocabulary, T64
- Review High-Frequency Words (Tier 2)
- Review Academic Vocabulary (Tier 2)

Fluency, T66
- Expression (Tier 2)

Comprehension, T66–T67
- Central Idea and Relevant Details (Tier 2)
- Self-Selected Reading

Independent/Collaborative Work See pages T3I–T3J.

Reading

Comprehension
- Expository Text
- Central Idea and Relevant Details
- Ask and Answer Questions

Fluency
Independent Reading

Phonics/Word Study

Phonics/Decoding
- Suffixes

Vocabulary
- Greek Roots

Writing

Extended Writing 1: Research Report
Self-Selected Writing
Grammar
- Clauses

Spelling
- Suffixes

Handwriting

ACADEMIC VOCABULARY
approximately, astronomical, calculation, criteria, diameter, evaluate, orbit, spheres

SPELLING
serious, furious, eruption, usually, direction, position, forgetful, comfortable, finally, destruction, apparently, completely, eventually, carefully, microscopic, allergic, scientific, safety, activity, sickness

Review *distance, ambulance, substance*
Challenge *aquatic, mathematics*
See pages T276–T277 for Differentiated Spelling Lists.

Reading

Lesson 3	Lesson 4	Lesson 5
Anchor Text, T28–T45 Read *When Is a Planet Not a Planet?* Take Notes About Text **Expand Vocabulary, T57**	**Anchor Text, T28–T45** Read *When Is a Planet Not a Planet?* Take Notes About Text **Expand Vocabulary, T57**	**Anchor Text, T28–T45** Reread *When Is a Planet Not a Planet?* **Expand Vocabulary, T57**

Writing

Lesson 3	Lesson 4	Lesson 5
	Extended Writing 1, T228–T229 Expert Model	**Extended Writing 1, T230–T231** Plan: Choose Your Topic
Writing Lesson Bank: Craft Minilessons, T260–T263		
Teacher and Peer Conferences		
Grammar Lesson Bank, T267 Clauses Talk About It **Spelling Lesson Bank, T277** Suffixes	**Grammar Lesson Bank, T267** Clauses Talk About It **Spelling Lesson Bank, T277** Suffixes	**Grammar Lesson Bank, T267** Clauses Talk About It **Spelling Lesson Bank, T277** Suffixes

On Level
Vocabulary, T72
- Review Academic Vocabulary
- Greek Roots

Comprehension, T73
- Review Central Idea and Relevant Details
- Self-Selected Reading

Beyond Level
Vocabulary, T78
- Review Domain-Specific Words
- Greek Roots

Comprehension, T79
- Review Central Idea and Relevant Details
- Self-Selected Reading 

English Language Learners
See ELL Small Group Guide, pp. 186–197

Content Area Connections

Content Area Reading
- Science, Social Studies, and the Arts

Research and Inquiry
- Scientific Knowledge Grows

Inquiry Space
- Options for Project-Based Learning

English Language Learners
See ELL Small Group Guide, pp. 186–197

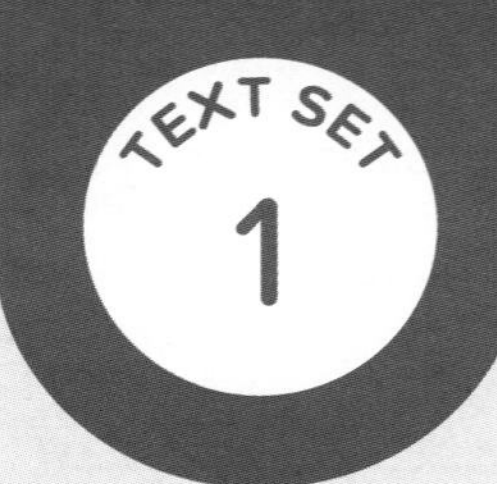

Week 2 Planner

Customize your own lesson plans at **my.mheducation.com**

Reading Suggested Daily Time (60+ mins)

READING LESSON GOALS

- **I can read and understand expository text.**
- **I can use text evidence to respond to expository text.**
- **I know how scientific knowledge changes over time.**

SMALL GROUP OPTIONS The designated lessons can be taught in small groups. To determine how to differentiate instruction for small groups, use Formative Assessment and Data Dashboard.

Writing Suggested Daily Time (30+ mins)

WRITING LESSON GOALS

I can write a research report.

	Lesson 6	Lesson 7
Reading	**Anchor Text, T28–T45** Reread *When Is a Planet Not a Planet?* **Respond to Reading, T46–T47** **Expand Vocabulary, T56**	**Paired Selection, T48–T49** Read "The Crow and the Pitcher" **Expand Vocabulary, T56**
Writing	**Extended Writing 1, T230–T231** Plan: Choose Your Topic	**Extended Writing 1, T232–T233** Plan: Relevant Evidence
	Writing Lesson Bank: Craft Minilessons, T260–T263	
	Teacher and Peer Conferences	
	Grammar Lesson Bank, T268 Complex Sentences Talk About It **Spelling Lesson Bank, T278** Homophones	**Grammar Lesson Bank, T268** Complex Sentences Talk About It **Spelling Lesson Bank, T278** Homophones

Teacher-Led Instruction

Differentiated Reading

Differentiated Genre Passages
- "Is There Life Out There?," T60–T61
- "Is There Life Out There?," T70–T71
- "Is There Life Out There?," T76–T77

Differentiated Skills Practice

Approaching Level

Phonics/Decoding, T63
- Decode Words with Homophones (Tier 2)
- Practice Words with Homophones

Vocabulary, T65
- Identify Related Words
- Greek Roots

Fluency, T66
- Accuracy and Phrasing 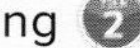

Comprehension, T67
- Review Central Idea and Relevant Details
- Self-Selected Reading

Independent/Collaborative Work See pages T3I–T3J.

Reading

Comprehension
- Expository Text
- Central Idea and Relevant Details
- Ask and Answer Questions

Fluency

Independent Reading

Phonics/Word Study

Phonics/Decoding
- Homophones

Vocabulary
- Greek Roots

Writing

Extended Writing 1: Research Report

Self-Selected Writing

Grammar
- Complex Sentences

Spelling
- Homophones

Handwriting

ACADEMIC VOCABULARY
approximately, astronomical, calculation, criteria, diameter, evaluate, orbit, spheres

SPELLING
sweet, suite, pray, prey, poll, pole, waste, waist, manor, manner, pier, peer, currant, current, presence, presents, council, counsel, stationery, stationary

Review *eruption, forgetful, allergic*
Challenge *kernel, colonel*
See pages T278–T279 for Differentiated Spelling Lists.

 LESSON 8	 LESSON 9	 LESSON 10
Reading		
Paired Selection, T48–T49 Reread "The Crow and the Pitcher" **Author's Craft, T50–T51** Figurative Language: Imagery **Phonics, T52–T53** Homophones **Expand Vocabulary, T57**	**Fluency, T53** Accuracy and Phrasing **Make Connections, T54** **Expand Vocabulary, T57**	**Show Your Knowledge, T55** **Progress Monitoring, T3K–T3L** **Expand Vocabulary, T57**
Writing		
Extended Writing 1, T232–T233 Plan: Relevant Evidence	**Extended Writing 1, T234–T235** Draft: Elaboration	**Extended Writing 1, T234–T235** Draft: Elaboration
Writing Lesson Bank: Craft Minilessons, T260–T263		
Teacher and Peer Conferences		
Grammar Lesson Bank, T269 Complex Sentences Talk About It **Spelling Lesson Bank, T279** Homophones	**Grammar Lesson Bank, T269** Complex Sentences Talk About It **Spelling Lesson Bank, T279** Homophones	**Grammar Lesson Bank, T269** Complex Sentences Talk About It **Spelling Lesson Bank, T279** Homophones

On Level
Vocabulary, T72
- Review Academic Vocabulary
- Greek Roots

Comprehension, T73
- Review Central Idea and Relevant Details
- Self-Selected Reading

Beyond Level
Vocabulary, T78
- Review Domain-Specific Words
- Greek Roots

Comprehension, T79
- Review Central Idea and Relevant Details
- Self-Selected Reading GIFTED and TALENTED

English Language Learners
See ELL Small Group Guide, pp. 186–197

Content Area Connections

Content Area Reading
- Science, Social Studies, and the Arts

Research and Inquiry
- Scientific Knowledge Grows

Inquiry Space
- Options for Project-Based Learning

English Language Learners
See ELL Small Group Guide, pp. 186–197

Independent and Collaborative Work

As you meet with small groups, the rest of the class completes activities and projects that allow them to practice and apply the skills they have been working on.

Student Choice and Student Voice

- Print the My Independent Work blackline master and review it with students. Identify the "Must Do" activities.
- Have students choose additional activities that provide the practice they need.
- Remind students to reflect on their learning each day.

Name ______ Unit 5 • Text Set 1

My Independent Work

	Reading	Phonics/Word Study	Writing
Center Activity Cards	Card: Activity:	Card: Activity:	Card: Activity:
Digital Activities my.mheducation.com	Activity:	Activity:	Activity:
Practice Pages	Content Area Reading:	Practice:	Practice:
Independent Choices	Independent Reading:	Activity:	Self-Selected Writing:

Grade 5 • My Independent Work 33

My Independent Work BLM

Reading

Independent Reading Texts

Students can choose a Center Activity Card to use while they read independently.

Classroom Library
A Black Hole Is NOT a Hole
Genre: Expository Text
Lexile: 900L

The Mighty Mars Rovers: The Incredible Adventures of Spirit and Opportunity
Genre: Expository Text
Lexile: 950L

Unit Bibliography
Have students self-select independent reading texts about scientific knowledge.

Leveled Texts Online
- Additional Leveled Readers in the **Leveled Reader Library Online** allow for flexibility.
- Six leveled sets of **Differentiated Genre Passages** in diverse genres are available.
- **Differentiated Texts** offer ELL students more passages at different proficiency levels.

Additional Literature
Literature Anthology
Global Warming, pp. 392–405
Genre: Expository Text

"When Volcanoes Erupt," pp. 408–411
Genre: Expository Text

Center Activity Cards

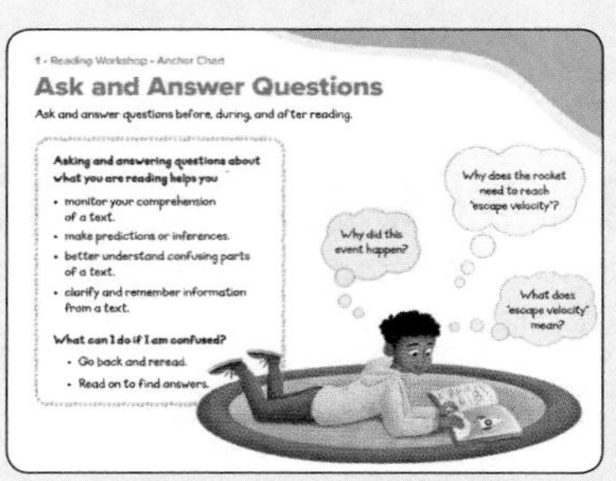

Ask and Answer Questions Card 1

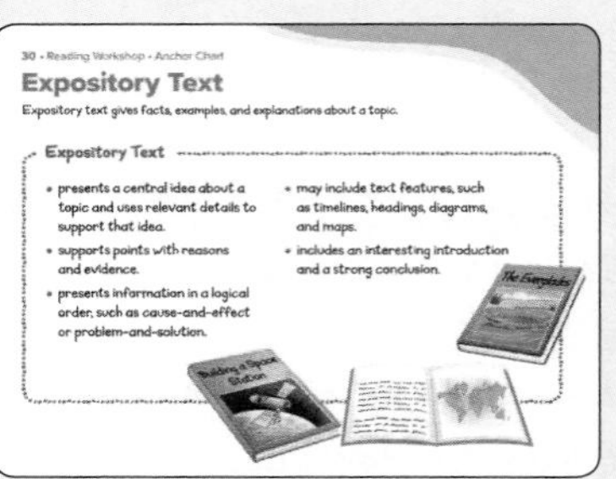

Expository Text Card 30

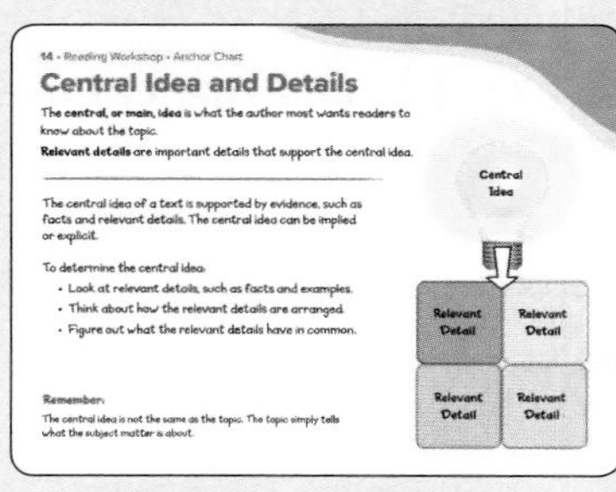

Central Idea and Details Card 14

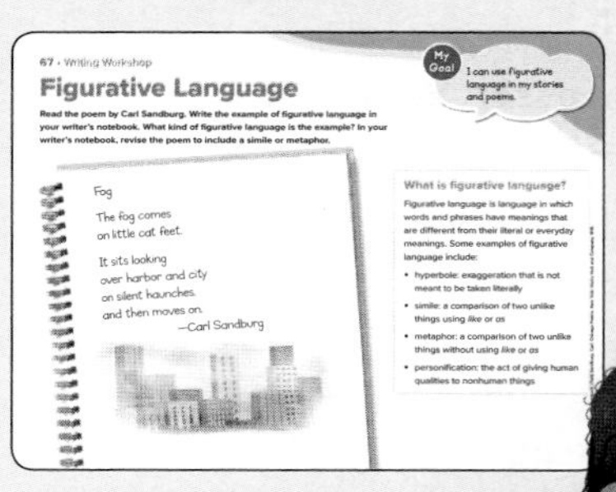

Figurative Language Card 67

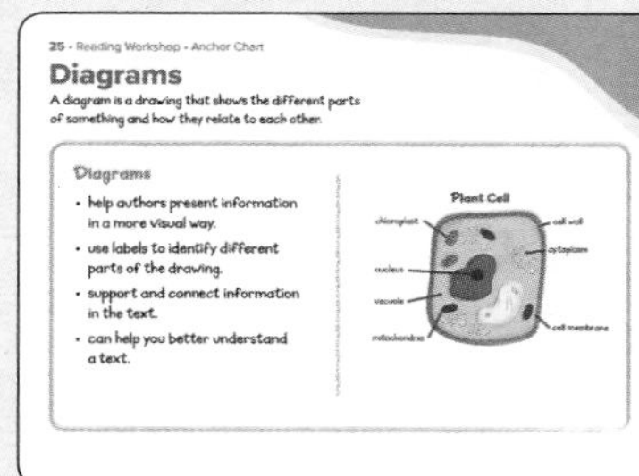

Diagrams Card 25

Digital Activities

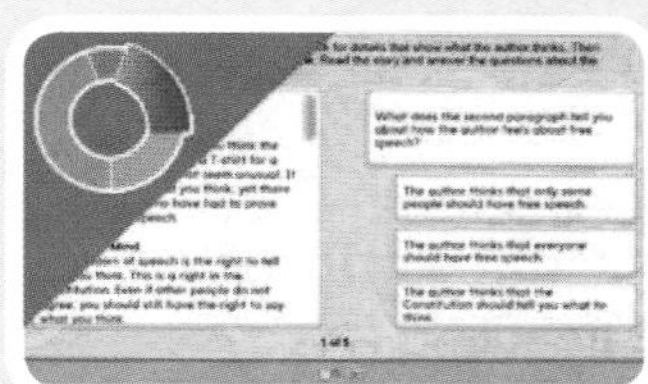

Comprehension

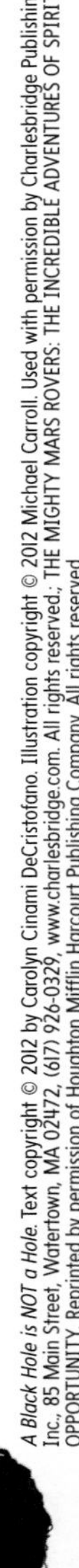

Phonics/Word Study

Center Activity Cards

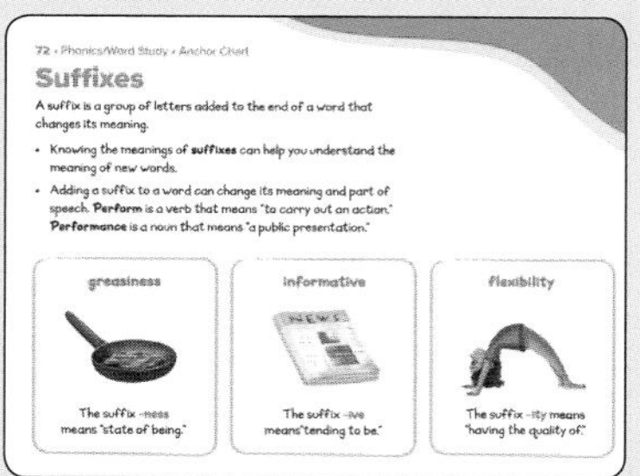
Suffixes Card 72

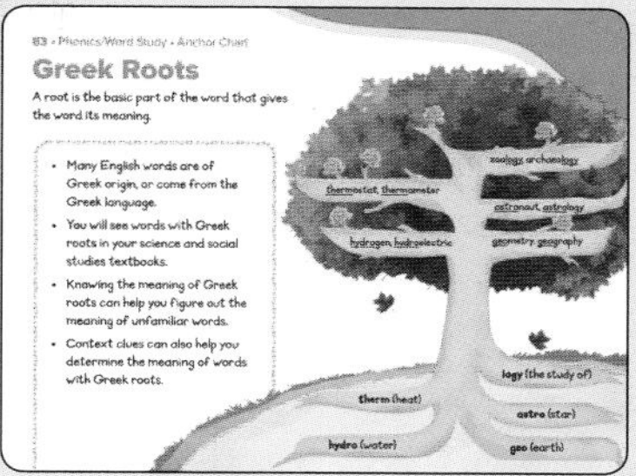
Greek Roots Card 83

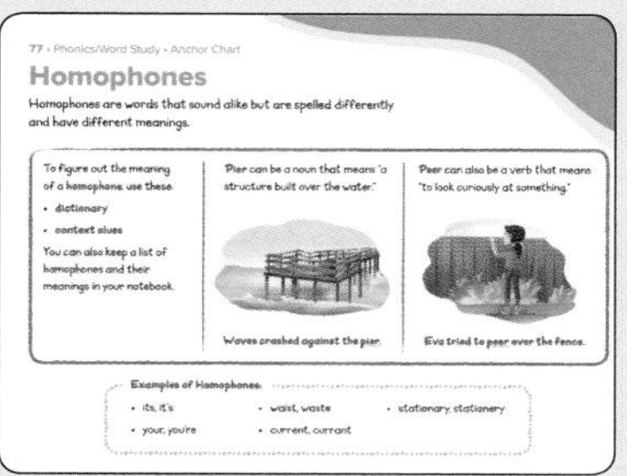
Homophones Card 77

Practice Book BLMs

Phonics: pages 247–247B, 250, 259–259B, 262

Vocabulary: pages 251–252, 263–264

Digital Activities

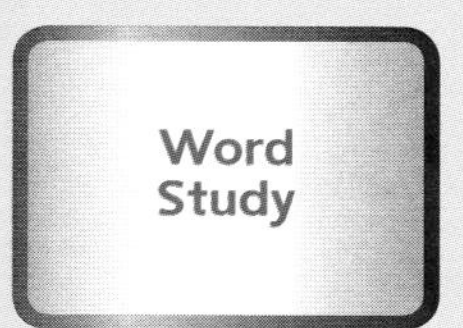

Phonics

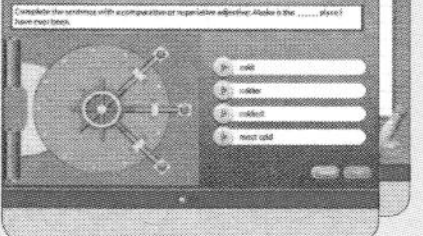
Vocabulary

Writing

Center Activity Cards

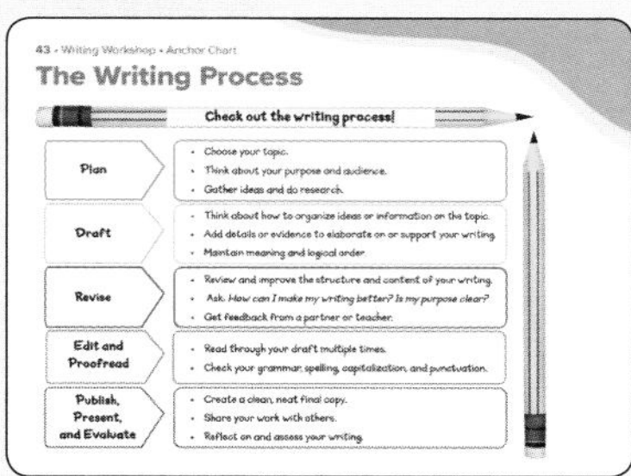
Writing Process Card 43

Research Report Card 46

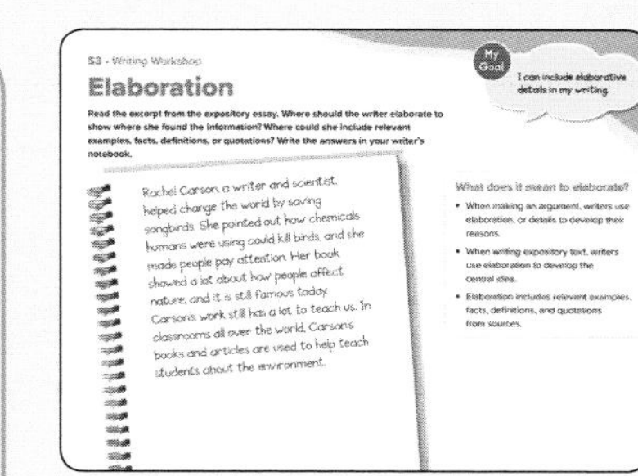
Elaboration Card 53

Self-Selected Writing

Share the following prompts.

- Describe the moon using descriptive words and metaphors.
- Explain some of the challenges that might be faced when exploring another planet.
- Write about a kid who lives in space. Describe the gadgets on his or her spacecraft.

Extended Writing

Have students continue developing their **research reports**.

Practice Book BLMs

Grammar: pages 241–245, 253–257
Spelling: pages 246–250, 258–262
Handwriting: pages 361–396

Digital Activities

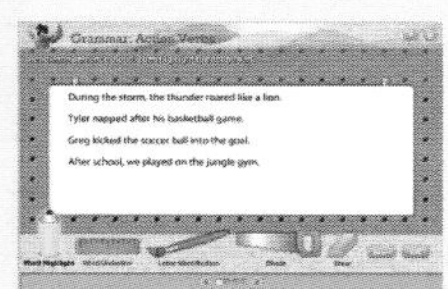
Grammar

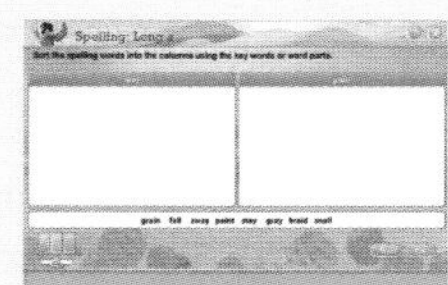
Spelling

Content Area Connections

Content Area Reading Blackline Masters
- Additional texts related to Science, Social Studies, and the Arts

Research and Inquiry
- Scientific Knowledge Grows

Inquiry Space
- Choose an activity

Progress Monitoring

Moving Toward Mastery

FORMATIVE ASSESSMENT
STUDENT CHECK-IN
CHECK FOR SUCCESS

For ongoing formative assessment, use students' self-assessments at the end of each lesson along with your own observations.

Assessing skills along the way . . .

SKILLS	HOW ASSESSED
Comprehension **Vocabulary**	Digital Activities, Rubrics
Text-Based Writing	Reading/Writing Companion: Respond to Reading
Grammar, Mechanics, Phonics, Spelling	Practice Book, Digital Activities including word sorts
Listening/Presenting/Research	Checklists
Oral Reading Fluency (ORF) Fluency Goal: 136–156 words correct per minute (WCPM) Accuracy Rate Goal: 95% or higher	Fluency Assessment

At the end of the text set . . .

SKILLS	HOW ASSESSED
Text Features: Diagrams **Central Idea and Relevant Details** **Figurative Language: Imagery**	Progress Monitoring
Greek Roots	

Making the Most of Assessment Results

Make data-based grouping decisions by using the following reports to verify assessment results. For additional student support options refer to the reteaching and enrichment opportunities.

ONLINE ASSESSMENT CENTER

- ***Gradebook***

DATA DASHBOARD

- ***Recommendations Report***
- ***Activity Report***
- ***Skills Report***
- ***Progress Report***
- ***Grade Card Report***

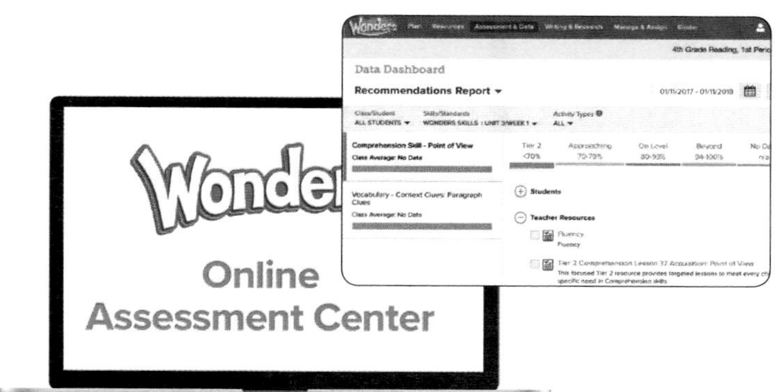

 Assign practice pages online for auto-grading.

TIER 2

Reteaching Opportunities with Intervention Online PDFs

IF STUDENTS SCORE . . .	THEN ASSIGN . . .
below 70% in **comprehension** . . .	lesson 150 on Using Diagrams in **Comprehension PDF.** lessons 55–57 on Central Idea and Details in **Comprehension PDF,** and/or lesson 128 on Imagery in **Comprehension PDF**
below 70% in **vocabulary** . . .	lesson 109 on Greek, Latin, and Other Roots in **Vocabulary PDF**
127–135 WCPM in **fluency** . . .	lessons from Section 1 or 7–10 of **Fluency PDF**
0–126 WCPM in **fluency** . . .	lessons from Sections 2–6 of **Fluency PDF**

Use the* Phonics/Word Study PDF *and* Foundational Skills Kit *for additional reteaching opportunities. Use the* Foundational Skills Kit *for students who need support with phonemic awareness and other early literacy skills.

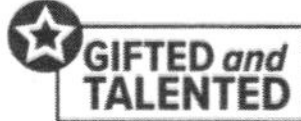

Enrichment Opportunities

Beyond Level small group lessons and resources include suggestions for additional activities in these areas to extend learning opportunities for gifted and talented students:

- ***Leveled Readers***
- ***Genre Passages***
- ***Vocabulary***
- ***Comprehension***
- ***Leveled Reader Library Online***
- ***Center Activity Cards***

OBJECTIVES

Engage effectively in a range of collaborative discussions (one-on-one, in groups, and teacher-led) with diverse partners, building on others' ideas and expressing their own clearly.

Come to discussions prepared, having read or studied required material; explicitly draw on that preparation and other information known about the topic to explore ideas under discussion.

Build background knowledge on changes in scientific knowledge.

ELA ACADEMIC LANGUAGE

- *ideas, knowledge, narrate, discuss*
- Cognates: *ideas, narrar, discutir*

DIGITAL TOOLS

Show the image during class discussion.

Discuss Concept

Watch Video

 **VOCABULARY**

research (*investigar*) to search for new information

technology (*tecnología*) machines or methods that are created to make life easier

evaluate (*evaluar*) to judge the worth of something

submersible (*submarino*) a type of underwater machine

Build Knowledge

Build Knowledge

How can scientific knowledge change over time?

Read the Essential Question on **Reading/Writing Companion** page 8. Explain that students will read expository texts that focus on scientific ideas and build knowledge about how these ideas have changed. They will use words to read, write, and talk about how scientific knowledge changes over time.

Watch the Video Play the video without sound first. Have partners narrate what they see. Then replay the video with sound as students listen.

Talk About the Video Have partners discuss how scientific knowledge changes over time.

Write About the Video Have students add their ideas to the Build Knowledge pages of their reader's notebooks.

Anchor Chart Begin a Build Knowledge anchor chart. Have volunteers share what they learned about how scientific knowledge changes over time. Record their ideas. Explain that students will add to the anchor chart after they read each text.

Build Knowledge

Then discuss the photograph of the deep sea submersible. Ask: *How can technology and new scientific discoveries change our understanding of a subject?* Have students discuss in pairs or groups.

Build Vocabulary

Model using the graphic organizer to write down words related to changes in scientific knowledge. Have partners continue the discussion and add the graphic organizer and new words to their reader's notebooks. Students will add words to the Build Knowledge pages in their notebooks as they read about how scientific knowledge changes throughout the text set.

Collaborative Conversations

Add New Ideas As students engage in partner, small-group, and whole-class discussions, encourage them to add personal contributions after listening and considering others' viewpoints. Remind students to

- connect their own ideas to things peers have said.
- make connections to personal experiences, ideas in texts, and society.
- generate questions before, during, and after discussions.

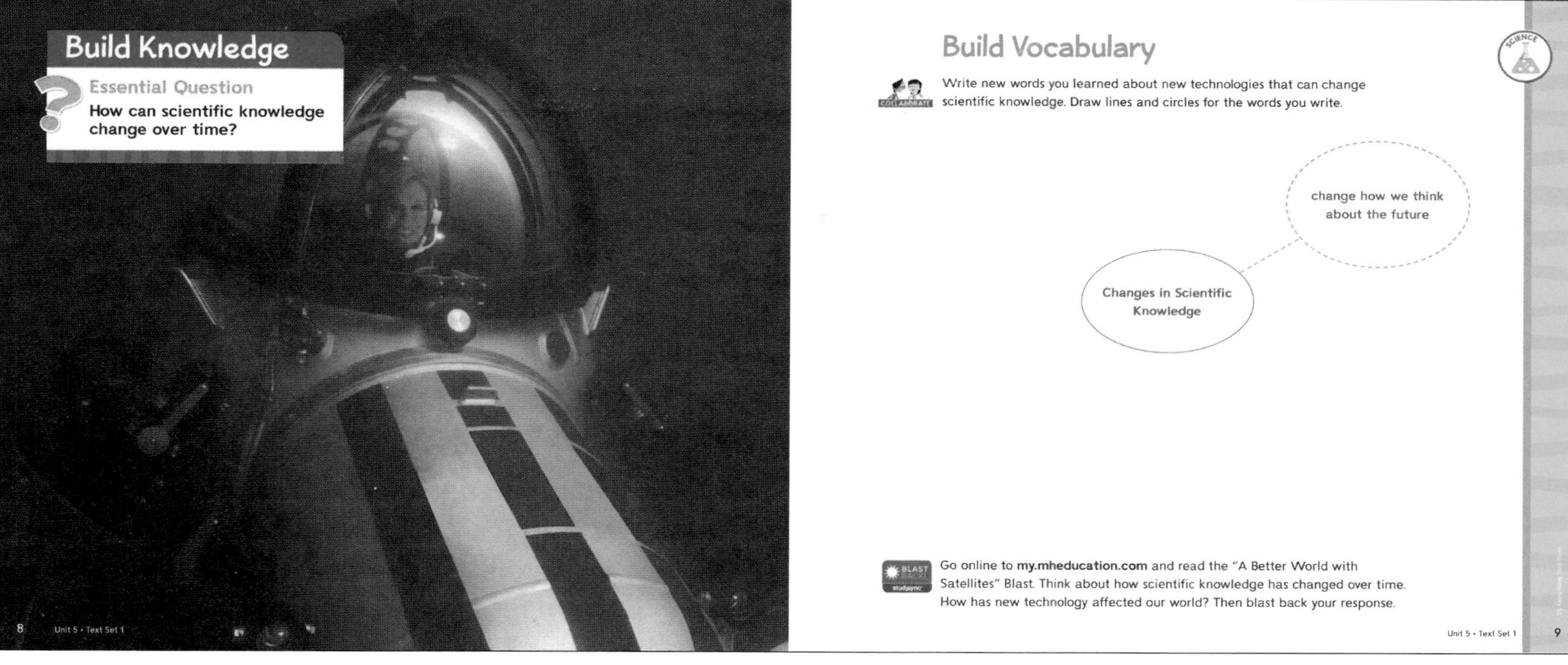

Build Knowledge
Essential Question
How can scientific knowledge change over time?
Build Vocabulary
Write new words you learned about new technologies that can change scientific knowledge. Draw lines and circles for the words you write.
change how we think about the future
Changes in Scientific Knowledge
Go online to my.mheducation.com and read the "A Better World with Satellites" Blast. Think about how scientific knowledge has changed over time. How has new technology affected our world? Then blast back your response.

Reading/Writing Companion, pp. 8–9

Share the Blast assignment, "A Better World with Satellites," with students. Point out that you will discuss their responses in the Make Connections lesson at the end of this text set.

English Language Learners

Use the following scaffolds to build knowledge and vocabulary. Teach the ELL Vocabulary, as needed.

Beginning

Describe the photograph of the submersible with students. Say: *Scientists use technology to research and learn more about a subject. What technology does the scientist in the photo use?* (a submersible) Help partners generate a list of words and phrases to describe how technology can help the scientist. Then have them respond using: Technology can help the scientist learn more about the ocean.

Intermediate

Use the photograph to talk about the submersible with students. Elicit that scientists use technology to research and learn more about a subject. Have partners generate a list of words and phrases to describe how technology can help the scientist in the photo and respond using: New technology can help the scientist _______.

Advanced/Advanced High

Discuss the photo with students. Have pairs describe how technology, such as the submersible, can help scientists learn more about a subject, using the terms *technology* and *research.* Then have them complete the graphic organizer.

NEWCOMER

To help students develop oral language and build vocabulary, use **Newcomer Cards 5–9** and the accompanying materials in the **Newcomer Teacher's Guide**. For thematic connection, use **Newcomer Cards 6** and **16** with the accompanying materials.

MY GOALS ROUTINE

What I Know Now

Read Goals Have students read the goals on Reading/Writing Companion page 10.

Reflect Review the key. Ask students to reflect on each goal and fill in the bars to show what they know now. Explain they will fill in the bars on page 11 at the end of the text set to show their progress.

LEARNING GOALS

We can actively listen to learn how scientific knowledge changes over time.

OBJECTIVES

Summarize a written text read aloud or information presented in diverse media and formats, including visually, quantitatively, and orally.

Use common, grade-appropriate Greek and Latin affixes and roots as clues to the meaning of a word.

Listen for a purpose.

Identify characteristics of expository text.

ELA ACADEMIC LANGUAGE

- *expository text, summarize*
- Cognate: *texto expositivo*

DIGITAL TOOLS

Read or play the Interactive Read Aloud.

Interactive Read Aloud

FORMATIVE ASSESSMENT

STUDENT CHECK-IN

Have partners talk about how our scientific understanding of the sun has changed over time. Then ask them to reflect using the Check-In routine.

Interactive Read Aloud

Connect to Concept: Now We Know

Tell students that scientific knowledge about the world can change as we acquire new information. Let students know that you will be reading aloud a passage that shows how our knowledge of the Sun has changed from ancient times to the present.

Preview Expository Text

Anchor Chart Explain that the text you will read aloud is expository text. Have students add characteristics of the genre to their Expository Text anchor chart and encourage them to add to it as they read more expository texts. Discuss these features of expository text:

- presents information in a logical order
- supports points with reasons and evidence
- may include text features such as subheadings
- uses certain text structures to organize information

Ask students to think about other texts that you have read or they have read independently that were expository text.

Read and Respond

Read the text aloud to students. Then reread it using the Teacher Think Alouds and Student Think Alongs on page T7 to build knowledge and model comprehension and the vocabulary strategy Greek Roots.

Summarize Have students summarize the most important information from "The Sun: Our Star" in their own words. Remind them to summarize texts in ways that maintain meaning and logical order.

Build Knowledge: Make Connections

Talk About the Text Have partners discuss how scientific knowledge changes over time.

Write About the Text Have students add their ideas to their Build Knowledge pages of their reader's notebooks.

Anchor Chart Record any new ideas on the Build Knowledge anchor chart.

Add to the Vocabulary List Have students write down any words they learned about how scientific knowledge changes over time in their reader's notebooks.

The Sun: Our Star

The Sun is vital to life on Earth. It provides the heat and warmth humans and other living things depend on for survival. Throughout history, people have recognized the Sun's importance and sought to understand it. As technology has become more sophisticated, so has our knowledge of the Sun.

Old Beliefs

In ancient times, people held many different beliefs about the Sun. According to the Greek myths, the Sun was a blazing chariot that the god Helios drove across the sky. Ancient Egyptians believed the sun god, Ra, sailed in a ship. The Chinese believed there were ten different suns when the world began.

Over time, mathematicians and astronomers developed a variety of theories about the Sun. However, by about the twelfth century, most Europeans believed that the Sun revolved around Earth, and that Earth was a stationary body at the center of the universe. (1)

New Ideas

In the sixteenth century, a man named Copernicus proposed that the Earth revolved around the Sun. Less than a century later, another man, Galileo, invented a telescope more powerful than any before it. Based in part on what he observed using his telescope, Galileo declared that Copernicus was correct. Earth indeed orbited the Sun. This idea was so offensive to people that Galileo was forced to live under house arrest for the rest of his life. (2)

Continuing Research

Through observation and experimentation, our knowledge of the Sun has grown. New technologies have led to new discoveries. Today we know that the Sun is a star among billions of other stars in our galaxy. It is composed of burning gases, and it is about 93 million miles from Earth. The Sun's radiation provides us with light and heat.

While we have learned a great deal about the Sun, there is more to discover. Scientists continue to study the Sun—our special star. (3)

(1) Teacher Think Aloud

I know that many English words have Greek roots. In the section "Old Beliefs" I read about how according to Greek myths, Helios was a god who drove a chariot across the sky. The Greek root *helio* means "sun," so this explains how the sun god got his name.

Student Think Along

Listen for more words with the Greek roots *-logy, -scope,* and *tele-* as I continue reading the text. Turn and talk with a partner about how identifying these roots can help you define unfamiliar words.

(2) Teacher Think Aloud

Asking and answering questions as I read helps to clarify my understanding of a text. As I get to the end of this paragraph, I wonder: Why was Galileo put under house arrest? I can reread to find text evidence and answer my question.

Student Think Along

As I reread this paragraph, listen for the reason Galileo was put under house arrest. Raise your hand when you hear the answer. Then discuss how Galileo and Copernicus's new ideas changed people's understanding of the sun.

(3) Teacher Think Aloud

At the end of the last section, I wonder: Why are scientists still studying the sun even though we've already learned so much about it? I can reread to determine why. The conclusion explains that we continue to discover new things about the sun over time as our ideas and technology change.

Student Think Along

What questions do you have about the text? Write down your questions. Then share them with a partner. Discuss what you have learned about how scientific knowledge changes over time.

"Changing Views of Earth"

Lexile 910L

LEARNING GOALS

We can read and understand expository text.

OBJECTIVES

Quote accurately from a text when explaining what the text says explicitly and when drawing inferences from the text.

Identify the author's purpose.

Determine two or more central, or main, ideas of a text and explain how they are supported by relevant, or key details; summarize the text.

Connect grade-level-appropriate science concepts with the history of science, science careers, and contributions of scientists.

Close Reading Routine

Read DOK 1–2

- Identify important ideas and details.
- Take notes and summarize.
- Use ACT prompts as needed.

Reread DOK 2–3

- Analyze the text, craft, and structure.
- Use the **Reread minilessons** and **prompts.**

Integrate DOK 3–4

- Integrate knowledge and ideas.
- Make text-to-text connections.
- Use the Integrate lesson.
- Complete the Show Your Knowledge task.
- Inspire action.

Read

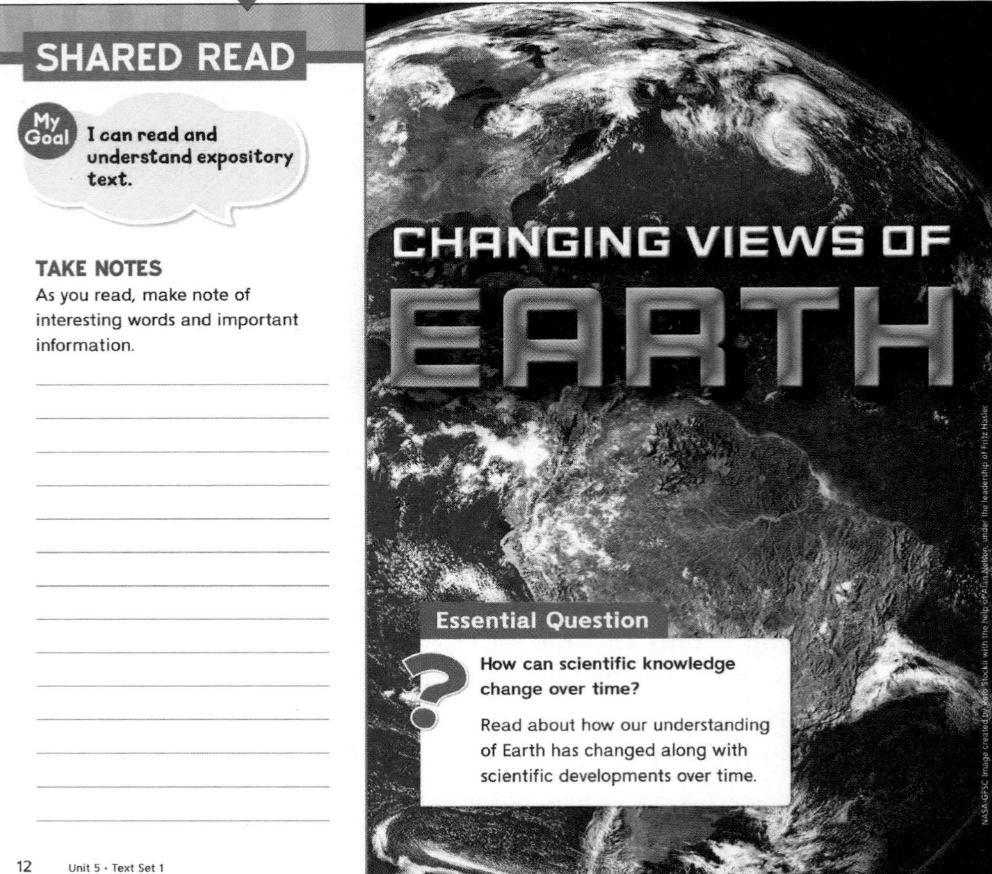

SHARED READ
My Goal
I can read and understand expository text.
TAKE NOTES
As you read, make note of interesting words and important information.
CHANGING VIEWS OF
EARTH
Essential Question
How can scientific knowledge change over time?
Read about how our understanding of Earth has changed along with scientific developments over time.
12 Unit 5 • Text Set 1

Reading/Writing Companion, pp. 12–13

Set a Purpose Before they begin, have students think about the Essential Question and what they know about how Earth has changed. Have students set a purpose for reading. Explain that after students preview the text, they should use the left column on page 12 to write a prediction about what they might learn. Have students list interesting words and key details from the text.

Focus on the Read prompts now. For additional support, use the extra prompts not included in the **Reading/Writing Companion.** Use the Reread prompts during the Craft and Structure lesson on pages T20–T21. Consider preteaching vocabulary to some students.

DIFFERENTIATED READING

Approaching Level Model how to preview the text and make a prediction. As a group, complete all Read prompts.

On Level Have partners do the Read prompts before you meet.

Beyond Level Discuss partners' responses to the Read prompts. Explain how the diagrams support the prompts.

English Language Learners Preteach the vocabulary. Have Beginning and Early-Intermediate ELLs listen to the selection summary, available in multiple languages, and use the **Scaffolded Shared Read**. For small group support, see the **ELL Small Group Guide**.

On the Ground, Looking Around

No matter where on Earth you go, people like to talk about the weather. This weekend's forecast may provide the main **criteria** for planning outdoor activities. Where does all that information about the weather come from? The ability to predict storms and droughts required centuries of scientific innovation. We had to look up at the skies to learn more about life here on Earth.

Long ago, humans based their knowledge on what they experienced with their eyes and ears. If people could heighten their senses, they might not feel so mystified by the events confronting them daily. For example, something as simple as the rising sun perplexed people for centuries. They believed that the Earth stayed in place while the Sun moved around it. This was called the geocentric model.

In the early 1600s, an Italian named Galileo pointed a new tool called the telescope toward the night sky. As a result of his heightened vision, he could see stars, planets, and other celestial **spheres** with new clarity. Each observation and **calculation** led him to support a radical new model of the solar system. In the heliocentric version proposed by the scientist Copernicus, the Sun did not **orbit** the Earth. The Earth orbited the Sun.

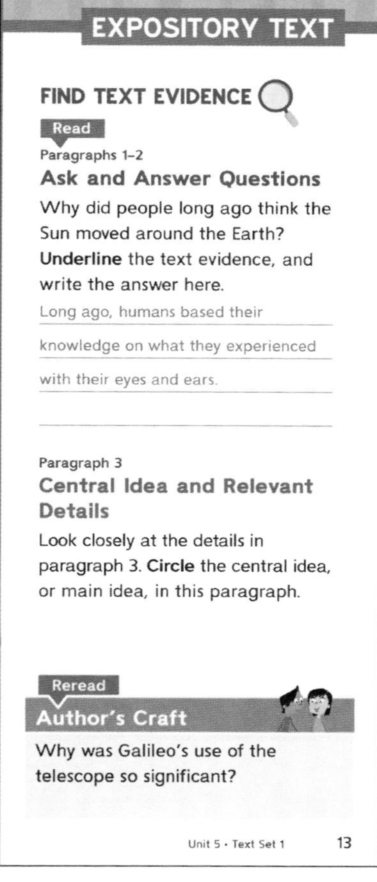

Galileo's telescope helped prove that Copernicus's heliocentric view was correct. ▶

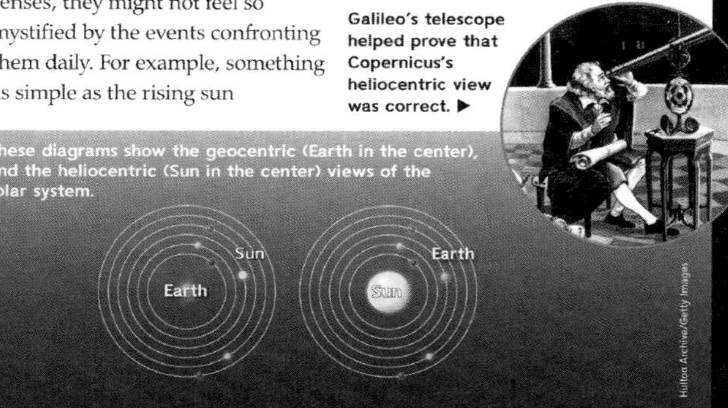

These diagrams show the geocentric (Earth in the center), and the heliocentric (Sun in the center) views of the solar system.

Hulton Archive/Getty Images

EXPOSITORY TEXT

FIND TEXT EVIDENCE

Read

Paragraphs 1–2

Ask and Answer Questions

Why did people long ago think the Sun moved around the Earth? **Underline** the text evidence, and write the answer here.

Long ago, humans based their knowledge on what they experienced with their eyes and ears.

Paragraph 3

Central Idea and Relevant Details

Look closely at the details in paragraph 3. **Circle** the central idea, or main idea, in this paragraph.

Reread

Author's Craft

Why was Galileo's use of the telescope so significant?

Unit 5 • Text Set 1 13

Ask and Answer Questions DOK 1

Paragraphs 1–2: *Why did people long ago think the Sun moved around the Earth?*

Think Aloud I read that long ago people based their knowledge on what they saw or heard. They thought that the Sun moved because it did not stay in the same position during the day. Have students skim ahead on this page and think of other questions they might have.

Central Idea and Relevant Details DOK 2

Paragraph 3: *What is the central idea in the third paragraph? What relevant details help you determine the central idea?*

Think Aloud I will look for text evidence to answer this question. I read in the third paragraph that Galileo first used a telescope in the early 1600s. That is important because for the first time he could see further than he could with just his eyes. The words, "As a result," signal that relevant details will follow. I read that the telescope heightened Galileo's vision and he could see stars, planets, and other celestial spheres with new clarity. The central idea is that Galileo's invention of the telescope helped us gain new knowledge about the solar system. Have students check to see if any of their questions have been answered.

Check for Understanding DOK 2

Page 13: Monitor students' understanding of how people made observations in the past, how Galileo's new tool affected this process, and what new discoveries came to light. Ask: *What new model of the solar system did Copernicus propose? How did it work?* (He proposed the heliocentric model. In this model, the Earth orbits the Sun rather than the Sun orbiting the Earth.) To emphasize why this was such a radical idea at the time, have students look at the diagram at the bottom of the page. Ask: *How are the sizes of the Earth and the Sun different in the two models?* (In the geocentric model, the Earth is slightly bigger than the Sun. In the heliocentric model, the Sun is much bigger than the Earth.)

ELL Spotlight on Language

Page 13, Paragraph 3 Read the paragraph. Check students' understanding of the word *observation.* Point out that *observe* is the root word. Say: Observe *is a verb, or an action word, that means "to watch someone or something carefully." When you add the affix* -tion *to the verb* observe, *it becomes a noun.* So, observation *means "something you have noticed by watching carefully."* Elicit examples of students' observations, such as those made in science class. Ask: *Can you identify another word with the affix* -tion *in this paragraph?* (calculation) *What action do you take to make a calculation?* (calculate)

Ask and Answer Questions DOK 1

Paragraphs 1–2: Read the first paragraph. *What question does the author ask?* (What if they could travel into the sky, where the weather actually happened?) Ask: *What is a question you have about measuring devices?* (Sample question: *How did kites and hot-air balloons change what scientists understood about weather patterns?*)

Greek Roots DOK 2

Paragraph 3: Read the first and second sentences in the third paragraph. Point out *atmosphere* and explain that the Greek root *atmos-* means "vapor, or gases," and *sphere* means "something that is shaped like a ball." Ask: *What does* atmosphere *mean?* (Gases that surround a spherical planet like Earth.)

Text Features: Diagram DOK 2

Remind students that authors often use different types of text features in expository texts. Ask: *Why did the author include the diagram?* (to give information about the different layers of Earth's atmosphere) *How does it help you understand why breakthroughs came fast and furiously when aircraft were used instead of kites and balloons?* (The diagram shows how much higher into the Earth's atmosphere the aircraft can travel.) *At what altitude do the Troposphere and Tropopause meet?* (10 km)

Read

SHARED READ

FIND TEXT EVIDENCE

Read

Paragraphs 1–2

Ask and Answer Questions

What question do you have about measuring devices? Write your question. **Underline** your answer.

Sample answer: The appropriate response text should be underlined.

Paragraphs 3–4

Central Idea and Relevant Details

Circle details that support the idea that using aircraft improves how we study weather.

Diagram

At what altitude do the Troposphere and Tropopause meet?

10 km

Reread

Author's Craft

Why did the author use the heading "In the Sky, Looking Down" for this section?

14 Unit 5 • Text Set 1

In the Sky, Looking Down

New technology allowed scientists to **evaluate** theories better than ever. Measuring devices such as the thermometer and barometer offered new insights into weather patterns. However, people were still limited to ground-based learning. What if they could travel into the sky, where the weather actually happened?

In the mid-1700s, some scientists sent measurement devices higher and higher. At first they used kites. Before long, hot-air balloons offered new ways to **transport** the tools—and sometimes scientists themselves—into the sky.

However, scientists were not satisfied studying the lower layers of Earth's atmosphere. The more they learned, the higher they wanted to go. They also wanted to obtain information more quickly and accurately. Kites and balloons were hard to control. As a result, they occasionally veered off course or got lost, taking their data with them.

The development of aircraft in the early 1900s promised safer ways to observe Earth's surface and the atmosphere above it. Kites and balloons could reach altitudes of **approximately** three kilometers. By comparison, airplanes lifted scientists to a height of five kilometers and more. Radio technology allowed scientists to transmit data from the air to the ground, where other scientists analyzed and compared information. Breakthroughs came fast and furiously. Still, scientists dreamed of reaching ever higher.

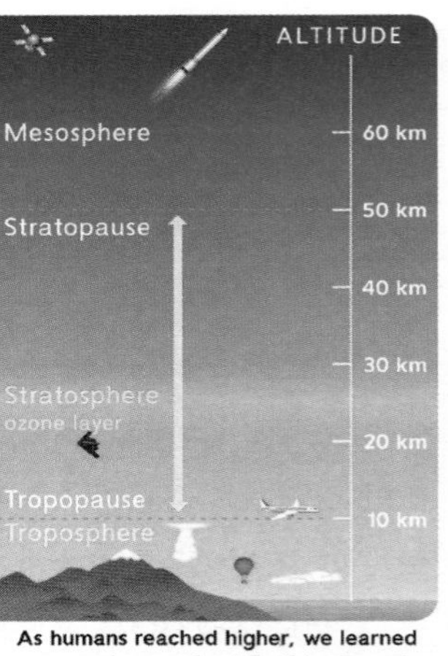

As humans reached higher, we learned more and more about Earth's atmosphere.

Reading/Writing Companion, pp. 14–15

Central Idea and Relevant Details DOK 2

Paragraphs 3–4: Reread the third and fourth paragraphs. Ask: *What was the problem with kites and balloons? What happened as a result?* (They were hard to control and veered off course, so the data they collected was often lost.) *What problem did the use of aircraft solve?* (Aircraft would not veer off course, and the data would not get lost.) *What effect did aircraft have on learning more about weather patterns?* (Aircraft could travel higher and use radio technology to transmit data.) *Use these details to determine the central idea.* (Central idea: The development of new technology made studying Earth's atmosphere more accurate.)

Access Complex Text

Prior Knowledge

Explain how scientific advances over time have helped meteorologists predict weather.

- 1643: Evangelista Torricelli invents the modern barometer to measure air pressure near Earth's surface.
- 1714: Daniel Gabriel Fahrenheit invents the modern thermometer to measure air temperature near Earth's surface.
- 1960: The first weather satellite is launched. Today's satellites gather data from Earth's atmosphere and view weather systems across the entire globe.

Out in Space, Looking Back Home

In the late twentieth century, advances in aeronautics led to more powerful rockets that lifted satellites into orbit around Earth. From these heights, scientists could study the composition and relative thinness of our layered atmosphere. Since meteorologists could analyze multiple factors at once, the accuracy of their weather predictions improved dramatically.

NASA launched dozens of satellites into orbit in the following years. Some stared back at Earth, while others peered deep into endless space. They gathered **astronomical** data about the ages of planets and galaxies. Sensors and supercomputers measured things such as Earth's **diameter** with incredible accuracy. Because of this technology, scientists could develop more reliable models about Earth's systems. For example, they could form theories to show how climate might change over time.

Space missions continue to venture farther from home. Even so, nothing compares to seeing Earth the old way, with our own eyes. Views of our planet from space inspire awe in nearly all people who have seen them, even in photographs. "With all the arguments . . . for going to the Moon," said astronaut Joseph Allen, "no one suggested that we should do it to look at the Earth. But that may in fact be the most important reason."

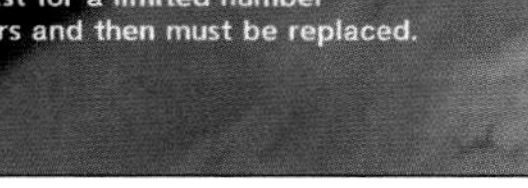

Satellites launched into orbit only last for a limited number of years and then must be replaced.

Summarize

Use your notes and the diagrams, photographs, and captions to write a short summary of the important information in "Changing Views of Earth."

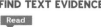

EXPOSITORY TEXT

FIND TEXT EVIDENCE

Read

Paragraphs 1–3

Greek Roots

How does the Greek root *photo*, meaning "light," help you understand more about how *photographs* are created?

Photographs are pictures made with cameras, so cameras must need to use light to create photographs.

Evaluate Information

Underline Joseph Allen's quote. Do you think Allen is qualified to say this? Why or why not?

Yes, Allen is qualified to say this because he is an astronaut who has seen Earth from space.

Reread

Author's Craft

Do you believe the ability to predict weather will continue to improve? Why or why not? Use text evidence in your answer.

Unit 5 • Text Set 1 15

Ask and Answer Questions DOK 1

Paragraph 1: Ask: *Why is it helpful to ask and answer questions when you read expository text?* (Answering questions helps you set a purpose for reading and helps you stay focused.) Remind students to use text evidence, including information in text features, to answer the question they asked about the first paragraph.

Greek Roots DOK 2

Paragraphs 2–3: Read the third sentence in paragraph 3 and point to the word *photograph*. Ask: *What two word parts are in* photograph? (*photo, graph*) Explain that *graph* was added to the Greek root, *photo*. Discuss how you can use your understanding of the meaning of Greek roots to figure out the meaning of the longer words. (Photographs are pictures made with cameras, so cameras must need to use light to create photographs.)

Evaluate Information DOK 2

Read the quote in the third paragraph. *What is Joseph Allen's profession?* (He is an astronaut.) *What do astronauts do?* (They travel into space.) *What do astronauts see that few people on Earth have ever seen?* (Earth from space) Explain that students should use what they know about Joseph Allen to determine if he is qualified to say what he said.

Summarize DOK 2

Analytical Writing **Quick Write** Have students briefly summarize the text in their reader's notebooks. Remind them only to include important information and to explain whether or not they were able to confirm the prediction they made before beginning the text.

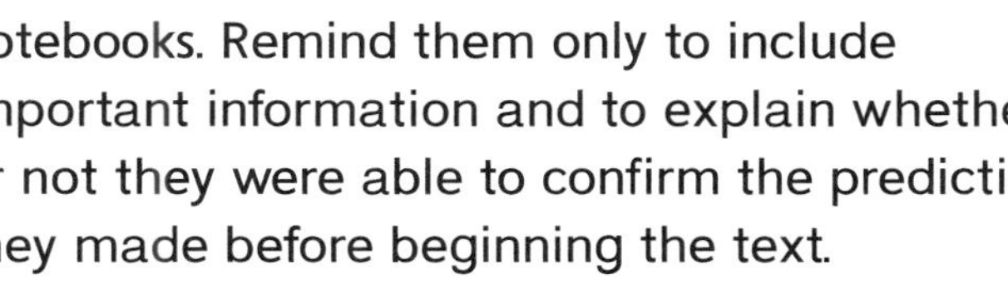

ELL Spotlight on Language

Page 14, Paragraph 4 Read the second sentence and point to the word *kilometer*. Explain that it combines the Greek root for thousand, *kilo*, with the word *meter* (cognate: *metro*), which measures length or distance. *How many meters is a kilometer?* (one thousand) Point to the diagram and explain that *km* is an abbreviation, or short form, of *kilometer*. Elicit altitudes from the diagram.

Connection of Ideas

Students may struggle to connect the diagram and text.

- According to the text, which inventions helped people measure weather from above the ground? (kites, balloons, airplanes, rockets, satellites)
- What additional information about these inventions does the diagram provide? (It indicates which levels in Earth's atmosphere some inventions could reach.)

FORMATIVE ASSESSMENT

STUDENT CHECK-IN

Have partners share their summaries from Reading/Writing Companion page 15. Ask them to reflect using the Check-In routine.

LEARNING GOALS

- We can use new vocabulary words to read and understand expository text.
- We can use Greek roots to figure out the meaning of unfamiliar words.

OBJECTIVES

Determine the meaning of words and phrases in a text relevant to a topic or subject area.

Determine or clarify the meaning of unknown and multiple-meaning words and phrases, choosing flexibly from a range of strategies.

Use common, grade-appropriate Greek and Latin affixes and roots as clues to the meaning of a word (e.g., *photograph, photosynthesis*).

ELA ACADEMIC LANGUAGE

- *root, interpret, define*
- Cognates: *interpretar, definir*

DIGITAL TOOLS

Visual Vocabulary Cards

TEACH IN SMALL GROUP

Academic Vocabulary

Approaching Level and **ELL** Preteach the words before students begin the Shared Read.

On Level Have students look up each word in the online **Visual Glossary.**

Beyond Level Have pairs compose an additional context sentence for each vocabulary word.

Reread

Academic Vocabulary

Use the routines on the **Visual Vocabulary Cards** to introduce each word.

If two things are **approximately** the same size, they are nearly or about the same size.

Cognate: *aproximadamente*

Something **astronomical** relates to outer space or astronomy.

Cognate: *astronómico*

When you make a **calculation**, you do math to find an answer.

Cognate: *cálculo*

Criteria are rules for judging something or making a decision.

Cognate: *criterios*

You can measure across the center of a circle to find its **diameter**.

Cognate: *diámetro*

When you **evaluate** something, you examine it again and again.

Cognate: *evaluar*

To **orbit** something is to move in a circle around it again and again.

Cognate: *orbitar*

Spheres are anything that is shaped like a ball or a globe.

Cognate: *esferas*

Encourage students to use their newly acquired vocabulary in their discussions and written responses about the texts in this text set.

Greek Roots

1 Explain

Remind students that a root is the basic part of a word that gives the word its meaning and that some words contain Greek roots. Explain that knowing the meaning of a root can help students interpret the meaning of unfamiliar words. Begin an anchor chart on Greek Roots.

2 Model

Model using the Greek roots *geo* ("earth") and *centric* ("center") to determine the meaning of geocentric ("centered around Earth") on **Reading/Writing Companion** page 13 of "Changing Views of Earth."

3 Guided Practice

Help student pairs use the given Greek roots to determine the meanings of *heliocentric* on page 13 and *thermometer* on page 14. Discuss how knowing the meaning of the root can help them define each word.

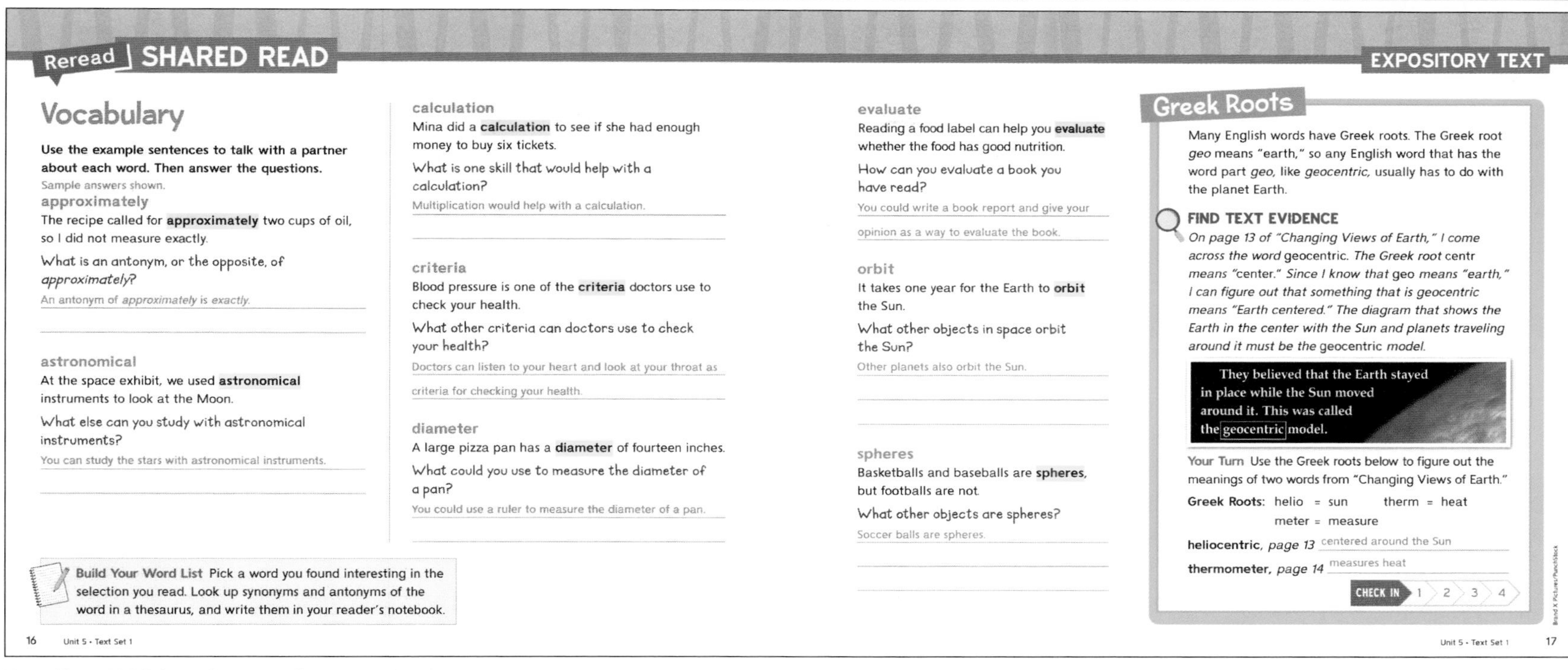

Reread | SHARED READ

EXPOSITORY TEXT

Vocabulary

Use the example sentences to talk with a partner about each word. Then answer the questions.

Sample answers shown.

approximately
The recipe called for **approximately** two cups of oil, so I did not measure exactly.
What is an antonym, or the opposite, of *approximately*?
An antonym of *approximately* is *exactly*.

astronomical
At the space exhibit, we used **astronomical** instruments to look at the Moon.
What else can you study with astronomical instruments?
You can study the stars with astronomical instruments.

calculation
Mina did a **calculation** to see if she had enough money to buy six tickets.
What is one skill that would help with a calculation?
Multiplication would help with a calculation.

criteria
Blood pressure is one of the **criteria** doctors use to check your health.
What other criteria can doctors use to check your health?
Doctors can listen to your heart and look at your throat as criteria for checking your health.

diameter
A large pizza pan has a **diameter** of fourteen inches.
What could you use to measure the diameter of a pan?
You could use a ruler to measure the diameter of a pan.

evaluate
Reading a food label can help you **evaluate** whether the food has good nutrition.
How can you evaluate a book you have read?
You could write a book report and give your opinion as a way to evaluate the book.

orbit
It takes one year for the Earth to **orbit** the Sun.
What other objects in space orbit the Sun?
Other planets also orbit the Sun.

spheres
Basketballs and baseballs are **spheres**, but footballs are not.
What other objects are spheres?
Soccer balls are spheres.

Build Your Word List Pick a word you found interesting in the selection you read. Look up synonyms and antonyms of the word in a thesaurus, and write them in your reader's notebook.

Greek Roots

Many English words have Greek roots. The Greek root *geo* means "earth," so any English word that has the word part *geo*, like *geocentric*, usually has to do with the planet Earth.

FIND TEXT EVIDENCE

On page 13 of "Changing Views of Earth," I come across the word geocentric. *The Greek root* centr *means "center." Since I know that* geo *means "earth," I can figure out that something that is geocentric means "Earth centered." The diagram that shows the Earth in the center with the Sun and planets traveling around it must be the* geocentric *model.*

They believed that the Earth stayed in place while the Sun moved around it. This was called the geocentric model.

Your Turn Use the Greek roots below to figure out the meanings of two words from "Changing Views of Earth."

Greek Roots: helio = sun therm = heat meter = measure

heliocentric, *page 13* centered around the Sun

thermometer, *page 14* measures heat

CHECK IN 1 2 3 4

16 Unit 5 • Text Set 1 Unit 5 • Text Set 1 17

Reading/Writing Companion, pp. 16–17

English Language Learners

Use the following scaffolds with **Guided Practice**. For small group support, see the **ELL Small Group Guide**.

Beginning

Read with students the last two sentences on page 13 of "Changing Views of Earth." Have them point to the word *heliocentric* and look at the heliocentric diagram on the page. *What do you see in the center of the diagram?* (the Sun) *What part of the word "*heliocentric*" looks like the word "*center*"?* (centric) Explain to them that "helio" is something related to the sun. Help partners define using: Heliocentric means the Sun is the center. Repeat with *thermometer* on page 14.

Intermediate

Display the word *heliocentric*. Circle the Greek roots and guide students to read them aloud. *What does the Greek root* centric *look like?* (center) The Greek root *centric* describes something that is in the center. Have them point to the diagram on page 13. *What do you see in the center?* (the Sun) Helio *means Sun.* In the heliocentric model, the Sun is in the center. Have partners use the Greek roots and context clues to figure out the meaning of *thermometer* on page 14.

Advanced/Advanced High

Have partners use Greek roots to determine the meaning of *heliocentric* on page 13 and *thermometer* on page 14. Have partners share how they determined the meanings of each.

BUILD YOUR WORD LIST

Students might choose *innovation* from page 13. Have them use a synonym or antonym to explore the meaning.

FORMATIVE ASSESSMENT

STUDENT CHECK-IN

Academic Vocabulary Ask partners to share two answers from Reading/Writing Companion pages 16-17.

Greek Roots Ask partners to share their Your Turn responses on page 17.

Have students use the Check-In routine to reflect and fill in the bars.

CHECK FOR SUCCESS

Rubric Use your online rubric to record student progress.

Can students identify and use Greek roots to determine the meanings of *heliocentric* and *thermometer?*

Small Group Instruction

If No:

- **Approaching** Reteach p. T65

If Yes:

- **On** Review p. T72
- **Beyond** Extend p. T78

LEARNING GOALS

We can ask and answer questions to understand expository text.

OBJECTIVES

Quote accurately from a text when explaining what the text says explicitly and when drawing inferences from the text.

Identify the author's purpose.

Ask and answer questions to increase understanding.

ELA ACADEMIC LANGUAGE

- *ask and answer questions, expository text, pose*
- Cognate: *texto expositivo*

Reread

Ask and Answer Questions

1 Explain

Explain to students that when they read expository texts, they should pause periodically to ask themselves questions about their reading.

- Explain that nonfiction authors often pose their own questions in the text. Such questions give readers clues about information that is to come. They also encourage readers to form their own questions in response.
- Point out that finding answers to questions gives readers a purpose for reading and helps them stay focused.
- Explain to students that if they are unable to answer their questions or those that the author poses, they should reread sections of the text they may have overlooked or misunderstood.

Anchor Chart Have a volunteer add any additional points about the strategy to the Ask and Answer Questions anchor chart.

2 Model

Identify the question posed by the author in the first paragraph: *Where does all that information about the weather come from?* Then model using your knowledge about how forecasters use scientific instruments to predict the weather to ask your own question: *What kinds of instruments do scientists use to make forecasts?* Demonstrate how reading **Reading/Writing Companion** pages 13 and 14, which describe advances in scientific instruments, helps you answer your question.

3 Guided Practice

Help students work with partners to ask a question about the section "Out in Space, Looking Back Home" on page 15. Encourage students to reread the section to identify evidence and details that help them find the answer. Guide partners to discuss how asking and answering a question helped them deepen their understanding of the information in the text and identify other sections of "Changing Views of Earth" about which they might want to ask and answer questions.

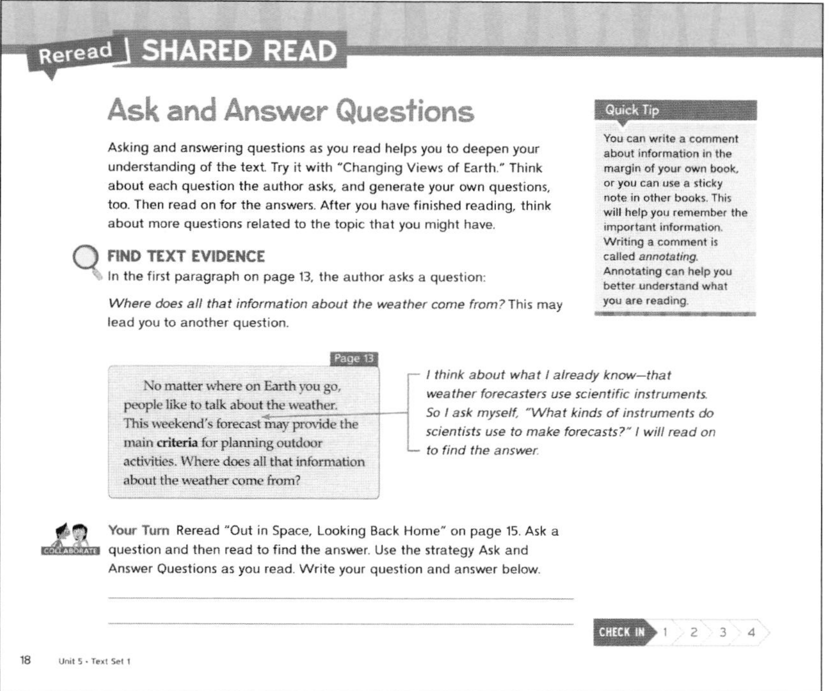
Reread | SHARED READ

Ask and Answer Questions

Asking and answering questions as you read helps you to deepen your understanding of the text. Try it with "Changing Views of Earth." Think about each question the author asks, and generate your own questions, too. Then read on for the answers. After you have finished reading, think about more questions related to the topic that you might have.

FIND TEXT EVIDENCE
In the first paragraph on page 13, the author asks a question:

Where does all that information about the weather come from? This may lead you to another question.

Page 13

No matter where on Earth you go, people like to talk about the weather. This weekend's forecast may provide the main **criteria** for planning outdoor activities. Where does all that information about the weather come from?

I think about what I already know—that weather forecasters use scientific instruments. So I ask myself, "What kinds of instruments do scientists use to make forecasts?" I will read on to find the answer.

Quick Tip

You can write a comment about information in the margin of your own book, or you can use a sticky note in other books. This will help you remember the important information. Writing a comment is called *annotating*. Annotating can help you better understand what you are reading.

COLLABORATE Your Turn Reread "Out in Space, Looking Back Home" on page 15. Ask a question and then read to find the answer. Use the strategy Ask and Answer Questions as you read. Write your question and answer below.

CHECK IN 1 2 3 4

18 Unit 5 • Text Set 1

Reading/Writing Companion, p. 18

HABITS OF LEARNING

I am part of a community of learners.

Asking and answering questions is a powerful learning tool that helps students connect with one another and build community. Remind students that active listening and knowing how to build upon other people's ideas are important ways of connecting with others.

English Language Learners

Use the following scaffolds with **Guided Practice**. For small group support, see the **ELL Small Group Guide**.

Beginning

Review with students how asking and answering questions can help them understand the text. Read paragraph 2 on page 15 of "Changing Views of Earth" with them. Help partners ask and answer questions about the satellites NASA launched: *How many* satellites *did NASA launch into orbit?* NASA launched dozens of satellites into orbit. *Did the satellites gather a lot of* data? (yes)

Intermediate

Review with students how asking and answering questions can help them understand the text. Have partners read paragraphs 1–2 on page 15 of "Changing Views of Earth." Ask: *What did NASA launch into orbit?* (satellites) Guide partners to ask and answer questions about the satellites: How many satelites did NASA launch into orbit? What data did the satellites gather from space? Have partners point to the text evidence that answers each question.

Advanced/Advanced High

Review the strategies of asking and answering questions with students. Have them read page 15 of "Changing Views of Earth." Allow pairs to take turns asking for information and answering the questions about the satellites NASA launched. Then have them support their answers with text evidence.

FORMATIVE ASSESSMENT

STUDENT CHECK-IN

Ask partners to share their Your Turn responses on Reading/Writing Companion page 18. Have them use the Check-In routine to reflect and fill in the bars.

CHECK FOR SUCCESS

Do students ask and answer questions? Do they find text evidence to answer the questions?

Small Group Instruction

If No:

- **Approaching** Reteach p. T58

If Yes:

- **On** Review p. T68
- **Beyond** Extend p. T74

Reread

Text Features: Diagrams

LEARNING GOALS

We can use diagrams to read and understand expository text.

OBJECTIVES

Interpret information presented visually, orally, or quantitatively (e.g., in charts, graphs, diagrams, time lines, animations, or interactive elements on Web pages) and explain how the information contributes to an understanding of the text in which it appears.

Identify characteristics of expository text.

ELA ACADEMIC LANGUAGE

- *expository text, headings, subheadings, photographs, diagrams*
- Cognates: *texto expositivo, fotografías, diagramas*

1 Explain

Share with students these characteristics of **expository text:**

- An expository text is a nonfiction text that presents factual information about a topic in a logical order.
- Authors of expository text support their points with reasons and evidence.
- An expository text often includes text features, such as headings and subheadings, that organize the information in it. Other text features, such as photographs and diagrams, enable readers to visualize ideas and information related to the text.

2 Model

Model how to identify "Changing Views of Earth" as an expository text in which facts are presented in a logical order. Read aloud dates in the text (such as *in the early 1600s* and *in the mid-1700s*) to show students how the author discusses inventions in the order they occurred. Then model using the diagram on **Reading/Writing Companion** page 14.

Diagrams Remind students that a diagram is a drawing that shows the different parts of something and how they relate to each other. Read aloud the caption of the diagram on page 14 and explain that this diagram shows layers of Earth's atmosphere and inventions that can reach each. Ask: *How does the diagram connect to information in the text?*

Anchor Chart Have a volunteer add this feature to the Expository Text anchor chart.

3 Guided Practice

Circulate as partners identify other examples of things that show the selection is expository text, including factual statements from the text, the use of headings and other text features, evidence presented to support a point, and examples of logical order. Then guide partners to turn to the diagrams on pages 13 and 14 and discuss how each supports their understanding of ideas in the text.

Independent Practice Have students read the online **Differentiated Genre Passage,** "Is There Life Out There?"

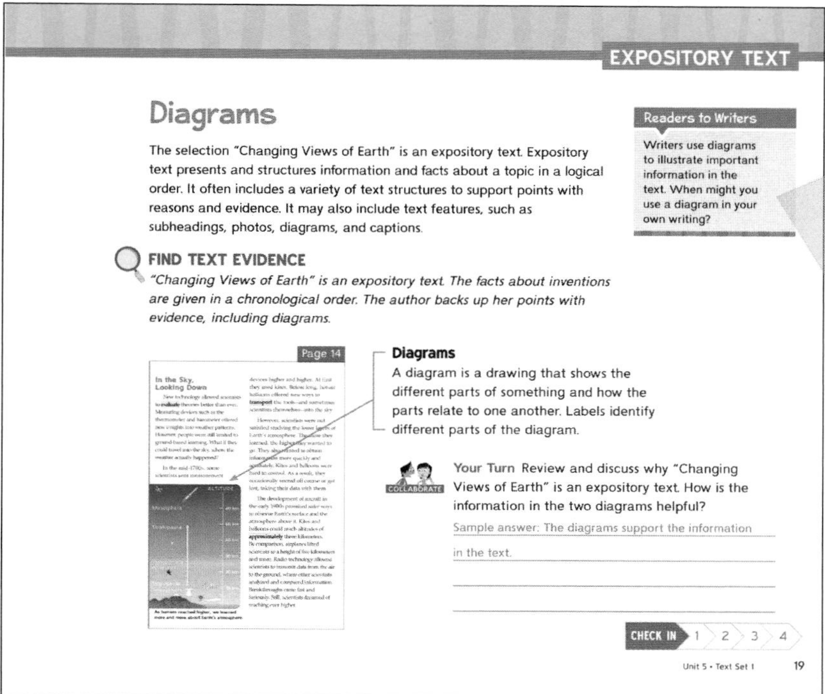

EXPOSITORY TEXT

Diagrams

The selection "Changing Views of Earth" is an expository text. Expository text presents and structures information and facts about a topic in a logical order. It often includes a variety of text structures to support points with reasons and evidence. It may also include text features, such as subheadings, photos, diagrams, and captions.

Readers to Writers

Writers use diagrams to illustrate important information in the text. When might you use a diagram in your own writing?

FIND TEXT EVIDENCE

"Changing Views of Earth" is an expository text. The facts about inventions are given in a chronological order. The author backs up her points with evidence, including diagrams.

Page 14

Diagrams

A diagram is a drawing that shows the different parts of something and how the parts relate to one another. Labels identify different parts of the diagram.

COLLABORATE

Your Turn Review and discuss why "Changing Views of Earth" is an expository text. How is the information in the two diagrams helpful?

Sample answer: The diagrams support the information in the text.

CHECK IN 1 2 3 4

Unit 5 • Text Set 1 19

Reading/Writing Companion, p. 19

Readers to Writers

Remind students that including diagrams in an expository text helps authors present information in a more visual way. Using diagrams also allows authors to include information that helps readers understand the ideas in the main text. Have students look back at the diagram on page 14. Ask: *What text on page 14 does this diagram help the author support? How does it give you a better understanding of this text?*

English Language Learners

Use the following scaffolds with **Guided Practice**. For small group support, see the **ELL Small Group Guide**.

Beginning

Read the last paragraph on page 13 of "Changing Views of Earth" with students. The paragraph starts with a factual statement about Galileo in the early 1600s. The image shows what Galileo's telescope looked like. *Talk to your partner about what the diagram shows.* The diagram shows the heliocentric and geocentric versions of our solar system. *Why is the diagram helpful?* The diagram supports the information in the text.

Intermediate

Have partners read the last paragraph on page 13 of "Changing Views of Earth." Ask: *Is the first sentence a factual statement?* (yes) *What is the statement?* Galileo was an Italian who pointed a telescope/new tool toward the night sky in the early 1600s. *What other text features do you see, and how are they helpful?* The diagram is a helpful text feature because ____.

Advanced/Advanced High

Have partners read page 13 and discuss the benefits of the text features (diagram, factual statements, heading). Then guide partners as they interpret and discuss how the diagram on page 14 helps them to better understand ideas in the text.

FORMATIVE ASSESSMENT

STUDENT CHECK-IN

Ask partners to share their Your Turn responses on Reading/Writing Companion page 19. Have them use the Check-In routine to reflect and fill in the bars.

CHECK FOR SUCCESS

Can students determine why "Changing Views of Earth" is an expository text? Can they explain why the information in the diagrams is helpful?

Small Group Instruction

If No:

- **Approaching** Reteach p. T60

If Yes:

- **On** Review p. T70
- **Beyond** Extend p. T76

LEARNING GOALS

We can read and understand expository text by identifying the central idea and relevant details.

OBJECTIVES

Determine two or more central, or main, ideas of a text and explain how they are supported by relevant, or key, details; summarize the text.

Draw evidence from literary or informational texts to support analysis, reflection, and research.

ELA ACADEMIC LANGUAGE

- *central idea, relevant details*
- Cognates: *idea central, detalles relevantes*

DIGITAL TOOLS

To differentiate instruction for key skills, use the results of the activity.

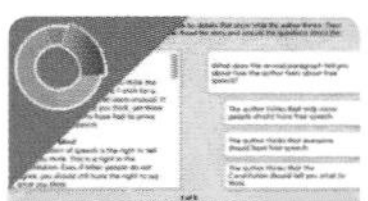

Reread

Central Idea and Relevant Details

1 Explain

Explain to students that the overall **central idea**, or main idea, of an expository text is what the author most wants readers to know about the topic. The topic, on the other hand, should not be confused with the central idea. The topic simply describes the subject matter of a text.

- Point out that while the text as a whole has a central idea, each section of the text also has a central idea.
- The central idea is supported by **relevant details**. Relevant details are important details that support the central idea. Not all details in a text may directly support the central idea.
- Sometimes the central idea is explicitly stated in the text, but often readers must look more closely at the relevant details in order to figure out the central idea.

Anchor Chart Add any new points to the Central Idea and Relevant Details anchor chart.

2 Model

Reread the section, "On the Ground, Looking Around" on **Reading/ Writing Companion** page 13. Model identifying the relevant details and listing them on the graphic organizer. Then model how to use the details to find the central idea on the page.

3 Guided Practice

Help pairs complete a graphic organizer for each remaining section of "Changing Views of Earth," identifying the relevant details and central ideas described. Then have students determine the central idea for the entire selection. Discuss the organizer with students as they complete each page.

Analytical Writing **Write About Reading: Summarize** Model how to use the details from the organizer to summarize how advancements in scientific knowledge have been so important to our understanding of Earth.

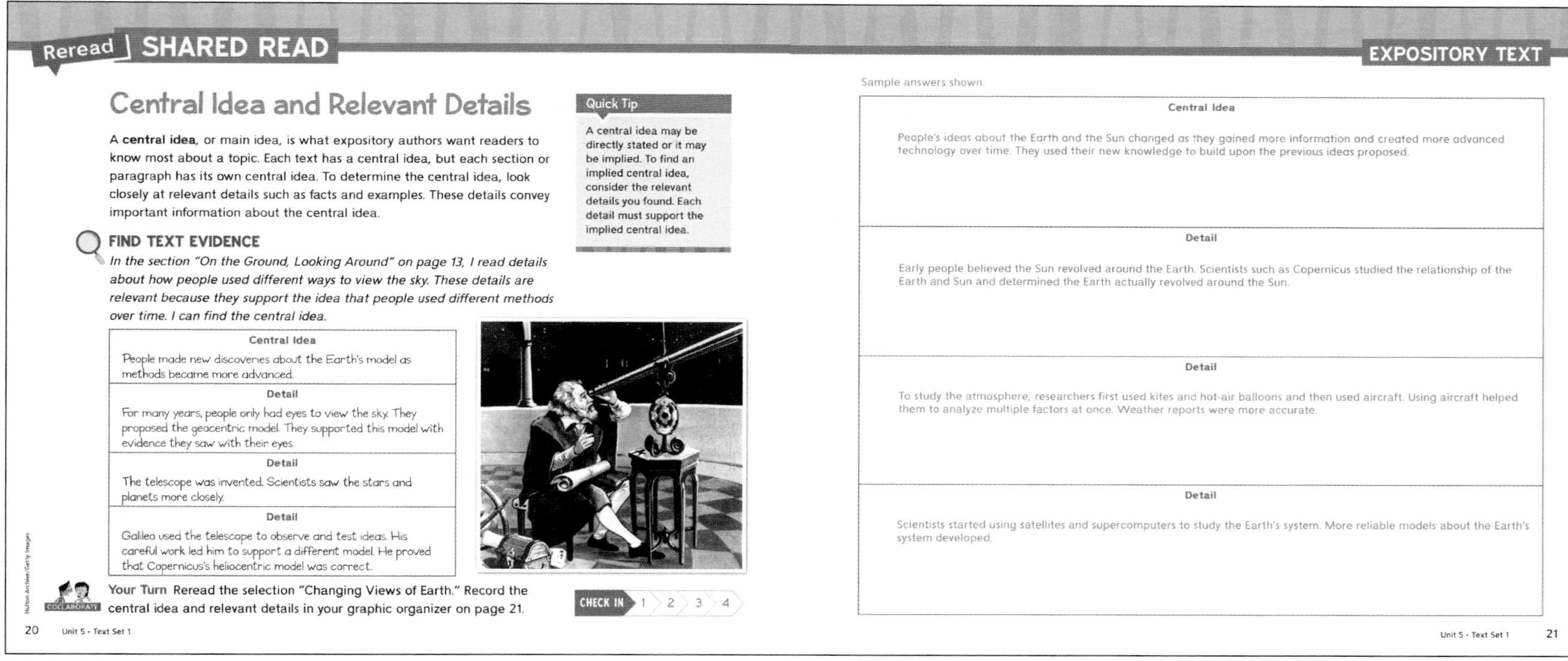

Reread | SHARED READ

EXPOSITORY TEXT

Central Idea and Relevant Details

A **central idea**, or main idea, is what expository authors want readers to know most about a topic. Each text has a central idea, but each section or paragraph has its own central idea. To determine the central idea, look closely at relevant details such as facts and examples. These details convey important information about the central idea.

Quick Tip

A central idea may be directly stated or it may be implied. To find an implied central idea, consider the relevant details you found. Each detail must support the implied central idea.

FIND TEXT EVIDENCE

In the section "On the Ground, Looking Around" on page 13, I read details about how people used different ways to view the sky. These details are relevant because they support the idea that people used different methods over time. I can find the central idea.

Central Idea
People made new discoveries about the Earth's model as methods became more advanced.
Detail
For many years, people only had eyes to view the sky. They proposed the geocentric model. They supported this model with evidence they saw with their eyes.
Detail
The telescope was invented. Scientists saw the stars and planets more closely.
Detail
Galileo used the telescope to observe and test ideas. His careful work led him to support a different model. He proved that Copernicus's heliocentric model was correct.

Hulton Archive/Getty Images

COLLABORATE

Your Turn Reread the selection "Changing Views of Earth." Record the central idea and relevant details in your graphic organizer on page 21.

CHECK IN 1 2 3 4

20 Unit 5 • Text Set 1

Sample answers shown.

Central Idea
People's ideas about the Earth and the Sun changed as they gained more information and created more advanced technology over time. They used their new knowledge to build upon the previous ideas proposed.
Detail
Early people believed the Sun revolved around the Earth. Scientists such as Copernicus studied the relationship of the Earth and Sun and determined the Earth actually revolved around the Sun.
Detail
To study the atmosphere, researchers first used kites and hot-air balloons and then used aircraft. Using aircraft helped them to analyze multiple factors at once. Weather reports were more accurate.
Detail
Scientists started using satellites and supercomputers to study the Earth's system. More reliable models about the Earth's system developed.

Unit 5 • Text Set 1 21

Reading/Writing Companion, pp. 20–21

English Language Learners

Use the following scaffolds with **Guided Practice**. For small group support, see the **ELL Small Group Guide**.

Beginning

Review central idea and relevant details with students. Reread with them the last paragraph on page 13 and the first two paragraphs on page 14 of "Changing Views of Earth." Help partners identify relevant details by asking: *Did early people believe the Sun revolved around the Earth?* (yes) *What did Copernicus find out?* Copernicus found out the Earth revolves around the Sun. Discuss the central idea with them. Then help them fill in their graphic organizer.

Intermediate

Review central idea and relevant details with students. Have partners reread pages 13-14 of "Changing Views of Earth." Ask: *What did early people believe about the Sun?* Early people believed ____. *What did Copernicus find out?* Copernicus found out ____. *Did people's ideas about the Sun and Earth change?* (yes) Then have them use the details to discuss the central idea and fill in the graphic organizer.

Advanced/Advanced High

Check the students' understanding of central idea and relevant details. Have pairs reread "Changing Views of Earth" and identify details that show how people's ideas about the Sun and Earth changed over time. Then have them complete the graphic organizer.

FORMATIVE ASSESSMENT

STUDENT CHECK-IN

Ask partners to share their graphic organizers on Reading/Writing Companion page 21. Have them reflect using the Check-In routine to fill in the bars.

CHECK FOR SUCCESS

Rubric Use your online rubric to record student progress.

Are students able to identify and list the central idea and relevant details on the graphic organize?

Small Group Instruction

If No:

- **Approaching** Reteach p. T67

If Yes:

- **On** Review p. T73
- **Beyond** Extend p. T79

LEARNING GOALS

We can reread to analyze craft and structure in expository text.

OBJECTIVES

Compare and contrast the overall structure (e.g., chronology, comparison, cause/effect, problem/solution) of events, ideas, concepts, or information in two or more texts.

Draw on information from multiple print or digital sources, demonstrating the ability to locate an answer to a question quickly or to solve a problem efficiently.

ELA ACADEMIC LANGUAGE

- *techniques, comparison, text structure*
- Cognates: *técnicas, comparación, estructura del texto*

TEACH IN SMALL GROUP

Approaching Level Use the scaffolded questions to guide students as they reread parts of "Changing Views of Earth." Have them make marks in the margin to indicate text evidence.

On Level Have partners share their answers after completing the Reread prompts.

Beyond Level Give partners the opportunity to individually answer the Reread prompts.

ELL Have Beginning and Early-Intermediate ELLs use the **Scaffolded Shared Read.**

Reread

Craft and Structure

Tell students that they will now reread parts of "Changing Views of Earth" and analyze the techniques the author used in writing the selection. Features like headings and diagrams, along with an effective text structure, can help an author present information in an expository text.

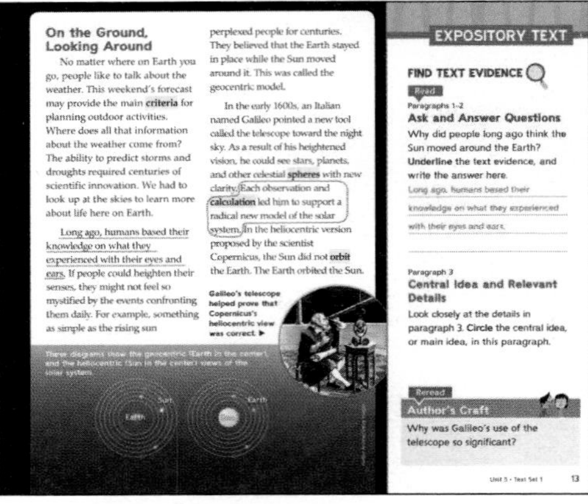

On the Ground, Looking Around

No matter where on Earth you go, people like to talk about the weather. This weekend's forecast may provide the main **criteria** for planning outdoor activities. Where does all that information about the weather come from? The ability to predict storms and droughts required centuries of scientific innovation. We had to look up at the skies to learn more about life here on Earth.

Long ago, humans based their knowledge on what they experienced with their eyes and ears. If people could heighten their senses, they might not feel so mystified by the events confronting them daily. For example, something as simple as the rising sun perplexed people for centuries. They believed that the Earth stayed in place while the Sun moved around it. This was called the geocentric model.

In the early 1600s, an Italian named Galileo pointed a new tool called the telescope toward the night sky. As a result of his heightened vision, he could see stars, planets, and other celestial **spheres** with new clarity. Each observation and **calculation** led him to support a radical new model of the solar system. In the heliocentric version proposed by the scientist Copernicus, the Sun did not **orbit** the Earth. The Earth orbited the Sun.

Galileo's telescope helped prove that Copernicus's heliocentric view was correct. ▶

EXPOSITORY TEXT

FIND TEXT EVIDENCE

Read

Paragraphs 1-2

Ask and Answer Questions

Why did people long ago think the Sun moved around the Earth? **Underline** the text evidence, and write the answer here.

Long ago, humans based their knowledge on what they experienced with their eyes and ears.

Paragraph 3

Central Idea and Relevant Details

Look closely at the details in paragraph 3. **Circle** the central idea, or main idea, in this paragraph.

Reread

Author's Craft

Why was Galileo's use of the telescope so significant?

Unit 5 • Text Set 1 13

Reading/Writing Companion, p. 13

AUTHOR'S CRAFT DOK 2

Reread the second paragraph on page 13 with students. Ask: *How did humans originally study Earth and space?* (They relied on their eyes and ears.) *What scientific advancement allowed humans to expand their study?* (The telescope was invented.)

ELL Use prompts such as the following to support the comparison shown in the diagrams: *What is at the center of the diagram on the left?* (the Earth) *What is at the center of the diagram on the right?* (the Sun) *According to the caption for the diagrams, which model has the Earth in the center?* (geocentric) *Which model has the Sun in the center?* (heliocentric)

Why was Galileo's use of the telescope so significant? (The telescope helped Galileo disprove the earlier belief about the Sun rotating around Earth. This suggests that advances in technology lead to new knowledge.)

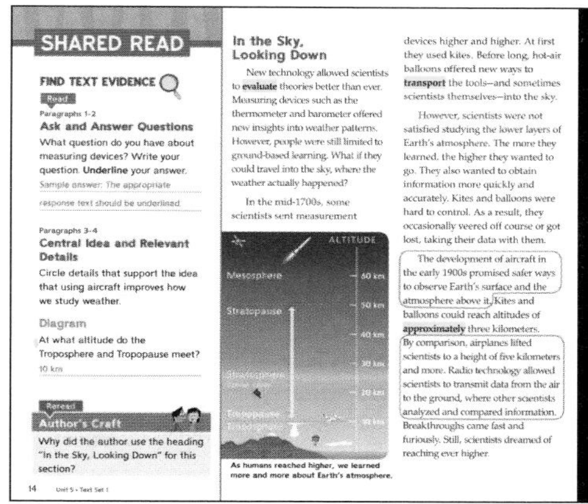

SHARED READ

FIND TEXT EVIDENCE

Read

Paragraphs 1-2

Ask and Answer Questions

What question do you have about measuring devices? Write your question. **Underline** your answer.

Sample answer: The appropriate response text should be underlined.

Paragraphs 3-4

Central Idea and Relevant Details

Circle details that support the idea that using aircraft improves how we study weather.

Diagram

At what altitude do the Troposphere and Tropopause meet?

10 km

Reread

Author's Craft

Why did the author use the heading "In the Sky, Looking Down" for this section?

In the Sky, Looking Down

New technology allowed scientists to **evaluate** theories better than ever. Measuring devices such as the thermometer and barometer offered new insights into weather patterns. However, people were still limited to ground-based learning. What if they could travel into the sky, where the weather actually happened?

In the mid-1700s, some scientists sent measurement devices higher and higher. At first they used kites. Before long, hot-air balloons offered new ways to **transport** the tools—and sometimes scientists themselves—into the sky.

However, scientists were not satisfied studying the lower layers of Earth's atmosphere. The more they learned, the higher they wanted to go. They also wanted to obtain information more quickly and accurately. Kites and balloons were hard to control. As a result, they occasionally veered off course or got lost, taking their data with them.

The development of aircraft in the early 1900s promised safer ways to observe Earth's surface and the atmosphere above it. Kites and balloons could reach altitudes of **approximately** three kilometers. By comparison, airplanes lifted scientists to a height of five kilometers and more. Radio technology allowed scientists to transmit data from the air to the ground, where other scientists analyzed and compared information. Breakthroughs came fast and furiously. Still, scientists dreamed of reaching ever higher.

As humans reached higher, we learned more and more about Earth's atmosphere.

14 Unit 5 • Text Set 1

Reading/Writing Companion, p. 14

AUTHOR'S CRAFT DOK 2

Reread the first two paragraphs of page 14. Ask: *How do they help you understand the focus of this section?* (The paragraphs discuss how scientists figured out how to send devices into the sky so that they could study weather where it actually happens.)

ELL *Reread the heading and the first two paragraphs on page 14. In what way was science still limited?* (It was ground-based.) What did scientists do in the 1700s? (started sending devices into the sky) *What does the question at the end of the first paragraph help explain?* (why scientists wanted to travel to the sky)

Why did the author use the heading "In the Sky, Looking Down" for this section? Explain your answer. (The focus of the section is on scientists sending devices into the sky to study the weather, so "In the Sky, Looking Down" is referring to those devices.)

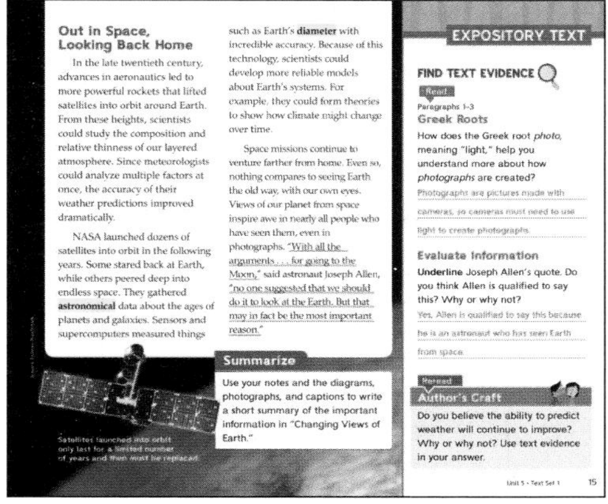

Out in Space, Looking Back Home

In the late twentieth century, advances in aeronautics led to more powerful rockets that lifted satellites into orbit around Earth. From these heights, scientists could study the composition and relative thinness of our layered atmosphere. Since meteorologists could analyze multiple factors at once, the accuracy of their weather predictions improved dramatically.

NASA launched dozens of satellites into orbit in the following years. Some stared back at Earth, while others peered deep into endless space. They gathered **astronomical** data about the ages of planets and galaxies. Sensors and supercomputers measured things such as Earth's **diameter** with incredible accuracy. Because of this technology, scientists could develop more reliable models about Earth's systems. For example, they could form theories to show how climate might change over time.

Space missions continue to venture farther from home. Even so, nothing compares to seeing Earth the old way, with our own eyes. Views of our planet from space inspire awe in nearly all people who have seen them, even in photographs. "With all the arguments . . . for going to the Moon," said astronaut Joseph Allen, "no one suggested that we should do it to look at the Earth. But that may in fact be the most important reason."

Satellites launched into orbit only last for a limited number of years and then must be replaced.

Summarize

Use your notes and the diagrams, photographs, and captions to write a short summary of the important information in "Changing Views of Earth."

EXPOSITORY TEXT

FIND TEXT EVIDENCE

Read

Paragraphs 1-3

Greek Roots

How does the Greek root *photo*, meaning "light," help you understand more about how *photographs* are created?

Photographs are pictures made with cameras, so cameras must need to use light to create photographs.

Evaluate Information

Underline Joseph Allen's quote. Do you think Allen is qualified to say this? Why or why not?

Yes, Allen is qualified to say this because he is an astronaut who has seen Earth from space.

Reread

Author's Craft

Do you believe the ability to predict weather will continue to improve? Why or why not? Use text evidence in your answer.

Unit 5 • Text Set 1 15

Reading/Writing Companion, p. 15

AUTHOR'S CRAFT DOK 3

Reread page 15. Ask: *How have advances in technology helped scientists learn more about Earth and space?* (In the first paragraph, the author says that more powerful rockets launched satellites that allowed scientists to study Earth's atmosphere. The author also says that using new technology caused scientists to develop "more reliable models about Earth's systems," as well as gather more information about space.)

Have partners scan the first paragraph for the word *since. Does the word* since *indicate a cause or an effect?* (a cause)

Do you believe the ability to predict weather will continue to improve? Why or why not? (Sample answer: Yes, I believe the ability to predict weather will continue to improve because the text points out how multiple factors improved meteorologists' ability to predict weather accurately and how new technology has allowed scientists to develop more reliable models.)

SYNTHESIZE INFORMATION

Explain that when you synthesize information, you gather information from different places and put it together. Synthesizing information can help you come to a new understanding about a topic.

Think Aloud On page 13, the last paragraph discusses the heliocentric model of the solar system, while the diagram at the bottom of the page shows a visual representation of it. I can synthesize the information from both the text and the diagram to understand that in Copernicus's heliocentric model, the Sun is in the center of the solar system and that Earth orbits the Sun, rather than the other way around.

Integrate

BUILD KNOWLEDGE: MAKE CONNECTIONS

Talk About the Text Have partners discuss how scientific knowledge changes over time.

Write About the Text Have students add ideas to the Build Knowledge pages of their reader's notebooks.

Anchor Chart Record any new ideas on the Build Knowledge anchor chart.

Add to the Vocabulary List Have students write down any words they learned about how scientific knowledge changes over time in their reader's notebooks.

FORMATIVE ASSESSMENT

STUDENT CHECK-IN

Have partners share their responses to one of the Reread prompts on Reading/Writing Companion pages 13–15. Ask them to use the Check-In routine.

LEARNING GOALS

We can use text evidence to respond to expository text.

OBJECTIVES

Determine two or more central, or main, ideas of a text and explain how they are supported by relevant, or key details; summarize the text.

Explain the relationships or interactions between two or more individuals, events, ideas, or concepts in a historical, scientific, or technical text based on specific information in the text.

ELA ACADEMIC LANGUAGE

- *prompt, analyze, sequence*
- Cognates: *analizar, secuencia*

TEACH IN SMALL GROUP

Approaching Level Have partners work through the selection together to gather details that support their points.

On Level Have students provide feedback to each other about their responses.

Beyond Level Have students develop a plan for incorporating any changes that partners have suggested.

ELL Group students of mixed proficiency levels to discuss and respond to the prompt.

Reread

Write About the Shared Read

Analyze the Prompt DOK 3

Read the prompt aloud: *What is the author's purpose for providing an in-depth look at the chronology of our study of Earth and space?* Ask: *What is the prompt asking?* (to determine the author's purpose for including a detailed chronology of the study of Earth and space) Say: *Let's reread to see how the text explains how and why people continued to demonstrate an interest in learning more about Earth and space. Doing this will help you make inferences that will aid you in your response.*

Analyze Text Evidence

Remind students that one text can reflect several different structures. In "Changing Views of Earth," the author uses a cause-and-effect text structure to describe how and why advances in scientific technology happened, but also lists the advances in chronological order, or in the order in which they happened. Phrases such as *long ago, at first,* and *before long,* as well as concrete dates, help to provide chronological information. In the **Reading/Writing Companion**, have students skim page 13 for the phrases *long ago* and *in the early 1600s.* Ask: *Why does the author go back this far into history?* (The author wants to show that humans have been interested in learning more about Earth and space for a very long time.) Ask: *How does the chronological order of events also show cause and effect?* (The order lets me know that each event was a cause for another event, creating a chain reaction of causes and effects.) Have students look for other clues in the text that help them establish a timeline of causes and effects and problems and solutions.

Respond

Direct student pairs to the sentence starters on Reading/Writing Companion page 22. Ask: *How does understanding the chronology of events help you understand why people have continued wanting to learn more and more about Earth and space?* As needed, model a response.

Think Aloud The text shows how, over time, new causes led to new effects. In the beginning, scientists studied space from the ground. But as they wanted to know more and more, they developed new devices to use in the air. Then, when these devices became less helpful than the scientists wanted, they developed newer, more useful ones again.

Analytical Writing Students should use the phrases in the sentence starters to form their responses. Their response should state the central idea and support that idea with relevant details from the text. Students may continue their responses on a separate piece of paper.

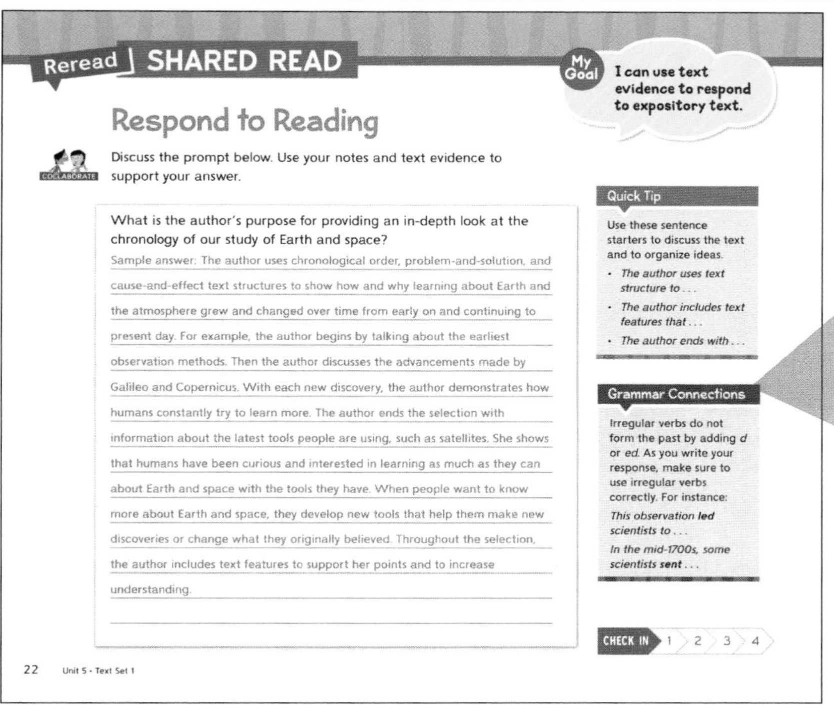

Reread | SHARED READ

My Goal: I can use text evidence to respond to expository text.

Respond to Reading

COLLABORATE

Discuss the prompt below. Use your notes and text evidence to support your answer.

What is the author's purpose for providing an in-depth look at the chronology of our study of Earth and space?

Sample answer: The author uses chronological order, problem-and-solution, and cause-and-effect text structures to show how and why learning about Earth and the atmosphere grew and changed over time from early on and continuing to present day. For example, the author begins by talking about the earliest observation methods. Then the author discusses the advancements made by Galileo and Copernicus. With each new discovery, the author demonstrates how humans constantly try to learn more. The author ends the selection with information about the latest tools people are using, such as satellites. She shows that humans have been curious and interested in learning as much as they can about Earth and space with the tools they have. When people want to know more about Earth and space, they develop new tools that help them make new discoveries or change what they originally believed. Throughout the selection, the author includes text features to support her points and to increase understanding.

Quick Tip

Use these sentence starters to discuss the text and to organize ideas.

- *The author uses text structure to . . .*
- *The author includes text features that . . .*
- *The author ends with . . .*

Grammar Connections

Irregular verbs do not form the past by adding *d* or *ed*. As you write your response, make sure to use irregular verbs correctly. For instance:

This observation ***led*** *scientists to . . .*

In the mid-1700s, some scientists ***sent*** *. . .*

CHECK IN 1 2 3 4

22 Unit 5 • Text Set 1

Reading/Writing Companion, p. 22

Grammar Connections

Students can use online **Grammar Handbook** page 462 to review and practice forming irregular verbs correctly.

English Language Learners

Use the following scaffolds with **Respond**.

Beginning

Read the prompt with students and discuss what they will write about. Reread with them sentences 1–2 in paragraph 3 on page 14 of "Changing Views of Earth." *Were the scientists satisfied or unsatisfied?* (unsatisfied) *What happened as they learned more?* They wanted to go higher. They wanted to go higher because they felt unsatisfied. Ask guiding questions to help partners discuss how this cause-and-effect relationship helps them better understand why people wanted to learn more about Earth and space.

Intermediate

Read the prompt and the Quick Tip box with students and discuss what they will write about. Have partners read paragraph 3 on page 14 of "Changing Views of Earth." *Why did scientists want to go higher?* They were not satisfied and wanted to learn more about Earth and space. Elicit partners to discuss how this cause-and-effect relationship helps them better understand people's desire to learn more about Earth and space.

Advance/Advanced High

Review the prompt and sentence starters on page 22 with students. Have them read pages 14–15 and identify the cause and effect of how new discoveries led to people to develop new tools Then have them respond using the sentence starters and the terms *Earth* and *space*.

NEWCOMER

Have students listen to the summaries of the **Shared Read** in their native language and then in English to help them access the text and develop listening comprehension. Help students ask and answer questions with a partner. Use these sentence frames: What is the text about? The text is about ___. Then continue the lessons in the **Newcomer Teacher's Guide**.

FORMATIVE ASSESSMENT

STUDENT CHECK-IN

Ask partners to share their responses on Reading/Writing Companion page 22. Have them use the Check-In routine to reflect and fill in the bars.

LEARNING GOALS

- We can decode words with suffixes.
- We can identify and read multisyllabic words.
- We can read fluently with expression.

OBJECTIVES

Know and apply grade-level phonics and word analysis skills in decoding words.

Use combined knowledge of all letter-sound correspondences, syllabication patterns, and morphology (e.g., roots and affixes) to read accurately unfamiliar multisyllabic words in context and out of context.

Read grade-level prose and poetry orally with accuracy, appropriate rate, expression, and automaticity on successive readings.

- Rate: 136–156 WCPM

ELA ACADEMIC LANGUAGE

- *expression*
- Cognate: *expresión*

TEACH IN SMALL GROUP

Word Study

Approaching Level and **ELL** Use the Tier 2 activity on page T62 before teaching the lesson.

On Level and **Beyond Level** As needed, use the Read Multisyllabic Words section.

ELL See page 5 in the **Language Transfers Handbook** for guidance in identifying sounds and symbols that may not transfer for speakers of certain languages.

Suffixes

1 Explain

Explain that a suffix is a letter or group of letters added to a base word or root that changes the word's meaning and can also change its part of speech. Review with students that the most common suffixes are *-s, -es* (plurals), *-ing* (present tense), and *-ed* (past tense).

2 Model

Write the following suffixes and sample words on the board. Model using the meaning of the suffix to determine the meaning of the sample word.

- *-ful,* means "full of"; forms an adjective
  The joyful children played in the snow.
- *-ion, -tion, -ation, -ition,* mean "act or process of"; forms a noun
  This book explains the *formation* of the mountain range.

  When these words become nouns, the final consonant changes sound. For example, the /t/ in *inspect* changes to /sh/ in *inspection.* Similarly, the /k/ in *politic* changes to /sh/ when *-ian* is added to form *politician.*
- *-less,* means "without"; forms an adjective
  The *careless* skater tripped and fell.
- *-ist,* means "person who"; forms a noun
  The *artist* used clay to make her sculpture.

3 Guided Practice

Write the following words on the board. Using the first word, model underlining the suffix and then reading the word. Have students underline the suffixes in the remaining words. Then have them read the words chorally and note the consonant sound change from /t/ or /k/ to /sh/ in the words *inspect* and *inspection* and *magic* and *magician.*

expression	inspection	chemist	discussion
helpful	violinist	description	fearful
creation	narration	healthful	biologist
admiration	stylist	fearless	thoughtful
magician	weightless	dentist	thankful

For practice with decoding suffixes, use **Practice Book** page 247 or online activities.

Read Multisyllabic Words

Transition to Longer Words Write the following word pairs on the board. Have students read the first word in each pair. Then model how to read the multisyllabic words with suffixes. Point out each suffix and any consonant changes as you read the words to help students gain awareness of these common word parts. Remind students when the suffix changes the spelling of a word.

educate, education	penny, penniless
prepare, preparation	science, scientist
beauty, beautiful	statistic, statistician
humor, humorless	purpose, purposeful
add, addition	piano, pianist
indent, indentation	resent, resentful

When finished, have students chorally read the words as you point to them in random order and at varying speeds. Have students use these words when writing and remind them to note any consonant change from /t/ or /k/ to /sh/.

Fluency

Expression

Explain/Model Review with students how reading with expression, or prosody, can help them better understand and enjoy what they read. Read aloud "On the Ground, Looking Around" from the **Reading/Writing Companion** page 13. Model using expression and show a clear differentiation of statements and questions. Read carefully, emphasizing suffixes to clarify meaning.

Practice/Apply Have partners alternate reading paragraphs in the passage, modeling the expression you used. Remind students that you will be listening for their use of expression as you monitor their reading during the week.

Daily Fluency Practice

Automaticity Students can practice reading with accuracy and appropriate rate to develop automaticity, using the online **Differentiated Genre Passage,** "Is There Life Out There?"

DIGITAL TOOLS

For more practice, have students use the phonics and fluency activities.

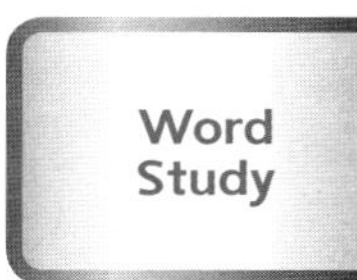

Suffixes

MULTIMODAL LEARNING

Use self-stick notes to mark the beginning and end of a short section of a reading passage. Choose sentences that have words with suffixes. Have partners read the section aloud to each other. As they read, have students underline words with suffixes. After reading, have students write the words and then have partners take turns saying the words aloud.

FORMATIVE ASSESSMENT

STUDENT CHECK-IN

Suffixes Ask partners to share three words with suffixes.

Multisyllabic Words Have partners read the following words: *careful, plentiful, selfless, election.*

Fluency Ask partners to read "Is There Life Out There?" fluently.

Have partners use the Check-In routine to reflect.

CHECK FOR SUCCESS

Can students decode words with suffixes? Can students read fluently and with expression?

Small Group Instruction

If No:

- **Approaching** Reteach pp. T62, T66
- **ELL** Develop p. T62

If Yes:

- **On** Apply p. T68
- **Beyond** Apply p. T74

LEARNING GOALS

- **We can use the research process to create a podcast.**
- **We can avoid plagiarism by paraphrasing information from sources.**

OBJECTIVES

Conduct short research projects that use several sources to build knowledge through investigation of different aspects of a topic.

Recall relevant information from experiences or gather relevant information from print and digital sources; summarize or paraphrase information in notes and finished work, and provide a list of sources.

Come to discussions prepared, having read or studied required material; explicitly draw on that preparation and other information known about the topic to explore ideas under discussion.

Follow agreed-upon rules for discussions and carry out assigned roles.

Pose and respond to specific questions by making comments that contribute to the discussion and elaborate on the remarks of others.

ELA ACADEMIC LANGUAGE

- *podcast, paraphrase, quote, cite, plagiarism*
- Cognate: *parafrasear*

TEACH IN SMALL GROUP

You may wish to teach the Research and Inquiry lesson during Small Group time. Have groups of mixed abilities complete the page and work on the podcast.

Scientific Knowledge Grows

Explain to students that for the next two weeks they will work collaboratively in large groups to research the Earth, Sun, and Moon. Students will create a podcast that explains how the relationships in the solar system have changed over time as technology improved. Discuss what students know about how our understanding of the Sun and Earth has changed over time based on the selections they've read in this text set.

Paraphrasing Before students begin, review paraphrasing and plagiarism. Have students look at the sample index cards on **Reading/Writing Companion** page 23. Remind them that when they research additional information using print and online sources, the source information will need to be paraphrased in their own words or directly quoted and cited to avoid plagiarism. Support them as they go through each step in the Research Process as outlined on page 23 to make their podcasts.

STEP 1 **Set a Goal** Guide students in focusing their research by writing down questions that they want to research about the Earth, Sun, and Moon. Offer feedback as students generate questions and decide what information they would like to include in their podcasts. Have them use an **Accordion Foldable®**, available online, to help organize their information.

STEP 2 **Identify Sources** Remind students to use reliable, credible sources. Point out that print and online science articles, journals, and databases may be good sources of information when researching how the relationship between the Earth, Sun, and Moon changed over time.

STEP 3 **Find and Record Information** Discuss plagiarism with students and how to avoid it. Remind them that plagiarism is copying the exact words an author uses and using them as your own. Point out that paraphrasing source information in their own words and giving credit to the author is one way to avoid plagiarism. Students can paraphrase by restating the author's ideas and opinions in their own words. They can also summarize the central idea of a source or use a direct quotation from the source. Review with students how to take notes and cite the sources they use to gather information for their podcasts.

STEP 4 **Organize and Synthesize Information** Show students how to organize the information that they want to include in the draft of their podcasts. Have them focus on why our understanding of the relationship between the Earth, Sun, and Moon has changed over time. Remind them to give credit to their sources.

STEP 5 **Create and Present** Review with students what information they should include in their podcasts. At the end of their podcast, have them cite the sources they used. Discuss options for sharing their presentations. Consider posting student podcasts to a classroom website.

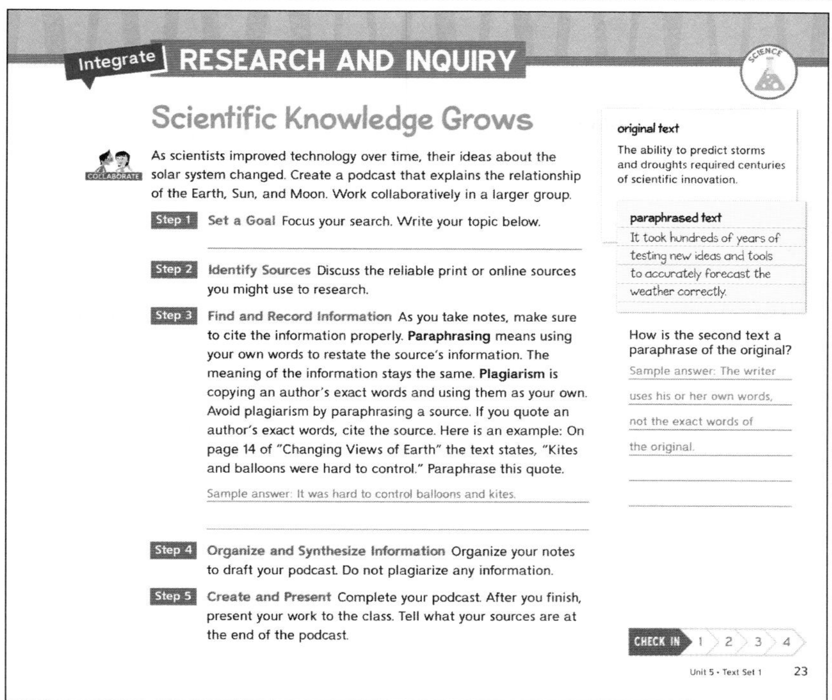

Integrate | RESEARCH AND INQUIRY

Scientific Knowledge Grows

As scientists improved technology over time, their ideas about the solar system changed. Create a podcast that explains the relationship of the Earth, Sun, and Moon. Work collaboratively in a larger group.

Step 1 **Set a Goal** Focus your search. Write your topic below.

Step 2 **Identify Sources** Discuss the reliable print or online sources you might use to research.

Step 3 **Find and Record Information** As you take notes, make sure to cite the information properly. **Paraphrasing** means using your own words to restate the source's information. The meaning of the information stays the same. **Plagiarism** is copying an author's exact words and using them as your own. Avoid plagiarism by paraphrasing a source. If you quote an author's exact words, cite the source. Here is an example: On page 14 of "Changing Views of Earth" the text states, "Kites and balloons were hard to control." Paraphrase this quote.

Sample answer: It was hard to control balloons and kites.

Step 4 **Organize and Synthesize Information** Organize your notes to draft your podcast. Do not plagiarize any information.

Step 5 **Create and Present** Complete your podcast. After you finish, present your work to the class. Tell what your sources are at the end of the podcast.

original text
The ability to predict storms and droughts required centuries of scientific innovation.

paraphrased text
It took hundreds of years of testing new ideas and tools to accurately forecast the weather correctly.

How is the second text a paraphrase of the original?
Sample answer: The writer uses his or her own words, not the exact words of the original.

CHECK IN 1 2 3 4

Unit 5 • Text Set 1 23

Reading/Writing Companion, p. 23

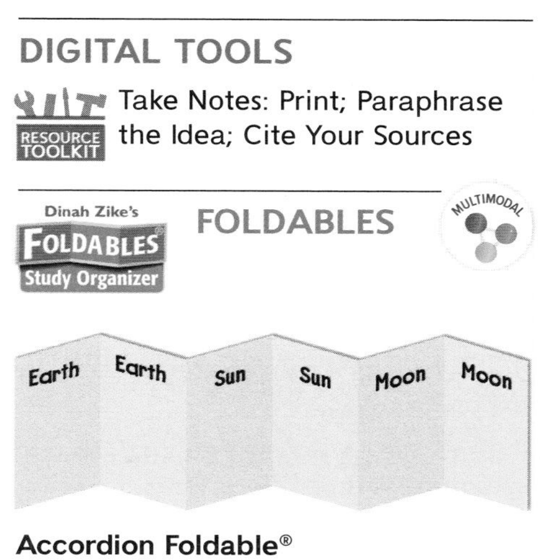

DIGITAL TOOLS

RESOURCE TOOLKIT Take Notes: Print; Paraphrase the Idea; Cite Your Sources

Dinah Zike's FOLDABLES Study Organizer

FOLDABLES

MULTIMODAL

Accordion Foldable®

English Language Learners

Use the following scaffolds with **Step 3**.

Beginning

Review how to paraphrase with students. Read the original text on page 23 with them. *This is the original text. These are the author's words.* Point to and read the paraphrased text. *This is the paraphrased text. Talk to your partner about how you know the second text is a paraphrase from the original.* Have them respond using: The writer uses his or her own words. Help partners gather information and paraphrase in their own words. Model how to take notes and cite sources. Check the students' notes and provide feedback as needed.

Intermediate

Review how to paraphrase with students. Have partners reread and discuss the original text and paraphrased text examples on page 23: The first paragraph is the original text. The second paragraph is paraphrased. The writer uses his or her own words. Then help partners take notes in their own words and cite sources. Check their notes and provide feedback as needed.

Advanced/Advanced High

Check the students' understanding of plagarism and paraphrasing. Have partners review the original and paraphrased text examples on page 23 and discuss how the writer paraphrased original text. Then guide partners to take notes in their own words and cite sources.

FORMATIVE ASSESSMENT

STUDENT CHECK-IN

Podcast Ask students to share their podcasts.

Paraphrasing Have students share an example of a source they used and how they paraphrased it.

Have students use the Check-In routine to reflect and fill in the bars on Reading/Writing Companion page 23.

When Is a Planet Not a Planet?

Lexile 980L

LEARNING GOALS

Read We can apply strategies and skills to read expository text.

Reread We can reread to analyze text, craft, and structure and compare texts.

Have students apply what they learned as they read.

What makes this text complex?

- Sentence Structure
- Specific Vocabulary
- Genre
- Connection of Ideas
- Purpose

Distinguish among objects in the Solar System, including the Sun, Earth, planets, moons, asteroids, comets, and discuss their interactions.

Close Reading Routine

Read DOK 1–2

- Identify important ideas and details.
- Take notes and summarize.
- Use ACT prompts as needed.

Reread DOK 2–3

- Analyze the text, craft, and structure.
- Use *Reading/Writing Companion*, pp. 24–26

Integrate DOK 3–4

- Integrate knowledge and ideas.
- Make text-to-text connections.
- Use the Integrate lesson.
- Complete the Show Your Knowledge task.
- Inspire action.

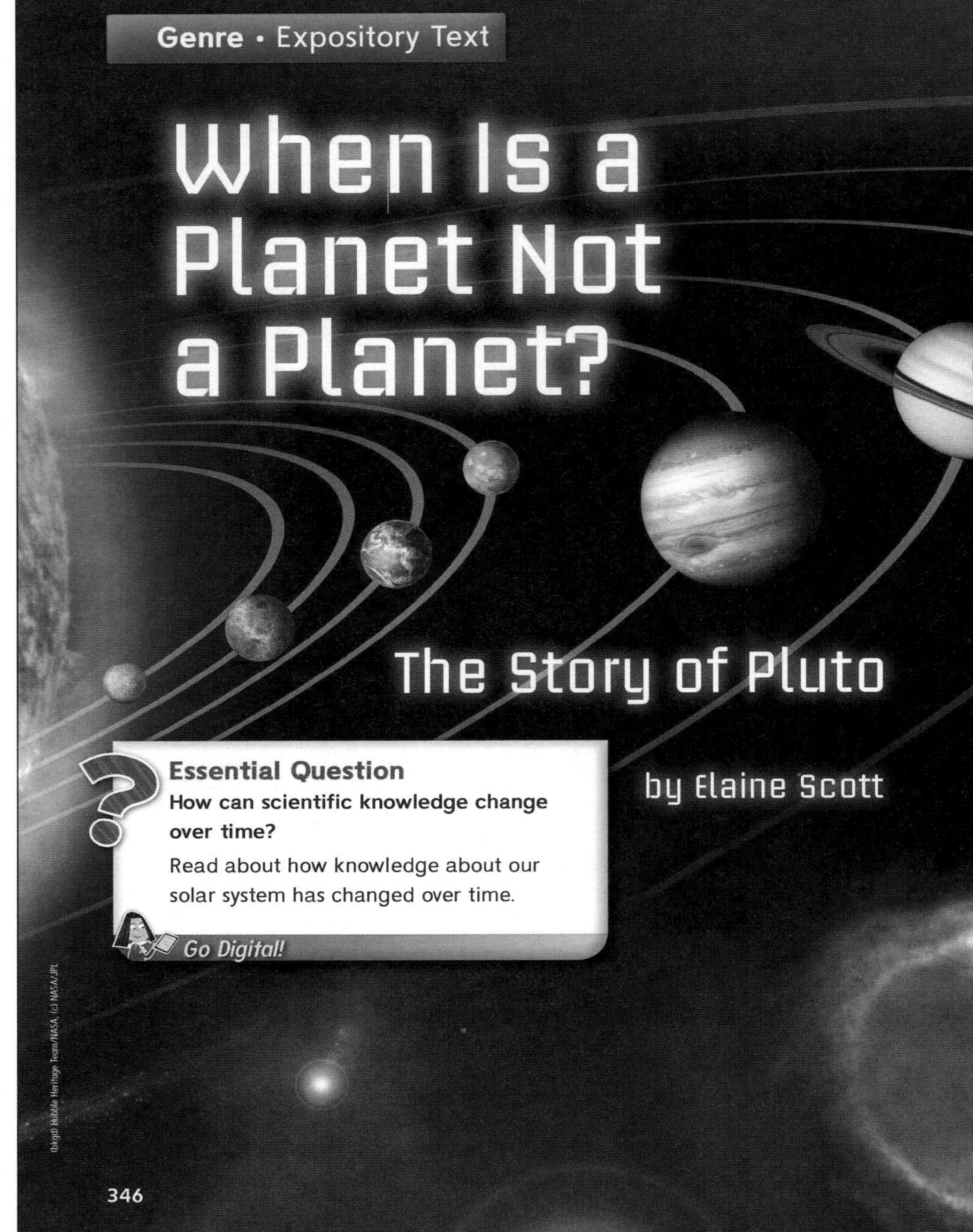

Genre • Expository Text
When Is a Planet Not a Planet?
The Story of Pluto
by Elaine Scott
Essential Question
How can scientific knowledge change over time?
Read about how knowledge about our solar system has changed over time.
Go Digital!
346

Literature Anthology, pp. 346-347

DIFFERENTIATED READING

You may wish to read the full selection aloud once with minimal stopping before you begin using the Read prompts.

Approaching Level Have students listen to the selection summary. Use the Reread prompts during Small-Group time.

On Level and Beyond Level Pair students or have them independently complete the Reread prompts on **Reading/ Writing Companion,** pages 24–26.

English Language Learners Have ELLs listen to the summary of the selection, available in multiple languages. See also **ELL Small Group Guide**.

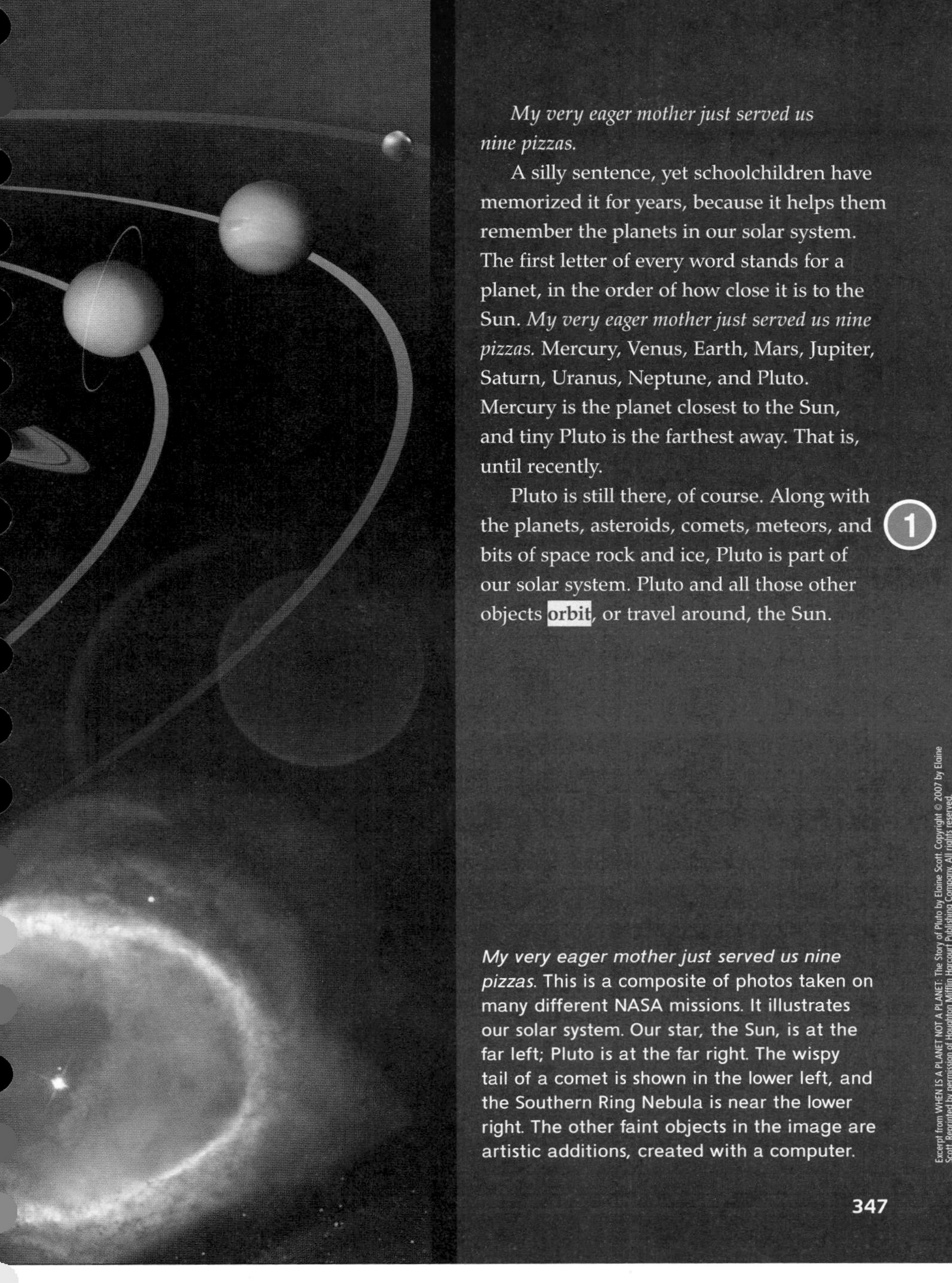

My very eager mother just served us nine pizzas.

A silly sentence, yet schoolchildren have memorized it for years, because it helps them remember the planets in our solar system. The first letter of every word stands for a planet, in the order of how close it is to the Sun. *My very eager mother just served us nine pizzas.* Mercury, Venus, Earth, Mars, Jupiter, Saturn, Uranus, Neptune, and Pluto. Mercury is the planet closest to the Sun, and tiny Pluto is the farthest away. That is, until recently.

Pluto is still there, of course. Along with the planets, asteroids, comets, meteors, and bits of space rock and ice, Pluto is part of our solar system. Pluto and all those other objects **orbit**, or travel around, the Sun. (1)

My very eager mother just served us nine pizzas. This is a composite of photos taken on many different NASA missions. It illustrates our solar system. Our star, the Sun, is at the far left; Pluto is at the far right. The wispy tail of a comet is shown in the lower left, and the Southern Ring Nebula is near the lower right. The other faint objects in the image are artistic additions, created with a computer.

347

Read

Set a Purpose Tell students to preview the text and set a purpose for reading. Remind them that setting a purpose can help them monitor their comprehension.

Note Taking: Use the Graphic Organizer

Analytical Writing Remind students to take notes as they read. Distribute copies of online Central Idea and Relevant Details **Graphic Organizer 7**. Have students add relevant details to determine the central idea of the selection.

1 Greek Roots DOK 2

Point out the word *asteroids* on page 347. Explain that it comes from the Greek root *aster-*, meaning "star," and the Greek suffix *-oid*, meaning "like." Have students look for words with the same root as they continue reading. (astronomical, astronomers)

ACT Access Complex Text

Sentence Structure

Point out the second sentence on page 347. Explain that sometimes an author may write in a conversational style. As part of this style, the author may omit parts of a sentence, such as the subject, which can be confusing to the reader.

- *Are there words missing in this sentence? Where?* (Yes, at the beginning, before "A silly sentence.")
- *What words could you add that would make a complete sentence?* (It is; It's)
- *What words could you add to the last sentence in the paragraph to make a full sentence?* (That is, Pluto was the farthest, until recently.)

Read

2 Central Idea and Relevant Details DOK 1

Why doesn't the old memory clue for planets—"My very eager mother just served us nine pizzas"—work anymore? (Pluto is no longer a planet, so the word "pizzas" must be eliminated from the sentence.)

3 Ask and Answer Questions DOK 1

Teacher Think Aloud As I read, I ask myself questions to make sure I understand the information in an expository text. When I read the word *nebula* in the second paragraph, I asked myself what it meant. I reread the first sentence, and I found out that a nebula is a space cloud.

Build Vocabulary on page 349

Have students add the Build Vocabulary words to their reader's notebook.

core: the central part of something

fuse: join together completely

swirled: spun around

Newcomer

Use the **Newcomer Online Visuals 5–9 and 20** with the accompanying prompts to help students expand vocabulary and language about measurements.

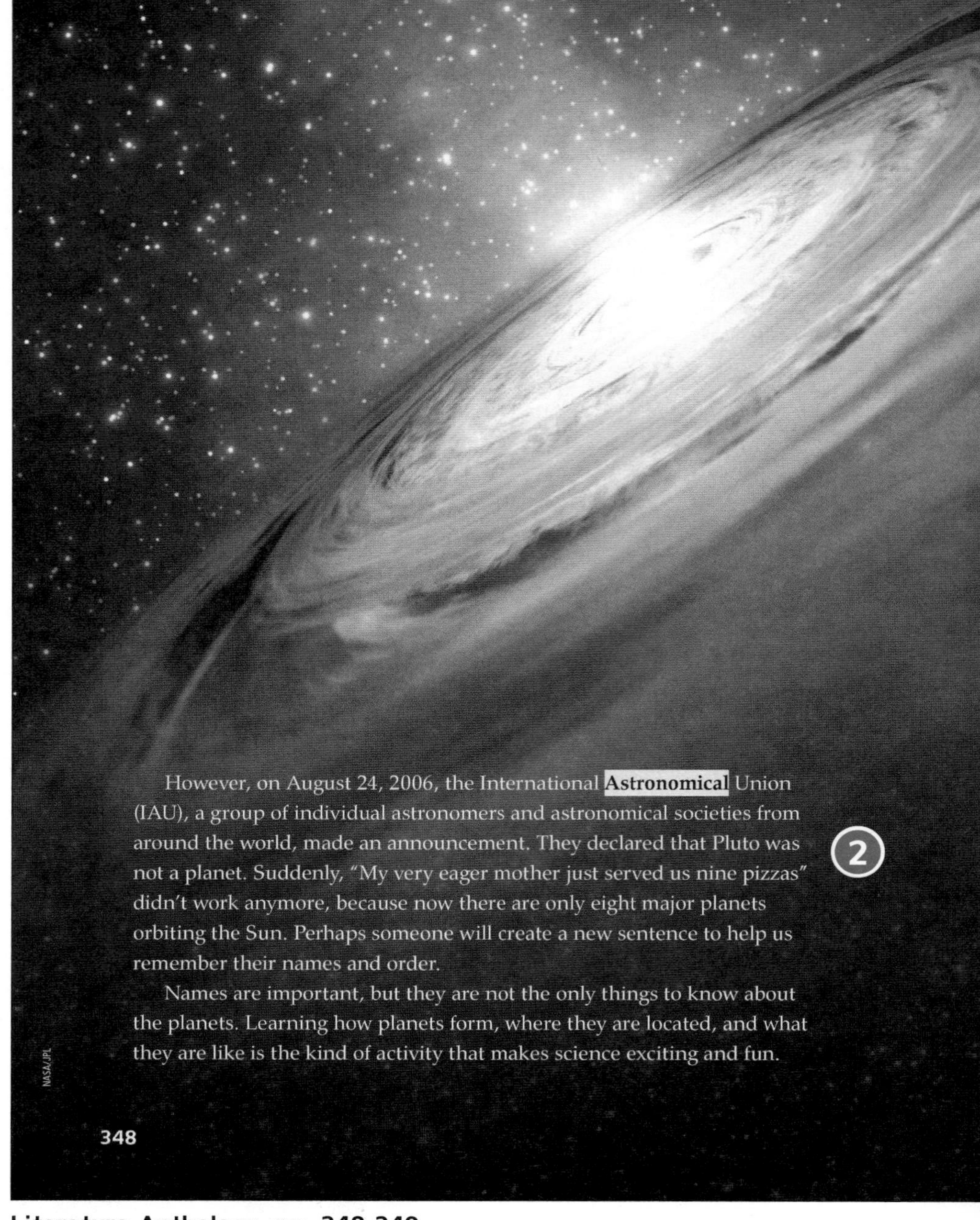

However, on August 24, 2006, the International **Astronomical** Union (IAU), a group of individual astronomers and astronomical societies from around the world, made an announcement. They declared that Pluto was not a planet. Suddenly, "My very eager mother just served us nine pizzas" didn't work anymore, because now there are only eight major planets orbiting the Sun. Perhaps someone will create a new sentence to help us remember their names and order. 2

Names are important, but they are not the only things to know about the planets. Learning how planets form, where they are located, and what they are like is the kind of activity that makes science exciting and fun.

NASA/JPL

348

Literature Anthology, pp. 348-349

Access Complex Text

Sentence Structure

Help students break down complex sentences to understand the subject and action. Guide them to identify the subject and verb in the first sentence on page 348.

- *What is the verb, or action, in the sentence?* (made)
- *What was made?* (an announcement)
- *Who made the announcement?* (the International Astronomical Union) *This is the subject.*

If students erroneously identify the subject as *group, astronomers,* or *societies,* review how these words are part of an appositive phrase. This phrase gives a description of the subject, the International Astronomical Union.

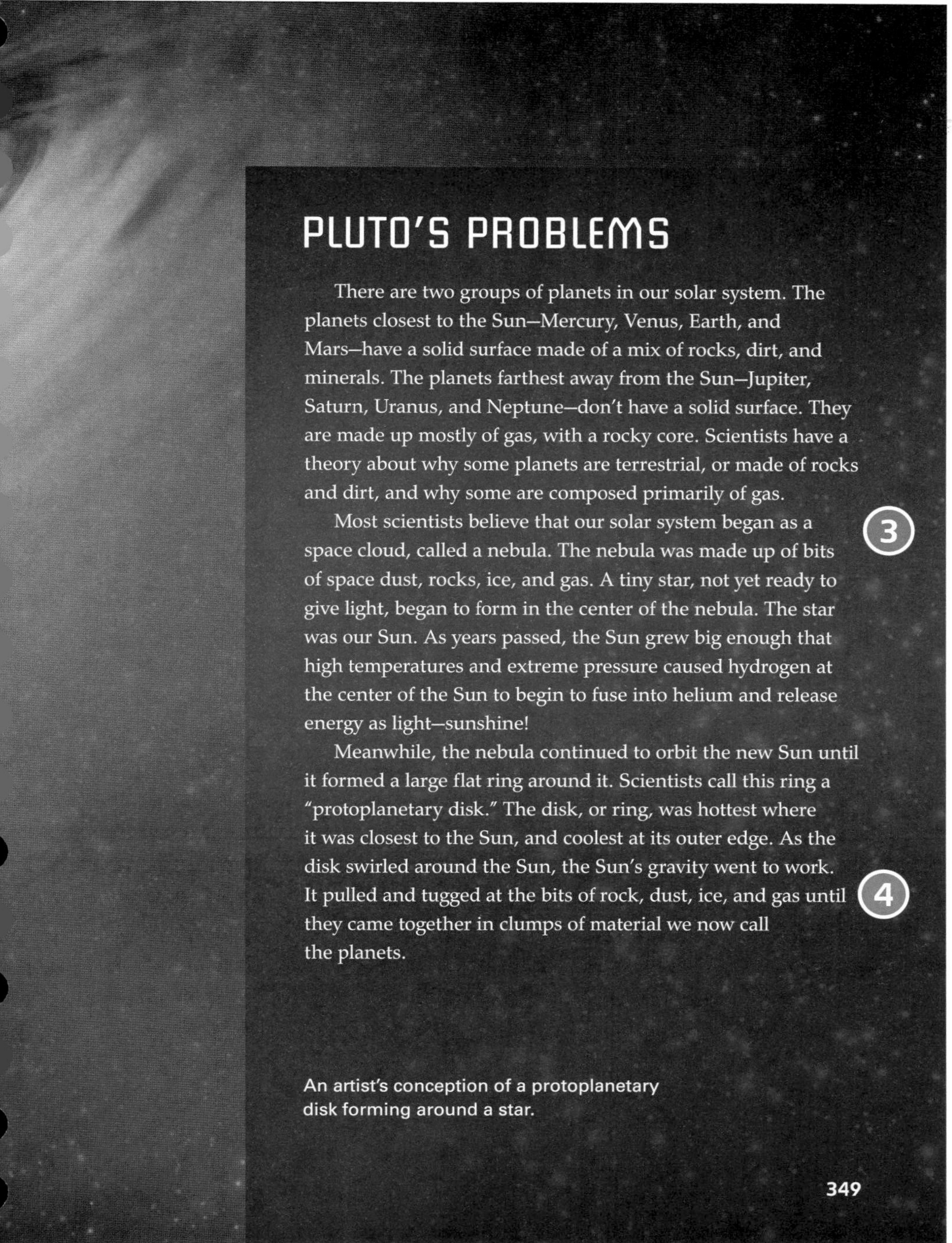

PLUTO'S PROBLEMS

There are two groups of planets in our solar system. The planets closest to the Sun—Mercury, Venus, Earth, and Mars—have a solid surface made of a mix of rocks, dirt, and minerals. The planets farthest away from the Sun—Jupiter, Saturn, Uranus, and Neptune—don't have a solid surface. They are made up mostly of gas, with a rocky core. Scientists have a theory about why some planets are terrestrial, or made of rocks and dirt, and why some are composed primarily of gas.

Most scientists believe that our solar system began as a space cloud, called a nebula. The nebula was made up of bits of space dust, rocks, ice, and gas. A tiny star, not yet ready to give light, began to form in the center of the nebula. The star was our Sun. As years passed, the Sun grew big enough that high temperatures and extreme pressure caused hydrogen at the center of the Sun to begin to fuse into helium and release energy as light—sunshine! 3

Meanwhile, the nebula continued to orbit the new Sun until it formed a large flat ring around it. Scientists call this ring a "protoplanetary disk." The disk, or ring, was hottest where it was closest to the Sun, and coolest at its outer edge. As the disk swirled around the Sun, the Sun's gravity went to work. It pulled and tugged at the bits of rock, dust, ice, and gas until they came together in clumps of material we now call the planets. 4

An artist's conception of a protoplanetary disk forming around a star.

349

Read

4 Central Idea and Relevant Details DOK 2

What is the central idea of the last paragraph on page 349? What relevant details support this central idea? Add the central idea and relevant details to your organizer.

Central Idea
The planets were formed around a "protoplanetary disk."
Detail
The disk swirled around the sun.
Detail
The sun's gravity pulled bits of rock, dust, ice, and gas together to form the planets.

Reread

Author's Purpose DOK 2

Reading/Writing Companion, p. 24

Reread page 349. What does this section describe? (It describes how scientists think the solar system formed.) How does the author use this section to support her ideas about Pluto? (Pluto didn't fit the theory of the solar system's development, which is what this section describes. Unlike the planets most distant from the Sun—Pluto is not made up of gas. It is solid, similar to the planets closest to the Sun.)

Spotlight on Language

Page 348, Paragraph 1 Point out and explain that "My very eager mother just served us nine pizzas" is an old memory clue. It helps us remember the planets in our solar system in order from the Sun. *The* M *in* My *stands for* Mercury. *The* V *in* very *stands for Venus.* The *E* in *eager* stands for Earth. *Pluto is no longer a planet. Which word needs to be taken out of the memory clue?* (pizzas)

Synthesize Information DOK 2

Explain Illustrations and captions give a visual presentation of the ideas in the text.

Discuss Reread the last paragraph on page 349. Discuss that the star in the illustration is like the Sun.

Apply *If this illustration represented the beginning of our solar system, where would Pluto have formed?* (on the edge of the disk)

Read

5 Genre: Expository Text DOK 2

Authors use text features such as captions to provide information about illustrations, photos, or diagrams. Turn to a partner and share what information you learn from the caption on page 350. How does this relate to the main text? (The caption tells that the photograph shows the Orion Nebula and explains that 153 stars with protoplanetary disks are forming new solar systems there. The caption relates to the information about the nebula that became a protoplanetary disk on page 349.)

6 Text Structure: Cause and Effect DOK 1

What caused astronomers to have a problem with Pluto? Paraphrase the text. (It didn't fit into the theory about how planets far from the Sun are formed.)

Build Vocabulary on page 350

terrestrial: relating to hard ground

NASA/JPL-Caltech/T. Megeath(University of Toledo & M. Robberto(STScI)

A small portion of the Orion Nebula, 1,500 light years away from Earth. At least 153 stars in this region have protoplanetary disks swirling around them, forming new solar systems. Scientists believe our solar system formed in just this way.

The planets that were closest to the Sun didn't keep much of their gas. The Sun's heat blasted it away, leaving behind solid **spheres** of matter, with only a little gas. Those spheres became the terrestrial planets—Mercury, Venus, Earth, and Mars. But on the outer edges of the disk, far away from the Sun's heat, it was much cooler. The clumps of rock and dirt there still had their thick layers of gas; they didn't burn away. The planets farthest from the Sun became the gas giants—Jupiter, Saturn, Uranus, and Neptune.

350

Literature Anthology, pp. 350–351

ACT Access Complex Text

Sentence Structure

Point out that a dash sets off information that explains the part of the sentence before it. On page 350, the author uses dashes to explain terrestrial planets and gas giants.

- *Which planets are terrestrial planets?* (Mercury, Venus, Earth, Mars) *Which planets are the gas giants?* (Jupiter, Saturn, Uranus, Neptune)

Specific Vocabulary

Point out the word *dense* on page 351.

- *Identify context clues to figure out what* dense *means.* (rocky core, made of rock, [not] made of gas) *What is another word for* dense*?* (thick, solid)

Have students use context clues to figure out the phrase *raised questions.* (made people ask questions)

6 Because astronomers still believed this theory about how our planets formed, they had a problem with Pluto. When it was first discovered in 1930, astronomers assumed Pluto was made of ice and gas because of its great distance from the sun. However, by 1987, Pluto had moved into a position that only occurs twice in its 248-year orbit and scientific instruments had improved. Astronomers were able to study Pluto and the light that reflected off it. Their instruments told them that Pluto was dense and must have a rocky core. That new information raised questions. If the planets closest to the Sun were rocky and the planets farthest away from the Sun were mostly made of gas, why was Pluto—the most distant planet of all—made of rock?

7

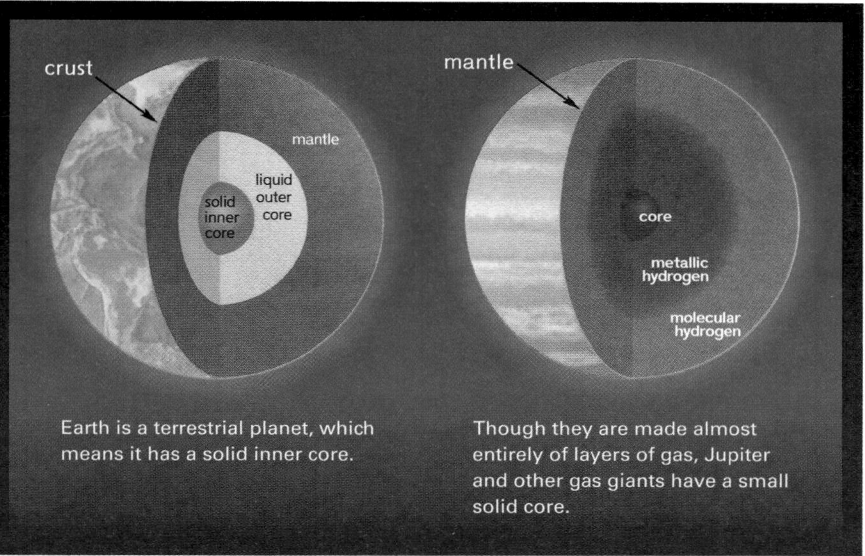

Earth is a terrestrial planet, which means it has a solid inner core.

Though they are made almost entirely of layers of gas, Jupiter and other gas giants have a small solid core.

Michelle Gengaro-Kokmen

351

Spotlight on Language

Page 351, Paragraph 1 Explain that pronouns are words that replace nouns, or names of people, places, and things. Then read the first two sentences. *The author uses the pronoun* it. Ask: *What noun does the pronoun refer to?* (Pluto) *How can you tell?* (*It* refers to Pluto because Pluto is singular and was mentioned earlier in the sentence.) Have partners identify pronouns and referents in the rest of the paragraph. For each pronoun, have students explain how they know which noun it refers to.

Read

7 Text Features: Diagram DOK 2

On page 351, what can you learn from the diagram about Earth and the gas giants that is not contained in the text? (The diagram shows the names of the layers of planets, such as crust and mantle, and where they are located in relation to each other; the types of gases present in a gas giant; and that Earth has a liquid outer core surrounding the solid inner core.)

STOP AND CHECK **DOK 1**

Ask and Answer Questions According to theory, why are some planets mostly made of gas and others mostly made of rock? (Planets close to the Sun are made of rock because heat from the Sun blasted away the gas. In the planets far away from the Sun, the gas didn't burn up because it was cooler.)

Build Vocabulary on page 351

theory: a scientific idea that explains facts or events

reflected: bounced off

Connect to Content

Inner and Outer Planets

The four planets closest to the Sun—Mercury, Venus, Earth, and Mars—are known as the inner planets. The planets farthest away from the Sun—Jupiter, Saturn, Uranus, and Neptune—are known as the outer planets. On pages 350–351, the author compares and contrasts several properties of the inner and outer planets, including their surfaces, climates, and origins. Have students evaluate the differences between inner and outer planets.

Read

8 Ask and Answer Questions DOK 1

 COLLABORATE **Teacher Think Aloud** There is a lot of information about orbits on this page. What questions can we ask to be sure we understand it?

Prompt students to apply the strategy in a Think Aloud by asking themselves questions about orbits and finding answers for their questions in the text. Have them turn to a partner and paraphrase what they read. Remind students that when they paraphrase, they reword the author's words.

Student Think Aloud The text says that an orbit is like a lane on a racetrack. How are they similar? As I keep reading, I see that each planet has its own path around the Sun, just like runners each have their own lane on a track.

Build Vocabulary on page 352

individual: for one person only

comets: frozen masses of dust and gas that move in a regular course around the sun

8 There were other questions as well. Pluto's orbit is different from the orbits of the planets. Think of an orbit as a lane on a racetrack. Just as runners have their own lanes on the track, each planet has its own orbit around the Sun. For the runners, all the lanes together make up the racetrack. For the planets, all their orbits, taken together, make up the "orbital plane." Just as runners don't run outside their individual lanes, planets don't travel around the Sun outside their individual orbits. Except for Pluto. Pluto crosses Neptune's orbit.

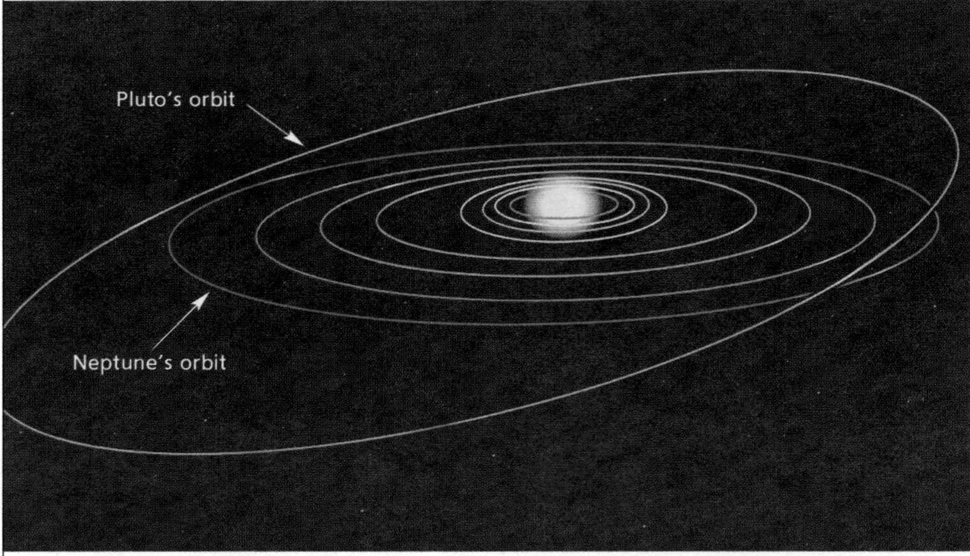

Michelle Gengaro-Kokmen

All of the planets, comets, and asteroids in the solar system are in orbit around the Sun. Their orbits line up with each other, creating an imaginary flat disk called the orbital plane. Pluto's orbit, which takes 248 Earth years to complete, brings it outside the orbital plane. For 20 years of each orbit, Pluto moves inside the orbit of Neptune, making Neptune farther from the sun than Pluto. Pluto was inside Neptune's orbit from 1979 to 1999.

352

Literature Anthology, pp. 352–353

ACT Access Complex Text

Genre

Diagrams are often included in expository text to give information visually. Remind students to use and interpret the information in the diagram on page 352 to help them understand text on page 353.

- Read aloud the second and third sentences on page 353, calling attention to the words "oval-shaped" and "stretched-out oblong."
- *How does the diagram help you understand these descriptions?* (The diagram shows the shapes of all the planets' orbits, making it obvious how the shape of Pluto's orbit is different.)
- *What does* oblong *mean?* ("a long stretched-out circle")

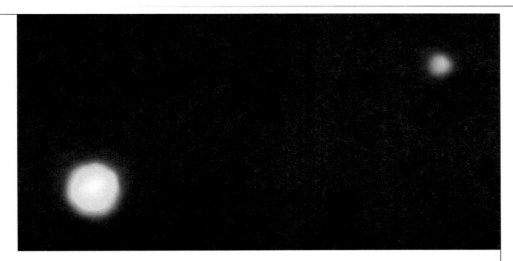

Pluto and its moon, Charon. Pluto was 2.6 billion miles from Earth when the Hubble Space Telescope took this photo.

Dr. R. Albrecht, ESA/ESO Space Telescope European Coordinating Facility; NASA

The shape of Pluto's orbit is different, too. The larger planets travel around the Sun in an oval-shaped orbit. Pluto's orbit is more of a stretched-out oblong. The other planets' orbits are level with the Sun. Pluto's is tilted. Comets' orbits are often tilted, so astronomers wondered, Could Pluto be a comet?

And of course there is Pluto's size. Astronomers knew Pluto was tiny when it was discovered in 1930. But because it was so far away, it was hard to see the planet clearly. Pluto appeared as a tiny dot of light in the night sky. Then telescopes improved. In 1976, American astronomer James Christy discovered that the tiny dot everyone thought was Pluto was really two objects: Pluto had a moon—Charon (CARE-en). Once astronomers discovered that Charon was separate from Pluto, they realized that Pluto was even smaller than they had originally thought. Pluto is only 1,440 miles in **diameter.** (Charon's diameter is 790 miles.) They began to ask, Is Pluto too small to be a planet? And since they had found Charon, they wondered, Were there more objects out there the size of Pluto? Were *they* planets, too? 9

353

Read

9 Central Idea and Relevant Details DOK 2

What are the relevant details on page 352 and the first paragraph of page 353? Use these details to determine the central idea. Add the central idea and relevant details to your organizer.

Central Idea
Pluto's orbit is unlike the orbits of other planets.
Detail
All of the planets but Pluto lie in the orbital plane and do not cross into other planets' "lanes."
Detail
Pluto crosses into Neptune's orbit.
Detail
The shape of Pluto's orbit is oblong, unlike that of the other planets whose orbits are circular.

ELL Spotlight on Language

Page 353, Paragraph 2 Guide partners as they read the paragraph and point to a signal word that shows sequence, or time order. (Then) Help students brainstorm other sequence words. (possible answers: first, finally, next, before, now, later) *These words help to connect events in time order.* Then have partners take turns using sequence words to talk about a time they discovered something or learned something new.

Connect to Content

Characteristics of Planets

On page 352, students read that one major characteristic all planets have in common is staying within a fixed orbit around the Sun. Have students explain how Pluto's orbit differs from the other planets' orbits and how this relates to its status as a planet.

Read

10 Ask and Answer Questions DOK 1

COLLABORATE Reread page 354. Ask yourself a question about the text. Then share your question with a partner and search together for the answer.

Student Think Aloud The fourth paragraph says that robots changed the way astronomers study the night sky. I wonder how things changed? As I continue reading, I find out that astronomers no longer have to stay up at night to watch the sky. Robots take photographs for them. The photos are sent to special computers.

Build Vocabulary on page 354

observatory: a building with telescopes and other equipment in it for studying space

peering: looking closely

captured: recorded, as in a photograph

FINDING PLANETS

In 1992, astronomers made an amazing discovery: 9.3 *billion* miles away from our sun is another region of space, shaped like a disk. Astronomers believe it contains approximately 70,000 icy objects, including Pluto.

This area of space was named the Kuiper Belt, after the Dutch-American astronomer Gerard Kuiper (KI-per) who lived from 1905 to 1973. In 1951, more than forty years before its discovery, Kuiper actually predicted that a region like this might exist.

Michael Brown, Chad Trujillo, and David Rabinowitz are planetary astronomers who study Kuiper Belt Objects, or KBOs. People often call these men "the Planet Finders." Together, they hunt for planets at the outer edges of our solar system using the Samuel Oschin Telescope at the Palomar Observatory in California. The Oschin telescope is a wide-field telescope, which means it views broad regions of the sky at once. When paired with a camera at the observatory, it can take pictures of these large areas.

In the past, astronomers had to spend their evenings peering through telescopes in order to study the night sky. Now things have changed. Robots control the Oschin telescope and its camera.

10 In the evenings, the cameras in the telescope at the Palomar Observatory are at work. They take three photographs over three hours of the part of the night sky the men want to study. Any object moving across the background of billions of stars and galaxies will be captured in pictures. The pictures are then sent from the telescope's cameras to a bank of ten computers at the California Institute of Technology. Next, the computers decide which objects appear to be moving and therefore might be a planet. Usually, the computers select about 100 objects; when the men arrive at work each morning, the pictures are ready for them to view.

354

Literature Anthology, pp. 354–355

Access Complex Text

Connection of Ideas

Tell students that on page 354, the author builds on previous ideas in each new paragraph.

- *The first paragraph tells about the discovery of a special region of space.*
- *What do we learn in the second paragraph that is related to the first paragraph?* (Kuiper predicted the existence of a region of space mentioned in the first paragraph.)
- *How does information about "the Planet Finders" in the third paragraph relate to the first two paragraphs?* (They are the people who look for planets in the Kuiper Belt.)

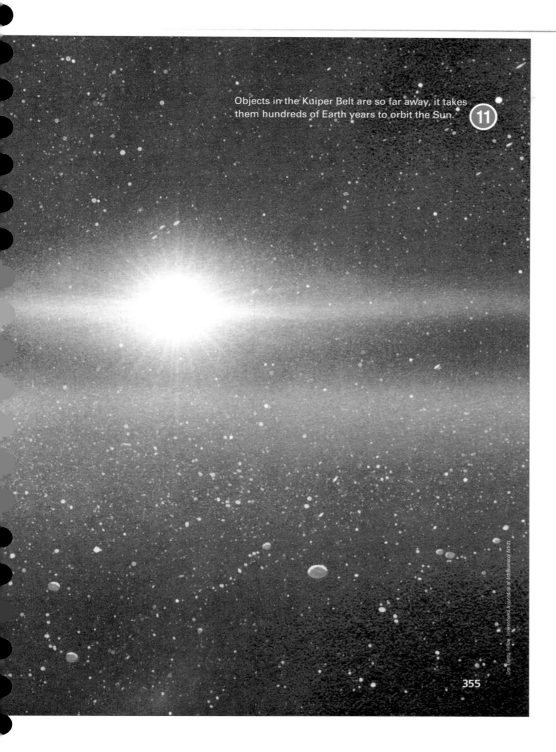

Objects in the Kuiper Belt are so far away, it takes them hundreds of Earth years to orbit the Sun. 11

Read

11 Genre: Expository Text DOK 2

COLLABORATE Expository text provides information and facts about a topic. Authors use text features to organize ideas and share information. Turn to a partner and discuss text features you find on pages 354 and 355. (I see the subheading "Finding Planets" and a photograph and caption.)

Reread

Author's Craft: Text Features DOK 2

Study the photo and reread the caption on page 355. How do they add to the information in the text on page 354? (The photo and caption help the reader visualize the Kuiper Belt and understand how difficult it is to locate a planet within this region.)

ELL Spotlight on Language

Page 354, Paragraph 3 Read the first three sentences of the paragraph. Point to the idiom *hunt for planets.* Explain that *hunting for* something can mean looking or searching for it. Ask: *What are the scientists doing?* (They are trying to find planets.) *Where are they trying to find the planets?* They are hunting at the outer edges of the solar system. *Talk to your partner about a time that you hunted for something.*

Sentence Structure

Help students understand the first sentence in paragraph two by removing descriptive phrases.

- *Restate the sentence using just the essential information.* (This area of space was named the Kuiper Belt after Gerard Kuiper.)
- *What do the omitted details tell about?* (They give additional facts about Gerard Kuiper.)

Read

12 Central Idea and Relevant Details DOK 2

Sometimes a central idea is not explicitly stated in the text; rather, it is implied. The relevant details should point to a central idea. Add the relevant details and central idea from page 357 to your organizer.

Central Idea
Scientists decided to create an official definition for the word "planet."
Detail
Astronomers disagreed over whether or not Eris could be classified as a planet.
Detail
Existing definitions of the word "planet" were problematic.
Detail
The IAU decided it was best to create three definitions.

Build Vocabulary on page 356 and 357

flaw: any fault or error

nicknamed: given another name in place of a formal name

verify: prove to be true

revealed: to show or announce

raging: out of control

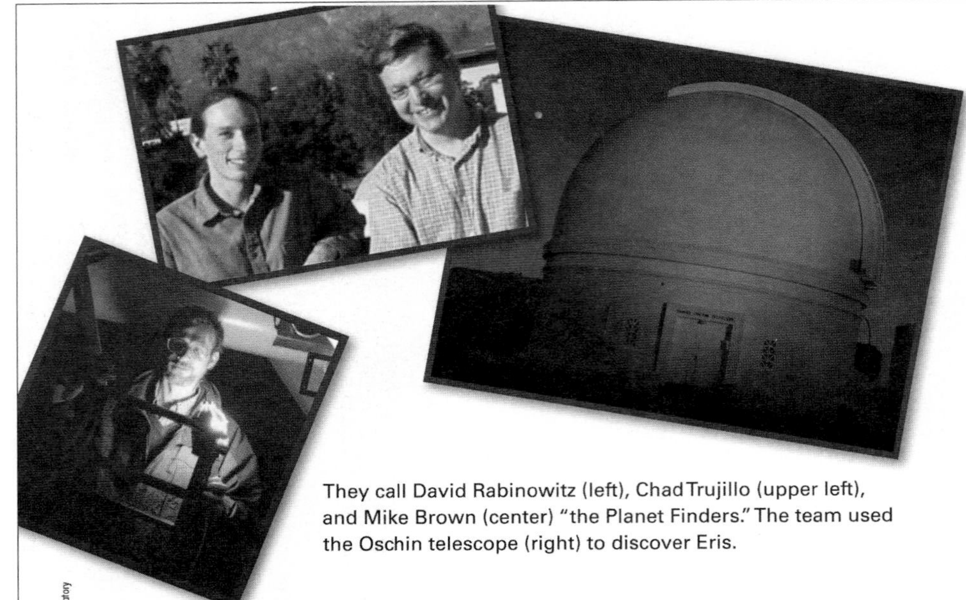

They call David Rabinowitz (left), Chad Trujillo (upper left), and Mike Brown (center) "the Planet Finders." The team used the Oschin telescope (right) to discover Eris.

Mike Brown says most of the objects he looks at on his computer screen are not planets. Many are caused by some kind of flaw in the telescope's camera. But every once in a while, an astronomer will get very lucky and something new and exciting will appear. That's how Mike and his team discovered 2003UB313, or Xena (ZEE-nah), as it was nicknamed, on October 21, 2003. Mike says, "The very first time I saw Xena on my screen, I thought that there was something wrong. It was too big and too bright. Then I did a **calculation** of how big it was and how far away it was. Xena is the most distant object ever seen in orbit around the Sun."

Pluto is 3.6 billion miles away, but Xena is 10 billion miles away and is approximately 400 miles bigger in diameter than Pluto. It takes Xena more than twice as long as Pluto to orbit the Sun.

Xena was always a nickname. On September 13, 2006, the newly discovered celestial body officially became Eris (AIR-is), for the Greek goddess of strife and discord. It seems an appropriate name, since there was a lot of strife and discord surrounding Eris. Was it a planet, or not?

356

Literature Anthology, pp. 356–357

Access Complex Text

Specific Vocabulary

Point out the words *strife* and *discord* in the last paragraph on page 356.

- *Identify context clues to figure out what* strife *and* discord *mean.* ("Was it a planet or not?" implies that scientists argued and disagreed about the discovery. On page 357, we find out they did argue about it. *Strife* and *discord* mean "a disagreement.")
- Have partners confirm their definitions in a dictionary. Point out that the two words are synonyms.

Discuss why scientists disagreed about Eris.

- *What was the problem with the dictionary definition of* planet*?* (It was too general. A "large body" wasn't specific enough.)

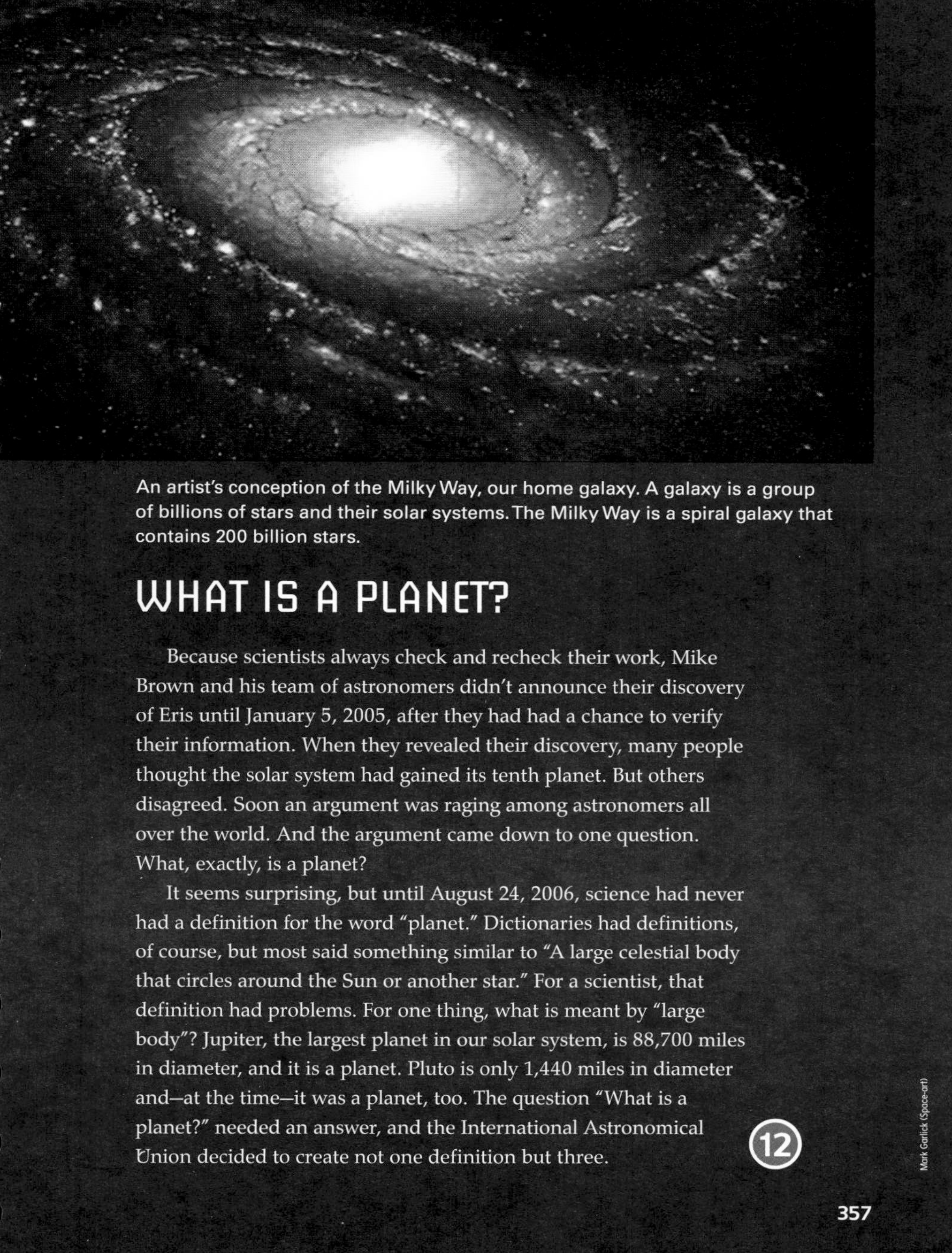

An artist's conception of the Milky Way, our home galaxy. A galaxy is a group of billions of stars and their solar systems. The Milky Way is a spiral galaxy that contains 200 billion stars.

WHAT IS A PLANET?

Because scientists always check and recheck their work, Mike Brown and his team of astronomers didn't announce their discovery of Eris until January 5, 2005, after they had had a chance to verify their information. When they revealed their discovery, many people thought the solar system had gained its tenth planet. But others disagreed. Soon an argument was raging among astronomers all over the world. And the argument came down to one question. What, exactly, is a planet?

It seems surprising, but until August 24, 2006, science had never had a definition for the word "planet." Dictionaries had definitions, of course, but most said something similar to "A large celestial body that circles around the Sun or another star." For a scientist, that definition had problems. For one thing, what is meant by "large body"? Jupiter, the largest planet in our solar system, is 88,700 miles in diameter, and it is a planet. Pluto is only 1,440 miles in diameter and—at the time—it was a planet, too. The question "What is a planet?" needed an answer, and the International Astronomical Union decided to create not one definition but three. (12)

Mark Garlick (Space-art)

357

Reread

Author's Craft: Text Features DOK 3

Reading/Writing Companion, p. 25

Look at the photos and reread the caption on page 356. What do you notice about the size of the telescope? (It is very large.) Why do you think having such a large telescope is necessary in studying space? (Possible response: Because objects in space are so far away, telescope lenses must be very powerful to see them. By making the telescopes so big, they are able to include the necessary parts to see images at a great distance.)

Author's Craft: Text Structure DOK 2

Reread page 356. What comparisons does the author make between Pluto and Eris? Why does she make these comparisons? (Pluto is 3.6 billion miles away, but Eris is 10 billion miles away. Eris is 400 miles bigger in diameter than Pluto. Both orbit the Sun, but Eris takes twice as long as Pluto to do so. This comparison suggests that Eris has many qualities of a planet.) Why was the discovery of Eris so significant? (This discovery raised questions about what constitutes a planet and forced astronomers to finally agree on a definition.)

Connection of Ideas

Remind students to connect pictures with the text.

- *How is the photograph of the Oschin telescope on page 356 connected to the text on page 354?* (Page 354 tells how astronomers used the telescope to take large pictures of the sky.)

English Language Learners

Non-verbal Cues Remind students that they can use non-verbal cues to share information when they are not able to do so verbally. Encourage students to pantomime, point to images, and draw diagrams and pictures to share information and answer questions: *Which image best shows why Pluto is different? How is it different?*

Read

⑬ Central Idea and Relevant Details DOK 2

What do the details in each paragraph on page 358 have in common? (They are all about the definition of a planet.) What is the central idea on this page? (The IAU made three rules used to decide whether a celestial body is a planet.)

⑭ Ask and Answer Questions DOK 1

Generate a question of your own about the definition of planets. For example, you might ask, "What is the difference between a planet and a dwarf planet?" Answer this question by paraphrasing the text. (A planet orbits the Sun, is round or nearly round, and is big enough to clear away objects in its path. A dwarf planet is also round and orbits the Sun, but it is not as big as a planet, so it doesn't have enough gravity to clear its path. A dwarf planet cannot be a moon or satellite of another planet.)

The IAU came up with three classes of objects that orbit the Sun: planets, dwarf planets, and small solar-system bodies.

The IAU decided that a celestial body is a planet if it:

1. orbits the Sun
2. is round or nearly round, because its gravity has pulled it into that shape
3. is big enough and has enough gravity to "clear the neighborhood" around its orbit

The first two qualifications for planethood, orbiting the Sun and a round shape, are easy to understand. The concept of "clearing the neighborhood" is a little more difficult.

⑬ It might help to think of planets as the schoolyard bullies of the solar system. In order to clear the neighborhood, a planet has to be big enough, and have enough gravity, to get rid of any celestial objects in its way. A large planet might clear its orbit by using its gravity to pull other, smaller, objects toward it and destroy them, the way asteroids are destroyed when they hit Earth.

NASA/JPL

A cosmic collision. Planets often "clear their neighborhoods" in this manner.

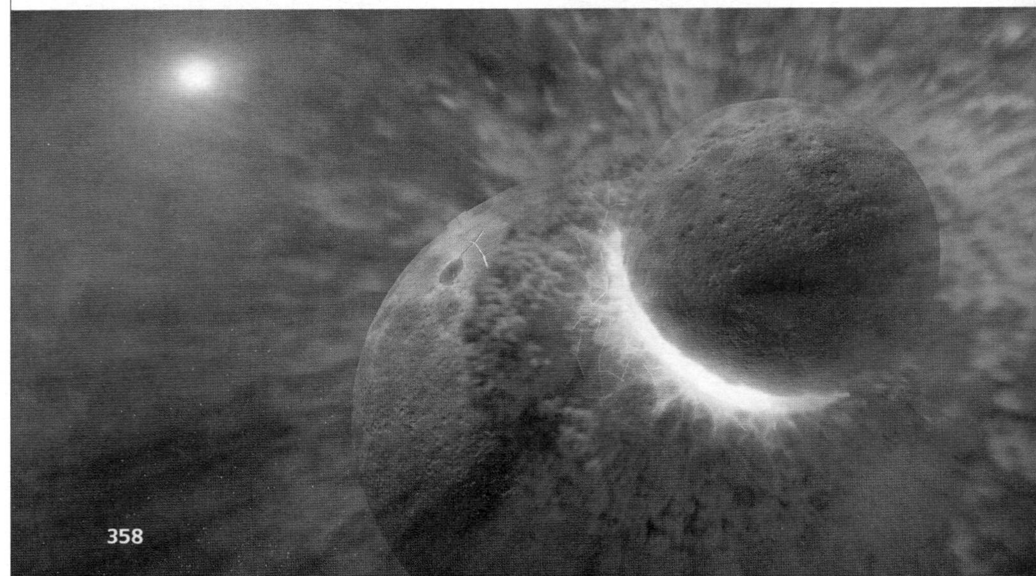

358

Literature Anthology, pp. 358–359

Access Complex Text

Genre

Help students connect the illustration and its caption on page 358 with the text in the last paragraph on that page.

- *What is happening in the picture?* (Two objects in space are colliding, and one is breaking apart.)
- *What sentence in the text describes the action shown in the illustration?* (the last sentence)

Connection of Ideas

Help students connect the term *celestial body* in paragraph two on page 358 to the existing definition of a planet on page 357.

- *How did scientists define a planet before? How is the new definition different?* (A planet was defined as a large celestial body; the new definition distinguishes planets from other celestial bodies.)

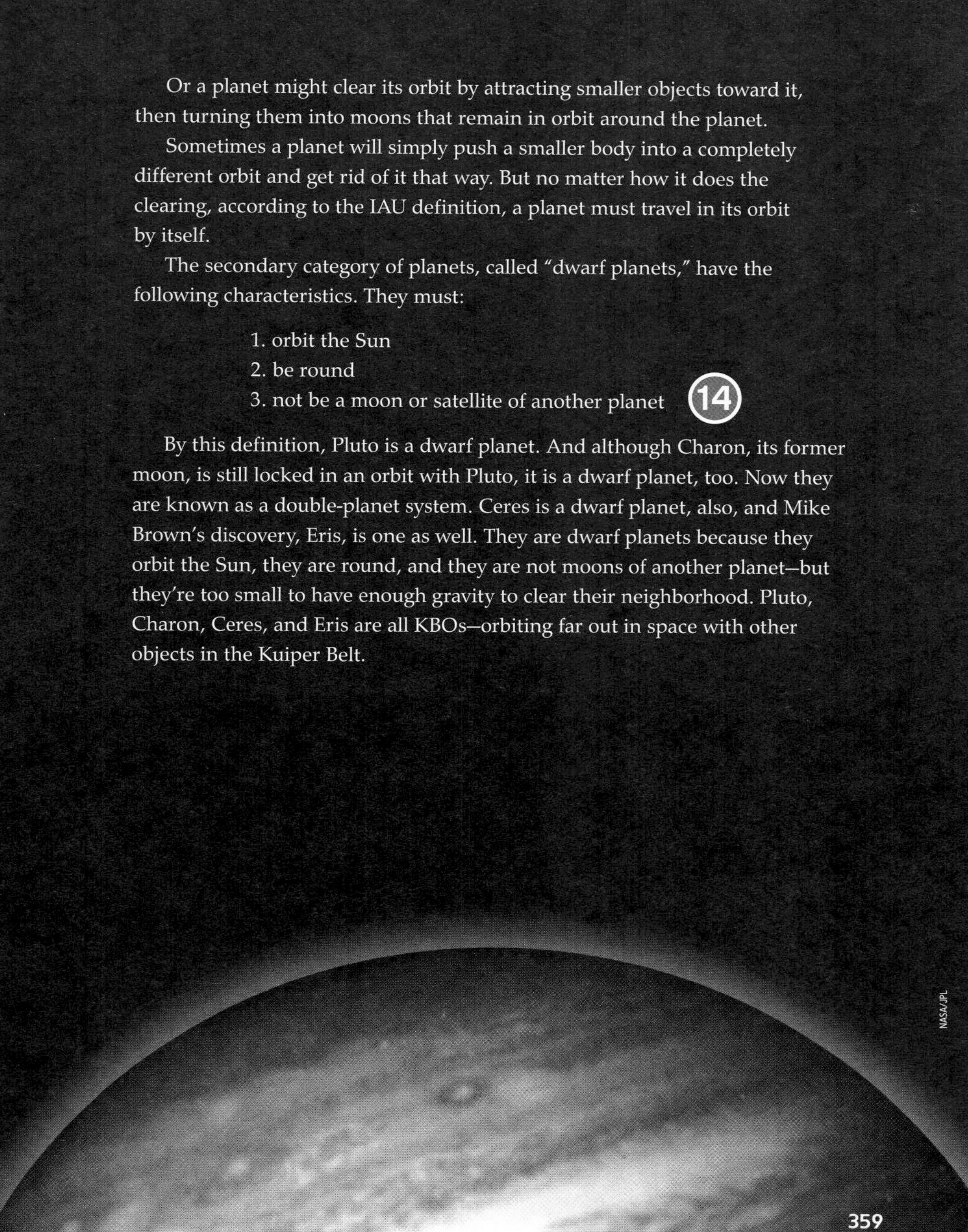

Or a planet might clear its orbit by attracting smaller objects toward it, then turning them into moons that remain in orbit around the planet.
Sometimes a planet will simply push a smaller body into a completely different orbit and get rid of it that way. But no matter how it does the clearing, according to the IAU definition, a planet must travel in its orbit by itself.
The secondary category of planets, called "dwarf planets," have the following characteristics. They must:
1. orbit the Sun
2. be round
3. not be a moon or satellite of another planet (14)
By this definition, Pluto is a dwarf planet. And although Charon, its former moon, is still locked in an orbit with Pluto, it is a dwarf planet, too. Now they are known as a double-planet system. Ceres is a dwarf planet, also, and Mike Brown's discovery, Eris, is one as well. They are dwarf planets because they orbit the Sun, they are round, and they are not moons of another planet—but they're too small to have enough gravity to clear their neighborhood. Pluto, Charon, Ceres, and Eris are all KBOs—orbiting far out in space with other objects in the Kuiper Belt.
NASA/JPL
359

STOP AND CHECK **DOK 1**

Ask and Answer Questions How does the size and gravity of a planet affect other objects around it? (A planet can attract objects to it and destroy them or turn them into moons, or it can push smaller bodies into another orbit.)

Reread

Author's Craft: Analogies DOK 2

Reread pages 358–359. The International Astronomical Union introduced the ability to "clear the neighborhood" as criteria for a planet. What comparison does the author make to help explain this concept? (She compares planets to schoolyard bullies.) How does this analogy help readers visualize the effect that large planets have on other celestial bodies? (Just as other kids either join with a bully or run away, the smaller objects in a planet's "neighborhood" will either be drawn to the planet or scattered by its gravity. In other words, a planet's gravitational pull is strong enough to push or pull any objects orbiting nearby.)

Spotlight on Idioms

Page 358, Paragraph 3 Point to the idiom *clear the neighborhood*. Explain that *neighborhood* can mean the area around or nearby something, not just a place where people live. Ask: *What characteristics must a planet have to make space around it?* (Must be big enough, must have enough gravity) *What other object is in Earth's neighborhood?* (The Moon) Have partners use the idiom to discuss the relative locations of places around the school.

Read

⑮ Make Inferences DOK 2

Reread the final paragraph on page 360. What can you infer about the number of planets in the future? (As "new information is discovered," the number of planets changes, as shown by the past. So the number might change again as more new information is discovered.) The author says, "And that is just in *our* solar system!" What is the author implying? (By italicizing *our*, the author implies that other solar systems in space may also have planets.)

⑯ Text Structure: Cause and Effect DOK 2

What will happen if the New Horizons spacecraft reaches Pluto and Charon? Paraphrase the text to explain the effect. (Instruments on the spacecraft will be able to get a close look at these distant worlds.) What will happen as scientists receive new data from the spacecraft? (They will learn more about how our solar system formed and what is at its outer edges.)

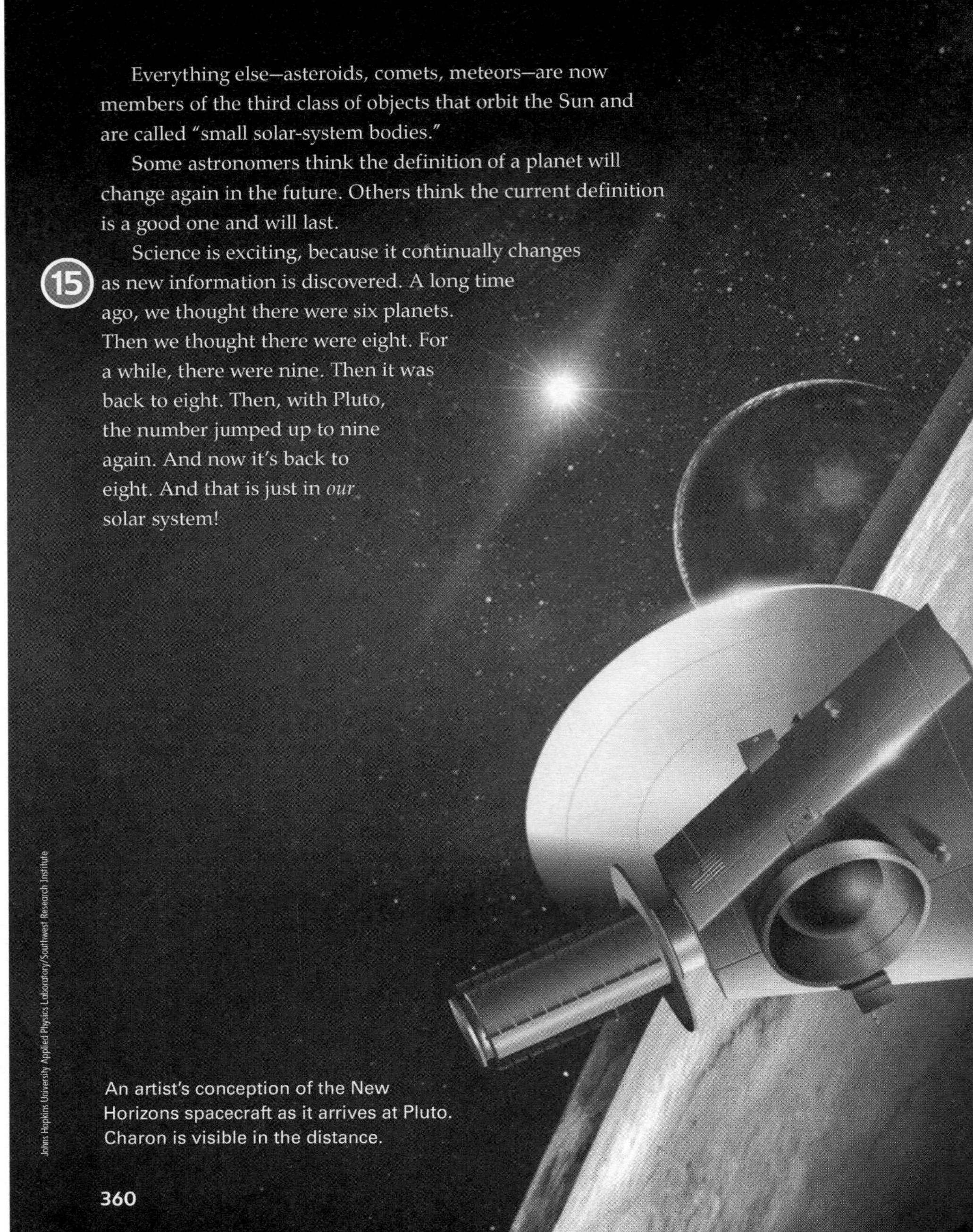

Everything else—asteroids, comets, meteors—are now members of the third class of objects that orbit the Sun and are called "small solar-system bodies."

Some astronomers think the definition of a planet will change again in the future. Others think the current definition is a good one and will last.

⑮ Science is exciting, because it continually changes as new information is discovered. A long time ago, we thought there were six planets. Then we thought there were eight. For a while, there were nine. Then it was back to eight. Then, with Pluto, the number jumped up to nine again. And now it's back to eight. And that is just in *our* solar system!

Johns Hopkins University Applied Physics Laboratory/Southwest Research Institute

An artist's conception of the New Horizons spacecraft as it arrives at Pluto. Charon is visible in the distance.

360

Literature Anthology, pp. 360–361

Access Complex Text

Purpose

Point out that the author concludes the selection by explaining that scientists have a great deal more to learn about planets.

- *On page 360, what changes does the author say might occur in the future?* (the definition of planet, the number of planets in our solar system)
- *On page 361, how does the author show readers how much more scientists have to learn?* (She includes many questions that don't yet have answers.)
- *What is the author's purpose for writing this selection?* (Readers can infer that the author may want to inspire future scientists.)

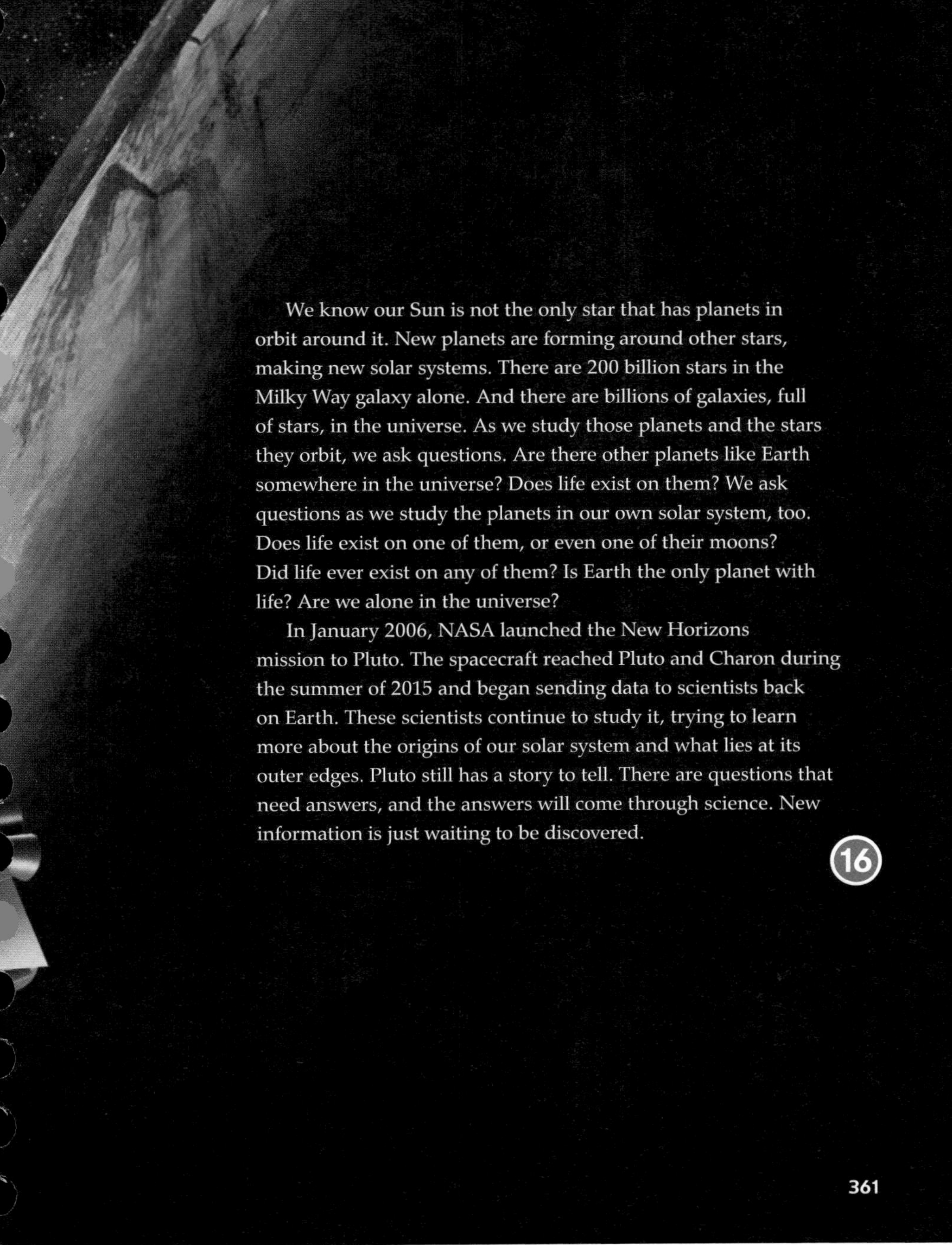

We know our Sun is not the only star that has planets in orbit around it. New planets are forming around other stars, making new solar systems. There are 200 billion stars in the Milky Way galaxy alone. And there are billions of galaxies, full of stars, in the universe. As we study those planets and the stars they orbit, we ask questions. Are there other planets like Earth somewhere in the universe? Does life exist on them? We ask questions as we study the planets in our own solar system, too. Does life exist on one of them, or even one of their moons? Did life ever exist on any of them? Is Earth the only planet with life? Are we alone in the universe?

In January 2006, NASA launched the New Horizons mission to Pluto. The spacecraft reached Pluto and Charon during the summer of 2015 and began sending data to scientists back on Earth. These scientists continue to study it, trying to learn more about the origins of our solar system and what lies at its outer edges. Pluto still has a story to tell. There are questions that need answers, and the answers will come through science. New information is just waiting to be discovered. (16)

361

ELL Spotlight on Language

Page 361, Paragraph 1 Help students understand that the questions the author mentions are rhetorical. Read the paragraph with students. Say: *Sometimes the author asks a question to give the reader information or to put an idea in the reader's mind. Does the author expect you to answer these questions?* (no) *A rhetorical question is a question the author does not expect the reader to answer.* Guide partners as they discuss what each question helps them understand. Provide sentence starters: Scientists are looking for ______. They want to find out if ______.

Read

Build Vocabulary on page 361

universe: all of space and everything in it

instruments: tools used to record data

beams: sends

STOP AND CHECK **DOK 1**

Reread Why do some astronomers think the definition of a planet will change in the future? (As we learn new information about space, definitions may change.)

Return to Purpose Review students' purpose for reading. Then ask partners to share how setting a purpose helped them understand the text.

Reread

Author's Craft: Text Features DOK 2

Reading/Writing Companion, p. 26

Study the artist's rendering on page 360 and read the caption. What advantages might an unmanned spacecraft have in discovering new information? (Possible response: An unmanned spacecraft can go to great distances that humans are unable to reach. This will allow them to send more data that may otherwise not be gathered.)

Read

Meet the Author DOK 2

Elaine Scott

Have students read the biography of the author. Ask:

- Why did Elaine Scott decide to write for children instead of adults?
- What sources did Elaine Scott use to write this story? Why did she use these sources?
- Which part of the selection did you find the most interesting? Why?

Author's Purpose DOK 2

To Inform: Remind students that the main purpose of most nonfiction is to give information. Students may say that Elaine Scott ends a paragraph with a question to get readers thinking about what the answer might be and to make them interested in reading on to find the answer.

Reread

Author's Craft: Text Features DOK 2

Elaine Scott incorporated the use of text features such as captions, diagrams, photographs, and illustrations to add to the text. Discuss how the diagram on page 351 helps the reader better understand the text. (The diagram on page 351 shows the layers of terrestrial planets and gas giants. By showing the layers in a visual model, it helps the reader visualize the different types of planets and how they compare to each other.)

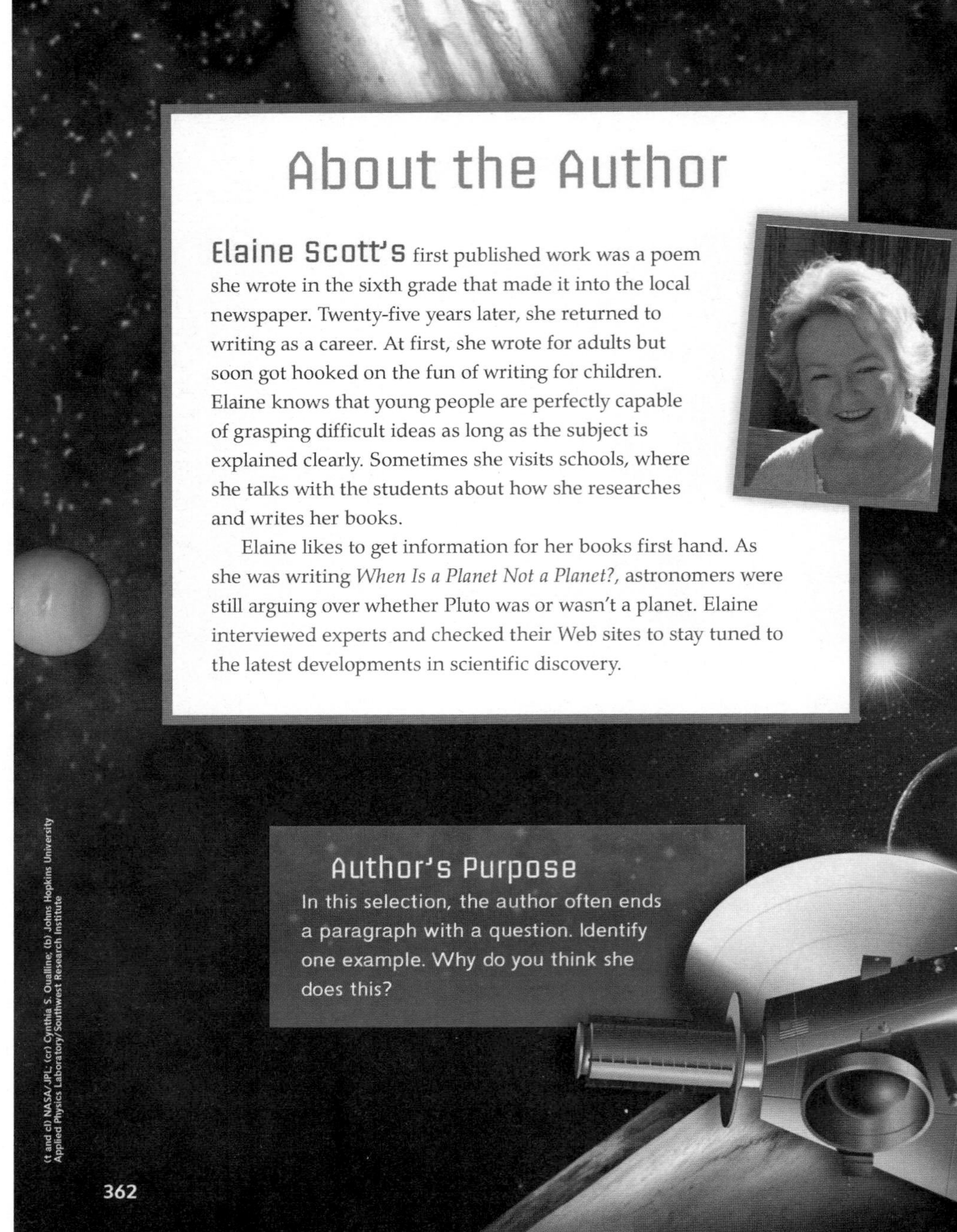

About the Author

Elaine Scott's first published work was a poem she wrote in the sixth grade that made it into the local newspaper. Twenty-five years later, she returned to writing as a career. At first, she wrote for adults but soon got hooked on the fun of writing for children. Elaine knows that young people are perfectly capable of grasping difficult ideas as long as the subject is explained clearly. Sometimes she visits schools, where she talks with the students about how she researches and writes her books.

Elaine likes to get information for her books first hand. As she was writing *When Is a Planet Not a Planet?*, astronomers were still arguing over whether Pluto was or wasn't a planet. Elaine interviewed experts and checked their Web sites to stay tuned to the latest developments in scientific discovery.

Author's Purpose
In this selection, the author often ends a paragraph with a question. Identify one example. Why do you think she does this?

362

Literature Anthology, p. 362

Spotlight on Language

Page 362, Paragraph 1 Explain that the word *grasping* is a verb that means "grabbing something." *Grasping* can also mean "understanding an idea." *Here, the word* grasping *means that Scott's readers understand the ideas explained in her books.* Ask students to share examples of difficult subjects or ideas that they have *grasped*. Provide sentence frames as necessary: I grasped the idea that _____. I grasp how to ______.

Read

Summarize

Tell students they will use information from their Central Idea and Relevant Details graphic organizers to summarize. As I read *When Is a Planet Not a Planet?,* I gathered information about how scientific knowledge changed over time and how that affected views on Pluto's status as a planet. To summarize, I will organize relevant details that help to determine the central idea.

Reread

Analyze the Text

After students summarize the selection, have them reread to develop a deeper understanding of the text and answer the questions on **Reading/Writing Companion** pages 24–26. For students who need support in citing text evidence, use the Reread prompts on pages T31–T44.

Integrate

Build Knowledge: Make Connections

Talk About the Text Have partners discuss the Essential Question: *How can scientific knowledge change over time?*

Write About the Text Then have students add their ideas to their Build Knowledge page of their reader's notebook.

Anchor Chart Record any new ideas on the Build Knowledge anchor chart.

Add to the Vocabulary List Have students write down any words they learned about how scientific knowledge changes over time in their reader's notebook.

Compare Texts DOK 4

Have students compare how the authors present information in "Changing Views of Earth" and *When Is a Planet Not a Planet?* Ask: What is similar about the way the author presents information in these two selections? What is different?

FORMATIVE ASSESSMENT

STUDENT CHECK-IN

Read Have partners tell each other relevant details from the text. Have them reflect using the Check-In routine.

Reread Have partners share responses and text evidence. Then ask them to use the Check-In routine to reflect and fill in the bars on Reading/Writing Companion pages 24–26.

LEARNING GOALS

We can use text evidence to respond to expository text.

OBJECTIVES

Determine two or more central, or main, ideas of a text and explain how they are supported by relevant, or key, details; summarize the text.

Explain how an author uses reasons and evidence to support particular points in a text, identifying which reasons and evidence support which point(s).

Identify the author's purpose.

ELA ACADEMIC LANGUAGE

- *prompt, organization, features*
- Cognate: *organización*

TEACH IN SMALL GROUP

● ● **Approaching Level** and **On Level** Have partners work together to plan and complete the response to the prompt.

● **Beyond Level** Ask students to respond to the prompt independently.

● **ELL** Group students of mixed proficiency levels to discuss and respond to the prompt.

Reread

Write About the Anchor Text

Analyze the Prompt DOK 3

Read the prompt aloud: *The author says that "new information is just waiting to be discovered." What kind of technology seems most useful for finding information about the universe? Support your answer with text evidence.* Ask: *What is the prompt asking you to write?* (to share an opinion about the best kind of technology for finding new information about the universe) Say: *Let's reread to see how the author uses examples to show the importance of technology in space exploration. Doing this will help us make inferences to aid us in answering the prompt.*

Analyze Text Evidence

Remind students that the cause-and-effect and problem-and-solution text structures in this selection help readers understand the importance and advancement of technology related to space exploration. Have students look at the caption in the **Literature Anthology** on page 347. Ask: *What technology was used to create the image of the solar system?* (Photography along with art renderings done on a computer.) Look at the diagram on page 352. Ask: *Which kind of technology do you think is better at providing a realistic representation of the solar system?* (Possible answer: The photographs are better because they are actual images.) Encourage students to look for more details about how technology is used in the study of the universe. Remind them to look in the captions as well as the main text.

Respond

Review pages 24–26 of the **Reading/Writing Companion**. Have partners or small groups refer to and discuss their completed charts and writing responses from those pages. Then direct students' attention to the sentence starters on page 27 of the Reading/Writing Companion. Have them use sentence starters to guide their responses.

Analytical Writing Students should focus on the ways the author describes how knowledge about our universe has been gained. Remind students to vary sentence structure by combining short sentences and adding phrases and clauses to others. Students may use additional paper to complete the assignment if needed.

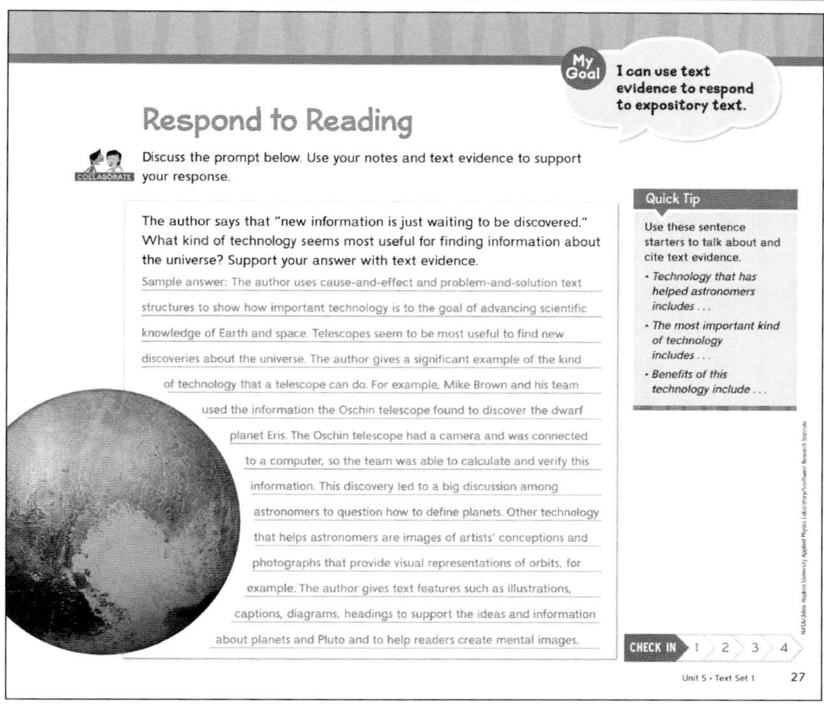

My Goal I can use text evidence to respond to expository text.

Respond to Reading

COLLABORATE Discuss the prompt below. Use your notes and text evidence to support your response.

The author says that "new information is just waiting to be discovered." What kind of technology seems most useful for finding information about the universe? Support your answer with text evidence.

Sample answer: The author uses cause-and-effect and problem-and-solution text structures to show how important technology is to the goal of advancing scientific knowledge of Earth and space. Telescopes seem to be most useful to find new discoveries about the universe. The author gives a significant example of the kind of technology that a telescope can do. For example, Mike Brown and his team used the information the Oschin telescope found to discover the dwarf planet Eris. The Oschin telescope had a camera and was connected to a computer, so the team was able to calculate and verify this information. This discovery led to a big discussion among astronomers to question how to define planets. Other technology that helps astronomers are images of artists' conceptions and photographs that provide visual representations of orbits, for example. The author gives text features such as illustrations, captions, diagrams, headings to support the ideas and information about planets and Pluto and to help readers create mental images.

Quick Tip

Use these sentence starters to talk about and cite text evidence.

- *Technology that has helped astronomers includes . . .*
- *The most important kind of technology includes . . .*
- *Benefits of this technology include . . .*

CHECK IN 1 2 3 4

NASA/Johns Hopkins University Applied Physics Laboratory/Southwest Research Institute

Unit 5 • Text Set 1 27

Reading/Writing Companion, p. 27

English Language Learners

Use the following scaffolds with **Respond**.

Beginning

Read the prompt with students and discuss what they will write about. Clarify the meaning of *universe.* (cognate: *universo*) Review their completed charts on **Reading/Writing Companion** pages 24–26. *What technology do scientists use to study space?* (telescopes) Then help partners respond using: I think telescopes seem the most useful for finding information about the universe. The author gives an example of how telescopes helped scientists discover dwarf planets.

Intermediate

Read the prompt with students and discuss what they will write about. Have partners review their completed charts on **Reading/Writing Companion** pages 24–26. Elicit partners to discuss what technology helps astronomers study space and look for examples the author provides. Then have them respond using: I think telescopes seem the most useful for _______. For example, the Oschin telescope helped _______ discover _______.

Advanced/Advanced High

Review the prompt and sentence starters on page 27 with students. Have pairs discuss their completed charts on pages 24–26. *What technology helps astronomers study space?* Guide pairs to share their answers. Then have them write using the sentence starters.

ELL NEWCOMERS

Have students listen to the summaries of the **Anchor Text** in their native language and then in English to help them access the text and develop listening comprehension. Help students ask and answer questions with a partner. Use these sentence frames: What is the text about? The text is about ____. Then have them complete the online **Newcomer Activities** individually or in pairs.

FORMATIVE ASSESSMENT

STUDENT CHECK-IN

Ask partners to share their responses on Reading/Writing Companion page 27. Have them use the Check-In routine to reflect and fill in the bars.

"The Crow and the Pitcher"

Lexile 640L

LEARNING GOALS

Read **We can apply strategies and skills to read a fable.**

Reread **We can reread to analyze text, craft, and structure and compare texts.**

Have students apply what they learned as they read.

ACT ***What makes this text complex?***

▶ **Sentence Structure**

Compare Texts DOK 4

As students read and reread "The Crow and the Pitcher," encourage them to take notes about the Essential Question: *How can scientific knowledge change over time?* Ask them how the moral of this fable compares to what they learned about Pluto in *When Is a Planet Not a Planet?*

Read

1 Ask and Answer Questions DOK 1

What question might you ask yourself to determine the crow's problem? (Possible answer: I asked why the crow was so happy to see a pitcher.) How did you find the answer to your question? (Possible answer: I reread the first sentence.)

Reread

Author's Message DOK 2

Reading/Writing Companion, p. 30

How do the crow's actions help convey the author's message? (The crow came up with a good plan to save his life.)

Genre • Fable
Compare Texts
Read about how a crow gains valuable new knowledge through a simple experiment.
A fable is a form of classical literature. It usually includes animals as characters and ends with a moral. Aesop was an ancient Greek storyteller who is credited with many fables, now known as Aesop's Fables. His criteria for a good tale seem simple: Tell a meaningful story and end with an unforgettable moral.
The Crow and the Pitcher
a retelling of an Aesop fable
A crow whose throat was parched and dry with thirst saw a pitcher in the distance. With great joy, he flew to it.
1
The crow found that the pitcher held a little water.
He stooped and he strained, but the water was too near the bottom of the pitcher. He could not reach it.
Next he tried to overturn the pitcher, thinking that he would be able to catch some of the water as it trickled out.
364

Literature Anthology, pp. 364–365

ACT Access Complex Text

Sentence Structure

Point out this complex sentence on page 364: *A crow, whose throat was parched and dry with thirst, saw a pitcher in the distance.* Explain that breaking apart complex sentences can give readers important information about characters.

- *What information do you learn from the dependent clause?* (The crow is very thirsty.)
- *What do you learn from the rest of the sentence?* (A pitcher is nearby. The crow might be able to drink from it.)

he tired crow was too weak
o knock over the pitcher. He
k a minute to **evaluate** the
tuation and devise a plan.
He collected as many stones as he could.
He dropped a stone into the pitcher with his beak. Then he peered into the pitcher.
could not tell if his plan was
rking yet, so he dropped
nother stone into the pitcher.
nd then he added another.
The crow looked again. "This experiment just might work!" he thought.
One by one the crow dropped stones into the pitcher until he brought the water within his reach and thus saved his life.
Moral: *Necessity is the mother of invention.*
Make Connections
How did the crow gain the knowledge that saved his life? ESSENTIAL QUESTION
How are the crow's methods similar to those you've read about in another selection? TEXT TO TEXT
365

Spotlight on Language

Page 365, Paragraph 1 Check for understanding of the first sentence. Gesture being weak and trying to knock something over. Have students look at the image that goes with the paragraph. *What do you think it means to evaluate the situation?* (think about how to solve a problem) *What did the crow do after it thought about how to solve the problem?* (devised a plan)

Read

Summarize

Guide students to summarize the selection.

Reread

Analyze the Text

After students summarize, have them reread and answer questions on pages 28–30 of the **Reading/Writing Companion**.

Integrate

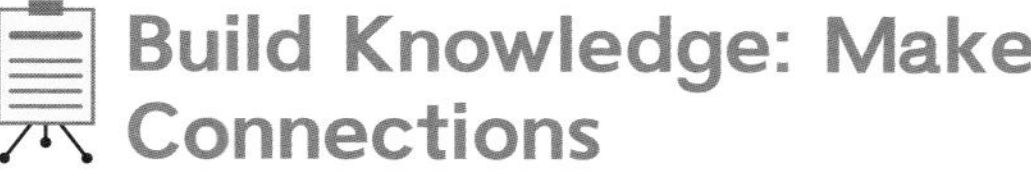

Build Knowledge: Make Connections

Talk About the Text Have partners discuss how scientific knowledge changes over time.

Write About the Text Have students add their ideas to their Build Knowledge pages of their reader's notebooks.

Anchor Chart Record any new ideas on the Build Knowledge anchor chart.

Compare Texts DOK 4

Text to Text Answer: Both the crow and the astronomers in *When Is a Planet Not a Planet?* carefully analyzed information to solve a problem. Evidence: Page 356: "But every once in a while, an astronomer will get very lucky and something new and exciting will appear." Page 365: "He could not tell if his plan was working yet, so he dropped another stone into the pitcher."

FORMATIVE ASSESSMENT

STUDENT CHECK-IN

Read Ask partners to share their summaries. Then have them reflect using the Check-In routine.

Reread Ask partners to share their responses on pages 28-30. Then have them use the Check-In routine to reflect and fill in the bars.

LEARNING GOALS

We can identify imagery to help us read and understand fables.

OBJECTIVES

Determine the meaning of words and phrases as they are used in a text, including figurative language such as metaphors and similes.

Interpret figurative language, including similes and metaphors, in context.

ELA ACADEMIC LANGUAGE

- *imagery, mood, characteristics, sensory*
- Cognates: *imaginería, características, sensorial*

Imagery

1 Explain

Have students turn to **Reading/Writing Companion** page 31. Share with students the following key characteristics of imagery.

- Writers use imagery to create sensory images for readers. The author could use figurative language to create sensory images that are unexpected or literal language that means exactly what it says. This allows readers to imagine seeing, hearing, feeling, smelling, or tasting what the writer describes.
- Imagery allows readers to better relate to and understand a character's experiences. Specific words help readers understand how a character feels.
- Adjectives, adverbs, and specific verbs and nouns can all create effective imagery.
- Imagery can affect the mood, or feeling, the author creates. Mood affects how readers feel as they read the text. A writer might set a dark, scary mood by using words like *blood-curdling* or *gruesome*.

2 Model

Model identifying effective imagery on page 28. Have students read the second paragraph. Point out the phrase *parched and dry with thirst*. Explain that this description helps the reader feel just how thirsty and desperate for water the crow is. Discuss why this imagery is more effective than simply stating that the crow is thirsty.

3 Guided Practice

Now have students identify words the author uses to create imagery in paragraph 4 on page 28. (*stooped and strained*) Ask: *How do these words help the author create an image in your mind?* (They help me feel how hard the crow has to work in order to try to reach the water in the pitcher.) *What mood do these words help the writer set and maintain?* (an anxious or desperate mood)

Have partners identify additional imagery used in the rest of the story on pages 28–29 and discuss what senses the writer is appealing to. Have them explain how the author's use of imagery affects the mood of the story. Then have pairs share their work with the class.

Allow students to enter their responses on Reading/Writing Companion page 31. Remind students to use a print or online dictionary to define difficult words.

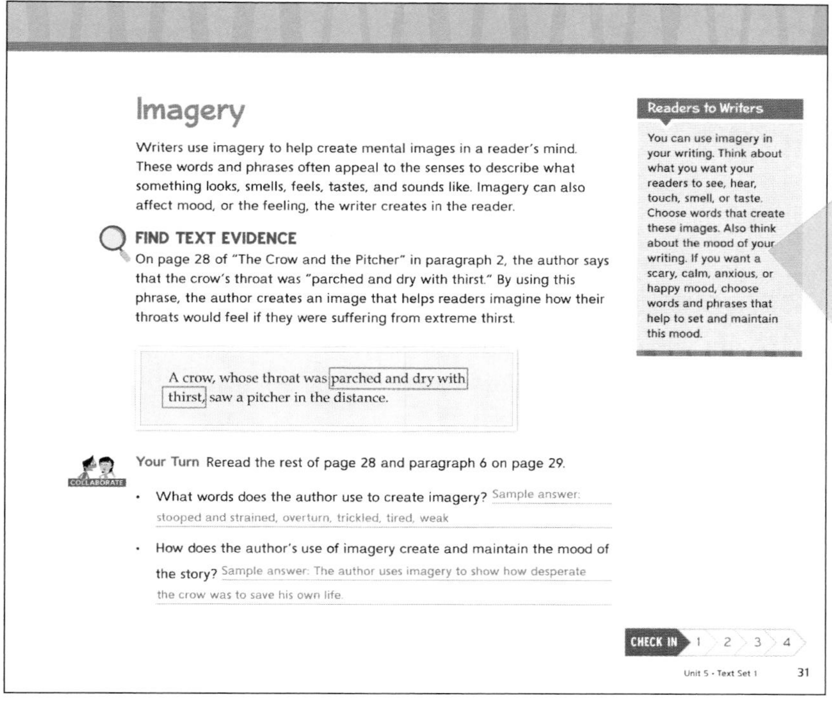

Imagery

Writers use imagery to help create mental images in a reader's mind. These words and phrases often appeal to the senses to describe what something looks, smells, feels, tastes, and sounds like. Imagery can also affect mood, or the feeling, the writer creates in the reader.

FIND TEXT EVIDENCE

On page 28 of "The Crow and the Pitcher" in paragraph 2, the author says that the crow's throat was "parched and dry with thirst." By using this phrase, the author creates an image that helps readers imagine how their throats would feel if they were suffering from extreme thirst.

A crow, whose throat was parched and dry with thirst, saw a pitcher in the distance.

COLLABORATE

Your Turn Reread the rest of page 28 and paragraph 6 on page 29.

- What words does the author use to create imagery? Sample answer: stooped and strained, overturn, trickled, tired, weak
- How does the author's use of imagery create and maintain the mood of the story? Sample answer: The author uses imagery to show how desperate the crow was to save his own life.

Readers to Writers

You can use imagery in your writing. Think about what you want your readers to see, hear, touch, smell, or taste. Choose words that create these images. Also think about the mood of your writing. If you want a scary, calm, anxious, or happy mood, choose words and phrases that help to set and maintain this mood.

CHECK IN 1 2 3 4

Unit 5 • Text Set 1 31

Reading/Writing Companion, p. 31

Readers to Writers

Point out that for authors to write effective imagery, they first visualize what they are describing and think about how they want their readers to feel. Then they carefully choose descriptive language. Have students revisit the imagery in "The Crow and the Pitcher." Ask: *Which words and phrases were most effective? How did they affect you?*

English Language Learners

Use the following scaffolds with **Guided Practice**.

Beginning

Review how to identify imagery with students. Reread the first sentence of paragraph 4 on page 28 with students. Use gestures to help you define and describe *stooped* and *strained*. *Stooping and straining looks hard.* Make gestures again to model as you say: *After stooping and straining for a long time, I feel tired.* Guide students to tell what the imagery describes. I read that the crow stooped and strained. *That helps me understand how the crow feels.* The crow feels tired.

Intermediate

Review how to identify imagery with students. Have pairs read paragraph 4 on page 28, using a dictionary to check the meanings of *stooped* and *strained* as needed. Have partners talk about what it would feel like to stoop and strain over and over. Imagining and seeing these actions in the image help me understand how the crow feels. The crow feels tired.

Advanced/Advanced High

Check the students' understanding of imagery. Have partners take turns reading paragraph 4 on page 28. Allow them to work together to identify what words the author uses to create imagery. Then have them explain what these words help them understand.

FORMATIVE ASSESSMENT

STUDENT CHECK-IN

Ask partners to share their Your Turn responses on Reading/Writing Companion page 31. Ask them to use the Check-In routine to reflect and fill in the bars.

LEARNING GOALS

- **We can decode homophones.**
- **We can identify and read multisyllabic words.**
- **We can read fluently with accuracy and phrasing.**

OBJECTIVES

Know and apply grade-level phonics and word analysis skills in decoding words.

Use combined knowledge of all letter-sound correspondences, syllabication patterns, and morphology to read accurately unfamiliar multisyllabic words in context and out of context.

Read grade-level prose and poetry orally with accuracy, appropriate rate, expression, and automaticity on successive readings.

Use the relationship between particular words to better understand each of the words.

- Rate: 136–156 WCPM

ELA ACADEMIC LANGUAGE

- *context, accuracy, phrasing*
- Cognate: *contexto*

TEACH IN SMALL GROUP

Word Study

Approaching Level and **ELL** Use the Tier 2 activity on page T63 before teaching the lesson.

On Level and **Beyond Level** As needed, use the Read Multisyllabic Words section only.

ELL See page 5 in the **Language Transfers Handbook** for guidance in identifying sounds and symbols that may not transfer for speakers of certain languages.

Homophones

1 Explain

Tell students that homophones are words that sound alike but are spelled differently and have different meanings, such as *ate* and *eight*. Explain that readers use context clues from words surrounding the homophone to determine its meaning.

2 Model

Write the following homophones on the board. Pronounce the homophones, and give possible definitions for each word in the pair. Then read the sentences, modeling how to use context clues to determine the meaning of the word.

- ***pear, pair***
  I pulled a **pear** from the tree and bit into the juicy fruit.
  I chose a **pair** of brown shoes to wear to school.
- ***hole, whole***
  I fell down and tore a **hole** in my jeans.
  This pie is so good, I could eat the **whole** thing!
- ***way, weigh***
  We took a wrong turn on the **way** to the soccer game.
  The judges at the fair will **weigh** my biggest pumpkin.

3 Guided Practice

Write the following homophones on the board. Guide students to come up with a definition and a sentence for each word.

seen	scene	right	write
cent	sent	buy	by
deer	dear	guest	guessed
you	ewe	sell	cell
break	brake	mail	male

For practice with decoding homophones, use **Practice Book** page 259 or online activities.

Read Multisyllabic Words

Transition to Longer Words Write the following homophones on the board. Have students read each word and use their knowledge of phonics patterns to decode each homophone.

Model how to determine the meaning of each word. Point to the word, read it aloud, and use it in a sentence that has context clues to the word's meaning. Then have students identify the context clues and provide a definition for the word.

weather	whether	principal	principle
cereal	serial	minor	miner
presents	presence	seller	cellar
friar	fryer	capitol	capital
ceiling	sealing	attendants	attendance
assistants	assistance	aloud	allowed

After you complete the activity, have students write their own sentences that include homophones from the list.

Fluency

Accuracy and Phrasing

Explain/Model Explain that reading with accuracy means reading each word as it appears on the page and pronouncing it correctly. Review how punctuation marks such as commas, periods, and question marks can help students break text into meaningful phrases. Read aloud the first two paragraphs of "In the Sky, Looking Down" from the **Reading/Writing Companion** page 14. Model reading with accuracy and pay particular attention to punctuation marks.

Practice/Apply Have partners alternate reading paragraphs in the passage, modeling the phrasing you used. Remind students that you will be listening for their accuracy and phrasing as you monitor their reading during the week.

Daily Fluency Practice

Automaticity Students can practice reading with accuracy and appropriate rate to develop automaticity using the online **Differentiated Genre Passage,** "Is There Life Out There?"

DIGITAL TOOLS

For more practice, have students use the phonics and fluency activities.

Homophones

MULTIMODAL LEARNING

Provide students with sentences that use homophones, such as *This is the best movie I've seen this year* and *The last scene in the drama was my favorite.* Have partners read the sentences aloud, identifying the homophone. Have them use context clues to determine the meaning of the homophone and then spell, write, and say the homophone in their own sentences.

FORMATIVE ASSESSMENT

STUDENT CHECK-IN

Homophones Ask partners to share three homophones.

Multisyllabic Words Have partners use the following words in a sentence: *morning, mourning.*

Fluency Ask partners to read "Is There Life Out There?" fluently.

Have partners use the Check-In routine to reflect.

CHECK FOR SUCCESS

Can students identify and read homophones? Can students read fluently?

Small Group Instruction

If No

- **Approaching** Reteach pp. T63, T66
- **ELL** Develop p. T63

If Yes

- **On** Apply pp. T68
- **Beyond** Apply pp. T74

LEARNING GOALS

We can compare the painting with the selections in this text set to build knowledge about how scientific knowledge changes over time.

OBJECTIVES

Draw on information from multiple print or digital sources, demonstrating the ability to locate an answer to a question quickly or to solve a problem efficiently.

Integrate information from several texts on the same topic in order to write or speak about the subject knowledgeably.

Close Reading Routine

Read DOK 1–2

- Identify important ideas and details.
- Take notes and summarize.
- Use ACT prompts as needed.

Reread DOK 2–3

- Analyze the text, craft, and structure.
- Use the ***Reading/Writing Companion***.

Integrate DOK 3–4

- Integrate knowledge and ideas.
- Make text-to-text connections.
- Use the Integrate/Make Connections lesson.
- Use ***Reading/Writing Companion***, page 32.
- Complete the Show Your Knowledge task.
- Inspire action.

FORMATIVE ASSESSMENT

STUDENT CHECK IN

Ask partners to share their response. Have them use the Check-In routine to reflect and fill in the bars on Reading/Writing Companion page 32.

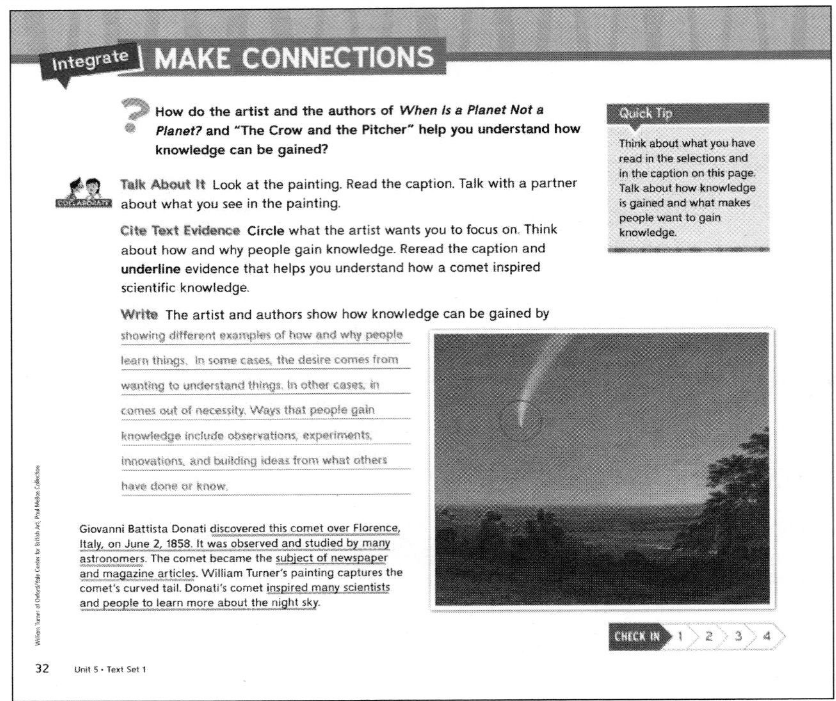

Integrate | MAKE CONNECTIONS

How do the artist and the authors of *When Is a Planet Not a Planet?* and "The Crow and the Pitcher" help you understand how knowledge can be gained?

COLLABORATE

Talk About It Look at the painting. Read the caption. Talk with a partner about what you see in the painting.

Cite Text Evidence **Circle** what the artist wants you to focus on. Think about how and why people gain knowledge. Reread the caption and **underline** evidence that helps you understand how a comet inspired scientific knowledge.

Write The artist and authors show how knowledge can be gained by showing different examples of how and why people learn things. In some cases, the desire comes from wanting to understand things. In other cases, in comes out of necessity. Ways that people gain knowledge include observations, experiments, innovations, and building ideas from what others have done or know.

Quick Tip

Think about what you have read in the selections and in the caption on this page. Talk about how knowledge is gained and what makes people want to gain knowledge.

Giovanni Battista Donati discovered this comet over Florence, Italy, on June 2, 1858. It was observed and studied by many astronomers. The comet became the subject of newspaper and magazine articles. William Turner's painting captures the comet's curved tail. Donati's comet inspired many scientists and people to learn more about the night sky.

William Turner of Oxford/Yale Center for British Art, Paul Mellon Collection

CHECK IN 1 2 3 4

32 Unit 5 • Text Set 1

Reading/Writing Companion, p. 32

Integrate

Make Connections

Talk About It DOK 3

Share and discuss students' responses to "A Better World with Satellites" Blast. Display the Build Knowledge anchor chart. Review the chart and have students read through their notes, annotations, and responses for each text. Then ask students to complete the Talk About It activity on **Reading/Writing Companion** page 32.

Cite Text Evidence

Guide students to see the connections between the painting of the comet on Reading/Writing Companion page 32 and the selections. Remind students to read the caption next to the painting and the Quick Tip on page 32.

Write

Students should refer to their notes on the chart as they respond to the writing prompt at the bottom of the page. When students have finished writing, have groups share and discuss their responses.

Build Knowledge: Make Connections

Talk About the Text Have partners discuss how scientific knowledge changes over time.

Write About the Text Have students add their ideas to their Build Knowledge pages of their reader's notebooks.

Anchor Chart Record any new ideas on the Build Knowledge anchor chart.

SHOW YOUR KNOWLEDGE

My Goal I know how scientific knowledge changes over time.

Write a Report

Think about what you learned about how we gain scientific knowledge. Why are scientists inspired to conduct new experiments or improve technology?

1. Look at your Build Knowledge notes in your reader's notebook.
2. Make a list of the ways scientists are inspired. Use evidence from the texts you read to support your ideas.
3. Use your ideas to write a report about why it is important to conduct experiments or improve technology even when we know something to be proven. Use the new vocabulary words you learned.

Unit 5 • Text Set 1 33

Reading/Writing Companion, p. 33

Integrate

Show Your Knowledge DOK 4

Write a Report

Explain to students that they will show how they built knowledge across the text set based on what they read by writing a report about scientific knowledge. Display the Build Knowledge anchor chart and ask: *How can scientific knowledge change over time?*

Step 1 Guide partners to review the Build Knowledge anchor chart and notes in their reader's notebook to discuss the prompt.

Step 2 Remind students that they have studied how scientists were inspired and how ideas about our world and universe have evolved over time. Have students make a list of the ways in which scientists were inspired from the selections, video, and listening passage.

Step 3 Have students use their ideas to write a report about the importance of conducting experiments or improving technology even when something has been proven. Encourage students to use words from their Build Knowledge vocabulary list.

Inspire Action

Share Your Report Have partners present their reports and display them in the classroom. Ask students to use sticky notes to post comments under the reports. Presenters can respond if they want.

What Are You Inspired to Do? Encourage partners to think of another way to respond to the texts. Ask: *What else do the texts inspire you to do?*

LEARNING GOALS

We can write a report to show the knowledge we built about how scientific knowledge changes over time.

OBJECTIVES

Report on a topic or text or present an opinion, sequencing ideas logically and using appropriate facts and relevant, descriptive details to support main ideas or themes; speak clearly at an understandable pace.

Include multimedia components (e.g., graphics, sound) and visual displays in presentations when appropriate to enhance the development of main ideas or themes.

ELA ACADEMIC LANGUAGE

- *technology*
- Cognate: *tecnología*

DIGITAL TOOLS

Show Your Knowledge Rubric

ELL ENGLISH LANGUAGE LEARNERS

Provide sentence frames for support. *It is important to conduct experiments because ___. Improving technology can help ___.*

MY GOALS ROUTINE

What I Learned

Review Goals Have students turn back to page 11 of the Reading/Writing Companion and review the goals for the text set.

Reflect Have students think about the progress they've made toward the goals. Review the key. Have students reflect and fill in the bars.

LEARNING GOALS

- We can build and expand on new vocabulary words.
- We can use Greek roots to figure out unfamiliar words.
- We can write using new vocabulary words.

OBJECTIVES

Use context (e.g., cause/effect relationships and comparisons in text) as a clue to the meaning of a word or phrase.

Use common, grade-appropriate Greek and Latin affixes and roots as clues to the meaning of a word (e.g., *photograph, photosynthesis*).

Expand vocabulary by adding inflectional endings and suffixes.

DIGITAL TOOLS

Vocabulary Activities

ENGLISH LANGUAGE LEARNERS

Pair students of different language proficiency levels to practice vocabulary. Have partners discuss different shades of meaning in words with similar meanings, such as *criteria* and *standards*.

FORMATIVE ASSESSMENT

STUDENT CHECK-IN

After each lesson, have partners share and reflect using the Check-In routine.

Connect to Words

Practice the target vocabulary.

1. **Approximately** how many people do you know?
2. Describe an **astronomical** object or phenomenon.
3. When might you make a **calculation**?
4. What **criteria** do you use when buying a gift?
5. Name three things that have a **diameter**.
6. **Evaluate** a recent meal you ate.
7. Would you like to **orbit** Earth? Why or why not?
8. Describe two different types of **spheres.**

Content Words

Help students generate different forms of this text set's words by adding, changing, or removing inflectional endings.

- Draw a four-column chart on the board. Write *orbit* in the first column. Then write *orbits, orbited,* and *orbiting* in the next three columns. Read aloud the words with students.
- Have students share sentences using each form of *orbit.*
- Students should add to the chart for *evaluate* and then share sentences using the different forms of the word.
- Have students copy the chart in their reader's notebooks.

See **Practice Book** page 251.

Build Vocabulary

- Display *innovation, centuries,* and *telescope.*
- Define the words and discuss their meanings with students.
- Write *innovate* under *innovation.* Have partners write other words with the same root and define them. Then have partners ask and answer questions using the words.
- Repeat with *centuries* and *telescope.*

Thesaurus

Have students use a thesaurus to find synonyms for target vocabulary. Provide sample sentences:

- The **criteria** to win the cake contest was based on taste and decoration.
- The artist was ready for the judge to **evaluate** her painting.
- The satellite was built to **orbit** Earth.
- The game requires a small **sphere** that is thrown from player to player.

See **Practice Book** page 263.

Spiral Review

Reinforce the Words

Review this text set's vocabulary words. Have students orally complete each sentence stem.

1. I am approximately ____.
2. The astronomical observatory is ____.
3. Her calculation was ____.
4. The diameter of a penny is about ____.
5. Planets orbit the ____.
6. Trina collects spheres made of ____.

Display the previous text set's vocabulary: *barren, expression, meaningful, plumes.* Have partners ask and answer questions for each word.

See **Practice Book** page 252.

Connect to Writing

- Have students write sentences in their reader's notebooks using the target vocabulary.
- Tell them to write sentences that provide word information they learned from this text set's readings.
- ELL Provide the Lesson 3 sentence stems 1–6 for students needing extra support.

Write Using Vocabulary

Have students write something they learned from this text set's words in their reader's notebooks. For example, they might write about how teachers *evaluate* their work.

Word Squares

Ask students to create Word Squares for each vocabulary word.

- In the first square, students write the word (e.g., *spheres*).
- In the second square, students write their own definition of the word and any related words, such as synonyms (e.g., *globes, orbs*).
- In the third square, students draw a simple illustration that will help them remember the word (e.g., drawing of a basketball).
- In the fourth square, students write nonexamples, including antonyms for the word (e.g., *oval, circle, ellipse, square, pyramid*).

Have partners discuss their squares.

Greek Roots

Elicit from students what Greek roots are and how they can be helpful.

- Display On Level **Differentiated Genre Passage** "Is There Life Out There?" Model using Greek roots to figure out the meaning of the word *photosynthesis*.
- Have students figure out the meaning of *astrobiology* in the first paragraph.
- Have students write the meanings in their reader's notebooks.

See **Practice Book** page 264.

Shades of Meaning

Help students generate words related to *approximately*. Draw a T-chart. Head the columns "Synonyms" and "Antonyms."

- Have partners generate words to add to the T-chart. Ask students to use a thesaurus.
- Add synonyms not included, such as *almost, around,* and *roughly*. Add antonyms, such as *exactly* and *precisely*.
- Ask students to copy the words in their reader's notebooks.

Morphology

Use *evaluate* for students to learn more words. Draw a T-chart. Write *evaluate* in the left column.

- In one column, write *-ion* and *-ive*. Discuss how suffixes change the meaning and parts of speech.
- Have students add the suffixes to *evaluate* and review meanings.
- Ask partners to do a search for other words with these suffixes.

Write Using Vocabulary

Have students use vocabulary words in their extended writing.

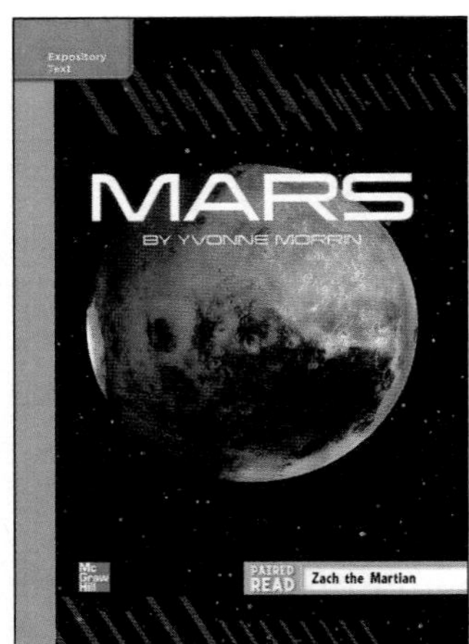

Lexile 700L

OBJECTIVES

Explain the relationships or interactions between two or more individuals, events, ideas, or concepts in a historical, scientific, or technical text based on specific information in the text.

Use context to or self-correct word recognition and understanding, rereading as necessary.

ELA ACADEMIC LANGUAGE

- *preview, predict, relevant, root*
- Cognates: *predecir, relevante*

Approaching Level

Leveled Reader: *Mars*

Preview and Predict

- Read the Essential Question with students: *How can scientific knowledge change over time?*
- Have students preview the title, table of contents, and first page of *Mars.* Students should predict what they think the selection will be about. Encourage them to make, confirm, or correct their predictions as they continue reading.

Review Genre: Expository Text

Tell students that this selection is expository text. Expository text provides factual information about a topic. Relevant details are organized logically and support the central idea. Features, such as photographs, captions, and diagrams, add information that might not be in the text. Have students identify features of expository text in *Mars.*

Close Reading

Note Taking Ask students to use a copy of the online Central Idea and Relevant Details **Graphic Organizer 7** as they read.

Pages 2–3 *Which Greek root helps you figure out the meaning of* astronomers? (*Astro* means "star." Astronomers are people who study stars or space.) Have students add this word in their reader's notebooks. *What questions have astronomers asked about Mars?* (What is it made of? How big is it? Is it hot or cold? Could it have life?)

Pages 4–6 *How are Mars and Earth alike? Work with a partner to answer, using the table on page 4.* (The length of their days is only about an hour apart.) *How do the lengths of their years differ?* (A year on Mars has almost twice as many days as a year on Earth.) *Which Greek root helps you figure out the meaning of* orbit *on page 6?* (*Orb* means "circle" or "ring." An orbit is a circular path.) Have students add this word in their reader's notebooks.

Pages 7–9 *How did the use of a telescope help Herschel?* (He identified polar ice caps.) *What was the effect of the incorrect translation of* canali*?* (People thought Martians made canals.) *How do Mars' moons differ from Earth's?* (Mars has two moons. They are smaller than Earth's moon and are oddly shaped.)

Pages 10–12 *Why are rovers and landers tested before they are used?* (They must land safely, carry out tests, communicate with Earth, and move over rough ground.)

Pages 13–16 *Turn to a partner and summarize the central idea of the text to answer the question in the Chapter 3 title, "Life on Mars?"* (Mars may be able to support life. Future missions will explore this possibility.) *What is the Goldilocks zone? Why is it important?* (It is the zone where life can exist because it is not too hot or too cold. Mars may be in this zone.)

Page 17 *What kind of equipment might an astronaut on Mars need?* (spacecraft, protective spacesuit) *Why?* (Mars is very far away, is very cold, and has an atmosphere mostly made up of carbon dioxide.)

Respond to Reading Revisit the Essential Question and ask students to complete the Text Evidence Questions on page 18.

Analytical Writing **Write About Reading** Check that students have correctly explained how studying Mars and improving technology have helped ideas about Mars change over time. Make sure they include details.

Fluency: Expression

Model Model reading page 2 with expression. Next, read the passage aloud and have students read along with you.

Apply Have students practice reading the passage with partners.

Paired Read: "Zach the Martian"

Make Connections: Write About It

Before reading, ask students to note that the genre of this text is science fiction. Then discuss the Essential Question. After reading, ask students to write connections between *Mars* and "Zach the Martian."

Leveled Reader

Build Knowledge

Talk About the Text Have partners discuss how scientific knowledge can change over time.

Write About the Text Have students add their ideas to the Build Knowledge pages of their reader's notebooks.

FOCUS ON SCIENCE

Students can extend their knowledge of Mars by completing the research and observation activity on page 24.

LITERATURE CIRCLES

Ask students to conduct a literature circle using the Thinkmark questions to guide the discussion. You may wish to have a whole-class discussion, using information from both selections in the Leveled Reader, about how scientific knowledge can change over time.

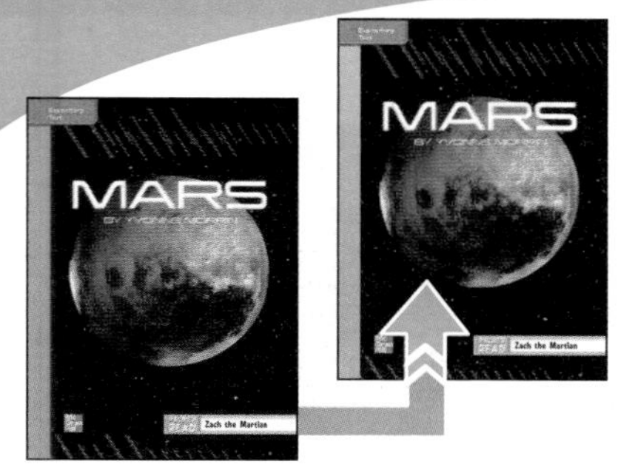

IF students read the Approaching Level fluently and answered the questions,

THEN pair them with students who have proficiently read the On Level and have students

- echo-read the On Level main selection.
- identify three traits of expository text.

The On Level challenges students by including more **domain-specific words** and **complex sentence structures**.

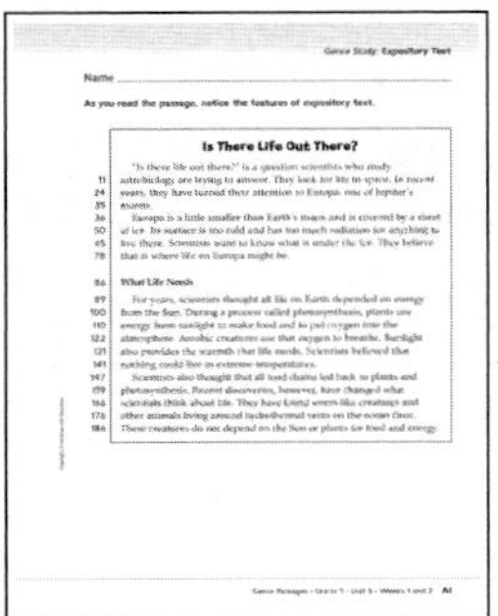

"Is There Life Out There?"
Lexile 790L

OBJECTIVES

Compare and contrast the overall structure (e.g., chronology, comparison, cause/effect, problem/solution) of events, ideas, concepts, or information in two or more texts.

Determine or clarify the meaning of unknown and multiple-meaning words and phrases based on grade 5 reading and content, choosing flexibly from a range of strategies.

Use common, grade-appropriate Greek and Latin affixes and roots as clues to the meaning of a word (e.g., *photograph, photosynthesis*).

ELA ACADEMIC LANGUAGE

- *expository text, compare, relevant, diagram, visualize*
- Cognates: *texto espositivo, comparar, relevante, diagrama, visualizar*

Approaching Level

Genre Passage: "Is There Life Out There?"

Build Background

- Read aloud the Essential Question: *How can scientific knowledge change over time?* Ask students to compare two expository texts they have read in this text set. Use the following sentence starters to help focus discussion.

  I read that scientists have learned...

  The effect of this seems to be...

- The online **Differentiated Genre Passage** "Is There Life Out There?" discusses one of Jupiter's moons, Europa. Remind students that Jupiter is much farther from the Sun than Earth is. Display a world map and point out Antarctica, noting that students will read about why this southernmost continent is important to the study of possible life on Europa.

Review Genre: Expository Text

Reiterate that expository text gives facts, examples, and explanations about a topic. Headings and subheadings organize text and tell what a section of text is about. Diagrams help readers visualize ideas and information.

Close Reading

Note Taking As students read the passage the first time, ask them to annotate the text. Have them note central ideas, relevant details, unfamiliar words, and questions they have. Then read again and use the following questions. Encourage students to cite text evidence from the selection.

Read

Genre: Expository Text Read paragraphs 1–2 on page A1. *Name two facts the author shares about Europa.* (Europa is one of Jupiter's moons. It is smaller than Earth's moon and is covered with ice.)

Greek Roots Locate the word *photosynthesis* in paragraph 3. *Which Greek root helps you understand its meaning?* (*Photo* means "light." Photosynthesis is the way plants use energy from sunlight to make food.)

Relevant Details Read paragraph 4. *What belief did scientists once have about how living things get food?* (Food supplies of living things depended on plants and photosynthesis.) *What changed their thinking?* (They found that living things near hydrothermal vents did not need plants or sunlight for food.)

Text Features: Diagram Look at the diagram on page A2. *What is above the vent?* (the ocean surface) *What is below the vent?* (mid ocean ridge)

Central Idea Read paragraph 2. *What effect did the discovery of chemosynthetic life have on scientists' thoughts about Europa?* (It caused scientists to think that life could possibly exist on Europa.)

COLLABORATE **Summarize** Have students use their notes to summarize reasons scientists think there might be life under Europa's ice.

Reread

Use the questions on page A3 to guide students' rereading of the passage.

Author's Craft Reread the first sentence. *What question does the author ask?* (Is there life out there?) *Why do you think the author started the passage with a question?* (Starting the passage with a question tells the reader what information to look for. The reader should look for information that answers the question "Is there life out there?")

Author's Craft *How does the diagram help you better understand hydrothermal vents?* (The diagram helps me understand where a hydrothermal vent might be in the ocean.)

Author's Craft Reread the last paragraph. *Why did the author include information about Lake Vostok in Antarctica?* (The author included information about Lake Vostok because like Europa's oceans, Lake Vostok sits miles beneath a frozen surface. If they find life in Lake Vostok, scientists may also find life on Europa. This possibility is one answer to the question asked at the beginning of the passage.)

Integrate

COLLABORATE **Make Connections** Connect "Is There Life Out There?" to other selections students have read. Have pairs cite text evidence and answer this question: *How do the authors help you know why people understand more about the world now?*

Compare Genres Display a two-column chart labeled *Then* and *Now*. Work with students to compare examples of how scientific knowledge has changed over time.

Build Knowledge

Talk About the Text Have partners discuss how scientific knowledge can change over time.

Write About the Text Have students add their ideas to the Build Knowledge pages of their reader's notebooks.

Differentiate and Collaborate

COLLABORATE **Be inspired** Have students think about "Is There Life Out There?" and other selections they have read. Ask: *What do the texts inspire you to do?* Use the following activities or have pairs of students think of a way to respond to the texts.

Make a Timeline Create a timeline that displays the scientific discoveries and advancements you've read about. Include the date of each discovery and a brief description of it. Add several well-known historical events to provide context for different time periods.

Write an Interview Script Write questions and responses for a news interview featuring a scientist from one of the texts. Include a question and an answer about how the person's scientific knowledge changed over time.

Readers to Writers

Using Text Features Remind students that authors often use subheads within a text to explain what a section is about. Have students reread the section with the subhead "What Life Needs" on page A1. Ask: *Why is this an appropriate subhead for this section? How does it help the author prepare readers for what they will learn?*

LEVEL UP

IF students read the Approaching Level fluently and answered the questions,

THEN pair them with students who have proficiently read the On Level. Have them

- partner-read the On Level passage.
- summarize a discovery identified in the text and explain how it has changed people's scientific knowledge.

Approaching Level

Word Study/Decoding

REVIEW WORDS WITH SUFFIXES

OBJECTIVES

Know and apply grade-level phonics and word analysis skills in decoding words.

Use combined knowledge of all letter-sound correspondences, syllabication patterns, and morphology (e.g., roots and affixes) to read accurately unfamiliar multisyllabic words in context and out of context.

Decode words with suffixes.

I Do Review that a suffix is a group of letters added to the end of a base word or root that changes that word's meaning and often its part of speech. Display the word *hope* and read it aloud. Remind students that *hope* is a noun. Then explain that the suffix *-ful* means "full of." Add *-ful* to the end of *hope*. Read *hopeful* aloud and explain that it is an adjective meaning "full of hope."

We Do Write the suffix *-less* on the board. Review that it means "without." Then write *hopeless* and read it aloud. Model using the meaning of the suffix to determine that *hopeless* means "without hope." Display the words *careful* and *careless*. Guide students to use the meaning of the suffix to define each word.

You Do Add the following examples: *joyful, joyless*. Have students identify each suffix, tell its meaning, and define the word in which it appears.

PRACTICE WORDS WITH SUFFIXES

OBJECTIVES

Know and apply grade-level phonics and word analysis skills in decoding words.

Use combined knowledge of all letter-sound correspondences, syllabication patterns, and morphology (e.g., roots and affixes) to read accurately unfamiliar multisyllabic words in context and out of context.

Practice words with suffixes.

I Do Write on the board: *cheerful, tireless, soloist, preparation*. Read each word aloud, identify each suffix and its meaning, and then define each word.

We Do Write *celebration, harmless, tasteful, reaction, exhibition,* and *scientist* on the board. Model how to decode and figure out the meaning of the first word. Then have students decode and define the remaining words. As necessary, help students identify and define the suffix in each word.

Display the following words. Read aloud the first word, identify the suffix and its meaning, and give the word's meaning.

faithful	cloudless	painful	competition	airless
addition	nameless	animation	flavorful	collection

You Do Have students read the remaining words aloud. Ask them to identify each suffix and its meaning and then define each word.

Afterward, point to the words in random order for students to read chorally.

REVIEW HOMOPHONES

TIER 2

OBJECTIVES

Know and apply grade-level phonics and word analysis skills in decoding words.

Decode homophones.

I Do Write *tale* and *tail* on the board. Explain that *tale* and *tail* are homophones, or words that sound alike but are spelled differently and have different meanings. Tell students that readers use context clues from the surrounding words to determine the meaning of a homophone. Use *tail* and *tale* in sentences that provide context clues about their meanings.

We Do Display this sentence: *I write with my right hand, but Tia uses her left.* Guide students to identify *write* and *right* as homophones. Discuss how to use context clues to figure out the meaning of each word.

You Do Add these sentences to the board: *I see a boat sailing on the sea. We guessed what time our guest would arrive at our home.* Have students identify the homophone pair in each sentence and use context clues to determine the meanings of each word in the pair.

PRACTICE HOMOPHONES

OBJECTIVES

Know and apply grade-level phonics and word analysis skills in decoding words.

Practice homophones.

I Do Write this homophone pair on the board: *overdo, overdue.* Read the words aloud and use each in a sentence. Then discuss the meaning of each word.

We Do Write these sentences: *Your concern about the test should lessen after you review the lesson. I would like to open the presents in your warm presence.* Model how to identify the homophones in the first sentence and how to use context clues to determine the meaning of each one. Then have students identify and define each homophone in the second sentence.

To provide additional practice, write these homophone pairs on the board: *weight, wait; forth, fourth; you, ewe; freeze, frees; flower, flour; patience, patients.* Read aloud the first pair and give the meaning of each word.

You Do Have students read aloud the remaining homophone pairs. Ask them to use a dictionary to find the meaning of each word. Point to the word pairs in random order for students to read chorally.

ELL For **ELL** students who need phonics and decoding practice, define words and help them use the words in sentences, scaffolding to ensure their understanding. See the **Language Transfers Handbook** for phonics elements that may not transfer from students' native languages.

Approaching Level

Vocabulary

REVIEW HIGH-FREQUENCY WORDS

TIER 2

OBJECTIVES

Acquire and use accurately grade-appropriate general academic and domain-specific words and phrases,including those that signal contrast, addition, and other logical relationships (e.g., *however, although, nevertheless, similarly, moreover, in addition*).

I Do Use **High-Frequency Word Cards** 161–180. Display one word at a time, following the routine:

Display the word. Read the word. Then spell the word.

We Do Ask students to state the word and spell the word with you. Model using the word in a sentence and have students repeat the sentence after you.

You Do Display the word. Ask students to say the word and spell it. When completed, quickly flip through the word card set as students chorally read the words. Provide opportunities for students to use the words in speaking and writing. For example, provide sentence starters, such as *I think that* _____. Ask students to write each word in their reader's notebooks.

REVIEW ACADEMIC VOCABULARY

OBJECTIVES

Acquire and use accurately grade-appropriate general academic and domain-specific words and phrases, including those that signal contrast, addition, and other logical relationships (e.g., *however, although, nevertheless, similarly, moreover, in addition*).

I Do Display each **Visual Vocabulary Card** and state the word. Explain how the photograph illustrates the word. State the example sentence and repeat the word.

We Do Point to the word on the card and read the word with students. Ask them to repeat the word. Engage students in structured partner talk about the image as prompted on the back of the vocabulary card.

You Do Display each visual in random order, hiding the word. Have students match the definitions and context sentences of the words to the visuals displayed.

You may wish to review high-frequency words with ELL students using the lesson above.

UNDERSTAND ACADEMIC VOCABULARY

OBJECTIVES

Acquire and use accurately grade-appropriate general academic and domain-specific words and phrases, including those that signal contrast, addition, and other logical relationships (e.g., *however, although, nevertheless, similarly, moreover, in addition*).

I Do Display the *approximately* **Visual Vocabulary Card** and ask: *If you know approximately how many people were at a party, do you know about or exactly how many people were there?*

Explain that if you know approximately how many, you don't know the exact number.

We Do Ask these questions. Help students explain their answers.

- Are people in an *astronomical* society interested in stars or animals?
- Would you do a *calculation* while swimming or doing math homework?
- Would you measure the *diameter* of a circle or a car?

You Do Have pairs respond to these questions and explain their answers:

- What are three planets that *orbit* the sun?
- Which are *spheres,* planets or boxes?
- Which has *criteria,* a diary entry or a scored essay?
- Who is qualified to *evaluate* a dance performance?

Have students pick words from their reader's notebooks and use an online thesaurus to find words with similar meanings.

GREEK ROOTS

OBJECTIVES

Determine or clarify the meaning of unknown and multiple-meaning words and phrases based on grade 5 reading and content, choosing flexibly from a range of strategies.

Use common, grade-appropriate Greek and Latin affixes and roots as clues to the meaning of a word (e.g., *photograph, photosynthesis*).

I Do Display the Approaching Level of "Is There Life Out There?" in the online **Differentiated Genre Passage.** Point to the word *astrobiology* in the first paragraph on page A1. Tell students they can use their knowledge of Greek roots to determine its meaning.

Think Aloud The Greek prefix *astro-* means "star," and the Greek root *bio* means "life." The suffix *-logy* means "the study of." I also see a context clue: "life in space." *Astrobiology* must be the study of life in space.

We Do Ask students to point to the word *photosynthesis* in paragraph three on page A1. Provide the Greek root *syntithenai* ("put together") and the Greek prefix *photo-* ("light") and discuss how these can help students tell the word's meaning. Write the definition of the word.

You Do Have students determine the meaning of *hydrothermal* (page A1, paragraph 4) and *chemosynthesis* (page A2, paragraph 1) using Greek roots: *therm* ("heat"), *hydro* ("water"), *chemo* ("chemical"), and *syntithenai* ("put together"). Students can write the words and their definitions in their reader's notebooks. They can use a dictionary to confirm word meanings.

Approaching Level

Fluency/Comprehension

FLUENCY

MULTIMODAL

TIER 2

OBJECTIVES

Read with sufficient accuracy and fluency to support comprehension.

Use context to confirm or self-correct word recognition and understanding, rereading as necessary.

Read fluently with accuracy.

I Do Explain that reading a selection out loud is not just about reading the words correctly. Readers should change the sound of their voice to help convey the meaning of what they read. Read the first two paragraphs of "Is There Life Out There?" in the Approaching Level online **Differentiated Genre Passage** page A1. Tell students to monitor your expression.

We Do Read the rest of the page aloud. Have students repeat each sentence after you, using the same expression. Explain that you used punctuation cues and your knowledge of word meanings to guide how you changed the sound of your voice.

You Do Have partners take turns reading sentences from the passage, focusing on their expression. Listen in and provide corrective feedback as needed by modeling proper fluency.

IDENTIFY RELEVANT DETAILS

OBJECTIVES

Explain the relationships or interactions between two or more individuals, events, ideas, or concepts in a historical, scientific, or technical text based on specific information in the text.

I Do Read aloud the second paragraph of "Is There Life Out There?" in the Approaching Level online **Differentiated Genre Passage** page A1. Write *Europa has a cold surface and a lot of radiation.* Tell students that this sentence is a relevant detail. It supports the central idea of the paragraph that since nothing can live on Europa's surface, scientists think life could possibly exist under the ice.

We Do Read the third paragraph on page A1 aloud. Ask questions, such as *What did scientists believe all life depended on? What new discoveries did they make that changed this thinking?* Guide students to find relevant details.

You Do Have partners read the rest of the passage. Then have them discuss how all of the relevant details support the central idea of the passage.

REVIEW CENTRAL IDEA AND RELEVANT DETAILS

OBJECTIVES

Determine two or more central, or main, ideas of a text and explain how they are supported by relevant, or key, details; summarize the text.

Model Remind students that authors of science and history texts organize their texts logically using relevant details to support the central idea.

We Do Choral-read the "What Life Needs" section of "Is There Life Out There?" in the Approaching Level online **Differentiated Genre Passage** page A1. Model identifying relevant details. For example, photosynthesis causes oxygen to be released into the atmosphere, which in turn causes aerobic creatures to be able to live and breathe. Then work with students to identify the central idea about what life needs to survive.

You Do Have partners use the relevant details explored in the text to summarize how the discovery of chemosynthetic life changed the way astrobiologists think about life on Earth and in space. Guide them in filling in a copy of online Central Idea and Relevant Details **Graphic Organizer 7**.

SELF-SELECTED READING

OBJECTIVES

Determine two or more central, or main, ideas of a text and explain how they are supported by relevant, or key, details; summarize the text.

Ask and answer questions to increase understanding of a text.

Read Independently

In this text set, students focus on these key aspects of informational text: how relevant details support a central idea, how to summarize the text using the central idea and relevant details, and how to identify an author's purpose. Guide students to apply what they have learned in this text set as well as in previous lessons as they read independently.

Have students choose an expository nonfiction book for sustained silent reading and set a purpose for reading that book. They can check the online **Leveled Reader Library** for selections. Remind students that:

- relevant details support the central, or main, idea(s).
- asking and answering questions can help them better understand and remember important information.

Have students record the main idea and details on **Graphic Organizer 7**. After students finish, they can conduct a Book Talk about what they read.

- Students should share their organizers and describe the main idea and relevant details they identified in the text.
- They should also tell the group any questions they asked themselves and how they answered them.

Lexile 900L

OBJECTIVES

Explain the relationships or interactions between two or more individuals, events, ideas, or concepts in a historical, scientific, or technical text based on specific information in the text.

Use context to or self-correct word recognition and understanding, rereading as necessary.

ELA ACADEMIC LANGUAGE

- *preview, predict, relevant, root*
- Cognates: *predecir, relevante*

On Level

Leveled Reader: *Mars*

Preview and Predict

- Have students read the Essential Question: *How can scientific knowledge change over time?*
- Have students preview the title, table of contents, and first page of *Mars*. Students should predict what they think the selection will be about. Encourage them to confirm or revise their predictions as they continue reading.

Review Genre: Expository Text

Tell students that this selection is expository text. Expository text provides factual information about a topic. Relevant details are organized logically and support the central idea. Features such as photographs, captions, and diagrams add information that might not be in the text. Have students identify features of expository text in *Mars*.

Close Reading

Note Taking Ask students to use a copy of online Central Idea and Relevant Details **Graphic Organizer 7** as they read.

Pages 2–3 *Which Greek root helps you figure out the meaning of* astronomers*?* (*Astro* means "star." Astronomers are people who study stars, or space.) Have students add this word in their reader's notebook. *Why might the Romans have called the planet "Mars"?* (Mars is the Roman god of war, and the planet's red color might have reminded them of blood in battle.)

Pages 4–6 *How are Mars and Earth similar and different? Use the text and table on page 4 to help you answer.* (Similar: Mars has seasons and an atmosphere. Its day is almost the same length as Earth's; Different: Mars is farther from the sun, has a smaller diameter, is much colder, and has a much longer year.) *Which Greek root helps you figure out the meaning of* orbit *on page 6?* (*Orb* means "circle" or "ring." An orbit is a circular path.) Have students add this word in their reader's notebook.

Pages 7–9 *What is one effect of the development of telescope technology?* (Astronomers observed features on the surface of Mars.) *What caused people to think Martians dug canals on Mars?* (The incorrect translation of the word *canali*.)

What discoveries did Asaph Hall make about Mars' moons? (Mars has two moons. They are smaller than Earth's moon and are irregularly shaped.)

Pages 10–12 *Why must lander and rover designs be tested first?* (They must land safely, have reliable energy supplies and communication devices, and move on rough terrain.)

Pages 13–16 *Summarize the central idea of the text to answer the question in the chapter title.* (Mars may have some of the conditions needed to support life. Future missions will explore the possibility.) *What discovery would be the best clue to finding life?* (water) *Why would humans need special transportation and protective suits to explore Mars?* (It's far away, it's cold, and its atmosphere is mostly carbon dioxide.)

Respond to Reading Revisit the Essential Question and ask students to complete the Text Evidence Questions on page 18.

Analytical Writing **Write About Reading** Check that students have correctly explained how observations and improving technology caused ideas about Mars to change over time. Make sure they include details from the text.

Fluency: Expression

Model Model reading page 5 with expression. Next, read the passage aloud and have students read along with you.

Apply Have students practice reading the passage with partners.

Paired Read: "Zach the Martian"

Make Connections: Write About It

Before reading, ask students to note that the genre of this text is science fiction. Discuss the Essential Question. Ask students to write connections between the texts.

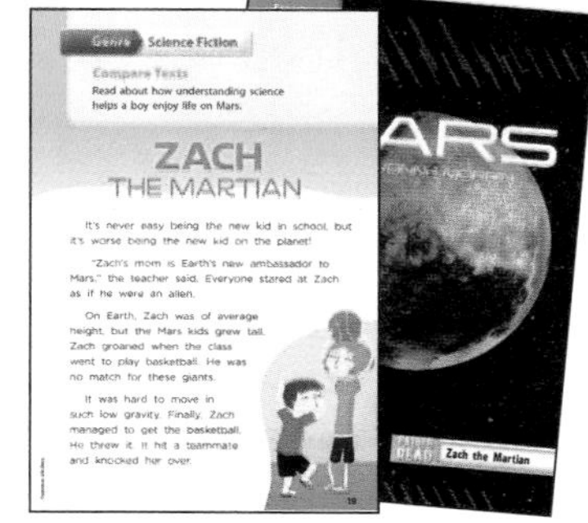

Leveled Reader

Build Knowledge

Talk About the Text Have partners discuss how scientific knowledge can change over time.

Write About the Text Have students add their ideas to the Build Knowledge pages of their reader's notebooks.

FOCUS ON SCIENCE

Students can extend their knowledge of Mars by completing the research and observation activity on page 24.

LITERATURE CIRCLES

Ask students to conduct a literature circle using the Thinkmark questions to guide the discussion. You may wish to have a whole-class discussion, using information from both selections in the Leveled Reader, about how scientific knowledge can change over time.

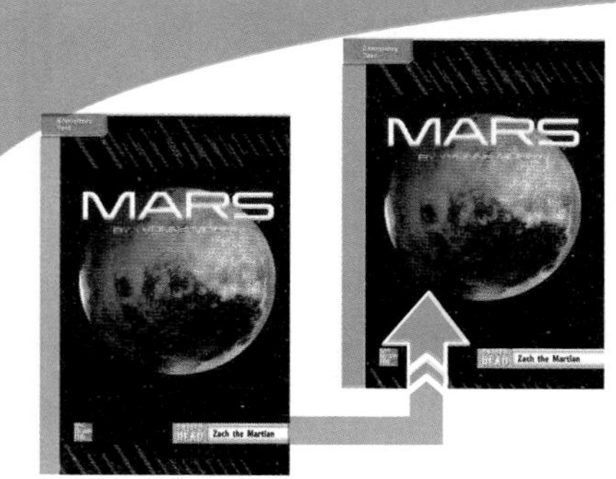

IF students read the On Level fluently and answered the questions,

THEN pair them with students who have proficiently read the Beyond Level and have students

- partner-read the Beyond Level main selection.
- identify three causes and effects.

Access Complex Text

The Beyond Level challenges students by including more **domain-specific words** and **complex sentence structures.**

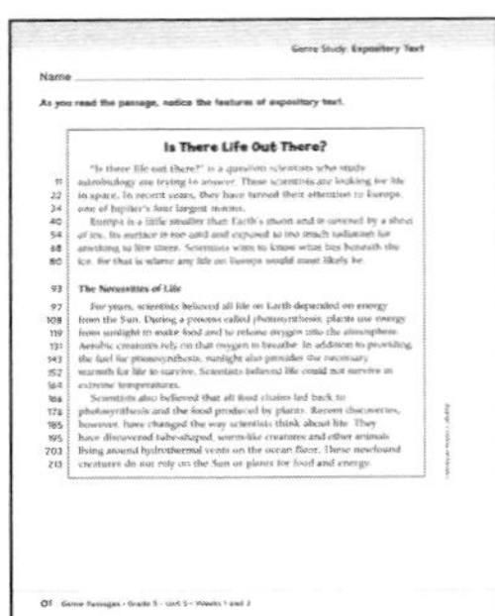

"Is There Life Out There?"
Lexile 910

OBJECTIVES

Compare and contrast the overall structure (e.g., chronology, comparison, cause/effect, problem/solution) of events, ideas, concepts, or information in two or more texts.

Determine or clarify the meaning of unknown and multiple-meaning words and phrases based on grade 5 reading and content, choosing flexibly from a range of strategies.

Use common, grade-appropriate Greek and Latin affixes and roots as clues to the meaning of a word (e.g., *photograph, photosynthesis*).

ELA ACADEMIC LANGUAGE

- *expository text, compare, relevant, diagram, visualize*
- Cognates: *texto espositivo, comparar, relevante, diagrama, visualizar*

On Level

Genre Passage: "Is There Life Out There?"

Build Background

- Read aloud the Essential Question: *How can scientific knowledge change over time?* Ask students to compare two expository texts they have read in this genre study. Use the following sentence starters to help focus discussion.

  I read that scientists have learned . . .

  The effect of this seems to be . . .

- The online **Differentiated Genre Passage** "Is There Life Out There?" references one of Jupiter's moons, Europa. Remind students that as the fifth planet from the Sun in our solar system, Jupiter is much farther from the Sun than Earth is. Discuss the effect this distance might have on the planet and its moon.

Review Genre: Expository Text

Remind students that expository text gives facts, examples, and explanations about a topic presented in a logical order. Text features, such as headings and subheadings, group related ideas within expository text, while diagrams, including labels and captions, help readers visualize ideas and information.

Close Reading

Note Taking As students read the passage the first time, ask them to annotate the text. Have them note central ideas, relevant details, unfamiliar words, and questions they have. Then read again and use the following questions. Encourage students to cite text evidence from the selection.

Read

Genre: Expository Text *How does page O1 indicate that this passage is expository text?* (It contains facts, examples, and explanations about possible life on Europa. A subhead organizes information about what life needs to survive.)

Greek Roots Read paragraph 4. *Which part of* hydrothermal *indicates that hydrothermal vents are found on the ocean floor?* (*hydro,* which means "water") *What does the Greek root* thermo *mean?* (*hot*) *What do these Greek roots tell you about the meaning of* hydrothermal? (It describes water that is heated.)

Relevant Details Read paragraph 4. *What changed the way scientists think about life?* (The discovery of creatures around hydrothermal vents made scientists realize that life could survive without plants or light from the Sun.)

Text Features: Diagrams *What does the diagram on page O2 help you understand?* (Hydrothermal vents sit below the ocean surface on top of a mid-ocean ridge.)

Central Idea Read paragraphs 3 and 4 on page O2. *Why do scientists think that life on Europa might be possible?* (Both oxygen and oceans could support life. Europa's atmosphere has oxygen, and it looks like there are oceans under its surface ice.)

COLLABORATE **Summarize** Have students use their notes to summarize how scientists' beliefs about life on Europa has changed.

Reread

Use the questions on page O3 to guide students' rereading of the passage.

Author's Craft *Why do you think the author chose to start the passage with a question?* (The question tells the reader to look for information about the possibility of life in space. It also makes the reader curious to learn more so they will have the answer to the question.)

Author's Craft *How does the diagram on page O2 help you better understand hydrothermal vents?* (The diagram shows me an example of where a hydrothermal vent is in the ocean.)

Author's Craft *The last paragraph has information about Lake Vostok in Antarctica. Why might the author have included this information?* (Lake Vostok exists miles beneath a frozen surface, so its environment is similar to Europa's. Finding life in Lake Vostok would mean it is possible that life exists on Europa. This possibility is one answer to the question asked at the beginning of the passage.)

Integrate

COLLABORATE **Make Connections** Have pairs connect "Is There Life Out There?" to other selections they have read as they answer this question: *How do the authors help you understand why people know more about the world now than they did years ago?*

Compare Genres Have students use a two-column chart labeled *Then* and *Now* to compare what they learned about how scientific knowledge has changed.

Build Knowledge

Talk About the Text Have partners discuss how scientific knowledge can change over time.

Write About the Text Have students add their ideas to the Build Knowledge pages of their reader's notebooks.

Differentiate and Collaborate

COLLABORATE **Be inspired** Have students think about "Is There Life Out There?" and other selections they have read. Ask: *What do the texts inspire you to do?* Use the following activities or have pairs of students think of a way to respond to the texts.

Make a Timeline Create a timeline that displays the scientific discoveries and advancements you've read about. Include the date of each discovery and a brief description of it. Add several well-known historical events to provide context for different time periods.

Write an Interview Script Write questions and responses for a news interview featuring a scientist from one of the texts. Include a question and an answer about how the person's scientific knowledge changed over time.

Readers to Writers

Using Text Features Remind students that authors often use subheads within a text to explain what a section is about. Have students reread the section with the subhead "The Necessities of Life" on page O1. Ask: *Why is this an appropriate subhead for this section? How does it help the author prepare readers for what they will learn?*

LEVEL UP

IF students read the On Level fluently and answered the questions,

THEN pair them with students who have proficiently read the Beyond Level. Have them

- partner-read the Beyond Level passage.
- summarize a discovery identified in the text and explain how it has changed people's scientific knowledge.

On Level

Vocabulary/Comprehension

REVIEW ACADEMIC VOCABULARY

MULTIMODAL

OBJECTIVES

Demonstrate understanding of figurative language, word relationships, and nuances in word meanings.

Use the relationship between particular words (e.g., synonyms, antonyms, homographs) to better understand each of the words.

I Do Use the **Visual Vocabulary Cards** to review the key selection words *approximately, calculation, criteria, evaluate, orbit,* and *spheres*. Point to each, read it aloud, and have students repeat.

We Do Read aloud the word set. Help students identify the word in each set that has almost the same meaning as the first word.

- *approximately, absolutely, nearly*
- *calculation, computation, explanation*
- *criteria, standards, cafeteria*

You Do Have students work in pairs to identify the word that has almost the same meaning as the first word.

- *evaluate, elevate, judge*
- *orbit, circle, delete*
- *spheres, cubes, globes*

Have students choose words from their reader's notebooks and use an online thesaurus to find synonyms and antonyms.

GREEK ROOTS

OBJECTIVES

Determine or clarify the meaning of unknown and multiple-meaning words and phrases based on grade 5 reading and content, choosing flexibly from a range of strategies.

Use common, grade-appropriate Greek and Latin affixes and roots as clues to the meaning of a word (e.g., *photograph, photosynthesis*).

I Do Remind students that they can use Greek roots to find the meanings of words. Point to *astrobiology* in the first paragraph of "Is There Life Out There?" On Level online **Differentiated Genre Passage** page O1.

Think Aloud The Greek prefix *astro-* and the root *bio* mean "star" and "life." The Greek suffix *-logy* means "the study of." I also see a context clue: "life in space." These clues tell me that *astrobiology* means "the study of life in space."

We Do Have students read paragraph 3 on page O1 and find *photosynthesis*. Help students find its meaning by pointing out the Greek root *syntithenai*, meaning "put together," and the Greek prefix *photo-*, meaning "light."

You Do Have pairs determine the meanings of *Aerobic* (page O1, paragraph 3), *hydrothermal* and *chemosynthesis* (page O2, paragraph 1). Note: *aero* ("air"), *bio* ("life"), *therm* ("heat"), *hydro* ("water"), and *chemo* ("chemical").

REVIEW CENTRAL IDEA AND RELEVANT DETAILS

OBJECTIVES

Determine two or more central, or main, ideas of a text and explain how they are supported by relevant, or key, details; summarize the text.

Model Review that authors of science and history texts organize their texts logically using relevant details to support the central idea.

We Do Have a volunteer read the second paragraph of "Is There Life Out There?" in the On Level online **Differentiated Genre Passage** page O1. Guide students to identify the central idea and relevant details.

You Do Have partners identify more relevant details to support the central idea by filling in a copy of online Central Idea and Relevant Details **Graphic Organizer 7**. Then have them explain how the discovery of chemosynthetic life affected how scientists began to view life on Earth and in space.

SELF-SELECTED READING

OBJECTIVES

Determine two or more central, or main, ideas of a text and explain how they are supported by relevant, or key, details; summarize the text.

Ask and answer questions to increase understanding of a text.

Read Independently

In this text set, students focus on how relevant details support a central idea, how to summarize the text using the central idea and relevant details, and how to identify an author's purpose. Guide students to apply what they have learned in this text set as well as in previous lessons as they read independently.

Have students choose an expository nonfiction book for sustained silent reading and set a purpose for reading that book. They can check the online **Leveled Reader Library** for selections. Remind students that:

- relevant details support the central, or main, idea(s).
- asking and answering questions can help them better understand and remember details in the text.

Have students record the main idea and details on **Graphic Organizer 7**.

- They can use the central idea and relevant details they identify to summarize the text.
- Ask students to share their reactions to the book with classmates.

You may want to include **ELL** students in On Level vocabulary and comprehension lessons. Offer language support as needed.

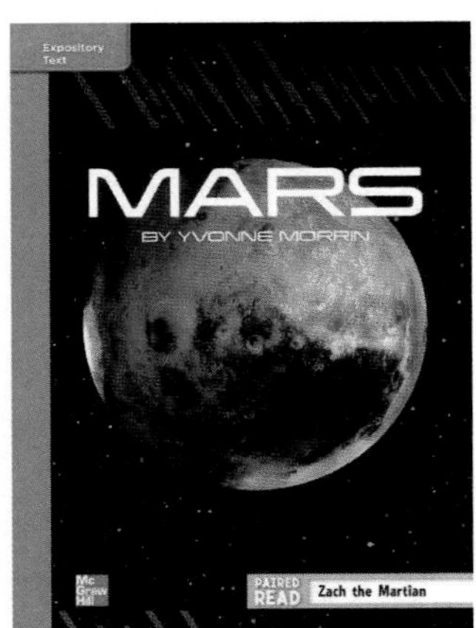

Lexile 970L

OBJECTIVES

Explain the relationships or interactions between two or more individuals, events, ideas, or concepts in a historical, scientific, or technical text based on specific information in the text.

Use context to or self-correct word recognition and understanding, rereading as necessary.

ELA ACADEMIC LANGUAGE

- *preview, predict, relevant, root*
- Cognates: *predecir, relevante*

Beyond Level

Leveled Reader: *Mars*

Preview and Predict

- Have students read the Essential Question: *How can scientific knowledge change over time?*
- Have students preview the title, table of contents, and first page of *Mars*. Then have them predict what they think the selection will be about. Encourage them to confirm or revise their predictions as they continue reading.

Review Genre: Expository Text

Tell students that this selection is expository text. Expository text provides factual information about a topic. Relevant details are organized logically and support the central idea. Features, such as photographs, captions, and diagrams, add information that might not be in the text. Have students identify features of expository text in *Mars*.

Close Reading

Note Taking Ask students to use a copy of online Central Idea and Relevant Details **Graphic Organizer 7** as they read.

Pages 2–3 *Which Greek root helps you figure out the meaning of* astronomers? (*Astro* means "star;" astronomers are people who study space.) Have students add this word in their reader's notebooks. *Why might the Greeks and Romans have named the planet after the god of war?* (The planet is red, reminding them of blood in battle.)

Pages 4–6 *Identify a similarity and a difference with Mars and Earth using the table on page 4.* (The days on Mars and Earth are a similar length; Mars is much colder than Earth.) *Look at the sidebar on page 5. How is the planet still associated with war?* (*Martial* comes from Mars, the Roman god of war.) *Which Greek root helps you figure out the meaning of* orbit *on page 6?* (*Orb* means "circle" or "ring." An orbit is a circular path.) Have students add this word to their reader's notebooks.

Pages 7–9 *Paraphrase the discoveries of some early Mars astronomers.* (Herschel found polar ice caps. Hall found and named the two moons.) *What was the effect of Kepler's use of mathematical calculations? Use the timeline to help you answer.* (Kepler figured out that all the planets move in elliptical orbits around the Sun.)

Pages 10–12 *Review the sidebar on page 11. How do natural features on Mars compare with those on Earth?* (Mars has taller mountains and longer canyons.) *How did we discover this?* (space missions)

Pages 13–16 *Summarize the central idea of the text to answer the question in the chapter title. Have a partner reread to verify your answer.* (Mars may be able to support life. Future missions will explore this.) *Why is discovering water so important?* (It could prove that there is life on Mars, since some things can survive without sunlight or oxygen.)

Page 17 *What aspects of Mars would cause human explorers to need special transportation and protective suits?* (Mars is far away, is cold, and has an atmosphere primarily made up of carbon dioxide.)

Respond to Reading Revisit the Essential Question and ask students to complete the Text Evidence Questions on page 18.

Analytical Writing **Write About Reading** Check that students have correctly explained how observations and improving technology have caused ideas about Mars to change. Make sure they include text details.

Fluency: Expression

Model Model reading page 2 with expression. Then read the passage aloud and have students read along with you.

Apply Have students practice reading the passage with partners.

Paired Read: "Zach the Martian"

Make Connections: Write About It

Before reading, ask students to note that the genre of this text is science fiction. Then discuss the Essential Question. After reading, ask students to write connections between the texts.

Leveled Reader

Build Knowledge

Talk About the Text Have partners discuss how scientific knowledge can change over time.

Write About the Text Have students add their ideas to the Build Knowledge pages of their reader's notebooks.

FOCUS ON SCIENCE

Students can extend their knowledge of Mars by completing the research and observation activity on page 24.

LITERATURE CIRCLES

Ask students to conduct a literature circle using the Thinkmark questions to guide the discussion. You may wish to have a whole-class discussion, on information learned from both selections in the Leveled Reader, about how scientific knowledge can change over time.

GIFTED AND TALENTED

Synthesize Have students choose one of the theories about Mars presented in the article and trace the changes in that theory over time as a result of new discoveries. Students should write a short paper that describes the original theory and explains the work scientists did to develop and change the theory. Challenge them to include a graphic organizer, such as a sequence chain or a timeline, to show the changes in the theory over time as a result of further scientific study.

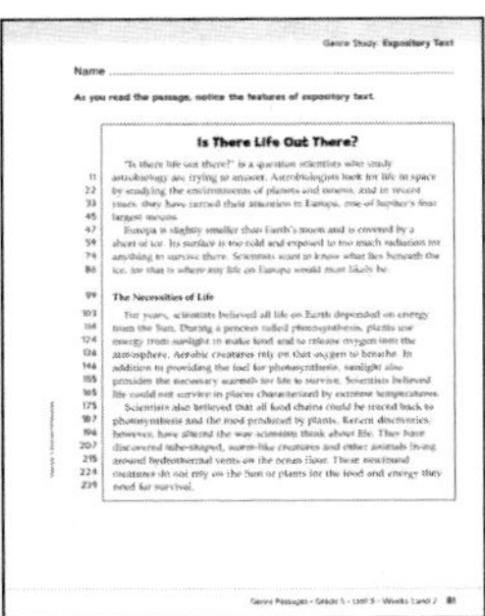

"Is There Life Out There?"
Lexile 990L

OBJECTIVES

Compare and contrast the overall structure (e.g., chronology, comparison, cause/effect, problem/solution) of events, ideas, concepts, or information in two or more texts.

Determine or clarify the meaning of unknown and multiple-meaning words and phrases based on grade 5 reading and content, choosing flexibly from a range of strategies.

Use common, grade-appropriate Greek and Latin affixes and roots as clues to the meaning of a word (e.g., *photograph, photosynthesis*).

ELA ACADEMIC LANGUAGE

- *expository text, compare, relevant, diagram, visualize*
- Cognates: *texto espositivo, comparar, relevante, diagrama, visualizar*

Beyond Level

Genre Passage: "Is There Life Out There?"

Build Background

- Read aloud the Essential Question: *How can scientific knowledge change over time?* Ask students to compare two expository texts they have read in this genre study. Use the following sentence starters to help focus discussion.

  I read that scientists have learned . . .
  The effect of this appears to be . . .

- The online **Differentiated Genre Passage** "Is There Life Out There?" references one of Jupiter's moons, Europa. Remind students that Jupiter is the fifth planet from the Sun in our solar system, and ask students how this knowledge helps them draw conclusions about the planet and its moon.

Review Genre: Expository Text

Remind students that expository text gives facts, examples, and explanations about a topic presented in a logical sequence. Text features, such as headings and subheadings, can indicate a connection among ideas in a section, while diagrams, labels, and captions help readers visualize ideas and information.

Close Reading

Note Taking As students read the passage the first time, ask them to annotate the text. Have them note central ideas, relevant details, unfamiliar words, and questions they have. Then read again and use the following questions. Encourage students to cite text evidence from the selection.

Read

Genre: Expository Text *Why is "Is There Life Out There?" expository text?* (It contains facts, examples, and explanations about the possibility of life on Europa. Subheads organize information about the knowledge related to the necessary components for life. A diagram about hydrothermal vents supports the text.)

Greek Roots Read paragraph 1 on page B1. *How does the Greek root* astro *help you understand why an astrobiologist would be interested in studying Europa?* (*Astro* refers to space. Astrobiology is the study of life in space, so an astrobiologist would want to study Europa because it is part of space.)

Relevant Details *Summarize the relevant details in paragraph 4.* (Scientists found that creatures around hydrothermal vents made food without the Sun or plants. This made the scientists reexamine the preconditions for life.)

Text Features: Diagrams *Examine the diagram on page B2. What can you infer about how water in a hydrothermal vent is warmed?* (It is likely warmed by chemicals found in the mid-ocean ridge.)

Central Idea Read paragraphs 3 and 4 on page B2. *Summarize scientists' hypothesis about life on Europa.* (Both oxygen and oceans could support life. Europa's atmosphere has oxygen, and it looks like there are oceans under its surface ice, so it's possible that Europa could support life.)

COLLABORATE **Summarize** Have students use their notes to summarize how scientists' ideas about life on Europa have changed over time.

Reread

Use the questions on page B3 to guide rereading.

Author's Craft *Why do you think the author chose to start the passage with a question?* (It sets the stage for the author to give information about the possibility of life on other planets and makes the reader curious to learn more and answer the question.)

Author's Craft *How does the diagram help you understand hydrothermal vents?* (It helps me visualize where hydrothermal vents are in the ocean.)

Author's Craft *Why do you think the author concluded the passage with information about Lake Vostok in Antarctica?* (Lake Vostok exists miles beneath a frozen surface, so it is possible it has an environment that is similar to Europa's. Finding life in Lake Vostok would support the idea that there might also be life on Europa. This possibility is one answer to the question asked at the beginning of the passage.)

Integrate

COLLABORATE **Make Connections** Have pairs connect "Is There Life Out There?" to other selections they have read as they answer this question: *How do the authors help you understand why people know more about the world now than they did years ago?*

Compare Genres Have students use a two-column chart labeled *Then* and *Now* to compare what they learned about how scientific knowledge has changed.

Build Knowledge

Talk About the Text Have partners discuss how scientific knowledge can change over time.

Write About the Text Have students add their ideas to the Build Knowledge pages of their reader's notebooks.

Differentiate and Collaborate

COLLABORATE **Be inspired** Have students think about "Is There Life Out There?" and other selections they have read. Ask: *What do the texts inspire you to do?* Use the following activities or have pairs of students think of ways to respond to the texts.

Make a Timeline Create a timeline that displays the scientific discoveries and advancements you've read about. Include the date of each discovery and a brief description of it. Add several well-known historical events to provide context for different time periods.

Write an Interview Script Write questions and responses for a news interview featuring a scientist from one of the texts. Include a question and an answer about how the person's scientific knowledge changed over time.

Readers to Writers

Using Text Features Remind students that authors often use subheads within a text to explain what a section is about. Have students reread the section with the subhead "The Necessities of Life" on page B1. Ask: *Why is this an appropriate subhead for this section? How does it help the author prepare readers for what they will learn?*

GIFTED AND TALENTED

Independent Study Have students synthesize their notes and the selections they read to create a travel guide to space. Encourage them to think about all the supplies they might need to bring as well as some of the places they will see. Ask them to self-evaluate and revise if necessary.

Beyond Level

Vocabulary/Comprehension

REVIEW DOMAIN-SPECIFIC WORDS

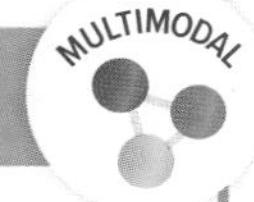

OBJECTIVES

Acquire and use accurately grade-appropriate general academic and domainspecific words and phrases, including those that signal contrast, addition, and other logical relationships (e.g., *however, although, nevertheless, similarly, moreover, in addition*).

Model Use the **Visual Vocabulary Cards** to review the meanings of the words *criteria* and *evaluate*. Use each word in a science-related sentence.

Write the words *environments* and *radiation* on the board and discuss the meanings with students. Then help students write sentences using these words.

Apply Have students work in pairs to review the meanings of the words *chemicals* and *oxygen*. Then have partners write sentences using the words.

GREEK ROOTS

OBJECTIVES

Determine or clarify the meaning of unknown and multiple-meaning words and phrases based on grade 5 reading and content, choosing flexibly from a range of strategies.

Use common, grade-appropriate Greek and Latin affixes and roots as clues to the meaning of a word (e.g., *photograph, photosynthesis*).

Model Read aloud the first three paragraphs of "Is There Life Out There?" in the Beyond Level online **Differentiated Genre Passage** page B1.

Think Aloud I want to know the meaning of *atmosphere* in the third paragraph. I see the Greek roots *atmos*, which means "vapor" and *sphaira*, meaning "globe." So *atmosphere* must mean "vapors or gases around Earth."

With students, reread the third paragraph on page B1. Help them figure out the meaning of *photosynthesis* by pointing out the Greek root *syntithenai* ("put together") and the Greek prefix *photo-* ("light").

Apply Have pairs of students read the rest of the passage. Ask them to use Greek roots to determine the meanings of the following words: *Aerobic* (page B1, paragraph 3), *hydrothermal* (page B1, paragraph 4), and *chemosynthesis* (page B2, paragraph 1). Note the following: *aero* ("air"), *bio* ("life"), *therm* ("heat"), *hydro* ("water"), and *chemo* ("chemical").

GIFTED and TALENTED **Independent Study** Challenge students to identify three other words explored this week that contain Greek roots and to identify their meanings. Have them write sentences in which the words are used appropriately.

Have students pick words from their reader's notebooks and use an online thesaurus to find synonyms and antonyms.

REVIEW CENTRAL IDEA AND RELEVANT DETAILS

OBJECTIVES

Determine two or more central, or main, ideas of a text and explain how they are supported by relevant, or key, details; summarize the text.

Review that authors of science and history texts organize their texts logically using relevant details to support a central idea.

Have students read the first two paragraphs of "Is There Life Out There?" in the Beyond Level online **Differentiated Genre Passage** page B1. Ask open-ended questions to facilitate discussion, such as *What is the central idea of this section? Which relevant details support it?*

Have students identify more relevant details to support the central idea in the rest of the passage as they independently fill in a copy of online Central Idea and Relevant Details **Graphic Organizer 7**. Then have partners use their work to explain why scientists continue to search for life in space.

SELF-SELECTED READING

OBJECTIVES

Determine two or more central, or main, ideas of a text and explain how they are supported by relevant, or key, details; summarize the text.

Ask and answer questions to increase understanding of a text.

Read Independently

In this text set, students focus on how relevant details support a central idea, how to summarize the text using the central idea and relevant details, and how to identify an author's purpose. Guide students to apply what they have learned in this text set as well as in previous lessons as they read independently.

Have students choose an expository nonfiction book for sustained silent reading. They can check the online **Leveled Reader Library** for selections.

- Have students record the central idea and details on **Graphic Organizer 7**.
- Remind them to ask and answer questions as they read to monitor their comprehension.

Encourage students to keep a reading journal. Suggest that they select books on topics that interest them.

- Students can write summaries of the books in their journals.
- Ask students to share with classmates an interesting fact they learned from the text.

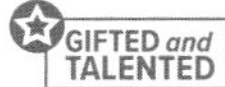

Independent Study Challenge students to discuss how their books relate to the weekly theme of now we know. Have students use all of their reading materials to compare the different ways our scientific knowledge has changed over time.

Student Outcomes

✓ Tested in *Wonders* Assessments

FOUNDATIONAL SKILLS

Phonics and Word Analysis

- Use knowledge of prefixes to decode words
- Use knowledge of suffixes *-less* and *-ness* to decode words

Fluency

- Read grade-level texts with accuracy, appropriate rate, expression, and automaticity

READING

Reading Literature

✓ Analyze how conflict and characterization contribute to the plot in a literary text
- Read and comprehend texts in the grades 4-5 text complexity band
- Summarize a text to enhance comprehension
- Write in response to texts

Reading Informational Text

✓ Explain how the text structure of compare and contrast contributes to the overall meaning of a text

Compare Texts

- Compare and contrast how authors present information on the same topic or theme

COMMUNICATION

Writing

Writing Process

✓ Write an expository text about a topic, using multiple sources and an organizational structure
- With guidance and support from peers and adults, develop and strengthen writing as needed by planning, revising, and editing

Speaking and Listening

- Report on a topic or text or present an opinion, sequencing ideas; speak clearly at an understandable pace

Conventions

Grammar

✓ Explain the function of adjectives
✓ Use correct capitalization and punctuation
✓ Identify adjectives that compare
✓ Use *more* and *most* correctly with adjectives

Spelling

- Spell words with prefixes
- Spell words with suffixes *-less* and *-ness*

Researching

- Conduct short research projects that use several sources to build knowledge through investigation of different aspects of a topic

Creating and Collaborating

- Add audio recordings and visual displays to presentations when appropriate
- With some guidance and support from adults, use technology to produce and publish writing

VOCABULARY

Academic Vocabulary

- Acquire and use grade-appropriate academic vocabulary

Vocabulary Strategy

✓ Use context clues to determine the meaning of unknown words and phrases, including idioms

 CONTENT AREA LEARNING

Historical and Cultural Analysis

- Analyze various issues and events of the 20th century, such as the Great Depression. **Social Studies**
- Explain how examples of art, music, and literature reflect the times during which they were created. **Social Studies**

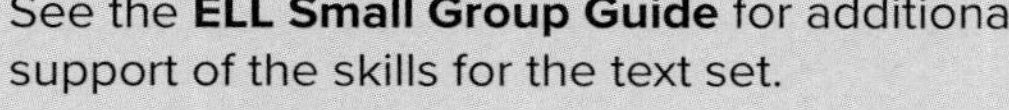

ELL Scaffolded supports for English Language Learners are embedded throughout the lessons, enabling students to communicate information, ideas, and concepts in English Language Arts and for social and instructional purposes within the school setting.

See the **ELL Small Group Guide** for additional support of the skills for the text set.

FORMATIVE ASSESSMENT

For assessment throughout the text set, use students' self-assessments and your observations.

Use the Data Dashboard to filter class, group, or individual student data to guide group placement decisions. It provides recommendations to enhance learning for gifted and talented students and offers extra support for students needing remediation.

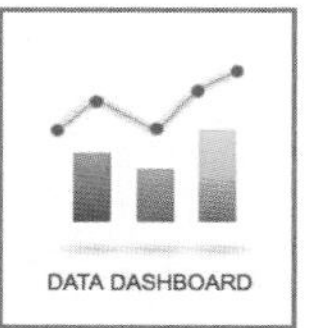

Develop Student Ownership

To build student ownership, students need to know what they are learning and why they are learning it, and to determine how well they understood it.

Students Discuss Their Goals

READING

TEXT SET GOALS

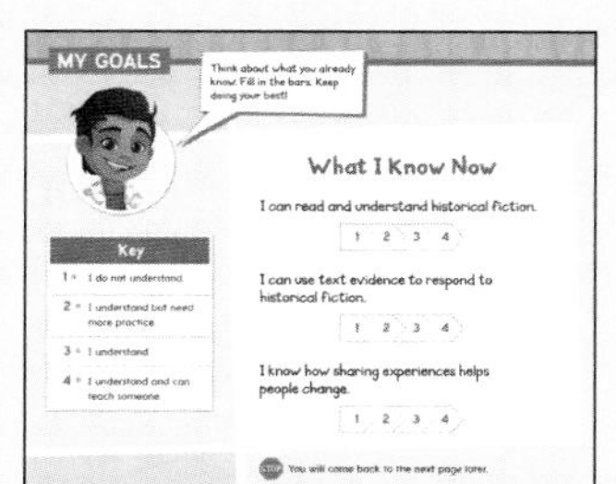

- I can read and understand historical fiction.
- I can use text evidence to respond to historical fiction.
- I know how sharing experiences helps people change.

Have students think about what they know and fill in the bars on **Reading/Writing Companion** page 36.

WRITING

EXTENDED WRITING GOALS

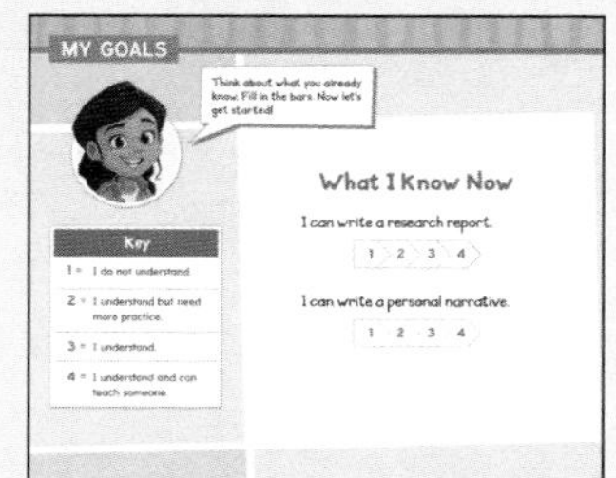

Extended Writing 1:

- I can write a research report.
- I can write a personal narrative.

Have students think about what they know and fill in the bars on **Reading/Writing Companion** page 84.

Students Monitor Their Learning

LEARNING GOALS

Specific learning goals identified in every lesson make clear what students will be learning and why. These smaller goals provide stepping stones to help students reach their Text Set and Extended Writing Goals.

CHECK-IN ROUTINE

The Check-In Routine at the close of each lesson guides students to self-reflect on how well they understood each learning goal.

Review the lesson learning goal.
Reflect on the activity.
Self-Assess by
- filling in the bars in the **Reading/Writing Companion**
- holding up 1, 2, 3, or 4 fingers

Share with your teacher.

Students Reflect on Their Progress

READING

TEXT SET GOALS

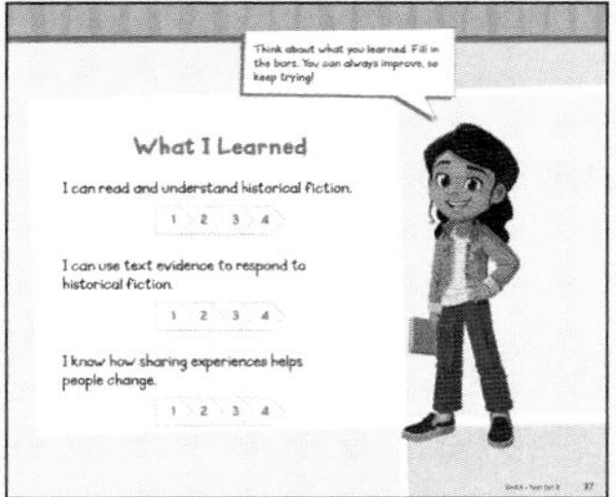

After completing the Show Your Knowledge task for the text set, students reflect on their understanding of the Text Set Goals by filling in the bars on **Reading/Writing Companion** page 37.

WRITING

EXTENDED WRITING GOALS

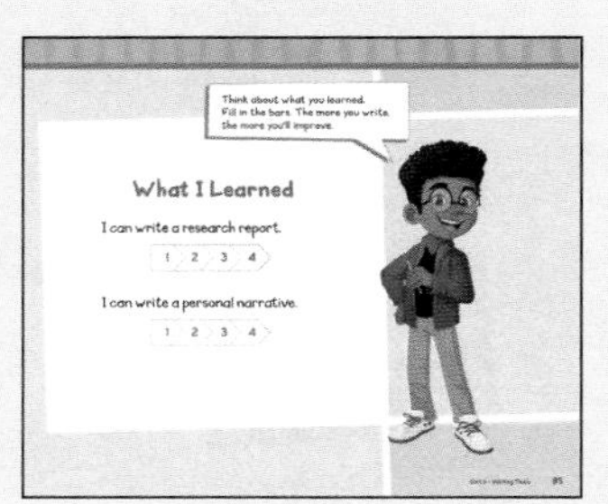

After completing their extended writing projects, students reflect on their understanding of the Extended Writing Goals by filling in the bars on **Reading/Writing Companion** page 85.

Build Knowledge

Shared Read
Reading/Writing Companion p. 38

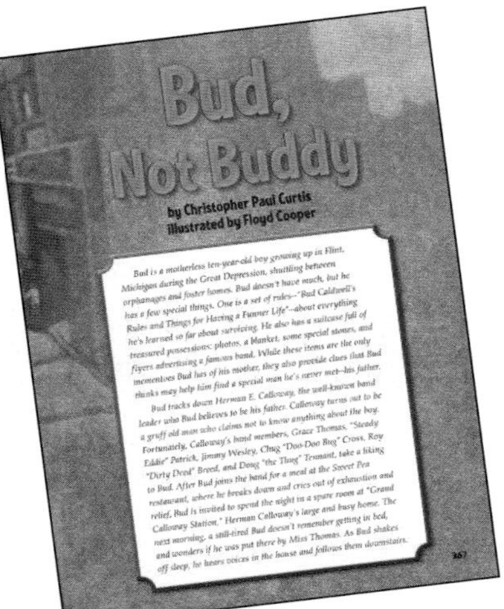

Anchor Text
Literature Anthology p. 367

Paired Selection
Literature Anthology p. 382

Essential Question

How do shared experiences help people adapt to change?

Video The Civil Conservation Corps was formed during the Great Depression to create jobs. Working together in the Corps restored people's pride.

Study Sync Blast Americans came together in many ways during the Great Depression. One program, the Federal Art Project, paid artists to make sculptures, paintings, and murals.

Interactive Read Aloud An immigrant boy adapts to his new country with the help of his cousin, who advises him that at first "you think you'll never fit in here, but you will."

Shared Read Despite the hardships of the Great Depression, the Rollet family puts on a performance that lifts everyone's spirit and makes the future seem bright.

Anchor Text Bud, a motherless boy, is adopted by a band of musicians that may include his father. The band helps him fit in and adjust to his new life as a musician.

Paired Selection During the Great Depression, music let listeners know they were not alone in their struggles. Jazz used upbeat rhythms to lift people's spirits.

Make Connections The photo and texts show how the shared experience of listening to music connects people emotionally and makes them more resilient.

Differentiated Sources

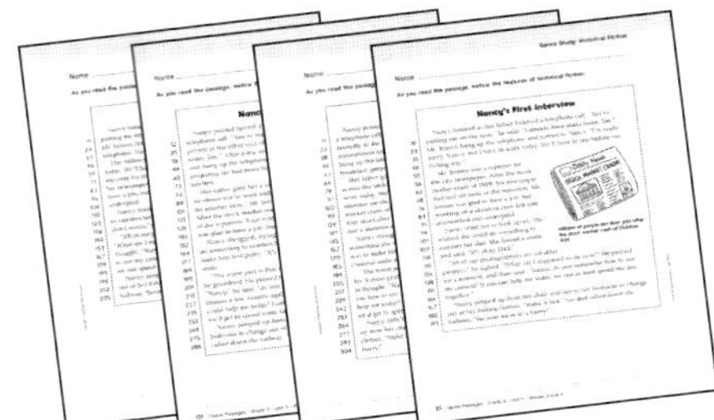

Leveled Readers

The Picture Palace Two boys find success trying to earn money by helping one another.

Hard Times A family finds a way to work together to stay together during the Great Depression.

Woodpecker Warriors A fire helps a man overcome his prejudices about the CCC.

Differentiated Genre Passages

A story of two different families that were impacted by the Great Depression.

Build Knowledge Routine

After reading each text, ask students to document what facts and details they learned to help answer the Essential Question of the text set.

Talk About the source.

Write About the source.

Add to the Class Anchor Chart.

- Add to your Vocabulary List.

Show Your Knowledge

Write Song Lyrics

Have students show how they built knowledge across the text set by writing song lyrics, Have students first think about the Essential Question: *How do shared experiences help people adapt to change?* Students will write song lyrics that describe the qualities the characters in the texts have in common that helped them triumph over their hardships and disappointments.

Social Emotional Learning

Relationships and Prosocial Behavior

Anchor Text: Students should exhibit behaviors that help others and understand how those cultivate meaningful relationships. Ask: *Why did the band members allow Bud to join them?*

Paired Selection: Prosocial behaviors are behaviors intended to help others. Have the class discuss how music can help people. Ask: *In what ways did the myriad musical styles of the Great Depression affect people?*

Roundtable Discussion: Compare and contrast some ways shared experiences, relationships, and prosocial behavior helped characters in *Bud, Not Buddy* and musicians during the Great Depression adapt to the challenges of the time.

TEXT SET 2

Explore the Texts

Essential Question: How do shared experiences help people adapt to change?

ACT

Access Complex Text (ACT) boxes throughout the text set provide scaffolded instruction for seven different elements that may make a text complex.

Teacher's Edition	Reading/Writing Companion	Literature Anthology	

"Starting Over" Interactive Read Aloud p. T87 Historical Fiction	"The Day the Rollets Got Their Moxie Back" Shared Read pp. 38–41 Historical Fiction	*Bud, Not Buddy* Anchor Text pp. 366–379 Historical Fiction	"Musical Impressions of the Great Depression" Paired Selection pp. 382–385 Expository Text
Qualitative			
Meaning/Purpose Low Complexity **Structure** Moderate Complexity **Language** Moderate Complexity **Knowledge Demands** Low Complexity	**Meaning/Purpose** Moderate Complexity **Structure** Moderate Complexity **Language** High Complexity **Knowledge Demands** Low Complexity	**Meaning/Purpose** Mid Complexity **Structure** Moderate Complexity **Language** High Complexity **Knowledge Demands** Moderate Complexity	**Meaning/Purpose** Moderate Complexity **Structure** Moderate Complexity **Language** Moderate Complexity **Knowledge Demands** Moderate Complexity
Quantitative			
Lexile 890L	**Lexile** 900L	**Lexile** 950L	**Lexile** 990L
Reader and Task Considerations			
Reader The structure demands and language features will be the most challenging. Provide background information about immigration, urbanization, and industrialization in the early 1900s.	**Reader** The knowledge demands and language features will be the most challenging. Discuss the Great Depression and the era's economic difficulties and joblessness.	**Reader** The knowledge demands will be challenging. Discuss the Depression and review the historical fiction genre. Use dictionaries to rephrase characters' slang.	**Reader** Students will not need background knowledge to understand the text but teachers might wish to discuss how music reflects its era.

Task The questions for the read aloud are supported by teacher modeling. The tasks provide a variety of ways for students to begin to build knowledge and vocabulary about the text set topic. The questions and tasks provided for the other texts are at various levels of complexity, ensuring that all students can interact with the text in meaningful ways.

Additional Texts

Classroom Library

SeeSaw Girl
Genre: Historical Fiction
Lexile: 810L

Bud, Not Buddy
Genre: Historical Fiction
Lexile: 950L

See **Classroom Library Lessons**

Content Area Reading BLMs

Additional online texts related to grade-level Science, Social Studies, and Arts content

Leveled Readers

(A) *The Picture Palace*

(O) *Hard Times*

(B) *Woodpecker Warriors*

(ELL) *Hard Times*

Qualitative

(A) **Meaning/Purpose** Low Complexity
Structure Moderate Complexity
Language Moderate Complexity
Knowledge Demands Low Complexity

(O) **Meaning/Purpose** Moderate Complexity
Structure Moderate Complexity
Language High Complexity
Knowledge Demands Moderate Complexity

(B) **Meaning/Purpose** Moderate Complexity
Structure Moderate Complexity
Language High Complexity
Knowledge Demands Moderate Complexity

(ELL) **Meaning/Purpose** Moderate Complexity
Structure Low Complexity
Language Moderate Complexity
Knowledge Demands Low Complexity

Quantitative

Lexile 710L

Lexile 830L

Lexile 900L

Lexile 520L

Reader and Task Considerations

Reader Students may not understand that in the past, going to the movies was less common than today, so it was very special.

Reader Students will need background knowledge of The Great Depression to better understand the story.

Reader Students will need background knowledge of The Great Depression to better understand the story.

Reader Students will need background knowledge of The Great Depression to better understand the story.

Task The questions and tasks provided for the Leveled Readers are at various levels of complexity, ensuring that all students can interact with the text in meaningful ways.

Differentiated Genre Passages

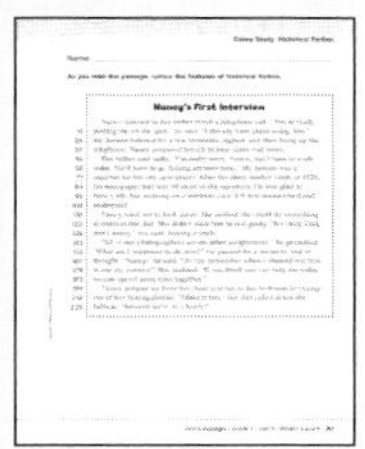

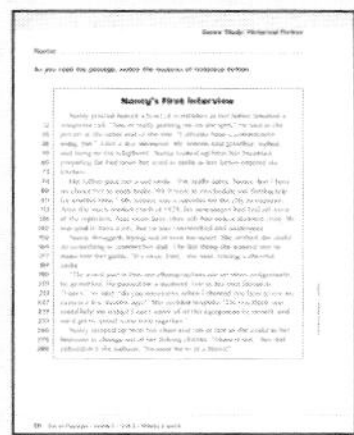

(A) "Nancy's First Interview"

(O) "Nancy's First Interview"

(B) "Nancy's First Interview"

(ELL) "Nancy's First Interview"

Qualitative

(A) **Meaning/Purpose** Low Complexity
Structure Low Complexity
Language Low Complexity
Knowledge Demands Low Complexity

(O) **Meaning/Purpose** Low Complexity
Structure Low Complexity
Language Moderate Complexity
Knowledge Demands Low Complexity

(B) **Meaning/Purpose** Low Complexity
Structure Low Complexity
Language Moderate Complexity
Knowledge Demands Moderate Complexity

(ELL) **Meaning/Purpose** Low Complexity
Structure Low Complexity
Language Moderate Complexity
Knowledge Demands Low Complexity

Quantitative

Lexile 670L

Lexile 720L

Lexile 820L

Lexile 710L

Reader and Task Considerations

Reader Students will need background knowledge of The Great Depression to better understand the story.

Reader Students will need background knowledge of The Great Depression to better understand the story.

Reader Students will need background knowledge of The Great Depression to better understand the story.

Reader Students will need background knowledge of The Great Depression to better understand the story.

Task The questions and tasks provided for the Differentiated Genre Passages are at various levels of complexity, ensuring that all students can interact with the text in meaningful ways.

Week 3 Planner

Customize your own lesson plans at **my.mheducation.com**

Reading Suggested Daily Time (60+ mins)

READING LESSON GOALS

- **I can read and understand historical fiction.**
- **I can use text evidence to respond to historical fiction.**
- **I know how sharing experiences helps people change.**

SMALL GROUP OPTIONS The designated lessons can be taught in small groups. To determine how to differentiate instruction for small groups, use Formative Assessment and Data Dashboard.

Writing Suggested Daily Time (30+ mins)

WRITING LESSON GOALS

I can write a research report.

Lesson 1	Lesson 2
Reading	
Introduce the Concept, T84–T85 Build Knowledge **Listening Comprehension, T86–T87** "Starting Over" **Shared Read, T88–T91** Read "The Day the Rollets Got Their Moxie Back" Quick Write: Summarize **Vocabulary, T92–T93** Academic Vocabulary Idioms **Expand Vocabulary, T136**	**Shared Read, T88–T91** Reread "The Day the Rollets Got Their Moxie Back" **Minilessons, T94–T101** Make, Confirm, and Revise Predictions Plot: Characterization Plot: Conflict Craft and Structure **Respond to Reading, T102–T103** **Phonics, T104–T105** Prefixes **Fluency, T105** Rate **Research and Inquiry, T106–T107** **Expand Vocabulary, T136**
Writing	
Extended Writing: Research Report	
Writing Lesson Bank: Craft Minilessons, T260–T263	
Teacher and Peer Conferences	
Grammar Lesson Bank, T270 Adjectives Talk About It **Spelling Lesson Bank, T280** Prefixes	**Grammar Lesson Bank, T270** Adjectives Talk About It **Spelling Lesson Bank, T280** Prefixes

SMALL GROUP

Teacher-Led Instruction

Differentiated Reading

Leveled Readers
- *The Picture Palace,* T138–T139
- *Hard Times,* T148–T149
- *Woodpecker Warriors,* T154–T155

Differentiated Skills Practice

Approaching Level
Phonics/Decoding, T142
- Decode Words with Prefixes
- Practice Words with Prefixes

Vocabulary, T144
- Review High-Frequency Words
- Review Academic Vocabulary

Fluency, T146
- Rate

Comprehension, T146–T147
- Plot: Conflict
- Self-Selected Reading

Independent/Collaborative Work

See pages T83G–T83H.

Reading

Comprehension
- Historical Fiction
- Plot: Conflict
- Make, Confirm, and Revise Predictions

Fluency
Independent Reading

Phonics/Word Study

Phonics/Decoding
- Prefixes

Vocabulary
- Idioms

Writing

Extended Writing 1: Research Report
Self-Selected Writing
Grammar
- Adjectives

Spelling
- Prefixes

Handwriting

ACADEMIC VOCABULARY
assume, guarantee, nominate, obviously, rely, supportive, sympathy, weakling

SPELLING
prewash, disable, discolor, mistaken, misunderstand, mistrust, incorrect, disconnect, preview, prejudge, misjudge, discomfort, dismount, disobey, injustice, preheats, dishonest, disapprove, inexpensive, indefinite

Review *presence, stationary, current*
Challenge *prehistoric, misbehave*
See pages T280–T281 for Differentiated Spelling Lists.

 LESSON 3	 LESSON 4	 LESSON 5
Reading		
Anchor Text, T108–T123 Read *Bud, Not Buddy* Take Notes About Text **Expand Vocabulary, T137**	**Anchor Text, T108–T123** Read *Bud, Not Buddy* Take Notes About Text **Expand Vocabulary, T137**	**Anchor Text, T108–T123** Reread *Bud, Not Buddy* **Expand Vocabulary, T137**
Writing		
		Extended Writing 1, T236–T237 Revise: Sentence Structure
Writing Lesson Bank: Craft Minilessons, T260–T263		
Teacher and Peer Conferences		
Grammar Lesson Bank, T271 Adjectives Talk About It **Spelling Lesson Bank, T281** Prefixes	**Grammar Lesson Bank, T271** Adjectives Talk About It **Spelling Lesson Bank, T281** Prefixes	**Grammar Lesson Bank, T271** Adjectives Talk About It **Spelling Lesson Bank, T281** Prefixes

On Level
Vocabulary, T152
- Review Academic Vocabulary
- Idioms

Comprehension, T153
- Review Plot: Conflict
- Self-Selected Reading

Beyond Level
Vocabulary, T158
- Review Domain-Specific Words
- Idioms GIFTED and TALENTED

Comprehension, T159
- Review Plot: Conflict
- Self-Selected Reading GIFTED and TALENTED

English Language Learners
See ELL Small Group Guide, pp. 198–209

Content Area Connections

Content Area Reading
- Science, Social Studies, and the Arts

Research and Inquiry
- Supporting One Another

Inquiry Space
- Options for Project-Based Learning

English Language Learners
See ELL Small Group Guide, pp. 198–209

Week 4 Planner

Customize your own lesson plans at
my.mheducation.com

60+ mins Reading Suggested Daily Time

READING LESSON GOALS

- **I can read and understand historical fiction.**
- **I can use text evidence to respond to historical fiction.**
- **I know how sharing experiences helps people change.**

SMALL GROUP OPTIONS The designated lessons can be taught in small groups. To determine how to differentiate instruction for small groups, use Formative Assessment and Data Dashboard.

30+ mins Writing Suggested Daily Time

WRITING LESSON GOALS

I can write a research report.

Lesson 6	Lesson 7
Reading	
Anchor Text, T108–T123 Reread *Bud, Not Buddy* **Respond to Reading, T124–T125** **Expand Vocabulary, T136**	**Paired Selection, T126–T129** Read "Musical Impressions of the Great Depression" **Expand Vocabulary, T136**
Writing	
Extended Writing 1, T236–T237 Revise: Sentence Structure	**Extended Writing 1, T238–T239** Peer Conferencing
Writing Lesson Bank: Craft Minilessons, T260–T263	
Teacher and Peer Conferences	
Grammar Lesson Bank, T272 Adjectives That Compare Talk About It **Spelling Lesson Bank, T282** Suffixes *-less* and *-ness*	**Grammar Lesson Bank, T272** Adjectives That Compare Talk About It **Spelling Lesson Bank, T282** Suffixes *-less* and *-ness*

SMALL GROUP

Teacher-Led Instruction

Differentiated Reading

Differentiated Genre Passages

- "Nancy's First Interview," T140–T141
- "Nancy's First Interview," T150–T151
- "Nancy's First Interview," T156–T157

Differentiated Skills Practice

Approaching Level

Phonics/Decoding, T143

- Decode Words with Suffixes *-less* and *-ness*
- Practice Words with Suffixes *-less* and *-ness*

Vocabulary, T145

- Identify Related Words
- Idioms

Fluency, T146

- Accuracy

Comprehension, T146–T147

- Review Plot: Conflict
- Transfer Knowledge of Standards

Independent/Collaborative Work

See pages T83G–T83H.

Reading

Comprehension

- Historical Fiction
- Plot: Conflict
- Make, Confirm, and Revise Predictions

Fluency

Independent Reading

Phonics/Word Study

Phonics/Decoding

- Suffixes *-less* and *-ness*

Vocabulary

- Idioms

Writing

Extended Writing 1: Research Report

Self-Selected Writing

Grammar

- Adjectives That Compare

Spelling

- Suffixes *-less* and *-ness*

Handwriting

ACADEMIC VOCABULARY
assume, guarantee, nominate, obviously, rely, supportive, sympathy, weakling

SPELLING
sadness, gladness, needless, harmless, darkness, fullness, stillness, hopeless, fearless, weakness, bottomless, foolishness, fondness, effortless, meaningless, emptiness, forgiveness, motionless, ceaseless, fierceness

Review *disobey, mistrust, preview*
Challenge *weightlessness, thoughtlessness*
See pages T282–T283 for Differentiated Spelling Lists.

Reading

Lesson 8	Lesson 9	Lesson 10
Paired Selection, T126–T129 Reread "Musical Impressions of the Great Depression" **Author's Craft, T130–T131** Text Structure: Compare and Contrast **Phonics, T132–T133** Suffixes *-less* and *-ness* **Expand Vocabulary, T137**	**Fluency, T133** Accuracy **Make Connections, T134** **Expand Vocabulary, T137**	**Show Your Knowledge, T135** **Progress Monitoring, T83I–T83J** **Expand Vocabulary, T137**

Writing

Lesson 8	Lesson 9	Lesson 10
Extended Writing 1, T240–T241 Edit and Proofread	**Extended Writing 1, T240–T241** Edit and Proofread	**Extended Writing 1, T242–T243** Publish, Present, and Evaluate
Writing Lesson Bank: Craft Minilessons, T260–T263		
Teacher and Peer Conferences		
Grammar Lesson Bank, T273 Adjectives That Compare Talk About It **Spelling Lesson Bank, T283** Suffixes *-less* and *-ness*	**Grammar Lesson Bank, T273** Adjectives That Compare Talk About It **Spelling Lesson Bank, T283** Suffixes *-less* and *-ness*	**Grammar Lesson Bank, T273** Adjectives That Compare Talk About It **Spelling Lesson Bank, T283** Suffixes *-less* and *-ness*

On Level
Vocabulary, T152
- Review Academic Vocabulary
- Idioms

Comprehension, T153
- Review Plot: Conflict
- Self-Selected Reading

Beyond Level
Vocabulary, T158
- Review Domain-Specific Words
- Idioms

Comprehension, T159
- Review Plot: Conflict
- Self-Selected Reading 

English Language Learners
See ELL Small Group Guide, pp. 198–209

Content Area Connections

Content Area Reading
- Science, Social Studies, and the Arts

Research and Inquiry
- Supporting One Another

Inquiry Space
- Options for Project-Based Learning

English Language Learners
See ELL Small Group Guide, pp. 198–209

Independent and Collaborative Work

As you meet with small groups, the rest of the class completes activities and projects that allow them to practice and apply the skills they have been working on.

Student Choice and Student Voice

- Print the My Independent Work blackline master and review it with students. Identify the "Must Do" activities.
- Have students choose additional activities that provide the practice they need.
- Remind students to reflect on their learning each day.

Name ________ Unit 5 • Text Set 2

My Independent Work

	Reading	Phonics/Word Study	Writing
Center Activity Cards	Card: Activity:	Card: Activity:	Card: Activity:
Digital Activities my.mheducation.com	Activity:	Activity:	Activity:
Practice Pages	Content Area Reading:	Practice:	Practice:
Independent Choices	Independent Reading:	Activity:	Self-Selected Writing:

34 Grade 5 • My Independent Work

My Independent Work BLM

Reading

Independent Reading Texts

Students can choose a Center Activity Card to use while they read independently.

Classroom Library
SeeSaw Girl
Genre: Historical Fiction
Lexile: 810L

Bud, Not Buddy
Genre: Historical Fiction
Lexile: 950L

Unit Bibliography
Have students self-select independent reading texts about how togetherness helps people.

Leveled Texts Online

- Additional Leveled Readers in the **Leveled Reader Library Online** allow for flexibility.
- Six leveled sets of **Differentiated Genre Passages** in diverse genres are available.
- **Differentiated Texts** offer ELL students more passages at different proficiency levels.

Additional Literature
Literature Anthology
Ida B, pp. 412–423
Genre: Realistic Fiction

"A Dusty Ride," pp. 426–429
Genre: Realistic Fiction

Center Activity Cards

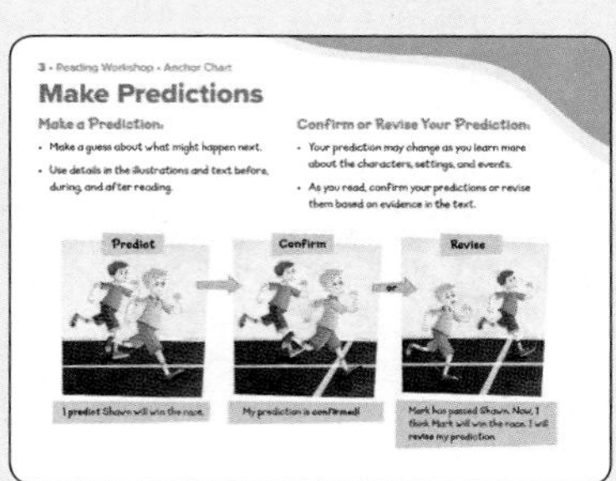

Make Predictions Card 3

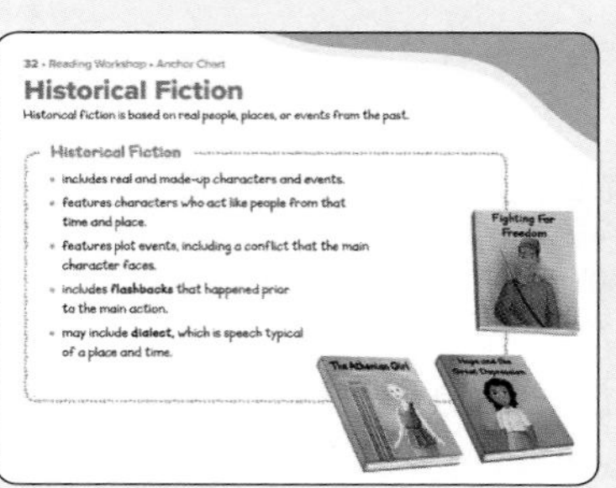

Historical Fiction Card 32

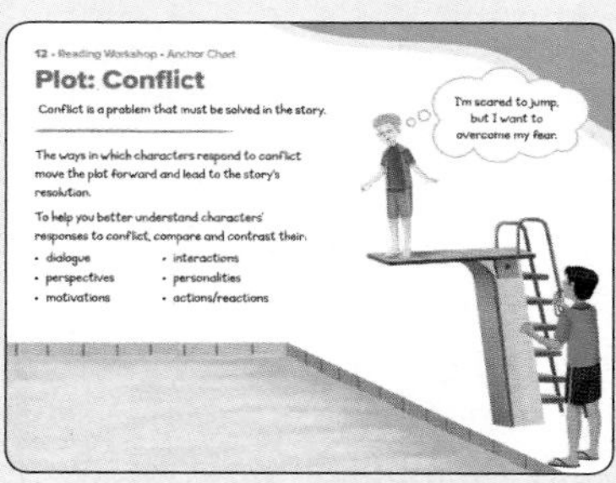

Plot: Conflict Card 12

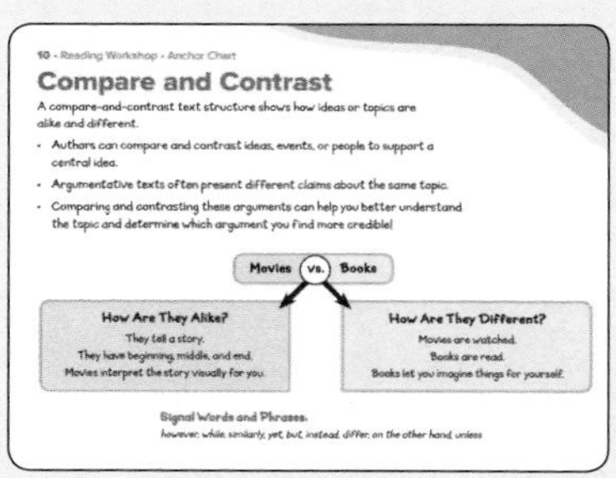

Compare and Contrast Card 10

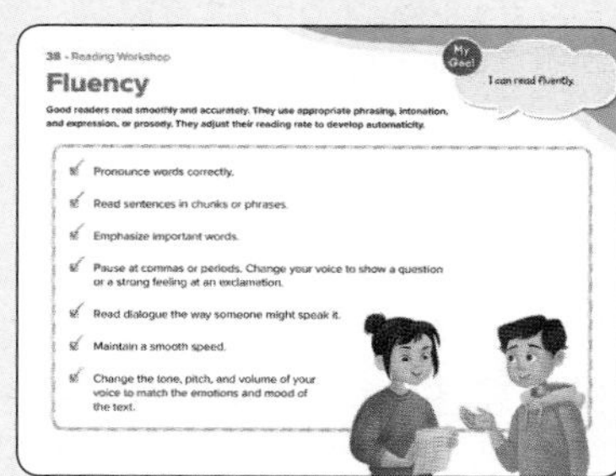

Fluency Card 38

Digital Activities

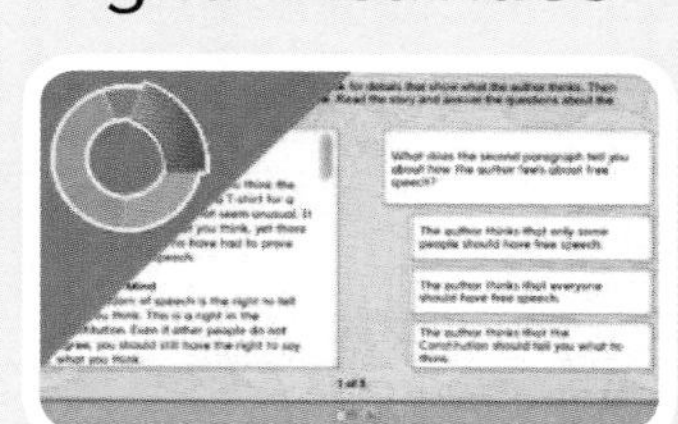

Comprehension

Phonics/Word Study

Center Activity Cards

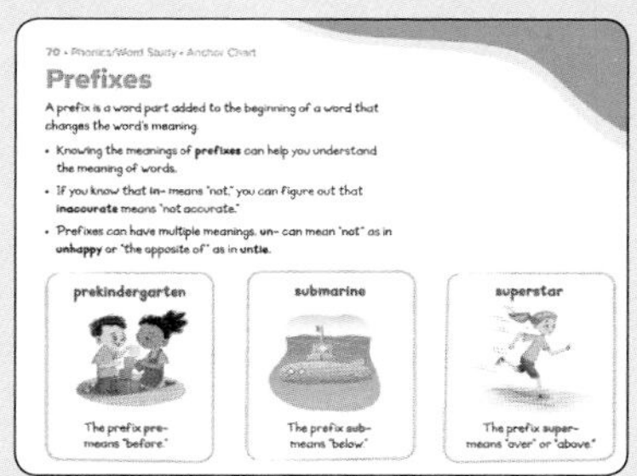

Prefixes Card 70

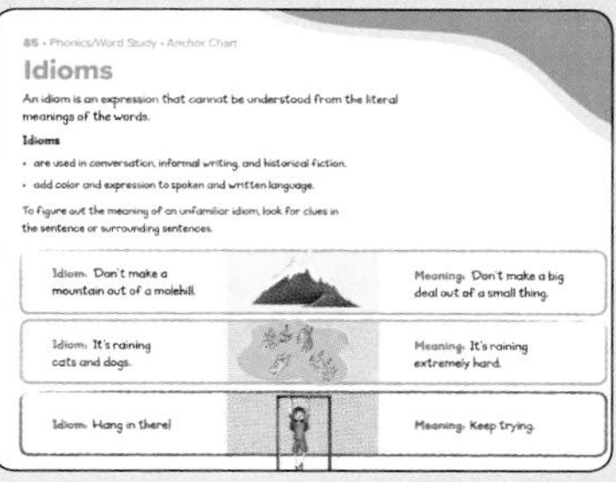

Idioms Card 85

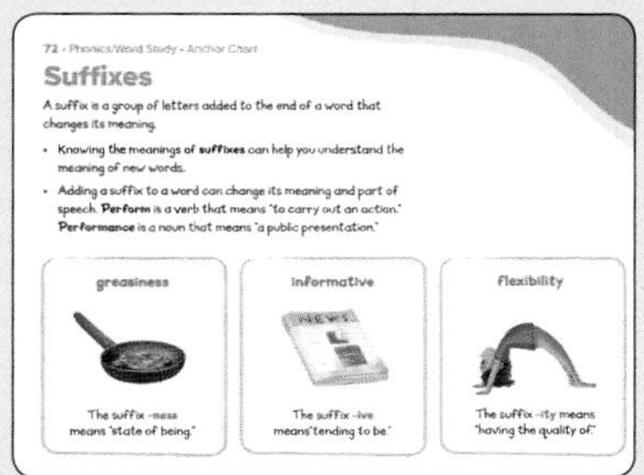

Suffixes Card 72

Practice Book BLMs

Phonics: pages 271–271B, 274, 283–283B, 286

Vocabulary: pages 275–276, 287–288

Digital Activities

Phonics

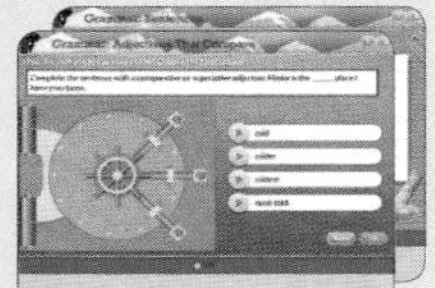
Vocabulary

Writing

Center Activity Cards

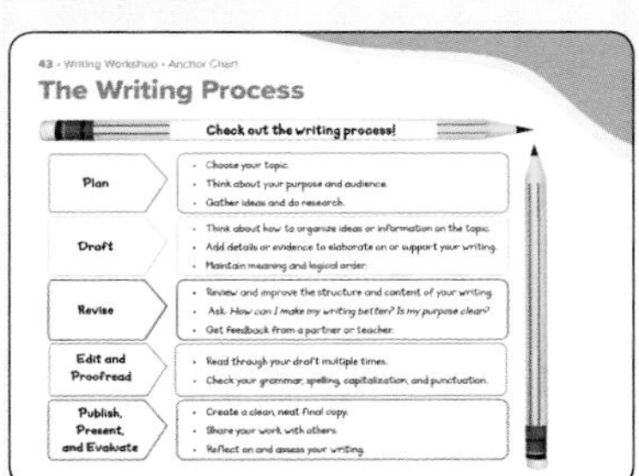

Writing Process Card 43

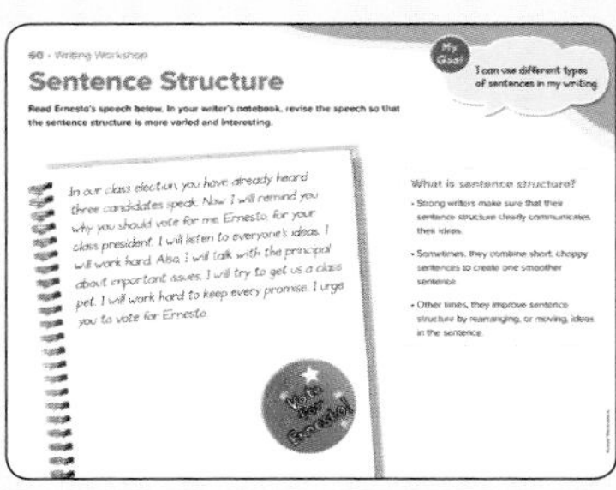

Sentence Structure Card 60

Extended Writing

Have students continue developing their **research reports**.

Practice Book BLMs

Grammar: pages 265–269, 277–281
Spelling: pages 270–274, 282–286
Handwriting: pages 361–396

Self-Selected Writing

Share the following prompts.

- Write a story about an orphan who has an adventure finding the perfect family to live with.
- Look at historic photographs of the Great Depression and write about what you see.
- Research and write about programs that helped families during the Great Depression.
- Choose a famous jazz musician and write about her or his life.
- Write about a historical fiction story that you have read. What did you learn about history from the story?

Digital Activities

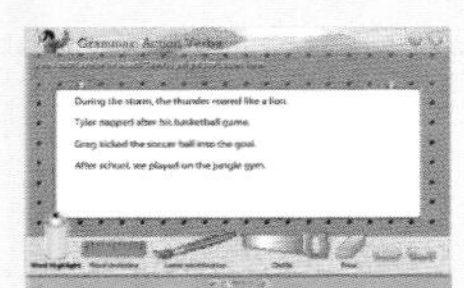
Grammar

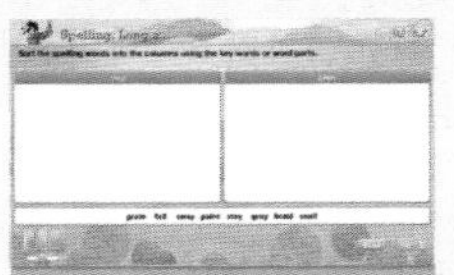
Spelling

Content Area Connections

Content Area Reading Blackline Masters

- Additional texts related to Science, Social Studies, and the Arts

Research and Inquiry

- Supporting One Another

Inquiry Space

- Choose an activity

Progress Monitoring

Moving Toward Mastery

FORMATIVE ASSESSMENT
STUDENT CHECK-IN
CHECK FOR SUCCESS

For ongoing formative assessment, use students' self-assessments at the end of each lesson along with your own observations.

Assessing skills along the way . . .

SKILLS	HOW ASSESSED
Comprehension **Vocabulary**	Digital Activities, Rubrics
Text-Based Writing	Reading/Writing Companion: Respond to Reading
Grammar, Mechanics, Phonics, Spelling	Practice Book, Digital Activities including word sorts
Listening/Presenting/Research	Checklists
Oral Reading Fluency (ORF) Fluency Goal: 136–156 words correct per minute (WCPM) Accuracy Rate Goal: 95% or higher	Fluency Assessment

At the end of the text set . . .

SKILLS	HOW ASSESSED
Plot: Characterization **Plot: Conflict** **Text Structure: Compare and Contrast**	Progress Monitoring
Idioms	

Making the Most of Assessment Results

Make data-based grouping decisions by using the following reports to verify assessment results. For additional student support options refer to the reteaching and enrichment opportunities.

ONLINE ASSESSMENT CENTER

- ***Gradebook***

DATA DASHBOARD

- ***Recommendations Report***
- ***Activity Report***
- ***Skills Report***
- ***Progress Report***
- ***Grade Card Report***

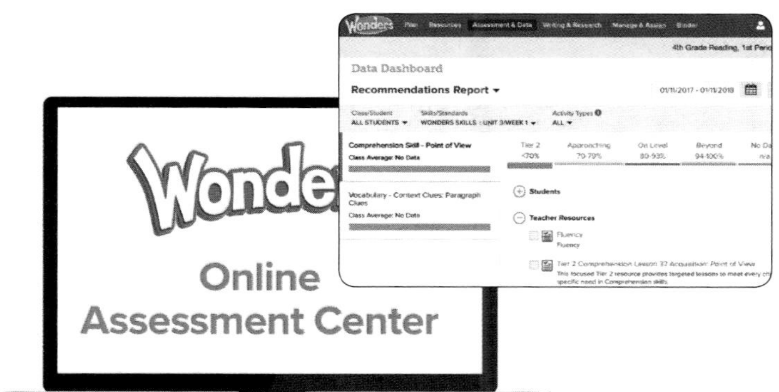

 Assign practice pages online for auto-grading.

TIER 2

Reteaching Opportunities with Intervention Online PDFs

IF STUDENTS SCORE . . .	THEN ASSIGN . . .
below 70% in **comprehension . . .**	lessons 25–27 on Character in **Comprehension PDF,** lessons 46–48 on Conflict and Resolution in **Comprehension PDF,** and/or lessons 79–81 on Compare and Contrast in **Comprehension PDF**
below 70% in **vocabulary . . .**	lesson 118 on Idioms, Adages, Proverbs in **Vocabulary PDF**
127–135 WCPM in **fluency . . .**	lessons from Section 1 or 7–10 of **Fluency PDF**
0–126 WCPM in **fluency . . .**	lessons from Sections 2–6 of **Fluency PDF**

Use the* Phonics/Word Study PDF *and* Foundational Skills Kit *for additional reteaching opportunities.
Use the* Foundational Skills Kit *for students who need support with phonemic awareness and other early literacy skills.

GIFTED *and* TALENTED

Enrichment Opportunities

Beyond Level small group lessons and resources include suggestions for additional activities in these areas to extend learning opportunities for gifted and talented students:

- ***Leveled Readers***
- ***Genre Passages***
- ***Vocabulary***
- ***Comprehension***
- ***Leveled Reader Library Online***
- ***Center Activity Cards***

OBJECTIVES

Engage effectively in a range of collaborative discussions (one-on-one, in groups, and teacher-led) with diverse partners, building on others' ideas and expressing their own clearly.

Follow agreed-upon rules for discussions and carry out assigned roles.

Build background knowledge about how people adapt to change.

ELA ACADEMIC LANGUAGE

- *discuss, collaboration*
- Cognates: *discutir, colaboración*

DIGITAL TOOLS

Show the image during class discussion. Then play the video.

Discuss Concept

Watch Video

Discuss Images

VOCABULARY

experienced (*experimentar*) to have something happen to you

kindness (*amabilidad*) the state of being nice to someone

adapt (*adaptarse*) change yourself to fit a new situation

Build Knowledge

Essential Question

How do shared experiences help people adapt to change?

Read the Essential Question on **Reading/Writing Companion** page 34. Tell students that they will read historical fiction texts that describe a difficult time in our country's history and build knowledge about how people adapt to change. They will use words to read, write, and talk about how shared experiences help people adapt to change.

Watch the Video Play the video without sound first. Have partners narrate what they see. Then replay the video with sound as students listen.

Talk About the Video Have partners discuss how shared experiences help people adapt to change.

Write About the Video Have students add their ideas to the Build Knowledge pages of their reader's notebooks.

Anchor Chart Begin a Build Knowledge anchor chart. Write the Essential Question at the top of the chart. Have volunteers share their ideas about adapting to change. Record their ideas. Explain that students will add to the anchor chart after they read each text.

Build Knowledge

Discuss the photograph of people waiting in line to receive assistance. Focus on ways that people can be supportive of others who are in difficult circumstances. Ask: *How were you supportive of others during a time of change? How did you rely on each other?* Have students discuss in pairs.

Build Vocabulary

Model using the graphic organizer to write down new words related to adapting to change. Have partners continue the discussion and add the graphic organizer and new words to their reader's notebooks. Students will add words to the Build Knowledge pages in their notebooks as they read about how people adapt to change throughout the text set.

Collaborative Conversations

Take On Discussion Roles As students engage in discussions, encourage them to take on roles to help keep the discussion on track that include

- a questioner who asks questions in order to keep the discussion moving.
- a recorder who takes notes and later reports to the class.
- a discussion monitor who keeps the group on topic and makes sure everyone gets a turn to talk.

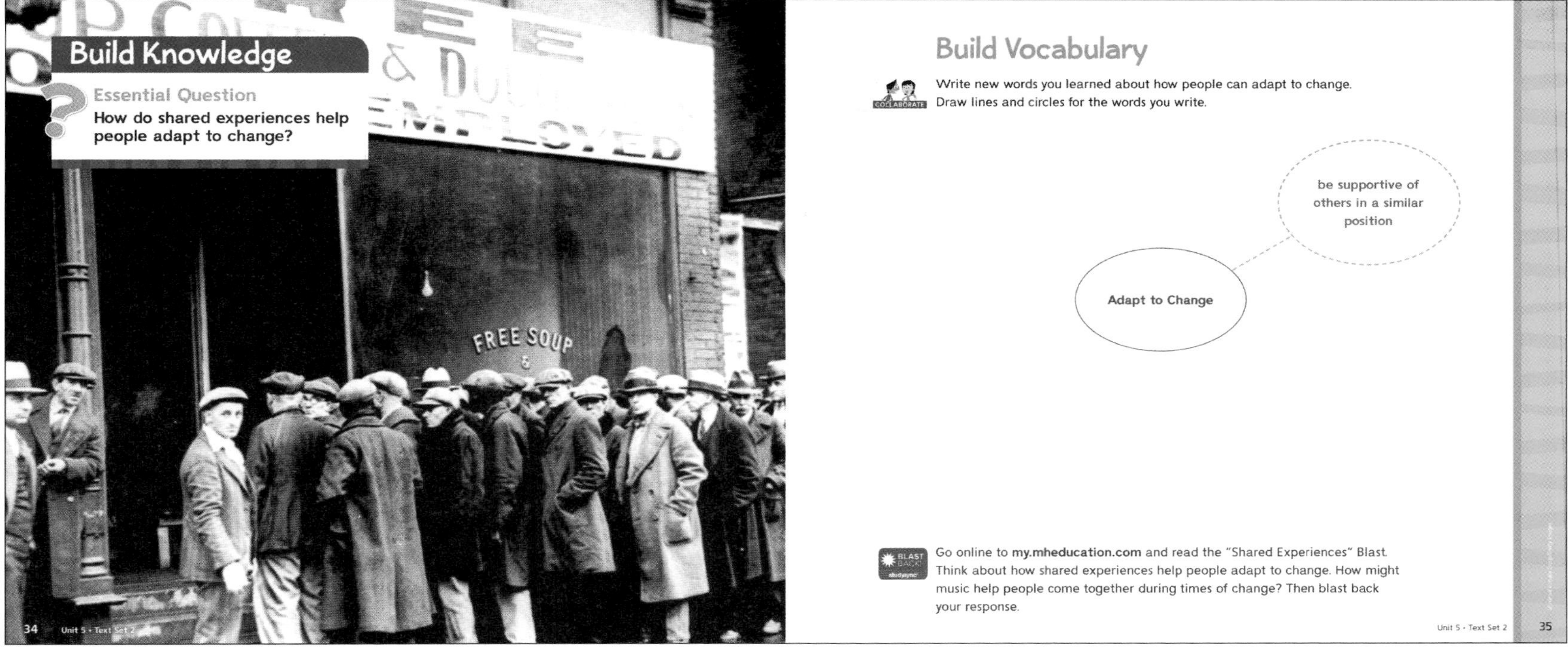

Reading/Writing Companion, pp. 34–35

Share the "Shared Experiences" Blast assignment with students. Point out that you will discuss their responses about solutions in the Make Connections lesson at the end of this text set.

English Language Learners

Use the following scaffolds to build knowledge and vocabulary. Teach the ELL Vocabulary, as needed.

Beginning

Describe the photograph with students. Use the sign "Free Soup" to help students understand *rely on: It means to need help. During the Depression many people lost their jobs.* What does the sign tell you? The men needed free soup. They had to rely on others.

Intermediate

Use the photograph to discuss what it means to *rely on. During the Depression many people lost their jobs. What does the sign show?* The men relied on others for free soup. Talk to your partner about a time you had to rely on someone. I had to rely on ______ to help me with ______.

Advanced/Advanced High

Check understanding of *rely on* and *supportive.* Have pairs use the words to discuss the sign: *What does the sign show you about the Depression?* Have partners discuss a time they relied on someone and explain how that person was supportive.

NEWCOMERS

To help students develop oral language and build vocabulary, use **Newcomer Cards 10-14** and the accompanying materials in the **Newcomer Teacher's Guide.** For thematic connection, use **Newcomer Cards 15 and 22** with the accompanying materials.

MY GOALS ROUTINE

What I Know Now

Read Goals Have students read the goals on Reading/Writing Companion page 36.

Reflect Review the key. Ask students to reflect on each goal and fill in the bars to show what they know now. Explain they will fill in the bars on page 37 at the end of the text set to show their progress.

LEARNING GOALS

We can actively listen to learn how shared experiences help people adapt to change.

OBJECTIVES

Summarize a written text read aloud or information presented in diverse media and formats, including visually, quantitatively, and orally.

Recognize and explain the meaning of common idioms, adages, and proverbs.

Listen for a purpose.

Identify characteristics of historical fiction.

ELA ACADEMIC LANGUAGE

- *historical fiction, characteristics*
- Cognate: *características*

DIGITAL TOOLS

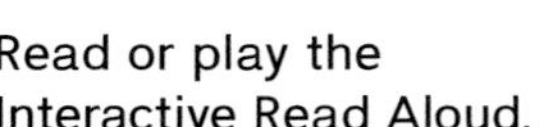

Read or play the Interactive Read Aloud.

Interactive Read Aloud

FORMATIVE ASSESSMENT

STUDENT CHECK-IN

Have partners discuss how Paulo helped Tomasso adapt to his new life in America. Ask them to reflect using the Check-In routine.

Interactive Read Aloud

Connect to Concept: Better Together

Tell students that people who share an experience can often help each other adapt to change. Let students know that you will be reading aloud a passage about a boy who has to adjust to living in a new place.

Preview Historical Fiction

Anchor Chart Explain that the text you will read is historical fiction. Start a Historical Fiction anchor chart and ask students to add characteristics of the genre to the chart. As they read more historical fiction stories, students may want to add to the chart. Discuss the features of historical fiction:

- includes events and settings typical of the period in which the story is set
- includes characters who speak and act like people from a particular time and place in the past
- often includes real as well as made-up people and events

Ask students to think about other texts that you have read or that they have read independently that were historical fiction.

Read and Respond

Read the text aloud to students. Then reread it using the Teacher Think Alouds and Student Think Alongs on page T87 to build knowledge and model comprehension and the vocabulary strategy, Idioms.

Summarize Have students summarize the plot and theme from "Starting Over." Remind them to summarize in ways that maintain meaning and sequential order.

Build Knowledge: Make Connections

Talk About the Text Have partners discuss how shared experiences can help people adapt to change.

Write About the Text Have students add their ideas to their Build Knowledge pages of their reader's notebooks.

Anchor Chart Record any new ideas on the Build Knowledge anchor chart.

Add to the Vocabulary List Have students write down any words they learned about adapting to change in their reader's notebooks.

Starting Over

Tomasso looked out over the ship's railing, trying to catch a glimpse of the city that would be his new home. After two weeks at sea, he and his parents had finally reached America. During the voyage, everyone was talking about what happened last month—the Titanic, which was supposed to be an unsinkable ship, had hit an iceberg and gone down. Luckily, the ship Tomasso and his family were traveling on had made the voyage successfully.

Tomasso and his parents were coming to America in search of opportunity. His aunt and uncle had immigrated to America from Italy two years earlier and opened a successful market. Soon, Tomasso and his parents would join them in New York City.

Tomasso was excited about his new home, especially because he would see his cousin, Paulo, but he was scared, too. He didn't speak English, he was already homesick for his village, and he missed the field where he and Paulo used to play "You Can't Catch Me," a game they had invented. Tomasso wondered about Paulo. Did he speak English? Where—and what—did he play now? (1)

As his family made their way through the city, Tomasso marveled at how busy and loud New York was! Noisy motorcars rattled up and down every block, horse-drawn carriages clattered and bounced over the cobblestoned streets, and men called out as they peddled food from large carts. It was like nothing he had ever experienced.

Finally, they arrived at their new home. Paulo and his family were waiting for them. "Hello," Paulo greeted him, and Tomasso's jaw dropped to the floor—Paulo was speaking English! (2)

"Come with me," Paulo laughed, switching to Italian. He led Tomasso down the street to a park.

"I know how you feel," said Paulo, "because I felt the same way when I first arrived. You think you'll never fit in here, but you will. When I feel homesick, I come to this park. Later, I'll start teaching you English, but right now, I bet you can't catch me!"

Tomasso grinned and began chasing Paulo. America was already starting to feel like home! (3)

(1) Teacher Think Aloud

Making predictions helps me monitor my comprehension. When I read fiction, I pay close attention to the characters and events. I wonder if Paulo will help Tomasso adapt to his new life. I predict that Paulo has learned English and will help Tomasso learn it.

Student Think Along

What problem does Tomasso have? How else might Paulo help? Listen as I reread the beginning, and make another prediction about how Paulo might help Tomasso.

(2) Teacher Think Aloud

Paying attention to how characters interact in a story increases my understanding. I notice the idiom, "Tomasso's jaw dropped to the floor." I wonder what this idiom means. I know that an idiom is a kind of figurative language, so its meaning is not literal.

Student Think Along

Listen as I reread this section. What is the meaning of "Tomasso's jaw dropped to the floor"? Discuss with a partner. What context clues helped you figure out the idiom?

(3) Teacher Think Aloud

After making a prediction, it is important to confirm or revise the prediction. As I finish the story, I see that my prediction was correct—Paulo is going to help Tomasso adapt to life in America by teaching him English.

Student Think Along

Look back at the prediction that you made at the beginning of the story. Was your prediction correct? How did Paulo help Tomasso adapt to his new life?

LESSON
1

"The Day the Rollets Got Their Moxie Back"

Lexile 900L

LEARNING GOALS

We can read and understand historical fiction.

OBJECTIVES

Determine a theme of a story, drama, or poem from details in the text, including how characters in a story or drama respond to challenges or how the speaker in a poem reflects upon a topic; summarize the text.

Compare and contrast two or more characters, settings, or events in a story or drama, drawing on specific details in the text.

Use knowledge of language and its conventions when writing, speaking, reading, or listening.

Compare and contrast the varieties of English used in stories, dramas, or poems.

 Analyze various issues and events of the 20th century, such as the Great Depression.

Close Reading Routine

Read DOK 1–2

- Identify important ideas and details.
- Take notes and summarize.
- Use ACT prompts as needed.

Reread DOK 2–3

- Analyze the text, craft, and structure.
- Use the **Reread minilessons** and **prompts.**

Integrate DOK 3–4

- Integrate knowledge and ideas.
- Make text-to-text connections.
- Use the Integrate lesson.
- Complete the Show Your Knowledge task.
- Inspire action.

Read

SHARED READ
My Goal I can read and understand historical fiction.
TAKE NOTES
As you read, make note of interesting words and important events.
38 Unit 5 • Text Set 2
The Day the Rollets Got Their Moxie Back
Essential Question
How do shared experiences help people adapt to change?
Read about how a family comes together during a period of great hardship in the United States.

Reading/Writing Companion, pp. 38–39

Set a Purpose Have students first preview the title and illustrations and ask questions about the characters, setting, and plot. Have them consider the Essential Question and what they know about how people adapt to changes they experience. Students should use the left column on page 38 to note their questions, as well as interesting words and key details from the text.

Focus on the Read prompts now. For more support, use the extra prompts not included in the **Reading/Writing Companion.** Use the Reread prompts during the Craft and Structure lesson on pages T100–T101. Preteach the vocabulary to some students.

DIFFERENTIATED READING

Approaching Level Model how to identify and note interesting words. Complete all Read prompts together.

On Level Have pairs finish the Read prompts before you meet.

Beyond Level Have partners discuss their responses to the Read prompts. Analyze how the illustrations support the prompts.

English Language Learners Preteach the vocabulary. Have Beginning/Early-Intermediate ELLs listen to the selection summary, available in multiple languages, and use the **Scaffolded Shared Read.** For small group support, see the **ELL Small Group Guide**.

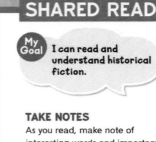

Sometimes, the thing that gets you through hard times comes like a bolt from the blue. That's what my older brother's letter was like, traveling across the country from a work camp in Wyoming. It was 1937, and Ricky was helping to build facilities for a new state park as part of President Roosevelt's employment program. Though the program created jobs for young men like Ricky, it hadn't helped our dad find work yet.

I imagined Ricky looking up at snowcapped mountains and sparkling skies, breathing in the smell of evergreens as his work crew turned trees into lumber and lumber into buildings. It almost made an 11-year-old **weakling** like me want to become a lumberjack.

Back in our New York City apartment, the air smelled like meatloaf and cabbage. Dad sat slantwise in his chair by the window, **obviously** trying to catch the last rays of sunlight rather than turn on a light. My older sister Ruth and I lay on the floor comparing the letters Ricky had sent us.

"Shirley, Ricky says they had a talent show, and he wore a grass skirt and did a hula dance while playing the ukulele!" Ruth reported with delight. "I'll bet he was the cat's pajamas!"

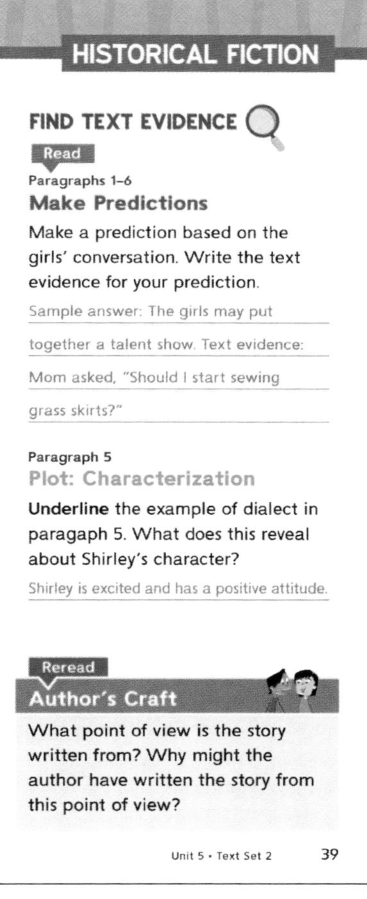

"It'd be swell to have our own talent show!" I replied.

"Should I start sewing grass skirts?" Mom asked from the kitchen, which was just the corner where someone had plopped down a stove next to a sink and an icebox. "Now come set the table. Dinner's almost ready."

HISTORICAL FICTION

FIND TEXT EVIDENCE

Read

Paragraphs 1–6

Make Predictions

Make a prediction based on the girls' conversation. Write the text evidence for your prediction.

Sample answer: The girls may put together a talent show. Text evidence: Mom asked, "Should I start sewing grass skirts?"

Paragraph 5

Plot: Characterization

Underline the example of dialect in paragagh 5. What does this reveal about Shirley's character?

Shirley is excited and has a positive attitude.

Reread

Author's Craft

What point of view is the story written from? Why might the author have written the story from this point of view?

Unit 5 • Text Set 2 39

Make Predictions DOK 2

Paragraphs 4–6: *What prediction can you make based on the girls' conversation?*

Think Aloud The girls seem to be excited about the talent show their brother Ricky participated in. When Shirley mentions how "swell" it would be if they had their own show, their mom responds by asking if she should start sewing grass skirts, like their brother wore in his talent show. This leads me to predict the girls are going to put on their own talent show. Have students predict what type of performance the girls might do for their talent show.

Plot: Characterization DOK 2

Paragraph 5: *Find an example of dialect in this paragraph. What does Shirley's use of dialect reveal about her character?*

Think Aloud I know that dialect refers to how people speak at a particular place and time. In paragraph 5, Shirley uses the word *swell* as part of her dialect. By using context clues, I can infer that this word has a positive connotation. This leads me to believe that Shirley is someone who tries to remain positive. She is also excited. Have students tell how the use of an exclamation point helps support their understanding of the dialect Ruth uses.

Check for Understanding DOK 2

Page 35: Monitor students' understanding of the story's characters, setting, and rising action up to this point. Ask: *Where are the girls, and where is their brother Ricky?* (The girls are at home in New York, and Ricky is constructing buildings at a work camp in Wyoming.) Clarify that students understand how Ricky and his family are communicating with each other. Ask: *How do the girls find out about Ricky's talent show? How do they feel about it?* (Ricky is sending letters home to his family in New York City, telling them about his life at the work camp in Wyoming. They are excited that he participated in the talent show.)

ELL Spotlight on Language

Page 39, Paragraph 5 Read the paragraph aloud. Explain that *It'd* is a contraction, which stands for *It would.* Reread the sentence using *It would* instead of *It'd* and using *great* as an appositive to *swell*: *It would be swell, or great, to have our own talent show! Have you ever heard the word* swell*? What does the word* swell *mean?* (great) *What are some other words that mean great, or swell?* (fantastic, excellent) Explain that not many people use the word *swell* any more. The author used this dialect to take the reader to the time of the story. (cognate: *dialecto*)

Plot: Conflict DOK 2

Paragraphs 1-3: Read the first paragraph. Ask: *What words describe how Dad is feeling?* ("sullen and spent") *What words describe Mom's voice?* ("rich with sympathy") Explain that one way to compare and contrast characters is to pay attention to words that describe how they are acting and feeling. *Compare Mom and Dad. What do the words* sullen *and* spent *and the words* rich with sympathy *tell about how the characters are feeling?* (Dad is feeling sad, and Mom is concerned about him.) Read the next two paragraphs. Identify words and phrases that will help students compare the characters. ("my frown," "sang," "fidgeted," "excited," "calm," and "atwitter") Help students use the text evidence to compare and contrast the character's attitudes at the dinner table. (Dad is quiet and does not talk. Mom tries to act cheerful. Ruth and Shirley are excited about the talent show, but Shirley is also nervous.)

Check for Understanding DOK 2

Paragraph 4: Read the first sentence. Describe how the sisters interact. (They are practicing a dance routine.) Using this information, what kind of inference can you make about their relationship? (It shows that they get along well.)

Read

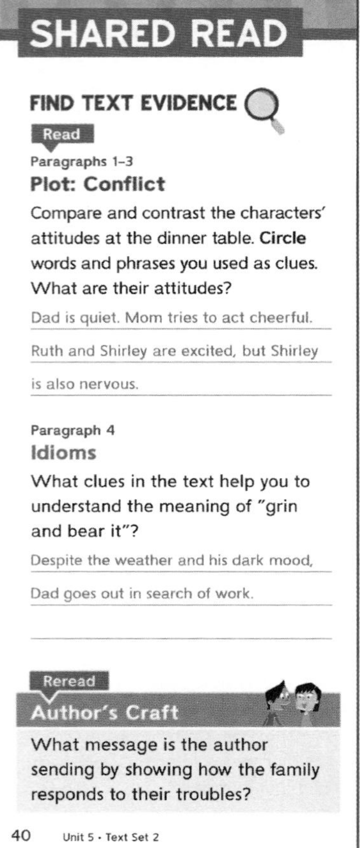

SHARED READ

FIND TEXT EVIDENCE

Read

Paragraphs 1–3

Plot: Conflict

Compare and contrast the characters' attitudes at the dinner table. **Circle** words and phrases you used as clues. What are their attitudes?

Dad is quiet. Mom tries to act cheerful.

Ruth and Shirley are excited, but Shirley is also nervous.

Paragraph 4

Idioms

What clues in the text help you to understand the meaning of "grin and bear it"?

Despite the weather and his dark mood, Dad goes out in search of work.

Reread

Author's Craft

What message is the author sending by showing how the family responds to their troubles?

40 Unit 5 • Text Set 2

Dad stayed where he was, sullen and spent. "Any jobs in the paper?" Mom asked, her voice rich with **sympathy**. Dad shook his head no. He had worked as an artist in the theater for years, but most productions were still strapped for cash. Dad sketched posters for shows that did get the green light, just to keep his skills sharp. He even designed posters for "Rollet's Follies" with Ruth and me depicted in watercolor costumes.

For dinner, Mom served a baked loaf of whatever ingredients she had that worked well together. From the reddish color, I could **assume** that she had snuck in beets. "I **guarantee** you'll like these beets," she said, reading my frown. "It's beet loaf, the meatless meat loaf," she sang as she served up slices.

Ruth fidgeted in her seat, still excited about the talent show. Though calm on the outside, inside I was all atwitter, too.

Over the next week, Ruth and I practiced our Hawaiian dance routine. Our parents worried about heating bills as cold weather settled in. One Saturday, my father decided to grin and bear it and grab some hot coffee at the local soup kitchen, where he hoped to hear about available jobs. Ruth and I begged to go along. Since the kitchen offered doughnuts and hot chocolate on weekends, he agreed.

Reading/Writing Companion, pp. 40–41

Idioms DOK 2

Paragraph 4: *What words and sentences on page 36 help you understand the meaning of the phrase "grin and bear it"?* (Dad is "sullen and spent" because he doesn't have a job; he is "worried about heating bills.") *Use text evidence to explain the meaning of "grin and bear it."* (Even though Dad is sullen and worried, he knows how important it is to keep searching for a job.) Discuss reasons why someone may "grin and bear" something.

Access Complex Text

Prior Knowledge

Historical fiction may use unfamiliar language and describe unfamiliar events. For example, the word *follies* was common during the 1930s. Help students determine its meaning.

Ask: *What was Dad doing to help Shirley and Ruth?* (Designing posters for his daughters' dance routine.)

Based on this, what is the meaning of follies? (Follies must mean a performance of some kind.)

During the 1930s, the United States experienced tough economic times and high unemployment rates. This period in history is known as the Great Depression. One of the ways people dealt with this hardship was through music, art, and theater. Follies such as Shirley's and Ruth's were quite common.

Most everyone in line was bundled up against the cold. Many of us had to **rely** on two or three threadbare layers. Like many other men, Dad bowed his head as if in shame.

The line moved slowly. Bored, Ruth began practicing her dance steps. I sang an upbeat tune to give her some music. Around us, downturned hats lifted to reveal frowns becoming smiles. Soon, folks began clapping along. Egged on by the **supportive** response, Ruth twirled and swayed like there was no tomorrow.

"Those girls sure have moxie!" someone shouted.

"They've got heart, all right!" offered another. "Why, they oughta be in pictures!"

"With performances like that, I'd **nominate** them for an Academy Award!" a woman called out.

"Those are my girls!" Dad declared, his head held high.

Everyone burst into applause. For those short moments, the past didn't matter, and the future blossomed ahead of us like a beautiful flower. I couldn't wait to write Ricky and tell him the news.

Summarize

Use your notes to orally summarize the plot and theme of this story.

HISTORICAL FICTION

FIND TEXT EVIDENCE

Read

Paragraphs 1–2

Plot: Conflict

Underline the words that show how the people's mood changes.

Paragraphs 3–7

Confirm Predictions

How accurate was your prediction?

Sample answer: The girls performed a dance routine for an audience, although not in a talent show.

Reread

Author's Craft

How does the author use imagery to show the father has changed by the end of the story?

Unit 5 • Text Set 2 41

Plot: Conflict DOK 2

Paragraphs 1–2: Read the first paragraph. Ask: *How are the people in line similar?* (bundled up against the cold; wear layers, bow their heads) Discuss the mood of the people waiting in line. (unhappy, tired, ashamed) Read the second paragraph. Ask: *What do Ruth and Shirley do while they are waiting in line? How do the people in line react?* (Ruth dances; Shirley sings. The people in line are frowning, but then start smiling.) Discuss how the people's mood has changed after the girls perform.

Sentence Structure

Remind students about the different kinds of sentences: declarative, interrogative, imperative, and exclamatory. Have them look at page 41 and list which kinds of sentences they see. (declarative, exclamatory) Ask: *What do you notice about the exclamatory sentences?* (They are part of dialogue.) *Why might an author want to write dialogue with exclamatory sentences?* (The exclamatory sentences convey a sense of excitement by the characters.)

Idioms DOK 2

Paragraph 2: Reread the last sentence. Ask: *Why is Ruth acting this way?* (because folks began clapping along) *What does "egged on" mean?* (encouraged)

Confirm Predictions DOK 1

Paragraphs 3–7: Read from the third paragraph to the end of the story. Ask: *How accurate was your prediction?* (Answers will vary.) Have students infer what Ricky might have thought about the girls' experience and explain their reasons with text evidence.

Summarize DOK 2

Analytical Writing **Quick Write** After their initial reads, have partners summarize the selection orally using their notes. Then have them write a summary in their reader's notebooks. Remind them to include details about the characters based on their interactions and responses to events. Students may decide to digitally record presentations of their summaries.

ELL Spotlight on Idioms

Page 41, Paragraph 1 Point to the image. *Do they look warm or cold?* (cold) *They are wearing layers of clothing.* Read the first two sentences of the paragraph, miming being "bundled up." *Which detail helps you understand the adjective* threadbare*?* (relied on two or three layers) *How does this word help you understand the situation?* (Shows characters don't have a lot of money.)

FORMATIVE ASSESSMENT

STUDENT CHECK-IN

Have partners share their summaries from Reading/Writing Companion page 41. Ask them to reflect using the Check-In routine.

LEARNING GOALS

- **We can use new vocabulary words to read and understand historical fiction.**
- **We can use context clues to figure out the meaning of idioms.**

OBJECTIVES

Demonstrate understanding of figurative language, word relationships, and nuances in word meaning.

Recognize and explain the meaning of common idioms, adages, and proverbs.

Consult reference materials, both print and digital, to find the pronunciation and determine or clarify the precise meaning of key words and phrases.

Use context as a clue to the meaning of a word or phrase.

ELA ACADEMIC LANGUAGE

- *idiom, expression, context clues*
- Cognate: *expresión*

DIGITAL TOOLS

Visual Vocabulary Cards

TEACH IN SMALL GROUP

Academic Vocabulary

Approaching Level and **ELL** Preteach the words before students begin the Shared Read.

On Level Have students look up words in the online **Visual Glossary**.

Beyond Level Have pairs write an additional context sentence for each vocabulary word.

Reread

Academic Vocabulary

Use the routines on the **Visual Vocabulary Cards** to introduce each word.

When you **assume** something, you take it for granted, or suppose it is so.

To **guarantee** is to make sure of something.
Cognate: *garantizar*

If you **nominate** someone, you suggest or propose that the person be chosen, such as a candidate for an office.
Cognate: *nominar*

If something is done **obviously**, it is easily seen or understood.
Cognate: *obviamente*

To **rely** is to trust or depend on someone or something.

When you are **supportive**, you provide approval, aid, or encouragement to others.

If you feel **sympathy** toward someone, you feel and understand their troubles.

A **weakling** is a person who lacks physical strength.

Encourage students to use their newly acquired vocabulary in their discussions and written responses about the texts in this text set.

Idioms

1 Explain

Explain that an **idiom** is a form of figurative language, so these expressions are not literal. Point out that authors may use idioms in historical fiction to make characters appear more realistic and to reflect the time period in which the story is set. To determine the meaning of an idiom, students can use surrounding words and sentences as context clues. Have students begin an Idioms anchor chart.

2 Model

Model using context clues to infer the meaning of the idiom *a bolt from the blue* in the first sentence on **Reading/Writing Companion** page 39. Point out that Ricky's letter, like a bolt of lightning from a blue sky, came unexpectedly, or seemingly from out of nowhere.

3 Guided Practice

Circulate as partners work to figure out the meanings of the idioms *the cat's pajamas* on page 39 and *get the green light* on page 40. Guide students to use context clues in the surrounding sentences to help them determine each idiom's meaning.

Reread | SHARED READ

HISTORICAL FICTION

Vocabulary

Use the example sentences to talk with a partner about each word. Then answer the questions.

Sample answers shown.

assume

Caitlyn could only **assume** the cat had broken the flowerpot since Pip was standing over the pieces.

What might you assume if you awaken to a major snowstorm on a school day?

You might assume that school will be closed.

guarantee

The weather forecaster can **guarantee** that it will rain soon because of the dark clouds approaching.

When else might you guarantee something?

You might guarantee your parents that you will clean your room when it is messy.

nominate

The team will **nominate** the best candidate for team captain.

When might you nominate a particular person for a task or position?

You might nominate someone to be class president.

obviously

The scarf was **obviously** too long for Marta.

What clothes are obviously wrong for a cold day?

Sandals and shorts are obviously wrong for a cold day.

rely

Calvin must **rely** on his notes in order to study.

When have you had to rely on someone else?

I had to rely on my big brother to pick me up from school.

Build Your Word List Circle the word *supportive* on page 41. In your reader's notebook, list its root word and related words. Then do the same with another word that uses the suffix *-ive*. Use an online or print dictionary to find more related words.

supportive

The audience's **supportive** applause boosted Clare's energy as she played her violin.

How else can you be supportive of a performer onstage?

You could listen quietly and attentively.

sympathy

Jamar's dad gave him **sympathy** when his team lost the game.

When else might you express sympathy to someone?

You might offer sympathy to someone if they didn't get a role they wanted in a play.

weakling

Being sick in bed made Emily feel like a **weakling**.

Why might being sick make someone feel like a weakling?

Someone might feel like a weakling if they are sick because they have no energy.

Idioms

An **idiom** is an expression that uses words in a creative way. Surrounding words and sentences can help you understand the meaning of an idiom.

FIND TEXT EVIDENCE

I'm not sure what the idiom a bolt from the blue *means on page 39. When I think of a "bolt," I think of lightning and how quickly and unpredictably it can strike. Letters often come unexpectedly, as if out of nowhere. That must be the meaning.*

Sometimes, the thing that gets you through hard times comes like a bolt from the blue. That's what my older brother's letter was like, traveling across the country from a work camp in Wyoming.

Your Turn Use context clues to explain the meanings of the following idioms from "The Day the Rollets Got Their Moxie Back."

the cat's pajamas, *page 39* an excellent performer

get the green light, *page 40* given permission to do something

CHECK IN 1 2 3 4

42 Unit 5 • Text Set 2 — Unit 5 • Text Set 2 43

Reading/Writing Companion, pp. 42–43

English Language Learners

Use the following scaffolds with **Guided Practice.** For small group support, see the **ELL Small Group Guide**.

Beginning

Read the first paragraph on **Reading/Writing Companion** page 40 with students. Point out the phrase *get the green light.* to them and say: *This phrase is an idiom. Does a green light mean "go" or "stop"?* (go) Only *some shows are performed for people. What happened to shows that* "get the green light"? Shows that get the green light are performed. Repeat the routine for *the cat's pajamas.*

Intermediate

Have partners read paragraph 4 on **Reading/Writing Companion** page 39. Write *the cat's pajamas* on the board and elicit that the phrase is an idiom. Ask: *What sentence(s) in the paragraph helps you figure out the meaning of the idiom?* ("Ricky says they had a talent show, and he wore a grass skirt and did a hula dance while playing the ukulele!") *Talk to your partner about the meaning of the idiom.* Repeat the routine for *got the green light.*

Advanced/Advanced High

Have partners work together to figure out the meaning of *the cat's pajamas* in the fourth paragraph on page 39. Guide partners as they discuss the context clues that helped them define the idiom. Then have partners work together to figure out the meaning of *get the green light* in the first paragraph on page 40.

BUILD YOUR WORD LIST

Students might choose the compound word *threadbare* from page 41. Have them use a thesaurus to find synonyms.

FORMATIVE ASSESSMENT

STUDENT CHECK-IN

Academic Vocabulary Ask partners to share two answers from Reading/Writing Companion pages 42–43.

Idioms Ask partners to share their Your Turn responses on page 43.

Have students use the Check-In routine to reflect and fill in the bars.

CHECK FOR SUCCESS

Rubric Use your online rubric to record student progress.

Can students use context clues to determine the meanings of the idioms *the cat's pajamas* and *get the green light?*

Small Group Instruction

If No:

- **Approaching** Reteach p. T145

If Yes:

- **On** Review p. T152
- **Beyond** Extend p. T158

Reread

Make, Confirm, and Revise Predictions

LEARNING GOALS

We can make, confirm, and revise predictions to understand historical fiction.

OBJECTIVES

Quote accurately from a text when explaining what the text says explicitly and when drawing inferences from the text.

Make, confirm, and revise predictions based on details in the text.

ELA ACADEMIC LANGUAGE

- *make predictions, historical fiction, confirm, revise*
- Cognates: *predicciones, ficción histórica, confirmar, revisar*

1 Explain

Remind students that when they read historical fiction, they should **make predictions** about what might happen next.

- Students should use details in the illustrations and text, such as expressions on the characters' faces or what characters do, say, and think, to help them predict what might happen later in the story.
- Knowing the characteristics of a particular genre can also help students make a prediction. For example, a mystery often involves a crime of some kind, while science fiction may take place in the future. Historical fiction often includes certain dialects and figurative language typical of the time period.
- As they continue reading, students should confirm their predictions or revise as necessary based on additional information in the text.

Tell students that making predictions gives readers a purpose and helps keep them actively engaged in a story.

Anchor Chart Have a volunteer add any additional points about the strategy to the Make Predictions anchor chart.

2 Model

Model using details in the title to make predictions about when the story takes place. Have them also make predictions about who the main characters are, and what kind of ending the story will have.

3 Guided Practice

Guide partners to describe what is happening in the illustration on **Reading/Writing Companion** page 40 and how the characters appear to be feeling based on their expressions. Encourage students to use these observations to make predictions about the characters. Help partners identify details in the last paragraph on page 40 as well as in subsequent pages of the story that help them confirm or revise their predictions.

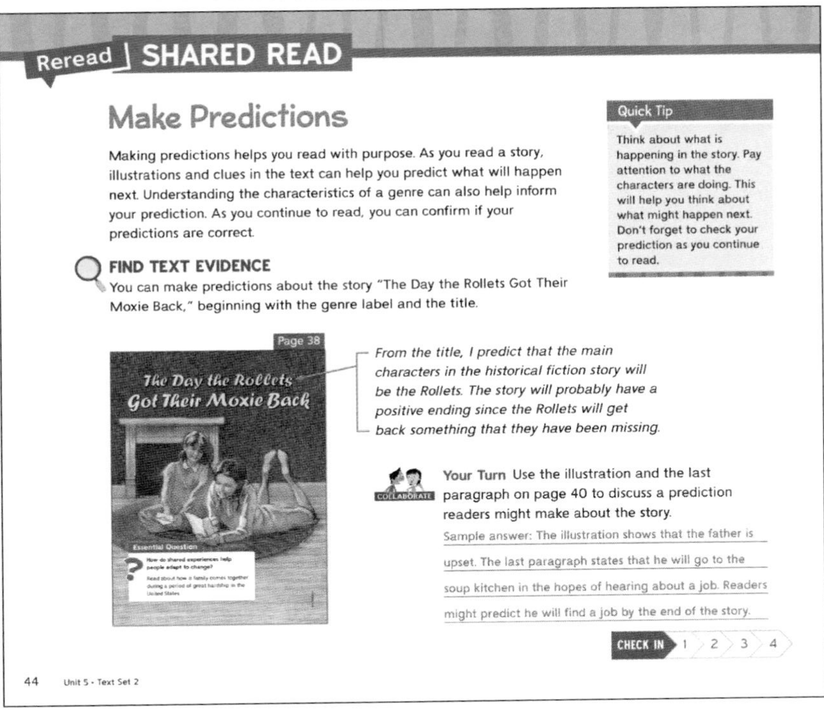
Reread | SHARED READ

Make Predictions

Making predictions helps you read with purpose. As you read a story, illustrations and clues in the text can help you predict what will happen next. Understanding the characteristics of a genre can also help inform your prediction. As you continue to read, you can confirm if your predictions are correct.

FIND TEXT EVIDENCE

You can make predictions about the story "The Day the Rollets Got Their Moxie Back," beginning with the genre label and the title.

Quick Tip

Think about what is happening in the story. Pay attention to what the characters are doing. This will help you think about what might happen next. Don't forget to check your prediction as you continue to read.

Page 38

The Day the Rollets Got Their Moxie Back

From the title, I predict that the main characters in the historical fiction story will be the Rollets. The story will probably have a positive ending since the Rollets will get back something that they have been missing.

Your Turn Use the illustration and the last paragraph on page 40 to discuss a prediction readers might make about the story.

Sample answer: The illustration shows that the father is upset. The last paragraph states that he will go to the soup kitchen in the hopes of hearing about a job. Readers might predict he will find a job by the end of the story.

CHECK IN 1 2 3 4

44 Unit 5 • Text Set 2

Reading/Writing Companion, p. 44

English Language Learners

Use the following scaffolds with **Guided Practice.** For small group support, see the **ELL Small Group Guide**.

Beginning

Reread the last paragraph on **Reading/Writing Companion** page 40 with students. Restate sentences as needed. Then help students use the illustrations to talk about how the characters feel. Ask: *Do you think the father feels happy or sad?* (sad) *Do you think he feels good or bad?* (bad) *What is a prediction you can make?* Have partners discuss and respond using: I can predict that _______.

Intermediate

Have partners use the illustration on **Reading/Writing Companion** page 40 to tell how the characters feel: The girls and the mother are smiling/happy. The father is upset. Then have them reread the last paragraph on page 40. *Where does the father decide to go? Why?* (soup kitchen; he hopes to hear of a job) *What can a reader predict?* A reader can predict that_______.

Advanced/Advanced High

Have pairs use the illustration on page 40 to describe the characters' feelings. Then have them reread the last paragraph on page 40 and ask each other questions about the characters: *Why is the father worried? Where does he decide to go? Why?* Have them discuss what a reader can predict using this information.

HABITS OF LEARNING

I use a variety of strategies when I read. Making predictions is one of a variety of reading strategies that enables students to interact with the text. Explain to students that making predictions helps them comprehend the text on a deeper level. Remind them to ask the following question as they read: *What do I think will happen next?*

FORMATIVE ASSESSMENT

STUDENT CHECK-IN

Ask partners to share their Your Turn responses on Reading/Writing Companion page 44. Have them use the Check-In routine to reflect and fill in the bars.

CHECK FOR SUCCESS

Do students make predictions about the characters based on the illustration?

Small Group Instruction

If No:

- **Approaching** Reteach p. T138

If Yes:

- **On** Review p. T148
- **Beyond** Extend p. T154

LEARNING GOALS

We can use characterization to read and understand historical fiction.

OBJECTIVES

Quote accurately from a text when explaining what the text says explicitly and when drawing inferences from the text.

Explain different characters' perspectives in a literary text.

Compare and contrast the varieties of English (e.g., dialects, registers) used in stories, dramas, or poems.

Demonstrate understanding of figurative language, word relationships, and nuances in word meanings.

ELA ACADEMIC LANGUAGE

- *historical fiction, characters, dialect*
- Cognates: *ficción histórica, dialecto*

Reread

Plot: Characterization

1 Explain

Share with students the following characteristics of **historical fiction**.

- Historical fiction features events and settings that are typical of a particular period in history.
- Characters in historical fiction speak and act like the people from a particular time and/or place in the past. This kind of speaking is known as dialect. The specific language that characters use also provides clues to their traits, or characterization. Additionally, it can reveal their attitude toward other characters, relationships, and events.
- Historical fiction often includes real as well as made-up people and events. For example, a story with made-up main characters might mention an actual historical figure, such as a president.

Explain to students that reading historical fiction can sometimes require some prior knowledge about the time and place of the story.

2 Model

Model using details from the story as well as dialect typical of a specific time and place in history to identify "The Day the Rollets Got Their Moxie Back" as historical fiction.

Dialect Remind students that characters sometimes use dialect, or speech typical of a time or place. This dialect may include words, phrases, and idioms that are no longer commonly used. It reveals how characters feel about certain things. On **Reading/Writing Companion** page 39, point out the idiom *the cat's pajamas*. Ask: *What present-day words mean the same things as* the cat's pajamas*? Why might the author of the story have included words like* the cat's pajamas? *What does this phrase reveal about Ruth?*

Anchor Chart Have a volunteer add these features to the Historical Fiction anchor chart.

3 Guided Practice

Guide students to work with partners to list another example of dialect in "The Day the Rollets Got Their Moxie Back." Partners should discuss what the example of dialect might mean and why the author might have included it in this historical fiction story. Guide partners to share and compare their findings with the class.

Independent Practice Have students read the online **Differentiated Genre Passage**, "Nancy's First Interview."

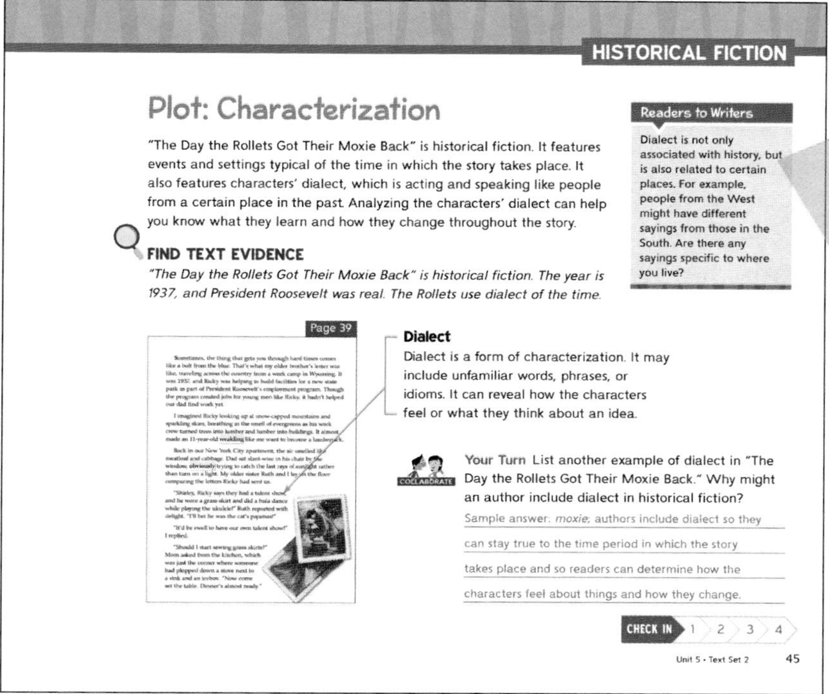
Plot: Characterization

"The Day the Rollets Got Their Moxie Back" is historical fiction. It features events and settings typical of the time in which the story takes place. It also features characters' dialect, which is acting and speaking like people from a certain place in the past. Analyzing the characters' dialect can help you know what they learn and how they change throughout the story.

FIND TEXT EVIDENCE

"The Day the Rollets Got Their Moxie Back" is historical fiction. The year is 1937, and President Roosevelt was real. The Rollets use dialect of the time.

Readers to Writers

Dialect is not only associated with history, but is also related to certain places. For example, people from the West might have different sayings from those in the South. Are there any sayings specific to where you live?

Dialect

Dialect is a form of characterization. It may include unfamiliar words, phrases, or idioms. It can reveal how the characters feel or what they think about an idea.

Your Turn List another example of dialect in "The Day the Rollets Got Their Moxie Back." Why might an author include dialect in historical fiction?

Sample answer: *moxie*; authors include dialect so they can stay true to the time period in which the story takes place and so readers can determine how the characters feel about things and how they change.

Reading/Writing Companion, p. 45

Readers to Writers

Remind students that including dialect in historical fiction adds flavor and interest by allowing a writer's characters to "sound" like they are really from the time and place in which the story is set. Writers of historical fiction often do a great deal of research to make sure they correctly use the dialect of a specific time and place. Ask: *Suppose "The Day the Rollets Got Their Moxie Back" was set in a rural area rather than a big city. How might the dialect be different?*

English Language Learners

Use the following scaffolds with **Guided Practice.** For small group support, see the **ELL Small Group Guide**.

Beginning

Review with students that dialect is a form of characterization. Read with them paragraphs 3–4 on page 41 of "The Day the Rollets Got Their Moxie Back." Remind them that *moxie* means *courage* or *determination* and that it was more commonly used during the time of the story's setting. Point to the image of the girls dancing. *Does it take courage to dance in front of people?* (cognate: *coraje*) (yes) Using this dialect helps take the reader to the time of the Great Depression.

Intermediate

Review with students that dialect is a form of characterization. Have partners read page 41 of "The Day the Rollets Got Their Moxie Back" and look at the image. Elicit that *moxie* means courage and determination. Say: *The word was more commonly used during the Great Depression. Talk to your partner about why the author uses this dialect.* The author includes this dialect so they can ______.

Advanced/Advanced High

Have partners read page 41 until they find an example of dialect: *moxie*. Have partners determine the meaning of the word using the image and the context. Remind them that the word *moxie* was used during the Great Depression. *Why does the author use this word?*

FORMATIVE ASSESSMENT

STUDENT CHECK-IN

Ask partners to share their Your Turn responses on Reading/Writing Companion page 45. Have them use the Check-In routine to reflect and fill in the bars.

CHECK FOR SUCCESS

Can students identify another example of dialect? Can they explain why the author might have used it?

Small Group Instruction

If No:

- **Approaching** Reteach p. T140

If Yes:

- **On** Review p. T150
- **Beyond** Extend p. T156

LEARNING GOALS

We can read and understand historical fiction by identifying the story's conflict.

OBJECTIVES

Quote accurately from a text when explaining what the text says explicitly and when drawing inferences from the text.

Explain different characters' perspectives in a literary text.

Compare and contrast two or more characters, settings, or events in a story or drama, drawing on specific details in the text (e.g., how characters interact).

Describe how a narrator's or speaker's point of view influences how events are described.

Explain different characters' perspectives in a literary text.

ELA ACADEMIC LANGUAGE

- *compare, contrast, situations*
- Cognates: *comparar, contrastar, situaciones*

DIGITAL TOOLS

To differentiate instruction for key skills, use the results of the activity.

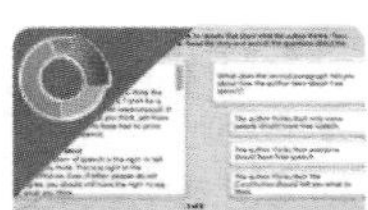

Reread

Plot: Conflict

1 Explain

Explain to students that historical fiction stories involve a conflict of some kind. Conflict involves a problem that must be solved. Conflicts often occur because of certain events, and sometimes a conflict occurs between characters. Identifying the characters' personalities and actions in a story can help readers better understand the conflict by learning how the characters respond to the problem.

- Explain that the characters' personalities and actions affect the events in a story, but they can also be changed by these events. Each character's response to the conflict moves the plot forward.
- To compare and contrast how characters respond to a story's conflict, students must review details in the text that reveal how the various characters are both similar and different. These details may include the characters' thoughts, feelings, words, actions, traits, and responses to events.
- By comparing and contrasting different characters, students can better understand the characters' relationships. These relationships can also help advance the plot and lead to conflict resolution.

Anchor Chart Have a volunteer add to the Plot anchor chart.

2 Model

Model identifying important details on **Reading/Writing Companion** page 40 that tell about the situations of different family members. Then model using the details on the graphic organizer on page 47 to compare and contrast how characters respond to the conflict in the story.

3 Guided Practice

Assist students in using the graphic organizer to record details about the characters' actions at the soup kitchen. Discuss each character as students complete the organizer.

Write About Reading: Compare and Contrast Have pairs write a summary of the ways in which the narrator's and Dad's feelings throughout the story are similar and different and how they relate to the story's conflict. Ask volunteers to share their summaries with the class. Provide feedback on the summary's effectiveness.

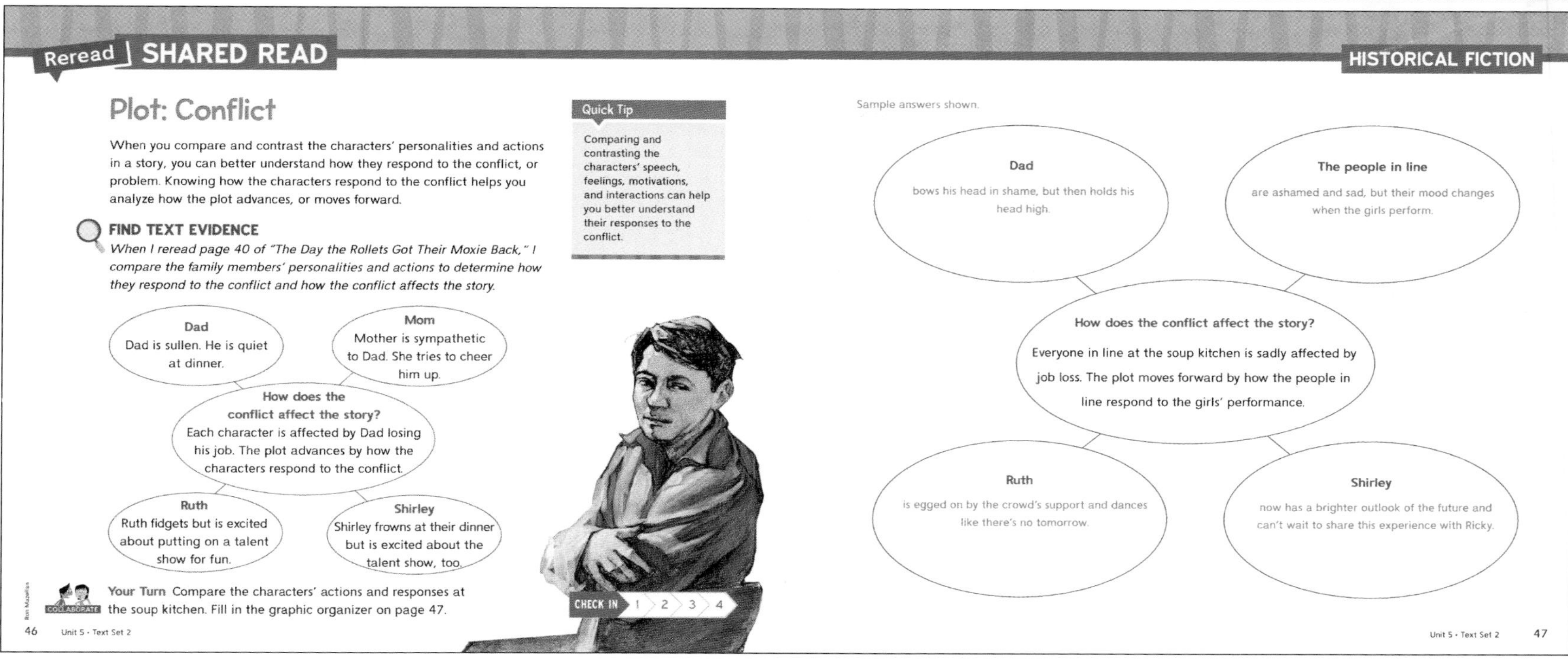
Reread | SHARED READ

HISTORICAL FICTION

Plot: Conflict

When you compare and contrast the characters' personalities and actions in a story, you can better understand how they respond to the conflict, or problem. Knowing how the characters respond to the conflict helps you analyze how the plot advances, or moves forward.

FIND TEXT EVIDENCE

When I reread page 40 of "The Day the Rollets Got Their Moxie Back," I compare the family members' personalities and actions to determine how they respond to the conflict and how the conflict affects the story.

Dad: Dad is sullen. He is quiet at dinner.

Mom: Mother is sympathetic to Dad. She tries to cheer him up.

How does the conflict affect the story? Each character is affected by Dad losing his job. The plot advances by how the characters respond to the conflict.

Ruth: Ruth fidgets but is excited about putting on a talent show for fun.

Shirley: Shirley frowns at their dinner but is excited about the talent show, too.

Quick Tip

Comparing and contrasting the characters' speech, feelings, motivations, and interactions can help you better understand their responses to the conflict.

Your Turn Compare the characters' actions and responses at the soup kitchen. Fill in the graphic organizer on page 47.

CHECK IN 1 2 3 4

Sample answers shown.

Dad: bows his head in shame, but then holds his head high.

The people in line: are ashamed and sad, but their mood changes when the girls perform.

How does the conflict affect the story? Everyone in line at the soup kitchen is sadly affected by job loss. The plot moves forward by how the people in line respond to the girls' performance.

Ruth: is egged on by the crowd's support and dances like there's no tomorrow.

Shirley: now has a brighter outlook of the future and can't wait to share this experience with Ricky.

46 Unit 5 • Text Set 2

Unit 5 • Text Set 2 47

Reading/Writing Companion, pp. 46–47

English Language Learners

Use the following scaffolds with **Guided Practice.** For small group support, see the **ELL Small Group Guide**.

Beginning

Reread the second paragraph on **Reading/Writing Companion** page 41 with students. Restate sentences as needed. *What is Ruth doing?* Ruth is dancing. Help students add the information to the graphic organizer. *What does Shirley do?* Shirley sings an upbeat song. Help students add this information to the graphic organizer. Continue with this approach through the remainder of the graphic organizer.

Intermediate

Have partners reread **Reading/Writing Companion** page 41, and look for words or phrases that tell how Ruth feels. Then have partners fill in the oval for Ruth in their graphic organizer. Have partners scan the text and share their words and phrases for the other characters in the graphic organizer.

Advanced/Advanced High

Have partners review the text on page 41, looking for words and phrases that describe each character's feelings. Have students use the words and phrases to fill out the graphic organizer. Then ask partners to take turns saying a word or phrase from the organizer and telling why they chose them for a particular box.

FORMATIVE ASSESSMENT

STUDENT CHECK-IN

Ask partners to share their graphic organizers on Reading/Writing Companion page 47. Have them use the Check-In routine to reflect and fill in the bars.

CHECK FOR SUCCESS

Rubric Use your online rubric to record student progress. Are students able to compare and contrast characters' actions and responses in the story to understand the conflict?

Small Group Instruction

If No:

- **Approaching** Reteach p. T147

If Yes:

- **On** Review p. T153
- **Beyond** Extend p. T159

Reread

Craft and Structure

LEARNING GOALS

We can reread to analyze craft and structure in historical fiction.

OBJECTIVES

Describe how a narrator's or speaker's point of view influences how events are described.

Explain different characters' perspectives in a literary text.

Describe how an author develops a character's perspective in a literary text.

Demonstrate understanding of figurative language, word relationships, and nuances in word meanings.

Interpret figurative language, including similes and metaphors, in context.

ELA ACADEMIC LANGUAGE

- *analyze, technique, perspective*
- Cognates: *analizar, técnica, perspectiva*

TEACH IN SMALL GROUP

Approaching Level Use the scaffolded questions provided to help students cite text evidence and answer the Reread prompts.

On Level Assist partners in completing the Reread prompts. Then have them share their answers.

Beyond Level Allow partners to discuss and answer the Reread prompts without guidance.

ELL Have Beginning and Early-Intermediate ELLs use the **Scaffolded Shared Read.**

Tell students that they will now reread parts of "The Day the Rollets Got Their Moxie Back" and analyze the techniques the author used in writing the selection. As they craft historical fiction, writers often use specific techniques to help readers better understand the plot details.

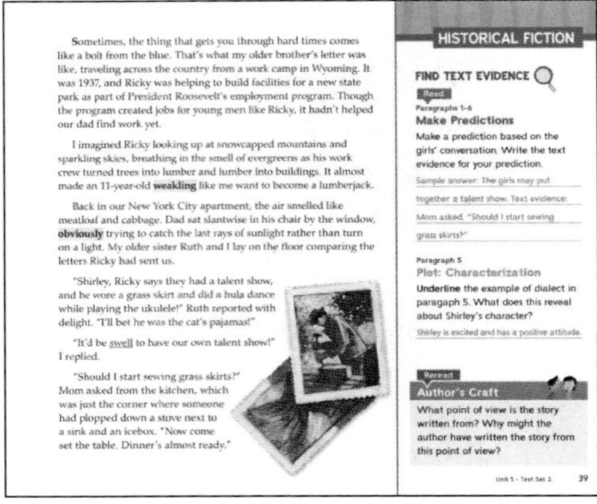

Sometimes, the thing that gets you through hard times comes like a bolt from the blue. That's what my older brother's letter was like, traveling across the country from a work camp in Wyoming. It was 1937, and Ricky was helping to build facilities for a new state park as part of President Roosevelt's employment program. Though the program created jobs for young men like Ricky, it hadn't helped our dad find work yet.

I imagined Ricky looking up at snowcapped mountains and sparkling skies, breathing in the smell of evergreens as his work crew turned trees into lumber and lumber into buildings. It almost made an 11-year-old **weakling** like me want to become a lumberjack.

Back in our New York City apartment, the air smelled like meatloaf and cabbage. Dad sat slantwise in his chair by the window, **obviously** trying to catch the last rays of sunlight rather than turn on a light. My older sister Ruth and I lay on the floor comparing the letters Ricky had sent us.

"Shirley, Ricky says they had a talent show, and he wore a grass skirt and did a hula dance while playing the ukulele!" Ruth reported with delight. "I'll bet he was the cat's pajamas!"

"It'd be swell to have our own talent show!" I replied.

"Should I start sewing grass skirts?" Mom asked from the kitchen, which was just the corner where someone had plopped down a stove next to a sink and an icebox. "Now come set the table. Dinner's almost ready."

HISTORICAL FICTION

FIND TEXT EVIDENCE

Read

Paragraphs 1-6

Make Predictions

Make a prediction based on the girls' conversation. Write the text evidence for your prediction.

Sample answer: The girls may put together a talent show. Text evidence: Mom asked, "Should I start sewing grass skirts?"

Paragraph 5

Plot: Characterization

Underline the example of dialect in paragaph 5. What does this reveal about Shirley's character?

Shirley is excited and has a positive attitude.

Reread

Author's Craft

What point of view is the story written from? Why might the author have written the story from this point of view?

Unit 5 · Text Set 2 39

Reading/Writing Companion, p. 39

AUTHOR'S CRAFT DOK 3

Review first- and third-person points of view prior to rereading page 39. Ask: *Who is the narrator when a story is told from a first-person point of view?* (a character in the story) *Who narrates a story told from a third-person point of view?* (an outside narrator) *How do these points of view affect what you learn about the characters and events?* (In a first-person point of view, readers learn only what the narrator knows about characters and events. A third-person omniscient point of view allows readers to learn what multiple characters are thinking and feeling.)

ELL Review the differences between pronouns used by a narrator in a first-person versus third-person point of view. Then reinforce students' understanding with prompts. *What pronoun does the narrator use to refer to herself in the second paragraph?* (I) *What does she call Ruth in the third paragraph?* ("my older sister") *What does this tell you about the point of view?* (It is first person.)

What point of view is the story written from? (It's written from the first-person point of view of Shirley Rollet, a young girl living in New York City with her family in 1937.) *Why might the author have written the story from this point of view?* (Possible answer: Describing events from Shirley's perspective helps the reader better understand her character. In addition, the author may have suspected that her audience would include younger readers, so writing from this point of view helps readers better relate to Shirley and her situation.)

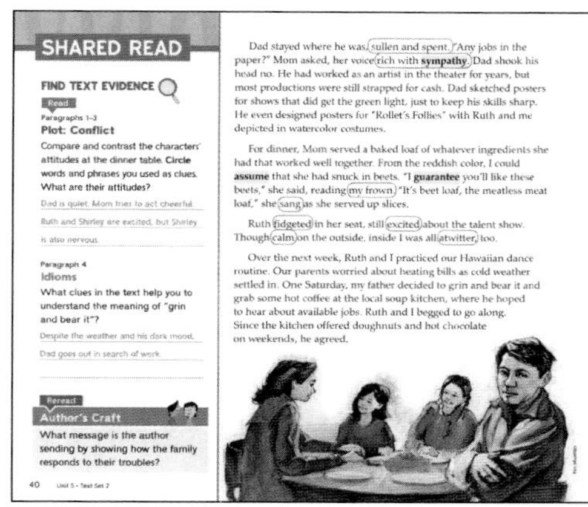

SHARED READ

FIND TEXT EVIDENCE

Read

Paragraphs 1–3

Plot: Conflict

Compare and contrast the characters' attitudes at the dinner table. **Circle** words and phrases you used as clues. What are their attitudes?

Dad is quiet. Mom tries to act cheerful.

Ruth and Shirley are excited, but Shirley is also nervous.

Paragraph 4

Idioms

What clues in the text help you to understand the meaning of "grin and bear it"?

Despite the weather and his dark mood, Dad goes out in search of work.

Reread

Author's Craft

What message is the author sending by showing how the family responds to their troubles?

Dad stayed where he was, sullen and spent. "Any jobs in the paper?" Mom asked, her voice rich with **sympathy**. Dad shook his head no. He had worked as an artist in the theater for years, but most productions were still strapped for cash. Dad sketched posters for shows that did get the green light, just to keep his skills sharp. He even designed posters for "Rollet's Follies" with Ruth and me depicted in watercolor costumes.

For dinner, Mom served a baked loaf of whatever ingredients she had that worked well together. From the reddish color, I could **assume** that she had snuck in beets. "I **guarantee** you'll like these beets," she said, reading my frown. "It's beet loaf, the meatless meat loaf," she sang as she served up slices.

Ruth fidgeted in her seat, still excited about the talent show. Though calm on the outside, inside I was all atwitter, too.

Over the next week, Ruth and I practiced our Hawaiian dance routine. Our parents worried about heating bills as cold weather settled in. One Saturday, my father decided to grin and bear it and grab some hot coffee at the local soup kitchen, where he hoped to hear about available jobs. Ruth and I begged to go along. Since the kitchen offered doughnuts and hot chocolate on weekends, he agreed.

40 Unit 5 • Text Set 2

Reading/Writing Companion, p. 40

AUTHOR'S CRAFT DOK 2

Reread paragraphs 2–4 on page 40 with students. Ask: ***What is similar about the ways the characters respond to the family's struggles?*** (They all respond positively. Mom tries to make the family a good dinner. Shirley and Ruth excitedly practice their dance routine. Even though he doesn't want to, Dad goes to the soup kitchen to hear about work.)

ELL Point out that Mom is singing in the last sentence of paragraph 2. Reread Mom's dialogue twice—in a "singing" voice and with a neutral expression. *In which version does Mom sound happier?* (the first) Have partners describe how Mom's attitude helps the family.

What message is the author sending by showing how the family responds to their troubles? (The author is showing that people don't have to respond negatively when times are difficult. The Rollet family does not have a lot of money, but each member tries to make the best of things.)

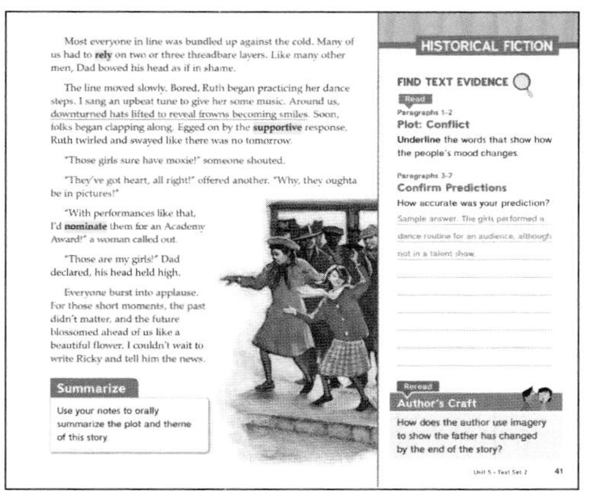

Most everyone in line was bundled up against the cold. Many of us had to **rely** on two or three threadbare layers. Like many other men, Dad bowed his head as if in shame.

The line moved slowly. Bored, Ruth began practicing her dance steps. I sang an upbeat tune to give her some music. Around us, downturned hats lifted to reveal frowns becoming smiles. Soon, folks began clapping along. Egged on by the **supportive** response, Ruth twirled and swayed like there was no tomorrow.

"Those girls sure have moxie!" someone shouted.

"They've got heart, all right!" offered another. "Why, they oughta be in pictures!"

"With performances like that, I'd **nominate** them for an Academy Award!" a woman called out.

"Those are my girls!" Dad declared, his head held high.

Everyone burst into applause. For those short moments, the past didn't matter, and the future blossomed ahead of us like a beautiful flower. I couldn't wait to write Ricky and tell him the news.

Summarize

Use your notes to orally summarize the plot and theme of this story.

HISTORICAL FICTION

FIND TEXT EVIDENCE

Read

Paragraphs 1–2

Plot: Conflict

Underline the words that show how the people's mood changes.

Paragraphs 3–7

Confirm Predictions

How accurate was your prediction?

Sample answer: The girls performed a dance routine for an audience, although not in a talent show.

Reread

Author's Craft

How does the author use imagery to show the father has changed by the end of the story?

Unit 5 • Text Set 2 41

Reading/Writing Companion, p. 41

AUTHOR'S CRAFT DOK 2

Reread page 41 with students. Ask: ***What words and phrases does the author use to help you understand how the father is feeling in paragraphs 1 and 6?*** (In paragraph 1, the author says that the father "bowed his head as if in shame" while in the soup kitchen line. In paragraph 6, after watching the girls perform, Dad has "his head held high," which indicates that he now feels proud.)

ELL Model the two examples of imagery as you say them: *bowed his head* and *his head held high*. Have partners describe the different feelings conveyed when bowing one's head versus holding one's head high.

How does the author use imagery to show the father has changed by the end of the story? (The author describes how the father holds his head before and after the girls dance. It helps readers understand that the father is proud of his girls and is now feeling more upbeat and optimistic about the future.)

MAKE INFERENCES

Explain that when you make inferences, you use text evidence and what you already know to come to conclusions that are not directly stated by the author. Making inferences can help you better understand characters and their struggles.

Think Aloud On page 41, I read that after the girls' performance, their father's attitude improved. I can infer that the father's family does what they can to help him feel better about the difficult time he is going through.

Integrate

BUILD KNOWLEDGE: MAKE CONNECTIONS

Talk About the Text Have partners discuss how the Rollets were able to adapt to change.

Write About the Text Have students add ideas to the Build Knowledge pages of their reader's notebooks.

Anchor Chart Record any new ideas on the Build Knowledge anchor chart.

Add to the Vocabulary List Have students write down any words they learned in their reader's notebooks about how shared experiences can help people adapt to change.

FORMATIVE ASSESSMENT

STUDENT CHECK-IN

Have partners share their responses to one of the Reread prompts on Reading/Writing Companion pages 39-41. Ask them to reflect using the Check-In routine.

Reread

Write About the Shared Read

LEARNING GOALS

We can use text evidence to respond to historical fiction.

OBJECTIVES

Quote accurately from a text when explaining what the text says explicitly and when drawing inferences from the text.

Explain different characters' perspectives in a literary text.

Compare and contrast two or more characters, settings, or events in a story or a drama, drawing on specific details in the text (e.g., how characters interact).

ELA ACADEMIC LANGUAGE

- *text evidence, response, compare, contrast*
- Cognates: *evidencia del texto, respuesta, comparar, contrastar*

TEACH IN SMALL GROUP

Approaching Level Have partners locate text evidence together as they form and support their conclusions.

On Level Have students write their first paragraphs independently. Then trade with partners and provide feedback before finalizing their answers.

Beyond Level Have students answer the Reread prompt independently.

ELL Group students of mixed proficiency levels to discuss and respond to the prompt.

Analyze the Prompt DOK 3

Read the prompt aloud. *Compare and contrast the characters' actions in this story. What does this story tell you about having a positive outlook? Provide text evidence in your answer.* Ask: *What is the prompt asking?* (to compare the characters and determine why having a positive outlook matters) Say: *Let's reread to see how certain actions cause changes in the way the characters in "The Day the Rollets Got Their Moxie Back" feel or respond to something. As we go through the story, we can note text evidence. Doing this will help you make inferences and write your response.*

Analyze Text Evidence

Remind students that an author makes it clear to readers how and why the characters change by **comparing and contrasting** characters' feelings and behaviors at different points in the story. As they reread, students should look for words and phrases that describe characters' thoughts, actions, and responses. In the **Reading/Writing Companion**, have students reread the first two sentences on page 39. Ask: *What effect does Ricky's letter have on the narrator?* (It helps her to get through hard times, or feel better when life is hard or challenging.) Have students continue rereading the rest of the page. Ask: *How do you know that the letter improves the narrator's mood?* (After reading the letter, she and her sister get excited about performing in their own talent show, just like their brother did.) Have students look for other examples in the text that show how simple actions change how characters feel.

Respond

Direct student pairs to the sentence starters on Reading/Writing Companion page 48. Ask: *How does examining the author's descriptions of the family members' moods help you understand the benefits of having a positive outlook?* As needed, model a response.

Think Aloud By examining the author's descriptions of the family members' moods throughout the story, and determining the reasons for changes in their moods, I can see why having a positive outlook is important. For example, when the girls and their father first arrive at the soup kitchen, the father feels bad. He's ashamed and "bows his head as if in shame." But after the girls do their dance, he holds his head high. That small action helps me understand that his feelings have changed. Now he feels proud of the girls and optimistic about their future.

Analytical Writing Students should use the phrases in the sentence starters to form their responses. Text evidence should support their response. Students may continue their responses on a separate piece of paper.

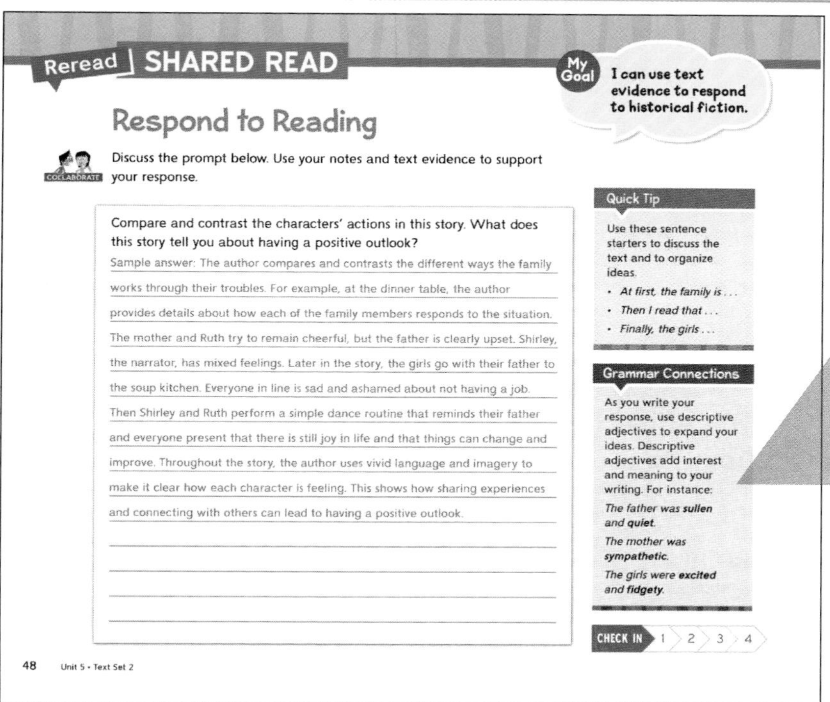

Reread | SHARED READ

My Goal: I can use text evidence to respond to historical fiction.

Respond to Reading

COLLABORATE Discuss the prompt below. Use your notes and text evidence to support your response.

Compare and contrast the characters' actions in this story. What does this story tell you about having a positive outlook?

Sample answer: The author compares and contrasts the different ways the family works through their troubles. For example, at the dinner table, the author provides details about how each of the family members responds to the situation. The mother and Ruth try to remain cheerful, but the father is clearly upset. Shirley, the narrator, has mixed feelings. Later in the story, the girls go with their father to the soup kitchen. Everyone in line is sad and ashamed about not having a job. Then Shirley and Ruth perform a simple dance routine that reminds their father and everyone present that there is still joy in life and that things can change and improve. Throughout the story, the author uses vivid language and imagery to make it clear how each character is feeling. This shows how sharing experiences and connecting with others can lead to having a positive outlook.

Quick Tip

Use these sentence starters to discuss the text and to organize ideas.

- *At first, the family is . . .*
- *Then I read that . . .*
- *Finally, the girls . . .*

Grammar Connections

As you write your response, use descriptive adjectives to expand your ideas. Descriptive adjectives add interest and meaning to your writing. For instance:

*The father was **sullen** and **quiet**.*

*The mother was **sympathetic**.*

*The girls were **excited** and **fidgety**.*

CHECK IN 1 2 3 4

48 Unit 5 • Text Set 2

Reading/Writing Companion, p. 48

Grammar Connections

Students can use online **Grammar Handbook** pages 466–468 to review and practice using descriptive adjectives.

English Language Learners

Use the following scaffolds with **Respond**.

Beginning

Read the prompt with students and discuss what they will write about. Reread **Reading/Writing Companion** page 40 and describe the illustration with them. Ask: *How does the father feel when they first arrive at the soup kitchen?* (bad) *How does the father feel after the girls dance?* (proud) Help partners to discuss what the story tells about having a positive outlook and respond using: The story tells that it is important to have a positive outlook.

Intermediate

Read the prompt with students and discuss what they will write about. Have partners reread **Reading/Writing Companion** page 40. Elicit them to describe what happens at the soup kitchen that changes the father's mood. Then to discuss what the story tells about having a positive outlook and respond using: At first, the father feels _____. After the girls do their dance, the father _____. The story tells that having a positive outlook can _____.

Advanced/Advanced High

Review the prompt and sentence starters on page 48 with students. Have partners describe how the father's mood changes from the beginning to the end of the story and use evidence from the text to explain why. Then have them respond using the sentence starters.

ELL NEWCOMERS

Have students listen to the summaries of the **Shared Read** in their native language and then in English to help them access the text and develop listening comprehension. Help students ask and answer questions with a partner. Use these *sentence frames:* What causes a problem for the family? The family's problem is that ____. Then continue the lessons in the **Newcomer Teacher's Guide**.

FORMATIVE ASSESSMENT

STUDENT CHECK-IN

Ask partners to share their response on Reading/Writing Companion page 48. Have them use the Check-In routine to reflect and fill in the bars.

LEARNING GOALS

- **We can identify and use words with prefixes.**
- **We can identify and read multisyllabic words.**
- **We can read fluently with an appropriate rate.**

OBJECTIVES

Know and apply grade-level phonics and word analysis skills in decoding words.

Use combined knowledge of all letter-sound correspondences, syllabication patterns, and morphology (e.g., roots and affixes) to read accurately unfamiliar multisyllabic words in context and out of context.

Read grade-level prose and poetry orally with accuracy, appropriate rate, expression, and automaticity on successive readings.

- Rate: 136–156 WCPM

ELA ACADEMIC LANGUAGE

- *rate*
- Cognate: *ritmo*

TEACH IN SMALL GROUP

Word Study

Approaching Level and **ELL** Use the Tier 2 activity on page T142 before teaching.

On Level As needed, use the Read Multisyllabic Words section only.

Beyond Level Use the Read Multisyllabic Words section only.

ELL See page 5 in the **Language Transfers Handbook** for guidance in identifying sounds and symbols that may not transfer for speakers of certain languages, and support in accommodating those students.

Prefixes

1 Explain

Remind students that a *prefix* is a group of letters added to the beginning of a word that changes the word's meaning.

Write the following prefixes and meanings on the board. Read each one aloud as you point to it.

- ***dis-***, often means "not," "absence of," or "opposite of"
- ***in-***, often means "not," or "opposite of"; other forms of *in-* are *im-* (before words that begin with *m* or *p,* as in *impossible*), *ir-* (before words that begin with *r,* as in *irregular*), and *il-* (before words that begin with *l,* as in *illogical*)
- ***mis-***, often means "wrong"
- ***pre-***, often means "before"

2 Model

Write the word *disappear* on the board. Do not say the word, but ask students to examine the word's parts. Then model how to use knowledge of prefixes to decode the word and figure out its meaning. Repeat the activity using the following words:

disagree	discontinue	inactive	immature
irregular	illegal	misbehave	preheat

3 Guided Practice

Write the following words on the board. Have students underline the prefix in each word, define the prefix, and then use its meaning to determine the meaning of the whole word.

distrust	disobey	disinterest	disarm
incorrect	immobile	irresponsible	illogical
miscount	misread	preset	precaution
disinterest	impolite	preview	mistreat

For practice with prefixes, use **Practice Book** page 271 or online activities.

Read Multisyllabic Words

Transition to Longer Words Write the following words on the board. Have students chorally read the prefixes in the first and third columns. Then have them underline the prefixes in the words in the second and fourth columns. Model how to read the words in the second column and how to determine their meaning based on the meaning of the prefixes. Then have students read and define the words in the fourth column.

dis-	disagreement	*dis-*	displacement
mis-	misunderstanding	*mis-*	misalignment
in-	inseparable	*ir-*	irreplaceable
im-	impersonal	*il-*	illegible
pre-	prefabricate	*pre-*	prejudgment

Fluency

Rate

Explain/Model Remind students that rate refers to the speed with which they read. Explain that reading too quickly or too slowly might make a text difficult to understand. Read aloud the first three paragraphs of "The Day the Rollets Got Their Moxie Back" from the **Reading/Writing Companion** page 39. Model reading first very quickly and then again at a more appropriate, measured rate. Ask students which rate made the text easier to understand.

Practice/Apply Have partners take turns reading the passage, modeling the rate you used.

Daily Fluency Practice

Automaticity Students can practice reading with accuracy and appropriate rate to develop automaticity using the online **Differentiated Genre Passage,** "Nancy's First Interview."

DIGITAL TOOLS

For more practice, have students use the phonics and fluency activities.

Prefixes

MULTIMODAL LEARNING

Write *dis-, in-, mis-, il-,* and *pre-* on one set of note cards. On another set of cards, write a variety of words that can be used with the prefixes, such as *honest, active, place, legal,* and *test.* Ask partners to take turns putting together a prefix card and a word card to make a new word. Have them read their new word and tell its meaning.

FORMATIVE ASSESSMENT

STUDENT CHECK-IN

Prefixes Have partners share three words with prefixes.

Mutlisyllabic Words Have partners add prefixes to the following words: *agreement, personal,* and *alignment.*

Fluency Ask partners to read "Nancy's First Interview" fluently.

Have partners reflect using the Check-In routine.

CHECK FOR SUCCESS

Can students identify multisyllabic words with prefixes? Can students read accurately at an appropriate rate?

Small Group Instruction

If No:

- **Approaching** Reteach pp. T142, T146
- **ELL** Develop p. T142

If Yes:

- **On** Apply p. T148
- **Beyond** Apply p. T154

LEARNING GOALS

- **We can use the research process to create a collage.**
- **We can identify primary and secondary sources.**

OBJECTIVES

Conduct short research projects that use several sources to build knowledge through investigation of different aspects of a topic.

Recall relevant information from experiences or gather relevant information from print and digital sources; summarize or paraphrase information in notes and finished work, and provide a list of sources.

Engage effectively in a range of collaborative discussions (one-on-one, in groups, and teacher-led) with diverse partners, building on others' ideas and expressing their own clearly.

ELA ACADEMIC LANGUAGE

- *primary source, secondary source, unbiased*
- Cognates: *fuente primaria, fuente secundaria*

TEACH IN SMALL GROUP

You may wish to teach the Research and Inquiry lesson during Small Group time. Have groups of mixed abilities complete the page and work on the collage.

Supporting One Another

Explain to students that for the next two weeks they will work collaboratively with a partner to research the Great Depression. They will create a collage in which they document the experiences of people during this time. Explain that the student groups should create a research plan to help decide what types of information to include in the collage.

Primary and Secondary Sources Review primary and secondary sources with students. Point out the following:

- Primary sources are firsthand accounts of an event. Examples include speeches, diaries, letters, interviews, and photographs.
- Secondary sources are secondhand accounts of an event. These accounts did not have direct involvement in the event. Examples include encyclopedias, textbooks, and magazine articles.
- Some secondary sources may include primary sources within them, such as a quote or a photograph directly related to the event.

Have students look at the Tech Tip on **Reading/Writing Companion** page 49. Support them as they go through each step in the Research Process as outlined on page 49 to make their collages.

STEP 1 **Set Research Goals** Review with students the causes of the Great Depression, and the various hardships that people faced during that time. Have students brainstorm a list of notable people from that era. Offer feedback as students generate questions and decide what kind of visuals and details they would like to include in their collages. Have them use an **Accordion Foldable®**, available online, to help organize their information.

STEP 2 **Identify Sources** Discuss the importance of using trustworthy and reliable sources when doing their research. Provide examples of sources that are credible, such as encyclopedias, news organizations, and government sites. Make sure students understand that not all encyclopedias and news organizations are reliable. If citing encyclopedias and news organizations, encourage them to cite from sources that have a long history of reporting factual, unbiased information.

STEP 3 **Find and Record Information** Review with students how to take notes and cite the sources they use to gather information for their collages. Have them create a bibliography.

STEP 4 **Organize and Synthesize Information** Show students how to organize the information that they want to add to their collages. Discuss how to integrate captions with their photos and any other visuals. Help them sketch out their collages before they create them.

STEP 5 **Create and Present** Review with students what they should include in their collages and have them make changes as necessary. Discuss options for presenting their work. Consider displaying them in the classroom.

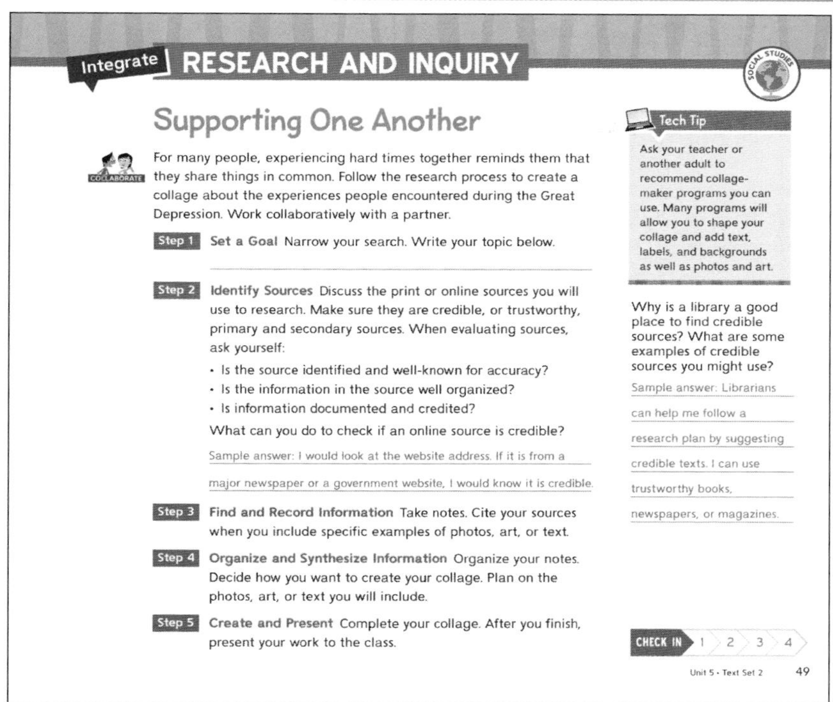

Integrate | RESEARCH AND INQUIRY

SOCIAL STUDIES

Supporting One Another

COLLABORATE

For many people, experiencing hard times together reminds them that they share things in common. Follow the research process to create a collage about the experiences people encountered during the Great Depression. Work collaboratively with a partner.

Step 1 **Set a Goal** Narrow your search. Write your topic below.

Step 2 **Identify Sources** Discuss the print or online sources you will use to research. Make sure they are credible, or trustworthy, primary and secondary sources. When evaluating sources, ask yourself:

- Is the source identified and well-known for accuracy?
- Is the information in the source well organized?
- Is information documented and credited?

What can you do to check if an online source is credible?

Sample answer: I would look at the website address. If it is from a major newspaper or a government website, I would know it is credible.

Step 3 **Find and Record Information** Take notes. Cite your sources when you include specific examples of photos, art, or text.

Step 4 **Organize and Synthesize Information** Organize your notes. Decide how you want to create your collage. Plan on the photos, art, or text you will include.

Step 5 **Create and Present** Complete your collage. After you finish, present your work to the class.

Tech Tip

Ask your teacher or another adult to recommend collage-maker programs you can use. Many programs will allow you to shape your collage and add text, labels, and backgrounds as well as photos and art.

Why is a library a good place to find credible sources? What are some examples of credible sources you might use?

Sample answer: Librarians can help me follow a research plan by suggesting credible texts. I can use trustworthy books, newspapers, or magazines.

CHECK IN 1 2 3 4

Unit 5 • Text Set 2 49

Reading/Writing Companion, p. 49

English Language Learners

Use the following scaffolds with **Step 3**.

Beginning

Review primary and secondary sources with students. Remind them that a credible source has information we can trust, and provide examples. Help partners find relevant information from credible sources and take notes in the **Accordion Foldable®**. Ask: *Is this information from a primary or secondary source?* (primary/secondary) Model how to cite sources and create a bibliography. Check the students' notes and provide feedback as needed.

Intermediate

Review primary and secondary sources with students. Have partners find relevant information from credible sources and take notes in the **Accordion Foldable®**. Ask: *Is this information from a primary or secondary source?* (primary/secondary) *Is the source credible? How can you tell?* I can tell the source is/is not credible because ____. Guide them to cite sources and create a bibliography. Check their notes and provide feedback as needed.

Advance/Advanced High

Check the students' understanding of primary and secondary sources. Have them find information from credible sources and take notes. Allow pairs to discuss what kind of sources they used and check if it is reliable. Remind them how to cite sources and create a bibliography.

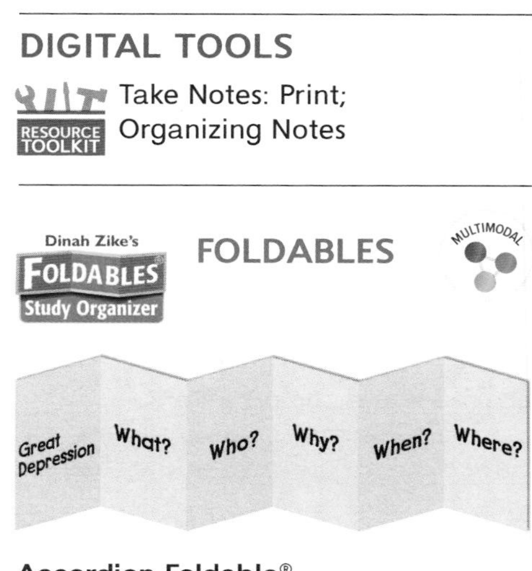

DIGITAL TOOLS

RESOURCE TOOLKIT Take Notes: Print; Organizing Notes

Dinah Zike's FOLDABLES Study Organizer

FOLDABLES

MULTIMODAL

Accordion Foldable®

FORMATIVE ASSESSMENT

STUDENT CHECK-IN

Collage Ask students to share their collages.

Primary and Secondary Sources Have students share an example of one primary source and one secondary source that they used in their collages.

Have students use the Check-In routine to reflect and fill in the bars on Reading/Writing Companion page 49.

Bud, Not Buddy

Lexile 950L

LEARNING GOALS

Read We can apply strategies and skills to read historical fiction.

Reread We can reread to analyze text, craft, and structure and compare texts.

Have students apply what they learned as they read.

ACT *What makes this text complex?*

- **Prior Knowledge**
- **Connection of Ideas**
- **Specific Vocabulary**
- **Genre**

Close Reading Routine

Read DOK 1–2

- Identify important ideas and details.
- Take notes and summarize.
- Use ACT prompts as needed.

Reread DOK 2–3

- Analyze the text, craft, and structure.
- Use *Reading/Writing Companion*, pp. 50-52.

Integrate DOK 3–4

- Integrate knowledge and ideas.
- Make text-to-text connections.
- Use the Integrate lesson.
- Complete the Show Your Knowledge task.
- Inspire action.

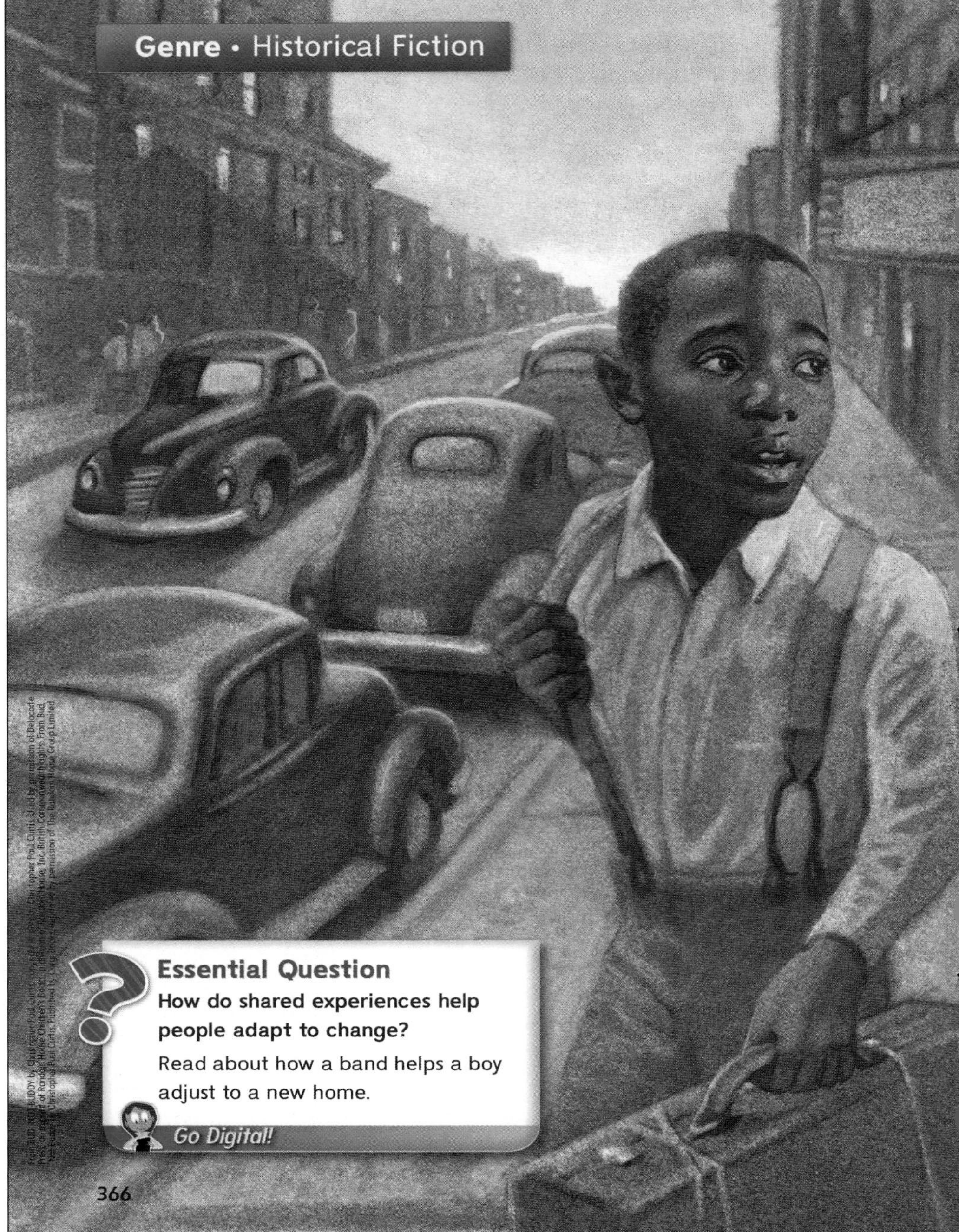

Genre • Historical Fiction
Essential Question
How do shared experiences help people adapt to change?
Read about how a band helps a boy adjust to a new home.
Go Digital!
366

Literature Anthology, pp. 366–367

DIFFERENTIATED READING

You may wish to read the full selection aloud once with minimal stopping before you begin using the Read prompts.

Approaching Level Have students listen to the selection summary. Use the Reread prompts during Small Group time.

On Level and **Beyond Level** Pair students or have them independently complete the Reread prompts on **Reading/ Writing Companion** pages 50-52.

English Language Learners Have ELLs listen to a summary of the selection, available in multiple languages. See also the **ELL Small Group Guide**.

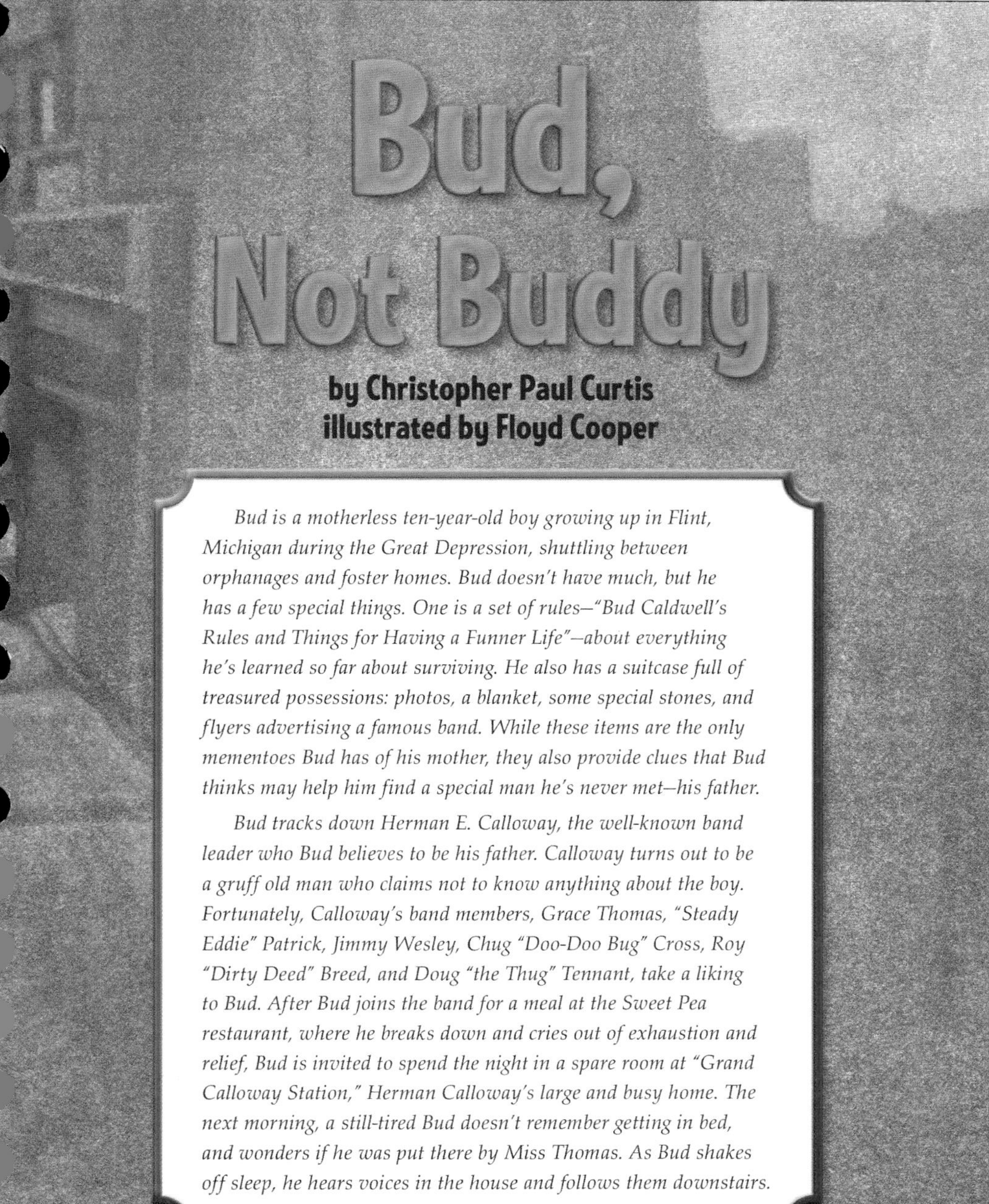

Bud, Not Buddy

by Christopher Paul Curtis
illustrated by Floyd Cooper

Bud is a motherless ten-year-old boy growing up in Flint, Michigan during the Great Depression, shuttling between orphanages and foster homes. Bud doesn't have much, but he has a few special things. One is a set of rules—"Bud Caldwell's Rules and Things for Having a Funner Life"—about everything he's learned so far about surviving. He also has a suitcase full of treasured possessions: photos, a blanket, some special stones, and flyers advertising a famous band. While these items are the only mementoes Bud has of his mother, they also provide clues that Bud thinks may help him find a special man he's never met—his father.

Bud tracks down Herman E. Calloway, the well-known band leader who Bud believes to be his father. Calloway turns out to be a gruff old man who claims not to know anything about the boy. Fortunately, Calloway's band members, Grace Thomas, "Steady Eddie" Patrick, Jimmy Wesley, Chug "Doo-Doo Bug" Cross, Roy "Dirty Deed" Breed, and Doug "the Thug" Tennant, take a liking to Bud. After Bud joins the band for a meal at the Sweet Pea restaurant, where he breaks down and cries out of exhaustion and relief, Bud is invited to spend the night in a spare room at "Grand Calloway Station," Herman Calloway's large and busy home. The next morning, a still-tired Bud doesn't remember getting in bed, and wonders if he was put there by Miss Thomas. As Bud shakes off sleep, he hears voices in the house and follows them downstairs.

367

Read

Set a Purpose Tell students to preview the text and set a purpose for reading. Remind them that setting a purpose can help them monitor their comprehension.

Note Taking: Use the Graphic Organizer

Analytical Writing Remind students to take notes as they read. Distribute copies of online **Graphic Organizer 10.** Have students fill in the graphic organizer to record details about the characters. They can also note words they don't understand and questions they have.

Reread

Author's Purpose DOK 2

Reread page 367. What is the name of Bud's set of rules? ("Bud Caldwell's Rules and Things for Having a Funner Life") Why did the author include this? (The author wants to show that because Bud has to keep track of ways to have more fun, his life of moving around must not be easy. Staying hopeful must require effort.)

Build Vocabulary on page 367

Have students add the Build Vocabulary words to their reader's notebook.

possessions: the things that a person owns

exhaustion: the state of being very tired

Access Complex Text

Prior Knowledge

Students may know little about the Great Depression, the historical period in which this story is set. Point out that the introduction on page 367 says that Bud grew up during the Great Depression. Elicit what students already know about this period in U.S. history. Supplement their prior knowledge with this information:

The Great Depression began in 1929 and ended around 1940. During that time, many people lost their jobs and homes. Thousands of children had to live in orphanages, sometimes because their families could not afford to care for them, or because their parents left them to find work. When possible, the children were placed in foster homes.

Read

❶ Idioms DOK 2

What is the meaning of the idiom, "so that's how the cookie's going to crumble," on page 368? (It means things will happen in a certain way. It refers to what Mr. Calloway plans to do about Bud.) What is another idiom on page 368? What does it mean? ("Making a break" means getting ready to leave suddenly.)

❷ Dialect DOK 2

Dialect is a specific way of speaking. Different regions of the country often have their own dialects, as have different groups throughout history. What is a synonym for dialect? (slang) What examples of dialect can you find on page 368? ("I'ma"; "uh-oh") What does "I'ma" mean? (It means "I am going to.")

❸ Make Predictions DOK 2

COLLABORATE **Teacher Think Aloud** As I read, I can use clues in the text to make predictions. I know that Bud has been in and out of orphanages and foster homes. I predict that Herman will find out Bud is telling the truth and will let him stay with the band. As I read, I will make, correct, and confirm my predictions.

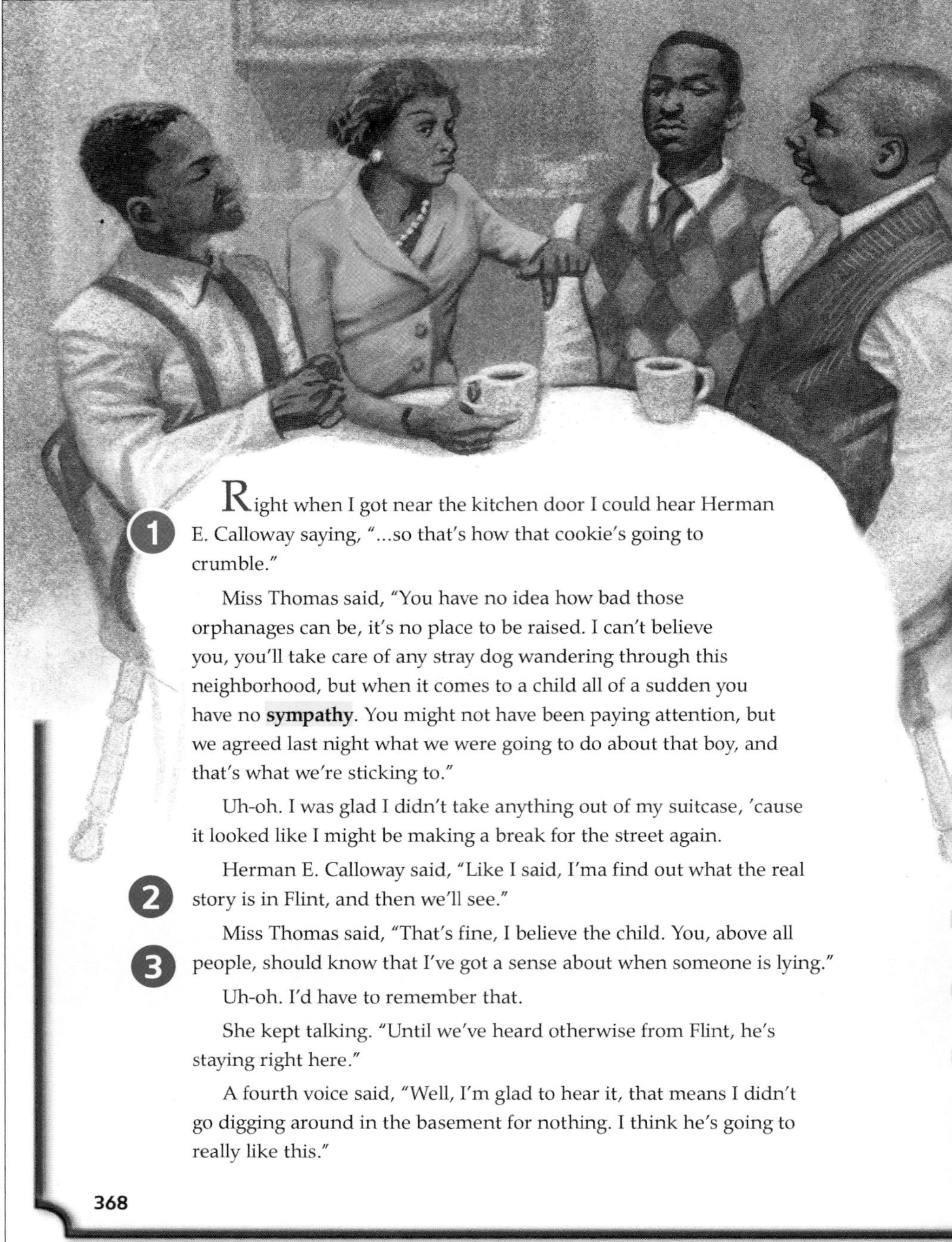

Right when I got near the kitchen door I could hear Herman E. Calloway saying, "...so that's how that cookie's going to crumble." ❶

Miss Thomas said, "You have no idea how bad those orphanages can be, it's no place to be raised. I can't believe you, you'll take care of any stray dog wandering through this neighborhood, but when it comes to a child all of a sudden you have no **sympathy**. You might not have been paying attention, but we agreed last night what we were going to do about that boy, and that's what we're sticking to."

Uh-oh. I was glad I didn't take anything out of my suitcase, 'cause it looked like I might be making a break for the street again.

Herman E. Calloway said, "Like I said, I'ma find out what the real story is in Flint, and then we'll see." ❷

Miss Thomas said, "That's fine, I believe the child. You, above all people, should know that I've got a sense about when someone is lying." ❸

Uh-oh. I'd have to remember that.

She kept talking. "Until we've heard otherwise from Flint, he's staying right here."

A fourth voice said, "Well, I'm glad to hear it, that means I didn't go digging around in the basement for nothing. I think he's going to really like this."

368

Literature Anthology, pp. 368–369

ACT Access Complex Text

Connection of Ideas

Help students connect the introduction on page 367 with the beginning of the story on page 368.

- *Why is the text on page 367 set in italics?* (It's a summary of what has happened before the story begins.)
- *Where is Bud at the start of the first scene?* (He is in Herman Calloway's house.)
- *Where was Bud before he met the band?* (in orphanages and foster homes in Flint, Michigan)
- *What are the adults talking about?* (whether Bud can stay with them or not)
- *Why does Bud think he might have to make a break for the street?* (If he can't stay with the band, he does not want to go back to the orphanage.)

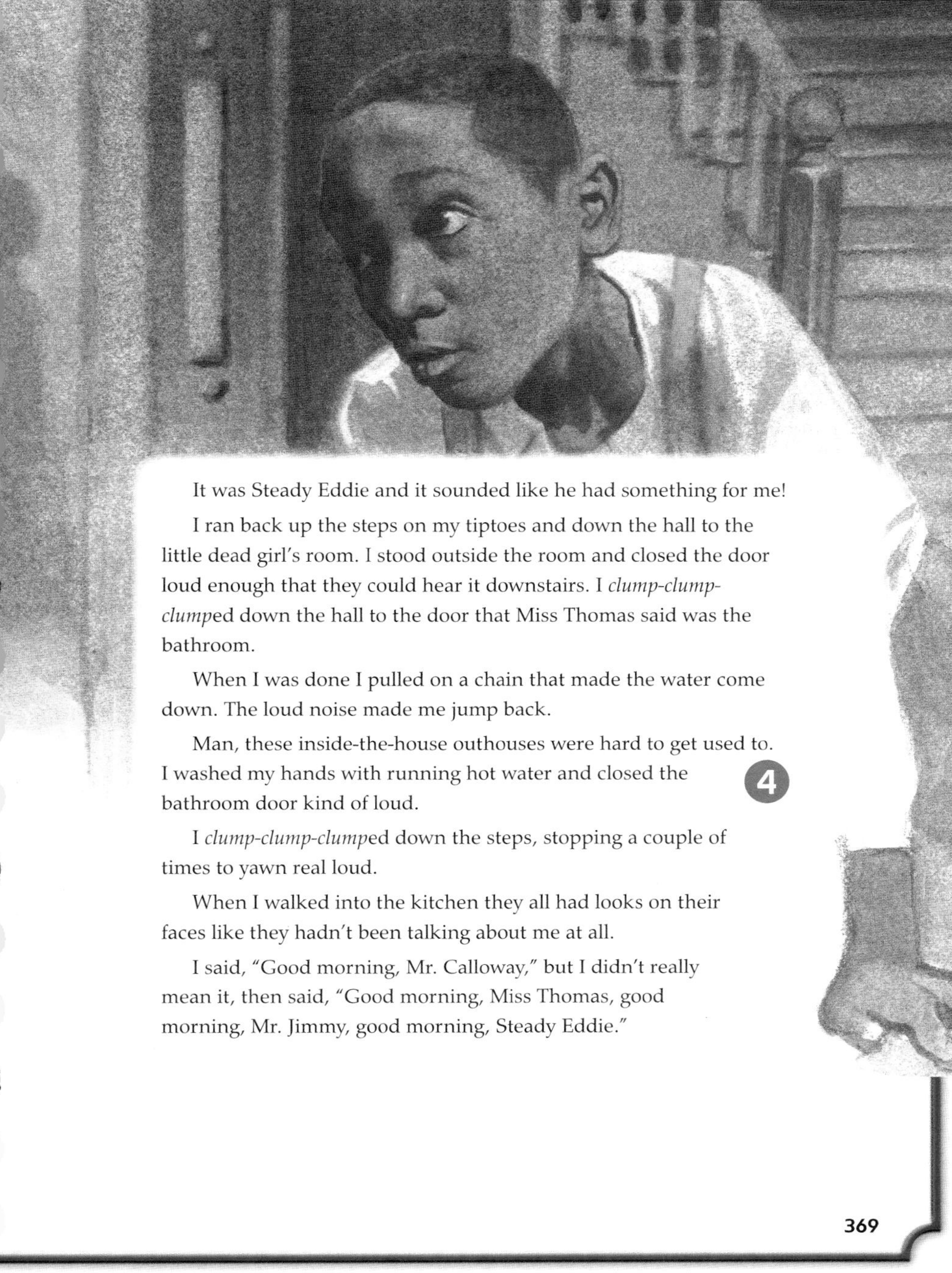

It was Steady Eddie and it sounded like he had something for me!

I ran back up the steps on my tiptoes and down the hall to the little dead girl's room. I stood outside the room and closed the door loud enough that they could hear it downstairs. I *clump-clump-clump*ed down the hall to the door that Miss Thomas said was the bathroom.

When I was done I pulled on a chain that made the water come down. The loud noise made me jump back.

Man, these inside-the-house outhouses were hard to get used to. I washed my hands with running hot water and closed the bathroom door kind of loud. 4

I *clump-clump-clump*ed down the steps, stopping a couple of times to yawn real loud.

When I walked into the kitchen they all had looks on their faces like they hadn't been talking about me at all.

I said, "Good morning, Mr. Calloway," but I didn't really mean it, then said, "Good morning, Miss Thomas, good morning, Mr. Jimmy, good morning, Steady Eddie."

369

Read

4 Genre: Historical Fiction DOK 1

What evidence tells you this is historical fiction? (Bud pulls a chain to make water come down into the toilet. He talks about "inside-the-house outhouses.")

STOP AND CHECK **DOK 2**

Make Predictions Why does Bud go back upstairs? (He wants to make sure the people downstairs know he is coming down.) What do you think Steady Eddie will give him? (a musical instrument because he is a musician)

Reread

Author's Craft: Characterization DOK 2

Reading/Writing Companion, p. 50

Reread pages 368–369. What does the author reveal about Bud through his responses to the conversation he overhears? (Bud wants to stay, but after hearing Mr. Calloway, he thinks about running away again. When the others defend Bud, he starts to feel more welcome, so he decides to stay. This shows that Bud is used to taking care of himself, but that he also wants his life to be more stable.)

Evaluate Information DOK 2

Explain Details can be used to evaluate Bud's reaction to the kitchen conversation.

Model I think Bud must be disappointed when he overhears the adults discussing whether or not he will be allowed to stay. He makes noises so that the adults don't know that he was secretly listening. I think Bud is used to hiding his behavior and thoughts from others.

Apply Ask students to evaluate more of Bud's actions that show how he reacts to the adults' conversation.

Spotlight on Idioms

Page 369, Paragraph 4 Clarify the meaning of *outhouse*. Read aloud the first sentence of the paragraph, modeling the exclamatory tone of *man*. Explain that the idiom "man" does not always directly address anybody. *"Man" can be used to express surprise or frustration. Which adjective phrase shows why the bathroom is strange for Bud?* (inside-the-house) Have partners practice using the idiom "man" to express surprise or frustration.

Read

5 Idioms DOK 2

What is the meaning of "what's the scoop?" ("What's happening?") What is the meaning of "cop a squat?" ("Have a seat.")

6 Plot: Conflict DOK 1

Compare everybody's response to Bud's arrival in the kitchen. (Everyone but Herman E. Calloway is pleasant to Bud.) Add this information to your graphic organizer to compare and contrast characters' actions.

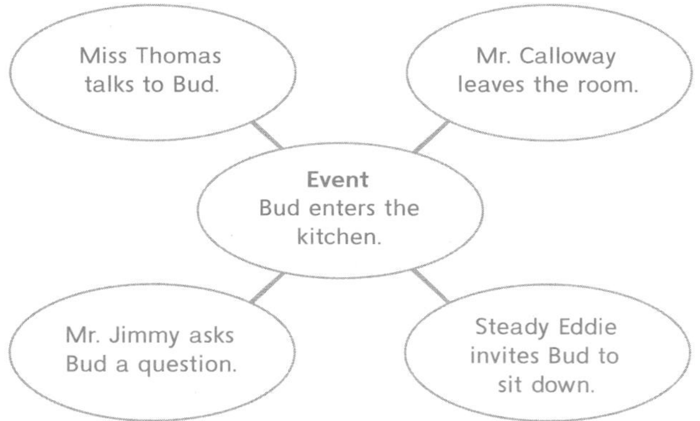

How does Mr. Calloway's reaction add to the story's conflict? (Mr. Calloway does not seem interested in interacting with Bud, so this creates tension in the story.)

I noticed right away that Miss Thomas didn't have all her diamond rings on, I guess it would've been hard sleeping with them flashing lights up at you, she must have to keep them closed up in a box that the sparkles can't get out of. I noticed too that even without the rings Miss Thomas still had to be the most beautiful woman in the world.

They smiled and said, "Good morning, Bud." All except Herman E. Calloway. He got up from the table and said, "I don't like the way Loudean is sounding, I'ma have a look at her plugs."

He went outside through a door at the back of the kitchen.

Miss Thomas said, "Bud, we'd just about given up on you. Do you usually sleep until after noon?"

After noon? Man, I couldn't believe it, I'd slept as long as those rich folks in the moving pictures!

"No, ma'am, that's the first time I ever did that."

She said, "I know you must be starving, but if you can hold out for another half hour or so Mr. Jimmy's going to make everyone's lunch. Think you can wait?"

"Yes, ma'am." A half hour wasn't nothing to wait, no matter how hungry you were.

Mr. Jimmy said, "So what's the scoop, little man?"

I didn't know what that meant so I said, "Nothing, sir."

Steady Eddie said, "How'd you sleep, kiddo?"

"Great, sir." Oops, I forgot I wasn't supposed to call the band men *sir*.

He said, "Cop a squat." He pointed at a chair. I guessed that
5 meant "sit down," so I did.

Miss Thomas said, "Were your ears burning last night, Bud?"

6 Man, all these Grand Rapids people really do talk funny. I only came from the other side of the state and it was like they talked some strange language out here. I said, "What, ma'am?"

She said, "There's an old saying that when people talk about you behind your back your ears start to get real warm, kind of like they were burning."

370

Literature Anthology, pp. 370–371

Access Complex Text

Connection of Ideas

Tell students that when they read fiction, they should try to connect the characters' actions to the characters' wants and needs. Have students recall what the adults said on pages 368–369 and connect it with their actions when Bud appears.

- *When Bud enters, Calloway says he needs to check the plugs on the car. Is this true? How do you know?* (Probably not; he's making an excuse to leave. Earlier, he made it clear he was not in favor of Bud staying.)
- *How do Miss Thomas and the band members treat Bud?* (They are kind and friendly. Earlier, Steady Eddie approved of Miss Thomas's suggestion that Bud stay with the band.)

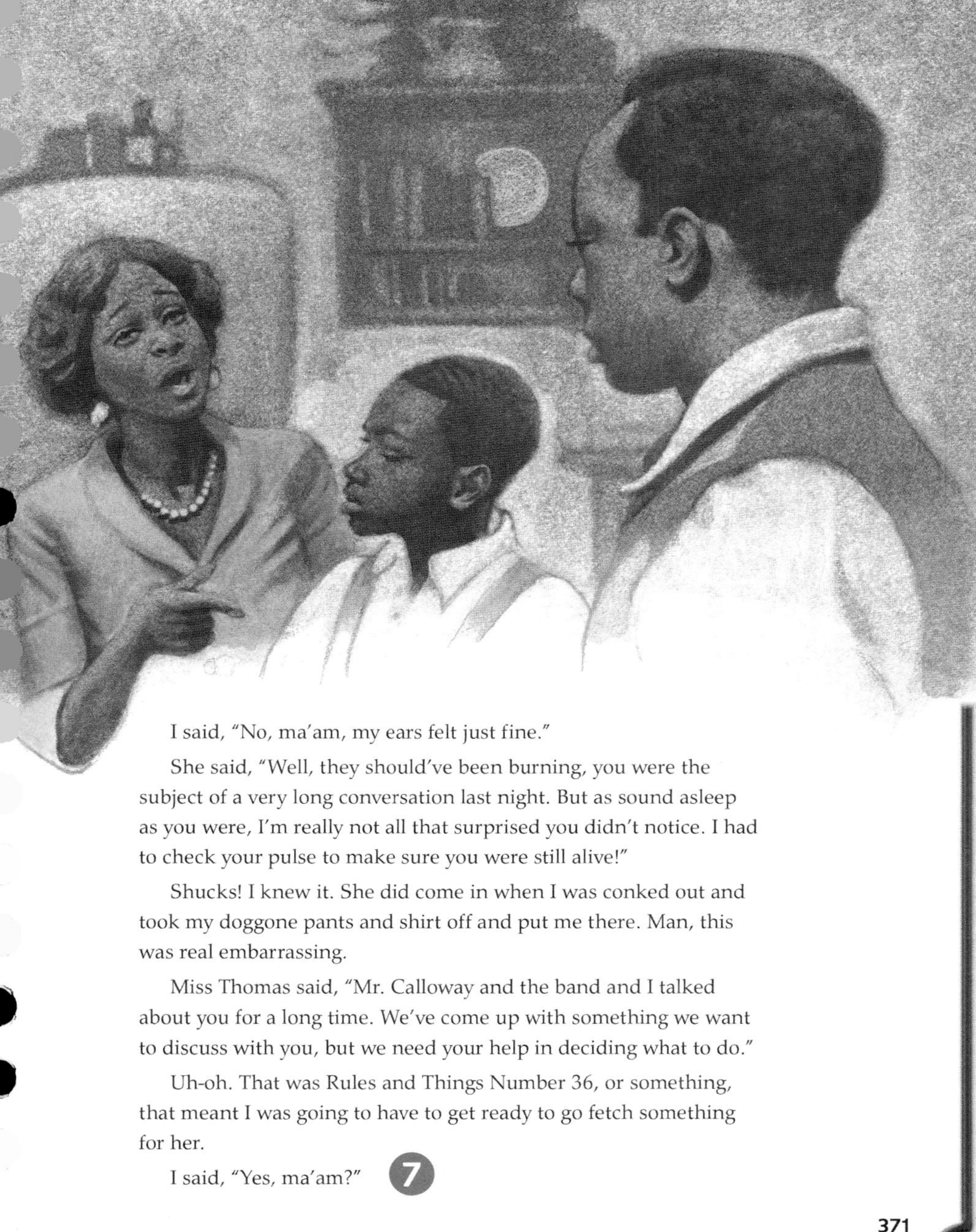

I said, "No, ma'am, my ears felt just fine."

She said, "Well, they should've been burning, you were the subject of a very long conversation last night. But as sound asleep as you were, I'm really not all that surprised you didn't notice. I had to check your pulse to make sure you were still alive!"

Shucks! I knew it. She did come in when I was conked out and took my doggone pants and shirt off and put me there. Man, this was real embarrassing.

Miss Thomas said, "Mr. Calloway and the band and I talked about you for a long time. We've come up with something we want to discuss with you, but we need your help in deciding what to do."

Uh-oh. That was Rules and Things Number 36, or something, that meant I was going to have to get ready to go fetch something for her.

I said, "Yes, ma'am?" 7

371

Read

7 Make Predictions DOK 2

COLLABORATE **Teacher Think Aloud** Miss Thomas says the adults need Bud's help in deciding what to do. Bud thinks he is going to have to fetch something. The clues I see don't lead me to make that prediction. I know that Miss Thomas wants to take care of him. I don't think she will put Bud to work. Do you think Bud is right? What help do you predict Miss Thomas wants from Bud?

Prompt students to apply the strategy in a Think Aloud. Have them turn to a partner and paraphrase Miss Thomas's dialogue and Bud's thoughts. Then have them predict what is going to happen next. Remind them to make, correct, or confirm their predictions as they continue reading.

Student Think Aloud I think Miss Thomas is going to ask if Bud wants to stay with the band. She said earlier, "he's staying right here." As I read more of the story, I will look for evidence to help me make, correct, or confirm my prediction.

Build Vocabulary on pages 370–371

sparkles: things that shine

fetch: to get something and bring it back

Spotlight on Idioms

Page 370, Paragraph 13 Point out that even the narrator, Bud, is having trouble understanding the idioms the other characters are using. Read the paragraph with students, and help them use context clues to understand the meaning of "cop a squat." Ask: *Does Bud know what "cop a squat" means?* (no) Act out what you do when you squat. *What did Mr. Jimmy point to?* (a chair) *How did that gesture help Bud understand what to do?* (Bud guessed that because Mr. Jimmy pointed to a chair "cop a squat" means to sit down.)

Newcomer

Use the **Newcomer Online Visuals** and their accompanying prompts to help students expand vocabulary and language about Feelings (12a-f), Family (13a-f), Home (14a-e), and Community (15a-d). Use the Conversation Starters, Speech Balloons, and the Games in the **Newcomer Teacher's Guide** to continue building vocabulary and developing oral and written language.

Read

8 Idioms DOK 2

What is the meaning of "split my face in half?" (a wide smile) What context clues did you use to help you figure it out? ("I'm going to assume that smile..."; "Before that grin gets stuck on your face...")

9 Plot: Characterization DOK 2

Why does Miss Thomas hold onto Bud's arms and tell him not to forget their conversation? (She knows he is happy to be with them, but he might not realize how hard it is to work with a band.) What does she think Bud might do if things get hard? (She is worried Bud will run away.) What information about Miss Thomas and Bud helps you make these inferences? Use text evidence. (Miss Thomas says to Bud, "this might get hard for you some of the time and I don't always travel with the band, so I don't want you to forget what I'm telling you." She says this because Bud has a history of running away.)

Build Vocabulary on pages 372–373

patient: able to calmly handle situations

godsend: something unexpected that is welcome and timely

She said, "We've got to talk to some people in Flint first, but if they say it's all right, we were hoping that you'd stay here at Grand Calloway Station for a while."

A gigantic smile split my face in half.

8 Miss Thomas said, "I'm going to **assume** that that smile means yes."

I said, "Yes, ma'am! Thank you, ma'am!"

Miss Thomas said, "Before that grin gets stuck on your face, let me tell you you're going to have lots of chores and things to take care of around here, Bud, you'll be expected to pull your own weight the best you can. We all like a very clean house and none of us are too used to having children around, so we're all going to have to learn to be patient with each other. There's one person in particular that you're going to have to be very patient with. Do you know who I mean?"

I sure did. "Yes, ma'am, it's Mr. Calloway."

She said, "Good boy, give him some time. He really needs help with a lot of different things, he swears someone's adding weight onto that bass fiddle of his every year, but he's just getting older. He can use some young, wiry hands to help him around. Think you can handle that?"

Now I knew for sure she'd looked at my legs, she must've thought I was a real **weakling**.

I said, "Yes, ma'am, my legs are a lot stronger than they look, most folks are surprised by that."

Miss Thomas said, "I don't doubt that at all, Bud. I'm not worried about your body being strong, I'm more concerned about your spirit. Lord knows Mr. Calloway is going to give it a test."

I said, "Yes, ma'am, my spirit's a lot stronger than it looks too, most folks are really surprised by that."

She smiled and said, "Very good, but you know what, Bud?"

"What, ma'am?"

"I knew you were an old toughie the minute I saw you."

I smiled again.

372

Literature Anthology, pp. 372–373

Access Complex Text

Connection of Ideas

Ask students to analyze the relationship between Miss Thomas and Bud. In particular, ask them to notice how they interact.

- *In what manner is Miss Thomas speaking to Bud on pages 372–373? How do you know?* (Miss Thomas is speaking to Bud very honestly and directly. She stares him right in the face and holds his arms.)
- *How does Miss Thomas feel toward Bud?* (motherly) *How do you know?* (She "looked right hard" in Bud's face, "just like Momma used to.")
- *Why do you think Miss Thomas feels this way about Bud?* (She knows that Bud is an orphan, and that it's difficult to grow up without a mother, so she wants to offer him as much support as she can.)

She said, "Our schedule's pretty heavy for the next couple of months, and then come September we'll have to see about school for you, but we'll be doing a lot of traveling right around Michigan, so I hope you don't mind long car trips."

"No, ma'am."

She said, "That's great, Bud. Something tells me you were a godsend to us, you keep that in mind all of the time, OK?"

"Yes, ma'am."

Then she did something that made me feel strange. She stood up, grabbed both my arms and looked right hard in my face, just like Momma used to, she said, "Really, Bud, I want you to always keep that in mind, this might get hard for you some of the time and I don't always travel with the band, so I don't want you to forget what I'm telling you."

I said, "No, ma'am, I won't." 

373

Reread

Author's Craft: Characterization

DOK 2

Reading/Writing Companion, p. 51

How does the author show how Bud will have to change to stay with the band? (Bud usually uses his rules to survive on his own. He has to use the band's rules now. The band expects him to pull his weight with chores and other things around the house. They also expect him to be patient with Mr. Calloway.) How do these expectations compare to Bud's original set of rules? How is he affected by this? (Bud's set of rules focus on survival in an unstable environment. This new set of rules is about surviving in a loving, family environment. This change causes Bud to initially feel uneasy, but he knows that he is strong.) Analyze the relationship between Bud and the band members as you read further.

ELL Spotlight on Language

Page 372, Paragraphs 1–2 Help students follow the dialogue by clarifying pronouns. Read the first paragraph on page 372 aloud. *To whom does the pronoun* they *refer?* (the people in Flint) *How do you know?* (plural, third person, appears right before *they)* *Who does the pronoun* you *in* you'd *refer to? How do you know?* (Bud; Miss Thomas is speaking to Bud; Bud is telling the story; *my* in the next sentence refers to Bud) Have partners identify pronoun references on the rest of the page.

Make Inferences — DOK 2

Explain Use earlier details in the text to help you make inferences about the band.

Model I know that this story takes place during the Great Depression when people did not have a lot of money. On page 368, Steady Eddie is relieved that he didn't go digging in the basement for nothing. He is happy that Bud will be staying with the band. Later, he gives Bud his alto sax case, something that means a lot to him. It is important to Steady Eddie, so Bud is excited to feel like part of a family.

Apply As students read, have them make inferences about the significance of Steady Eddie's gift to Bud.

Read

⑩ Dialect DOK 1

What examples of dialect can you find on page 374? (In the first paragraph, Steady Eddie says "your'n." In the middle of the page, Eddie talks about something not being "copacetic.")

⑪ Plot: Conflict DOK 2

Bud says he wasn't sure if he liked the way the talk with Steady Eddie was going. What might he think Steady Eddie wanted to do? (Bud might have thought that Steady Eddie wanted to take away his things and his suitcase.) How does Bud feel about Steady Eddie after seeing the gift? (He is thankful and appreciative.) How does the way Steady Eddie treat Bud compare to the way Miss Thomas treats him? (Both Steady Eddie and Miss Thomas are kind to Bud. Miss Thomas offers to take care of Bud, and Steady Eddie gives him a new suitcase.) Continue to analyze the relationships of and conflicts among Bud and the band members as you read.

Steady Eddie said, "Since you're going to be part of the family there's some things we've got to talk about. Now I've noticed the tight grip you keep on that old suitcase of your'n. I need to know how attached to it you are."

"I carry it with me everywhere I go 'cause all my things are in there." I wasn't sure if I liked the way this talk was going.

Steady Eddie said, "That's what I need to know, are you attached to the suitcase, or is it the things inside that are important?"

I'd never thought about that before, I'd always thought of the suitcase and the things inside together.

I said, "The things I got from my mother are the most important."

He said, "Good, 'cause if you're going to be traveling with us
⑩ it just wouldn't look too copacetic for you to be carrying that ratty old bag."

He reached under the kitchen table and pulled out one of those funny-looking suitcases that the band kept all their instruments in. This one looked like a baby one to his.

He put it on the table, opened it and said, "Since you're going to be traveling with Herman E. Calloway and the Worthy Swarthys, which is known far and wide as a very classy band, it's only fitting that you quit carrying your things in that cardboard suitcase.

"This is my old alto saxophone case, I've been hanging on to it for three years now, ever since the horn got stole right off the stage in Saginaw, but it doesn't look like I'm ever gonna get it back, so I figured you might as well keep your momma's things in it."

⑪ Wow! "Thank you, Steady Eddie!"

374

Literature Anthology, pp. 374–375

Access Complex Text

Specific Vocabulary

Read aloud the sixth paragraph on page 374. Explain that the word *copacetic* is an American slang word that was mostly used during the early- to mid-1900s meaning "fine, excellent, or highly satisfactory." The author's use of *copacetic* in the story adds to the historical accuracy and authenticity of the text.

- *What modern slang word could the author use in place of the word* copacetic*?* (Possible responses: cool, awesome)
- *Why is the word* copacetic *a better choice than the word* good*?* (It is a more interesting word, and it is specific to the character because it shows that Steady Eddie talks to Bud like he would with one of his bandmates.)

I pulled my new case over to me. The inside of it had a great big dent where Steady Eddie's saxophone used to go, now there wasn't anything in it but a little raggedy pink towel. The case had some soft smooth black stuff all over the inside of it, it covered everything, even the dent. There was a real old smell that came out of it too, like dried-up slobber and something dead. It smelled great! 

The back kitchen door opened and I thought Herman E. Calloway was coming back in to ruin everybody's fun, but it was the rest of the band.

Everybody said hello, poured themselves some coffee, then sat down at the table.

Doo-Doo Bug said, "I see Mr. C's got Loudean's carburetor tore down again, anything wrong?"

Miss Thomas said, "There's lots wrong, but not with that car."

They all laughed so I joined in too.

I patted my new case and said, "This here's my case now, I'm going to be going around with you."

They smiled and Dirty Deed said, "So we hear. Glad to have you on board, partner."

375

Read

12 Similes DOK 2

Reread the first paragraph on page 375. What two things are being compared? (The smell from the saxophone case is being compared to "dried-up slobber" and "something dead.") Is this a simile or a metaphor? How do you know? (It is a simile because it uses the word *like* in the comparison.)

Build Vocabulary on page 375

ruin: destroy or spoil something

carburetor: a part of a car that is necessary for the engine to work properly

Reread

Author's Craft: Dialogue DOK 2

Miss Thomas says, "There's lots wrong, but not with that car." What does she mean? What text evidence supports your understanding? (She means that the car isn't the problem. The problem is that Mr. Calloway isn't getting along well with the rest of the band, and he and Miss Thomas disagree about having Bud stay with the band. The band members seem to be in favor of having Bud stay with them. Bud mentions that Mr. Calloway will "ruin everybody's fun.")

ELL Spotlight on Idioms

Page 374, Paragraph 7 Read the paragraph aloud, and point to the images on pages 374 and 375 to show the type of suitcase Bud is talking about. Read the second sentence again, and ask: *Is Bud talking about a real baby here?* (No.) *What does Bud mean when he says that the suitcase "looks like a baby one to his"?* (Bud means that the suitcase is small compared to Steady Eddie's.) Have students talk about other things that are "baby" compared to larger things.

Read

⓭ Plot: Conflict DOK 1

Compare the characters' reactions after Steady Eddie gives Bud a gift. (Bud is excited and grateful. Steady Eddie says he'll have to practice. The Thug wants to give Bud a nickname. Miss Thomas isn't interested.) Add the information to your organizer.

Bud is excited and grateful.
Steady Eddy tells Bud about practice.
Event
Bud gets a recorder.
The Thug wants to give Bud a name.
Miss Thomas is not interested.

How does this show the story's conflict is headed toward a resolution? (Bud is learning to trust people and is excited to take an active role in the band.)

STOP AND CHECK **DOK 1**

Confirm or Revise Predictions What does Steady Eddie give Bud? (a recorder) How does this make Bud feel? (Bud feels grateful and excited to learn music. The illustration is a clue that shows he is happy.)

Steady Eddie said, "I was just about to tell him some of the things Herman E. Calloway requires of anybody in his band."

The Thug said, "Otherwise known as Herman E. Calloway's Rules to **Guarantee** You Have No Female Companionship, No Alcohol, and No Fun at All."

"Rule number one, practice two hours a day."

Mr. Jimmy said, "That's a good one."

Steady Eddie said, "So I got you this, Bud."

Steady Eddie had another present for me! This was a long, brown, skinny wooden flute. I was going to have to learn music!

He said, "It's called a recorder. Once you've developed a little wind, and some tone and a embouchure we'll move on to something a little more complicated."

Those must've been more of those Grand Rapids words 'cause they sure weren't like any American talk I ever heard before.

I said, "Thank you!"

376

Literature Anthology, pp. 376–377

Access Complex Text

Specific Vocabulary

Point out that the author uses musical terms that give the story a more authentic feel. Explain the meaning of each musical term.

- *A recorder is a wind instrument, similar to a flute, usually made of wood or plastic. The player blows into the mouthpiece and opens or closes the finger holes to make music.*
- Point to the recorder in the illustration on page 376. Say: *Show me how you would play a recorder.*
- Tone *is the sound of an instrument or voice.*
- Embouchure *is the position and use of the lips, tongue, and teeth in playing a wind instrument.*

Steady Eddie said, "Don't thank me until you've been through a couple of hours of blowing scales. We'll see if you're still grateful then."

The Thug said, "Now all that's left is to give little stuff here a name."

Miss Thomas said, "You know, I don't like the way Loudean's been sounding, I think I'm gonna go check the air in the trunk." She picked her coffee up and started to leave the kitchen. 13

Doo-Doo Bug said, "You don't have to leave, Miss Thomas."

"Darling, I know that, it's just that this is one of those man things that you all think is so mysterious and special that I have absolutely no interest in. The only thing I can hope is that the process has improved since you four were given your names." Then she left the room.

As soon as she was gone Steady Eddie told me, "Hand me your ax and stand up, Bud." I was starting to catch on to this Grand Rapids talk, I remember that a ax was a instrument. I handed Steady my recorder and stood up in front of him.

He said, "Uh-uh, she was right, this is mysterious and special, so that grin's got to go, brother."

I tried to tie down my smile.

Steady said, "Mr. Jimmy, you're the senior musician here, would you proceed?"

Mr. Jimmy said, "Gentlemen, the floor's open for names for the newest member of the band, Bud-not-Buddy."

They started acting like they were in school. The Thug raised his hand and Mr. Jimmy pointed at him.

Thug said, "Mr. Chairman, in light of the boy's performance last night at the Sweet Pea, I **nominate** the name Waterworks Willie."

Shucks, I was hoping they'd forgot about that.

Mr. Jimmy said, "You're out of order, Douglas."

Steady raised his hand. "Mr. Chairman, this boy's **obviously** going to be a musician, he slept until twelve-thirty today, so I propose that we call him Sleepy."

Mr. Jimmy said, "The name Sleepy is before the board, any comments?" 14

377

- *Scales are a series of notes in ascending or descending order. Why do musicians practice playing scales?* (to get better and faster)
- Invite students who play an instrument to share additional information with the class.

Read

14 Make Predictions DOK 2

Reread the last five paragraphs on page 377. Turn to a partner and say a name you predict the band might give Bud. Look for details in the story that may help you.

Student Think Aloud Mr. Jimmy said Thug was referring to the time Bud cried, so I think they'll give Bud a positive name that reflects his bravery or resourcefulness. I'll read on to see what name they give him and confirm or correct my prediction.

Build Vocabulary on page 377

mysterious: hard to explain

senior: highest ranking

chairman: a person who is in charge of a meeting

Reread

Author's Purpose DOK 2

Reread page 376. What new rule does Bud have? (He has to practice two hours a day.) Why did the author include this new rule in the story? (For Bud, it signals a new sense of himself as a musician and shows how the chaos of his old life is settling into stability.)

ELL Spotlight on Language

Page 376, Paragraphs 6–7 Explain the words: *tone, flute,* and *embouchure* (cognates: *tono, flauta*). Have a volunteer demonstrate high and low tones. Mime playing a flute. Explain how embouchure involves the use of the lips, tongue, and teeth. Have partners list other wind instruments that use embouchure.

Read

15 Plot: Conflict DOK 2

What name does each band member suggest? Add this to your organizer.

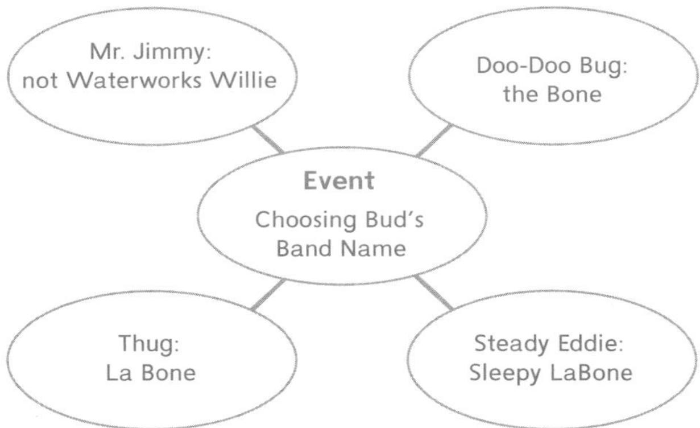

Compare the illustration on page 366 with the one on page 379. How do the illustrations show the story's conflict is resolved? (In the first illustration, Bud was alone and looked worried. In the final illustration, he is happy and part of a family.)

STOP AND CHECK DOK 1

Summarize How do the band members decide Bud's new name? (They think of words to describe Bud's characteristics and qualities, and then compromise and combine two words into a name.) How does Bud feel about the new name? (He likes the name.)

Dirty Deed said, "Too simple. I think we need something that lets folks know about how slim the boy is."

Doo-Doo Bug said, "How about the Bone?"

Steady said, "Not enough class, he needs something so people will know right off that the boy's got class."

Mr. Jimmy said, "How do you say *bone* in French? French always makes things sound a lot classier."

The Thug said, "That's easy, *bone* in French is *la bone*."

Doo-Doo Bug said, "*La bone*, nah, it don't have a ring to it."

Steady Eddie said, "I got it, we'll compromise. How about Sleepy LaBone?"

I couldn't tie the smile down anymore, that was about the best name I'd ever heard in my life!

15 Mr. Jimmy said, "Let me try it out. Ladies and gentlemen, thank you very much for coming out on this cold November night, this night that will live in history, this night that for the first time on any stage anywhere, you have listened to the smooth saxophonical musings of that prodigy of the reed, Mr. Sleepy LaBone!"

The whole crowd broke out clapping.

The Thug said, "What can I say but *bang*!"

Dirty Deed said, "You nailed him!"

Doo-Doo Bug said, "That is definitely smooth."

Steady said, "My man!"

Mr. Jimmy said, "Kneel down, young man."

I got down on one knee.

Mr. Jimmy tapped me on the head three times with my recorder and said, "Arise and welcome to the band, Mr. Sleepy LaBone."

I got off my knee and looked at my bandmates.

Sleepy LaBone. Shucks, that was the kind of name that was enough to make you forget folks had ever called you Buddy, or even Clarence. That was the kind of name that was enough to make you practice *four* hours every day, just so you could live up to it!

378

Literature Anthology, pp. 378–379

Access Complex Text

Genre

Reread page 378 aloud with students. Point out the author's use of slang in the dialogue. Note that after the band gives Bud his name, they slip into slang that was typical of the time period. Have students look up the definition of each man's comment in an online resource and rephrase it in standard modern English.

- Thug: "What can I say but bang!" (I think that's great!)
- Doo-Doo Bug: "That is definitely smooth." (That name sounds good.)
- Steady Eddie: "My man!" (You're all right with me!)

Read

Build Vocabulary on page 378

class: very fine style

musings: inspirations

prodigy: a child who is amazingly talented

Reread

Author's Craft: Characterization

DOK 2

Reading/Writing Companion, p. 52

Reread page 378. How does the author help you understand how Bud changes as he becomes part of the band? (The author reveals the changes in Bud through his interaction with the band. Bud doesn't mind being teased, and he likes his new name. It makes him want to "practice four hours every day!") How does this show that he has changed during the story? (His pride in his new name and hopes of living up to it contrast with his earlier thoughts about just keeping out of trouble and finding a way to survive. He is no longer an orphan; he is now part of a family.)

Return to Purpose Review students' purpose for reading. Then ask partners to share how setting a purpose helped them understand the text.

Spotlight on Language

Page 378, Paragraphs 1-8 Read the paragraphs with students. Then point to *compromise* in paragraph 7. Explain that a compromise is an agreement that combines ideas from both sides. *How do Steady Eddie and Doo-Doo Bug reach a compromise?* (They both come up with a name for Bud, so Steady Eddie takes part of each of their ideas to give Bud a new name.) *Which detail shows you how Bud feels about the compromise?* (smiles, says it's the best name he's heard in his life) Have partners discuss a compromise they have made.

Read

Meet the Author DOK 2

Christopher Paul Curtis

Have students read the biographies of the author and the illustrator. Ask:

- How might Christopher Paul Curtis's experiences with his own grandfather have helped him write this story?
- How do Floyd Cooper's illustrations help you visualize the story?
- Which helped you to better understand the story, the words or the illustrations? Explain.

Author's Purpose DOK 2

To Entertain: Review that the author's purpose is to entertain, but he may have had more reasons. Students may say that he wrote to inform readers about life during the Great Depression or to write about his family's history. He names the jazz band leader in *Bud, Not Buddy,* after his grandfather.

Reread

Author's Craft: Dialogue DOK 2

Christopher Paul Curtis uses figurative language as part of the dialogue throughout the story. Why is the use of this language appropriate? (*Bud, Not Buddy* is a historical fiction story written in a different era where people used slang and particular figures of speech related to that time period.)

Illustrator's Craft DOK 2

Have students review Floyd Cooper's illustrations throughout the story and discuss how they add to the author's characterization. Have students use this sentence frame:

This illustration shows characterization because . . .

Use text evidence to support your idea.

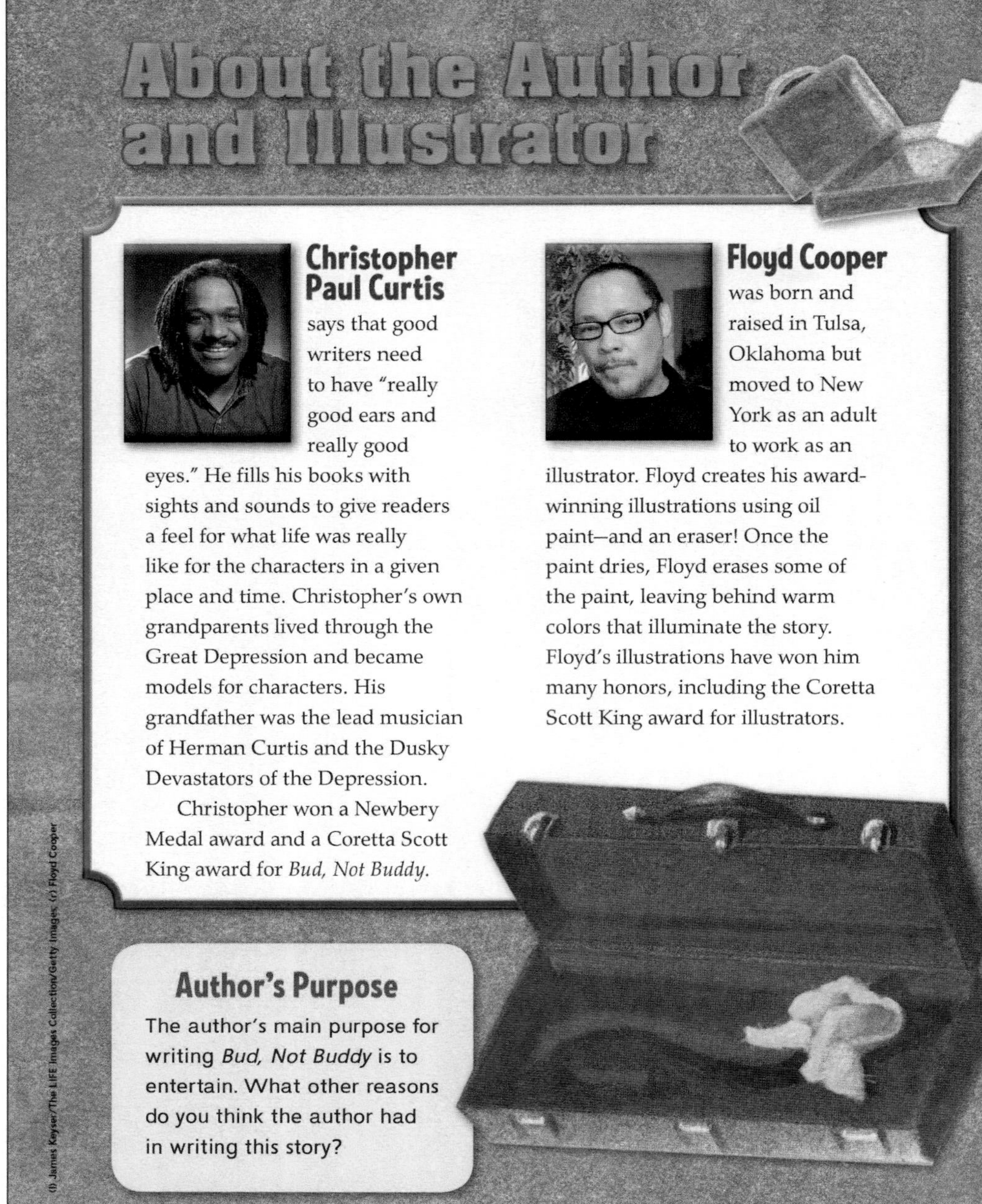

About the Author and Illustrator

Christopher Paul Curtis says that good writers need to have "really good ears and really good eyes." He fills his books with sights and sounds to give readers a feel for what life was really like for the characters in a given place and time. Christopher's own grandparents lived through the Great Depression and became models for characters. His grandfather was the lead musician of Herman Curtis and the Dusky Devastators of the Depression.

Christopher won a Newbery Medal award and a Coretta Scott King award for *Bud, Not Buddy*.

Floyd Cooper was born and raised in Tulsa, Oklahoma but moved to New York as an adult to work as an illustrator. Floyd creates his award-winning illustrations using oil paint—and an eraser! Once the paint dries, Floyd erases some of the paint, leaving behind warm colors that illuminate the story. Floyd's illustrations have won him many honors, including the Coretta Scott King award for illustrators.

Author's Purpose

The author's main purpose for writing *Bud, Not Buddy* is to entertain. What other reasons do you think the author had in writing this story?

(l) James Keyser/The LIFE Images Collection/Getty Images; (r) Floyd Cooper

380

Literature Anthology, p. 380

English Language Learners

Synonyms and Circumlocution Remind students that they can ask for synonyms to help clarify words, expressions, or phrases they do not understand. *What is another way of saying "illuminate the story"?* Explain that "illuminate" means "light up." Tell students warm colors are usually shades of red, yellow, and orange. *Warm colors remind us of warm things, like the sun.* Show examples of warm colors. *Cool colors are greens and blues.* Have partners look back at the illustrations in the story and describe how Cooper uses warm colors to illuminate the story.

Read

Summarize

Tell students they will use information from their graphic organizers to summarize the most important details of the story. As I read *Bud, Not Buddy,* I gathered information about how becoming a member of the band helps Bud adapt to life at Grand Calloway Station. To summarize, I will restate the most important details of the plot that help me reach this conclusion.

Reread

Analyze the Text

After students read and summarize the selection, have them reread to develop a deeper understanding of the story and answer the questions on **Reading/ Writing Companion** pages 50–52. For students who need support in citing text evidence, use the Reread prompts on pages T109–T122.

Integrate

Build Knowledge: Make Connections

Talk About the Text Have partners discuss the Essential Question: *How do shared experiences help people adapt to change?*

Write About the Text Have students add their ideas to their Build Knowledge page of their reader's notebook.

Anchor Chart Record any new ideas on the Build Knowledge anchor chart.

Add to the Vocabulary List Have students write down any words in their reader's notebook that they learned about how shared experiences help people adapt to change.

Compare Texts DOK 4

Have students compare how the authors present information in "The Day the Rollets Got Their Moxie Back" and *Bud, Not Buddy*. Ask: *What is similar about how shared experiences helped the characters adapt to change in "The Day the Rollets Got Their Moxie Back" and* Bud, Not Buddy*? What is different?*

FORMATIVE ASSESSMENT

STUDENT CHECK-IN

Read Have partners tell each other important details from the text. Then have them reflect using the Check-In routine.

Reread Have partners share responses and text evidence. Then ask them to use the Check-In routine to reflect and fill in the bars on Reading/Writing Companion pages 50–52.

LEARNING GOALS

We can use text evidence to respond to historical fiction.

OBJECTIVES

Describe in depth a character, setting, or event in a story or drama, drawing on specific details in the text (e.g., a character's thoughts, words, or actions).

Compare and contrast two or more characters, settings, or events in a story or drama, drawing on specific details in the text (e.g., how characters interact).

ELA ACADEMIC LANGUAGE

- *develop, conflict, perspective*
- Cognates: *conflicto, perspectiva*

TEACH IN SMALL GROUP

Approaching Level and **On Level** Have partners work together to plan and complete the response to the prompt.

Beyond Level Ask students to respond to the prompt independently.

ELL Group students of mixed proficiency levels to discuss and respond to the prompt.

Reread

10 mins

Write About the Anchor Text

Analyze the Prompt DOK 3

Read the prompt aloud: *What is the meaning behind Bud's original set of rules? How do they affect Bud's experiences as the story progresses?* Ask: *What is the prompt asking you to do?* (to explain the meaning behind Bud's set of rules and how they affect Bud as the story progresses) Say: *Let's reread to see how the author characterizes Bud and reveals his perspective over the course of the story. This will help us make inferences to answer the prompt.*

Analyze Text Evidence

Remind students that characters develop over the course of the story and that their perspectives are revealed by what they think, say, and do. Have students look at **Literature Anthology** page 371. Read the last three paragraphs. Ask: *What does Rules and Things Number 36 mean?* (It means that when Miss Thomas says she needs help deciding something, Bud thinks it means he has to go fetch something.) Read page 376 and ask: *What new rule does Bud learn?* (He learns that a musician in Mr. Calloway's band must practice for two hours a day.) *What event is learning this rule tied to?* (Bud is asked to travel with the band and receives an instrument of his own.) *Explain how being in the band has changed Bud.* (Being in the band has changed Bud because he has to learn to trust the band and become part of a family. He doesn't need to survive by himself.) Encourage students to look for more text evidence that shows how Bud's rules change and why the changes are significant.

Respond

Review pages 50–52 of the **Reading/Writing Companion.** Have partners or small groups refer to and discuss their completed charts and writing responses from those pages. Then direct students' attention to the sentence starters on page 53 of the Reading/Writing Companion. Have them use sentence starters to guide their responses.

Analytical Writing Students should focus on Bud's original set of rules that he follows at the beginning of the story and explain how and why those rules change. They should use text evidence in their response to support their ideas about why this is important. Students should focus on the development of Bud's character and how his interactions with the band members affects his perspective and advances the plot. Remind students to vary sentence structure by combining short sentences and adding phrases and clauses to others. Students may use additional paper to complete the assignment if needed.

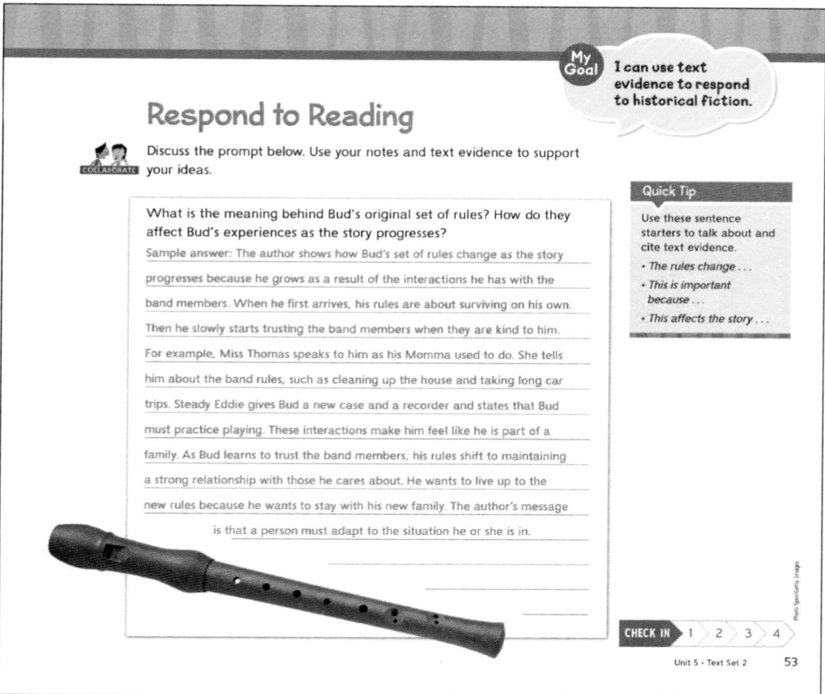

My Goal I can use text evidence to respond to historical fiction.

Respond to Reading

COLLABORATE Discuss the prompt below. Use your notes and text evidence to support your ideas.

What is the meaning behind Bud's original set of rules? How do they affect Bud's experiences as the story progresses?

Sample answer: The author shows how Bud's set of rules change as the story progresses because he grows as a result of the interactions he has with the band members. When he first arrives, his rules are about surviving on his own. Then he slowly starts trusting the band members when they are kind to him. For example, Miss Thomas speaks to him as his Momma used to do. She tells him about the band rules, such as cleaning up the house and taking long car trips. Steady Eddie gives Bud a new case and a recorder and states that Bud must practice playing. These interactions make him feel like he is part of a family. As Bud learns to trust the band members, his rules shift to maintaining a strong relationship with those he cares about. He wants to live up to the new rules because he wants to stay with his new family. The author's message is that a person must adapt to the situation he or she is in.

Quick Tip

Use these sentence starters to talk about and cite text evidence.

- *The rules change . . .*
- *This is important because . . .*
- *This affects the story . . .*

CHECK IN 1 2 3 4

Unit 5 • Text Set 2 53

Reading/Writing Companion, p. 53

English Language Learners

Use the following scaffolds with **Respond.**

Beginning

Restate the prompt: *Think about Bud's rules at the beginning of the story. Let's think about how those rules changed.* Have partners use details from their completed charts on **Reading/Writing Companion** pages 50–52 to talk about the rules. Help partners respond to the prompt: At first, Bud doesn't have a family. He has rules to keep out of trouble. At the end of the story, Bud feels like he's part of a family. His new rules are about helping and practicing with the band.

Intermediate

Read the prompt with students and discuss what they will write about. Have partners review their completed charts on Reading/Writing Companion pages 50–52 and use the sentence starters to discuss the prompt. Help them respond using: The author shows how Bud grows through his relationship with the band members. In the beginning, his rules are about surviving on his own. By the end, he trusts the band members. He feels like part of a family.

Advanced/Advanced High

Have partners review their completed charts on pages 50–52. Have partners take turns telling Bud's rules and why he formed them. Have partners use the sentence starters on page 53 to discuss why Bud has new rules at the end, why it's important, and how it affects the story.

ELL NEWCOMER

Have students listen to summaries of the **Anchor Text** in their native language and then in English to help them access the text and develop listening comprehension. Help students ask and answer questions with a partner. Use these *sentence frames*: Who is the main character? The main character is ____. Then have them complete the online **Newcomer Activities** individually or in pairs.

FORMATIVE ASSESSMENT

STUDENT CHECK-IN

Ask partners to share their response on Reading/Writing Companion page 53. Have them use the Check-In routine to reflect and fill in the bars.

"Musical Impressions of the Great Depression"

Lexile 990L

LEARNING GOALS

Read **We can apply strategies and skills to read expository text.**

Reread **We can reread to analyze text, craft, and structure and compare texts.**

Have students apply what they learned as they read.

What makes this text complex?

▶ **Specific Vocabulary**

Explain how examples of art, music, and literature reflect the times during which they were created.

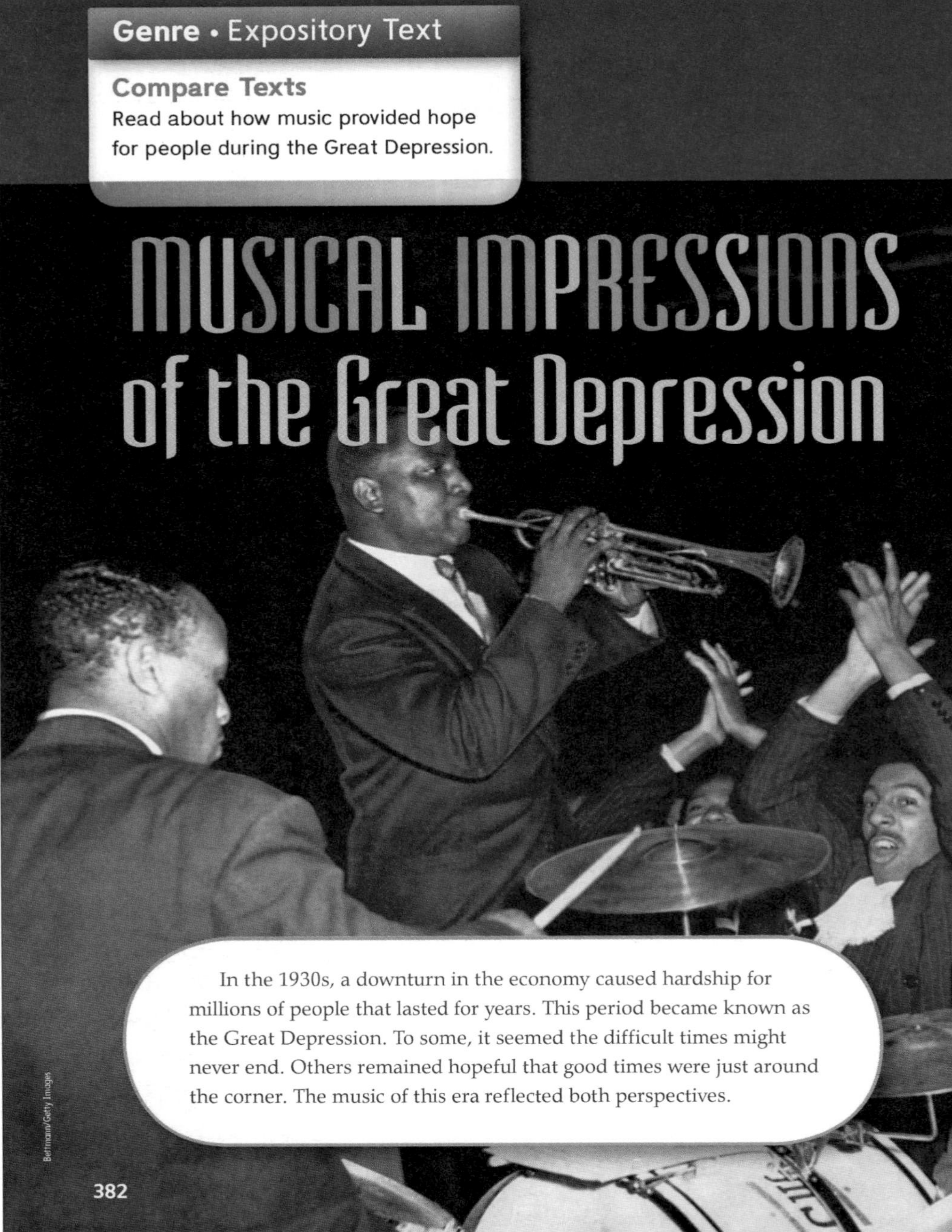

Genre • Expository Text
Compare Texts
Read about how music provided hope for people during the Great Depression.
MUSICAL IMPRESSIONS of the Great Depression
In the 1930s, a downturn in the economy caused hardship for millions of people that lasted for years. This period became known as the Great Depression. To some, it seemed the difficult times might never end. Others remained hopeful that good times were just around the corner. The music of this era reflected both perspectives.
382

Literature Anthology, pp. 382–383

Compare Texts DOK 4

Analytical Writing

As students read "Musical Impressions of the Great Depression," encourage them to take notes and think about the Essential Question: *How do shared experiences help people adapt to change?* Tell students to think about how different kinds of music united people from all over the country during this time of hardship. Then compare it to what they learned in *Bud, Not Buddy*. Students should discuss how these texts are similar and different.

Access Complex Text

Specific Vocabulary

Point out that a *stock market* is a system that allows people to put money into, or invest in, companies by buying stock. If a company does well, the stock price rises. If it does poorly or fails, the value of the stock falls. In 1929, the stock market collapsed and many people lost a lot of money. This collapse triggered a decade of widespread poverty—the Great Depression.

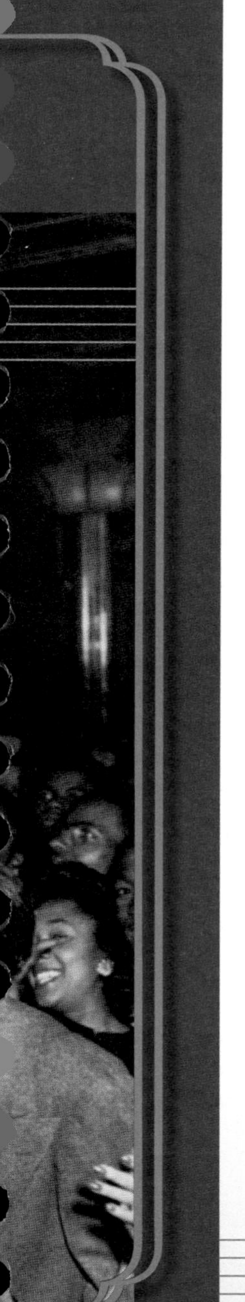

The Great Depression

After a decade of prosperity called the Roaring Twenties, economic progress in the United States changed abruptly. In October of 1929, the stock market collapsed and left thousands of investors broke. In turn, many companies laid off workers that they could no longer afford to pay. Around the same time, a massive drought destroyed crops and also left many farmers penniless. With so few resources, people across the country struggled to get by. 1

Sympathy through Song

Many songs of the 1930s, particularly in folk and country music, recounted people's stories of loss and hardship. The songwriter Woody Guthrie followed farm workers who traveled west to California hoping to find work. He saw that they often encountered new and tougher challenges. Guthrie expressed **sympathy** for them through songs like "Dust Bowl Blues" and "Goin' Down the Road Feeling Bad." He hoped to restore people's sense of dignity.

Meanwhile, across the country, The Carter Family performed similar songs, such as "Worried Man Blues," describing life in the Appalachian Mountains where resources were scarce. Listeners found comfort in the knowledge that they were not alone in their struggles.

During the 1930s, bands like this one (left) lifted people's spirits. Woody Guthrie (right) toured the country and composed songs about the challenges people faced.

Eric Schaal/The LIFE Picture Collection/Getty Images

383

Read

1 Central Idea and Relevant Details

DOK 2

What is the central idea of the section, "The Great Depression?" (The economy of the United States struggled after the stock market crash of 1929.)

Build Vocabulary on pages 382–383

economy: the wealth of a nation
drought: a long period of time without rain
recounted: told about or narrated
restore: to bring back

Reread

Author's Purpose DOK 2

Reread the section titled "The Great Depression" on page 383. Why did the author mention the decade of prosperity called the Roaring Twenties? (The author wanted to show that people and companies were surprised by and unprepared for the stock market crash. Because the economy had been extremely strong the previous decade, most people and companies probably expected it to remain strong and did not anticipate an economic crisis. This made things even worse.)

Read aloud the first two sentences on page 383.

- *Point out that prosperity comes from the word* prosper, *which means "to do very well." What happens to many businesses in a time of prosperity?* (They make a lot of money.)
- *"The Roaring Twenties" refers to a decade, a period of ten years. Which decade does it refer to?* (1920s)

Spotlight on Idioms

Page 383, Paragraph 1 Say: *"Few resources" refers to little money and not much food. "Struggle to get by" describes how people who don't have resources work hard to find jobs and feed their families. What are other resources people need?* (water, clothes, shelter) Ask partners to tell how people might struggle to get by to get those resources.

Read

❷ Text Structure: Problem and Solution DOK 2

What major challenge did African Americans face? (African Americans were faced with high unemployment. This reminded some people of earlier times of slavery.)

Build Vocabulary on page 385

promoted: encouraged

preserved: saved

Reread

Author's Purpose DOK 2

Reading/Writing Companion, p. 56

What is the author's purpose for writing this selection? (The author wanted to inform the reader about how people found comfort through music during the hardships of the Great Depression.)

Author's Craft: Idioms DOK 2

What does the author mean by saying "people left their problems behind them and escaped onto the dance floor?" (Swing music was "upbeat" and had "positive rhythms" that people could dance to. It lifted their spirits.)

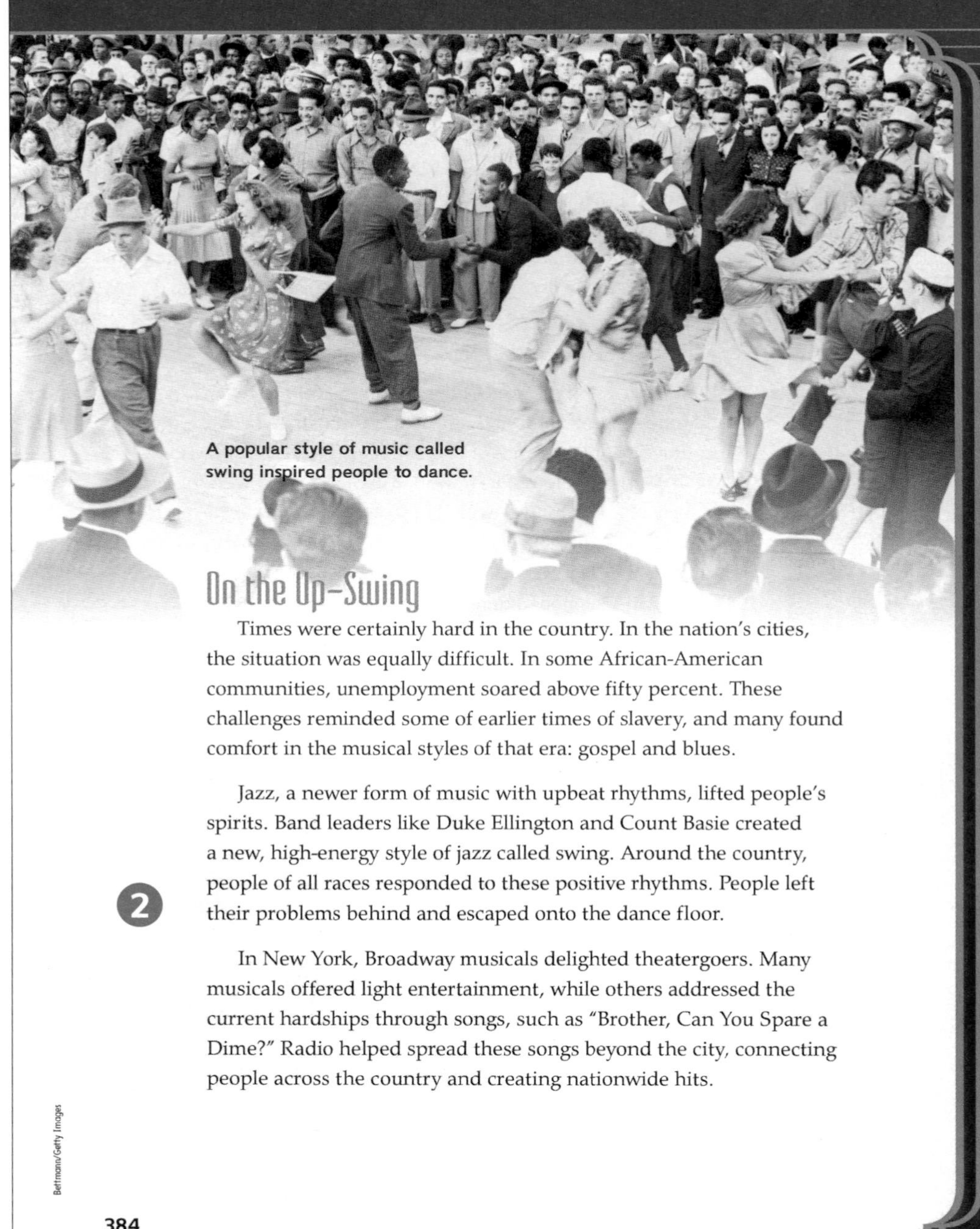

A popular style of music called swing inspired people to dance.

On the Up-Swing

Times were certainly hard in the country. In the nation's cities, the situation was equally difficult. In some African-American communities, unemployment soared above fifty percent. These challenges reminded some of earlier times of slavery, and many found comfort in the musical styles of that era: gospel and blues.

2 Jazz, a newer form of music with upbeat rhythms, lifted people's spirits. Band leaders like Duke Ellington and Count Basie created a new, high-energy style of jazz called swing. Around the country, people of all races responded to these positive rhythms. People left their problems behind and escaped onto the dance floor.

In New York, Broadway musicals delighted theatergoers. Many musicals offered light entertainment, while others addressed the current hardships through songs, such as "Brother, Can You Spare a Dime?" Radio helped spread these songs beyond the city, connecting people across the country and creating nationwide hits.

Bettmann/Getty Images

384

Literature Anthology, pp. 384–385

Access Complex Text

Specific Vocabulary

Help students understand terms from the section "Reaction from the Government."

- Legislation *means "law" or "lawmaking." What part of the word can help you remember this?* (The first part of the word is the same as in legal.)
- Explain that a federal project is one that is run by the national government. In the United States, each city and state has its own government, but the federal government is for the whole country.
- *What does the author mean by "federally supported concerts"?* (The term refers to concerts paid for by the U.S. government.)

Reaction from the Government

While some blamed the government for hard times, President Franklin Delano Roosevelt (FDR) created programs the public could **rely** on for assistance and new opportunities. This legislation became known as the New Deal. As part of a program called the Works Progress Administration, FDR initiated the Federal Music Project in 1935. His wife, Eleanor, promoted its main goals. These were to help musicians find work and to **guarantee** all people access to the arts, regardless of their financial situation.

Eleanor Roosevelt (standing, center) supported the work of musicians.

Before long, federally supported concerts and shows played on the radio and in music halls across the country. Throughout the nation, teachers provided free voice and instrument lessons to help promote participation and music appreciation. The government's **supportive** programs also paid musicians to travel and record styles of folk music from different regions. These recordings were preserved in our country's Library of Congress.

By the end of the 1930s, the hardest days of the Great Depression had passed. Times had been tough, but music had offered a way for people to share their fears and keep up their hopes. The music remains a legacy of this era that has inspired musicians to this day.

A poster for a government-funded performance

(a) Bettmann/Getty Images; (b) Library of Congress, Prints and Photographs Division LC-DIG-ppmsca-31186

Make Connections

How did the shared experience of music help people adapt to the changes caused by the Great Depression? ESSENTIAL QUESTION

How have characters in a story helped each other adapt to a change? How are their actions similar to the way people helped each other get through the Great Depression? TEXT TO TEXT

385

English Language Learners

Page 384, Paragraph 2 Help students understand "upbeat rhythms" and "lifted people's spirits." Tell students that here "upbeat rhythms" means fun or cheerful music. Explain that to "lift someone's spirit" means to make them happier. *Why did people need to have their spirits lifted during the depression?* (Sample answer: many people did not have jobs, times were hard.) Then ask, *what music lifts your spirits? Why?*

Read

Summarize

Guide students to summarize the selection.

Reread

Analyze the Text

After students read and summarize, have them reread and answer questions on pages 54–56 of the **Reading/Writing Companion.**

Integrate

Build Knowledge: Make Connections

Talk About the Text Have partners discuss how people adapt to change.

Write About the Text Have students add their ideas to their Build Knowledge pages of their reader's notebooks.

Anchor Chart Record any new ideas on the Build Knowledge anchor chart.

Add to the Vocabulary List Have students write down any words in their reader's notebooks that they learned about how shared experiences help people adapt to change.

Compare Texts DOK 4

Text to Text Answer: In the Great Depression, music helped people feel less alone. Evidence: In *Bud, Not Buddy,* Bud is happy when he becomes a member of the band. In "Musical Impressions of the Great Depression," programs were created to help musicians.

FORMATIVE ASSESSMENT

STUDENT CHECK-IN

Read Ask partners to share their summaries. Then have them reflect using the Check-In routine.

Reread Ask partners to share their responses on Reading/Writing Companion pages 54–56. Have them use the Check-In routine to reflect and fill in the bars.

LEARNING GOALS

We can identify text structure to help us read and understand expository text.

OBJECTIVES

Compare and contrast the overall structure of events, ideas, concepts, or information in two or more texts.

Determine or clarify the meaning of unknown and multiple-meaning words and phrases based on grade 5 reading and content, choosing flexibly from a range of strategies.

Consult reference material, both print and digital, to find the pronunciation and determine or clarify the precise meaning of key words and phrases.

Acquire and use accurately grade-appropriate general academic and domain-specific words and phrases, including those that signal contrast, addition, and other logical relationships.

ELA ACADEMIC LANGUAGE

- *text structure, compare, contrast, similarities, differences*
- Cognates: *estructura del texto, comparar, contrastar, diferencias*

Reread

Text Structure: Compare and Contrast

1 Explain

Have students turn to **Reading/Writing Companion** page 57. Share the following key points of a compare-and-contrast text structure.

- An author uses a compare-and-contrast text structure to organize similarities and differences about a central idea or concept. Within a text, authors might compare and contrast ideas, events, or people by explaining how those ideas, events, or people are alike and how they are different.
- Authors use key words that tell you something is being compared or contrasted. Words such as *like, also, in the same way, similarly, as well as, too,* and *equally* show that the author is comparing, or discussing the ways in which things are alike.
- Words such as *although, however, yet, but, instead, differ, on the other hand,* and *unless* show that the author is contrasting, or discussing the ways in which things are different.
- Comparing and contrasting to support a central idea helps an author clarify the idea for readers.

2 Model

Model identifying an example of compare-and-contrast text structure on page 55. Have students read paragraph 3. Point out the word *equally* in the second sentence. Explain that this word indicates that two things are similar. The comparison supports the idea that *everyone* struggled during this time—those who lived in the country as well as city residents. Discuss what other words can show a similarity between ideas.

3 Guided Practice

Guide students to reread paragraphs 1 and 2 on page 54. Ask: *Whose music is the focus of the first paragraph?* (Woody Guthrie) *What was the purpose of his music?* (Guthrie felt sympathy for farm workers traveling to find work in California, and he wanted his music to make them feel better about themselves.)

Have partners reread the second paragraph to identify the focus and purpose of the Carter family. Then have pairs discuss how the author compares and contrasts the two examples, noting any signal words used. Finally, have pairs identify the central idea, discussing the ways in which the compare-and-contrast text structure helps the author support ideas about people's struggles in the 1930s.

Allow students time to enter their responses on Reading/Writing Companion page 57.

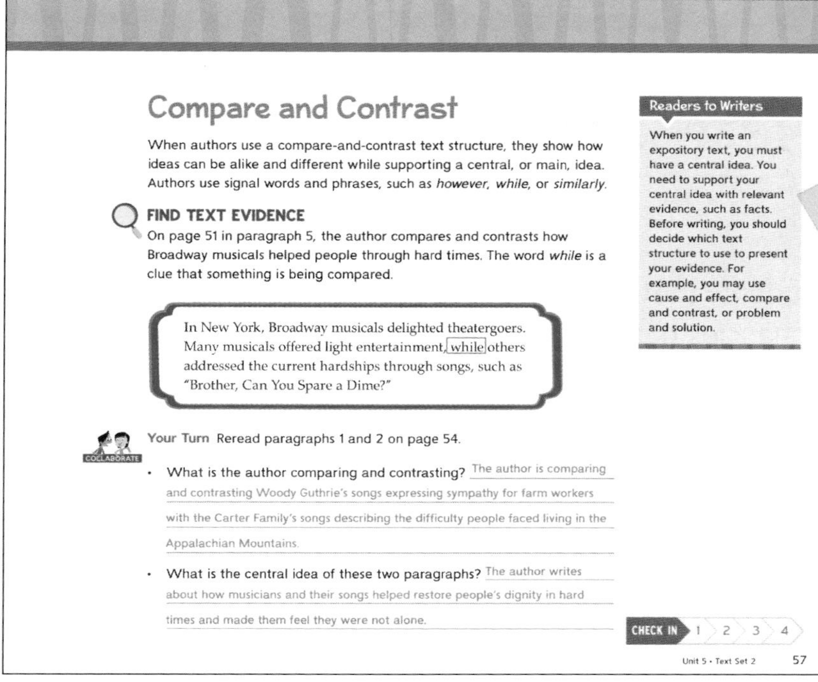

Compare and Contrast

When authors use a compare-and-contrast text structure, they show how ideas can be alike and different while supporting a central, or main, idea. Authors use signal words and phrases, such as *however, while,* or *similarly.*

FIND TEXT EVIDENCE

On page 51 in paragraph 5, the author compares and contrasts how Broadway musicals helped people through hard times. The word *while* is a clue that something is being compared.

> In New York, Broadway musicals delighted theatergoers. Many musicals offered light entertainment, while others addressed the current hardships through songs, such as "Brother, Can You Spare a Dime?"

Readers to Writers

When you write an expository text, you must have a central idea. You need to support your central idea with relevant evidence, such as facts. Before writing, you should decide which text structure to use to present your evidence. For example, you may use cause and effect, compare and contrast, or problem and solution.

COLLABORATE

Your Turn Reread paragraphs 1 and 2 on page 54.

- What is the author comparing and contrasting? The author is comparing and contrasting Woody Guthrie's songs expressing sympathy for farm workers with the Carter Family's songs describing the difficulty people faced living in the Appalachian Mountains.
- What is the central idea of these two paragraphs? The author writes about how musicians and their songs helped restore people's dignity in hard times and made them feel they were not alone.

CHECK IN 1 2 3 4

Unit 5 • Text Set 2 57

Reading/Writing Companion, p. 57

Readers to Writers

Remind students that authors of informational texts use text structure to present evidence for their central idea. Have them turn to "On the Up-Swing" on **Literature Anthology** page 384 of "Musical Impressions of the Great Depression." Say: *Identify the text structure that describes people's reactions to the new forms of music. How does this structure present evidence to support the author's central idea?*

English Language Learners

Use the following scaffolds with **Guided Practice.**

Beginning

Reread the first sentence on page 54 with students. Say: *Hardships are difficult things people have to do.* Then, use photos to help them describe the hardships people endured: During the Great Depression, people lived through many hardships. Guthrie sang about farm workers who had to travel far west to look for work. *Talk about how Guthrie's music could make the workers feel better about themselves.*

Intermediate

Have partners reread paragraphs 1–2 on page 54. Ask them to look up the word *hardship* in a dictionary. Have students define *hardship* in their own words and give examples of the hardships people had to live through during the Great Depression. Have partners talk of the hardships the Carter family sang about and compare and contrast their focus to Guthrie's.

Advanced/Advanced High

Have partners reread paragraph 1–2 on page 54 and then discuss the hardships that people endured during the Great Depression. Have students describe the types of music in the text and how each type could have helped people feel better.

FORMATIVE ASSESSMENT

STUDENT CHECK-IN

Ask partners to share their Your Turn responses on Reading/Writing Companion page 57. Then have them use the Check-In routine to reflect and fill in the bars.

LEARNING GOALS

- **We can identify and use words with the suffixes *-less* and *-ness*.**
- **We can identify and read multisyllabic words.**
- **We can read fluently with accuracy.**

OBJECTIVES

Know and apply grade-level phonics and word analysis skills in decoding words.

Use combined knowledge of all letter-sound correspondences, syllabication patterns, and morphology (e.g., roots and affixes) to read accurately unfamiliar multisyllabic words in context and out of context.

Use context to confirm or self-correct word recognition and understanding, rereading as necessary.

- Rate: 136–156 WCPM

ELA ACADEMIC LANGUAGE

- *suffix, define, accuracy*
- Cognates: *sufijo, definir*

TEACH IN SMALL GROUP

Word Study

Approaching Level Use the Tier 2 activity on page T143 before teaching the lesson.

On Level and **Beyond Level** As needed, use the Read Multisyllabic Words section only.

ELL See page 5 in the **Language Transfers Handbook** for guidance in identifying sounds and symbols that may not transfer for speakers of certain languages.

OPTION 10 mins

Suffixes *-less* and *-ness*

1 Explain

Review with students that a suffix is a word part added to the end of a word. A suffix changes the word's meaning as well as its part of speech.

Write the following suffixes and meanings on the board. Review the suffix *-less* and introduce the suffix *-ness* by reading each suffix, its meaning, and the sample word.

- ***-less***, means "without"
  thankless
- ***-ness***, means "state of being"
  kindness

Explain that *thankless* is an adjective that means "without thanks," and *kindness* is a noun that means "state of being kind."

2 Model

Write the following words on the board. Point to the first word, and model how to use knowledge of the suffix meaning to decode the word and figure out its meaning. Repeat the activity using the remaining words:

goodness	tireless	happiness
fearless	careless	ageless

3 Guided Practice

Write the following words on the board. Have students underline the suffix in each word, define the suffix, and then use its meaning to determine the meaning of the whole word.

darkness	hopeless	stainless	greatness
toothless	seamless	sweetness	gentleness
skinless	thoughtless	calmness	treeless
wingless	dryness	hairless	rightness
bitterness	clueless	brightness	colorless

For practice with suffixes, use **Practice Book** page 283 or online activities.

Read Multisyllabic Words

Transition to Longer Words Write on the board the following words with more than one suffix. Have students read a base word in the first column. Then model how to read the longer words in the second and third columns. To help students gain awareness of suffixes as common word parts, circle the suffix or suffixes added to each word.

help	helpless	helplessness
self	selfless	selflessness
worth	worthless	worthlessness
time	timeless	timelessness
use	useless	uselessness

To review prefixes and suffixes, guide students to decode the following words: *unhappiness, hopefulness, healthfulness, unkindness.*

Fluency

Accuracy

Explain/Model Explain that reading with accuracy means reading each word as it appears on the page and pronouncing words correctly. Read aloud the first four paragraphs of "The Day the Rollets Got Their Moxie Back" from the **Reading/Writing Companion** page 35. Model reading with accuracy.

Practice/Apply Have partners take turns reading page 35. As one student reads, have the other student follow along, checking for accuracy. Afterward, have students review any skipped or mispronounced words. Remind students that you will be listening for accuracy as you monitor their reading during the week.

Daily Fluency Practice

Automaticity Students can practice reading with accuracy and appropriate rate to develop automaticity using the online **Differentiated Genre Passage,** "Nancy's First Interview."

DIGITAL TOOLS

For more practice, have students use the phonics and fluency activities.

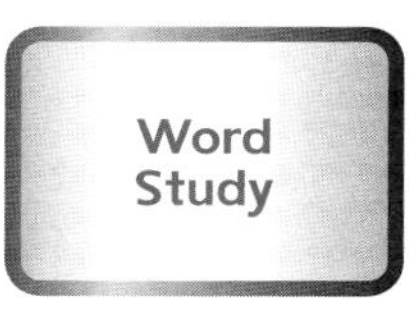

Suffixes

MULTIMODAL LEARNING

Record yourself reading aloud the **Differentiated Genre Passage** "Nancy's First Interview." Have small groups listen to the recording and then read aloud with it as they track the text with a finger. Have them answer the questions, *Did I say each word with the recording? Did I pause meaningfully between phrases and for punctuation marks along with the recording? Did I read fluently?*

FORMATIVE ASSESSMENT

STUDENT CHECK-IN

Suffixes Have partners share three words with the suffixes *-less* and *-ness.*

Mutlisyllabic Words Have partners add suffixes to the following words: *end, weak,* and *careless.*

Fluency Ask partners to read "Nancy's First Interview" fluently.

Have partners reflect using the Check-In routine.

CHECK FOR SUCCESS

Can students read words with suffixes *-less* and *-ness*? Can students read fluently?

Small Group Instruction

If No:

- **Approaching** Reteach pp. T143, T146
- **ELL** Develop p. T143

If Yes:

- **On** Apply p. T148
- **Beyond** Apply p. T154

LEARNING GOALS

We can compare the photo with the selections in this text set to build knowledge about how shared experiences help people adapt to change.

OBJECTIVES

Analyze how visual and multimedia elements contribute to the meaning, tone, or beauty of a text.

Integrate information from several texts on the same topic in order to write or speak about the subject knowledgeably.

Close Reading Routine

Read DOK 1–2

- Identify important ideas and details.
- Take notes and summarize.
- Use ACT prompts as needed.

Reread DOK 2–3

- Analyze the text, craft, and structure.
- Use the ***Reading/Writing Companion***.

Integrate DOK 3–4

- Integrate knowledge and ideas.
- Make text-to-text connections.
- Use the Integrate/Make Connections lesson.
- Use ***Reading/Writing Companion***, p. 58.
- Complete the Show Your Knowledge task.
- Inspire action.

FORMATIVE ASSESSMENT

STUDENT CHECK-IN

Ask partners to share their response. Have them use the Check-In routine to reflect and fill in the bars on Reading/Writing page 58.

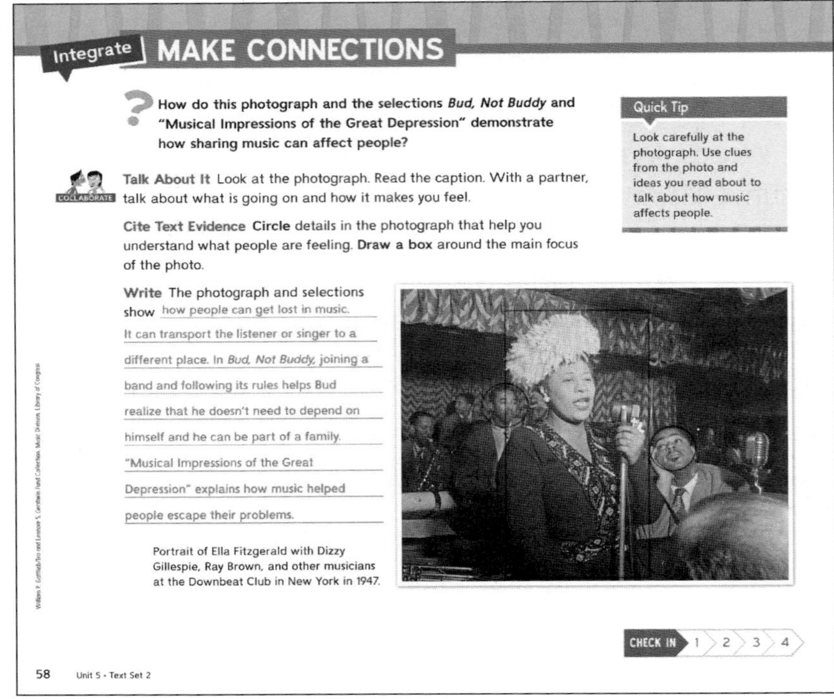
Integrate | MAKE CONNECTIONS

How do this photograph and the selections *Bud, Not Buddy* and "Musical Impressions of the Great Depression" demonstrate how sharing music can affect people?

COLLABORATE **Talk About It** Look at the photograph. Read the caption. With a partner, talk about what is going on and how it makes you feel.

Cite Text Evidence **Circle** details in the photograph that help you understand what people are feeling. **Draw a box** around the main focus of the photo.

Write The photograph and selections show how people can get lost in music. It can transport the listener or singer to a different place. In *Bud, Not Buddy,* joining a band and following its rules helps Bud realize that he doesn't need to depend on himself and he can be part of a family. "Musical Impressions of the Great Depression" explains how music helped people escape their problems.

Quick Tip

Look carefully at the photograph. Use clues from the photo and ideas you read about to talk about how music affects people.

Portrait of Ella Fitzgerald with Dizzy Gillespie, Ray Brown, and other musicians at the Downbeat Club in New York in 1947.

CHECK IN 1 2 3 4

58 Unit 5 • Text Set 2

Reading/Writing Companion, p. 58

Integrate

Make Connections DOK 4

Talk About It

Share and discuss students' responses to the "Shared Experiences" blast. Display the Build Knowledge anchor chart. Review the chart and have students read through their notes, annotations, and responses for each text. Then ask students to complete the Talk About It activity on **Reading/Writing Companion** page 58.

Cite Text Evidence

Guide students to see the connections between the photograph on Reading/Writing Companion page 58 and the selections in this text set. Remind students to read the photograph's caption and the Quick Tip.

Write

Students should refer to their notes on the chart as they respond to the writing prompt at the bottom of the page. When students have finished, have groups share and discuss their responses.

Build Knowledge: Make Connections

Talk About the Text Have partners discuss how shared experiences can help people adapt to change.

Write About the Text Have students add their ideas to their Build Knowledge pages of their reader's notebooks.

Anchor Chart Record any new ideas on the Build Knowledge anchor chart.

SHOW YOUR KNOWLEDGE

My Goal: I know how sharing experiences helps people change.

Write Song Lyrics

Many characters you read about used music to help them cope during the Great Depression. What qualities do they share that helped them triumph over their hardships and disappointments?

1. Look at your Build Knowledge notes in your reader's notebook.
2. Write song lyrics that describe the qualities the characters have in common that helped them triumph over the hardships and disappointments of the time.
3. Use examples from the texts you read. Use the new vocabulary words you learned.

Think about what you learned in this text set. Fill in the bars on page 37.

Unit 5 • Text Set 2 59

Reading/Writing Companion, p. 59

Integrate

10 mins

Show Your Knowledge DOK 4

Write Song Lyrics

Explain to students that they will show how they built knowledge across the text set based on what they read by writing song lyrics about how shared experiences help people adapt to change. Display the Build Knowledge anchor chart and ask: *How has a shared experience helped you adapt to change?*

COLLABORATE

Step 1 Guide partners to review the Build Knowledge anchor chart and notes in their reader's notebook to discuss the prompt.

Step 2 Discuss some of the character traits likely to help people adapt to change. Ask students to write examples from the text sets and to also include examples from the video and listening passage.

Step 3 Encourage students to think about what musical qualities make songs enjoyable, such as rhyme, meter, and repetition, and to consider this when writing their own song lyrics. Prompt students to use words from their Build Knowledge vocabulary list in their reader's notebook.

Inspire Action

Share Your Song Lyrics Have partners present their song lyrics and display them. Students can use sticky notes to post comments under the song lyrics on display. Presenters can respond if they want.

What Are You Inspired to Do? Have students talk about the texts they read this week. Ask: *What else do the texts inspire you to do?*

LEARNING GOALS

We can write song lyrics to show the knowledge we built about how shared experiences help people adapt to change.

OBJECTIVES

Write routinely over extended time frames and shorter time frames for a range of discipline-specific tasks, purposes, and audiences.

Come to discussions prepared, having read or studied required material; explicitly draw on that preparation and other information known about the topic to explore ideas under discussion.

ELA ACADEMIC LANGUAGE

- *character traits, rhyme, meter*
- Cognates: *rima, métrica*

DIGITAL TOOLS

RUBRIC

Show Your Knowledge Rubric

ENGLISH LANGUAGE LEARNERS

Provide sentence frames for support. *Some character traits that help people adapt to change are ____. For example, we read about ____.*

MY GOALS ROUTINE

What I Learned

Review Goals Have children turn back to Reading/Writing Companion page 37 and review the goals for the text set.

Reflect Have students think about the progress they've made toward the goals. Review the key. Then have students reflect and fill in the bars.

LEARNING GOALS

- **We can build and expand on new vocabulary words.**
- **We can use context clues to figure out the meanings of idioms.**
- **We can write using new vocabulary words.**

OBJECTIVES

Demonstrate understanding of figurative language, word relationships, and nuances in word meanings.

Recognize and explain the meaning of common idioms, adages, and proverbs.

Use the relationship between particular words (e.g., synonyms, antonyms, homographs) to better understand each of the words.

Expand vocabulary by adding inflectional endings and suffixes.

DIGITAL TOOLS

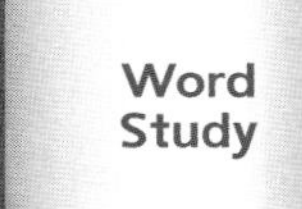

ENGLISH LANGUAGE LEARNERS

Pair students of different language proficiency levels to practice vocabulary. Have partners discuss how to build vocabulary by adding endings to roots such as *weak*.

FORMATIVE ASSESSMENT

STUDENT CHECK-IN

After each lesson, have partners share and reflect using the Check-In routine.

Connect to Words

Practice the target vocabulary.

1. What do you **assume** will happen this week?
2. Why do stores **guarantee** their products?
3. Whom would you **nominate** as the nicest person you know?
4. Describe a time when you were **obviously** wrong.
5. Whom do you **rely** on?
6. Who is **supportive** of you?
7. When do people usually feel **sympathy**?
8. When might someone feel like a **weakling**?

Related Words

Help students generate different forms of this text set's words by adding, changing, or removing inflectional endings.

- Draw a four-column chart on the board. Write *assume* in the first column. Then write *assumes, assumed,* and *assuming* in the other columns. Read aloud the words with students.
- Have students share sentences using each form of *assume*.
- Students should add to the chart for *guarantee, nominate,* and *rely* and share sentences using the different forms of the words.
- Have students copy the chart in their reader's notebooks.

See **Practice Book** page 275.

Build Vocabulary

- Display *employment, productions,* and *economic.*
- Define the words and discuss their meanings with students.
- Write *employ* under *employment.* Have partners write other words with the same root and define them. Then have partners ask and answer questions using the words.
- Repeat with *productions* and *economic.*

Puns

Remind students that puns use words or phrases in funny ways to suggest different meanings. Write: *Alaska is a cool place.* Discuss why the sentence has different possible meanings.

- Have partners brainstorm puns.
- Have students write their puns in their reader's notebooks.

See **Practice Book** page 287.

Spiral Review

Lesson 3 Reinforce the Words

Review the vocabulary words from last text set and this one. Have students orally complete each sentence stem.

1. Don't assume someone is a weakling because ____.
2. I guarantee that we will finish the ____.
3. The class will nominate Carlos for ____.
4. He obviously felt sympathy for Lisa because ____.

Display the previous text set's vocabulary words: *approximately, astronomical, calculation, diameter, orbit, spheres*. Have partners ask and answer questions using each of the words.

See **Practice Book** page 276.

Option Lesson 4 Connect to Writing

- Have students write sentences in their reader's notebooks using this text set's vocabulary.
- Tell them to write sentences that provide word information they learned from this text set's readings.
- ELL Provide the Lesson 3 sentence stems 1-4 for students needing extra support.

Write Using Vocabulary

Have students write something they learned from this text set's words in their reader's notebooks. For example, they might write about how people need to be *supportive* of each other and to *rely* on one another when going through a difficult time.

Option Lesson 5 Word Squares

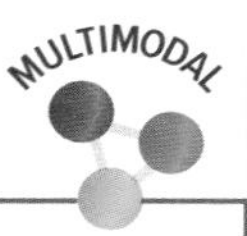

Ask students to create Word Squares for each vocabulary word.

- In the first square, students write the word (e.g., *guarantee*).
- In the second square, students write their own definition of the word and any related words, such as synonyms (e.g., *promise, assure, pledge*).
- In the third square, students draw a simple illustration that will help them remember the word (e.g., drawing of two people shaking hands).
- In the fourth square, students write nonexamples, including antonyms for the word (e.g., *disregard, undermine*).

Have partners discuss their squares.

Lesson 8 Idioms

Explain that idioms cannot be understood literally.

- Display On Level **Differentiated Genre Passage** "Nancy's First Interview." Model how to figure out the meaning of the idiom "putting me on the spot" in the first paragraph on page O1.
- Have pairs figure out the meaning of "She's a chip off the old block" in the last paragraph on page O2.
- Have students write the meanings of the idioms in their reader's notebooks.

See **Practice Book** page 288.

Option Lesson 9 Shades of Meaning

Help students generate synonyms for *rely*. Draw a word web. Write *rely* in the center circle.

- Have partners generate words to add to the word web. Ask students to use a thesaurus.
- Add words and phrases not included, such as *depend, trust in, count on, be sure of*.
- Ask students to copy the words in their reader's notebooks.

Option Lesson 10 Morphology

Draw a T-chart. Write *nominate* in the left column.

- In the right column of the T-chart, write *-ion* and *-or*. Discuss how the suffixes change the meaning and part of speech.
- Then add the suffixes to *nominate*. Review the meanings.
- Ask partners to do a search for other words with these suffixes.

Write Using Vocabulary

Have students use vocabulary words in their extended writing.

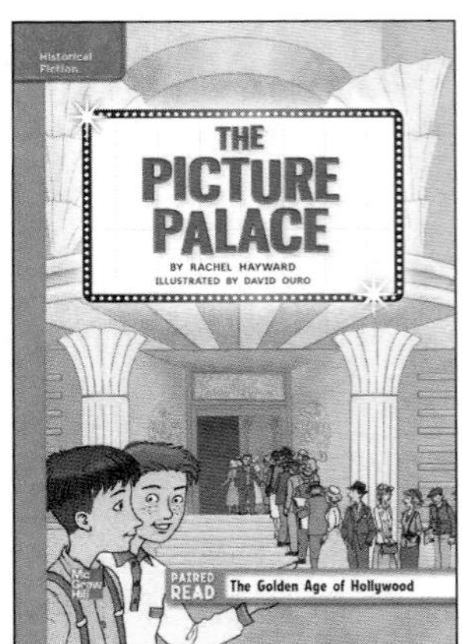

Lexile 710L

OBJECTIVES

Quote accurately from a text when explaining what the text says explicitly and when drawing inferences from the text.

Compare and contrast two or more characters, settings, or events in a story or drama, drawing on specific details in the text (e.g., how characters interact).

Read grade-level prose and poetry orally with accuracy, appropriate rate, expression, and automaticity on successive readings.

ELA ACADEMIC LANGUAGE

- *historical fiction, compare, contrast, characters, idiom*
- Cognates: *ficción histórica, comparar, contrastar*

Approaching Level

Leveled Reader: *The Picture Palace*

Preview and Predict

- Read the Essential Question: *How do shared experiences help people adapt to change?*
- Have students preview the title, table of contents, and first page of *The Picture Palace*. Students should consider the characteristics of historical fiction and use the illustrations to predict what they think the selection will be about. Tell them they should try to make, confirm, or correct their predictions as they read.

Review Genre: Historical Fiction

Tell students this text is historical fiction. Historical fiction features settings that could have existed and events that could have taken place during a particular period in history. The characters act and talk like people from that particular time and place. Historical fiction often contains both real and made-up events and characters. As students read, have them identify features of historical fiction in *The Picture Palace*.

Close Reading

Note Taking Ask students to use **Graphic Organizer 10** as they read.

Pages 2–4 *Compare and contrast the impact the stock market crash had on Frank's family and Joey's family.* (Frank's father lost his job and had to get a lower-paying one, and the family had to sell their house. Still, they have an apartment and enough food. Joey's family is evicted because they are unable to pay rent.) *What does the idiom "cute as a bug's ear" mean?* (It must mean "very cute or sweet." Mrs. Fisher thinks that Joey is a nice boy.) Have students add this idiom in their reader's notebooks.

Pages 5–7 *Compare and contrast the ways Frank and Joey respond to Marie.* (Frank says he is too busy, but Joey stops to play with her.) *Turn to a partner and make a prediction about how the window washing will turn out.* (The boys will make enough money to go to the movies.)

Pages 8–10 *Turn to a partner and tell if your prediction matched the text or how you revised it.* (It did not match the text, because no one wanted their help. I now think they will win the money at Bank Night.)

Paraphrase how the boys respond to the conflict. (They try to wash windows in a wealthier part of town. When the man's papers scatter, Joey quickly collects them.) *What does the idiom "you shred it, wheat" mean?* (Joey agrees with Frank, so it must mean "you're right.") Have students add this idiom in their reader's notebooks.

Pages 11–13 *Why does Frank tell Joey to "go low"?* (It will make it easier to get through the crowd.) *Turn to a partner and make a prediction about Joey's success.* (Joey will win the money.)

Pages 14–15 *Did your prediction match the text, or did you need to revise it?* (It matched; Joey wins the money.) *What happens afterward?* (He gets a job delivering papers.) *How does the boys' shared experience help them adapt to change?* (They find success by helping each other.)

Respond to Reading Revisit the Essential Question and ask students to complete the Text Evidence Questions on page 16.

Write About Reading Check that students have described a change Joey might have to make to start work early daily.

Fluency: Rate

Model Model reading page 4 with appropriate rate, or speed. Then read the passage aloud and have students read along.

Apply Have students practice reading the passage with partners.

Paired Read: "The Golden Age of Hollywood"

Make Connections: Write About It

Before reading, ask students to note that the genre of this text is expository text. Then discuss the Essential Question. After reading, ask students to write about connections between *The Picture Palace* and "The Golden Age of Hollywood."

Leveled Reader

Build Knowledge

Talk About the Text Have partners discuss how shared experiences can help people adapt to change.

Write About the Text Have students add their ideas to the Build Knowledge pages of their reader's notebooks.

FOCUS ON GENRE

Have students complete the activity on page 20 to learn how historical settings can be used to tell a story.

LITERATURE CIRCLES

Ask students to conduct a literature circle using the Thinkmark questions to guide the discussion. You may wish to have a whole-class discussion, using both selections in the Leveled Reader, about how shared experiences help people adapt to change.

LEVEL UP

IF students read the Approaching Level fluently and answered the questions,

THEN pair them with students who have proficiently read the On Level and have students

- echo-read the On Level main selection.
- identify two aspects that help them know that the story is historical fiction.

ACT Access Complex Text

The On Level challenges students by including more **idioms** and **complex sentence structures**.

"Nancy's First Interview"
Lexile 670L

OBJECTIVES

Compare and contrast two or more characters, setting, or events in a story or drama, drawing on specific details in text (e.g., how characters interact).

Determine the meaning of words and phrases as they are used in a text, including figurative language such as metaphors and similes.

Demonstrate understanding of figurative language, word relationships, and nuances in word meanings.

ELA ACADEMIC LANGUAGE

- *compare, contrast, characters, idiom, dialect*
- Cognates: *comparar, contrastar, dialecto*

Approaching Level

Genre Passage: "Nancy's First Interview"

Build Background

- Read aloud the Essential Question: *How do shared experiences help people adapt to change?* Ask students to compare two characters from the historical fiction texts they have read in this text set. Provide the following sentence starters:

  I read that the Great Depression was . . .

  This helps me understand that the characters . . .

- Tell students that after the stock market crashed in 1929, many lost their jobs, including migrant workers, who had to move to new locations to find work. Let students know that the online **Differentiated Genre Passage** "Nancy's First Interview" portrays the experiences of two families during the Great Depression, one of which includes migrant workers. Use the photograph and caption on page A2 to make predictions about the story.

Review Genre: Historical Fiction

Remind students that historical fiction features characters, settings, and plot events that are similar to those from a certain period in history. Historical fiction can include real as well as made-up events and characters.

Close Reading

Note Taking As students read the passage the first time, ask them to annotate the text and note relevant details, unfamiliar words, and questions they have. Then read again and use text evidence to answer the questions.

Read

Idioms Read paragraph 1 on page A1. *What does Mr. Jenson mean when he says that the caller is "putting him on the spot"?* (The caller is forcing him to make a hard choice.) *Why does this create a problem for Mr. Jenson?* (He already has plans with Nancy.)

Genre: Historical Fiction Read the second paragraph on page A1. *What detail helps you know that this story is historical fiction?* (The story takes place after the stock market crash of 1929.)

Plot: Conflict Read paragraph 3 on page A1. *Compare and contrast how Nancy and her father react to their plans being canceled.* (Mr. Jenson is sad and disappointed. Nancy is disappointed, too, but forces a smile.)

Plot: Characterization Read paragraph 4 on page A2. *Find an example of dialect the author uses.* (Mr. Jenson calls the Carters "you folks.")

Plot: Conflict Read paragraph 8 on page A2. *How did Nancy first feel when she met the Carters?* (She felt guilty that she lived in a larger house.) *How have her feelings changed?* (She now realizes that her family is a lot like the Carters because they support each other.)

COLLABORATE **Summarize** Have students use their notes to summarize how the historical setting influenced the story's characters and plot events.

Reread

Use the questions on page A3 to guide students' rereading of the passage.

Author's Craft Reread the third paragraph on page A1. *Why has Nancy's fishing trip been canceled?* (Her dad has to work.) *How do you know she is disappointed about not being able to go fishing?* (The author describes Nancy's actions. For example, the author writes, "Nancy tried not to look upset" and forced "a smile.")

Author's Craft Reread the third paragraph on page A2. *What does this paragraph help you understand about the Carters?* (The author describes how little the Carters have and how hard their life is now.)

Author's Craft Reread paragraph 9 on page A2. *"Y'all" is an example of dialect. Why do you think the author uses dialect in this story?* (The author wanted the Carters to sound like people from a particular place.)

Integrate

COLLABORATE **Make Connections** Guide students to recognize connections between "Nancy's First Interview" and other selections they have read. Guide partners to look for evidence that helps them identify how the authors help readers understand why people find it easier to get through difficult experiences together.

Compare Texts Write *Shared Experiences* in the center circle of a word web. Guide students to complete the outer circles with what they've learned about how people deal with these experiences.

Build Knowledge

Talk About the Text Have partners discuss how shared experiences can help people adapt to change.

Write About the Text Have students add their ideas to the Build Knowledge pages of their reader's notebooks.

Differentiate and Collaborate

COLLABORATE **Be inspired** Guide students to think about "Nancy's First Interview" and other selections they have read. Ask: *What do the texts inspire you to do?* Use the following activities or have pairs of students think of a way to respond to the texts.

Create a Correspondence Write a series of letters between two friends who live during the time of the Great Depression. Your letters should reflect the ways the friends help each other get through the experience.

Design a Poster Think about an event that a community in 1929 might have planned to help people. Create a poster that shows how the event would bring people together.

Readers to Writers

Word Choice Remind students that descriptive words help authors create a picture in readers' minds. Have students reread the third paragraph on page A2. Ask: *What words does the author use to describe the Carter's home? How do these words help you imagine what it's like?*

LEVEL UP

IF students read the Approaching Level fluently and answered the questions,

THEN pair them with students who have proficiently read the On Level. Have them

- partner read the On Level passage.
- summarize how Nancy has changed by the end of the story.

Approaching Level

Word Study/Decoding

REVIEW WORDS WITH PREFIXES

OBJECTIVES

Know and apply grade-level phonics and word analysis skills in decoding words.

Use combined knowledge of all letter-sound correspondences, syllabication patterns, and morphology (e.g., roots and affixes) to read accurately unfamiliar multisyllabic words in context and out of context.

Decode words with prefixes.

I Do Review with students that a prefix is a group of letters added to the beginning of a word that changes that word's meaning. Write the verbs *place* and *view* on the board and review their meanings. Then add the prefix *mis-* to *place* and the prefix *pre-* to *view* to create new words: *misplace, preview*. Explain how the meaning of each prefix ("wrong," "before") changes the meaning of the original word.

We Do Write the words *miscount* and *precook* on the board. Read the words aloud and underline each prefix. Tell what each word means, emphasizing the meaning of the prefix. Then write these words on the board: *misuse, predate*. Guide students to identify each prefix and use its meaning to determine the meaning of each word.

You Do Add the following examples to the board: *misbehave, prewash*. Have students identify each prefix, tell its meaning, and give the meaning of each word.

PRACTICE WORDS WITH PREFIXES

OBJECTIVES

Know and apply grade-level phonics and word analysis skills in decoding words.

Use combined knowledge of all letter-sound correspondences, syllabication patterns, and morphology (e.g., roots and affixes) to read accurately unfamiliar multisyllabic words in context and out of context.

Practice words with prefixes.

I Do Write *imbalance, disable,* and *incomplete* on the board. Read the words aloud, identify each prefix and its meaning, and define each word.

We Do Write the words *immature, disappoint,* and *insincere* on the board. Help students identify and define each prefix and then use this information to determine the meaning of each word.

Display the following words. Read aloud the first word, identify the prefix, and give the word's meaning.

incapable	irregular	disconnect
preseason	impossible	misunderstand

You Do Have students read the remaining words aloud. Ask them to identify each prefix and define each word. Afterward, point to the words in random order for students to read chorally.

REVIEW SUFFIXES

TIER 2

OBJECTIVES

Know and apply grade-level phonics and word analysis skills in decoding words.

Use combined knowledge of all letter-sound correspondences, syllabication patterns, and morphology (e.g., roots and affixes) to read accurately unfamiliar multisyllabic words in context and out of context.

Decode words with suffixes *-less* and *-ness*.

I Do Review that a suffix is a group of letters added to the end of a base word that changes that word's meaning. Remind students that *-less* is a suffix that means "without" and *-ness* is a suffix that means "state of being."

We Do Write the words *careless* and *goodness* on the board. Read each word aloud and model using the meaning of the suffix to determine that *careless* means "without care" and *goodness* means "state of being good." Then write the words *clueless* and *happiness* on the board. Guide students to use the meaning of the suffix to define each word.

You Do Write *hopeless* and *kindness* on the board. Have students identify the suffix, tell its meaning, and define each word.

PRACTICE WORDS WITH SUFFIXES *-less* AND *-ness*

OBJECTIVES

Know and apply grade-level phonics and word analysis skills in decoding words.

Use combined knowledge of all letter-sound correspondences, syllabication patterns, and morphology (e.g., roots and affixes) to read accurately unfamiliar multisyllabic words in context and out of context.

Practice words with suffixes *-less* and *-ness*.

I Do Write these words on the board: *darkness, harmless*. Read the words aloud, identify each suffix and its meaning, and give the meaning of each word.

We Do Display the words *illness, forgiveness, powerless,* and *worthless*. Model how to determine the meaning of the first word using the suffix. Then have students determine the meaning of each of the remaining words.

To provide additional practice, write the following words on the board. Read aloud the first word, identify the suffix, and give the word's meaning.

boldness	freshness	aimless	dizziness
cloudless	bossiness	cordless	odorless

You Do Have students read aloud the remaining words. Ask them to identify each suffix and give the meaning of each word. Afterward, point to the words in random order for students to read chorally.

ELL For **ELL** students who need phonics and decoding practice, define words and help them use the words in sentences, scaffolding to ensure their understanding. See the **Language Transfers Handbook** for phonics elements that may not transfer from students' native languages.

Approaching Level

Vocabulary

REVIEW HIGH-FREQUENCY WORDS

TIER 2

OBJECTIVES

Acquire and use accurately grade-appropriate general academic and domain-specific words and phrases, including those that signal contrast, addition, and other logical relationships (e.g., *however, although, nevertheless, similarly, moreover, in addition*).

I Do Use **High-Frequency Word Cards** 181–200. Display one word at a time, following the routine:

Display the word. Read the word. Then spell the word.

We Do Ask students to state the word and spell the word with you. Model using the word in a sentence and have students repeat the sentence after you.

You Do Display the word. Ask students to say the word and spell it. When completed, quickly flip through the word card set as students chorally read the words. Provide opportunities for students to use the words in speaking and writing. For example, provide sentence starters, such as *I want some* ____. Ask students to write each word in their reader's notebooks.

REVIEW ACADEMIC VOCABULARY

OBJECTIVES

Acquire and use accurately grade-appropriate general academic and domain-specific words and phrases, including those that signal contrast, addition, and other logical relationships (e.g., *however, although, nevertheless, similarly, moreover, in addition*).

I Do Display each **Visual Vocabulary Card** and state the word. Explain how the photograph illustrates the word. State the example sentence and repeat the word.

We Do Point to the word on the card and read the word with students. Ask them to repeat the word. Engage students in structured partner talk about the image as prompted on the back of the vocabulary card.

You Do Display each visual in random order, hiding the word. Have students match the definitions and context sentences of the words to the visuals displayed.

You may wish to review high-frequency words with ELL students using the lesson above.

UNDERSTAND ACADEMIC VOCABULARY

OBJECTIVES

Acquire and use accurately grade-appropriate general academic and domain-specific words and phrases, including those that signal contrast, addition, and other logical relationships (e.g., *however, although, nevertheless, similarly, moreover, in addition*).

I Do Display the *assume* **Visual Vocabulary Card**. Ask: *What would you assume if someone was crying?* Explain that you would assume, or suppose, that the person was upset.

We Do Ask these questions and help students respond and explain their answers:

- What is something you might *guarantee* your parents?
- Who would you *nominate* for class president?
- Why should exit signs be *obviously* marked?

You Do Have pairs respond to these questions and explain their answers:

- When have you felt *sympathy* for a friend?
- What might you tell a friend who feels like a *weakling*?
- Who is someone you *rely* on?
- What might a *supportive* coach say to you?

Have students pick words from their reader's notebooks and use an online thesaurus to find words with similar meanings.

IDIOMS

OBJECTIVES

Demonstrate understanding of figurative language, word relationships, and nuances in word meanings.

Recognize and explain the meaning of common idioms, adages, and proverbs.

I Do Display the Approaching Level of "Nancy's First Interview" in the online **Differentiated Genre Passages**. Read aloud the first and second paragraphs on page A1. Point to the idiom *skeleton crew*. Tell students that they can look for context clues to figure out the meaning of the idiom.

Think Aloud I'm not sure what *skeleton crew* means. In the sentence before, I learn that Mr. Jenson's newspaper laid off most of its reporters. Later in this sentence, I learn that Mr. Jenson is overworked. I think *skeleton crew* means "just enough workers to keep a business running."

We Do Have students read the idiom *make it fast* in the fifth paragraph on page A1. Have students figure out the idiom's meaning by looking for context clues. Point out the context clue *"we're in a hurry!"*

You Do Have students use clues to find the meaning of other idioms in the selection using clues from the passage. Have students write the idioms and their definitions in their reader's notebooks.

Approaching Level

Fluency/Comprehension

FLUENCY

OBJECTIVES

Read with sufficient accuracy and fluency to support comprehension.

Read grade-level prose and poetry orally with accuracy, appropriate rate, expression, and automaticity on successive readings.

I Do Explain that good readers read at an appropriate rate, or speed. They vary their rate based on the genre they are reading and the difficulty of the text. They pause at appropriate places by using punctuation clues. Read the first two paragraphs of "Nancy's First Interview" in the Approaching Level online **Differentiated Genre Passage** page A1. Tell students to listen for your rate to indicate the meaning of what you read.

We Do Read the rest of the page aloud and have students repeat each sentence after you, matching your rate. Point out that you pause at punctuation marks and at the ends of phrases, rather than running all of your words together.

You Do Have partners take turns reading sentences from the passage. Remind them to focus on their rate. Provide corrective feedback as needed by modeling proper fluency.

IDENTIFY IMPORTANT DETAILS ABOUT CHARACTERS

TIER 2

OBJECTIVES

Quote accurately from a text when explaining what the text says explicitly and when drawing inferences from the text.

I Do Remind students to pay attention to what characters do and say and how they respond to story events. Read aloud the first three paragraphs of "Nancy's First Interview" in the Approaching Level online **Differentiated Genre Passages,** page A1. Identify important details about the main characters. Although Mr. Jenson is unhappy, he agrees to work when he gets the call. Nancy is sad that her father has to work, but she understands and tries not to make him feel guilty.

We Do Have students read the fourth and fifth paragraphs on page A1. Ask: *Which details show how the characters respond to events?* Guide students to identify that Mr. Jenson thinks of a way to turn a negative situation into a positive one and that Nancy is quick to follow his lead.

You Do Have students read the rest of the passage and identify important details about the characters. Review the details students identify and help them explain why they are relevant.

REVIEW PLOT: CONFLICT

OBJECTIVES

Quote accurately from a text when explaining what the text says explicitly and when drawing inferences from the text.

Compare and contrast two or more characters, settings, or events in a story or drama, drawing on specific details in the text (e.g., how characters interact).

I Do Review with students that story characters can be similar to or different from each other. Comparing and contrasting characters helps readers understand how characters relate to and react to the conflict in a story.

We Do Read the first three paragraphs of "Nancy's First Interview" in the Approaching Level online **Differentiated Genre Passages,** page A1, together. Model how to compare and contrast the ways that Nancy and her father respond to the story's conflict. Point out that while both characters are unhappy that they can't go fishing, they try to do what they think is right.

You Do Have students read the rest of the passage and identify similarities and differences between the characters. Ask them to discuss how the characters' feelings and actions affect story events and how story events affect them in turn.

SELF-SELECTED READING

OBJECTIVES

Quote accurately from a text when explaining what the text says explicitly and when drawing inferences from the text.

Compare and contrast two or more characters, settings, or events in a story or drama, drawing on specific details in the text (e.g., how characters interact).

Make, confirm, and revise predictions based on details in the text.

Read Independently

In this text set, students focus on these key aspects of fiction: how setting, events, conflict, and characterization contribute to the plot and how to summarize the plot. Guide students to apply what they have learned in this text set as well as in previous lessons as they read independently.

Have students choose a historical fiction book for sustained silent reading and set a purpose for reading that book. Students can check the online **Leveled Reader Library** for selections. Remind students that:

- paying attention to the setting, events, conflict, and characterization can help them better understand the plot in a story.
- they can use clues in the story to make predictions about what will happen next.

Have students use **Graphic Organizer 10** to record how each character responds to an important event. After they finish, they can conduct a Book Talk about the books they read.

- Students should share their organizers and the most interesting historical detail they learned from reading the texts.
- They should also tell the group about any predictions they revised after reading on and learning new details.

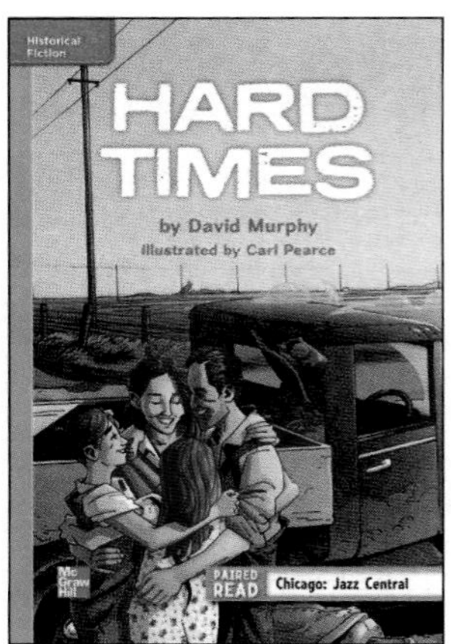

Lexile 830L

OBJECTIVES

Quote accurately from a text when explaining what the text says explicitly and when drawing inferences from the text.

Compare and contrast two or more characters, settings, or events in a story or drama, drawing on specific details in the text (e.g., how characters interact).

Read grade-level prose and poetry orally with accuracy, appropriate rate, and expression on successive readings.

ELA ACADEMIC LANGUAGE

- *historical fiction, compare, contrast, characters, idiom*
- Cognates: *ficción histórica, comparar, contrastar*

On Level

Leveled Reader: *Hard Times*

Preview and Predict

- Have students read the Essential Question: *How do shared experiences help people adapt to change?*
- Have students preview the title, table of contents, and first page of *Hard Times.* Students should use the characteristics of historical fiction and the illustrations to predict what they think the selection will be about. Tell them they should try to make, confirm, or correct their predictions as they read.

Review Genre: Historical Fiction

Tell students this text is historical fiction. Historical fiction features settings that could have existed and events that could have taken place during a particular period in history. The characters act and talk like people from that particular time and place. Historical fiction often contains both real and made-up events and characters. As students read, have them identify features of historical fiction in *Hard Times.*

Close Reading

Note Taking Ask students to use a copy of online Plot: Conflict **Graphic Organizer 10** as they read.

Pages 2–3 *How is this birthday different for the twins than their birthday four years ago?* (Now, four years after the Great Depression began, their family is having a hard time making payments on their farm.)

Pages 4–6 *What does John think of each of his twin children?* (Ruth is fiery and impulsive. Ritchie is serious and responsible.) *Paraphrase the family's discussion.* (They discuss ways to earn money to keep the farm. They eventually agree with Ruth's suggestion that John go to Chicago and find work sketching portraits.) *Turn to a partner and predict if this plan will be a success.* (Yes, John's portraits will earn enough money to make the payments on the farm.) *What does the idiom "spit it out" mean?* (Since Ruth says she has an idea, "spit it out" must mean "say it.") Have students add this idiom in their reader's notebook.

Pages 7–9 *Compare and contrast Ruth and Ritchie's behavior and personalities.* (Ritchie eats slowly and carefully and is calm. Ruth eats quickly and messily and has a jealous temper.)

Pages 10–11 *What prediction did you make when you read about the rattlesnake?* (Ritchie will help Ruth escape.) *Did your prediction match the text?* (Yes. Ritchie tells her to back away slowly.) *How does Ritchie know what to do?* (He read about rattlesnakes in his father's almanac.)

Pages 12–15 *Turn to a partner and describe how Ruth reacts to their parents' decision to move to Chicago.* (Ruth says she loves the farm and doesn't want to move. When John explains that they can move back eventually, she calls attention to Ritchie's idea for making money.) *Do you think the family will be successful in Chicago? Why or why not?* (They will be successful because John will make portraits and Ritchie will sell his cookbook.) *How does the family's shared experience help them adapt to change?* (They all work together so they can stay together.)

Respond to Reading Revisit the Essential Question and ask students to complete the Text Evidence Questions on page 16.

Analytical Writing **Write About Reading** Check that students have correctly compared and contrasted Ruth's and Ritchie's reactions to the rattlesnake and described what these reactions reveal about their personalities.

Fluency: Rate

Model Model reading page 4 with appropriate rate, or speed. Then read the passage aloud and have students read along.

Apply Have students practice reading the passage with partners.

Paired Read: "Chicago: Jazz Central"

Make Connections: Write About It

Before reading, ask students to note that the genre of this text is expository text. Then discuss the Essential Question. After reading, ask students to make connections between *Hard Times* and "Chicago: Jazz Central."

Leveled Reader

Build Knowledge

Talk About the Text Have partners discuss how shared experiences help people adapt to change.

Write About the Text Have students add their ideas to the Build Knowledge pages of their reader's notebooks.

FOCUS ON GENRE

Have students complete the activity on page 20 to learn how historical settings can be used to tell a story.

LITERATURE CIRCLES

Ask students to conduct a literature circle using the Thinkmark questions to guide the discussion. You may wish to have a whole-class discussion, using both selections in the Leveled Reader, about how shared experiences help people adapt to change.

IF students read the On Level fluently and answered the questions,

THEN pair them with students who have proficiently read the Beyond Level and have students

- partner read the Beyond Level main selection.
- describe techniques the author uses to convey a specific time and place in history.

Access Complex Text

The Beyond Level challenges students by including more **idioms** and **complex sentence structures.**

"Nancy's First Interview"
Lexile 720L

OBJECTIVES

Compare and contrast two or more characters, setting, or events in a story or drama, drawing on specific details in text (e.g., how characters interact).

Determine the meaning of words and phrases as they are used in a text, including figurative language such as metaphors and similes.

Demonstrate understanding of figurative language, word relationships, and nuances in word meanings.

ELA ACADEMIC LANGUAGE

- *compare, contrast, characters, idiom, dialect*
- Cognates: *comparar, contrastar, dialecto*

On Level

Genre Passage: "Nancy's First Interview"

Build Background

- Read aloud the Essential Question: *How do shared experiences help people adapt to change?* Ask students to compare two characters from the historical fiction texts they have read in this text set. Use these sentence starters:

  I read that the Great Depression was . . .

  This helps me understand that the characters . . .

- Tell students that after the stock market crashed in 1929, many lost their jobs, including migrant workers, who had to move to new places to find work. Let students know that the online **Differentiated Genre Passage** "Nancy's First Interview" portrays the experiences of two families during the Great Depression, one of which includes migrant workers. Use the photograph and caption on page O2 to make predictions about the story.

Review Genre: Historical Fiction

Review that historical fiction features characters and settings that are typical of a certain period in history. Elements such as dialect help authors create characters from that particular time and place. Historical fiction can feature real as well as fictional characters and events.

Close Reading

Note Taking As students read the passage the first time, ask them to annotate the text and note relevant details, unfamiliar words, and questions they have. Then read again and use text evidence to answer the questions.

Read

Genre: Historical Fiction Read paragraph 2 on page O1. *How does this paragraph help you identify the story's genre?* (It says that the story is set four years after the stock market crash of 1929, so the genre is historical fiction.)

Idioms Read paragraph 4 on page O1. *What does the idiom "lost in his own thoughts" mean?* (concentrating on something very hard) *Why does the author use this idiom?* (Mr. Jenson wants to spend time with Nancy, and he's trying to decide whether he can rely on her to help him with his work.)

Plot: Conflict Read paragraph 1 on page O2. *How has the stock market crash affected the Carters and Jensons differently?* (Mr. Jenson was able to keep his job, but the Carter family had to leave their home in search of work.)

Plot: Characterization Read paragraph 8 on page O2. *How does the author use dialect?* (Mr. Carter uses the phrase "I reckon" to mean "I think.")

Plot: Conflict Read paragraph 9 on page O2. *How do Nancy's feelings about the Carters change?* (Nancy realizes the Carters are like her family because they supported each other during difficult times.)

COLLABORATE **Summarize** Have students use their notes to summarize how the historical setting influenced the story's characters and plot events.

Reread

Use the questions on page O3 to guide students' rereading of the passage.

Author's Craft Reread paragraph 3 on page O1. *How does the author let the reader know Nancy's feelings?* (The author describes Nancy's actions. For example: "Nancy shrugged, trying not to look too upset." She forces a "cheerful smile." This shows she is disappointed but doesn't want her father to know.)

Author's Craft Reread paragraph 3 on page O2. *Why do you think the author included this paragraph?* (This paragraph describes where the Carters are living and what they own. They don't have many belongings, and what they do have is in bad shape. This helps show how hard their life is now.)

Author's Craft *"Y'all" is an example of dialect. Why might the author have used dialect in this story?* (The author wanted the Carters to sound like they could be from Oklahoma during the Depression.)

Integrate

COLLABORATE **Make Connections** Have partners explore connections between "Nancy's First Interview" and other selections they have read. Have them cite evidence that helps them identify how the authors help readers understand why people find it easier to get through difficult experiences together.

Compare Texts Have pairs write *Shared Experiences* in the center circle of a word web. Have them complete the outer circles with the effects that shared experiences can have on people's abilities to get through difficult times.

Build Knowledge

Talk About the Text Have partners discuss how shared experiences help people adapt to change.

Write About the Text Have students add their ideas to the Build Knowledge pages of their reader's notebooks.

Differentiate and Collaborate

COLLABORATE **Be Inspired** Guide students to think about "Nancy's First Interview" and other selections they have read. Ask: *What do the texts inspire you to do?* Use the following activities or have pairs of students think of a way to respond to the texts.

Create a Correspondence Write a series of letters between two friends who live during the time of the Great Depression. Your letters should reflect the ways the friends help each other get through the experience.

Design a Poster Think about an event that a community in 1929 might have planned to help people. Create a poster that shows how the event would bring people together.

Readers to Writers

Word Choice Remind students that descriptive language helps authors create a picture in readers' minds. Ask students to reread the third paragraph on page O2. Ask: *What words does the author use to describe the Carter's home? How do these words help you visualize what their home is like?*

LEVEL UP

IF students read the On Level fluently and answered the questions,

THEN pair them with students who have proficiently read the Beyond Level. Have them

- partner read the Beyond Level passage.
- summarize how Nancy has changed by the end of the story.

On Level

Vocabulary/Comprehension

REVIEW ACADEMIC VOCABULARY

OBJECTIVES

Acquire and use accurately grade-appropriate general academic and domain-specific words and phrases, including those that signal contrast, addition, and other logical relationships (e.g., *however, although, nevertheless, similarly, moreover, in addition*).

I Do Use the **Visual Vocabulary Cards** to review the key selection words *assume, guarantee, nominate, obviously, sympathy,* and *weakling*. Point to each word, read it aloud, and have students repeat it.

We Do Ask these questions. Help students explain their answers.

- If you *assume* something is true, do you know for certain or do you suppose it is true?
- What is something you might *guarantee* your teacher?
- Would you *nominate* a dishonest person or an honest person?

You Do Have students work in pairs to respond to these questions and explain their answers:

- How would you *obviously* show your excitement?
- Would you feel *sympathy* for a team that lost a soccer match?
- Would a *weakling* struggle to carry a heavy object?

Have students pick words from their reader's notebook and use an online thesaurus to find words with similar meanings.

IDIOMS

OBJECTIVES

Demonstrate understanding of figurative language, word relationships, and nuances in word meanings.

Recognize and explain the meaning of common idioms, adages, and proverbs.

I Do Remind students to use context clues to figure out the meanings of idioms in "Nancy's First Interview" in the On Level online **Differentiated Genre Passage** pages O1–O2.

Think Aloud I know that *skeleton crew* in paragraph 2 on page O1 is an idiom. In the sentence before, I learn that Mr. Jenson's newspaper laid off many reporters. Then I learn that he is overworked. I think *skeleton crew* means "just enough workers to keep a business running."

We Do Have students read the fifth paragraph on page O1, with the idiom *Make it fast*. Help them use the context clue *"we're in a hurry!"*

You Do Have students work in pairs to determine the meanings of the idioms *cost an arm and a leg* (page O2, paragraph 6) and *a chip off the old block* (page O2, last paragraph) as they read the rest of the selection.

REVIEW PLOT: CONFLICT

OBJECTIVES

Quote accurately from a text when explaining what the text says explicitly and when drawing inferences from the text.

Compare and contrast two or more characters, settings, or events in a story or drama, drawing on specific details in the text (e.g., how characters interact).

I Do Review with students that characters in a story may be similar or different from one another. Comparing and contrasting characters helps you understand the relationships of and conflicts among characters, how characters affect events in a story, and how characters are changed by these events.

We Do Have a volunteer read the first three paragraphs of "Nancy's First Interview" in the On Level online **Differentiated Genre Passage** page O1. Model identifying how Mr. Jenson responds to the story's conflict. Then work with students to compare and contrast Nancy's response with Mr. Jenson's.

You Do Have partners compare and contrast how different characters respond to events in the rest of the passage. Ask pairs to explain how the characters' feelings and actions influence story events and are also changed by them.

SELF-SELECTED READING

OBJECTIVES

Quote accurately from a text when explaining what the text says explicitly and when drawing inferences from the text.

Compare and contrast two or more characters, settings, or events in a story or drama, drawing on specific details in the text (e.g., how characters interact).

Make, confirm, and revise predictions based on details in the text.

Read Independently

In this text set, students focus on how setting, events, conflict, and characterization contribute to the plot and how to summarize the plot. Guide students to apply what they have learned in this text set as well as in previous lessons as they read independently.

Have students choose a historical fiction book for sustained silent reading. They can check the online **Leveled Reader Library** for selections. Remind students that:

- paying attention to the setting, events, conflict, and characterization can help them better understand the plot in a story.
- they can use clues in the story to make predictions about what will happen next.

Encourage students to select books about historical periods that interest them.

- As students read, have them use **Graphic Organizer 10** to record how each character responds to an important event in the story.
- They can use the organizer to help them write a summary of the book.
- Ask students to share their reactions about the book with classmates.

You may want to include ELL students in On Level vocabulary and comprehension lessons. Offer language support as needed.

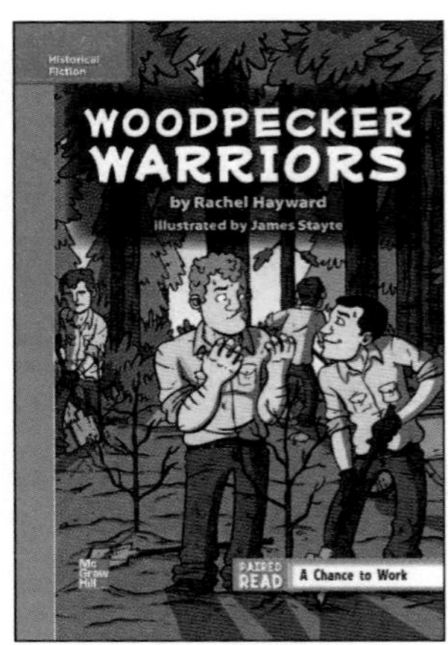

Lexile 900L

OBJECTIVES

Quote accurately from a text when explaining what the text says explicitly and when drawing inferences from the text.

Compare and contrast two or more characters, settings, or events in a story or drama, drawing on specific details in the text (e.g., how characters interact).

Read grade-level prose and poetry orally with accuracy, appropriate rate, and expression on successive readings.

ELA ACADEMIC LANGUAGE

- *historical fiction, make predictions, compare, contrast, characters, idiom*
- Cognates: *ficción histórica, predicciones, comparar, contrastar*

Beyond Level

Leveled Reader: *Woodpecker Warriors*

Preview and Predict

- Have students read the Essential Question: *How do shared experiences help people adapt to change?*
- Have students preview the title, table of contents, and first page of *Woodpecker Warriors*. Students should use the characteristics of historical fiction and the illustrations to predict what they think the selection will be about. Ask them to make, confirm, or correct their predictions as they read.

Review Genre: Historical Fiction

Tell students this text is historical fiction. Historical fiction features settings that could have existed and events that could have taken place during a particular period in history. The characters act and talk like people from that particular time and place. Historical fiction often contains both real and made-up events and characters. Have students identify features of historical fiction in *Woodpecker Warriors*.

Close Reading

Note Taking Ask students to use a copy of the online Plot: Conflict **Graphic Organizer 10** as they read.

Pages 2–5 *What does the idiom "make tracks" mean? Use context clues to help you answer.* (Since Jim and June need to make grocery deliveries, it must mean "move quickly.") Have students add this idiom in their reader's notebooks. *How do June and Uncle Dan differ in the way they greet Archie and Bob? Why?* (June is polite, but Uncle Dan is rude. Uncle Dan thinks Archie and Bob are taking jobs from local men.) *Turn to a partner and predict if Uncle Dan's attitude will change.* (Yes, something will happen to change his mind about the CCC workers.)

Pages 6–9 *Turn to a partner and tell if your prediction matched the text.* (Not yet. Uncle Dan is still unfriendly. I will keep reading to see if I need to revise my prediction.) *Compare and contrast Archie's and Bob's personalities and feelings about the CCC.* (Bob is outgoing and complains about the hard work. Archie is quiet and enjoys life in the camp.)

Pages 10–11 *Compare how Mr. Taylor and Uncle Dan treat Archie.* (Mr. Taylor is friendly, but Uncle Dan is still rude.)

What suggestion does Archie make to Uncle Dan? How does Dan respond? (Archie suggests that Uncle Dan work with the CCC. Uncle Dan scoffs at the idea.) *Do you want to revise your prediction about Uncle Dan's feelings? Why?* (No. He might still change his mind.)

Pages 12–15 *Turn to a partner and summarize the events in a logical order related to the fire.* (The workers and the townsmen work together to put out the fire. Uncle Dan and Archie cut down a dangerous tree. Uncle Dan changes his mind about the CCC workers after seeing how they helped.) *Turn to a partner and explain how the shared experience helped Uncle Dan adapt to change.* (Uncle Dan learned to overcome his prejudices about the CCC and appreciate the chance to work with Archie.)

Respond to Reading Revisit the Essential Question and ask students to complete the Text Evidence Questions on page 16.

Analytical Writing **Write About Reading** Check that students have correctly compared and contrasted the characters of June and Jim. Make sure they include details that support their descriptions.

Fluency: Rate

Model Model reading page 4 with appropriate rate, or speed. Then read the passage aloud and have students read along.

Apply Have students practice reading the passage with partners.

Paired Read: "A Chance to Work"

Make Connections: Write About It

Before reading, ask students to note that the genre of this text is expository text. Then discuss the Essential Question. After reading, ask students to write about connections between what they learned from *Woodpecker Warriors* and "A Chance to Work."

Leveled Reader

Build Knowledge

Talk About the Text Have partners discuss how shared experiences help people adapt to change.

Write About the Text Have students add their ideas to the Build Knowledge pages of their reader's notebooks.

FOCUS ON GENRE

Have students complete the activity on page 20 to learn how historical settings can be used to tell a story.

LITERATURE CIRCLES

Ask students to conduct a literature circle using the Thinkmark questions to guide the discussion. You may wish to have a whole-class discussion, using both selections in the Leveled Reader, about how shared experiences help people adapt to change.

GIFTED AND TALENTED

Synthesize Have students write a dialogue between Uncle Dan and Archie that takes place six months later. The dialogue should focus on how their shared experience at the fire helped each of them adapt to the changes taking place in the town and in the country as a whole. The dialogue should also include details about their experiences since the time of the fire. Encourage students to research the time period to help them create more authentic dialogues.

"Nancy's First Interview"
Lexile 820L

OBJECTIVES

Compare and contrast two or more characters, setting, or events in a story or drama, drawing on specific details in text (e.g., how characters interact).

Determine the meaning of words and phrases as they are used in a text, including figurative language such as metaphors and similes.

Demonstrate understanding of figurative language, word relationships, and nuances in word meanings.

ELA ACADEMIC LANGUAGE

- *compare, contrast, characters, idiom, dialect*
- Cognates: *comparar, contrastar, dialecto*

Beyond Level

Genre Passage: "Nancy's First Interview"

Build Background

- Read aloud the Essential Question *How do shared experiences help people adapt to change?* Ask students to compare two characters from the historical fiction texts they have read in this text set. Use these sentence starters:

  I read that the Great Depression was . . .

  This helps me understand that the characters . . .

- Tell students that after the stock market crashed in 1929, many people lost their jobs, including migrant workers, who had to move to new locations to find work. Let students know that the online **Differentiated Genre Passage** "Nancy's First Interview" portrays the experiences of two families during the Great Depression, one of which includes migrant workers. Use the photograph and caption on page O2 to make predictions about the story.

Review Genre: Historical Fiction

Review that historical fiction features characters and settings that are typical of a certain period in history. Elements such as dialect help authors create characters from that particular time and place. Historical fiction can feature real as well as fictional characters and events.

Close Reading

Note Taking As students read the passage the first time, ask them to annotate the text and note relevant details, unfamiliar words, and questions they have. Then read again and use text evidence to answer the questions.

Read

Genre: Historical Fiction Read paragraph 2 on page B1. *How does the author combine real and fictional elements in this paragraph?* (The characters are fictional, but the stock market crash of 1929 actually happened.)

Plot: Conflict Read paragraph 1 on page B2. *Compare and contrast how the stock market crash has affected the Carter and Jenson families.* (Both families have struggled because of the crash. Mr. Jenson was able to keep his job, but the Carter family had to leave their home in search of work.)

Idioms Read paragraph 6 on page B2. *What does the idiom "cost an arm and a leg" mean? Use context to help you.* (Mr. Carter says he lost his farm when costs rose, so it must mean "cost a lot of money.")

Plot: Characterization Read paragraph 8 on page B2. *How does the author use dialect in this paragraph?* (Mr. Carter uses the phrase "I reckon" to mean "I think.") Why is the dialect effective? (It makes Mr. Carter sound like he might have lived on an Oklahoma farm in the 1930s.)

Plot: Conflict Read paragraph 9 on page B2. *How does Nancy change by the end of the story?* (Nancy realizes that the Carters are like her family because they support each other during difficult times.)

COLLABORATE **Summarize** Have students use their notes to summarize how the historical setting influenced the story's characters and plot events.

Reread

Use the questions on page B3 to guide students' rereading of the passage.

Author's Craft Reread the third paragraph on page B1. *How does the author let the readers know Nancy's feelings?* (The author describes Nancy's actions. For example, "Nancy shrugged, trying not to look too upset." She plasters "a cheerful smile on her face." This shows she is disappointed but doesn't want her father to know.)

Author's Craft Reread the third paragraph on page B2. *Why do you think the author included this paragraph?* (This paragraph describes where the Carters are living and what they own. They don't have many belongings, and what they have is in bad shape. For example, their kitchen table is wobbly. This helps show how hard their life is now.)

Author's Craft *"Y'all" is an example of dialect. Why might the author have used dialect in this story?* (The author wanted the Carters to sound like they could be from Oklahoma during the Depression.)

Integrate

COLLABORATE **Make Connections** Have pairs explore connections between "Nancy's First Interview" and other selections they have read. Have them cite evidence to explain how the authors show how people find it easier to get through difficult experiences together.

Compare Genres Have pairs write *Shared Experiences* in the center of a word web. Have them add details that explain how people deal with difficult times.

Build Knowledge

Talk About the Text Have partners discuss how shared experiences help people adapt to change.

Write About the Text Have students add their ideas to the Build Knowledge pages of their reader's notebooks.

Differentiate and Collaborate

COLLABORATE **Be inspired** Guide students to think about "Nancy's First Interview" and other selections they have read. Ask: *What do the texts inspire you to do?* Use the following activities or have pairs of students think of a way to respond to the texts.

Create a Correspondence Write a series of letters between two friends who live during the time of the Great Depression. Your letters should reflect the ways the friends help each other get through the experience.

Design a Poster Think about an event that a community in 1929 might have planned to help people. Create a poster that shows how the event would bring people together.

Readers to Writers

Word Choice Remind students that descriptive language helps authors create pictures in readers' minds. Ask students to reread the third paragraph on page B2. Ask: *Which words does the author use to describe the Carter's home? How do these words help you visualize what their home is like?*

GIFTED AND TALENTED

Independent Study Have students synthesize details about the effects the Great Depression had on people and events during the 20th century. Then have students think about how those effects would be different if the Great Depression were to occur today. Have them write a newspaper article or script for a news program that reflects the effects on people, technology, the economy, and so on.

● Beyond Level

Vocabulary/Comprehension

REVIEW DOMAIN-SPECIFIC WORDS

OBJECTIVES

Acquire and use accurately grade-appropriate general academic and domain-specific words and phrases, including those that signal contrast, addition, and other logical relationships (e.g., *however, although, nevertheless, similarly, moreover, in addition*).

Model Use the **Visual Vocabulary Cards** to review the meanings of the words *rely* and *supportive*. Use each word in a context sentence.

Write the words *enroll* and *foremen* on the board and discuss the meanings with students. Then help students write a context sentence for each word.

Apply Have students work in pairs to find the meanings of the words *obligation* and *remorse*. Then have partners write sentences using the words.

IDIOMS

OBJECTIVES

Demonstrate understanding of figurative language, word relationships, and nuances in word meanings.

Recognize and explain the meaning of common idioms, adages, and proverbs.

Model Read aloud the first two paragraphs of "Nancy's First Interview" in the Beyond Level online **Differentiated Genre Passage** page B1.

Think Aloud When I read the second paragraph on page B1, I am unsure of the meaning of the idiom *skeleton crew*. In the previous sentence, I learned that Nancy's father was overworked. I think *skeleton crew* means "just enough workers to keep a business running."

With students, read aloud the fifth paragraph. Help them figure out the meaning of *make tracks*.

Apply Have pairs of students read the rest of the passage. Ask them to use context clues to determine the meanings of the following idioms: *cost an arm and a leg* (page B2, paragraph 6), and *a chip off the old block* (page B2, last paragraph).

Independent Study Challenge students to identify three additional examples of idioms they know of or have encountered in other books. Have them draw a picture of the literal meaning of the expression and the figurative meaning. Then have them use each idiom in an original sentence that shows its meaning.

Have students repeat the activity by finding idioms in their reader's notebooks and using an online website to look for idioms.

REVIEW PLOT: CONFLICT

OBJECTIVES

Quote accurately from a text when explaining what the text says explicitly and when drawing inferences from the text.

Compare and contrast two or more characters, settings, or events in a story or drama, drawing on specific details in the text (e.g., how characters interact).

Model Review with students that characters in a story may be similar or different. Comparing and contrasting characters helps readers understand how characters affect events and how characters are changed by the conflict.

Have students read the first two paragraphs of "Nancy's First Interview" in the Beyond Level online **Differentiated Genre Passage** page B1. Ask open-ended questions to facilitate discussion, such as: *How do the characters respond to events? How are their responses similar or different?* Students should support their answers with details from the selection.

Apply Have students identify similarities and differences in the way the characters respond to conflict in the passage as they independently fill in a copy of the online Plot: Conflict **Graphic Organizer 10**. Then have partners use their work to explain how the characters' actions and feelings both affect story events and are changed by them.

SELF-SELECTED READING

OBJECTIVES

Quote accurately from a text when explaining what the text says explicitly and when drawing inferences from the text.

Compare and contrast two or more characters, settings, or events in a story or drama, drawing on specific details in the text (e.g., how characters interact).

Make, confirm, and revise predictions based on details in the text.

Read Independently

In this text set, students focus on how setting, events, conflict, and characterization contribute to the plot and how to summarize the plot. Guide students to apply what they have learned in this text set as well as in previous lessons as they read independently.

Have students choose a historical fiction book for sustained silent reading. They can check the online **Leveled Reader Library** for selections. As they choose, they should consider their purpose for reading.

- As students read, have them use **Graphic Organizer 10** to record how each character responds to an important event in the story.
- Remind them to make, confirm, and revise predictions as they read.

Encourage students to keep a reading journal. Suggest that they select books about historical periods that interest them.

- Students can write summaries of the books in their journals.
- Ask students to share their reactions to the books with classmates.

Independent Study Challenge students to discuss how their books relate to the weekly theme of people being better together. Have students use all of their reading materials to compare ways that shared experiences help people adapt to change.

Student Outcomes

✓ Tested in *Wonders* Assessments

FOUNDATIONAL SKILLS

Phonics and Word Analysis

- Use knowledge of the suffix *-ion* to decode words

Fluency

- Read grade-level texts with accuracy, appropriate rate, expression, and automaticity

READING

Reading Literature

✓ Explain how charts and headings contribute to the understanding of a text
✓ Analyze an author's perspective in an informational text
✓ Track the development of an argument, identifying the specific claim(s), evidence, and reasoning
- Read and comprehend texts in the grades 4-5 text complexity band
- Summarize a text to enhance comprehension
- Write in response to texts

Compare Texts

✓ Analyze how an author's use of figurative language, such as puns, contributes to meaning in a text
- Compare how two texts are similar and different
- Compare and contrast how authors present information on the same topic or theme

COMMUNICATION

Writing

Writing Process

✓ Write a personal narrative with a logical sequence of events and effective use of description
- With guidance and support from peers and adults, develop and strengthen writing as needed by planning, revising, and editing

Speaking and Listening

- Report on a topic or text or present an opinion, sequencing ideas; speak clearly at an understandable pace

Conventions

Grammar

✓ Use *good* and *bad* to make comparisons
✓ Use irregular comparative forms correctly

Spelling

- Spell words with the suffix *-ion*

Researching

- Conduct short research projects that use several sources to build knowledge through investigation of different aspects of a topic

Creating and Collaborating

- Add audio recordings and visual displays to presentations when apppropriate
- With some guidance and support from adults, use technology to produce and publish writing

VOCABULARY

Academic Vocabulary

- Acquire and use grade-appropriate academic vocabulary

Vocabulary Strategy

✓ Apply knowledge of root words to determine the meaning of unfamiliar words

CONTENT AREA LEARNING

Diversity and Evolution of Living Organisms

- Predict the effects of changes in ecosystems caused by living organisms, including humans. **Science**

ELL Scaffolded supports for English Language Learners are embedded throughout the lessons, enabling students to communicate information, ideas, and concepts in English Language Arts and for social and instructional purposes within the school setting.

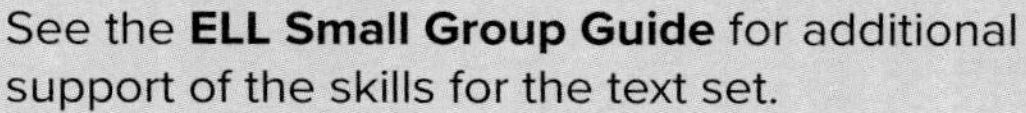

See the **ELL Small Group Guide** for additional support of the skills for the text set.

FORMATIVE ASSESSMENT

For assessment throughout the text set, use students' self-assessments and your observations.

Use the Data Dashboard to filter class, group, or individual student data to guide group placement decisions. It provides recommendations to enhance learning for gifted and talented students and offers extra support for students needing remediation.

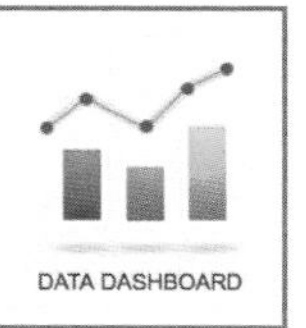

Develop Student Ownership

To build student ownership, students need to know what they are learning and why they are learning it, and to determine how well they understood it.

Students Discuss Their Goals

READING

TEXT SET GOALS

- I can read and understand argumentative text.
- I can use text evidence to respond to argumentative text.
- I know how natural events and human activities affect the environment.

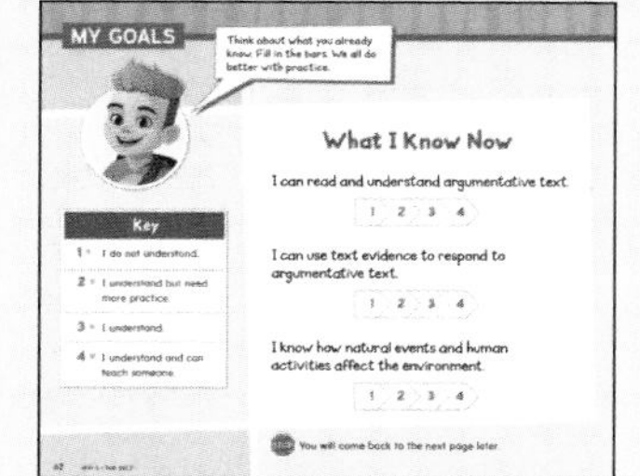

Have students think about what they know and fill in the bars on **Reading/Writing Companion** page 62.

WRITING

EXTENDED WRITING GOALS

Extended Writing 2:

- I can write a research report.
- I can write a personal narrative.

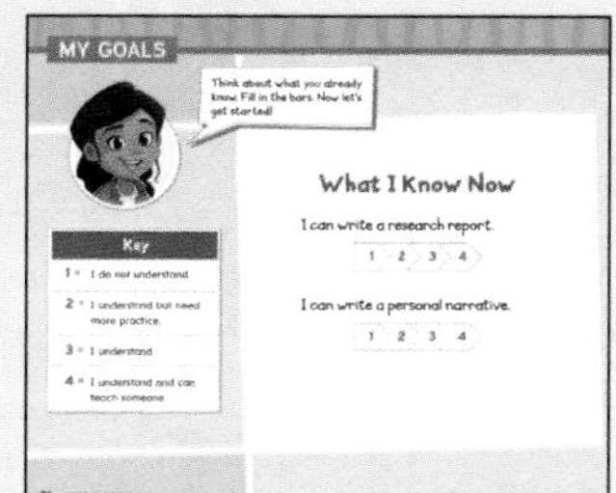

Have students think about what they know and fill in the bars on **Reading/Writing Companion** page 84.

Students Monitor Their Learning

LEARNING GOALS

Specific learning goals identified in every lesson make clear what students will be learning and why. These smaller goals provide stepping stones to help students reach their Text Set and Extended Writing Goals.

CHECK-IN ROUTINE

The Check-In Routine at the close of each lesson guides students to self-reflect on how well they understood each learning goal.

Review the lesson learning goal.
Reflect on the activity.
Self-Assess by

- filling in the bars in the **Reading/Writing Companion**
- holding up 1, 2, 3, or 4 fingers

Share with your teacher.

Students Reflect on Their Progress

READING

TEXT SET GOALS

After completing the Show Your Knowledge task for the text set, students reflect on their understanding of the Text Set Goals by filling in the bars on **Reading/Writing Companion** page 63.

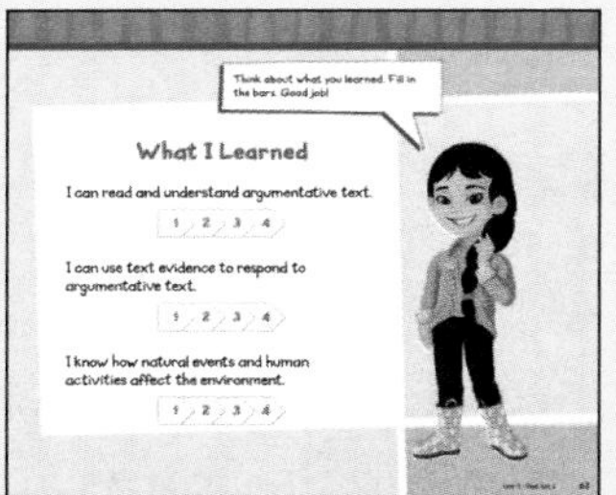

WRITING

EXTENDED WRITING GOALS

After completing their extended writing projects, students reflect on their understanding of the Extended Writing Goals by filling in the bars on **Reading/Writing Companion** page 85.

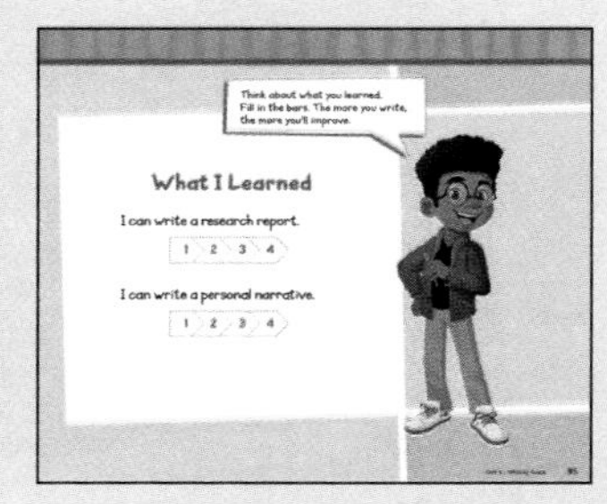

Build Knowledge

Shared Read
Reading/Writing Companion p. 64

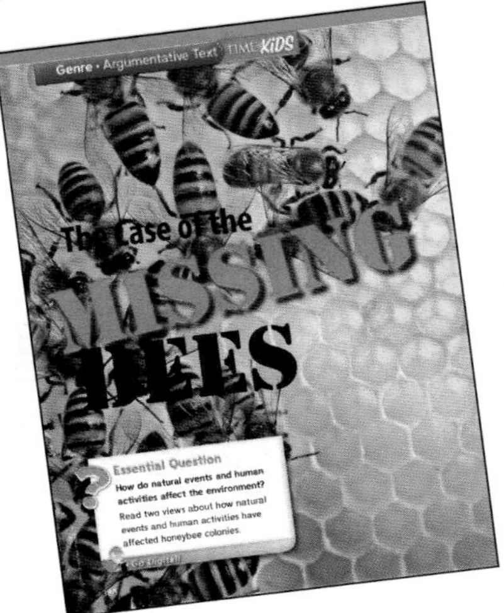

Anchor Text
Literature Anthology p. 386

Paired Selection
Literature Anthology p. 390

Essential Question 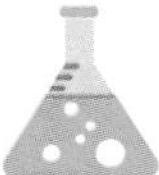

How do natural events and human activities affect the environment?

Video Human mistakes and natural disasters can cause dangerous results, such as wildfires that destroy homes, vegetation, and wildlife. We must work with nature to live safely in any environment.

BLAST BACK! studysync

Study Sync Blast Humans have had a major impact on the fast-disappearing rainforest. If we don't think about how we can preserve the rainforest, many plants and animals will go extinct.

Interactive Read Aloud Dams provide us with cheap electricity and water; they help control flooding. However, building dams also damages the environment. Dams destroy wildlife habitats, hurt fish, and release dangerous gases.

Shared Read Two viewpoints are presented: one argument focuses on the benefits of plants and animals from other places, while the other argues that nonnative species damage the environment and threaten endangered species.

Anchor Text Two authors debate the reason behind declining bee populations. The first argument claims a fungus and a virus are to blame, while the second points to pesticides.

Paired Selection Honeybees were imported from Europe about 400 years ago. If they disappear, our crops and economy will suffer.

Make Connections A poem expresses how kindness to animals connects us with the environment and helps wildlife. Nature will in turn help us.

Differentiated Sources

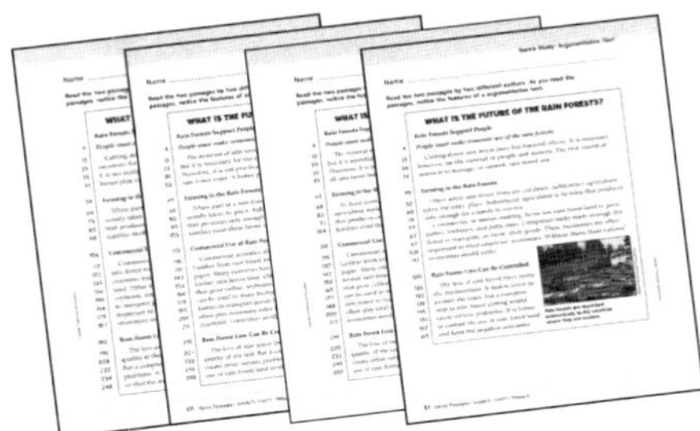

Leveled Readers

The settlers of The Great Plains plowed large areas of land for agriculture, disrupting the ecology of the land and leading to the Dust Bowl. They also hunted some species of animals until almost none were left.

Differentiated Genre Passages

Two arguments about rain forests are presented: one claims that rain forests support people economically, while the other claims people must preserve the rain forest.

Build Knowledge Routine

After reading each text, ask students to document what facts and details they learned to help answer the Essential Question of the text set.

Talk About the source.

Write About the source.

Add to the Class Anchor Chart.

- Add to your Vocabulary List.

Show Your Knowledge

Write an Editorial

Have students show how they built knowledge across the text set by writing an editorial. Students should start by thinking about the Essential Question: *How do natural events and human activities affect the environment?* Students will write an editorial that will explain why it is important to prioritize habitat conservation.

Social Emotional Learning

Curiosity

Anchor Text: Encourage curiosity by inviting students to ask questions and explore what they found most interesting. Ask: *What else would you like to know about bees? Why else might they be disappearing?*

Paired Selection: The motivation to learn comes from an internal drive. Nurture this drive by allowing students to continue to seek answers. Ask: *What foods that you eat are pollinated by bees?*

Roundtable Discussion: Compare and contrast *The Case of the Missing Bees* and "Busy, Beneficial Bees." Ask: *Why is it important to learn about bees? How do our actions affect them? Is there anything we can do to help the bees?*

Explore the Texts

Essential Question: How do natural events and human activities affect the environment?

> Access Complex Text (ACT) boxes throughout the text set provide scaffolded instruction for seven different elements that may make a text complex.

Teacher's Edition	Reading/Writing Companion	Literature Anthology	
	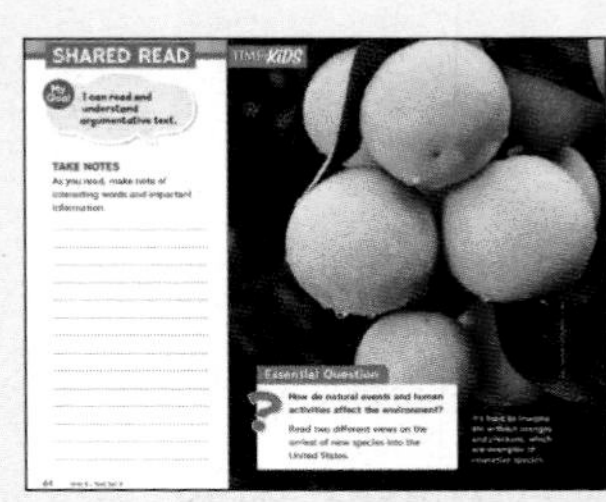		
"Dams: Harnessing the Power of Water" Interactive Read Aloud p. T167 Argumentative Text	**"Should Plants and Animals from Other Places Live Here?"** Shared Read pp. 64–67 Argumentative Text	***The Case of the Missing Bees*** Anchor Text pp. 386–389 Argumentative Text	**"Busy, Beneficial Bees"** Paired Selection pp. 390–391 Expository Text
Qualitative			
Meaning/Purpose Moderate Complexity **Structure** Moderate Complexity **Language** Low Complexity **Knowledge Demands** Moderate Complexity	**Meaning/Purpose** Moderate Complexity **Structure** Moderate Complexity **Language** Moderate Complexity **Knowledge Demands** Low Complexity	**Meaning/Purpose** Moderate Complexity **Structure** Moderate Complexity **Language** Moderate Complexity **Knowledge Demands** Moderate Complexity	**Meaning/Purpose** Moderate Complexity **Structure** Low Complexity **Language** Moderate Complexity **Knowledge Demands** Moderate Complexity
Quantitative			
Lexile 950L	**Lexile** 930L	**Lexile** 950L	**Lexile** 980L
Reader and Task Considerations			
Reader The language and knowledge demands will be challenging. Discuss the benefits and drawbacks of hydroelectric dams. Help students parse the meaning of complex sentences.	**Reader** The knowledge demands and language features will be challenging. Students will need to know certain types of animals to recognize those harmful to the environment.	**Reader** Sentence constructions will be most challenging to students. Break down complex structures to help students comprehend meaning.	**Reader** Students will not need background knowledge to understand the text.

Task The questions for the read aloud are supported by teacher modeling. The tasks provide a variety of ways for students to begin to build knowledge and vocabulary about the text set topic. The questions and tasks provided for the other texts are at various levels of complexity, ensuring that all students can interact with the text in meaningful ways.

Additional Texts

Content Area Reading BLMs

Additional online texts related to grade-level Science, Social Studies, and Arts content

Leveled Readers

(A) ***The Great Plains***	(O) ***The Great Plains***	(B) ***The Great Plains***	**(ELL)** *The Great Plains*
Qualitative			
Meaning/Purpose Moderate Complexity	**Meaning/Purpose** Moderate Complexity	**Meaning/Purpose** Moderate Complexity	**Meaning/Purpose** Moderate Complexity
Structure Moderate Complexity	**Structure** Moderate Complexity	**Structure** Moderate Complexity	**Structure** Moderate Complexity
Language Low Complexity	**Language** Low Complexity	**Language** Low Complexity	**Language** Low Complexity
Knowledge Demands Moderate Complexity	**Knowledge Demands** Moderate Complexity	**Knowledge Demands** High Complexity	**Knowledge Demands** Moderate Complexity
Quantitative			
Lexile 760L	**Lexile** 910L	**Lexile** 1020L	**Lexile** 830L
Reader and Task Considerations			
Reader Students will not need background knowledge to understand the text.	**Reader** Students will not need background knowledge to understand the text.	**Reader** Students will not need background knowledge to understand the text.	**Reader** Students will not need background knowledge to understand the text.

Task The questions and tasks provided for the Leveled Readers are at various levels of complexity, ensuring that all students can interact with the text in meaningful ways.

Differentiated Genre Passages

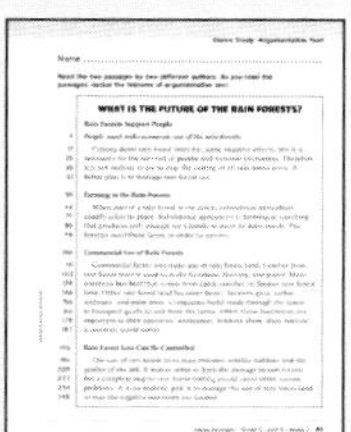	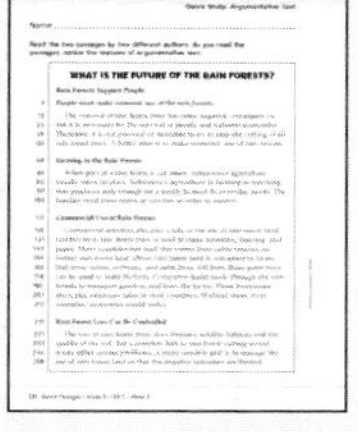	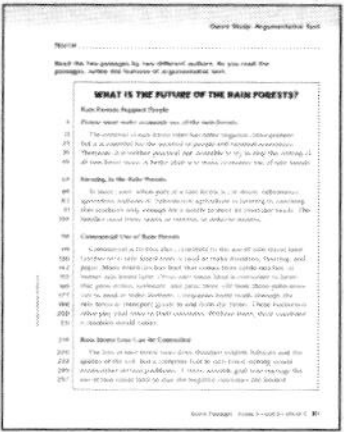	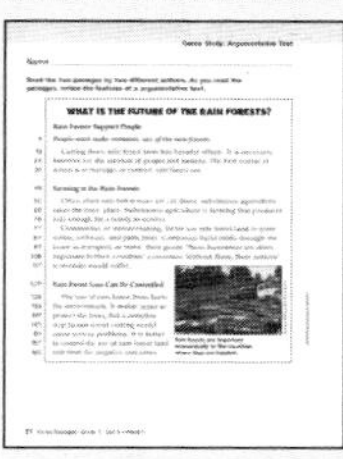
(A) "What Is the Future of the Rain Forests?"	**(O)** "What Is the Future of the Rain Forests?"	**(B)** "What Is the Future of the Rain Forests?"	**(ELL)** "What Is the Future of the Rain Forests?"
Qualitative			
Meaning/Purpose Moderate Complexity	**Meaning/Purpose** Moderate Complexity	**Meaning/Purpose** Moderate Complexity	**Meaning/Purpose** Moderate Complexity
Structure Moderate Complexity	**Structure** Moderate Complexity	**Structure** Moderate Complexity	**Structure** Moderate Complexity
Language Low Complexity	**Language** Low Complexity	**Language** Low Complexity	**Language** Low Complexity
Knowledge Demands Moderate Complexity	**Knowledge Demands** Moderate Complexity	**Knowledge Demands** Moderate Complexity	**Knowledge Demands** Moderate Complexity
Quantitative			
Lexile 840L	**Lexile** 920L	**Lexile** 970L	**Lexile** 860L
Reader and Task Considerations			
Reader Students will not need background knowledge to understand the text.	**Reader** Students will not need background knowledge to understand the text.	**Reader** Students will not need background knowledge to understand the text.	**Reader** Students will not need background knowledge to understand the text.

Task The questions and tasks provided for the Differentiated Genre Passages are at various levels of complexity, ensuring that all students can interact with the text in meaningful ways.

Week 5 Planner

Customize your own lesson plans at **my.mheducation.com**

READING LESSON GOALS

- **I can read and understand argumentative text.**
- **I can use text evidence to respond to argumentative text.**
- **I know how natural events and human activities affect the environment.**

SMALL GROUP OPTIONS The designated lessons can be taught in small groups. To determine how to differentiate instruction for small groups, use Formative Assessment and Data Dashboard.

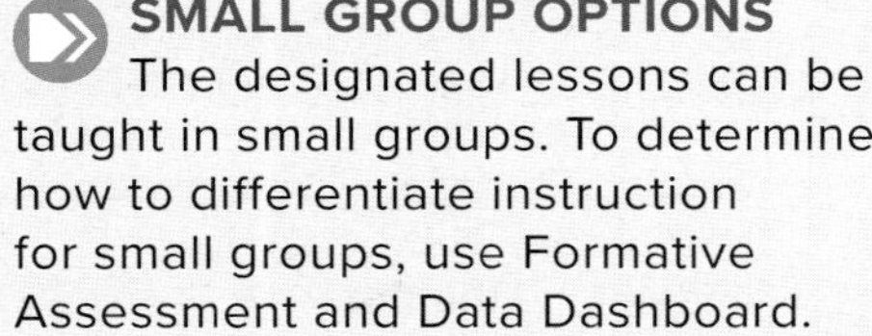

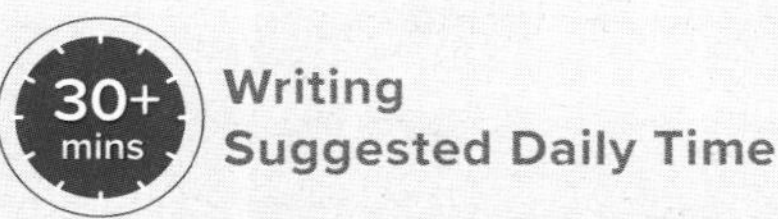

WRITING LESSON GOALS

I can write a personal narrative.

LESSON 1	LESSON 2
Reading	
Introduce the Concept, T164–T165 Build Knowledge **Listening Comprehension, T166–T167** "Dams: Harnessing the Power of Water" **Shared Read, T168–T171** Read "Should Plants and Animals from Other Places Live Here?" Quick Write: Summarize **Vocabulary, T172–T173** Academic Vocabulary Root Words **Expand Vocabulary, T200**	**Shared Read, T168–T171** Reread "Should Plants and Animals from Other Places Live Here?" **Minilessons, T174–T181** Ask and Answer Questions Text Features: Charts and Headings Author's Perspective Craft and Structure **Respond to Reading, T182–T183** **Phonics, T184–T185** Suffix *-ion* **Fluency, T185** Accuracy and Rate **Research and Inquiry, T186–T187** **Expand Vocabulary, T200**
Writing	
Extended Writing 2: Personal Narrative	
Writing Lesson Bank: Craft Minilessons, T260–T261, T264–T265	
Teacher and Peer Conferences	
Grammar Lesson Bank, T274 Comparing with *Good* and *Bad* Talk About It **Spelling Lesson Bank, T284** Suffix *-ion*	**Grammar Lesson Bank, T274** Comparing with *Good* and *Bad* Talk About It **Spelling Lesson Bank, T284** Suffix *-ion*

SMALL GROUP

Teacher-Led Instruction

Differentiated Reading

Leveled Readers

- *The Great Plains,* T202–T203
- *The Great Plains,* T212–T213
- *The Great Plains,* T218–T219

Differentiated Skills Practice

Approaching Level

Phonics/Decoding, T206–T207
- Decode and Build Words with Suffix *-ion* (Tier 2)
- Practice Words with Suffix *-ion*

Vocabulary, T208–T209
- Review High-Frequency Words (Tier 2)
- Review Academic Vocabulary (Tier 2)
- Answer Yes/No Questions
- Root Words

Fluency, T210
- Accuracy and Rate (Tier 2)

Comprehension, T210–T211
- Identify and Review Author's Perspective
- Self-Selected Reading

Independent/Collaborative Work See pages T163E–T164F.

Reading

Comprehension
- Argumentative Text
- Author's Perspective
- Ask and Answer Questions

Fluency

Independent Reading

Phonics/Word Study

Phonics/Decoding
- Suffix *-ion*

Vocabulary
- Root Words

Writing

Extended Writing 2: Personal Narrative

Self-Selected Writing

Grammar
- Comparing with *Good* and *Bad*

Spelling
- Suffix *-ion*

Handwriting

ACADEMIC VOCABULARY
agricultural, declined, disorder, identify, probable, thrive, unexpected, widespread

SPELLING
impress, impression, elect, election, locate, location, confuse, confusion, correct, correction, discuss, discussion, concentrate, concentration, estimate, estimation, decorate, decoration, exhaust, exhaustion

Review *hopeless, fearless, forgiveness*
Challenge *conclude, conclusion*
See pages T284–T285 for Differentiated Spelling Lists.

 LESSON 3	 LESSON 4	 LESSON 5
Reading		
Anchor Text, T188–T191 Read and Reread *The Case of the Missing Bees* Take Notes About Text **Respond to Reading, T192–T193** **Expand Vocabulary, T201**	**Paired Selection, T194–T195** Read and Reread "Busy, Beneficial Bees" **Author's Craft, T196–T197** Figurative Language: Puns **Expand Vocabulary, T201**	**Make Connections, T198** **Show Your Knowledge, T199** **Progress Monitoring, T163G–T163H** **Expand Vocabulary, T201**
Writing		
	Extended Writing 2, T244–T249 Expert Model; Plan	**Extended Writing 2, T250–T251** Draft: Description
Writing Lesson Bank: Craft Minilessons, T260–T261, T264–T265		
Teacher and Peer Conferences		
Grammar Lesson Bank, T275 Comparing with *Good* and *Bad* Talk About It **Spelling Lesson Bank, T285** Suffix *-ion*	**Grammar Lesson Bank, T275** Comparing with *Good* and *Bad* Talk About It **Spelling Lesson Bank, T285** Suffix *-ion*	**Grammar Lesson Bank, T275** Comparing with *Good* and *Bad* Talk About It **Spelling Lesson Bank, T285** Suffix *-ion*

On Level
Vocabulary, T216
- Review Vocabulary Words
- Root Words

Comprehension, T217
- Review Author's Perspective
- Self-Selected Reading

Beyond Level
Vocabulary, T222
- Review Domain-Specific Words
- Root Words

Comprehension, T223
- Review Author's Perspective
- Self-Selected Reading GIFTED and TALENTED

English Language Learners
See ELL Small Group Guide, pp. 210–221

Content Area Connections

Content Area Reading
- Science, Social Studies, and the Arts

Research and Inquiry
- Environmental Changes

Inquiry Space
- Options for Project-Based Learning

English Language Learners
See ELL Small Group Guide, pp. 210–221

Independent and Collaborative Work

As you meet with small groups, the rest of the class completes activities and projects that allow them to practice and apply the skills they have been working on.

Student Choice and Student Voice

- Print the My Independent Work blackline master and review it with students. Identify the "Must Do" activities.
- Have students choose additional activities that provide the practice they need.
- Remind students to reflect on their learning each day.

Name ________ Unit 5 • Text Set 3

My Independent Work

	Reading	Phonics/Word Study	Writing
Center Activity Cards	Card: Activity:	Card: Activity:	Card: Activity:
Digital Activities (my.mheducation.com)	Activity:	Activity:	Activity:
Practice Pages	Content Area Reading:	Practice:	Practice:
Independent Choices	Independent Reading:	Activity:	Self-Selected Writing:

Grade 5 • My Independent Work 35

My Independent Work BLM

Reading

Independent Reading Texts

Students can choose a Center Activity Card to use while they read independently.

Classroom Library
A Black Hole is NOT a Hole
Genre: Expository Text
Lexile: 900L

The Mighty Mars Rovers: The Incredible Adventures of Spirit and Opportunity
Genre: Expository Text
Lexile: 950L

Unit Bibliography
Have students self-select independent reading texts about scientific viewpoints.

Leveled Texts Online

- Additional Leveled Readers in the **Leveled Reader Library Online** allow for flexibility.
- Six leveled sets of **Differentiated Genre Passages** in diverse genres are available.
- **Differentiated Texts** offer ELL students more passages at different proficiency levels.

Additional Literature
Differentiated Genre Passages
Genres: Personal Narrative, Social Studies Article, Fable, Myth, Legend, Tall Tale

Center Activity Cards

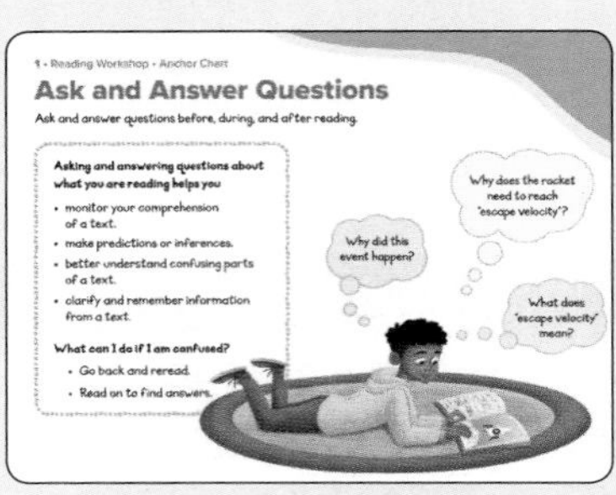

Ask and Answer Questions Card 1

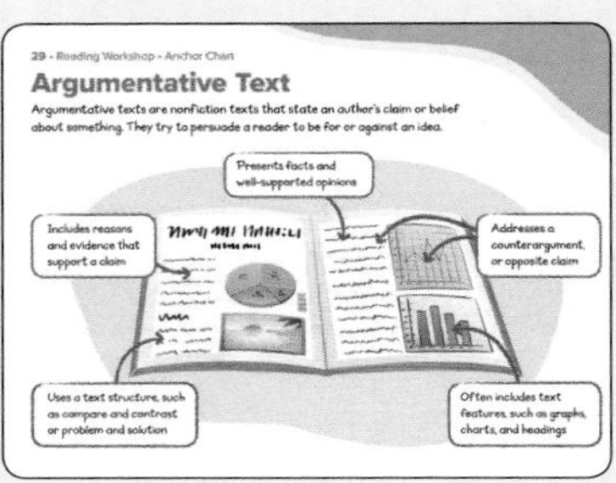

Argumentative Text Card 29

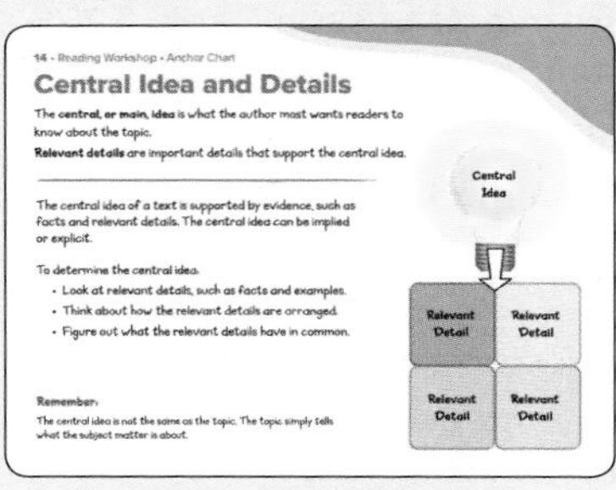

Central Idea and Details Card 14

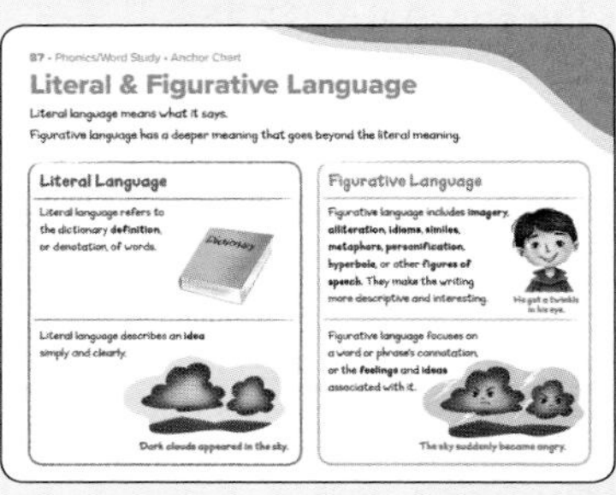

Literal & Figurative Language Card 87

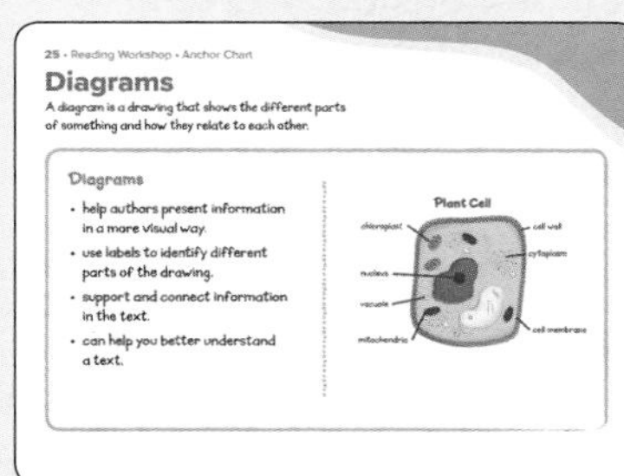

Diagrams Card 25

Digital Activities

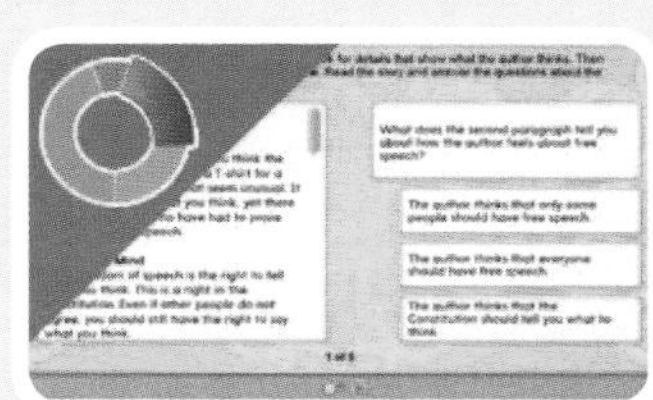

Comprehension

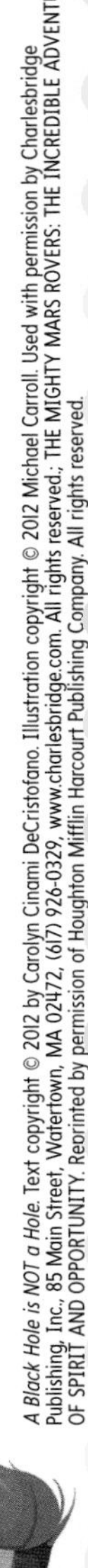

Phonics/Word Study

Center Activity Cards

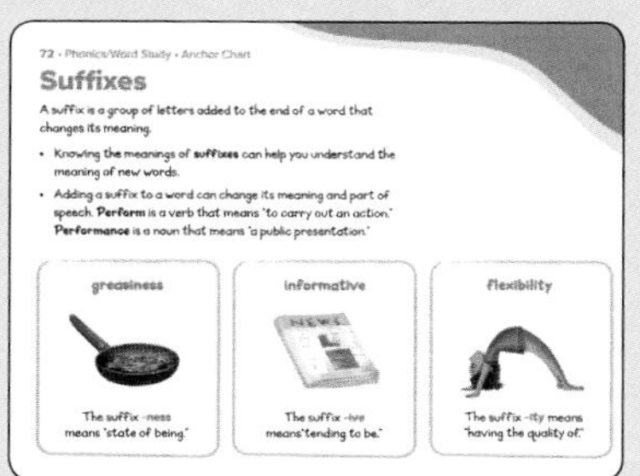
Suffixes Card 72

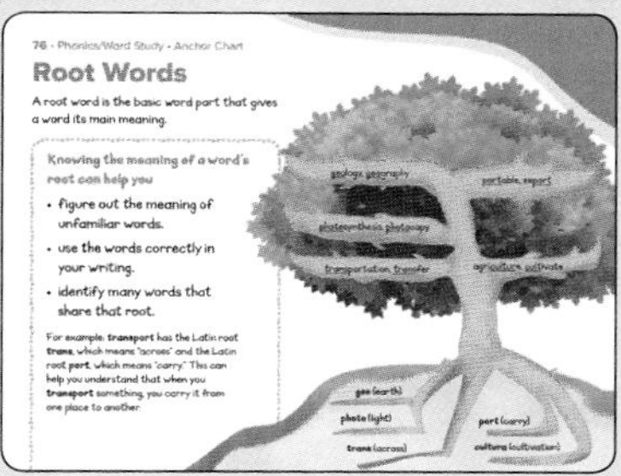
Root Words Card 76

Practice Book BLMs

Phonics: pages 295–295B, 298

Vocabulary: pages 299–300

Digital Activities

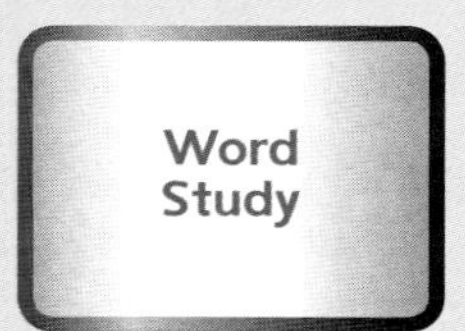

Phonics

Vocabulary

Writing

Center Activity Cards

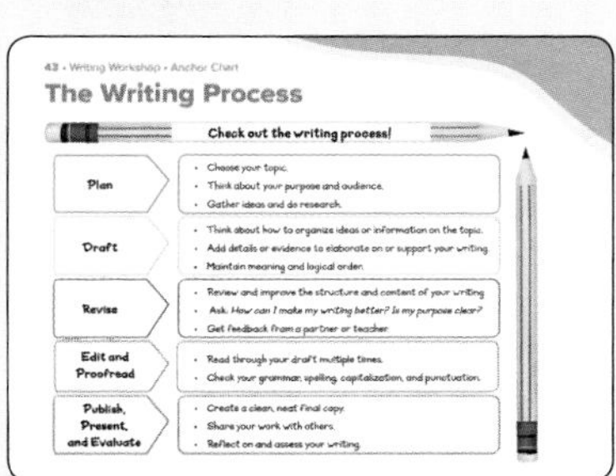
Writing Process Card 43

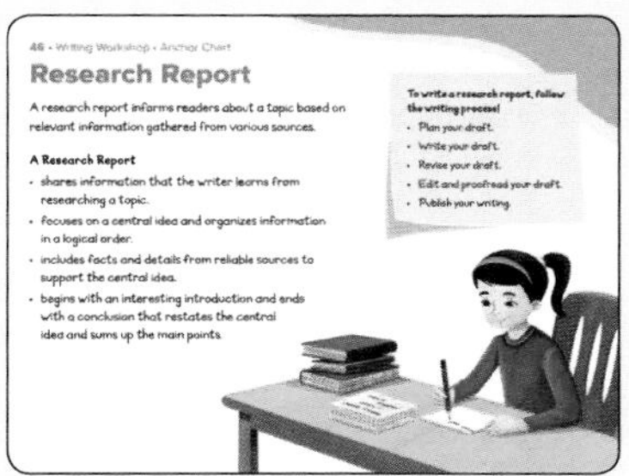
Research Report Card 46

Self-Selected Writing

Share the following prompts.

- If you could be any animal, what would you be? What do you like about that animal?
- Imagine that a helpful plant species is being threatened. How could you try to save it?
- What do you appreciate most about nature?
- Write about a goal that you have. Why do you want to accomplish this goal?

Extended Writing

Have students continue developing their **personal narratives.**

Practice Book BLMs

Grammar: pages 289–293
Spelling: pages 294–298
Handwriting: pages 361–396

Digital Activities

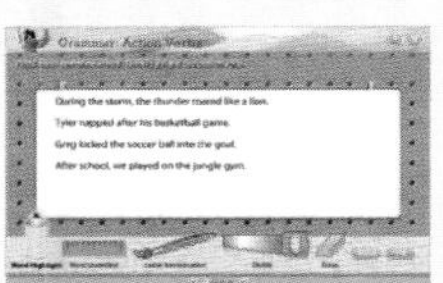
Grammar

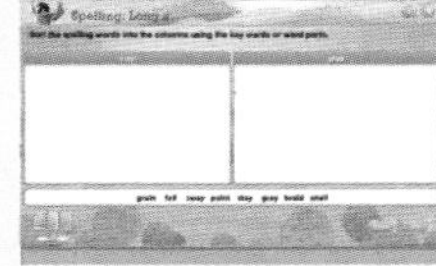
Spelling

Content Area Connections

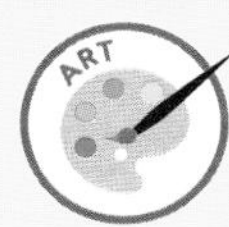

Content Area Reading Blackline Masters
- Additional texts related to Science, Social Studies, and the Arts

Research and Inquiry
- Environmental Changes

Inquiry Space
- Choose an activity

Progress Monitoring

Moving Toward Mastery

FORMATIVE ASSESSMENT
- STUDENT CHECK-IN
- CHECK FOR SUCCESS

For ongoing formative assessment, use students' self-assessments at the end of each lesson along with your own observations.

Assessing skills along the way . . .

SKILLS	HOW ASSESSED
Comprehension **Vocabulary**	Digital Activities, Rubrics
Text-Based Writing	Reading/Writing Companion: Respond to Reading
Grammar, Mechanics, Phonics, Spelling	Practice Book, Digital Activities including word sorts
Listening/Presenting/Research	Checklists
Oral Reading Fluency (ORF) Fluency Goal: 136–156 words correct per minute (WCPM) Accuracy Rate Goal: 95% or higher	Fluency Assessment

At the end of the text set . . .

SKILLS	HOW ASSESSED
Text Features: Charts and Headings **Author's Perspective** **Figurative Language: Puns**	Progress Monitoring
Root Words	

Making the Most of Assessment Results

Make data-based grouping decisions by using the following reports to verify assessment results. For additional student support options refer to the reteaching and enrichment opportunities.

ONLINE ASSESSMENT CENTER

- ***Gradebook***

DATA DASHBOARD

- ***Recommendations Report***
- ***Activity Report***
- ***Skills Report***
- ***Progress Report***
- ***Grade Card Report***

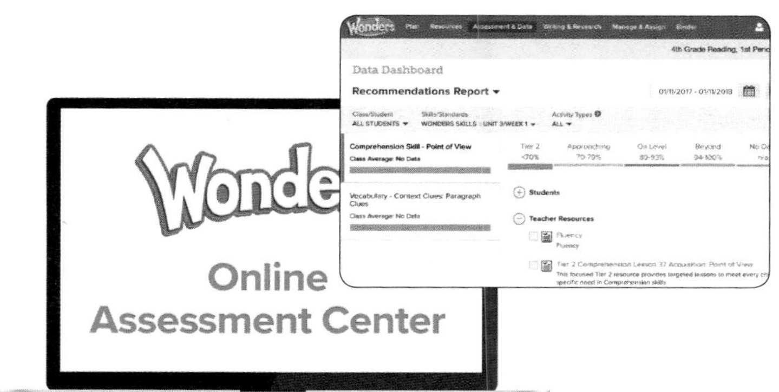

Assign practice pages online for auto-grading.

TIER 2

Reteaching Opportunities with Intervention Online PDFs

IF STUDENTS SCORE . . .	THEN ASSIGN . . .
below 70% in **comprehension . . .**	lessons 140 and 142 on Headings and Using Charts in **Comprehension PDF,** lessons 61–63 on Author's Perspective in **Comprehension PDF,** and/or lesson 130 on Figurative Language in **Comprehension PDF**
below 70% in **vocabulary . . .**	lesson 109 on Greek, Latin, and Other Roots in **Vocabulary PDF**
127–135 WCPM in **fluency . . .**	lessons from Section 1 or 7–10 of **Fluency PDF**
0–126 WCPM in **fluency . . .**	lessons from Sections 2–6 of **Fluency PDF**

Use the* Phonics/Word Study PDF *and* Foundational Skills Kit *for additional reteaching opportunities. Use the* Foundational Skills Kit *for students who need support with phonemic awareness and other early literacy skills.

Enrichment Opportunities

Beyond Level small group lessons and resources include suggestions for additional activities in these areas to extend learning opportunities for gifted and talented students:

- ***Leveled Readers***
- ***Genre Passages***
- ***Vocabulary***
- ***Comprehension***
- ***Leveled Reader Library Online***
- ***Center Activity Cards***

OBJECTIVES

Engage effectively in a range of collaborative discussions (one-on-one, in groups, and teacher-led) with diverse partners, building on others' ideas and expressing their own clearly.

Review the key ideas expressed and draw conclusions in light of information and knowledge gained from the discussions.

Build background knowledge on scientific viewpoints.

ELA ACADEMIC LANGUAGE

- *graphic organizer, collaborative*
- Cognate: *colaborativo*

DIGITAL TOOLS

Show the images during class discussion.

Discuss Concept

Watch Video

VOCABULARY

native (*originario*) growing in a place where it is usually found

area (*zona*) place

environment (*ambiente*) the place and the things around something

Build Knowledge

Essential Question

How do natural events and human activities affect the environment?

Have students read the Essential Question on page 60 of the **Reading/ Writing Companion.** Tell them they will build knowledge on how natural events and human actions affect plants and animals in different ways. They will use words to read, write, and talk about these concepts.

Watch the Video Play the opener video without sound first. Have partners narrate what they see. Then replay the video with sound as students listen.

Talk About the Video Have partners discuss how natural events and human activities affect the environment.

Write About the Video Have students add their ideas to the Build Knowledge pages of their reader's notebooks.

Anchor Chart Begin a Build Knowledge anchor chart. Write the Essential Question at the top of the chart. Have volunteers share their ideas about how natural events and human activities affect the environment. Record their ideas. Explain that students will add to the anchor chart after they read each text.

Build Knowledge

Discuss the photograph of the beekeeper. Ask: *Is this beekeeper in an agricultural or an urban environment? Why might the beekeeper be working in this environment?* Have students discuss in pairs or groups.

Build Vocabulary

Model using the graphic organizer to write down new words related to nature and the environment. Have partners continue the discussion and add the graphic organizer and new words to their reader's notebooks. Students will add words to the Build Knowledge pages in their notebooks as they read more about nature and the environment.

Collaborative Conversations

Listen Carefully As students engage in discussions, encourage them to follow discussion rules. Remind students to

- always look at the person who is speaking.
- respect others by not interrupting them.
- repeat peers' ideas to check understanding.
- draw conclusions based on knowledge gained in the discussion.

Reading/Writing Companion, pp. 60–61

Share the "Leaving a Trace" Blast assignment with students. Point out that you will discuss their responses about human impact on the environment in the Make Connections lesson at the end of this text set.

English Language Learners

Use the following scaffolds to build knowledge and vocabulary. Teach the ELL Vocabulary, as needed.

Beginning

Point to the photograph. Explain that taking care of bees can help the environment. *Bees help plants to thrive, or do well. What can you do to help the environment?* Help partners brainstorm activities that can help the environment. Use their responses to create sentence frames to further a discussion on the topic.

Intermediate

Point to the photograph. *This man is affecting the urban environment. Have you ever done something that helped an environment? Talk to your partner about what you did to affect the environment.* Discuss the difference between an agricultural and an urban environment.

Advanced/Advanced High

Have partners work together to explain how and why they once helped something thrive in the environment. Make sure partners describe their actions, the urban or agricultural setting, and how and why they helped something in that setting thrive.

 NEWCOMERS

To reinforce students' development of oral language and vocabulary, review **Newcomer Cards 5-14** and the accompanying materials in the **Newcomer Teacher's Guide**.

MY GOALS ROUTINE

What I Know Now

Read Goals Have students read the goals on Reading/Writing Companion page 62.

Reflect Review the key. Ask students to reflect on each goal and fill in the bars to show what they know now. Explain they will fill in the bars on page 63 at the end of the text set to show their progress.

LEARNING GOALS

We can actively listen to learn how natural events and human activities affect the environment.

OBJECTIVES

Analyze multiple accounts of the same event or topic, noting important similarities and differences in the point of view they represent.

Explain an author's perspective, or point of view, toward a topic in an informational text.

Use combined knowledge of all letter-sound correspondences, syllabication patterns, and morphology to read accurately unfamiliar multisyllabic words in context and out of context.

Summarize a written text read aloud or information presented in diverse media and formats, including visually, quantitatively, and orally.

Listen for a purpose.

Identify characteristics of persuasive articles.

ELA ACADEMIC LANGUAGE

- *persuade, perspective*
- Cognates: *persuadir, perspectiva*

DIGITAL TOOLS

Read or play the Interactive Read Aloud.

Interactive Read Aloud

FORMATIVE ASSESSMENT

STUDENT CHECK-IN

Have partners discuss the pros and cons of dams. Then ask students to reflect using the Check-In routine.

Interactive Read Aloud

Connect to Concept: Scientific Viewpoints

Remind students that scientists do not always agree on the best way to solve a problem. Point out that scientists on different sides of a controversial topic or issue will use evidence to defend their perspectives. Tell students that the selection you will read aloud presents two opposing perspectives on the benefits and drawbacks of dams.

Preview Argumentative Text

Anchor Chart Explain that the text you will read aloud is argumentative text. Add these features to your Argumentative Text anchor chart.

- attempts to persuade readers to agree with author's perspective
- opinions supported with facts
- may include facts to negate a counter argument
- may include text features, such as headers, captions, and labels

Ask students to think about other texts you have read aloud or they have read independently that were argumentative texts.

Read and Respond

Read the text aloud to students. Then reread it using the Teacher Think Alouds and Student Think Alongs on page T167 to build knowledge and model comprehension and the vocabulary strategy Root Words.

Summarize Have students summarize in their own words the most relevant information from "Dams: Harnessing the Power of Water." Remind students to ask and answer questions in ways that help them summarize the text.

Build Knowledge: Make Connections

Talk About the Text Have partners discuss how natural events and human activities affect the environment.

Write About the Text Have students add their ideas to their Build Knowledge pages of their reader's notebooks.

Anchor Chart Record any new ideas on the Build Knowledge anchor chart.

Add to the Vocabulary List Have students write in their reader's notebooks any words they learned about how natural events and human activities affect the environment.

Dams: Harnessing the Power of Water

Point: *The world depends on dams.*

Dams have long provided people with a way to control the flow and supply of water. They also give us an efficient way to produce electricity. (1)

Dams Produce Hydroelectric Power

Dams provide power plants with moving water to make electricity. Since the water is free, hydropower produces electricity inexpensively. Hydroelectric plants release few greenhouse gases, as they do not burn fossil fuels.

Dams Supply Water and Control Flooding

When a river is dammed, it creates an artificial lake called a reservoir. The water in a reservoir can be used to irrigate crops and for activities such as drinking and cooking.

Flood-control dams store a river's overflow in the reservoir. This keeps the excess water from flooding homes and destroying farm animals and crops.

Dams are indispensable to modern life. Thanks to dams, we have a reliable source of water. (2)

Counterpoint: *The destructive impact of dams on the environment outweighs their benefits.*

Despite the benefits provided by dams, they are not the answer to the world's need for cheap, renewable energy.

Dams Can Harm Wildlife

Damming a river and creating a reservoir floods the land, drowning some wildlife and destroying habitats. Building a dam requires constructing roads and power lines, which also causes the destruction of natural habitats.

When a river is dammed, its water flow changes. This keeps some fish from swimming upstream to breed.

Reservoirs Emit Greenhouse Gases

Scientific studies show that some reservoirs from dams release large amounts of methane and carbon dioxide. These gases contribute to climate change.

Without a better understanding of how dams impact the environment, dams will continue to create more problems than they solve. (3)

(1) Teacher Think Aloud

Asking and answering questions helps me monitor my comprehension. After reading the first paragraph, I wonder: How do dams produce electricity? The text says dams "provide power plants with moving water to make electricity."

Student Think Along

What questions can help you understand how natural events and human activities affect the environment? Share your questions with a partner. Listen for answers as I continue reading.

(2) Teacher Think Aloud

I'm not sure what the word *indispensable* means, but I know the root *dispense* can mean "to throw something away." I can infer that *indispensable* has to do with not throwing something away. When I check, I find that it means "necessary," which is something that should not be thrown away.

Student Think Along

As I reread this section, listen for other words with roots that can help you understand them, such as *inexpensively* and *renewable*. Examine these with your partner.

(3) Teacher Think Aloud

After reading the counterpoint, I ask myself: Why are dams not the answer? When I read on, I discover that dams can destroy habitats, disrupt fish breeding, and produce damaging gases.

Student Think Along

What other questions do you have about the counterpoint argument? Share your thoughts with a partner. Listen as I finish the passage. What did you learn about the ways natural events and human activities affect the environment? Discuss with your partner.

LESSON 1

"Should Plants and Animals from Other Places Live Here?"

Lexile 930L

LEARNING GOALS

We can read and understand argumentative text.

OBJECTIVES

Determine two or more central, or main, ideas of a text and explain how they are supported by relevant, or key details; summarize the text.

Explain how an author uses reasons and evidence to support particular points in a text, identifying which reasons and evidence support which point(s).

Engage effectively in a range of collaborative discussions with diverse partners, building on others' ideas and expressing their own clearly.

Pose and respond to specific questions by making comments that contribute to the discussion and elaborate on the remarks of others.

 Predict the effects of changes in ecosystems caused by living organisms, including humans.

Close Reading Routine

Read DOK 1–2

- Identify important ideas and details.
- Take notes and summarize.
- Use ACT prompts as needed.

Reread DOK 2–3

- Analyze the text, craft, and structure.
- Use the **Reread minilessons** and **prompts.**

Integrate DOK 3–4

- Integrate knowledge and ideas.
- Make text-to-text connections.
- Use the Integrate lesson.
- Complete the Share Your Knowledge task.
- Inspire action.

Read

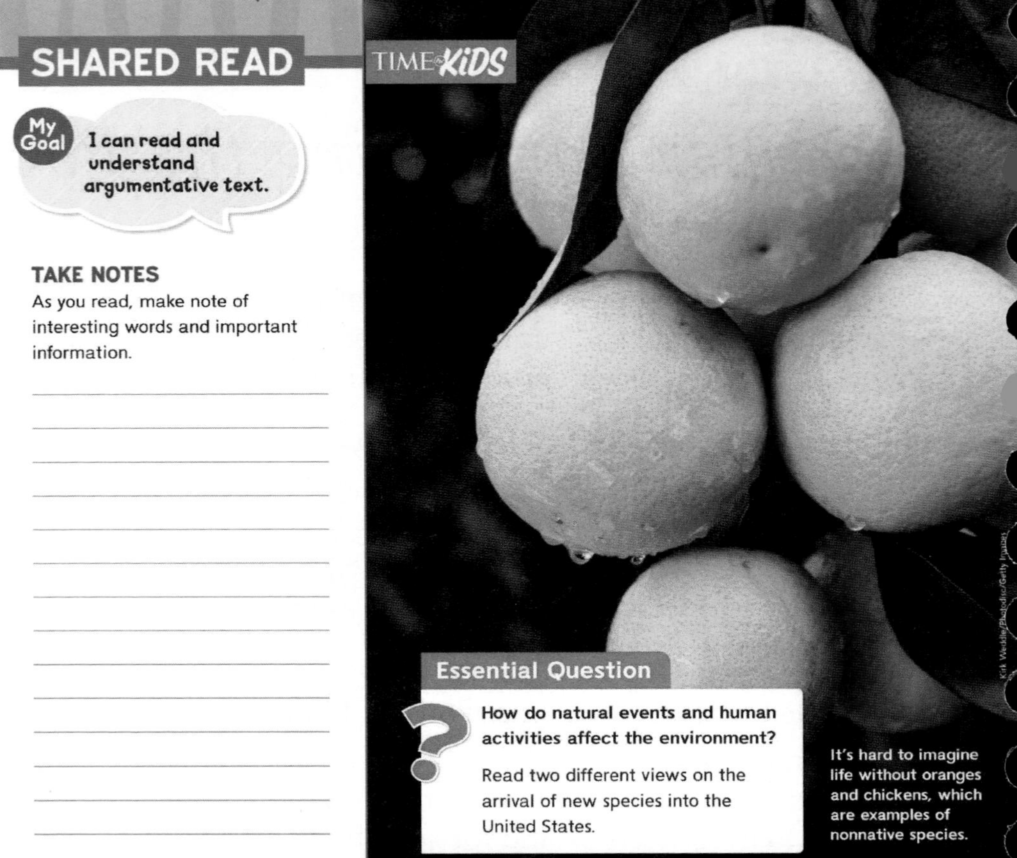

SHARED READ

My Goal: I can read and understand argumentative text.

TAKE NOTES

As you read, make note of interesting words and important information.

Essential Question

How do natural events and human activities affect the environment?

Read two different views on the arrival of new species into the United States.

It's hard to imagine life without oranges and chickens, which are examples of nonnative species.

64 Unit 5 • Text Set 3

Reading/Writing Companion, pp. 64–65

Set a Purpose Before students begin, have them think about the Essential Question and what they know about the ways human activity can affect the environment. Then preview the text and set a purpose for reading. Explain that students should use the left column of page 64 to note questions they have, interesting words they find, and key details from the text.

Focus on the Read prompts now. For additional support, use the extra prompts not included in the **Reading/Writing Companion.** Use the Reread prompts during the Craft and Structure lesson on pages T180–T181. Preteach vocabulary to students as needed.

DIFFERENTIATED READING

Approaching Level Help students find interesting words and key ideas. Complete all Read prompts with the group.

On Level Have partners complete the Read prompts independently.

Beyond Level Have partners share their responses to the Read prompts and discuss how the chart supports the prompts.

English Language Learners Preteach the vocabulary. Have Beginning/Early-Intermediate ELLs listen to the selection summary, available in multiple languages. Use the **Scaffolded Shared Read**. See also the **ELL Small Group Guide.**

Should Plants and Animals from Other Places Live Here?

New Arrivals Welcome

Nonnative species are good for the economy—and they taste good, too!

Some of America's important recent inhabitants are plants and animals. Called *nonnative species*, these creatures arrive here from other regions or countries. Nonnative species are known as *invasive* when they harm the environment, our health, or the economy. Invasive species often take over a **widespread** area and overwhelm native wildlife. The population of some native species has **declined** because of a few newcomers, but the news is not all bad. We would be a lot worse off without some of them.

In Florida, for example, about 2,000 species of familiar plants and animals are nonnative. These include oranges, chickens, and sugarcane. In fact, 90 percent of farm sales can be traced directly to nonnative species.

Nonnative species help to control insects and other pests that harm crops. Some scientists **identify** a pest's natural enemy and bring in nonnative enemy species, such as insects, to kill the pests. Killing the pests is a good thing, and an even better result is that pesticide use is reduced. Vedalia beetles were transported here from Australia to eat insects that killed citrus fruit. The beetles completed their mission without any side effects. They also help keep citrus farmers in business!

Not all new arrivals benefit humans. However, many nonnative species are just what the doctor ordered. Many of the dogs and cats we love so much originated in other parts of the world. Would you want to ban Labrador retrievers and Siamese cats? Creatures like these surely make our lives and our nation better!

ARGUMENTATIVE TEXT

FIND TEXT EVIDENCE 

Read

Paragraphs 1–2

Author's Perspective

Write the author's perspective about nonnative species.

Some nonnative species are more helpful than harmful.

Underline the details that support this claim.

Paragraphs 3–4

Ask and Answer Questions

Write a question you can ask to check your understanding about the plan to control insects and pests. Circle the answer.

Questions will vary. The appropriate response text should be circled.

Reread

Author's Craft 

Why does the author talk about both invasive nonnative species and helpful nonnative species?

Author's Perspective DOK 2

Paragraphs 1–2: *What is the author's perspective about nonnative species? How does the author support this perspective?*

Think Aloud When I read the text under "New Arrivals Welcome," I realize that it answers the question in the title. I know that nonnative species were brought into an area from somewhere else. The text says they are "good for the economy," so I think the author believes they are helpful. The author also says "we would be a lot worse off" without some nonnative species. Discuss why the word *invasive* is used to describe nonnative species, given the author's perspective.

Ask and Answer Questions DOK 1

Paragraphs 3–4: *What question might you ask about the plan to control insects and other pests?*

Think Aloud Paragraph 3 says that scientists sometimes introduce a nonnative species to do something beneficial, like controlling pests that damage crops. But can scientists predict whether or not that species might end up being invasive? That seems like a big risk to take. As I read, I'll look for details that explain if this ever happens. Have students evaluate any impact the details have on the author's perspective.

Check for Understanding DOK 2

Page 65: Monitor students' understanding of the importance of controlling the population of nonnative species. Ask: *Using information in the text, what can you infer about how nonnative species can be beneficial?* (The text suggests that nonnative species can be beneficial as long as their numbers don't get out of control. Problems occur when nonnative species become invasive.) *What are some of the different ways nonnative species benefit us?* (They provide us with food, such as oranges. Nonnative animals like Vedalia beetles help protect some crops from destruction by other insects. Nonnative breeds of dogs and cats provide companionship.)

ELL Spotlight on Idioms

Page 65, Paragraph 4 Read the paragraph aloud. Remind students that some nonnative species can benefit and be good for humans. *What do you think the idiom* just what the doctor ordered *means?* (It means a really good thing at a good time.) *Talk to your partner about which words in the paragraph let you know the meaning of the idiom. Would you consider dogs and cats* just what the doctor ordered*? Why or why not?*

Author's Perspective DOK 2

Paragraphs 1–3: Read the first three paragraphs. *Which word helps you understand how the author feels about nonnative species?* ("Threaten" tells me that the author thinks nonnative species are dangerous.) Have students identify details that support this perspective.

Root Words DOK 2

Paragraph 3: Reread the last sentence. *Use context clues and the Greek root* micro, *meaning "small," to define* microbe. (A microbe is a small living thing.) Discuss how microbes can cause lung disorders.

Author's Perspective DOK 2

Paragraph 4: *Compare the author's perspective with that of the author of "New Arrivals Welcome."* (The author of "New Arrivals Welcome" thinks nonnative species can be helpful. This author says that introducing them can be dangerous. That tells me the authors have different perspectives.)

Ask and Answer Questions DOK 1

Paragraph 4: Have students write a question and use text evidence to answer it. Ask: *How could asking a question help you understand the effect of invasive species on the environment?* (It could help me clarify whether the effect is positive or negative.)

Read

SHARED READ

FIND TEXT EVIDENCE 

Read

Paragraphs 1–4

Author's Perspective

Write the author's claim about nonnative species.

The author believes that nonnative species can threaten our country.

Underline specific examples the author gives to support this claim.

Paragraph 5

Root Words

How does the Latin root *clus,* meaning "to shut," help you know what *conclusion* means?

Sample answer: "Shut" is like "close" or "end" so a conclusion is a final statement.

Reread

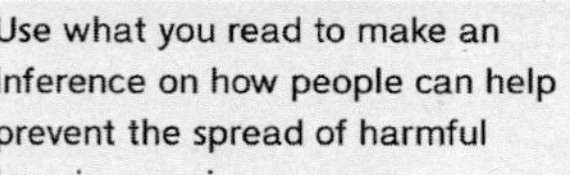

Use what you read to make an inference on how people can help prevent the spread of harmful invasive species.

66 Unit 5 • Text Set 3

TIME KIDS

A Growing Problem

Thousands of foreign plant and animal species threaten our country.

Visitors to the Florida Everglades expect to see alligators, not pythons. These huge snakes are native to Southeast Asia. But about 150,000 of the reptiles are crawling through the Everglades. The **probable** reason they got there is that pet owners dumped the snakes in the wild. Now the nonnative pythons have become a **widespread** menace, threatening to reduce the population of endangered native species.

Some nonnative species may be useful, but others are harmful to the nation. It costs the U.S. more than $120 billion each year to repair the damage these species cause to the environment. The trouble occurs when nonnative species become invasive. Invasive species are a nuisance just about everywhere in the nation. For example, the Asian carp, which was introduced unintentionally to the U.S., has been able to **thrive** in the Mississippi River and now threatens the Great Lakes ecosystem. Because of its large appetite, the population of native fish has gone down.

Some germs are also invasive species, and they are especially harmful to humans. One, the avian influenza virus, came to the U.S. carried by birds. This microbe can cause a serious lung **disorder** in infected people.

Some **agricultural** experts have introduced nonnative species on purpose to improve the environment. However, this can sometimes create **unexpected** problems. A hundred years ago, melaleuca trees were brought to Florida from Australia to stabilize swampy areas. Now millions of the trees blanket the land, crowding out native plants and harming endangered plants and animals.

The facts about this alien invasion lead to one conclusion: We must remove invasive species and keep new ones from our shores.

Reading/Writing Companion, pp. 66–67

Root Words DOK 2

Paragraph 5: Read the fifth paragraph and point out the word *conclusion*. Ask: *How does the Latin root* clus, *meaning "to shut," help you define the word?* (When you shut something, you close, or end, it. So a *conclusion* is an ending.) *Why might the author state a conclusion at this point in the article?* (It's the end of the article, so the conclusion "closes" it.)

Access Complex Text

Genre

Draw students' attention to connected ideas in the first two paragraphs of "A Growing Problem" to help clarify the author's perspective. Ask: *What two nonnative species are mentioned in these paragraphs?* (pythons, Asian carp) *What problem are both animals causing in local ecosystems?* (They kill or crowd out native animals.) *How does this damage affect the country?* (It costs billions of dollars to repair.) *Is the author's perspective on nonnative species positive or negative?* (negative)

Nonnative Species: Benefits and Costs

Over the years, about 50,000 nonnative species have entered the U.S. These four examples show the positive and negative impacts they can have.

SPECIES	NATIVE LAND	WHEN AND HOW INTRODUCED TO U.S.	POSITIVE IMPACT	NEGATIVE IMPACT
Horse	Europe	Early 1500s, on purpose	Used for work, transportation, and recreation	Made large-scale wars possible
Kudzu	Asia	Early 1800s, on purpose	Stops soil erosion	Crowds out native plants
Olives	Middle East and Europe	Early 1700s, on purpose, cultivation began in 1800s	Major food and cooking oil source, important industry in California	Uses much of the limited supply of water in California
Mediterranean Fruit Fly	Sub-Saharan Africa	1929 (first recorded), accidentally	May be a food source for creatures such as spiders	Destroys 400 species of plants, including citrus and vegetable crops

This community is trying to control the invasive melaleuca plant that has taken over this marsh.

Summarize

Use your notes to summarize the central ideas of the opposing arguments presented in the selection. Be sure to include the relevant reasons and details that support these arguments.

ARGUMENTATIVE TEXT

FIND TEXT EVIDENCE

Read

Charts and Headings

Look at the chart. Which species do you think had more of an impact on people than on the environment? Explain your answer.

Sample answer: The horse made large-scale wars possible, which would have disrupted where and how people lived.

Reread

Author's Craft

Why do you think this chart was used to end the selection?

Unit 5 • Text Set 3 67

Ask and Answer Questions DOK 1

Paragraph 1: Read the introduction above the chart. Ask: *What information does this paragraph provide?* (It tells how many nonnative species have entered the country. It also lets me know that the chart lists both positive and negative effects of four of them.) *What is one question you could ask about this information?* (Possible answer: About how many nonnative species have entered the U.S. over the years?) Discuss with students which places the nonnative species featured in the chart originally came from.

Connection of Ideas

Connect the chart and the two texts. Ask: *What kinds of animals and plants are listed in the first column of the chart?* (nonnative species) *Are these examples mentioned in either of the two argumentative texts?* (no) *What view of nonnative species does the chart provide support for—positive, negative, or both?* (both) *Why is the chart a helpful feature?* (Readers can evaluate the benefits and costs of nonnative species more objectively.)

Text Features: Charts and Headings DOK 2

Chart: Remind students that charts can help authors present information in organized ways. They can also provide information not included in the main text. Ask: *How do the headings across the top and down the left side help you understand the information in the chart?* (The headings indicate categories of information included in the chart.) *Which species do you think had more of an impact on people than on the environment?* (Possible response: The horse made large-scale wars possible. This disrupted where and how people lived.) *How is the chart helpful to the authors of both texts?* (The first author can use the positive impacts of nonnative species, while the second author can use the negative impacts.)

Summarize DOK 2

Analytical Writing **Quick Write** After their initial reads, have partners summarize the selections orally using their notes. Then have them write summaries in their reader's notebooks. Remind them to summarize both perspectives and to include only the most important information. Students may decide to digitally record presentations of summaries.

ELL Spotlight on Language

Page 66, Paragraph 2 Read the paragraph aloud. Point out the words *For example* in the fifth sentence. Say: *Authors use the phrase* for example *when they are giving more information about a topic. What idea does this sentence give information about?* (invasive species are nuisances) Have partners discuss other phrases that authors use when giving examples. (such as, for instance, like)

FORMATIVE ASSESSMENT

STUDENT CHECK-IN

Have partners share their summaries from Reading/Writing Companion page 67. Ask them to reflect using the Check-In routine.

LEARNING GOALS

- We can use new vocabulary words to read and understand argumentative text.
- We can use root words to help us figure out the meaning of unfamiliar words.

OBJECTIVES

Use common, grade-appropriate Greek and Latin affixes and roots as clues to the meaning of a word (e.g., *photograph, photosynthesis*).

Acquire and use accurately grade-appropriate general academic and domain-specific words and phrases, including those that signal contrast, addition, and other logical relationships (e.g., *however, although, nevertheless, similarly, moreover, in addition*).

ELA ACADEMIC LANGUAGE

- *root, determine, clarify*
- Cognates: *determinar, aclarar*

DIGITAL TOOLS

Visual Vocabulary Cards

Academic Vocabulary

Approaching Level and **ELL** Preteach the words before the Shared Read.

On Level Have students use the online **Visual Glossary** to define each word.

Beyond Level Have pairs use each vocabulary word in an additional sentence.

Reread

Academic Vocabulary

Use the routines on the **Visual Vocabulary Cards** to introduce each word.

Something that is **agricultural** has to do with farms or farming.
Cognate: *agricultura*

If something **declined**, it grew weaker or smaller in number.

A **disorder** is a sickness or an ailment.

If you can **identify** something, you can tell exactly what it is.
Cognate: *identificar*

Something that is **probable** is likely to happen or be true.
Cognate: *probable*

If crops **thrive**, they are successful and strong.

Something **unexpected** is not planned for or predicted.

If something is **widespread**, it is happening on a broad scale.

Encourage students to use their newly acquired vocabulary in their discussions and written responses about the texts in this text set.

Root Words

1 Explain

Explain that a **root word**, or root, gives a word its main meaning. Roots often come from a Latin or Greek word. Applying knowledge of roots can help readers determine the meanings of unfamiliar words. Have students add to the Root Words anchor chart.

2 Model

Model how to determine the meaning of the word *invasive* in the first paragraph on page 65 of the **Reading/Writing Companion**. Point out that *vas* and *vad* both come from a Latin word meaning "to go." Something that is *invasive* goes into areas beyond its boundaries.

3 Guided Practice

Guide pairs to use the meanings of the roots *nativus,* and *avis* to determine the meanings of the words *nonnative* on page 65 and *avian* on page 66. Encourage partners to see if the meanings they determine from the roots make sense in context. Have students use a print or digital resource to determine the origin of these words.

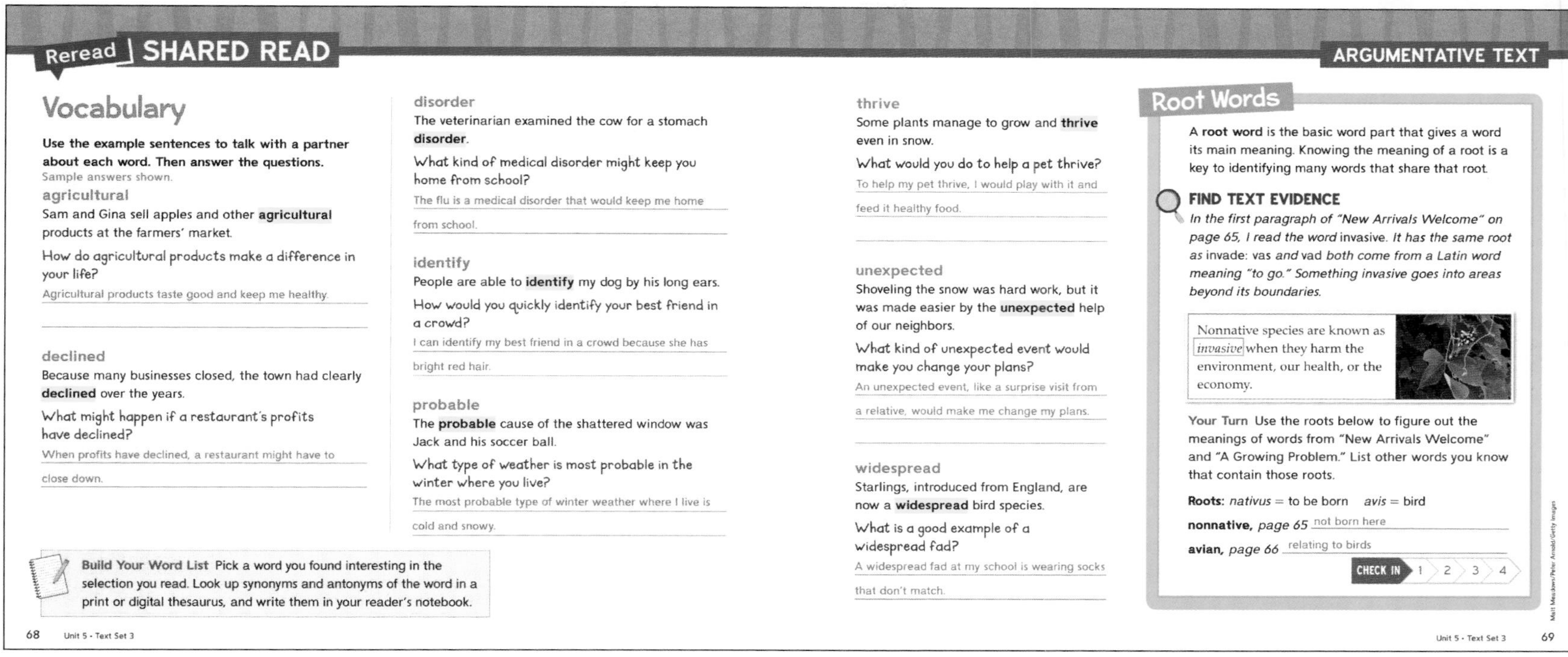

Reread | SHARED READ

ARGUMENTATIVE TEXT

Vocabulary

Use the example sentences to talk with a partner about each word. Then answer the questions.

Sample answers shown.

agricultural

Sam and Gina sell apples and other **agricultural** products at the farmers' market.

How do agricultural products make a difference in your life?

Agricultural products taste good and keep me healthy.

declined

Because many businesses closed, the town had clearly **declined** over the years.

What might happen if a restaurant's profits have declined?

When profits have declined, a restaurant might have to close down.

disorder

The veterinarian examined the cow for a stomach **disorder**.

What kind of medical disorder might keep you home from school?

The flu is a medical disorder that would keep me home from school.

identify

People are able to **identify** my dog by his long ears.

How would you quickly identify your best friend in a crowd?

I can identify my best friend in a crowd because she has bright red hair.

probable

The **probable** cause of the shattered window was Jack and his soccer ball.

What type of weather is most probable in the winter where you live?

The most probable type of winter weather where I live is cold and snowy.

thrive

Some plants manage to grow and **thrive** even in snow.

What would you do to help a pet thrive?

To help my pet thrive, I would play with it and feed it healthy food.

unexpected

Shoveling the snow was hard work, but it was made easier by the **unexpected** help of our neighbors.

What kind of unexpected event would make you change your plans?

An unexpected event, like a surprise visit from a relative, would make me change my plans.

widespread

Starlings, introduced from England, are now a **widespread** bird species.

What is a good example of a widespread fad?

A widespread fad at my school is wearing socks that don't match.

Build Your Word List Pick a word you found interesting in the selection you read. Look up synonyms and antonyms of the word in a print or digital thesaurus, and write them in your reader's notebook.

Root Words

A **root word** is the basic word part that gives a word its main meaning. Knowing the meaning of a root is a key to identifying many words that share that root.

FIND TEXT EVIDENCE

In the first paragraph of "New Arrivals Welcome" on page 65, I read the word invasive. *It has the same root as* invade: vas *and* vad *both come from a Latin word meaning "to go." Something invasive goes into areas beyond its boundaries.*

Nonnative species are known as invasive when they harm the environment, our health, or the economy.

Your Turn Use the roots below to figure out the meanings of words from "New Arrivals Welcome" and "A Growing Problem." List other words you know that contain those roots.

Roots: *nativus* = to be born *avis* = bird

nonnative, *page 65* not born here

avian, *page 66* relating to birds

CHECK IN 1 2 3 4

68 Unit 5 • Text Set 3

Unit 5 • Text Set 3 69

Reading/Writing Companion, pp. 68–69

English Language Learners

Use the following scaffolds with **Guided Practice**. For small group support, see the **ELL Small Group Guide**.

Beginning

Read the third paragraph on page 66 with students, and explain that viruses often live inside of animals, including humans (cognates: *virus, animales*). *Have you ever had the influenza virus, or the flu?* Reread the second sentence in the paragraph. *The Latin root* avis *means bird. Where do you think the avian influenza virus lives?* I think it lives inside of birds.

Intermediate

Tell students that the Latin root *avis* means bird. Have partners read the third paragraph on page 66 and work together to come up with a definition for the word *avian*. The word avian must mean ____. Have partners work together to use a print or digital resource to find the origin of the word *avian*.

Advanced/Advanced High

Tell students that the Latin root *nativus* means *to be born*. Have partners read the first paragraph on page 65 and work to determine the meanings of *native* and *nonnative* and explain why they think that. Then have partners repeat this routine with *avian* on page 66. Have partners use a dictionary or online resource to find the origin of the words *native* and *nonnative*.

BUILD YOUR WORD LIST

Students might choose *stabilize* from page 66. Have them find synonyms and antonyms to explore its meaning.

FORMATIVE ASSESSMENT

STUDENT CHECK-IN

Academic Vocabulary Ask partners to share two answers from Reading/Writing Companion pages 68-69.

Root Words Ask partners to share their Your Turn responses on page 69.

Have them use the Check-In routine to reflect and fill in the bars.

CHECK FOR SUCCESS

Rubric Use your online rubric to record student progress.

Can students identify roots within a word and use the meanings of the roots to define *nonnative* and *avian*?

Small Group Instruction

If No:

- **Approaching** Reteach p. T209

If Yes:

- **On** Review p. T216
- **Beyond** Extend p. T222

LEARNING GOALS

We can ask and answer questions to understand argumentative text.

OBJECTIVES

Determine two or more central, or main, ideas of a text and explain how they are supported by relevant, or key details; summarize the text.

Explain an author's perspective, or point of view, toward a topic in an informational text.

Ask and answer questions to increase understanding.

ELA ACADEMIC LANGUAGE

- *ask and answer questions, argumentative text*
- Cognate: *texto argumentativo*

Ask and Answer Questions

10 mins

1 Explain

Explain to students that they can monitor their comprehension of an argumentative text by asking and answering questions about it.

- Remind students to regularly pause and then ask themselves questions about what they just read.
- If students are confused about a paragraph or section, they should reread it. They may need to reread the section or paragraph more than once to discover the answers to their questions.

Point out that students should ask questions before they read as a way of setting a purpose for reading. They should then ask and answer questions about each section while they read and about the entire text after they finish reading.

Anchor Chart Have a volunteer add any additional points about the strategy to the Ask and Answer Questions anchor chart.

2 Model

Model how to ask and answer questions using the argumentative text "New Arrivals Welcome." For example, after completing the first paragraph on **Reading/Writing Companion** page 65, you might ask yourself, *How do nonnative species arrive here from other regions?* When you read the third paragraph, you understand that "some scientists . . . bring in nonnative enemy species" to control pests.

3 Guided Practice

Help pairs ask and answer a question about "A Growing Problem" on page 66. For example, suggest that students ask themselves, *What are some invasive species in the United States? What is the author's perspective on invasive species?* Remind students to reread and identify details that help them answer their questions. To ensure their understanding of the text, guide partners as they take turns asking each other questions and rereading for answers.

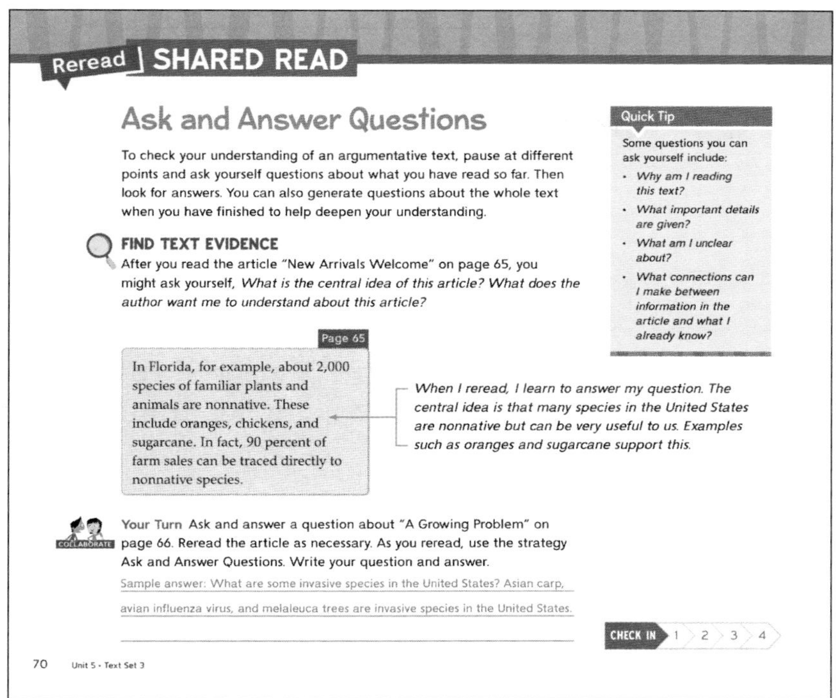

Reread | SHARED READ

Ask and Answer Questions

To check your understanding of an argumentative text, pause at different points and ask yourself questions about what you have read so far. Then look for answers. You can also generate questions about the whole text when you have finished to help deepen your understanding.

FIND TEXT EVIDENCE
After you read the article "New Arrivals Welcome" on page 65, you might ask yourself, *What is the central idea of this article? What does the author want me to understand about this article?*

Page 65

In Florida, for example, about 2,000 species of familiar plants and animals are nonnative. These include oranges, chickens, and sugarcane. In fact, 90 percent of farm sales can be traced directly to nonnative species.

When I reread, I learn to answer my question. The central idea is that many species in the United States are nonnative but can be very useful to us. Examples such as oranges and sugarcane support this.

Quick Tip

Some questions you can ask yourself include:

- *Why am I reading this text?*
- *What important details are given?*
- *What am I unclear about?*
- *What connections can I make between information in the article and what I already know?*

COLLABORATE

Your Turn Ask and answer a question about "A Growing Problem" on page 66. Reread the article as necessary. As you reread, use the strategy Ask and Answer Questions. Write your question and answer.

Sample answer: What are some invasive species in the United States? Asian carp, avian influenza virus, and melaleuca trees are invasive species in the United States.

CHECK IN 1 2 3 4

70 Unit 5 • Text Set 3

Reading/Writing Companion, p. 70

English Language Learners

Use the following scaffolds with **Guided Practice.** For small group support, see the **ELL Small Group Guide**.

Beginning

Restate the suggested questions students will ask themselves as they read, and help them answer the questions: *The United States has some invasive species. What are they?* Read the last two paragraphs on page 66. Melaleuca trees are invasive species in Florida. *The author has a strong perspective about invasive species in the United States. What is it?* Have pairs reread the last sentence on page 60, and talk about what the author thinks of invasive species. The author thinks we need to remove all invasive species.

Intermediate

Restate the suggested questions partners will ask themselves as they read: *There are some invasive species in the United States. What are they? What is the author's perspective on invasive species? Reread the last two paragraphs on page 66, and ask and answer these questions with your partner.* (Melaleuca trees; the author wants to get rid of all invasive species)

Advanced/Advanced High

Have each partner skim page 66 to come up with two questions to ensure their partner's understanding of the text. Have partners reread the page together, asking and answering each other's questions using the terms *invasive species* and *author's perspective.*

HABITS OF LEARNING

I think critically about what I am reading.

Understanding how to ask and answer questions about texts helps students learn this key habit of learning. Remind students to ask the following question about anything they read in school and outside of the classroom: *Does this fit with what I already know?*

FORMATIVE ASSESSMENT

STUDENT CHECK-IN

Ask partners to share their Your Turn responses on Reading/Writing Companion page 70. Have them use the Check-In routine to reflect and fill in the bars.

CHECK FOR SUCCESS

Can students ask and answer questions about part or all of the text? Do they reread as needed to answer their questions?

Small Group Instruction

If No:

- **Approaching** Reteach p. T202

If Yes:

- **On** Review p. T212
- **Beyond** Extend p. T218

Reread

Text Features: Charts and Headings

LEARNING GOALS

We can use charts and headings to read and understand argumentative text.

OBJECTIVES

Analyze multiple accounts of the same event or topic, noting important similarities and differences in the point of view they represent.

Explain an author's perspective, or point of view, toward a topic in an informational text.

Interpret information presented visually, orally, or quantitatively (e.g., in charts, graphs, diagrams, time lines, animations, or interactive elements on Web pages) and explain how the information contributes to an understanding of the text in which it appears.

ELA ACADEMIC LANGUAGE

- *argumentative text, persuade, opinions, chart, heading*
- Cognates: *texto argumentativo, persuadir, opiniones*

1 Explain

Share with students the following key characteristics of **argumentative texts**.

- Argumentative texts try to persuade readers to support an author's perspective. The author's perspective reveals his or her attitude on a topic or issue.
- Authors of argumentative texts support their perspectives with facts and relevant details. They may also use facts to argue against positions that oppose their own.
- Argumentative texts typically include text features, such as headings and charts, to organize information and data. These text features support the author's perspective.

2 Model

Identify text evidence and text features that indicate that "New Arrivals Welcome" and "A Growing Problem" are argumentative texts. Point out that the titles and headings in these articles reveal the authors' perspectives on nonnative species. Each article contains facts that support each author's perspective.

Chart Direct students' attention to the chart on **Reading/Writing Companion** page 67. Explain that the chart organizes information so it can be easily analyzed and compared. With students, read the title of the chart, "Nonnative Species: Benefits and Costs," and identify the heading of each row and column. Ask: *How does this chart help you analyze the authors' different perspectives on nonnative species?*

Headings Point out that the last two column headings in the chart—"Positive Impact" and "Negative Impact"—make it easy to compare the positive and negative effects of each nonnative species.

Anchor Chart Have a volunteer add these features to the Argumentative Text anchor chart.

3 Guided Practice

Guide pairs as they analyze information in the chart on Reading/ Writing Companion page 67 and identify one species that has a mostly positive impact and one that has a mostly negative impact. Have partners discuss how each author could use facts in the chart to support his or her perspective. Then have students share and compare their findings with the class.

Independent Practice Have students read the online **Differentiated Genre Passage**, "What Is the Future of the Rain Forests?"

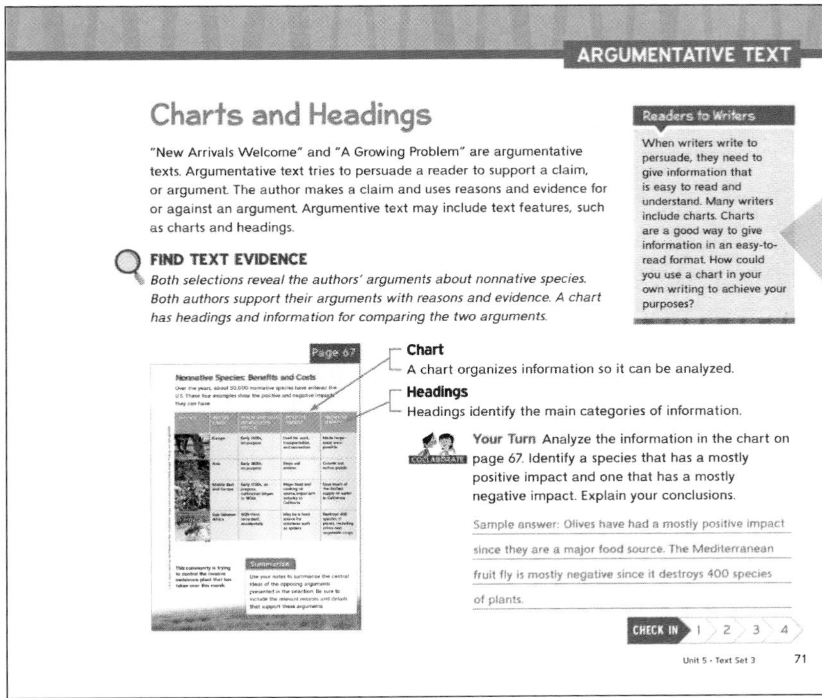
ARGUMENTATIVE TEXT

Charts and Headings

"New Arrivals Welcome" and "A Growing Problem" are argumentative texts. Argumentative text tries to persuade a reader to support a claim, or argument. The author makes a claim and uses reasons and evidence for or against an argument. Argumentive text may include text features, such as charts and headings.

FIND TEXT EVIDENCE

Both selections reveal the authors' arguments about nonnative species. Both authors support their arguments with reasons and evidence. A chart has headings and information for comparing the two arguments.

Readers to Writers

When writers write to persuade, they need to give information that is easy to read and understand. Many writers include charts. Charts are a good way to give information in an easy-to-read format. How could you use a chart in your own writing to achieve your purposes?

Page 67

Chart
A chart organizes information so it can be analyzed.

Headings
Headings identify the main categories of information.

COLLABORATE **Your Turn** Analyze the information in the chart on page 67. Identify a species that has a mostly positive impact and one that has a mostly negative impact. Explain your conclusions.

Sample answer: Olives have had a mostly positive impact since they are a major food source. The Mediterranean fruit fly is mostly negative since it destroys 400 species of plants.

CHECK IN 1 2 3 4

Unit 5 • Text Set 3 71

Reading/Writing Companion, p. 71

Readers to Writers

Remind students that including charts in an argumentative text helps authors present factual information that is easy for readers to analyze and interpret. Have students look back at the chart on page 67. Ask: *How could an author use the information on kudzu to support a negative opinion? How could the information be used to support a positive opinion?*

English Language Learners

Use the following scaffolds with **Guided Practice.** For small group support, see the **ELL Small Group Guide**.

Beginning

Point to the horse in the chart on page 67, and ask if any students have ever ridden a horse. Read the information for the horse with students. (cognates: *impacto, positivo, negativo, transportación*) Help partners discuss whether they think the horse has a mostly positive impact or a mostly negative impact. Explain that *mostly* means *for the most part.* The horse has a lot of positive/negative impacts because it _______.

Intermediate

Have students work in pairs to review the information on the horse and kudzu in the chart on page 67. Guide them to use the information in the chart to state which species has a mostly positive impact and which has a mostly negative impact. The impact of horses/kudzu is mostly _______ because _______. *Talk to your partner about how one of the authors could use one of these species as an example.*

Advanced/Advanced High

Have partners read the chart on page 67. Have partners identify one species on the page that has a mostly positive impact and one that has a mostly negative impact. Have partners explain to each other how they arrived to these conclusions and talk about which author could use which species as an example.

FORMATIVE ASSESSMENT

STUDENT CHECK-IN

Ask partners to share their Your Turn responses on Reading/Writing Companion page 71. Have them use the Check-In routine to reflect and fill in the bars.

CHECK FOR SUCCESS

Can students determine why "New Arrivals Welcome" and "A Growing Problem" are argumentative texts? Can they explain how headings and charts help authors of argumentative texts support their opinions?

Small Group Instruction

If No:

- **Approaching** Reteach p. T204

If Yes:

- **On** Review p. T214
- **Beyond** Extend p. T220

LEARNING GOALS

We can read and understand argumentative text by Identifying authors' perspectives.

OBJECTIVES

Analyze multiple accounts of the same event or topic, noting important similarities and differences in the point of view they represent.

Explain how an author uses reasons and evidence to support particular points in a text, identifying which reasons and evidence support which point(s).

Explain an author's perspective, or point of view, toward an argumentative text.

ELA ACADEMIC LANGUAGE

- *perspective, position, reasons, evidence, negative, positive*
- Cognates: *posición, razones, evidencia, negativo, positivo*

DIGITAL TOOLS

To differentiate instruction for key skills, use the results of the activity.

Reread

Author's Perspective

1 Explain

Explain to students that an author of an argumentative text shares his or her perspective, or point of view, toward an issue or topic.

- Authors of argumentative text use details, descriptions, reasons, and evidence to support their perspectives and make it more likely that readers will agree with it. They can also use facts to challenge an idea that does not support their own perspective.
- Word choice and an understanding of nuance can help readers understand an author's perspective. Some words, such as *toxic* and *dangerous*, have a negative connotation, whereas other words, such as *benefits* and *cuddly*, have a positive connotation.
- Point out that examining details, descriptions, reasons, evidence, and word choice can help students identify the author's perspective and decide whether or not they agree with it.

Anchor Chart Have a volunteer add these features to the Author's Perspective anchor chart.

2 Model

Identify word choices in the title, in the heading following the title, and in the text of "A Growing Problem" on Reading/Writing Companion page 66 that reveal the author's perspective. Then use the details listed on the graphic organizer to determine the author's negative perspective toward nonnative species.

3 Guided Practice

Help pairs to identify important details in "New Arrivals Welcome" on Reading/Writing Companion page 65 and record them in their graphic organizers. Ask partners to use these details to determine the author's perspective about nonnative species.

Analytical Writing **Write About Reading: Summary** Ask each pair to work together to summarize the reasons and evidence the author of "New Arrivals Welcome" provides to support his or her perspective about nonnative species. Then ask partners to tell which article's reasons and evidence they found more convincing and why. Have them share their views in a class discussion.

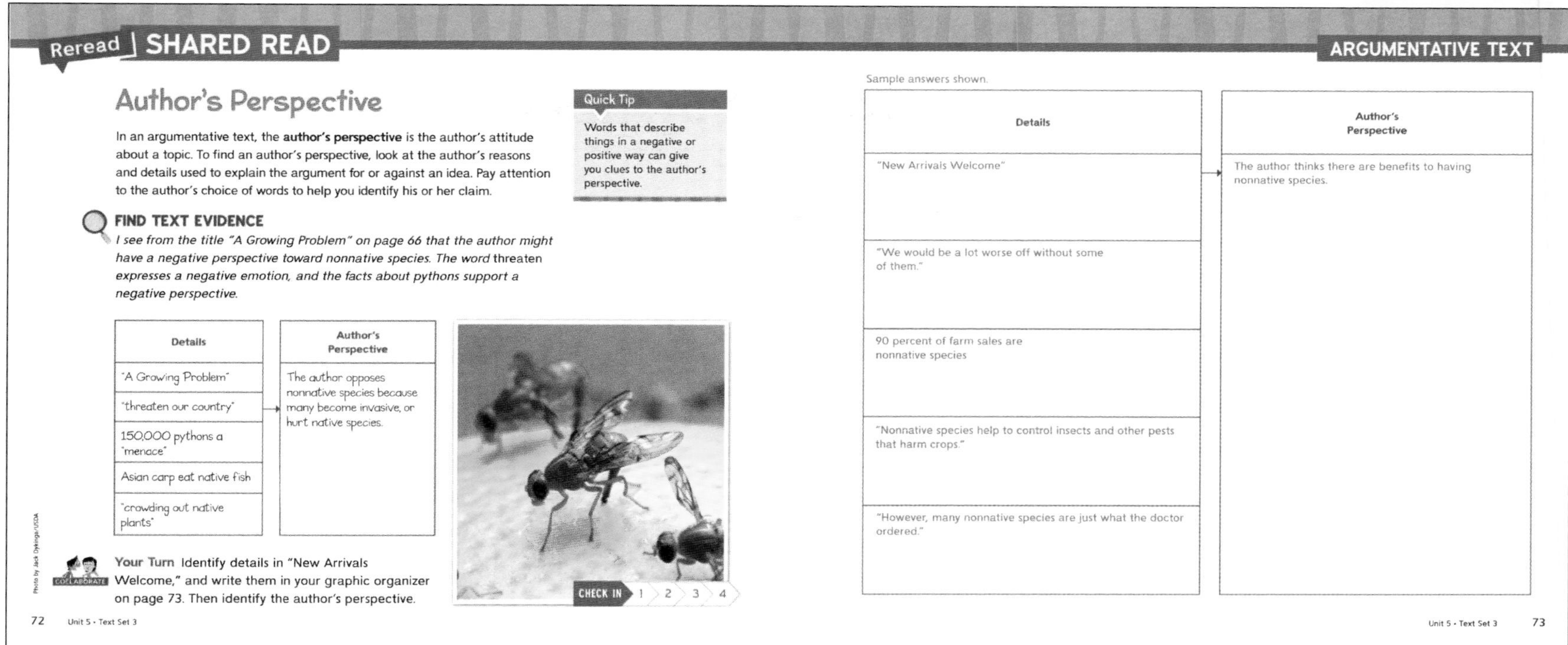

Reread | SHARED READ

ARGUMENTATIVE TEXT

Author's Perspective

In an argumentative text, the **author's perspective** is the author's attitude about a topic. To find an author's perspective, look at the author's reasons and details used to explain the argument for or against an idea. Pay attention to the author's choice of words to help you identify his or her claim.

Quick Tip

Words that describe things in a negative or positive way can give you clues to the author's perspective.

FIND TEXT EVIDENCE

I see from the title "A Growing Problem" on page 66 that the author might have a negative perspective toward nonnative species. The word threaten *expresses a negative emotion, and the facts about pythons support a negative perspective.*

Details	Author's Perspective
"A Growing Problem"	The author opposes nonnative species because many become invasive, or hurt native species.
"threaten our country"	
150,000 pythons a "menace"	
Asian carp eat native fish	
"crowding out native plants"	

Photo by Jack Dykinga/USDA

COLLABORATE **Your Turn** Identify details in "New Arrivals Welcome," and write them in your graphic organizer on page 73. Then identify the author's perspective.

CHECK IN 1 2 3 4

72 Unit 5 • Text Set 3

Sample answers shown.

Details	Author's Perspective
"New Arrivals Welcome"	The author thinks there are benefits to having nonnative species.
"We would be a lot worse off without some of them."	
90 percent of farm sales are nonnative species	
"Nonnative species help to control insects and other pests that harm crops."	
"However, many nonnative species are just what the doctor ordered."	

Unit 5 • Text Set 3 73

Reading/Writing Companion, pp. 72–73

English Language Learners

Use the following scaffolds with **Guided Practice**. For small group support, see the **ELL Small Group Guide**.

Beginning

Review with students how to identify author's perspective. Read the head and subhead of "New Arrivals Welcome" on page 65 with students. Say: *Does the author think new arrivals are good or bad?* (good) *How do you know?* Have students point to the word *good* found in the subhead twice. Read the second paragraph on page 65. Florida has many nonnative species like oranges, chickens, and sugarcane. Help partners fill in the graphic organizer on page 73.

Intermediate

Review with students how to identify the author's perspective. Have partners read "New Arrivals Welcome" on page 65 and identify the positive details about nonnative species, adding the details to the graphic organizer. *What is the author's perspective?* The author believes that many nonnative species are good for the economy. Then have partners fill in their graphic organizer on page 73.

Advanced/Advanced High

Guide partners to identify the author's perspective and details that help readers point of view in "New Arrivals Welcome" on page 65. Have them record the details in their graphic organizers and then share the details they found with the class.

FORMATIVE ASSESSMENT

STUDENT CHECK-IN

Ask partners to share their graphic organizers on Reading/Writing Companion page 72. Have them use the Check-In routine to reflect and fill in the bars.

CHECK FOR SUCCESS

Rubric Use your online rubric to record student progress.

Are students able to identify relevant details in an argumentative text and use them to determine the author's perspective?

Small Group Instruction

If No:

- **Approaching** Reteach p. T211

If Yes:

- **On** Review p. T217
- **Beyond** Extend p. T223

LEARNING GOALS

We can reread to analyze craft and structure in argumentative text.

OBJECTIVES

Draw on information from multiple print or digital sources, demonstrating the ability to locate an answer to a question quickly or to solve a problem efficiently.

Explain how an author uses reasons and evidence to support particular points in a text, identifying which reasons and evidence support which point(s).

Identify the author's purpose.

ELA ACADEMIC LANGUAGE

- *techniques, express, viewpoint, opposing*
- Cognates: *técnicas, expresar*

TEACH IN SMALL GROUP

Approaching Level Use the prompts to guide students as they reread parts of "Should Plants and Animals from Other Places Live Here?" Have them mark the margins to indicate text evidence.

On Level Help partners complete the Reread prompts and share their answers.

Beyond Level Allow students to work independently or in pairs to answer the Reread prompts.

ELL Have Beginning and Early-Intermediate ELLs use the **Scaffolded Shared Read.**

Reread

Craft and Structure

10 mins

Tell students they will now reread parts of "Should Plants and Animals from Other Places Live Here?" and analyze the techniques the authors used in writing each argument. When authors write argumentative texts, they typically express and support their perspectives with facts and evidence. They sometimes address opposing perspectives.

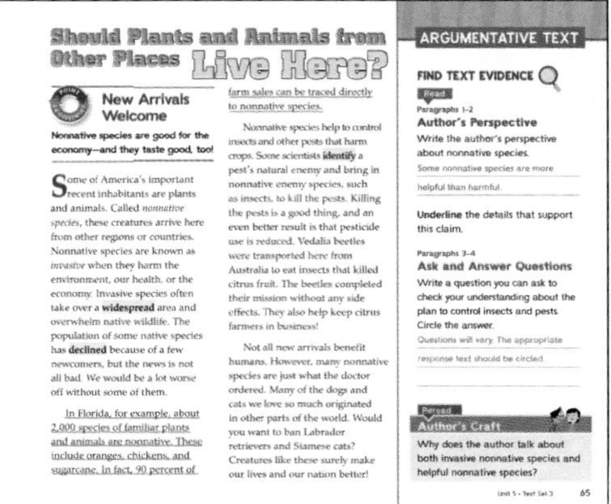

Should Plants and Animals from Other Places Live Here?

New Arrivals Welcome

Nonnative species are good for the economy—and they taste good, too!

Some of America's important recent inhabitants are plants and animals. Called *nonnative species*, these creatures arrive here from other regions or countries. Nonnative species are known as *invasive* when they harm the environment, our health, or the economy. Invasive species often take over a **widespread** area and overwhelm native wildlife. The population of some native species has **declined** because of a few newcomers, but the news is not all bad. We would be a lot worse off without some of them.

In Florida, for example, about 2,000 species of familiar plants and animals are nonnative. These include oranges, chickens, and sugarcane. In fact, 90 percent of farm sales can be traced directly to nonnative species.

Nonnative species help to control insects and other pests that harm crops. Some scientists **identify** a pest's natural enemy and bring in nonnative enemy species, such as insects, to kill the pests. Killing the pests is a good thing, and an even better result is that pesticide use is reduced. Vedalia beetles were transported here from Australia to eat insects that killed citrus fruit. The beetles completed their mission without any side effects. They also help keep citrus farmers in business!

Not all new arrivals benefit humans. However, many nonnative species are just what the doctor ordered. Many of the dogs and cats we love so much originated in other parts of the world. Would you want to ban Labrador retrievers and Siamese cats? Creatures like these surely make our lives and our nation better!

ARGUMENTATIVE TEXT

FIND TEXT EVIDENCE

Read

Paragraphs 1-2

Author's Perspective

Write the author's perspective about nonnative species.

Some nonnative species are more helpful than harmful.

Underline the details that support this claim.

Paragraphs 3-4

Ask and Answer Questions

Write a question you can ask to check your understanding about the plan to control insects and pests. Circle the answer.

Questions will vary. The appropriate response text should be circled.

Reread

Author's Craft

Why does the author talk about both invasive nonnative species and helpful nonnative species?

Unit 5 • Text Set 3 65

Reading/Writing Companion, p. 65

AUTHOR'S CRAFT DOK 2

Reread the first paragraph on page 65 with students. Ask: *What point does the author make about invasive species in this paragraph?* (The author explains that invasive species can be harmful, but also points out that not all nonnative species are invasive and that some benefit us.)

ELL Have pairs reread the third sentence in the first paragraph on page 65. An invasive species is a type of nonnative species. An invasive species is harmful in some way. Reread the last two sentences of the paragraph. The author points out that some nonnative species that are not invasive can be helpful to us.

Why does the author talk about both invasive nonnative species and helpful nonnative species? (The author wants to address opposing perspectives. The author admits that the problem with invasive species is real, but also emphasizes that some nonnative species are useful.)

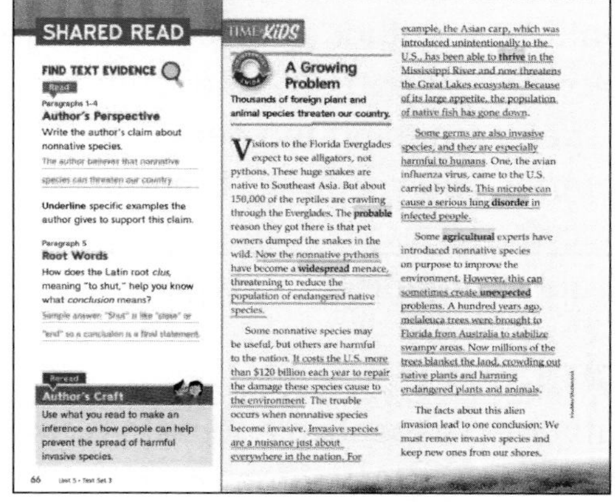

SHARED READ

FIND TEXT EVIDENCE

Read

Paragraphs 1-4

Author's Perspective

Write the author's claim about nonnative species.

The author believes that nonnative species can threaten our country.

Underline specific examples the author gives to support this claim.

Paragraph 5

Root Words

How does the Latin root *clus*, meaning "to shut," help you know what *conclusion* means?

Sample answer: "Shut" is like "close" or "end" so a conclusion is a final statement.

Reread

Author's Craft

Use what you read to make an inference on how people can help prevent the spread of harmful invasive species.

66 Unit 5 • Text Set 3

TIME KIDS

A Growing Problem

Thousands of foreign plant and animal species threaten our country.

Visitors to the Florida Everglades expect to see alligators, not pythons. These huge snakes are native to Southeast Asia. But about 150,000 of the reptiles are crawling through the Everglades. The **probable** reason they got there is that pet owners dumped the snakes in the wild. Now the nonnative pythons have become a **widespread** menace, threatening to reduce the population of endangered native species.

Some nonnative species may be useful, but others are harmful to the nation. It costs the U.S. more than $120 billion each year to repair the damage these species cause to the environment. The trouble occurs when nonnative species become invasive. Invasive species are a nuisance just about everywhere in the nation. For example, the Asian carp, which was introduced unintentionally to the U.S., has been able to **thrive** in the Mississippi River and now threatens the Great Lakes ecosystem. Because of its large appetite, the population of native fish has gone down.

Some germs are also invasive species, and they are especially harmful to humans. One, the avian influenza virus, came to the U.S. carried by birds. This microbe can cause a serious lung **disorder** in infected people.

Some **agricultural** experts have introduced nonnative species on purpose to improve the environment. However, this can sometimes create **unexpected** problems. A hundred years ago, melaleuca trees were brought to Florida from Australia to stabilize swampy areas. Now millions of the trees blanket the land, crowding out native plants and harming endangered plants and animals.

The facts about this alien invasion lead to one conclusion: We must remove invasive species and keep new ones from our shores.

Reading/Writing Companion, p. 66

AUTHOR'S CRAFT DOK 2

Reread the first four paragraphs of page 66. Ask: *How did the python become an invasive species?* (Pets were dumped in the wild.) *What did the introduction of the Asian carp and avian virus have in common with the python?* (They were also introduced accidentally.) *How was the introduction of the melaleuca tree different?* (It was introduced on purpose.)

ELL Have partners locate *unintentionally* in paragraph 2. Explain that it means *not done on purpose* or *accidentally. Did people introduce, or bring, the Asian carp species to the U.S. accidentally?* (Yes.) *How do you know?* The author states that it was introduced unintentionally.

Use what you read to make an inference on how people can help prevent the spread of harmful invasive species. (Possible response: People can be responsible and not dump their nonnative animals into the wild. The government can be more selective about which species to introduce.)

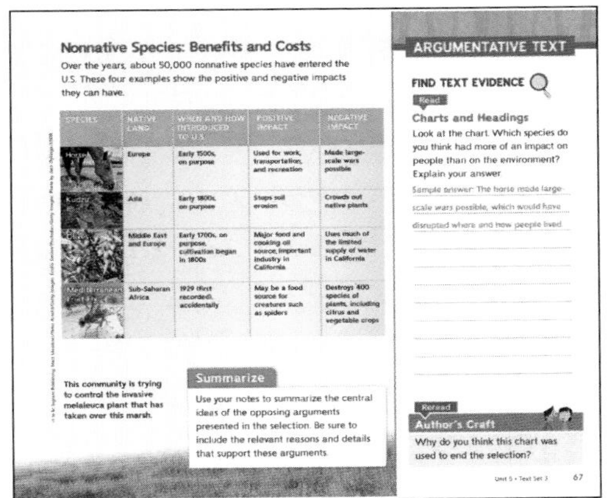

Nonnative Species: Benefits and Costs

Over the years, about 50,000 nonnative species have entered the U.S. These four examples show the positive and negative impacts they can have.

SPECIES	NATIVE LAND	WHEN AND HOW INTRODUCED TO U.S.	POSITIVE IMPACT	NEGATIVE IMPACT
Horse	Europe	Early 1500s, on purpose	Used for work, transportation, and recreation	Made large-scale wars possible
Kudzu	Asia	Early 1800s, on purpose	Stops soil erosion	Crowds out native plants
[illegible]	Middle East and Europe	Early 1700s, on purpose, cultivation began in 1800s	Major food and cooking oil source; important industry in California	Uses much of the limited supply of water in California
Mediterranean [illegible]	Sub-Saharan Africa	1929 (first recorded), accidentally	May be a food source for creatures such as spiders	Destroys 400 species of plants, including citrus and vegetable crops

This community is trying to control the invasive melaleuca plant that has taken over this marsh.

Summarize

Use your notes to summarize the central ideas of the opposing arguments presented in the selection. Be sure to include the relevant reasons and details that support these arguments.

ARGUMENTATIVE TEXT

FIND TEXT EVIDENCE

Read

Charts and Headings

Look at the chart. Which species do you think had more of an impact on people than on the environment? Explain your answer.

Sample answer: The horse made large-scale wars possible, which would have disrupted where and how people lived.

Reread

Author's Craft

Why do you think this chart was used to end the selection?

Unit 5 • Text Set 3 67

Reading/Writing Companion, p. 67

AUTHOR'S CRAFT DOK 2

Review the features of a chart before rereading page 67. Ask: *How does the chart support information from both "New Arrivals Welcome" and "A Growing Problem"?* (It includes examples of positive impacts of nonnative species, which is the focus of "New Arrivals Welcome," as well as negative impacts of invasive species, which "A Growing Problem" describes.)

ELL Have students locate the word *Positive* in the fourth column heading. *Something positive is good.* (cognate: *positivo*) *Which article says that nonnative species can be good?* ("New Arrivals Welcome") Repeat by making a connection between the *Negative* column and "A Growing Problem." (cognate: *negativo*)

Why do you think this chart was used to end the selection? (Possible answer: It supports both articles by summarizing both the positive and negative impacts of nonnative species. This helps readers evaluate both articles.)

EVALUATE INFORMATION

Explain that when you evaluate information, you think about how significant or important it is. Evaluating information can help you determine whether you agree or disagree with an author's perspective.

Think Aloud After reading both articles in "Should Plants and Animals from Other Places Live Here?," I was still undecided about which author's argument was more convincing. So I evaluated the information in the *Positive Impact* and *Negative Impact* columns of the chart. To me, negative impacts like large scale wars and the destruction of many species outweigh the positive impacts in the chart. Evaluating this information convinced me that I agreed with the second author's perspective.

Integrate

BUILD KNOWLEDGE: MAKE CONNECTIONS

Talk About the Text Have partners discuss how nonnative species can be both helpful and harmful.

Write About the Text Have students add ideas to the Build Knowledge pages of their reader's notebooks.

Anchor Chart Record any new ideas on the Build Knowledge anchor chart.

Add to the Vocabulary List Have students write down any words they learned about how natural events and human activities affect the environment in their reader's notebooks.

FORMATIVE ASSESSMENT

STUDENT CHECK-IN

Have partners share their responses to one of the Reread prompts on Reading/Writing Companion pages 65–67. Ask them to reflect using the Check-In routine.

Reread

Write About the Shared Read

LEARNING GOALS

We can use text evidence to respond to argumentative text.

OBJECTIVES

Explain how an author uses reasons and evidence to support particular points in a text, identifying which reasons and evidence support which point(s).

Identify the author's purpose.

Explain an author's perspective, or point of view, toward a topic in an informational text.

Introduce a topic or text clearly, state an opinion, and create an organizational structure in which ideas are logically grouped to support the writer's purpose.

Provide logically ordered reasons that are supported by facts and details.

ELA ACADEMIC LANGUAGE

- *argument, reason, support, evidence*
- Cognates: *argumento, razón, evidencia*

TEACH IN SMALL GROUP

Approaching Level Have pairs gather evidence that supports each argument presented, and decide which is more convincing.

On Level Have pairs exchange completed opinion statements and provide feedback.

Beyond Level Have partners work together to develop step-by-step guidance for evaluating evidence.

ELL Group students of mixed proficiency levels to discuss and respond to the prompt.

Analyze the Prompt DOK 3

Read the prompt aloud: *Did you find one author's argument more convincing than the other? Explain your answer.* Ask: *What is the prompt asking?* (to evaluate whether one author did a better job of arguing a perspective) Say: *Let's reread to see how each author organized and presented information. As we go through the two arguments, we can note text evidence. This will help you write your response.*

Analyze Text Evidence

Remind students that an author generally presents a specific perspective in an argument and supports it with reasons, facts, and relevant evidence. Students should look for a statement that conveys a perspective along with relevant details that support it. Have students reread the first paragraph on page 65 in the **Reading/Writing Companion**. Ask: *Which sentence best conveys the author's perspective about nonnative species?* ("We would be a lot worse off without some of them.") *What are some examples the author provides in the second paragraph to support this perspective?* (The author mentions oranges, chickens, and sugarcane as examples of useful nonnative species.) Have students look for other examples the author provides as support. Then have students identify the perspective and relevant evidence of the second author on page 66.

Respond

Direct student pairs to the sentence starters on Reading/Writing Companion page 74. Ask: *How does closely studying the way each author presents information help you determine which author did a better job presenting their perspective?* As needed, model a response.

Think Aloud The use of the word "harmful" in the first sentence of the second paragraph of "A Growing Problem" makes a strong impression, and the author supports it by mentioning the costs associated with the harm caused by nonnative species. The author also begins the text by describing how 150,000 pythons are now "crawling through the Everglades," and then mentions other examples of nonnative species that have caused damage in different ways. These examples help me understand the dangers the species present.

Analytical Writing Students should use the phrases in the sentence starters to form their responses. Their responses should state their opinion and provide reasons for it. Specific and relevant evidence from the text should also support the opinion. Students may continue to write their responses on a separate piece of paper.

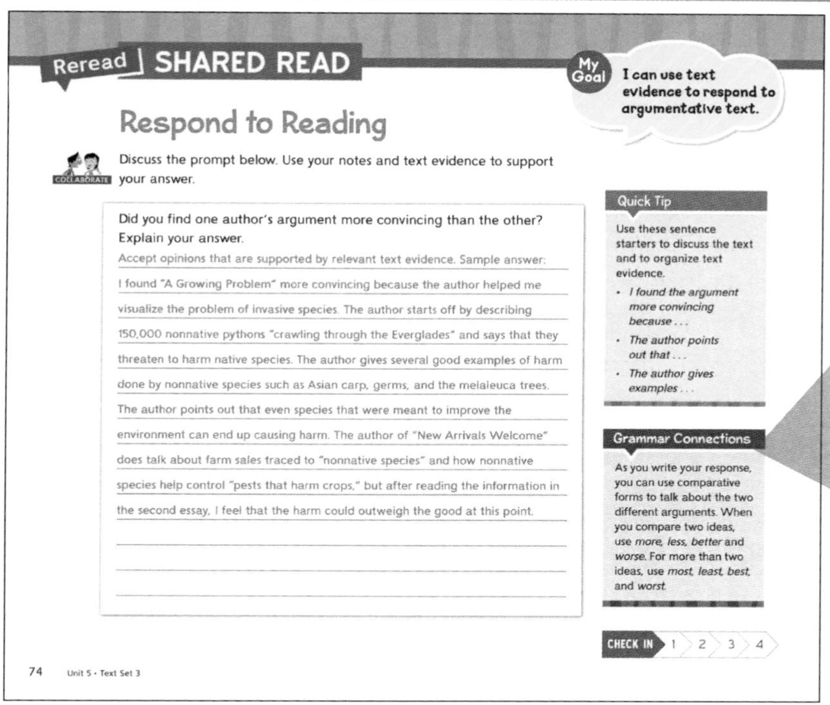
Reread | SHARED READ

My Goal: I can use text evidence to respond to argumentative text.

Respond to Reading

COLLABORATE Discuss the prompt below. Use your notes and text evidence to support your answer.

Did you find one author's argument more convincing than the other? Explain your answer.

Accept opinions that are supported by relevant text evidence. Sample answer: I found "A Growing Problem" more convincing because the author helped me visualize the problem of invasive species. The author starts off by describing 150,000 nonnative pythons "crawling through the Everglades" and says that they threaten to harm native species. The author gives several good examples of harm done by nonnative species such as Asian carp, germs, and the melaleuca trees. The author points out that even species that were meant to improve the environment can end up causing harm. The author of "New Arrivals Welcome" does talk about farm sales traced to "nonnative species" and how nonnative species help control "pests that harm crops," but after reading the information in the second essay, I feel that the harm could outweigh the good at this point.

Quick Tip

Use these sentence starters to discuss the text and to organize text evidence.

- *I found the argument more convincing because . . .*
- *The author points out that . . .*
- *The author gives examples . . .*

Grammar Connections

As you write your response, you can use comparative forms to talk about the two different arguments. When you compare two ideas, use *more, less, better* and *worse*. For more than two ideas, use *most, least, best,* and *worst*.

CHECK IN 1 2 3 4

74 Unit 5 • Text Set 3

Reading/Writing Companion, p. 74

Grammar Connections

Students can use online **Grammar Handbook** pages 467 and 468 to review and practice using comparative adjectives and forms of *more* and *most,* and *good* and *bad.*

English Language Learners

Use these scaffolds with **Respond** to help students prepare to write.

Beginning

Restate the prompt on page 74: *Was one article more convincing, or better, than the other? What are some examples you liked in the article?* I think "A Growing Problem"/"New Arrivals Welcome" is more convincing. The author gives examples about _____ . The author points out that _____. *Talk to your partner about why you found the article more convincing, or better.*

Intermediate

Check students' understanding of the prompt on page 74. Say: *An article that gives good examples to support its argument is more convincing.* Have partners review their graphic organizers to find convincing arguments with examples they liked from either author. Then guide them to respond using the sentence starters on page 74: I found the argument more convincing because _____. The author give examples of _____.

Advanced/Advanced High

Have students read the prompt. Review what it means to be *convincing,* as needed. Ask: *Which article is more convincing to you? Why?* Have partners discuss their answers before completing the sentence starters on page 74.

ELL NEWCOMERS

Have students listen to the summaries of the **Shared Read** in their native language and then in English to help them access the text and develop listening comprehension. Help students ask and answer questions with a partner. Use these sentence frames: *What question does this text ask? This text asks* ___. Then continue the lessons in the **Newcomer Teacher's Guide**.

FORMATIVE ASSESSMENT

STUDENT CHECK-IN

Ask partners to share their responses on Reading/Writing Companion page 74. Have them use the Check-In routine to reflect and fill in the bars.

LEARNING GOALS

- **We can decode words with the suffix *-ion.***
- **We can identify and read multisyllabic words.**
- **We can read fluently with accuracy and rate.**

OBJECTIVES

Know and apply grade-level phonics and word analysis skills in decoding words.

Use combined knowledge of all letter-sound correspondences, syllabication patterns, and morphology to read accurately unfamiliar multisyllabic words in context and out of context.

Read grade-level prose and poetry orally with accuracy, appropriate rate, expression, and automaticity on successive readings.

- Rate: 136–156 WCPM

ELA ACADEMIC LANGUAGE

- *suffix, accuracy, rate*
- Cognate: *ritmo*

TEACH IN SMALL GROUP

Word Study

Approaching Level and **ELL** Use Tier 2 activity on page T206 before teaching.

On Level As needed, use the Guided Practice section.

Beyond Level As needed, use only Multisyllabic Words.

ELL See page 5 in the **Language Transfers Handbook** for guidance in identifying sounds and symbols that may not transfer for speakers of certain languages, and support in accommodating those students.

OPTION 10 mins

Suffix *-ion*

1 Explain

Review with students that a suffix is a word part that is added to the end of a base word or root. The suffix *-ion* is added to certain words to change them from verbs to nouns. Write this example on the board:

narrate (verb) **narration** (noun)

2 Model

Write the following words on the board: *correction, imitation, donation.*

Pronounce each word and explain that each one is a noun made up of a base word and the suffix *-ion.* Identify the base words as the verbs *correct, imitate,* and *donate.* Model determining the meaning of *correction* by connecting it with the verb *correct.* Emphasize how the consonant sound at the end of the base word changes from /t/ to /sh/ when *-ion* is added. Repeat the process with *imitation* and *donation.* Point out that when the base word ends in an *e,* as in *imitate* and *donate,* the *e* is dropped before *-ion* is added.

Next, write the words *mission, notion,* and *fusion* on the board. Read each word aloud, emphasizing the /sh/ and /zh/ sounds. Explain that when the letter *s* is followed by *y, i,* or *u* in the middle of words, it may be pronounced /zh/ or /sh/ as in *measure* and *fission.* When the letter *i* follows *c, s, ss, sc,* or *t* in the last part of a word, it is usually silent and the consonants represent the /sh/ sound as in *nation, delicious,* and *conscious.*

3 Guided Practice

Write the following words with the suffix *-ion* on the board. Have students underline the suffix in each word and identify its beginning sound as /sh/ or /zh/. Then have them chorally read the words.

action	production	confusion	revision
devotion	pollution	emotion	rotation
eviction	restriction	creation	medication

Help pairs of students determine the meanings of the words in the list. Remind them to connect the meaning of the verb to the related noun with the *-ion* suffix.

For practice with decoding and encoding, use **Practice Book** page 295 or online activities.

Read Multisyllabic Words

Transition to Longer Words To help students transition to longer words with the suffix *-ion,* write the following four- and five-syllable words on the board. Have students use their knowledge of word parts to decode these longer words.

generation	appreciation	concentration
recollection	aggravation	remediation
disintegration	proposition	replication
population	interrogation	duplication

Model how to determine the meaning of the first word by covering the suffix with your finger and displaying only the base word. Define the base word, and then uncover the suffix. Connect the meaning of the verb to the longer word to determine its meaning. Then have students use these steps to define the remaining words.

Fluency

Accuracy and Rate

Explain/Model Review with students that reading words accurately and at a slower rate may help them read selections with unfamiliar terms. Model reading page 65 of "Should Plants and Animals from Other Places Live Here?" in the **Reading/Writing Companion**. Use punctuation and phrases to help pace your reading for meaning and for rate. Pronounce words that might be unfamiliar to students clearly, accurately, and slowly as students follow along.

Practice/Apply Have partners take turns reading the paragraphs on page 65, modeling the accuracy and rate that you used. Remind students that you will be listening for their accuracy and rate as you monitor their reading during the week.

Daily Fluency Practice

Automaticity Students can practice reading with accuracy and appropriate rate to develop automaticity using the online **Differentiated Genre Passage**, "What Is the Future of the Rain Forests?"

DIGITAL TOOLS

For more practice, use the word study and fluency activities.

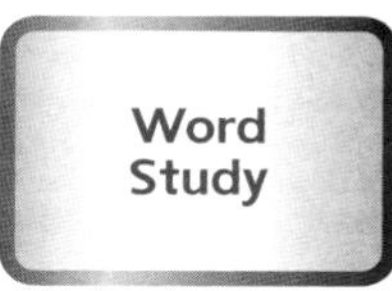

MULTIMODAL LEARNING

Write words with the suffix *-ion,* such as *transition, precision, satisfaction, possession,* and *recreation,* on note cards or strips of paper. Read aloud the words with students. Then have them use scissors or folding to break the words into word parts. Have them decode each word part and then read the longer word aloud.

FORMATIVE ASSESSMENT

STUDENT CHECK-IN

Suffix *-ion* Ask partners to share three words with the suffix *-ion.*

Multisyllabic Words Have partners read the following words: *generation, remediation, duplication.*

Fluency Ask partners to read "What Is the Future of the Rain Forests?" fluently.

Have partners reflect using the Check-In routine.

CHECK FOR SUCCESS

Can students decode multisyllabic words with the suffix *-ion*? Can students read with reasonable accuracy and at an appropriate rate?

Small Group Instruction

If No:

- **Approaching** Reteach pp. T206, T210
- **ELL** Develop p. T206

If Yes:

- **On** Apply p. T212
- **Beyond** Apply p. T218

LEARNING GOALS

We can use the research process to create a mock blog report.

OBJECTIVES

Conduct short research projects that use several sources to build knowledge through investigation of different aspects of a topic.

Recall relevant information from experiences or gather relevant information from print and digital sources; summarize or paraphrase information in notes and finished work, and provide a list of sources.

Come to discussions prepared, having read or studied required material; explicitly draw on that preparation and other information known about the topic to explore ideas under discussion.

Follow agreed-upon rules for discussions and carry out assigned roles.

Include multimedia components and visual displays in presentations when appropriate to enhance the development of main ideas or themes.

ELA ACADEMIC LANGUAGE

- *multimedia, digital*

TEACH IN SMALL GROUP

You may wish to teach the Research and Inquiry lesson during Small Group time. Have groups of mixed abilities complete the page and work on the blog report.

Environmental Changes

Explain to students that for the next week they will work collaboratively in large groups to research one nonnative species. They will create a mock blog report in which they will explain or predict the nonnative species' effect on its ecosystem. Explain that the student groups should create a research plan to help decide what types of information to include in the report.

Multimedia Elements Share a few examples of blog reports from the Internet. Ask students to note any digital elements they notice. Point out particular features, such as photographs, videos, and audio. Discuss how these digital elements enhance a blog.

Have students look at the example on **Reading/Writing Companion** page 75. Discuss the ways this example is informative. Support students as they go through each step in the research process outlined on page 75 to make their blog reports.

STEP 1 **Set a Goal** Explain to students that when some nonnative species arrive from other places, they may have different effects on their new environment. Have students brainstorm a list of nonnative species and confirm or revise that list with a quick Internet search. Offer feedback as students generate questions and decide what details they would like to include in their blog reports. Have them use a **Four-Door Foldable®**, available online, to help organize their information.

STEP 2 **Identify Sources** Remind students to use reliable, credible sources. Point out that print and online databases may be good sources of information when researching nonnative species.

STEP 3 **Find and Record Information** Review with students how to take notes and cite the sources they use to gather information for their blog reports.

STEP 4 **Organize and Synthesize Information** Show students how to organize the information they want to include in their blog reports. Remind them to explain why changes in the environment help or harm a species' survival.

STEP 5 **Create and Present** Review with students what they should include in their blog report and have them make changes as necessary. Remind them to include multimedia elements to enhance their presentations. Discuss options for presenting their blog reports. Consider sharing them on a classroom Internet page.

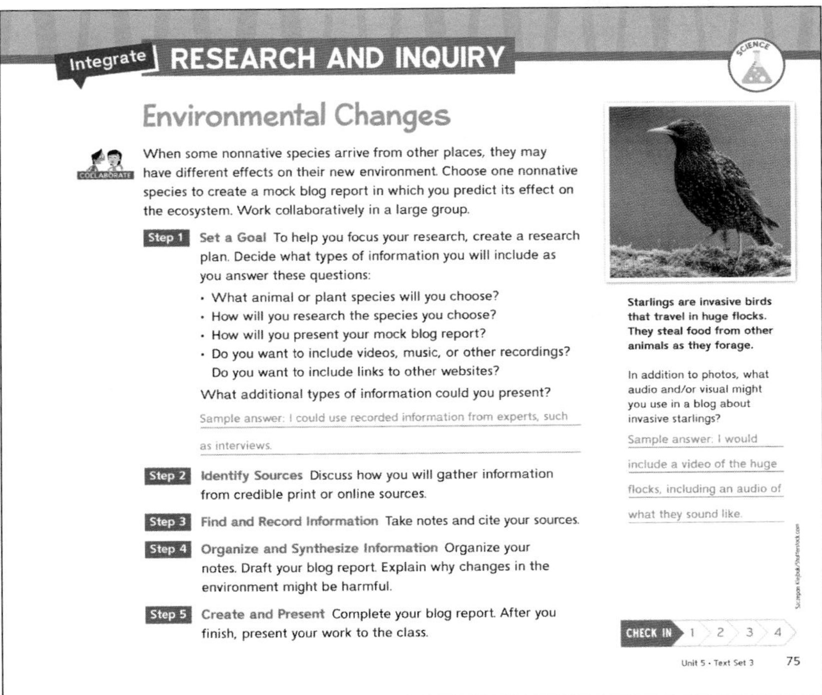

Integrate **RESEARCH AND INQUIRY**

SCIENCE

Environmental Changes

COLLABORATE

When some nonnative species arrive from other places, they may have different effects on their new environment. Choose one nonnative species to create a mock blog report in which you predict its effect on the ecosystem. Work collaboratively in a large group.

Step 1 **Set a Goal** To help you focus your research, create a research plan. Decide what types of information you will include as you answer these questions:

- What animal or plant species will you choose?
- How will you research the species you choose?
- How will you present your mock blog report?
- Do you want to include videos, music, or other recordings? Do you want to include links to other websites?

What additional types of information could you present?

Sample answer: I could use recorded information from experts, such as interviews.

Step 2 **Identify Sources** Discuss how you will gather information from credible print or online sources.

Step 3 **Find and Record Information** Take notes and cite your sources.

Step 4 **Organize and Synthesize Information** Organize your notes. Draft your blog report. Explain why changes in the environment might be harmful.

Step 5 **Create and Present** Complete your blog report. After you finish, present your work to the class.

Starlings are invasive birds that travel in huge flocks. They steal food from other animals as they forage.

In addition to photos, what audio and/or visual might you use in a blog about invasive starlings?

Sample answer: I would include a video of the huge flocks, including an audio of what they sound like.

CHECK IN 1 2 3 4

Unit 5 • Text Set 3 75

Reading/Writing Companion, p. 75

English Language Learners

Use the following scaffolds with **Step 5**.

Beginning

What is the purpose of a blog? The purpose of a blog is to share information. *You will create a blog as a way to share interesting information about a nonnative species.* Verify students' understanding of *blog* and *nonnative*. Display an example of a blog. Guide students in identifying and naming elements of the blog, such as facts, audio elements, videos, and links to other related websites.

Intermediate

Have partners talk about what they think the purpose of a blog is. Say: *You will be creating a blog report to share information about a nonnative species.* Display an example of a blog. Have partners discuss and identify the elements that make a blog interesting and informative: The blog I read had ____. This element was interesting because ____.

Advanced/Advanced High

Display an example of a blog. Have partners list the elements that make those blogs interesting and informative. Ask them to select which elements they will use in their blogs and explain why each element is important.

DIGITAL TOOLS

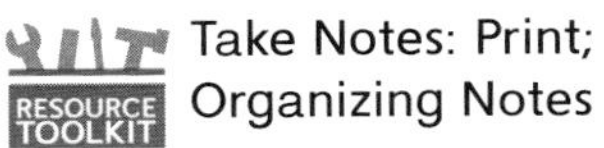

Take Notes: Print; Organizing Notes

FOLDABLES

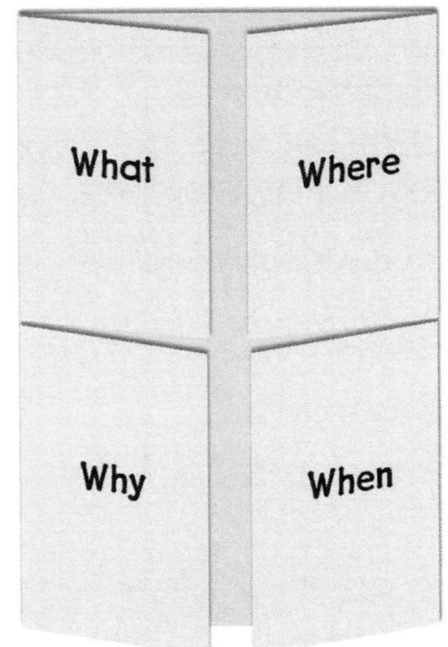

Four-Door Foldable®

FORMATIVE ASSESSMENT

STUDENT CHECK-IN

Blog Report Ask students to share their mock blog reports.

Multimedia Elements Have students share an example of a multimedia element they used.

Have students use the Check-In routine to reflect and fill in the bars on Reading/Writing Companion page 75.

The Case of the Missing Bees

Lexile 950L

LEARNING GOALS

Read We can apply strategies and skills to read argumentative text.

Reread We can reread to analyze text, craft, and structure and compare texts.

Have students apply what they learned as they read.

What makes this text complex?

- Organization
- Sentence Structure

Predict the effects of changes in ecosystems caused by living organisms, including humans.

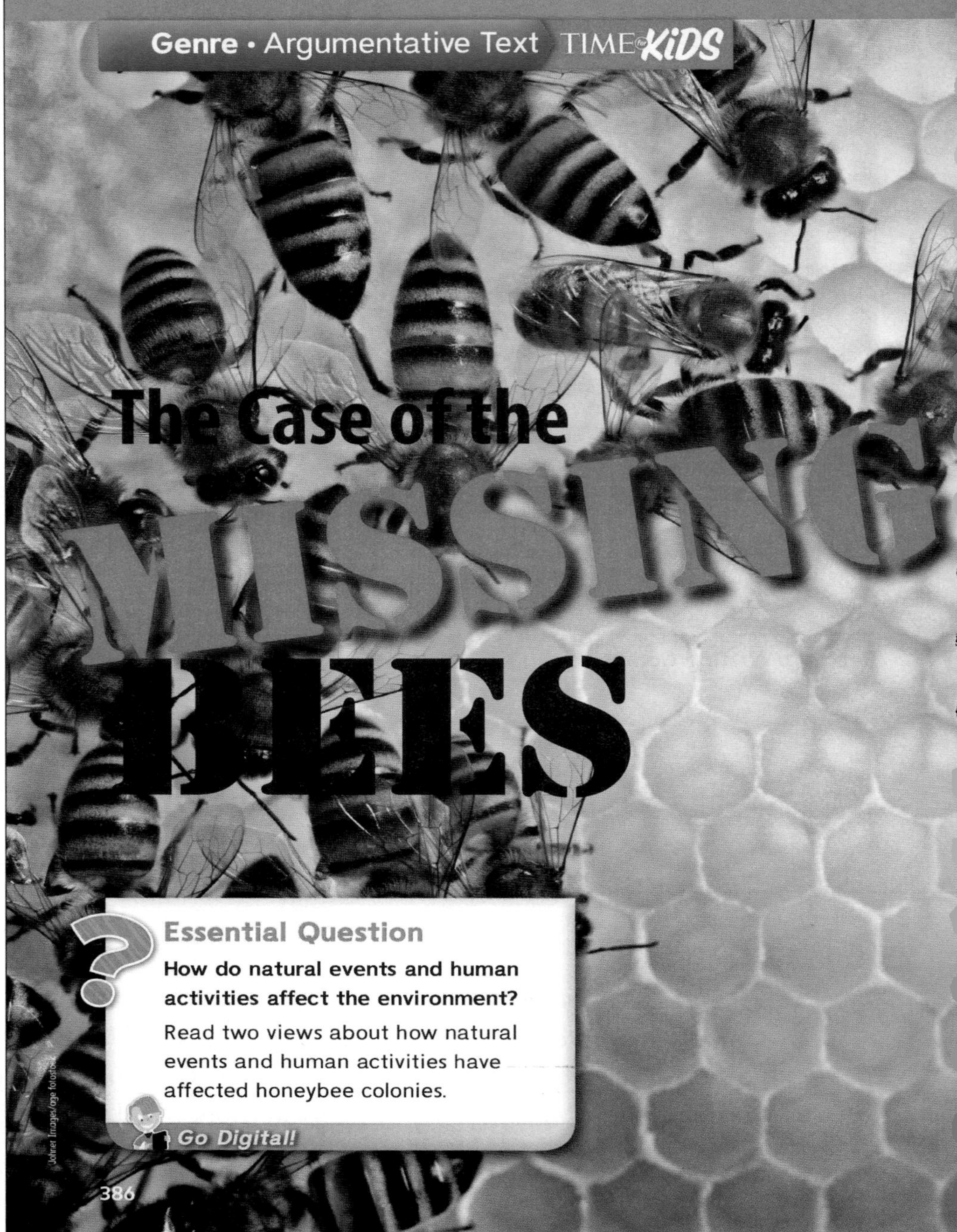

Genre • Argumentative Text TIME KiDS
The Case of the
MISSING
BEES
Essential Question
How do natural events and human activities affect the environment?
Read two views about how natural events and human activities have affected honeybee colonies.
Go Digital!
386

Literature Anthology, pp. 386–387

Close Reading Routine

Read DOK 1–2

- Identify important ideas and details.
- Take notes and summarize.
- Use ACT prompts as needed.

Reread DOK 2–3

- Analyze the text, craft, and structure.
- Use *Reading/Writing Companion*, pp. 76–77.

Integrate DOK 4

- Integrate knowledge and ideas.
- Make text-to-text connections.
- Use the Integrate lesson.
- Complete the Show Your Knowledge task.
- Inspire action.

DIFFERENTIATED READING

You may wish to read the full selection aloud once with minimal stopping before you begin using the Read prompts.

Approaching Level Have students listen to the selection summary. Use the Reread prompts during Small Group time.

On Level and Beyond Level Pair students or have them independently complete the Reread prompts on **Reading/ Writing Companion** pages 76–77.

English Language Learners Have ELLs listen to the summary of the selection, available in multiple languages. See also the **ELL Small Group Guide**.

A Germ of an Idea

An infection seems to have caused the decline of honeybee populations.

1

Where have all the honeybees gone? Over the past few years, billions of honeybees have disappeared. They fly away from their colonies and seem to never return. This **widespread** problem is called Colony Collapse **Disorder** (CCD). It's the main reason the honeybee population in the U.S. today has **declined** to half of what it was 50 years ago. Because one-third of crops in the U.S. require honeybees to help pollinate them, some experts predict CCD could create an **agricultural** catastrophe.

What's responsible for the **unexpected** disappearance? There are several suspects, including stress on bees from overcrowded hives, lack of pollen, parasites, and pesticides. Scientists have yet to identify any one of these as the definite cause of CCD. But recently, researchers have found two **probable** causes: a fungus and a virus. A fungus is an organism that breaks down matter; some fungi can cause infection. A virus is a microbe, or germ.

A Deadly Combination

Bees infected with either the fungus or the virus separately could become sick, but they probably would survive. Bees infected with the fungus and the virus at the same time would most certainly die. That is what scientists who did research in Montana concluded. They tested samples of empty hives against hives that **thrive**, a control group that was unaffected by CCD. They compared their findings and discovered the virus and fungus in every empty hive they tested.

Though the fungus and virus combination is the most probable cause so far, investigations into CCD continue. Other scientists are investigating whether CCD could have been caused by a combination of many factors: pesticides, parasites, fungus, and virus. Each of these can weaken a bee's immune system and make it sick. A combination could be deadly.

Only when scientists find the cause of CCD can they find the cure to saving the bees.

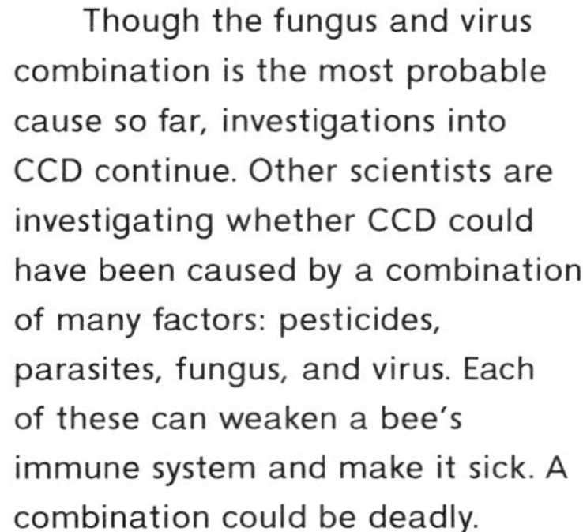

387

Access Complex Text

Organization

In "A Germ of an Idea," a cause-and-effect relationship is discussed in relation to the problem of the decreasing honeybee population.

- *What are some possible causes of this problem?* (a fungus, a virus, pesticides, and parasites) *What additional effect could this problem have?* (Crops could suffer without bees to pollinate them.)

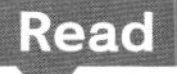

Read

Set a Purpose Tell students to preview the text and set a purpose for reading. Remind them that setting a purpose can help them monitor comprehension.

Use the Graphic Organizer

Analytical Writing Distribute copies of online Author's Perspective **Graphic Organizer 8**. Tell students to take notes as they read.

1 Author's Perspective DOK 1

What is the author's perspective? (An infection has caused the decline of honeybees.)

STOP AND CHECK **DOK 1**

Ask and Answer Questions According to the author, why are honeybees disappearing? (The likely cause is a fungus and a virus.)

Reread

Author's Purpose DOK 2

Reading/Writing Companion, p. 76

Why does the author begin the selection with a question? (The author wants readers to be curious about disappearing honeybees.)

Make Inferences **DOK 2**

Explain Authors use questions to get readers to read on to find the answers.

Model Asking can make readers aware that honeybees are missing.

Apply *How else in the article does the author use this technique?* (Another question is asked in the second paragraph.)

ELL English Language Learners

Request Assistance Remind students of expressions to request assistance: *Can you repeat it, please? Can you explain that part?*

Read

2 Author's Perspective DOK 2

According to the author of this article, what may cause CCD? (pesticides) Add the information to your organizer.

Details		Author's Perspective
Researchers found one pesticide that is harmful to bees.	→	Pesticides should be cut back because they may cause CCD.
Even small amounts can affect bee behavior.		
Sick bees might get lost and never return to the colony.		
Scientists found 50 different chemicals in hives hit by CCD.		

Reread

Author's Craft: Text Features DOK 2

Reading/Writing Companion, p. 77

Reread pages 388–389. How does the author's use of headings help you understand his or her perspective about pesticides? (Two of the author's headings focus on the use of pesticides. This repetition suggests that the author believes pesticides are harmful to bees.)

Build Vocabulary on page 388

reduction: less of something

Farmers use pesticides to keep away insects that will damage crops. Some pesticides can harm beneficial insects, like honeybees.

COUNTERPOINT

Pointing to Pesticides

Lately, honeybees have not been very busy. Are pesticides to blame?

It's a honey of a mystery. In recent years, beekeepers in many countries have lost thousands of colonies and billions of bees. The insects would suddenly disappear and not return to their hives. About 30 percent of the honeybee colonies that die are due to this condition, called Colony Collapse Disorder (CCD). Unfortunately, the reduction in the bee population could affect the country's food production. That's because honeybees pollinate crops of flowering plants. Without these insects, the production of fruits and vegetables would be threatened.

The Unusual Suspects 2

Most scientists believe the probable cause of CCD is a fungus or a virus, working alone or in combination. But some experts have reached a different conclusion. Their main suspect is pesticides. Pesticides are chemicals sprayed on crops to keep away pests. Researchers in France managed to **identify** one pesticide as harmful to bees. This has led other scientists to investigate how other pesticides affect bees.

Pesticides can be absorbed by pollen that the bees consume or that drifts into the hive. Some studies have shown that even small amounts of certain pesticides can affect bee behavior, such as how they search for flower nectar. Sick bees may not be able to figure out where they're going, get lost, and never return to their colonies. This would explain the decline in honeybee populations.

388

Literature Anthology, pp. 388–389

ACT Access Complex Text

Sentence Structure

Help students break down complex sentence structures in the article, such as the second and third sentences in paragraph two of "The Unusual Suspects." Ask: *What happens when bees "get lost?"* (They are unable to return to their colonies.) *Why does this matter?* (Fewer bees means less pollination.)

ELL Spotlight on Language

Page 389, Paragraph 1 Read aloud the second sentence in paragraph 1. Point out the conjunction *but*. Explain that the conjunction signals a contrast between the ideas that come before and after it. Ask: *What was the study unable to confirm?* (that the pesticides directly caused CCD) *What will scientists continue to do anyway?* (research to see if the pesticides are partly to blame)

TIME for KIDS

Are Pesticides to Blame?

A study of hives hit by CCD in Florida and California found 50 different human-made chemicals in the samples. The study could not confirm that the pesticides had directly caused CCD, but other scientists are still investigating whether pesticides are at least partly to blame. At the least, the chemicals may weaken bees enough to allow infection by a virus or a fungus. Until scientists know the exact cause of the honeybee disappearance, the use of these harsh poisons should be cut back.

Respond to the Text

1. Use details from the selection to summarize. SUMMARIZE
2. Think about how each argumentative article is organized. Which author's style is more convincing? Why? WRITE
3. What do you think caused the bees to disappear? Support your answer with reasons. How could people help honeybees? TEXT TO WORLD

Beekeepers examine hives to make sure the honeybee colonies are healthy.

389

Integrate

Build Knowledge: Make Connections

Talk About the Text Have partners discuss the Essential Question: How do natural events and human activities affect the environment?

Write About the Text Then have students add their ideas to their Build Knowledge page of their reader's notebook.

Anchor Chart Record any new ideas on the Build Knowledge anchor chart.

Read

Summarize

Guide students to use the information from the Author's Perspective **Graphic Organizer 8** to summarize.

Return to Purpose Review students' purpose for reading. Then ask partners to share how setting a purpose helped them understand the text.

Reread

Analyze the Text

After students summarize the selection, have them reread to develop a deeper understanding by answering the questions on pages 76–77 of the **Reading/Writing Companion**. For students who need support in citing text evidence, use the scaffolded instruction from the Reread prompts on pages T189–T190.

Integrate

Compare Texts DOK 4

Have students compare how the authors present information on pesticides affecting the environment in "Should Plants and Animals from Other Places Live Here?" and *The Case of the Missing Bees*. Ask: What is similar in the two readings? What is different about the way information is presented in the two readings?

FORMATIVE ASSESSMENT

STUDENT CHECK-IN

Read Have partners share their graphic organizers and summaries. Then have them reflect using the Check-In routine.

Reread Have partners share responses and text evidence on Reading/Writing Companion pages 76-77. Then have them use the Check-In routine to reflect and fill in the bars.

LEARNING GOALS

We can use text evidence to respond to argumentative text.

OBJECTIVES

Explain how an author uses reasons and evidence to support particular points in a text, identifying which reasons and evidence support which point(s).

Compare and contrast the overall structure events, ideas, concepts, or information in two or more texts.

Explain an author's perspective, or point of view, toward an argumentative text.

Identify the author's claim.

Introduce a topic or text clearly, state an opinion, and create an organizational structure in which ideas are logically grouped to support the writer's purpose.

ELA ACADEMIC LANGUAGE

- *argument, organization, convincing, perspective*
- Cognates: *argumento, organización, convincente, perspectiva*

TEACH IN SMALL GROUP

Respond to Reading

Approaching Level and **On Level** Have partners work together to plan and complete the response to the prompt.

Beyond Level Ask students to respond to the prompt independently.

ELL Group students of mixed proficiency levels to discuss and respond to the prompt.

Reread

Write About the Anchor Text

Analyze the Prompt DOK 3

Read the prompt aloud: *Think about how each argumentative article is organized. Which author's style is more convincing and why?* Ask: *What is the prompt asking you to do?* (to analyze the way the authors organize details in each argumentative text, and then determine whose organization is more effective) Say: *Let's reread each text to fully understand how the organization of each text and the techniques the authors use, including thought-provoking questions and the use of headings, support each author's perspective and help us answer the prompt.*

Analyze Text Evidence

Remind students that to determine an author's perspective in argumentative text, readers can examine the author's evidence and reasoning. Have students look at **Literature Anthology** page 387. Read the page and ask: *How does the author begin this text?* (The author begins by asking a question about what has happened to honeybees.) *How does that help the author organize the text that follows?* (It allows the author to answer the question and explain why honeybees have been disappearing.) Then turn to pages 388–389. Ask: *What text features does this author use? How are they helpful in organizing the text?* (The author uses headings, photos, and captions. The headings categorize the information the author presents about pesticides.) Encourage students to look for more text evidence. Then have them craft a short response.

Respond

Review pages 76–77 of the **Reading/Writing Companion.** Have partners or small groups refer to and discuss their completed charts and writing responses from those pages. Then direct students' attention to the sentence starters on page 78 of the Reading/Writing Companion. Have them use sentence starters to guide their responses.

Analytical Writing Students should focus on the argument each author makes and how well he or she organizes the text to best support a perspective. Students can compare and contrast how the authors organize and present their ideas, as well as how thoroughly each argument is supported with factual evidence and examples. This analysis should allow students to evaluate which author's argument they found more convincing and how the organization of the argument and supporting facts contributed to its effectiveness. Remind students to vary sentence structure by combining short sentences and adding phrases and clauses to others. Students may use additional paper to complete the assignment if needed.

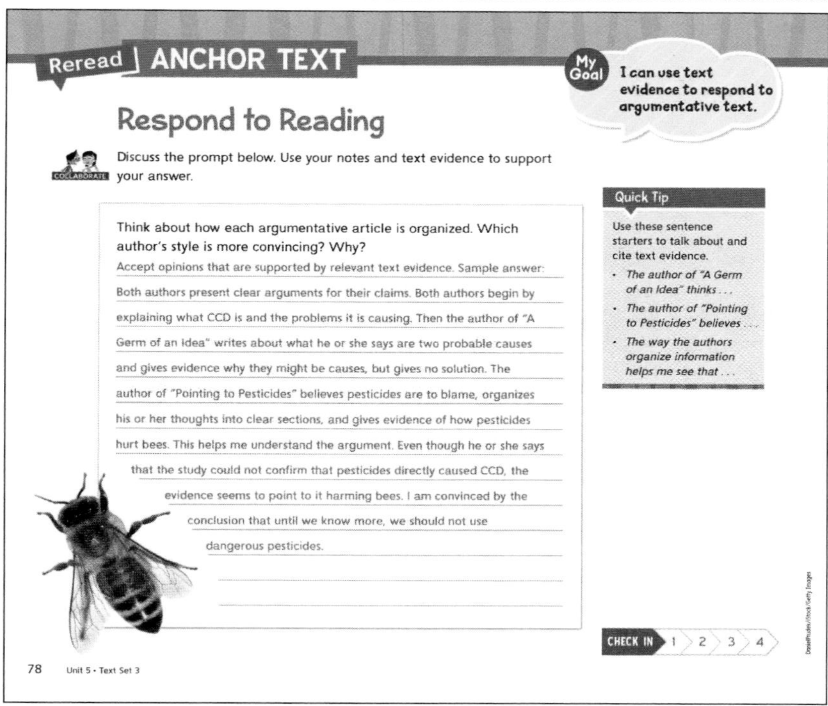

Reread | ANCHOR TEXT

My Goal: I can use text evidence to respond to argumentative text.

Respond to Reading

COLLABORATE Discuss the prompt below. Use your notes and text evidence to support your answer.

Think about how each argumentative article is organized. Which author's style is more convincing? Why?

Accept opinions that are supported by relevant text evidence. Sample answer: Both authors present clear arguments for their claims. Both authors begin by explaining what CCD is and the problems it is causing. Then the author of "A Germ of an Idea" writes about what he or she says are two probable causes and gives evidence why they might be causes, but gives no solution. The author of "Pointing to Pesticides" believes pesticides are to blame, organizes his or her thoughts into clear sections, and gives evidence of how pesticides hurt bees. This helps me understand the argument. Even though he or she says that the study could not confirm that pesticides directly caused CCD, the evidence seems to point to it harming bees. I am convinced by the conclusion that until we know more, we should not use dangerous pesticides.

Quick Tip

Use these sentence starters to talk about and cite text evidence.

- *The author of "A Germ of an Idea" thinks . . .*
- *The author of "Pointing to Pesticides" believes . . .*
- *The way the authors organize information helps me see that . . .*

CHECK IN 1 2 3 4

78 Unit 5 • Text Set 3

Reading/Writing Companion, p. 78

English Language Learners

Use the following scaffolds with **Respond**.

Beginning

Restate the prompt on page 78: *Each persuasive article is organized differently. Which organization do you like the most? Why?* Review the students' completed charts on pages 76–77. Then help partners respond using: I think the author of "Pointing to Pesticides" is more convincing. The author believes that pesticides are killing the bees. The way the author organizes information helps me see that _____.

Intermediate

Read the prompt with students and discuss with them the information they will use to write. Have pairs review their completed charts on pages 76–77. Elicit them to describe how each author organizes and present his or her ideas and discuss which argument is more convincing: I think the author of _____ is more convincing. The author believes that _____. The way the author organizes information helps me see that _____.

Advanced/Advanced High

Review the prompt and sentence starters on page 78 with students. Have them review their completed charts on pages 76–77. Allow pairs to describe each author's perspective and how the authors help them understand possible causes of CDC. Then have them decide which argument is more convincing and respond using the sentence starters.

NEWCOMERS

Have students listen to the summaries of the **Anchor Text** in their native language and then in English to help them access the text and develop listening comprehension. Help students ask and answer questions with a partner. Use these sentence frames: *What is the topic of these argumentative texts?* These argumentative texts are about ___. Then have them complete the online **Newcomer Activities** individually or in pairs.

FORMATIVE ASSESSMENT

STUDENT CHECK-IN

Ask partners to share their responses on Reading/Writing Companion page 78. Have them reflect using the Check-In routine to fill in the bars.

"Busy, Beneficial Bees"

Lexile 980L

LEARNING GOALS

Read We can apply strategies and skills to read expository text.

Reread We can reread to analyze text, craft, and structure and compare texts.

Have students apply what they learned as they read.

What makes this text complex?

▶ Purpose

Predict the effects of changes in ecosystems caused by living organisms, including humans.

Analytical Writing Compare Texts DOK 4

As students read and reread "Busy, Beneficial Bees," encourage them to think about the Essential Question. They will compare this text to *The Case of the Missing Bees.*

Read

1 Ask and Answer Questions DOK 1

How do honeybees help agriculture? (Pollen gets carried to another plant. This pollination makes plants able to produce fruit and seeds.)

Reread

Author's Craft: Text Features DOK 2

Reading/Writing Companion, p. 80

What information does the table on page 79 give? (dependency between crops and honeybees) Why is the table included? (It reinforces the importance of honeybees.)

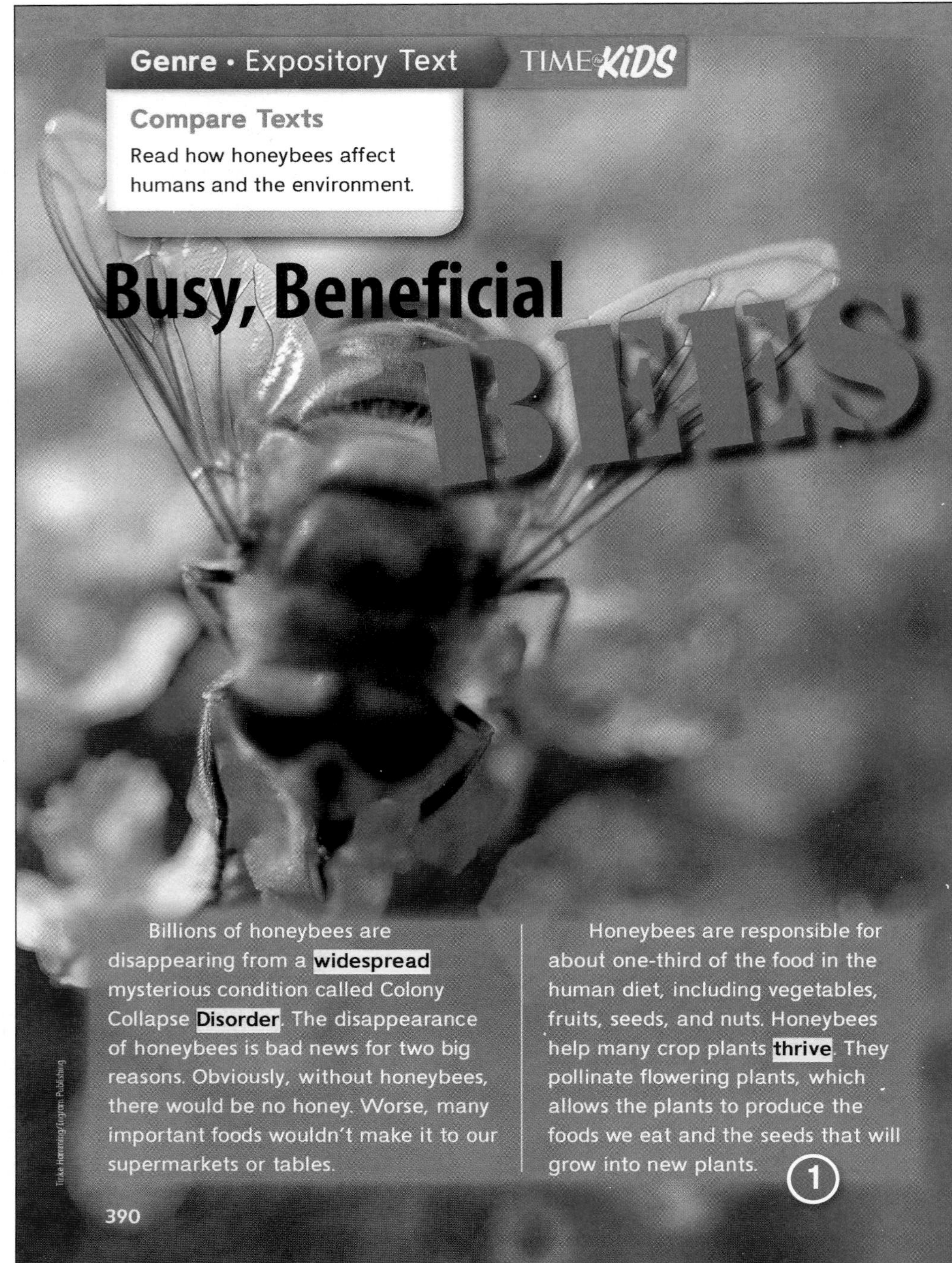

Genre • Expository Text
TIME KIDS
Compare Texts
Read how honeybees affect humans and the environment.
Busy, Beneficial
BEES
Billions of honeybees are disappearing from a widespread mysterious condition called Colony Collapse Disorder. The disappearance of honeybees is bad news for two big reasons. Obviously, without honeybees, there would be no honey. Worse, many important foods wouldn't make it to our supermarkets or tables.
Honeybees are responsible for about one-third of the food in the human diet, including vegetables, fruits, seeds, and nuts. Honeybees help many crop plants thrive. They pollinate flowering plants, which allows the plants to produce the foods we eat and the seeds that will grow into new plants.
1
390

Literature Anthology, pp. 390–391

Access Complex Text

Purpose

Clarify that the purpose of the text is to inform.

- *How is this text different from the previous articles on honeybees?* (It's not an argumentative text. Its purpose is to give facts about honeybees and the human diet.)
- *How do the photograph and diagram support this purpose?* (The photo shows pollination in action. The chart gives details about how bees help crops.)

Crops Depend on Honeybees	Crop	Dependence on Insect Pollination	Proportion That Are Honeybees
Many crops depend on insects to pollinate them. For some crops, honeybees make up a large percentage of those pollinators.	Alfalfa, hay & seed	100%	60%
	Apples	100%	90%
	Almonds	100%	100%
	Citrus	20-80%	10-90%
	Cotton	20%	90%
	Soybeans	10%	50%
Numbers based on estimates. Source: Compiled by Congressional Research Service using values reported in R. A. Morse, and N.W. Calderone, *The Value of Honey Bees as Pollinators of U.S. Crops in 2000, March 2000*, Cornell University.	Broccoli	100%	90%
	Carrots	100%	90%
	Cantaloupe	80%	90%

Honeybees use nectar from flowers to make honey, their winter food source. When the bees visit flowers to get nectar, tiny grains of pollen cling to their bodies. The bees carry the pollen from flower to flower and plant to plant. This process of pollination makes flowers turn into fruits. For farmers, this means a harvest!

Honeybees were brought to the U.S. from Europe about 400 years ago for **agricultural** purposes. Beekeepers today still maintain hives. Some sell honey. Others may rent hives to farmers to pollinate crops. In addition to honeybees, there are about 4,000 species of native "wild" bees in North America that also pollinate flowering plants. Most of these bees do not live in colonies and have not been affected by CCD.

In the U.S., honeybees pollinate about $15 billion worth of crops a year. That's on top of the $150 million worth of honey they produce annually. Although some crops can be pollinated by other nectar-feeding insects, many crops depend specifically on honeybees for pollination. Without honeybees, our crops and our economy would really feel the sting!

Make Connections

How do honeybees affect the environment? ESSENTIAL QUESTION

Think of an agricultural activity you've read about that affects the environment. How are the effects of beekeeping different? TEXT TO TEXT

391

Spotlight on Language

Page 391, Table Confirm the meaning of crops. Explain that the table provides information about the importance of insects, especially honeybees, for growing crops. Have students point to the headings at the top of each column. *How are these headings like the headings that appear in a text?* (They are not complete sentences; Each word is capitalized.) Direct students' attention to the numbers under the headings. *What does the symbol after each number mean?* (percent) (Cognate: *por ciento*)

Read

2 Author's Perspective DOK 2

What is the author's perspective about honeybees? (They are essential to farming and our food supply.) Which sentence on page 391 best states the author's perspective? ("Without honeybees, our crops and our economy would really feel the sting!")

Summarize

Guide students to summarize the selection.

Reread

Analyze the Text

After students read and summarize, have them reread and answer questions on pages 79–80 of the **Reading/Writing Companion**.

Integrate

Build Knowledge: Make Connections

Talk About the Text Have partners discuss how honeybees affect the environment.

Write About the Text Have students add their ideas to their Build Knowledge pages of their reader's notebooks.

Anchor Chart Record any new ideas on the Build Knowledge anchor chart.

Compare Texts DOK 4

Text to Text Answer: Pesticides hurt the honeybee population; beekeeping helps it. Evidence: Page 389: the cons of pesticides. Page 391: how beekeepers help farmers.

FORMATIVE ASSESSMENT

STUDENT CHECK-IN

Read Ask partners to share their summaries. Then have them reflect using the Check-In routine.

Reread Have partners share their responses on Reading/Writing Companion pages 79-80. Then have them use the Check-In routine to reflect and fill in the bars.

LEARNING GOALS

We can identify puns to help us read and understand expository text.

OBJECTIVES

Consult reference materials, both print and digital, to find the pronunciation and determine or clarify the precise meaning of key words and phrases.

Demonstrate understanding of figurative language, word relationships, and nuances in word meanings.

Recognize and explain the meaning of common idioms, adages, and proverbs.

ELA ACADEMIC LANGUAGE

- *expression, pun, message*
- Cognates: *expresión, mensaje*

Reread

Puns

1 Explain

Have students turn to **Reading/Writing Companion** page 81. Explain that authors choose words carefully to create a specific effect and to convey a stronger message. Choosing interesting words and phrases also helps create text that engages readers and makes them want to read more.

- A pun, or a play on words, is a funny or clever expression that reflects two different meanings of a word or phrase. For example, "Fish are smart because they live in schools" is a pun that uses an unexpected meaning of the word *schools.* When referring to fish, the meaning of *schools* is normally "groups." However, the pun also uses the meaning "place of learning" in relation to the fish.
- Authors use puns when they want to entertain readers and make them laugh. Since puns get readers to really think about the meanings of a word or phrase, they can also help an author convey a message to readers.

2 Model

Model identifying the use of puns on page 79 of the Reading/Writing Companion. Have students read the paragraph. Point out the phrase "feel the sting" in the last sentence and discuss its meaning. Then connect the phrase to the word *honeybees* and its impact on the meaning of the phrase "feel the sting." Discuss whether or not students think the author would have chosen the phrase if the text was not about honeybees.

3 Guided Practice

Now have students connect the meaning of the pun to the author's message. Ask: *What are two meanings of "feel the sting"?* (It can refer to an actual bee sting or to an emotion caused by something unpleasant.) *What does the pun help you understand about the value the author puts on honeybees?* (The author thinks it would be difficult to grow crops or make money without them.) Have pairs discuss the meaning of the pun and why it is effective at how it relates to the central idea. Then have students share their work with the class.

Allow students time to enter their responses on Reading/Writing Companion page 81. Remind them to use a print or online dictionary to find specific meanings of words in puns.

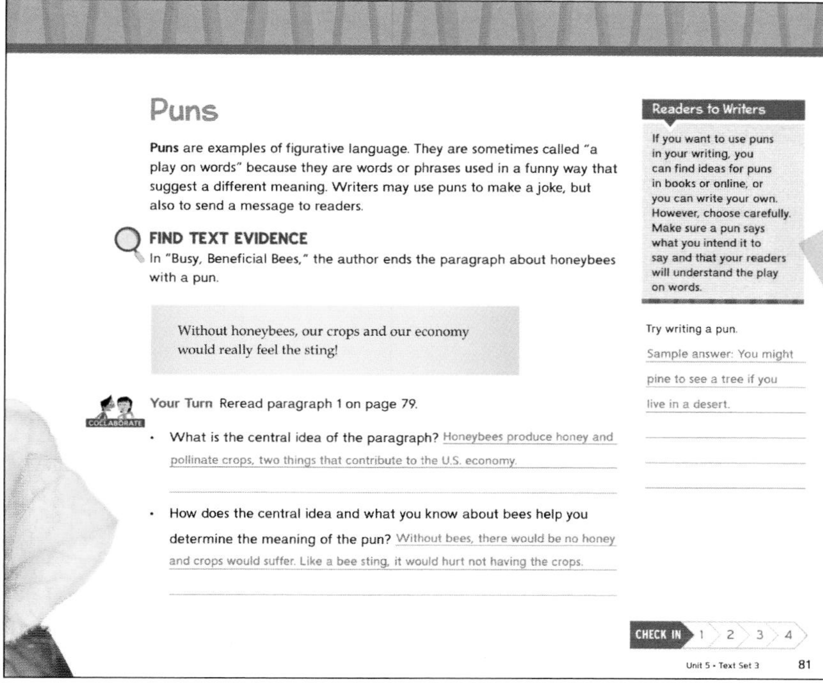

Puns

Puns are examples of figurative language. They are sometimes called "a play on words" because they are words or phrases used in a funny way that suggest a different meaning. Writers may use puns to make a joke, but also to send a message to readers.

FIND TEXT EVIDENCE

In "Busy, Beneficial Bees," the author ends the paragraph about honeybees with a pun.

> Without honeybees, our crops and our economy would really feel the sting!

Readers to Writers

If you want to use puns in your writing, you can find ideas for puns in books or online, or you can write your own. However, choose carefully. Make sure a pun says what you intend it to say and that your readers will understand the play on words.

Try writing a pun.

Sample answer: You might pine to see a tree if you live in a desert.

COLLABORATE

Your Turn Reread paragraph 1 on page 79.

- What is the central idea of the paragraph? Honeybees produce honey and pollinate crops, two things that contribute to the U.S. economy.
- How does the central idea and what you know about bees help you determine the meaning of the pun? Without bees, there would be no honey and crops would suffer. Like a bee sting, it would hurt not having the crops.

CHECK IN 1 2 3 4

Unit 5 • Text Set 3 81

Reading/Writing Companion, p. 81

Readers to Writers

Reiterate that a pun can restate an author's message or point of view in a way that is engaging, but also allows the reader to keep the importance of the topic and message in mind. Have students reread the last sentence in the paragraph on page 79. Have pairs compare it to a more direct statement of the author's message and discuss how effectively each conveys the author's perspective.

ELL English Language Learners

Use the following scaffolds with **Guided Practice.**

Beginning

Review puns with students. Write *feel the sting* on the board. Mime the action of being stung by a bee. Say: *Bees are helpful. But a bee sting hurts a lot. We feel pain when bees sting us.* Then read the last sentence of the paragraph on page 79 with students. Check their understanding of *crops* and *economy*. Say: *If there are no bees, the crops and economy will suffer. What will people feel?* (pain)

Intermediate

Say: *A bee sting hurts. When you* feel the sting, *you feel pain and you suffer.* Have partners read the paragraph on page 79 and point to the sentence that says the crops and the economy would *feel the sting.* Elicit them to discuss what they know about bees to determine the meaning of the pun. Then have them respond using: If there are no bees, there would be no honey and crops would suffer. Not having crops would hurt, like a bee sting.

Advanced/Advanced High

Have partners read the paragraph on page 79 and discuss the meaning of *"feel the sting."* (something that causes pain or makes you suffer) *What will happen to the crops and the economy if there are no honeybees?* Help students recognize that there will be negative consequences. *Enter your responses on page 81.*

FORMATIVE ASSESSMENT

STUDENT CHECK-IN

Ask partners to share their Your Turn responses on Reading/Writing Companion page 81. Have them use the Check-In routine to reflect and fill in the bars.

LEARNING GOALS

We can compare the poem with the selections in this text set to build knowledge about how we affect the environment.

OBJECTIVES

Draw on information from multiple print or digital sources, demonstrating the ability to locate an answer to a question quickly or to solve a problem efficiently.

Draw evidence from literary or informational texts to support analysis, reflection, and research.

Apply grade 5 Reading standards to informational texts.

Close Reading Routine

Read DOK 1–2

- Identify important ideas and details.
- Take notes and summarize.
- Use ACT prompts as needed.

Reread DOK 2–3

- Analyze the text, craft, and structure.
- Use the ***Reading/Writing Companion***.

Integrate DOK 3–4

- Integrate knowledge and ideas.
- Make text-to-text connections.
- Use the Integrate/Make Connections lesson.
- Use the ***Reading/Writing Companion***, p. 82.
- Complete the Show Your Knowledge task.
- Inspire action.

FORMATIVE ASSESSMENT

STUDENT CHECK-IN

Ask partners to share their response. Have them use the Check-In routine to reflect and fill in the bars on Reading/Writing Companion p. 82.

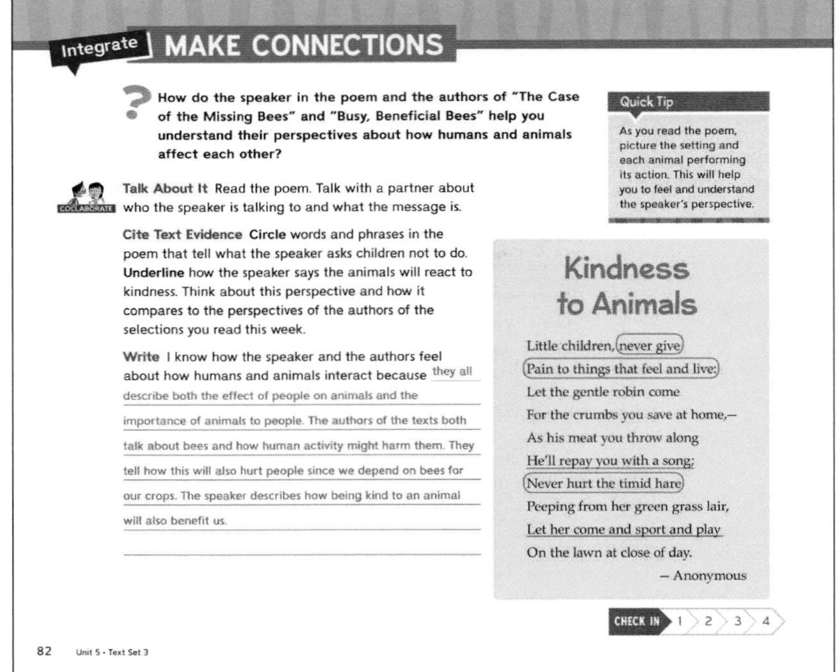

Integrate | MAKE CONNECTIONS

How do the speaker in the poem and the authors of "The Case of the Missing Bees" and "Busy, Beneficial Bees" help you understand their perspectives about how humans and animals affect each other?

COLLABORATE

Talk About It Read the poem. Talk with a partner about who the speaker is talking to and what the message is.

Cite Text Evidence **Circle** words and phrases in the poem that tell what the speaker asks children not to do. **Underline** how the speaker says the animals will react to kindness. Think about this perspective and how it compares to the perspectives of the authors of the selections you read this week.

Write I know how the speaker and the authors feel about how humans and animals interact because they all describe both the effect of people on animals and the importance of animals to people. The authors of the texts both talk about bees and how human activity might harm them. They tell how this will also hurt people since we depend on bees for our crops. The speaker describes how being kind to an animal will also benefit us.

Quick Tip

As you read the poem, picture the setting and each animal performing its action. This will help you to feel and understand the speaker's perspective.

Kindness to Animals

Little children, never give
Pain to things that feel and live;
Let the gentle robin come
For the crumbs you save at home,–
As his meat you throw along
He'll repay you with a song;
Never hurt the timid hare
Peeping from her green grass lair,
Let her come and sport and play
On the lawn at close of day.

– Anonymous

CHECK IN 1 2 3 4

82 Unit 5 • Text Set 3

Reading/Writing Companion, p. 82

Integrate

Make Connections DOK 4

Talk About It

Share and discuss students' responses to the "Leaving a Trace" blast. Display the Build Knowledge anchor chart. Below that, draw a chart with headings for all the texts students have read. Review the chart and have students read through their notes, annotations, and responses for each text. Then ask students to complete the Talk About It activity on **Reading/Writing Companion** page 82.

Cite Text Evidence

Guide students to see the connections between the poem on Reading/Writing Companion page 82 and the selections. Remind students to read the Quick Tip on page 82.

Write

Students should refer to their notes on the chart as they respond to the writing prompt on the page. When students have finished writing, have groups share and discuss their responses.

Build Knowledge: Make Connections

Talk About the Text Have partners discuss how people affect nature.

Write About the Text Have students add their ideas to the Build Knowledge pages of their reader's notebooks.

Anchor Chart Record any new ideas on the Build Knowledge anchor chart.

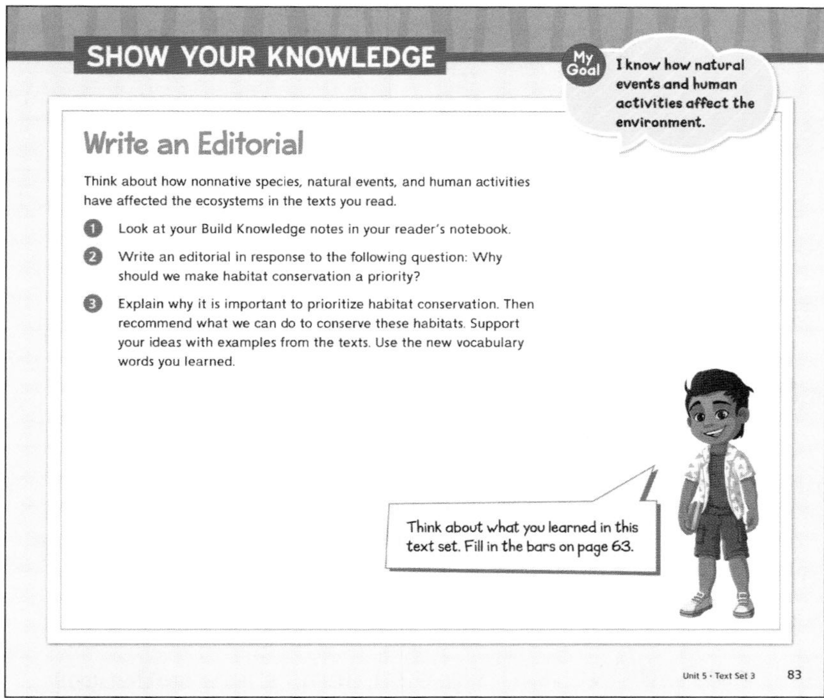

SHOW YOUR KNOWLEDGE

My Goal: I know how natural events and human activities affect the environment.

Write an Editorial

Think about how nonnative species, natural events, and human activities have affected the ecosystems in the texts you read.

1. Look at your Build Knowledge notes in your reader's notebook.
2. Write an editorial in response to the following question: Why should we make habitat conservation a priority?
3. Explain why it is important to prioritize habitat conservation. Then recommend what we can do to conserve these habitats. Support your ideas with examples from the texts. Use the new vocabulary words you learned.

Think about what you learned in this text set. Fill in the bars on page 63.

Unit 5 • Text Set 3 83

Reading/Writing Companion, p. 83

Integrate

10 mins

Show Your Knowledge DOK 4

Write an Editorial

COLLABORATE

Explain that students will show how they built knowledge across the text set by writing an editorial in response to the following question: Why should we make habitat conservation a priority? Display the Build Knowledge anchor chart and ask: *How do natural events and human activities affect the environment?*

Step 1 Guide partners to review the Build Knowledge anchor chart in their reader's notebooks to discuss the prompt.

Step 2 Have students think about how nonnative species, natural events, and human activities have affected the ecosystems discussed in this text set. Remind them to include evidence and examples from the texts, videos, and listening passages.

Step 3 Tell students their editorials should explain why habitat conservation is important. Have them suggest ideas for conserving these environments. Prompt students to use words from their Build Knowledge vocabulary lists in their reader's notebooks.

Inspire Action

Share Your Editorial Have students present their editorials to the class. Ask students in the audience to write down questions and things they find interesting. After the presentations, students can use sticky notes to post comments under the editorials on display. Presenters can read the comments and post sticky note responses.

LEARNING GOALS

We know how natural events and human activities affect the environment.

OBJECTIVES

Read with sufficient accuracy and fluency to support comprehension.

Read grade-level text with purpose and understanding.

ELA ACADEMIC LANGUAGE

- *editorial, evidence*
- Cognates: *editorial, evidencia*

DIGITAL TOOLS

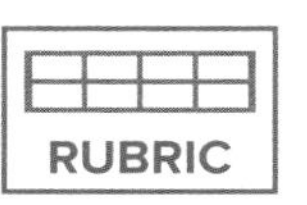

RUBRIC

Show Your Knowledge Rubric

ENGLISH LANGUAGE LEARNERS

Provide sentence frames for support. *Nonnative species/natural events/ human activities ____ the ecosystems. Habitat conservation is important because ____.*

MY GOALS ROUTINE

What I Learned

Review Goals Have students turn back to Reading/Writing Companion page 63 and review the goals for the text set.

Reflect Have students think about the progress they've made toward the goals. Review the key. Then have students reflect and fill in the bars.

LEARNING GOALS

- **We can build and expand on new vocabulary words.**
- **We can use root words to find the meanings of new words.**
- **We can write using new vocabulary words.**

OBJECTIVES

Determine or clarify the meaning of unknown and multiple-meaning words and phrases, choosing flexibly from a range of strategies.

Use context (e.g., cause/effect relationships and comparisons in text) as a clue to the meaning of a word or phrase.

Use common, grade-appropriate Greek and Latin affixes and roots as clues to the meaning of a word (e.g., *photograph, photosynthesis*).

DIGITAL TOOLS

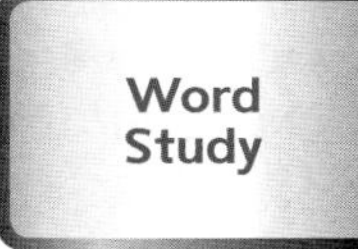

Vocabulary Activities

ENGLISH LANGUAGE LEARNERS

Pair students of different language proficiency levels to practice vocabulary. Have partners discuss the morphology of some of the vocabulary words: *agricultural* and *probable*.

FORMATIVE ASSESSMENT

STUDENT CHECK-IN

After each lesson, have partners share and reflect using the Check-In routine.

Connect to Words

Practice the target vocabulary.

1. What are some **agricultural** products?
2. If your health **declined**, what would you do?
3. Describe a common medical **disorder**.
4. What are some things that scientists **identify**?
5. Is it **probable** that the sun will rise tomorrow? Why or why not?
6. What do plants need to **thrive**?
7. Has anything **unexpected** happened to you lately?
8. How might a song become **widespread**?

Build Vocabulary

- Display *investigate, conclusion,* and *population.*
- Define the words and discuss their meanings with students.
- Write *investigated* under *investigate*. Have partners write other words with the same root and define them. Then have partners ask and answer questions using the words.
- Repeat with *conclusion* and *population.*

Related Words

Help students generate different forms of target words by adding, changing, or removing inflectional endings.

- Draw a four-column chart on the board. Write *thrive* in the first column. Then write *thrives, thrived,* and *thriving* in the next three columns. Read aloud the words with students.
- Have students share sentences using each form of *thrive.*
- Students should add to the chart for *declined* and *identify*, and then share sentences using different forms of the words.
- Have students copy the chart in their reader's notebooks.

See **Practice Book** page 299.

Context Clues

- Remind students that context clues are words or phrases that help a reader figure out unknown words. Some context clues show cause and effect.
- Display this sentence: *Liam was so insistent about joining the team that I couldn't say no.*
- Have partners discuss the meaning of *insistent*. Have students write the meaning in their reader's notebooks.

Spiral Review

LESSON 3 Reinforce the Words

Have students orally complete each sentence stem.

1. There was widespread panic when ____.
2. If you have a sleeping disorder, you might ____.
3. Maria got an unexpected call from ____.
4. The town's economy declined after the ____ closed.
5. It is probable that I will ____.
6. Kevin had to identify his lost ____ in order to pick it up.

Display the previous text set's vocabulary words: *assume, guarantee, nominate, obviously, sympathy, weakling.* Have partners ask and answer questions using each of the words.

Root Words

Remind students that root words can help them find the meanings of unknown words as they read.

- Display On Level **Differentiated Genre Passage** "What Is the Future of the Rain Forests?" Read paragraph 2 on page O1. Model using root words to figure out the meaning of *subsistence.*
- Have pairs use root words to figure out the meanings of other unfamiliar words in the passage. They can confirm meanings in a print or online dictionary.

See **Practice Book** page 300.

OPTION LESSON 4 Connect to Writing

- Have students write sentences in their reader's notebooks using the target vocabulary.
- Tell them to write sentences that provide context to show what the words mean.
- ELL Provide the Day 3 sentence stems 1–6 for students needing extra support.

Write Using Vocabulary

Have students write something they learned from the target words in their reader's notebooks. For example, they might write about an *unexpected* gift they received or something that is *probable* to happen in the near future.

Shades of Meaning

Help students generate words related to *disorder,* meaning "illness." Draw a word web and write *disorder* in the center.

- Have partners generate related words, such as synonyms, to add to the outer circles. Ask students to use a thesaurus.
- Add words not included, such as *syndrome, malady, ailment,* and *condition.*
- Ask students to copy the words in their reader's notebooks.

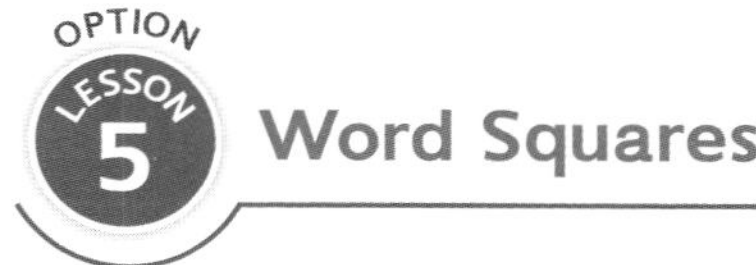

OPTION LESSON 5 Word Squares

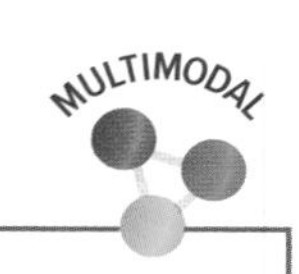

Ask students to create Word Squares for each vocabulary word.

- In the first square, students write the word (e.g., *agricultural*).
- In the second square, students write a definition and any related words, such as synonyms (e.g., *rural, farming*).
- In the third square, students draw a simple sketch that will help them remember the word (e.g., a farm with crops and a barn).
- In the fourth square, students write nonexamples, including antonyms for the word (e.g., *urban, metropolitan*).

Have partners discuss their squares.

Morphology

Draw a T-chart. Write *probable* in the left column. In the right column, write *suffixes.*

- Discuss how the suffixes *-y* and *-ity* change the meaning or part of speech of *probable.*
- Have students write *probably* and *probability.* Discuss the meanings of the words.

Write Using Vocabulary

Have students use vocabulary words in their extended writing.

Lexile 760L

OBJECTIVES

Quote accurately from a text when explaining what the text says explicitly and when drawing inferences from the text.

Explain how an author uses reasons and evidence to support particular points in a text, identifying which reasons and evidence support which point(s).

Explain an author's perspective, or point of view, toward a topic in an informational text.

ELA ACADEMIC LANGUAGE

- *argumentative, convince, perspective, evidence*
- Cognates: *convencer, evidencia*

Approaching Level

Leveled Reader: *The Great Plains*

Preview and Predict

- Read the Essential Question with students: *How do natural events and human activities affect the environment?*
- Have students preview the title, table of contents, and first page of *The Great Plains.* Students should use information in the text and images to predict what they think the selection will be about.

Review Genre: Expository Text

Tell students that this selection is an expository text. It gives factual information and often contains text features, such as diagrams, maps, charts, and photographs. Authors may also reveal their purpose or perspective in an expository text. Have students identify features of an expository text in *The Great Plains.*

Close Reading

Note Taking Ask students to use a copy of online Author's Perspective **Graphic Organizer 8** as they read.

Pages 2–3 Point out the word *ecosystems* on page 2. *The root word* eco *comes from a Latin word meaning "house."* Systems *means "a group of things that work together." Use the meanings of* eco *and* systems *to define* ecosystems. ("a group of living things in one habitat") Have students add this word in their reader's notebooks. *What effect did settlers have on the environment of the Great Plains?* (They converted large areas of land for agriculture; they hunted some species of animals until almost none were left.)

Pages 4–5 *What forces have shaped the land in the Great Plains?* (Streams carried rocks and soil from the Rockies and built up mounds of earth; water heading to the ocean dug out canyons and wore down hills.) Point out the word *biodiversity. The root word* bio *means "life."* Diversity *means a "variety." What does biodiversity mean?* ("a variety of life") Have students add this word in their reader's notebooks.

Pages 6–7 *What question might you ask after reading page 6?* (Which animals adapted to live in the grasslands, and which did not?) *What answer do you determine after rereading?* (bison; mammoth)

Pages 8–11 *Did Native Americans greatly impact the environment?* (no) *How did fur traders affect the environment?* (Numbers of some animals, such as beavers, declined.) *What activity created disorder in the ecology of the grasslands?* (plowing up large areas to plant crops)

Pages 12–13 *What evidence supports the author's perspective that crossbred crops are better for the Great Plains?* (Crossbred crops don't need chemicals to grow well.) *How have perspectives about prairie fires changed?* (Now people think they help the ecology of the area.)

Pages 14–17 *What is the first step to restore an animal population?* (make sure there is enough food) *What does the author think should be done to restore the ecology of the Great Plains?* (do more research)

Respond to Reading Revisit the Essential Question and ask students to complete the Text Evidence questions on page 18.

Analytical Writing **Write About Reading** Check that students have correctly identified the author's perspective and identified details that support it.

Fluency: Accuracy and Rate

Model Model reading page 13 with accuracy and appropriate rate. Then reread the page aloud and have students read along with you.

Apply Have students practice reading the passage with a partner.

Paired Read: "Save the Great Plains Wolves"

Make Connections: Write About It

Before reading, ask students to note that the genre of this text is argumentative text. Then discuss the Essential Question. After reading, ask students to write connections between the perspectives in *The Great Plains* and "Save the Great Plains Wolves."

Leveled Reader

Build Knowledge

Talk About the Text Have partners discuss how natural events and human activities affect the environment.

Write About the Text Have students add their ideas to the Build Knowledge pages of their reader's notebooks.

FOCUS ON SCIENCE

Students can extend their knowledge of life science by completing the activity on page 24.

LITERATURE CIRCLES

Ask students to conduct a literature circle using the Thinkmark questions to guide the discussion. You may wish to have a whole-class discussion, using both selections in the Leveled Reader, about how natural events and human activities affect the environment.

IF students read the Approaching Level fluently and answered the questions,

THEN pair them with students who have proficiently read the On Level and have students

- echo-read the On Level main selection.
- use self-stick notes to mark details that identify the author's perspective.

Access Complex Text

The On Level challenges students by including more **domain-specific words** and **complex sentence structures.**

Genre Study: Argumentative Text

Name ____________

Read the two passages by two different authors. As you read the passages, notice the features of argumentative text.

WHAT IS THE FUTURE OF THE RAIN FORESTS?

Rain Forests Support People

People must make economic use of the rain forests.

Cutting down rain forest trees has some negative effects, but it is necessary for the survival of people and national economies. Therefore, it is not realistic to try to stop the cutting of all rain forest trees. A better plan is to manage rain forest use.

Farming in the Rain Forests

When part of a rain forest is cut down, subsistence agriculture usually takes its place. Subsistence agriculture is farming or ranching that produces only enough for a family to meet its daily needs. The families need these farms in order to survive.

Commercial Use of Rain Forests

Commercial farms also make use of rain forest land. Lumber from rain forest trees is used to make furniture, flooring, and paper. Many countries buy beef that comes from cattle ranches on former rain forest land. Other rain forest land becomes farms. Farmers grow coffee, soybeans, and palm trees. Companies build roads through the forest to transport goods to and from the farms. Often these businesses are important to their countries' economies. Without them, their nations' economies would suffer.

Rain Forest Loss Can Be Controlled

The loss of rain forest trees does threaten wildlife habitats and the quality of the soil. It makes sense to limit the damage to rain forests. But a complete stop to rain forest cutting would cause other serious problems. A more realistic goal is to manage the use of rain forest land so that the negative outcomes are limited.

Genre Passages · Grade 5 · Unit 5 · Week 5 A1

"What Is the Future of the Rain Forests?"
Lexile 840L

OBJECTIVES

Explain how an author uses reasons and evidence to support particular points in a text, identifying which reasons and evidence support which point(s).

Explain an author's perspective, or point of view, toward a topic in an informational text.

Integrate information from several texts on the same topic in order to write or speak about the subject knowledgeably.

Determine or clarify the meaning of unknown and multiple-meaning words and phrases based on Grade 5 reading and content, choosing flexibly from a range of strategies.

Use common, grade-appropriate Greek and Latin affixes and roots as clues to the meaning of a word (e.g., *photograph, photosynthesis*).

ELA ACADEMIC LANGUAGE

- *perspective, evidence, root, heading*
- Cognate: *evidencia*

Approaching Level

Genre Passage: "What Is the Future of the Rain Forests?"

Build Background

- Read aloud the Essential Question: *How do natural events and human activities affect the environment?* Have students consider texts they've read in this text set and compare two environmental effects brought about by nature or by human activity. Focus discussion with these sentence starters:

  I read that humans/nature . . .

  This affected the environment because . . .

- Explain that the online **Differentiated Genre Passage** "What Is the Future of the Rain Forests?" is about ecosystems that receive a lot of rain and have many different kinds of plants and animals. Review the meanings of *ecosystem* and *biofuels* with students.

Review Genre: Argumentative Text

Reiterate that argumentative texts include an author's perspective about an issue. Authors support their perspectives with reasons, factual evidence, examples, and details. Headings, charts, and other text features help organize and present information.

Close Reading

Note Taking As students read the passage the first time, ask them to annotate the text. Have them note central ideas, relevant details, unfamiliar words, and questions they have. Then read again and use the following questions.

Read

Genre: Argumentative Text *How does the title of this text help you understand what the authors' arguments will be about?* (The title tells me that they will be about what should happen to rain forests in the future.)

Author's Perspective Read paragraphs 1–2. *In the author's opinion, should people be allowed to cut down trees?* (yes) *Why does the author think this?* (cutting down trees helps people and national economies survive)

Root Words Locate the word *transport* in paragraph 3. *This word contains the Latin root* trans, *which means "across" and the Latin root* port, *which means "carry." How does this help you understand the meaning of* transport? (It tells me that when you transport something, you carry it from one place to another.)

Text Features: Charts and Headings Look at the heading "Rain Forests and the Variety of Life" on page A2. *What does this heading tell you about what you will read?* (that this section will be about the different living things that can be found in rain forests)

Author's Perspective Read page A2. *What is the author's perspective about rain forests?* (People need to preserve rain forests to help protect Earth.) *Find a reason in paragraph 4 that supports this perspective.* (rain forests keep the air cleaner and reduce the risk of global warming)

COLLABORATE **Summarize** Have pairs summarize each author's perspective and supporting reasons and details.

Reread

Use the questions on page A3 to guide students' rereading of the passage.

Author's Craft Reread "Commercial Use of Rain Forests" on page A1. *How does the author help you understand the commercial use of rain forest land?* (The author gives examples of different commercial uses of rain forest land. The author also says that these are important to countries' economies.)

Author's Craft Reread the section "Earth's Water Cycle and Rain Forests" on page A2. *Why does the author describe the water cycle in the rain forest?* (to explain how global rainfall patterns might change as rain forests disappear)

Author's Craft *What did the headings help you understand?* (what each section is about)

Integrate

COLLABORATE **Make Connections** Guide students to think about the Essential Question and how it relates to "What Is the Future of the Rain Forests?" and another text they read in this text set. Have partners work together to cite evidence and respond to this question: *How has human activity affected nature?*

Compare Texts Draw a T-chart and label the columns with the titles of the texts students chose. Help students compare how each text helps readers understand how humans affect nature.

Build Knowledge

Talk About the Text Have partners discuss how natural events and human activities affect the environment.

Write About the Text Have students add their ideas to the Build Knowledge pages of their reader's notebooks.

Differentiate and Collaborate

COLLABORATE **Be Inspired** Have students think about "What Is the Future of the Rain Forests?" and other selections they have read. Ask: *What do the texts inspire you to do?* Use the following activities or have pairs of students think of ways to respond to the texts.

Hold a Debate Choose an issue discussed in this text set and organize a debate with classmates. Form two groups and have each group prepare an argument in support of one side of the issue. Ask a teacher or other classmates to moderate your debate and decide which argument is more convincing.

Write an Editorial What can you and your community do to help the environment? Write an editorial for your school or local newspaper explaining your ideas.

Readers to Writers

Supporting Evidence Remind students that authors use evidence, such as facts, details, and examples, to support their perspective. Ask students to reread paragraph 3 on page A2. Ask: *What supporting evidence does the author use? How does this evidence help make the author's perspective more convincing?*

LEVEL UP

IF students read the Approaching Level fluently and answered the questions,

THEN pair them with students who have proficiently read the On Level. Have them

- partner-read the On Level passage.
- explain how the authors' perspectives about the rain forests differ.

Approaching Level

Word Study/Decoding

REVIEW SUFFIX *-ion*

OBJECTIVES

Know and apply grade-level phonics and word analysis skills in decoding words.

Use combined knowledge of all letter-sound correspondences, syllabication patterns, and morphology (e.g., roots and affixes) to read accurately unfamiliar multisyllabic words in context and out of context.

Decode words with *-ion*.

I Do Review with students that *-ion* is a common suffix that, when added to certain verbs, changes them to nouns. Write the word pair *act/action* on the board. Explain that the verb *act* changes to the noun *action* when the suffix *-ion* is added. Review that *-tion* is usually pronounced *shun* (as in *action*).

We Do Write the word pair *create/creation* on the board and read it aloud, stressing the /sh/ sound as you pronounce *creation*. Point out that when the verb ends in an *e*, as in *create*, the *e* is dropped when the suffix *-ion* is added. Guide students to determine the meaning of the noun *creation*.

You Do Write the words *donation* and *permission* on the board. Have students pronounce each word correctly and underline the suffix. Remind them that *-tion* and *-ssion* are usually pronounced *shun*. Ask students to determine the meanings of *donation* and *permission* by connecting them to the verbs *donate* and *permit*.

BUILD WORDS WITH SUFFIX *-ion*

OBJECTIVES

Know and apply grade-level phonics and word analysis skills in decoding words.

Use combined knowledge of all letter-sound correspondences, syllabication patterns, and morphology (e.g., roots and affixes) to read accurately unfamiliar multisyllabic words in context and out of context.

Build words with *-ion*.

I Do Explain that students will build new words by combining verbs with the suffix *-ion*. On the board, write the suffix *-ion* and the following verbs: *construct, subtract, confuse, correct*.

We Do Work with students to combine the verbs and the suffix to build nouns. Have them chorally read the words *construction, subtraction, confusion,* and *correction*. Remind students that *-sion* is usually pronounced *zhun*, as in *confusion*, but *-tion* is usually pronounced *shun*, as in *construction, subtraction,* and *correction*. Point out that the *e* in *confuse* is dropped when *-ion* is added. Then guide students to use the meanings of the verbs to determine the meanings of the nouns.

You Do Write the verbs *concentrate, decorate,* and *revise* on the board. Have partners build nouns by adding the suffix *-ion* to each. Ask them to write each new word and then pronounce it.

PRACTICE WORDS WITH SUFFIX *-ion*

OBJECTIVES

Know and apply grade-level phonics and word analysis skills in decoding words.

Use combined knowledge of all letter-sound correspondences, syllabication patterns, and morphology (e.g., roots and affixes) to read accurately unfamiliar multisyllabic words in context and out of context.

Practice words with *-ion*.

I Do Write these words on the board: *appreciation, television*. Read the words aloud, underlining the *-ion* suffixes with your finger as you read. Emphasize the difference between the /sh/ and /zh/ pronunciations in the words.

We Do Write the words *division* and *discussion* on the board. Model how to pronounce the word *division*, underlining the *-ion* with your finger. Have students repeat the word. Then have students pronounce the word *discussion*. Lead students to identify the difference between the /zh/ and /sh/ pronunciations in the two words.

To provide additional practice, write these words on the board. Read aloud the first word and underline *-ion*.

omission	conclusion	decision
donation	education	equation
session	explosion	confusion
imitation	action	infection

You Do Have students read aloud the remaining words. Ask them to point out the *-ion* in each word and to tell whether the sound preceding it is /sh/ or /zh/. Have partners determine the meaning of each noun by connecting it to the meaning of the related verb.

Afterward, point to the words in the list in random order for students to read chorally.

ELL For **ELL** students who need phonics and decoding practice, define words and help them use the words in sentences, scaffolding to ensure their understanding. See the **Language Transfers Handbook** for phonics elements that may not transfer from students' native languages.

Approaching Level

Vocabulary

REVIEW HIGH-FREQUENCY WORDS

TIER 2

OBJECTIVES

Acquire and use accurately grade-appropriate general academic and domain-specific words and phrases, including those that signal contrast, addition, and other logical relationships (e.g., *however, although, nevertheless, similarly, moreover, in addition*).

I Do Review words from **High-Frequency Word Cards** 161–200. Display one word at a time, following the routine:

Display the word. Read the word. Then spell the word.

We Do Ask students to state the word and spell the word with you. Model using the word in a sentence and have students repeat after you.

You Do Display the word. Ask students to say the word and then spell it. When completed, quickly flip through the word card set as students chorally read the words. Provide opportunities for students to use the words in speaking and writing. For example, provide sentence starters, such as *I think that* ____. Ask students to write each word in their reader's notebooks.

REVIEW ACADEMIC VOCABULARY

OBJECTIVES

Acquire and use accurately grade-appropriate general academic and domain-specific words and phrases, including those that signal contrast, addition, and other logical relationships (e.g., *however, although, nevertheless, similarly, moreover, in addition*).

I Do Display each **Visual Vocabulary Card** and state the word. Explain how the photograph illustrates the word. State the example sentence and repeat the word.

We Do Point to the word on the card and read the word with students. Ask them to repeat the word. Engage students in structured partner talk about the image, as prompted on the back of the vocabulary card.

You Do Display each visual in random order, hiding the word. Have students match the definitions and context sentences of the words to the visuals displayed.

You may wish to review high-frequency words with ELL students using the lesson above.

UNDERSTAND ACADEMIC VOCABULARY

OBJECTIVES

Acquire and use accurately grade-appropriate general academic and domain-specific words and phrases, including those that signal contrast, addition, and other logical relationships (e.g., *however, although, nevertheless, similarly, moreover, in addition*).

I Do Display the *agricultural* **Visual Vocabulary Card** and ask: *Which would you describe as an agricultural tool, a wrench or a shovel?* Explain that a shovel would be an agricultural tool because it is used for farming.

We Do Ask these questions. Help students explain their answers.

- If sales *declined,* would a store make more money or less money?
- If a person has a *disorder,* is that person sick or healthy?
- What characteristics help you *identify* a bear?

You Do Have students work in pairs to respond to these questions and explain their answers:

- Which is *probable,* finding a penny or a buried treasure?
- If plants *thrive,* are they healthy or sick?
- Which is *unexpected,* winning a raffle or having homework?
- Which is more *widespread,* a sickness at home or at school?

Have students pick words from their reader's notebooks and write the definitions of the words and a sentence using each word.

ROOT WORDS

OBJECTIVES

Determine or clarify the meaning of unknown and multiple-meaning words and phrases based on grade 5 reading and content, choosing flexibly from a range of strategies.

Use common, grade-appropriate Greek and Latin affixes and roots as clues to the meaning of a word (e.g., *photograph, photosynthesis*).

I Do Display "What Is the Future of the Rain Forests?" in the Approaching Level online **Differentiated Genre Passage** page A1. Read aloud the first paragraph. Point to the word *survival.* Tell students they can use their knowledge of word roots to help them figure out the meaning of the word.

Think Aloud The Latin root *vivere* means "live." Words with *viv* and *vivi* usually have something to do with life. I think *survival* means "to stay alive." When I use this meaning in the sentence, it makes sense.

We Do Ask students to point to the word *agriculture* in the second paragraph on page A1. With students, discuss how to use the Latin roots *agri,* meaning "field," and *cultura,* meaning "cultivation," to figure out the meaning of the word. Write the definition of the word.

You Do Have students determine the meanings of *Commercial, transport* (page A1, paragraph 3), and *reside* (page A2, paragraph 2) by using context clues and word roots (*merc*: "merchandise"; *portare*: "to carry"; *sedere*: "to sit"). Then have students write the words and their definitions in their reader's notebooks. They can use a dictionary to confirm word meanings.

Approaching Level

Fluency/Comprehension

FLUENCY

OBJECTIVES

Read grade-level prose and poetry orally with accuracy, appropriate rate, expression, and automaticity on successive readings.

Read fluently with good expression and phrasing.

I Do Explain that good readers recognize words and read them accurately. They vary their reading rate, or speed, slowing down to understand more complex text. Read the first two paragraphs of "What Is the Future of the Rain Forests?" in the Approaching Level online **Differentiated Genre Passage** page A1. Tell students to monitor your accuracy and listen for how you vary your reading rate.

We Do Read the rest of the page aloud and have students repeat each sentence after you, matching your rate. Explain that you monitored your rate, reading neither too fast nor too slow, to ensure that you read accurately.

You Do Have partners take turns reading sentences from the passage. Remind them to focus on their accuracy and rate. Provide corrective feedback as needed by modeling proper fluency.

IDENTIFY AUTHOR'S PERSPECTIVE

OBJECTIVES

Analyze multiple accounts of the same event or topic, noting important similarities and differences in the point of view they represent.

Explain an author's perspective, or point of view, toward a topic in an informational text.

Explain how an author uses reasons and evidence to support particular points in a text, identifying which reasons and evidence support which point(s).

I Do Review that authors of argumentative texts include reasons and evidence as support for their perspective, or attitude, on a topic. Facts, opinions, details, and word choices in the text provide clues about the author's perspective.

We Do Read aloud the first paragraph of "What Is the Future of the Rain Forests?" in the online Approaching Level **Differentiated Genre Passage** page A1. Point out that each sentence expresses an opinion. Explain that the author's powerful word choices, such as *necessary for the survival of people, not realistic,* and *better plan,* reveal the author's perspective that it is necessary to cut down some rain forest trees.

You Do Have students read the rest of "Rain Forests Support People." After each paragraph, they should list details and word choices that help convey the author's perspective.

REVIEW AUTHOR'S PERSPECTIVE

OBJECTIVES

Explain how an author uses reasons and evidence to support particular points in a text, identifying which reasons and evidence support which point(s).

Explain an author's perspective, or point of view, toward a topic in an informational text.

Determine an author's point of view or purpose in a text and explain how it is conveyed in the text.

I Do Review that authors of argumentative texts have a certain perspective, or attitude, on a topic. Examining facts, opinions, details, and word choices in the text can help readers determine the author's perspective.

We Do Read the first paragraph of "What Is the Future of the Rain Forests?" in the online Approaching Level **Differentiated Genre Passage** page A1. Refer to the list of word choices and details the students have already compiled. Model how to use them to determine the author's perspective. Work with students to determine the author's perspective in the second section of the passage.

You Do Have pairs read page A2 of "What Is the Future of the Rain Forest?" After each section, have them identify facts, opinions, details, and word choices and then use these to determine the author's perspective.

SELF-SELECTED READING

OBJECTIVES

Determine an author's point of view or purpose in a text and explain how it is conveyed in the text.

Explain how an author uses reasons and evidence to support particular points in a text, identifying which reasons and evidence support which point(s).

Explain an author's perspective, or point of view, toward a topic in an informational text.

Ask and answer questions to increase understanding.

Read Independently

Have students choose a nonfiction book or article for independent reading. Students can read a **Classroom Library** book or check the online **Leveled Reader Library** or **Unit Bibliography** for selections. Guide students to apply what they learned in this text set. Remind them that:

- the central idea is the most important point the author makes about the topic. Relevant details support the central idea.
- the author's perspective is how the author feels about the topic.
- diagrams, charts, headings, and other text features give important information.

Have students record the author's perspective on Author's Perspective **Graphic Organizer 8** as they read independently. Students can choose activities from Reading **Center Activity Cards** to help them apply skills to the text as they read. After they finish, they can choose a Book Talk activity to talk about the texts they read. Offer assistance and guidance with self-selected assignments.

Lexile 910L

OBJECTIVES

Quote accurately from a text when explaining what the text says explicitly and when drawing inferences from the text.

Explain how an author uses reasons and evidence to support particular points in a text, identifying which reasons and evidence support which point(s).

Explain an author's perspective, or point of view, toward a topic in an informational text.

ELA ACADEMIC LANGUAGE

- *perspective, argumentative, convince, evidence*
- Cognates: *convencer, evidencia*

On Level

Leveled Reader: *The Great Plains*

Preview and Predict

- Read the Essential Question with students: *How do natural events and human activities affect the environment?*
- Have students preview the title, table of contents, and first page of *The Great Plains.* Students should use information in the text and images to predict what they think the selection will be about.

Review Genre: Expository Text

Tell students this selection is an expository text. It gives factual information and often contains text features, such as diagrams, maps, charts, and photographs. Authors may also reveal their purpose or perspective in an expository text. Have students identify features of an expository text in *The Great Plains.*

Close Reading

Note Taking Ask students to use a copy of online Author's Perspective **Graphic Organizer 8** as they read.

Pages 2–3 *The root word* eco *comes from a Latin word meaning "house." What does* ecosystems *mean?* ("a group of living things in one habitat") Have students add this word in their reader's notebooks. *What question might you ask after reading this section?* (How did settlers affect the environment of the Great Plains?) *What answer might you determine after rereading?* (They converted large areas for agriculture; they hunted some species of animals until there were almost none left.)

Pages 4–7 *How did streams and rivers affect the land on their way to the ocean?* (Water cut into rock, dug out canyons, and wore down hills.) *The root word* bio *means "life."* Diversity *means "a variety." What does* biodiversity *mean?* ("a variety of life") Have students add this word in their reader's notebooks. *How would a drought likely affect wildlife near streams in the Great Plains?* (Frogs and crustaceans could die; birds, beavers, and raccoons could be forced to leave the area.)

Pages 8–10 *How did the arrival of Spanish explorers and, later, European fur traders affect wildlife populations?* (More bison were killed; numbers of some animal species, such as beavers, declined drastically.)

Pages 11–12 *What question might you ask as you read page 11?* (What effects did chemicals in fertilizers and pesticides have?) *How might you answer it?* (They killed beneficial and harmful insects.)

Pages 13–15 *What evidence supports the author's perspective that crops crossbred with grasses are better for the Great Plains ecosystems?* (They don't need a lot of fertilizers and pesticides.) *How have people's views about prairie fires changed?* (People now see them as helpful.)

Pages 16–17 *Paraphrase the author's perspective about restoring the ecology of the Great Plains.* (It is a complicated task. Because all the ecosystems are closely linked, it can be difficult to tell which plant or animal species should be restored first. More research is needed.)

Respond to Reading Revisit the Essential Question and ask students to complete the Text Evidence questions on page 18.

Analytical Writing **Write About Reading** Check that students have correctly identified the author's perspective and the details that support it.

Fluency: Accuracy and Rate

Model Model reading page 11 with accuracy and appropriate rate. Then reread the page aloud and have students read along with you.

Apply Have students practice reading the passage with partners.

Paired Read: "Save the Great Plains Wolves"

Make Connections: Write About It

Before reading, ask students to note that the genre of this text is argumentative text. Then discuss the Essential Question. After reading, ask students to write about connections among the text's perspectives.

Leveled Reader

Build Knowledge

Talk About the Text Have partners discuss how natural events and human activities affect the environment.

Write About the Text Have students add their ideas to the Build Knowledge pages of their reader's notebooks.

FOCUS ON SCIENCE

Students can extend their knowledge of life science by completing the activity on page 24.

LITERATURE CIRCLES

Ask students to conduct a literature circle using the Thinkmark questions to guide the discussion. You may wish to have a whole-class discussion, using the Leveled Reader selections, about how natural events and human activities affect the environment.

IF students read the On Level fluently and answered the questions,

THEN pair them with students who have proficiently read the Beyond Level and have students

- partner-read the Beyond Level main selection.
- make a list of details that help them identify the author's perspective.
- make a list of questions while reading the selection and then reread for answers.

ACT Access Complex Text

The Beyond Level challenges students by including more **domain-specific words** and **complex sentence structures.**

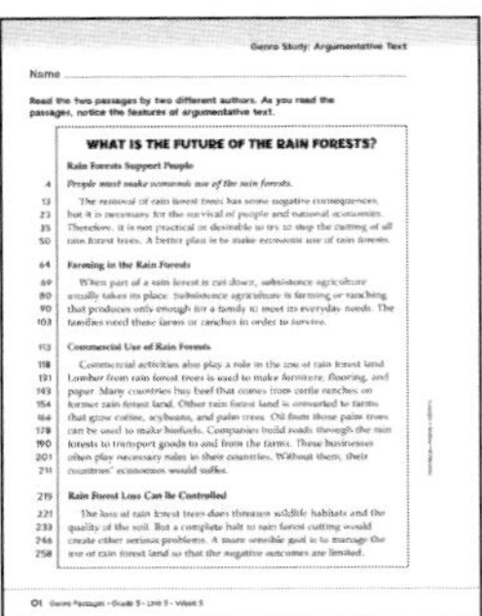

"What Is the Future of the Rain Forests?"
Lexile 920L

OBJECTIVES

Explain how an author uses reasons and evidence to support particular points in a text, identifying which reasons and evidence support which point(s).

Integrate information from several texts on the same topic in order to write or speak about the subject knowledgeably.

Determine or clarify the meaning of unknown and multiple-meaning words and phrases based on Grade 5 reading and content, choosing flexibly from a range of strategies.

Use common, grade-appropriate Greek and Latin affixes and roots as clues to the meaning of a word (e.g., *photograph, photosynthesis*).

ELA ACADEMIC LANGUAGE

- *perspective, evidence, root, heading*
- Cognate: *evidencia*

On Level

Genre Passage: "What Is the Future of the Rain Forests?"

Build Background

- Read aloud the Essential Question: *How do natural events and human activities affect the environment?* Have students consider texts they've read in this text set and compare two environmental effects brought about by nature or by human activity. Focus discussion with these sentence starters:

  I read that humans/nature . . .

  This affected the environment because . . .

- Explain that the online **Differentiated Genre Passage** "What Is the Future of Rain Forests?" is about ecosystems that receive heavy rainfall and are home to a large variety of plants and animals. Rain forests are located near the equator and cover nearly 16 percent of Earth's land surface. Review the meanings of *ecosystem* and *biofuels* with students.

Review Genre: Argumentative Text

Reiterate that argumentative texts include an author's perspective about an issue. Authors support their perspectives with reasons, factual evidence, examples, and details. Headings, charts, and other text features help organize and present information.

Close Reading

Note Taking As students read the passage the first time, ask them to annotate the text. Have them note central ideas, relevant details, unfamiliar words, and questions they have. Then read again and use the following questions.

Read

Genre: Argumentative Text *How does the title of this text set up an argument between the two authors?* (The authors will express different opinions about the answer to the question in the title.)

Author's Perspective Read paragraph 1 on page O1. *Why does the author point out that removing rain forest trees has some negative consequences?* (This is an opposing idea that the author wants to challenge.)

Root Words Find *transport* in paragraph 3 on page O1. *This word contains the Latin root* trans, *which means "across" and the Latin root* port, *which means "carry." How does this help you understand the meaning of* transport? (It tells me that when you transport something, you carry it from one place to another.)

Text Features: Charts and Headings Read the heading, "Rain Forests and Biodiversity," on page O2. *Why do you think the author used this heading?* (The heading identifies something the author feels is affected by rain forests: living things.)

Author's Perspective Read the rest of page O2. *How does this author's perspective differ from that of the previous author?* (This author thinks that cutting down rain forests will do long-term damage.)

COLLABORATE **Summarize** Have pairs summarize each author's perspective and supporting reasons and details.

Reread

Use the questions on page O3 to guide students' rereading of the passage.

Author's Craft Reread "Commercial Use of Rain Forests" on page O1. *How does the author help you understand the role of commercial activities in the use of rain forest land?* (The author gives examples of commercial use of rain forest land, and points out that without these businesses, economies would suffer.)

Author's Craft Read the headings. *How are they helpful to the reader?* (The headings introduce the points that support the author's perspective.)

Author's Craft *How does the author of "The World Needs Rain Forests" organize the information to help you understand the author's perspective?* (The author makes a statement about why people must save the rain forest and then shows understanding of an opposing view but argues against it. The author also gives different reasons the rain forest must be saved.)

Integrate

COLLABORATE **Make Connections** Have students think about how the Essential Question relates to "What Is the Future of the Rain Forests?" and other texts they read. Tell pairs to work with a partner to cite text evidence and answer this question: *How has human activity affected nature?*

Compare Texts Have partners draw a T-chart labeled with the titles of the texts they chose and use the chart to compare what they learned in each text about how humans affect nature.

Build Knowledge

Talk About the Text Have partners discuss how natural events and human activities affect the environment.

Write About the Text Have students add their ideas to the Build Knowledge pages of their reader's notebooks.

Differentiate and Collaborate

COLLABORATE **Be Inspired** Have students think about "What Is the Future of the Rain Forests?" and other selections they have read. Ask: *What do the texts inspire you to do?* Use the following activities or have students think of a way to respond to the texts.

Hold a Debate Choose an issue discussed in this text set and organize a debate with classmates. Form two groups and have each group prepare an argument in support of one side of the issue. Ask a teacher or other classmates to moderate your debate and decide which argument is more convincing.

Write an Editorial What can you and your community do to help the environment? Write an editorial for your school or local newspaper explaining your ideas. Share your editorial.

Readers to Writers

Supporting Evidence Remind students that authors use evidence, such as facts, details, and examples, to support their perspectives. Ask students to reread paragraph 4 on page O2. Ask: *What supporting evidence does the author use? How does this evidence help make the author's perspective more convincing?*

LEVEL UP

IF students read the On Level fluently and answered the questions,

THEN pair them with students who have proficiently read the Beyond Level. Have them

- partner-read the Beyond Level passage.
- summarize why each author holds a specific perspective about rain forests.

On Level

Vocabulary/Comprehension

REVIEW ACADEMIC VOCABULARY

OBJECTIVES

Acquire and use accurately grade-appropriate general academic and domainspecific words and phrases, including those that signal contrast, addition, and other logical relationships (e.g., *however, although, nevertheless, similarly, moreover, in addition*).

I Do Use the **Visual Vocabulary Cards** to review the key selection words *declined, disorder, identify, probable, unexpected,* and *widespread*. Point to each word, read it aloud, and have students chorally repeat it.

We Do Ask these questions. Help students to explain their answers.

- What might a store owner do if his or her profits *declined*?
- What *disorder* would you like to find a cure for?
- What characteristics can help people *identify* bears?

You Do Have students work in pairs to respond and explain their answers.

- What is a *probable* question someone might ask you tonight?
- How would you feel if your teacher gave an *unexpected* quiz?
- What is a *widespread* problem you have heard about?

Have students choose words from their reader's notebooks, write a definition for each word, and use each word in a sentence.

ROOT WORDS

OBJECTIVES

Determine or clarify the meaning of unknown and multiple-meaning words and phrases based on Grade 5 reading and content, choosing flexibly from a range of strategies.

Use common, grade-appropriate Greek and Latin affixes and roots as clues to the meaning of a word (e.g., *photograph, photosynthesis*).

I Do Remind students they can often figure out the meaning of a word by using their knowledge of word roots. Read aloud the first paragraph of "What Is the Future of the Rain Forests?" in the On Level online **Differentiated Genre Passage** page O1.

Think Aloud The word *survival* in the first paragraph contains the Latin root *vivere*, which means "live." I think *survival* means "to stay alive." This meaning makes sense in the sentence.

We Do Have students read the second paragraph on page O1, where they encounter *agriculture*. Help students figure out the definition by pointing out the Latin root *agri,* meaning "field," and *cultura*, meaning "cultivation."

You Do Have pairs determine the meanings of *Commercial* and *transport* (page O1, paragraph 3), *reside* (page O2, paragraph 2), and *perspective* (page O2, paragraph 5) by using context clues and word roots (*merc:* "merchandise"; *portare:* "to carry"; *sedere:* "to sit"; *specere:* "to look at").

REVIEW AUTHOR'S PERSPECTIVE

OBJECTIVES

Analyze multiple accounts of the same event or topic, noting important similarities and differences in the point of view they represent.

Explain an author's perspective, or point of view, toward a topic in an informational text.

Explain how an author uses reasons and evidence to support particular points in a text, identifying which reasons and evidence support which point(s).

I Do Review that authors of argumentative texts have a certain perspective, or attitude, on a topic. Examining facts, opinions, details, and word choices in the text can help readers determine the author's perspective.

We Do Display "What Is the Future of the Rain Forests?" in the On Level online **Differentiated Genre Passage** page O1. Have a volunteer read the first selection "Rain Forests Support People." Have students record relevant facts, opinions, details, and word choices. Model using these to determine the author's perspective about rain forests.

You Do Have pairs read the next selection "The World Needs Rain Forests" on page O2. Tell them to stop after each section and identify relevant facts, opinions, details, and word choices. They should use them to determine the author's perspective in each section and in the text as a whole.

SELF-SELECTED READING

OBJECTIVES

Determine an author's point of view or purpose in a text and explain how it is conveyed in the text.

Explain how an author uses reasons and evidence to support particular points in a text, identifying which reasons and evidence support which point(s).

Ask and answer questions to increase understanding.

Read Independently

Have students choose a nonfiction book or article for independent reading. Students can read a **Classroom Library** book or check the online **Leveled Reader Library** or **Unit Bibliography** for selections. Guide students to apply what they learned in this text set. Remind them to

- look for the central idea and relevant details.
- think about the author's perspective, or how the author feels about the topic.
- pay attention to diagrams, charts, headings, and other text features.

Before they read, have students preview the text, noting headings and other text features. Remind them to reread difficult sections as needed.

Students can choose activities from Reading **Center Activity Cards** to help them apply skills to the text as they read. After they finish, they can choose a Book Talk activity to talk about the texts they read.

You may want to include **ELL** students in On Level vocabulary and comprehension lessons. Offer language support as needed.

Lexile 1020L

OBJECTIVES

Quote accurately from a text when explaining what the text says explicitly and when drawing inferences from the text.

Explain how an author uses reasons and evidence to support particular points in a text, identifying which reasons and evidence support which point(s).

Explain an author's perspective, or point of view, toward a topic in an informational text.

ELA ACADEMIC LANGUAGE

- *perspective, argumentative, convince, evidence*
- Cognates: *convencer, evidencia*

Beyond Level

Leveled Reader: *The Great Plains*

Preview and Predict

- Read the Essential Question with students: *How do natural events and human activities affect the environment?*
- Have students preview the title, table of contents, and first page of *The Great Plains.* Students should use information in the text and images to predict what they think the selection will be about.

Review Genre: Expository Text

Tell students that this selection is an expository text. It gives factual information and often contains text features such as diagrams, maps, charts, and photographs. Authors may also reveal their purpose or perspective in an expository text. Have students identify features of an expository text in *The Great Plains.*

Close Reading

Note Taking Ask students to use a copy of online Author's Perspective **Graphic Organizer 8** as they read.

Pages 2–7 *Identify a word with the root* eco, *which comes from a Latin word meaning "house," and identify the meaning of the word.* (*ecosystems*: "a group of living things in one habitat") *What natural events have affected the Great Plains?* (droughts, blizzards, wildfires) *What human activities have affected them?* (converting large areas for agriculture, hunting some species to near extinction) *What does biodiversity mean? Use the root word* bio, *meaning "life," to answer.* ("variety of life") Have students add this word as well as *ecosystems* in their reader's notebook. *How do droughts affect wildlife near streams?* (Frogs and crustaceans may die; beavers and raccoons may be forced to leave the area.)

Pages 8–11 *What question did you ask on page 9?* (What effect did fur trappers have on wildlife?) *What answer did you identify?* (They reduced numbers of some species, such as beavers.) *Why are roots and grasses important to the ecology of the Great Plains?* (They hold soil in place and reduce erosion.) *What caused the Dust Bowl in the 1930s?* (Crops, which replaced grasslands, died in droughts, leading to a dust storm.)

Pages 12–13 *What evidence supports the author's perspective that crops crossbred with prairie grasses are better for the natural ecosystems of the Great Plains?* (They don't need a lot of fertilizers and pesticides; they regrow when harvested; their deep roots prevent soil erosion.)

Pages 13–17 *Paraphrase the change in people's perspectives about prairie fires.* (At one time, people tried to put out prairie fires. Now, people believe fires are beneficial to the land.) *What question did you have while reading this section?* (Why don't farmers like prairie dogs?) *What answer did you determine?* (Livestock can trip in their burrows and become injured.) *What is the author's perspective about restoring the ecology of the Great Plains?* (It is complicated, because all the ecosystems are closely linked. More research needs to be conducted.)

Respond to Reading Revisit the Essential Question and ask students to complete the Text Evidence questions on page 18.

Analytical Writing **Write About Reading** Check that students have correctly identified the author's perspective and identified details that support it.

Fluency: Accuracy and Rate

Model Model reading page 9 with reasonable accuracy and appropriate rate. Then reread the page aloud and have students read along with you.

Apply Have students practice reading the passage with partners.

Paired Read: "Save the Great Plains Wolves"

Make Connections: Write About It

Before reading, ask students to note that the genre of this text is argumentative text. Then discuss the Essential Question. After reading, ask students to make connections between the perspectives conveyed in *The Great Plains* and "Save the Great Plains Wolves."

Leveled Reader

Build Knowledge

Talk About the Text Have partners discuss how natural events and human activities affect the environment.

Write About the Text Have students add their ideas to the Build Knowledge pages of their reader's notebooks.

FOCUS ON SCIENCE

Students can extend their knowledge of life science by completing the activity on page 24.

LITERATURE CIRCLES

Ask students to conduct a literature circle using the Thinkmark questions to guide the discussion. You may wish to have a whole-class discussion, using information from both selections in the Leveled Reader, about how natural events and human activities affect the environment.

GIFTED AND TALENTED

Synthesize Have students conduct research, using both print and Internet sources, to identify other examples of species that conservationists seek to protect or increase in the Great Plains. Have partners choose a species, explain why it is endangered or why its population needs to be restored, and describe what strategies scientists think can help the species survive. Have students present their research in the format of a brochure, including both text and images as support.

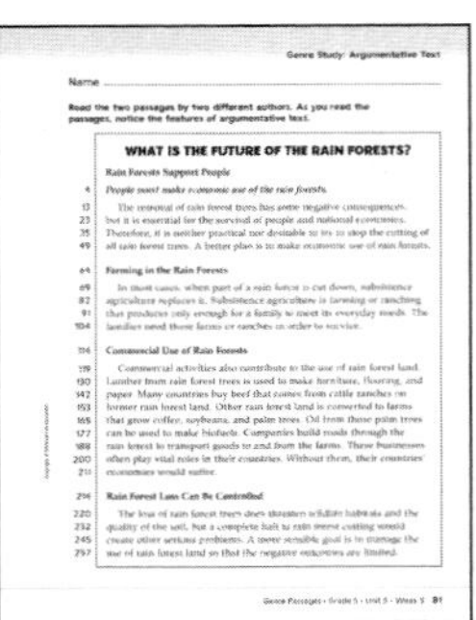

"What Is the Future of the Rain Forests?"
Lexile 970L

OBJECTIVES

Explain how an author uses reasons and evidence to support particular points in a text, identifying which reasons and evidence support which point(s).

Integrate information from several texts on the same topic in order to write or speak about the subject knowledgeably.

Determine or clarify the meaning of unknown and multiple-meaning words and phrases based on Grade 5 reading and content, choosing flexibly from a range of strategies.

Use common, grade-appropriate Greek and Latin affixes and roots as clues to the meaning of a word (e.g., *photograph, photosynthesis*).

ELA ACADEMIC LANGUAGE

- *perspective, evidence, root, heading*
- Cognate: *evidencia*

Beyond Level

Genre Passage: "What Is the Future of the Rain Forests?"

Build Background

- Read aloud the Essential Question: *How do natural events and human activities affect the environment?* Have students consider texts they've read in this text set and compare two environmental effects brought about by nature or by human activity. Focus discussion with these sentence starters:

  I read that humans/nature . . .

  This affected the environment because . . .

- Tell students that the online **Differentiated Genre Passage** "What Is the Future of Rain Forests?" is about ecosystems that receive heavy rainfall and are home to a large variety of plant and animal species. Review the meanings of *ecosystem* and *biofuels* with students.

Review Genre: Argumentative Text

Reiterate that argumentative texts include an author's perspective about an issue. Authors support their perspectives with reasons, factual evidence, examples, and details. Headings, charts, and other text features organize and present information.

Close Reading

Note Taking As students read the passage the first time, ask them to annotate the text. Have them note central ideas, relevant details, unfamiliar words, and questions they have. Then read again and use the following questions.

Read

Genre: Argumentative Text *Why is "What Is the Future of Rain Forests?" an argumentative text?* (Each author clearly states a claim and supports it with reasons, factual evidence, and details. Headings support reasons.)

Author's Perspective Read the first two paragraphs. *State the author's perspective and one piece of evidence that supports it.* (The author thinks that people must make economic use of the rain forests. A reason to support this is that cutting down rain forests allows for farms or ranches that families need.)

Root Words Locate the word *transport* in paragraph 3 on page B1. *This word contains the Latin root* trans, *which means "across" and the Latin root* port, *which means "carry." How does this help you understand the meaning of* transport? (It tells me that when you transport something, you carry it from one place to another.)

Author's Perspective Read paragraph 1 on page B2. *What opposing perspective does the author acknowledge?* (that cutting down rain forests may benefit some economies) *Why do you think the author mentions this perspective?* (to present evidence to support his or her own claim)

Text Features: Charts and Headings Look at the heading "Earth's Water Cycle and Rain Forests" on page B2. *What does it tell the reader about this section?* (This section will be about the water cycle and the role rain forests play.)

COLLABORATE **Summarize** Have pairs summarize each author's perspective and supporting reasons and choose the one they found more convincing.

Reread

Use the questions on page B3 to guide students' rereading of the passage.

Author's Craft Reread the section "Commercial Use of Rain Forests" on page B1. *How does the author help you understand the role of commercial activities in the use of rain forest land?* (The author gives many examples about the different commercial uses of rain forest land and explains that these businesses play a vital role in the economy.)

Author's Craft Reread the headings. *Do you think they are helpful to the reader?* (They are helpful because they introduce the topics that support each author's claim.)

Author's Craft *How does the organization of "The World Needs Rain Forests" help you understand the author's perspective?* (The author explains why the rain forest must be saved and then presents an opposing view but argues against it.)

Integrate

COLLABORATE **Make Connections** Have students think about the Essential Question and how it relates to "What Is the Future of the Rain Forests?" and another text they read. Tell pairs to work with a partner to cite text evidence and respond to this question: *How has human activity affected nature?*

Compare Texts Have partners draw a T-chart with the titles of the texts they chose to compare what they learned in each text about how humans affect nature.

Build Knowledge

Talk About the Text Have partners discuss how natural events and human activities affect the environment.

Write About the Text Have students add their ideas to the Build Knowledge pages of their reader's notebooks.

Differentiate and Collaborate

COLLABORATE **Be Inspired** Have students think about "What Is the Future of the Rain Forests?" and other selections they have read. Ask: *What do the texts inspire you to do?* Use the following activities or have pairs of students think of ways to respond to the texts.

Hold a Debate Choose an issue discussed in this text set and organize a debate with classmates. Form two groups and have each group prepare an argument in support of one side of the issue. Ask a teacher or other classmates to moderate your debate and decide which argument is more convincing.

Write an Editorial What can you and your community do to help the environment? Write an editorial for your school or local newspaper explaining your ideas. Share your editorial.

Readers to Writers

Supporting Evidence Remind students that authors use evidence, such as facts, details, and examples, to support their perspectives. Ask students to reread the fourth paragraph on page B2. Ask: *What evidence does the author use to support his or her perspective? How does this evidence make the author's perspective more convincing?*

GIFTED AND TALENTED

Independent Study Have students synthesize their notes and the selections they read to create a plan for making people more aware of one of the issues they've read about. Their plan should include a specific message they want to convey, as well as ideas for sharing that message with others. Have partners review each other's plans and provide feedback as needed.

Beyond Level

Vocabulary/Comprehension

REVIEW DOMAIN-SPECIFIC WORDS

OBJECTIVES

Acquire and use accurately grade-appropriate general academic and domain-specific words and phrases, including those that signal contrast, addition, and other logical relationships.

Model Use the **Visual Vocabulary Cards** to review the meanings of the words *agricultural* and *thrive*. Use each word in a context sentence.

Write the words *endangers* and *biodiversity* on the board and read them aloud. Discuss the meanings with students. Then help students write sentences using these words.

Apply Have students work in pairs to review the meanings of the words *biofuels, converted,* and *vital*. Then have partners write sentences using the words.

ROOT WORDS

OBJECTIVES

Determine or clarify the meaning of unknown and multiple-meaning words and phrases based on Grade 5 reading and content, choosing flexibly from a range of strategies.

Use common, grade-appropriate Greek and Latin affixes and roots as clues to the meaning of a word (e.g., *photograph, photosynthesis*).

Model Read aloud the second paragraph of "What Is the Future of the Rain Forests?" in the Beyond Level online **Differentiated Genre Passage** page B1.

Think Aloud I am uncertain about the meaning of *agriculture*. I see two Latin roots—*agri*, which means "field," and *cultura*, which means "cultivation." Based on this and context clues, I think that *agriculture* means "the science of cultivating the soil."

With students, read the first paragraph on page B1. Help them figure out the meaning of *survival* by using the Latin root *vivere*, which means "live."

Apply Have pairs use word roots and context clues to determine the meanings of *Commercial* and *transport* (page B1, paragraph 3), *reside* (page B2, paragraph 2), *absorbing* (page B2, paragraph 4), and *perspective* (page B2, paragraph 5).

Independent Study Challenge students to identify other words with the root *vivere* or *sedere*. Have them list as many words as they can find and then choose three to use in sentences that contain context clues. Have partners trade papers and determine the meanings of the words. Have students add the words and the definitions to their reader's notebooks.

REVIEW AUTHOR'S PERSPECTIVE

OBJECTIVES

Analyze multiple accounts of the same event or topic, noting important similarities and differences in the point of view they represent.

Explain an author's perspective, or point of view, toward a topic in an informational text.

Explain how an author uses reasons and evidence to support particular points in a text, identifying which reasons and evidence support which point(s).

Model Review that authors of argumentative texts have a certain perspective, or attitude, on a topic. Examining facts, opinions, details, and word choices in a text can help readers determine an author's perspective.

Display "What Is the Future of the Rain Forests?" in the Beyond Level online **Differentiated Genre Passage** page B1. Have students read the first section of "Rain Forests Support People." Ask open-ended discussion questions, such as *What does the author think about rain forests? Which words or phrases give you clues?* Students should support their responses with text evidence.

Apply Have students read "The World Needs Rain Forests" on page B2 and identify important facts, opinions, details, and word choices as they independently fill in a copy of online Author's Perspective **Graphic Organizer 8.** Have partners discuss how the author's perspective in "The World Needs Rain Forests" differs from that in "Rain Forests Support People" and which they found most convincing.

SELF-SELECTED READING

OBJECTIVES

Determine an author's point of view or purpose in a text and explain how it is conveyed in the text.

Explain how an author uses reasons and evidence to support particular points in a text, identifying which reasons and evidence support which point(s).

Ask and answer questions to increase understanding.

Read Independently

Have students choose a nonfiction book or article for independent reading. Students can read a **Classroom Library** book or check the online **Leveled Reader Library** or **Unit Bibliography** for selections. Guide students to apply what they learned in this text set by identifying the central idea and relevant details, thinking about the author's perspective, and paying attention to any diagrams, charts, headings, or other text features.

Students can choose activities from Reading **Center Activity Cards** to help them apply skills to the text as they read. After they finish, they can choose a Book Talk activity to talk about the texts they read.

Independent Study Challenge students to discuss how their books relate to the key concept of scientific viewpoints. Then ask students to discuss the different ways that natural events and human activities affect the environment.

Notes

Extended Writing 1

Research Report

Writing Prompt: Write a research report about one scientific advancement of the twenty-first century and why it is important.

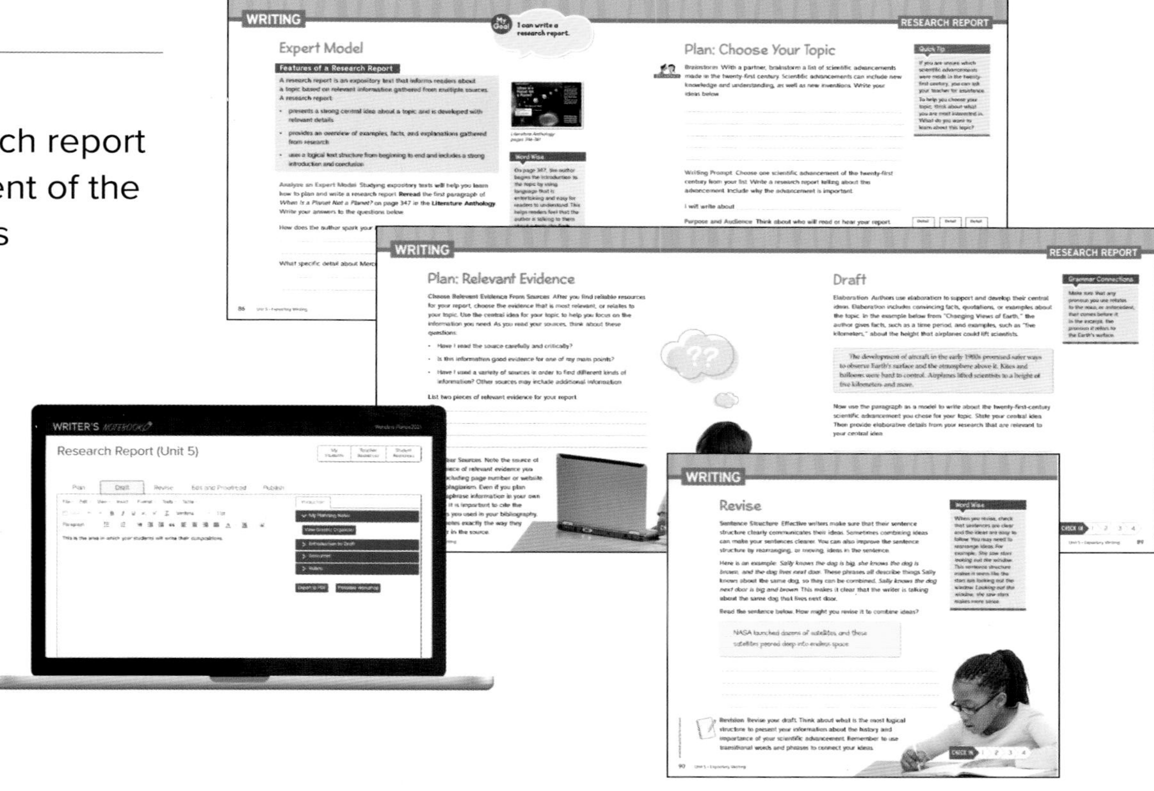

Extended Writing 2

Personal Narrative

Writing Prompt: Write a personal narrative about an event in your life that had a positive impact on the environment.

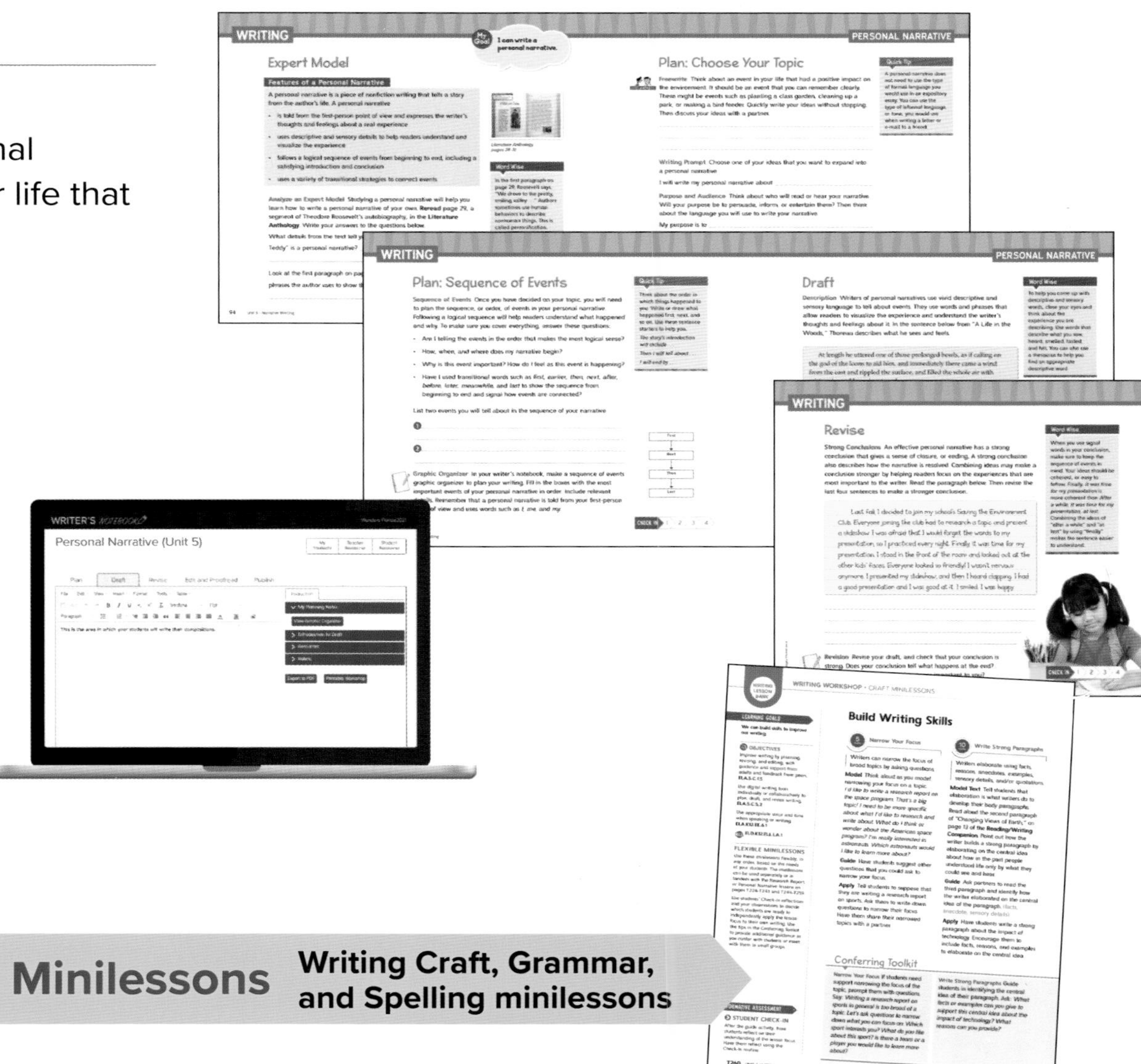

Flexible Minilessons Writing Craft, Grammar, and Spelling minilessons

Extended Writing

Research Report

Extended Writing Goals

- I can write a research report.

Start off each Extended Writing Project with a Writing Process minilesson or choose a Craft minilesson from the Writing Craft Lesson Bank. As you confer with students, the rest of your students write independently or collaboratively or confer with peers.

Writing Process Minilessons

During Writing Process minilessons, students first analyze an expert model, and then answer a writing prompt, going through each step of the writing process to develop a research report.

- Expert Model
- Plan: Choose Your Topic
- Plan: Relevant Evidence
- Draft: Elaboration
- Revise: Sentence Structure
- Peer Conferencing
- Edit and Proofread
- Publish, Present, and Evaluate

Independent and Collaborative Writing

- Provide time during writing for students to work collaboratively with partners and independently on their own writing.
- Use this time for teacher and peer conferencing.

Flexible Minilessons

Choose from the following minilessons to focus on areas where your students need support.

Writing Craft Lesson Bank

Narrow Your Focus T260
Write Strong Paragraphs T260
Use Formal or Informal Language? T261
Revise for Pronoun-Antecedent Agreement T261
Write a Strong Conclusion T261
Evaluate Sources T262
Avoid Plagiarism T262
Write an Engaging Introduction T263
Organize Information Chronologically T263
Use Domain-Specific Vocabulary T263

Grammar Lesson Bank

Clauses T266
Appositives T267
Complex Sentences T268
Commas with Clauses T269
Adjectives T270
Capitalization and Punctuation T271
Adjectives That Compare T272
Using *More* and *Most* T273

Spelling Lesson Bank

Suffixes T276–T277
Homophones T278–T279
Differentiated Spelling Lists T276, T278
Prefixes T280–T281
Suffixes *-less* and *-ness* T282–T283
Differentiated Spelling Lists T280, T282

Suggested Pacing

Students can develop their writing over four weeks, taking time to analyze an expert model and then work through the writing process to write their own research reports. Adjust the pacing to address your students' needs.

Weeks 1–2 BEGIN RESEARCH REPORTS

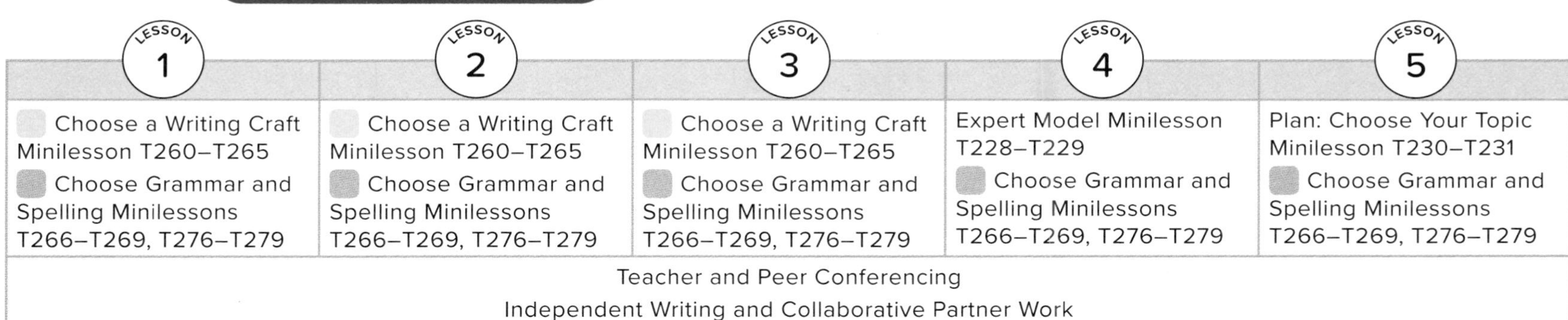

Lesson 1	Lesson 2	Lesson 3	Lesson 4	Lesson 5
Choose a Writing Craft Minilesson T260–T265 Choose Grammar and Spelling Minilessons T266–T269, T276–T279	Choose a Writing Craft Minilesson T260–T265 Choose Grammar and Spelling Minilessons T266–T269, T276–T279	Choose a Writing Craft Minilesson T260–T265 Choose Grammar and Spelling Minilessons T266–T269, T276–T279	Expert Model Minilesson T228–T229 Choose Grammar and Spelling Minilessons T266–T269, T276–T279	Plan: Choose Your Topic Minilesson T230–T231 Choose Grammar and Spelling Minilessons T266–T269, T276–T279
Teacher and Peer Conferencing Independent Writing and Collaborative Partner Work				

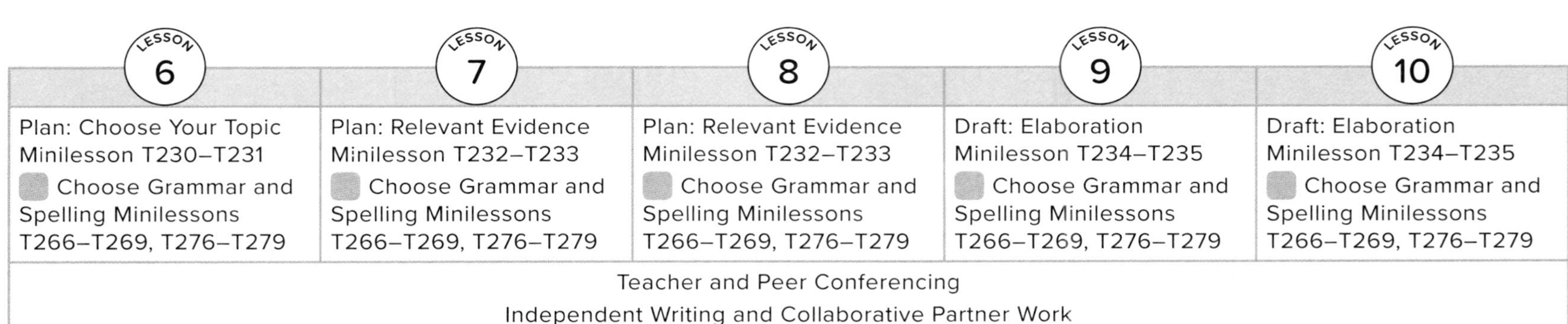

Lesson 6	Lesson 7	Lesson 8	Lesson 9	Lesson 10
Plan: Choose Your Topic Minilesson T230–T231 Choose Grammar and Spelling Minilessons T266–T269, T276–T279	Plan: Relevant Evidence Minilesson T232–T233 Choose Grammar and Spelling Minilessons T266–T269, T276–T279	Plan: Relevant Evidence Minilesson T232–T233 Choose Grammar and Spelling Minilessons T266–T269, T276–T279	Draft: Elaboration Minilesson T234–T235 Choose Grammar and Spelling Minilessons T266–T269, T276–T279	Draft: Elaboration Minilesson T234–T235 Choose Grammar and Spelling Minilessons T266–T269, T276–T279
Teacher and Peer Conferencing Independent Writing and Collaborative Partner Work				

Weeks 3–4 DEVELOP RESEARCH REPORTS

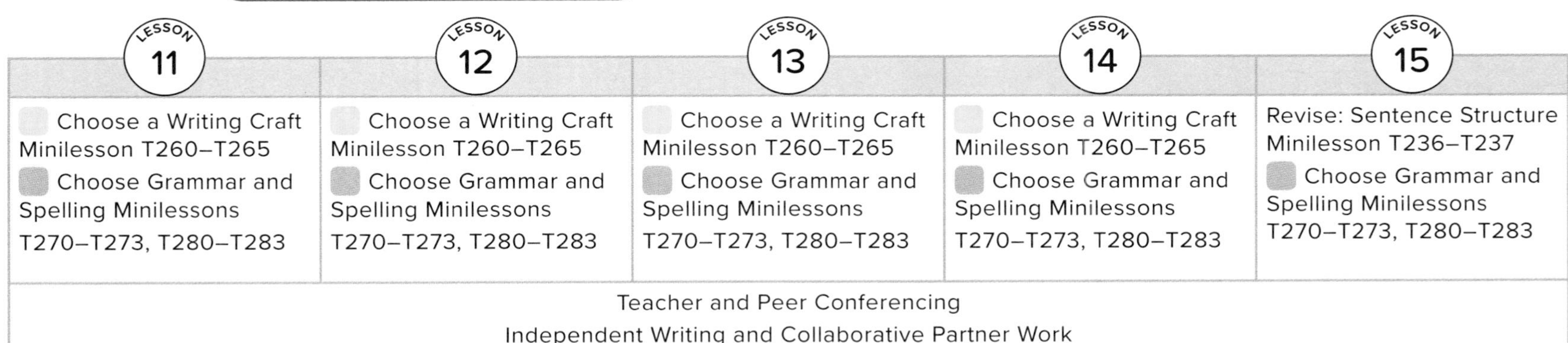

Lesson 11	Lesson 12	Lesson 13	Lesson 14	Lesson 15
Choose a Writing Craft Minilesson T260–T265 Choose Grammar and Spelling Minilessons T270–T273, T280–T283	Choose a Writing Craft Minilesson T260–T265 Choose Grammar and Spelling Minilessons T270–T273, T280–T283	Choose a Writing Craft Minilesson T260–T265 Choose Grammar and Spelling Minilessons T270–T273, T280–T283	Choose a Writing Craft Minilesson T260–T265 Choose Grammar and Spelling Minilessons T270–T273, T280–T283	Revise: Sentence Structure Minilesson T236–T237 Choose Grammar and Spelling Minilessons T270–T273, T280–T283
Teacher and Peer Conferencing Independent Writing and Collaborative Partner Work				

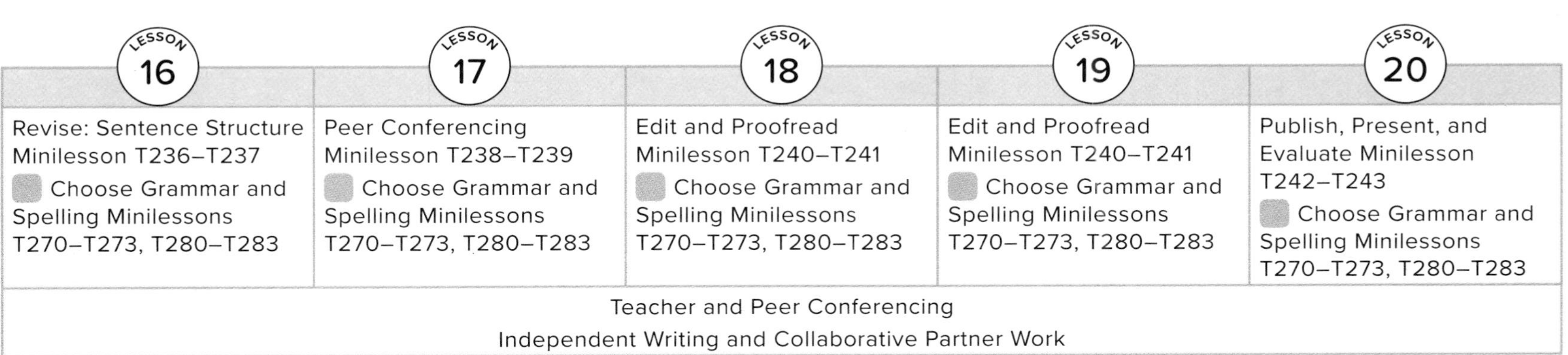

Lesson 16	Lesson 17	Lesson 18	Lesson 19	Lesson 20
Revise: Sentence Structure Minilesson T236–T237 Choose Grammar and Spelling Minilessons T270–T273, T280–T283	Peer Conferencing Minilesson T238–T239 Choose Grammar and Spelling Minilessons T270–T273, T280–T283	Edit and Proofread Minilesson T240–T241 Choose Grammar and Spelling Minilessons T270–T273, T280–T283	Edit and Proofread Minilesson T240–T241 Choose Grammar and Spelling Minilessons T270–T273, T280–T283	Publish, Present, and Evaluate Minilesson T242–T243 Choose Grammar and Spelling Minilessons T270–T273, T280–T283
Teacher and Peer Conferencing Independent Writing and Collaborative Partner Work				

Extended Writing

Personal Narrative

Extended Writing Goals

- I can write a personal narrative.

Start off each Extended Writing Project with a Writing Process minilesson or choose a Craft minilesson from the Writing Craft Lesson Bank. As you confer with students, the rest of your students write independently or collaboratively or confer with peers.

Writing Process Minilessons

During Writing Process minilessons, students first analyze an expert model and then answer a writing prompt, going through each step of the writing process to develop a personal narrative.

- Expert Model
- Plan: Choose Your Topic
- Plan: Sequence
- Draft: Description
- Revise: Strong Conclusions
- Peer Conferences
- Edit and Proofread
- Publish, Present, and Evaluate

Independent and Collaborative Writing

- Provide time during writing for students to work collaboratively with partners and independently on their own writing.
- Use this time for teacher and peer conferencing.

Flexible Minilessons

Choose from the following minilessons to focus on areas where your students need support.

Writing Craft Lesson Bank

Narrow Your Focus T260
Write Strong Paragraphs T260
Use Formal or Informal Language T261
Revise for Pronoun Agreement T261
Write a Strong Conclusion T261
Express Thoughts and Feelings T264
Establish a Point of View T264
Write Strong Hooks T265
Include Dialogue T265
Use Time-Order Words and Phrases T265

Grammar Lesson Bank

Comparing with *Good* and *Bad* T274
Irregular Comparative Forms T275

Spelling Lesson Bank

Suffix *-ion* T284–T285
Differentiated Spelling Lists T284

Suggested Pacing

Students can develop their writing over two weeks, taking time to analyze an expert model and then work through the writing process to write their own personal narratives. Adjust the pacing to address your students' needs.

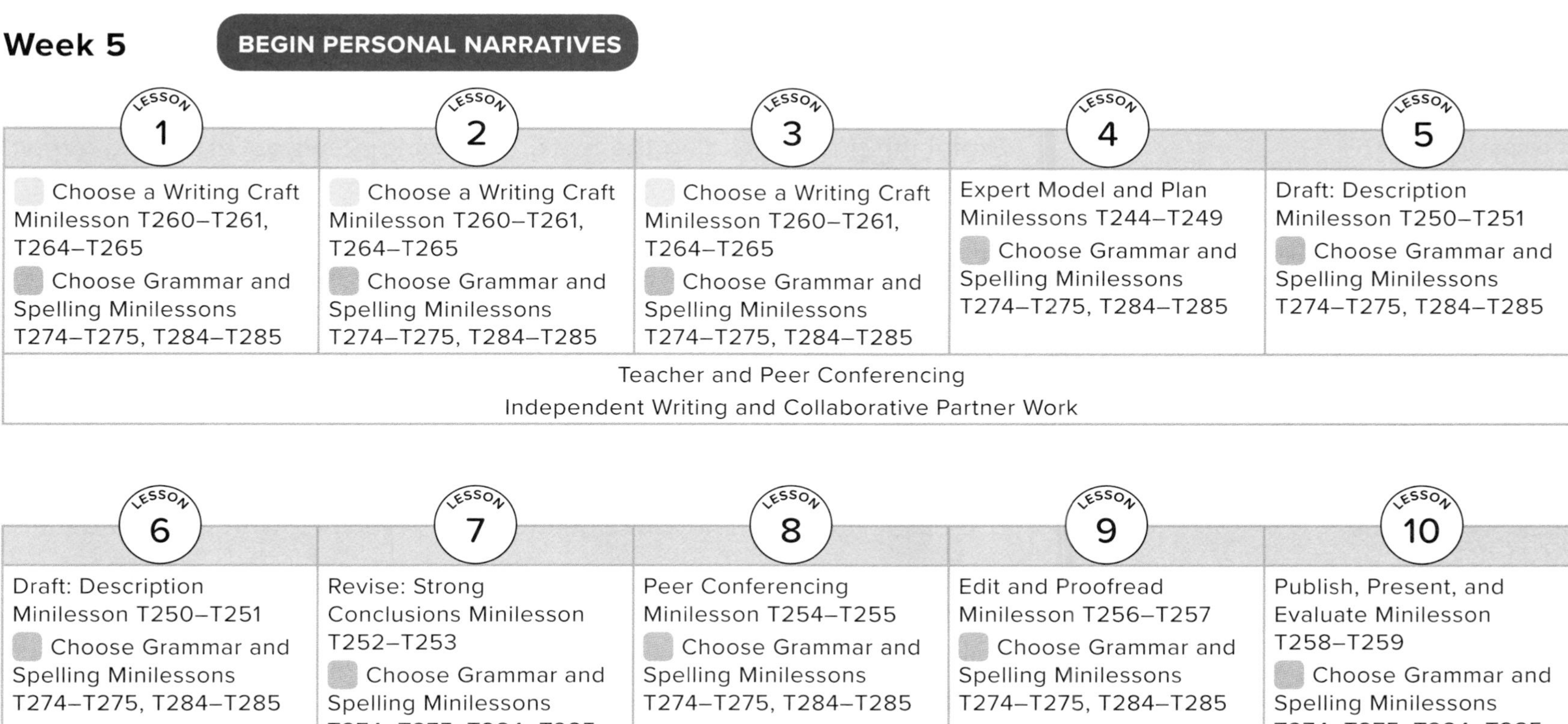

Week 5 — BEGIN PERSONAL NARRATIVES

LESSON 1	LESSON 2	LESSON 3	LESSON 4	LESSON 5
Choose a Writing Craft Minilesson T260–T261, T264–T265 Choose Grammar and Spelling Minilessons T274–T275, T284–T285	Choose a Writing Craft Minilesson T260–T261, T264–T265 Choose Grammar and Spelling Minilessons T274–T275, T284–T285	Choose a Writing Craft Minilesson T260–T261, T264–T265 Choose Grammar and Spelling Minilessons T274–T275, T284–T285	Expert Model and Plan Minilessons T244–T249 Choose Grammar and Spelling Minilessons T274–T275, T284–T285	Draft: Description Minilesson T250–T251 Choose Grammar and Spelling Minilessons T274–T275, T284–T285
Teacher and Peer Conferencing Independent Writing and Collaborative Partner Work				

LESSON 6	LESSON 7	LESSON 8	LESSON 9	LESSON 10
Draft: Description Minilesson T250–T251 Choose Grammar and Spelling Minilessons T274–T275, T284–T285	Revise: Strong Conclusions Minilesson T252–T253 Choose Grammar and Spelling Minilessons T274–T275, T284–T285	Peer Conferencing Minilesson T254–T255 Choose Grammar and Spelling Minilessons T274–T275, T284–T285	Edit and Proofread Minilesson T256–T257 Choose Grammar and Spelling Minilessons T274–T275, T284–T285	Publish, Present, and Evaluate Minilesson T258–T259 Choose Grammar and Spelling Minilessons T274–T275, T284–T285
Teacher and Peer Conferencing Independent Writing and Collaborative Partner Work				

Week 6 — DEVELOP PERSONAL NARRATIVES

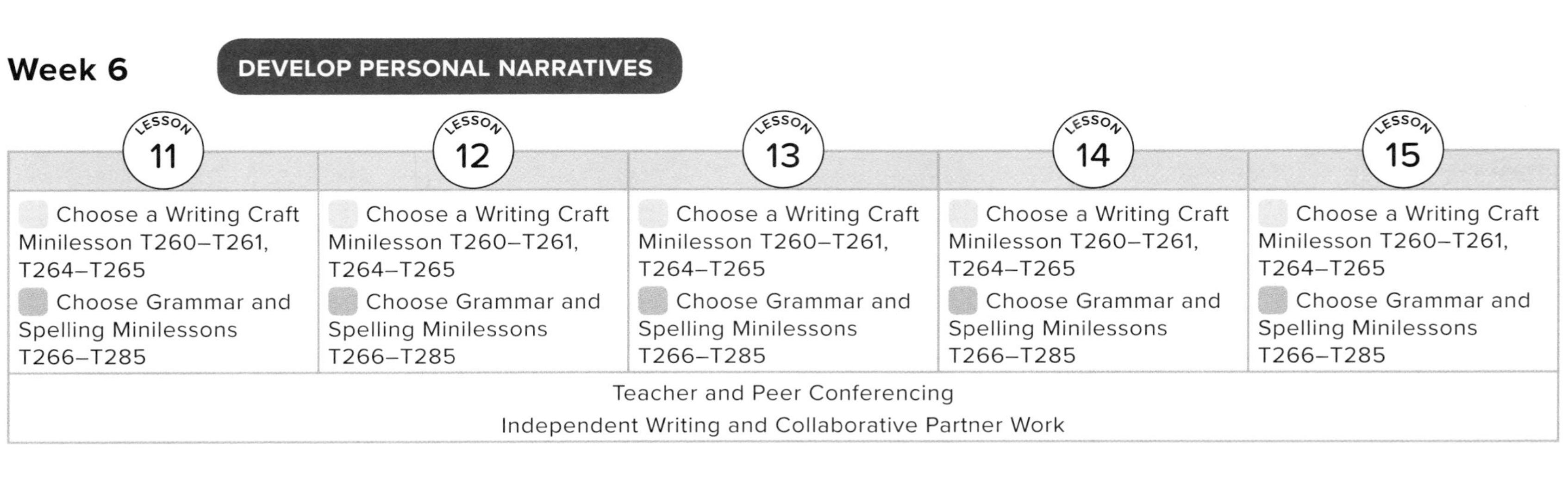

LESSON 11	LESSON 12	LESSON 13	LESSON 14	LESSON 15
Choose a Writing Craft Minilesson T260–T261, T264–T265 Choose Grammar and Spelling Minilessons T266–T285	Choose a Writing Craft Minilesson T260–T261, T264–T265 Choose Grammar and Spelling Minilessons T266–T285	Choose a Writing Craft Minilesson T260–T261, T264–T265 Choose Grammar and Spelling Minilessons T266–T285	Choose a Writing Craft Minilesson T260–T261, T264–T265 Choose Grammar and Spelling Minilessons T266–T285	Choose a Writing Craft Minilesson T260–T261, T264–T265 Choose Grammar and Spelling Minilessons T266–T285
Teacher and Peer Conferencing Independent Writing and Collaborative Partner Work				

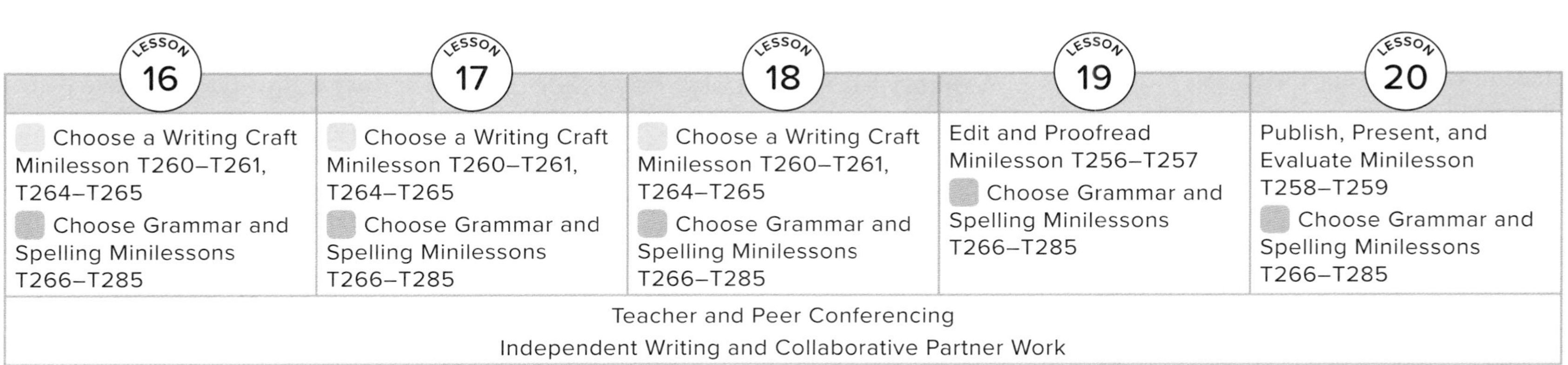

LESSON 16	LESSON 17	LESSON 18	LESSON 19	LESSON 20
Choose a Writing Craft Minilesson T260–T261, T264–T265 Choose Grammar and Spelling Minilessons T266–T285	Choose a Writing Craft Minilesson T260–T261, T264–T265 Choose Grammar and Spelling Minilessons T266–T285	Choose a Writing Craft Minilesson T260–T261, T264–T265 Choose Grammar and Spelling Minilessons T266–T285	Edit and Proofread Minilesson T256–T257 Choose Grammar and Spelling Minilessons T266–T285	Publish, Present, and Evaluate Minilesson T258–T259 Choose Grammar and Spelling Minilessons T266–T285
Teacher and Peer Conferencing Independent Writing and Collaborative Partner Work				

MY GOALS ROUTINE

Read Have students read the first goal on Reading/Writing Companion page 84.

Reflect Have students review the Key to help them assess what they know now. Then have them fill in the bars.

LEARNING GOALS

We can identify features of a research report.

OBJECTIVES

Determine two or more central, or main, ideas of a text and explain how they are supported by relevant, or key, details; summarize the text.

Orient the reader by establishing a situation and introducing a narrator and/or characters; organize an event sequence that unfolds naturally.

Apply grade 5 Reading standards to informational texts.

ELA ACADEMIC LANGUAGE

- *research report, reliable, analyze*
- Cognate: *analizar*

DIFFERENTIATED READING

Approaching Level Plan: Help students use the Internet to identify potential topics and develop research questions. Demonstrate how to cite print and digital sources.

Beyond Level Plan: Have students create an annotated bibliography.

ELL For additional support in writing a research report, see the **ELL Small Group Guide**.

Expert Model

Features of a Research Report

Explain that after reading the texts, "Changing Views of Earth" and *When Is a Planet Not a Planet?*, students will prepare to write a research report. Discuss texts students have read that use research to explain a topic.

Point out that a research report is a type of expository text. It presents facts, details, and other information about a specific topic from a variety of reliable sources. Make sure students understand that they will conduct research to plan and write their own reports.

Anchor Chart Have a volunteer list these features on a Research Report anchor chart.

- It has a strongly maintained central idea developed with relevant details.
- It provides an overview of facts and specific details gathered from a variety of credible sources during research.
- It organizes information in a logical way from beginning to end, including a strong introduction and conclusion.

Analyze an Expert Model

Explain that analyzing a research report will help students learn how to plan and write a research report. Writers often begin research reports with an interesting fact about the topic that will grab readers' interest.

Reread the first paragraph of **Literature Anthology** page 347. Ask: *What is unusual or unexpected about the way the author begins the selection?* (A sentence about a mother making pizza is unexpected in an expository text about planets.)

Build on students' responses. Tell them that a research report should be a piece of writing that engages as well as informs readers. Ask: *How did the author's first sentence affect you? What questions did it make you ask?* (Possible answer: The sentence surprised me. It made me ask, "What does this sentence mean? How does it apply to planets and science?") Have students answer the first question on page 86 of the **Reading/ Writing Companion**.

Then focus on the second paragraph. Ask: *What specific detail about Mercury and Pluto does the author give?* (Mercury is the planet closest to the Sun, and Pluto is the farthest away.) *What question does the final sentence want the reader to ask?* (What has happened recently to the planets?) Have students complete the rest of page 86.

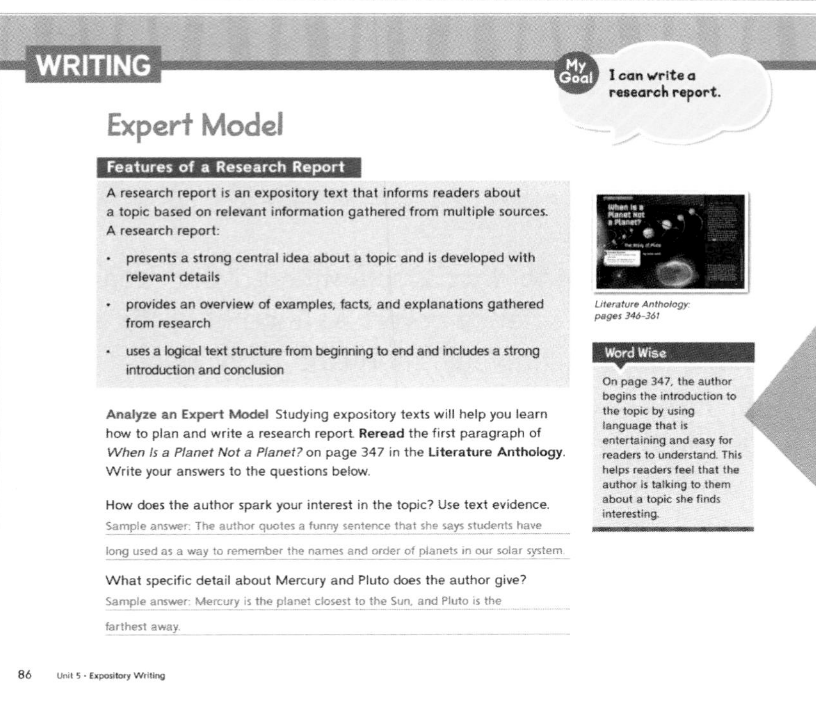
WRITING

My Goal: I can write a research report.

Expert Model

Features of a Research Report

A research report is an expository text that informs readers about a topic based on relevant information gathered from multiple sources. A research report:

- presents a strong central idea about a topic and is developed with relevant details
- provides an overview of examples, facts, and explanations gathered from research
- uses a logical text structure from beginning to end and includes a strong introduction and conclusion

Literature Anthology: pages 346–361

Word Wise

On page 347, the author begins the introduction to the topic by using language that is entertaining and easy for readers to understand. This helps readers feel that the author is talking to them about a topic she finds interesting.

Analyze an Expert Model Studying expository texts will help you learn how to plan and write a research report. **Reread** the first paragraph of *When Is a Planet Not a Planet?* on page 347 in the **Literature Anthology**. Write your answers to the questions below.

How does the author spark your interest in the topic? Use text evidence.

Sample answer: The author quotes a funny sentence that she says students have long used as a way to remember the names and order of planets in our solar system.

What specific detail about Mercury and Pluto does the author give?

Sample answer: Mercury is the planet closest to the Sun, and Pluto is the farthest away.

86 Unit 5 • Expository Writing

Reading/Writing Companion, p. 86

Word Wise

Explain how authors write introductions that not only engage the reader, but also clearly communicate information in a direct way. This keeps the reader interested. Discuss various ways that authors might "hook" their audience.

English Language Learners

Use the following scaffolds with **Analyze an Expert Model**.

Beginning

Read the first paragraphs on page 347 in the **Literature Anthology** with students. Restate sentences as needed. *What is the sentence about?* The sentence is about a mother serving pizza. *Does this make you want keep reading? Why or why not?* I want to keep/stop reading because the sentence is funny. Read the second paragraph. Restate sentences as needed. *Which planet is closet to the Sun?* (Mercury) *Which planet is farthest from the Sun?* (Pluto)

Intermediate

Have partners read the first paragraph on page 347 in the **Literature Anthology**. *Does this sentence make you want to read more? Why?* Elicit them to explain their answers. Then have them read the second paragraph on page 347. *What does it say about Mercury and Pluto?* Mercury is the planet closest to the Sun. Pluto is the planet furthest from the Sun.

Advance/Advanced High

Have partners reread the first two paragraphs on page 347 of the **Literature Anthology**. Have students state the topic and then work with a partner to talk about how the author introduces it. *How does the writer engage the reader?* Have students restate what they learned about Mercury and Pluto with others.

ELL NEWCOMERS

To help students develop their writing, display the **Newcomer Cards** and **Newcomer Online Visuals**, and ask questions to help them discuss the images. Provide sentence starters. For example: What do you see? I see a/an ___. What are they doing? They are ___. Have students point to the image as they ask and answer. Then have them write the sentences in their notebooks. Throughout the extended writing project, help students develop their writing by adding to and revising their sentences.

FORMATIVE ASSESSMENT

STUDENT CHECK-IN

Have partners share one feature of a research report. Then have them reflect using the Check-In routine.

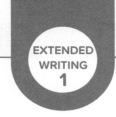

LEARNING GOALS

We can choose a topic to write a research report.

OBJECTIVES

With guidance and support from peers and adults, develop and strengthen writing as needed by planning.

With some guidance and support from adults, use technology, including the Internet, to produce and publish writing as well as to interact and collaborate with others; demonstrate sufficient command of keyboarding skills to type a minimum of two pages in a single sitting.

Write routinely over extended time frames and shorter time frames for a range of discipline-specific tasks, purposes, and audiences.

ELA ACADEMIC LANGUAGE

- *purpose, audience, inform*
- Cognates: *audiencia, informar*

DIGITAL TOOLS

 Model Graphic Organizer

Plan: Choose Your Topic

Brainstorm

Have partners or small groups meet to discuss scientific advances made in the 21st century. Remind them that science covers a range of areas, such as the environment, computers and technology, medicine, and space exploration. Encourage students to make connections to their own lives by focusing on scientific developments that interest them or affect them personally. Have them write their ideas on **Reading/Writing Companion** page 87.

Writing Prompt

Each student should choose one of the scientific advancements they identified and write a research report that focuses on how scientists developed this advancement. Have students record on page 87 the scientific advancement they selected.

Purpose and Audience

Tell students that thinking about their purpose and audience will help them plan their research and writing. Make sure students understand that their primary purpose for writing a research report is to inform—although they will also want to engage their readers as the author of *When Is a Planet Not a Planet?* does. Remind students that thinking about the people who will be reading their research reports—teachers, classmates, or family members—will help them ask useful questions about their topic and focus their research.

Plan

Tell students that before they can write their reports, they must make a research plan. They will need to ask questions about the topic and then research the information so they can explain it well. Say: *An author begins his or her research by asking questions about the topic. What do you already know about your topic? What do you want to know? What do you think your readers will already know or want to know?* Note that research usually leads to more questions.

Have students formulate a central idea from their topic and use online Central Idea and Relevant Details **Graphic Organizer 7** to plan their research and writing. Have them write the central idea at the bottom of the organizer. Tell them they will add relevant details later and may even need to revise their central idea after they research.

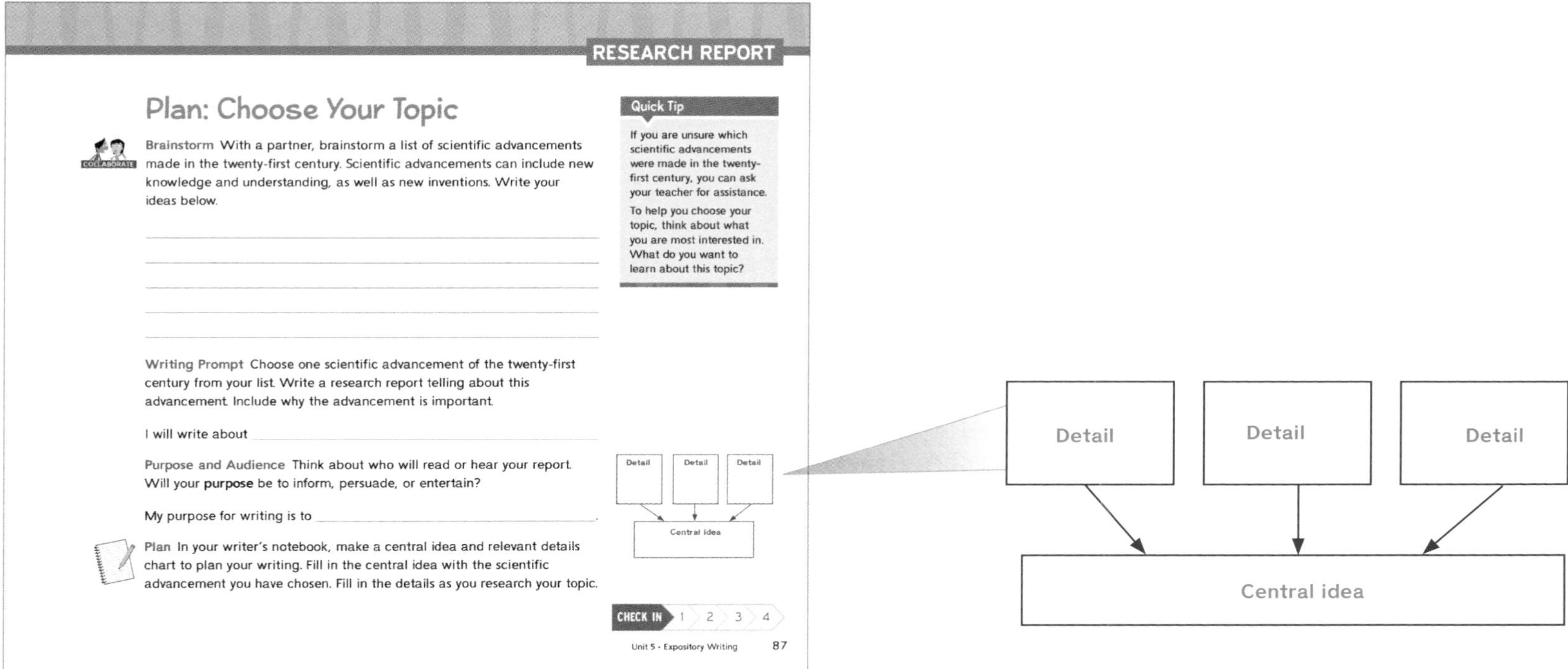

RESEARCH REPORT

Plan: Choose Your Topic

Brainstorm With a partner, brainstorm a list of scientific advancements made in the twenty-first century. Scientific advancements can include new knowledge and understanding, as well as new inventions. Write your ideas below.

Writing Prompt Choose one scientific advancement of the twenty-first century from your list. Write a research report telling about this advancement. Include why the advancement is important.

I will write about ________

Purpose and Audience Think about who will read or hear your report. Will your **purpose** be to inform, persuade, or entertain?

My purpose for writing is to ________.

Plan In your writer's notebook, make a central idea and relevant details chart to plan your writing. Fill in the central idea with the scientific advancement you have chosen. Fill in the details as you research your topic.

Quick Tip

If you are unsure which scientific advancements were made in the twenty-first century, you can ask your teacher for assistance.

To help you choose your topic, think about what you are most interested in. What do you want to learn about this topic?

CHECK IN 1 2 3 4

Unit 5 • Expository Writing 87

Reading/Writing Companion, p. 87

English Language Learners

Use the following scaffolds with **Brainstorm**, **Purpose and Audience**, and **Plan**. For additional support, see the **ELL Small Group Guide**.

Beginning

Brainstorm Read the Brainstorm prompt with students. Help them brainstorm a list of some 21st century advancements, such as smartphones, tablets, and self-driving cars. *Have any of these advancements affected or helped you?* (yes) Help students to answer the following: *Which advancement do you want to know more about? What would you like to know?* **Purpose and Audience** Review with students that they should use formal language for a research report.

Intermediate

Purpose and Audience Have partners describe their purpose for writing the research report: My purpose for writing is to inform. *Will you use formal or informal language to write your expository text?* (formal) *Talk to your partner about why you will use formal language.* **Plan** Have pairs read the Quick Tip box and use the last question to help them generate and focus their central idea.

Advanced/Advanced High

Purpose and Audience Have students discuss how their research reports will inform their readers and if they will use formal or informal language and why. **Plan** Have partners with similar topics talk about the central idea and details they will put in their charts.

TEACHER CONFERENCES

As students plan, hold teacher conferences with individual students.

Step 1: Talk About Strengths
Point out strengths in the research plan: *The questions you have are specific and will help you narrow your focus.*

Step 2: Focus on Skills
Give feedback on how the student uses the graphic organizer: *Some of the relevant details in your organizer don't support your central idea. Try replacing them with details that do.*

Step 3: Make Concrete Suggestions
Provide specific direction to help students plan. Then have students meet with you to review progress.

FORMATIVE ASSESSMENT

STUDENT CHECK-IN

Have partners share their topic and plan. Ask them to use the Check-In routine to reflect and fill in the bars on Reading/Writing Companion page 87.

LEARNING GOALS

We can use relevant evidence to plan a research report.

OBJECTIVES

With guidance and support from peers and adults, develop and strengthen writing as needed by planning.

With some guidance and support from adults, use technology, including the Internet, to produce and publish writing as well as to interact and collaborate with others; demonstrate sufficient command of keyboarding skills to type a minimum of two pages in a single sitting.

Conduct short research projects that use several sources to build knowledge through investigation of different aspects of a topic.

Draw evidence from literary or informational texts to support analysis, reflection, and research. Apply grade 5 Reading standards to informational texts.

Write routinely over extended time frames and shorter time frames for a range of discipline-specific tasks, purposes, and audiences.

Use underlining, quotation marks, or italics to indicate titles of works.

ELA ACADEMIC LANGUAGE

- *relevant, resource, plagiarism, paraphrase, cite*
- Cognates: *relevante, plagio, parafrasear, citar*

DIGITAL TOOLS

Paraphrase the Idea (Tutorial); Evaluate Sources for Relevance (Tutorial); Search with Keywords (Tutorial)

10 mins

Plan: Relevant Evidence

Choose Relevant Evidence from Sources

Using Reliable Sources Tell students that reliable sources are sources they can count on to be accurate, up-to-date, and written by experts. Say: *Choosing reliable sources helps you make sure your information is correct and current.* Make sure students interact thoughtfully with their sources by asking the questions on page 88 in the **Reading/Writing Companion**. Then share these tips:

- Consult a variety of print and digital sources.
- Focus on encyclopedia, science journals and magazines, as well as websites created by scientific institutions.
- Give priority to websites that end in *.edu* or *.org*.
- Choose sources that are current.
- Check three sources for facts to be sure they are accurate.

Citing Sources Remind students to credit all sources used for research. For books the format is: Author's last name, First name. City of Publication: Publisher, Copyright date. Remind students that when they cite a book in their research report, they should italicize or underline the title. For Web sources: "Name of this page." Name of website. Website's Internet address. Date they visited the site.

Identifying Relevant Evidence Share these questions to help students test if information they find in their sources is relevant:

- Is this information directly related to my topic?
- Does this information help me understand my topic?
- Will this information help me explain my topic to readers?

Say: *As you research, you might find information that's interesting, but not relevant to your topic.* Ask: *Why wouldn't you want to include irrelevant evidence in your research report?* (It won't help me explain the topic. It might confuse readers if it's not related to my topic.)

Have students list two pieces of relevant evidence for their report on page 88. Remind them to add relevant details to their graphic organizer.

Take Notes

Once students have chosen their sources, remind them of the importance of careful note-taking and source citation. Say: *To present another person's ideas or words as your own is called plagiarism. Avoid plagiarism by paraphrasing information in your notes and including the source information.* Have partners practice paraphrasing information from a source and writing its bibliographical citation.

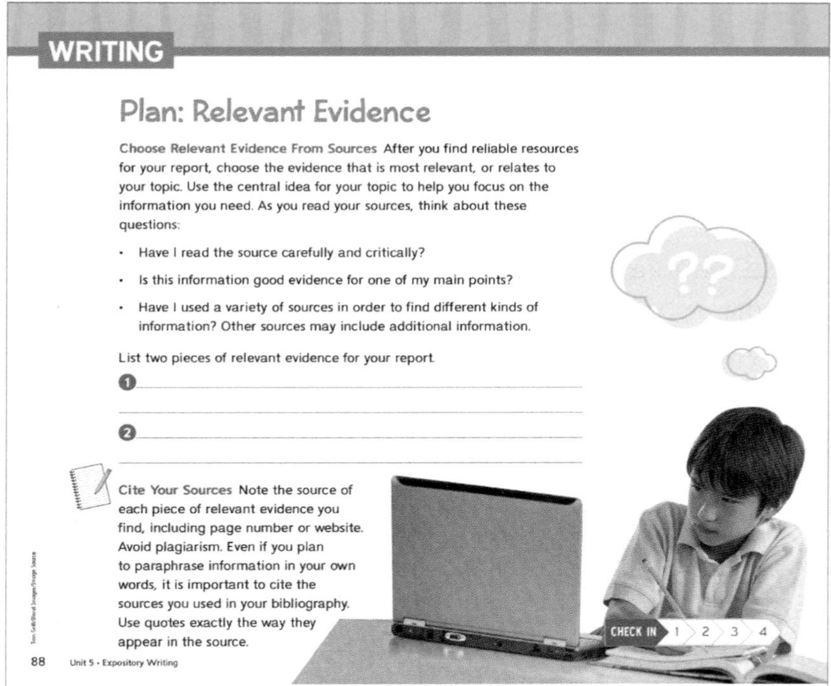

WRITING

Plan: Relevant Evidence

Choose Relevant Evidence From Sources After you find reliable resources for your report, choose the evidence that is most relevant, or relates to your topic. Use the central idea for your topic to help you focus on the information you need. As you read your sources, think about these questions:

- Have I read the source carefully and critically?
- Is this information good evidence for one of my main points?
- Have I used a variety of sources in order to find different kinds of information? Other sources may include additional information.

List two pieces of relevant evidence for your report.

1 ____________________

2 ____________________

Cite Your Sources Note the source of each piece of relevant evidence you find, including page number or website. Avoid plagiarism. Even if you plan to paraphrase information in your own words, it is important to cite the sources you used in your bibliography. Use quotes exactly the way they appear in the source.

CHECK IN 1 2 3 4

88 Unit 5 • Expository Writing

Reading/Writing Companion, p. 88

English Language Learners

Use the following scaffolds with **Choose Relevant Evidence from Sources**. For additional support, see the **ELL Small Group Guide**.

Beginning

Check for understanding of *reliable sources, accurate, up-to-date, information,* and *experts* (cognates: *información, expertos*). *Reliable sources give information we can trust.* Help partners describe where they can find reliable sources: We can find information on the Internet. We can trust scientific journals and magazines. We can also trust scientific websites that end in .edu or .org.

Intermediate

Check for understanding of *reliable sources*. Have pairs work together as they state their topic and generate a list of words that seem relevant to their topic. *Work with your partner to explain why each word is relevant to the topic:* This word is related to my topic ________ because ________.

Advanced/Advanced High

Have partners discuss how to choose reliable sources. Then have partners select two pieces of relevant evidence for their report and explain how it relates to their topic. Encourage students to use language from the paraphrasing exercise in their explanations.

MULTIMODAL LEARNING

Have students print out their reliable resources. Have them use colored pencils or different colored highlighters to take notes or annotate the printed resources, finding information to include in their research reports. Students may color-code their notes to keep their information from sources organized and clear.

FORMATIVE ASSESSMENT

STUDENT CHECK-IN

Have partners share their graphic organizer. Ask them to use the Check-In routine to reflect and fill in the bars on Reading/Writing Companion page 88.

LEARNING GOALS

We can draft a research report.

OBJECTIVES

Determine two or more central, or main, ideas of a text and explain how they are supported by relevant, or key, details; summarize the text.

Develop the topic with facts, definitions, concrete details, quotations, or other information and examples related to the topic.

Draw evidence from literary or informational texts to support analysis, reflection, and research.

Apply grade 5 Reading standards to informational texts.

Write routinely over extended time frames and shorter time frames for a range of discipline-specific tasks, purposes, and audiences.

ELA ACADEMIC LANGUAGE

- *draft, relevant, support, elaboration*
- Cognates: *relevante, elaboración*

DIGITAL TOOLS

Draft Student Model

Outline to Draft

Draft

Elaboration

Discuss how writers use elaboration to support and develop the central idea of a research report.

Have students reread the paragraph from "Changing Views of Earth" on page 89 of the **Reading/Writing Companion**. Ask for volunteers to identify the sentence that states the central idea and the sentences that elaborate on and support on this idea in the paragraph. Students should recognize that the central idea in this paragraph is conveyed in the first sentence: "The development of aircraft in the early 1900s promised safer ways to observe Earth's surface and the atmosphere above it." The other sentences in the paragraph present details that support and elaborate on this central idea.

- Elaborative details include facts, definitions, quotations, or examples. For instance, in the paragraph, the author included facts, such as the time period of the early 1900s, and specific details, such as "five kilometers," about the height that airplanes could lift scientists.
- Facts and specific details clearly elaborate on the central ideas and also make the text more interesting to read.

Have students use the paragraph from "Changing Views of Earth" as a model for their own paragraphs. They should begin by stating a central idea about the scientific advancement of the twenty-first century that they chose as a topic. They should be sure to use elaborative details in their paragraphs to help their readers better understand their central idea.

Write a Draft

Remind students they will be writing about a scientific advancement of the twenty-first century. Have students review the graphic organizer they created in the Plan phase as they write their drafts. Remind students to use elaboration to make the writing more interesting for the reader and to help readers better understand their central idea. Make sure students either write legibly in print or cursive in their writer's notebook or type accurately on-screen. Remind them to indent their paragraphs. Circulate to check their work.

Pair students to identify the elaborative details in each other's drafts and discuss how these details make the paragraph more interesting.

RESEARCH REPORT

Draft

Elaboration Authors use elaboration to support and develop their central ideas. Elaboration includes convincing facts, quotations, or examples about the topic. In the example below from "Changing Views of Earth," the author gives facts, such as a time period, and examples, such as "five kilometers," about the height that airplanes could lift scientists.

> The development of aircraft in the early 1900s promised safer ways to observe Earth's surface and the atmosphere above it. Kites and balloons were hard to control. Airplanes lifted scientists to a height of five kilometers and more.

Now use the paragraph as a model to write about the twenty-first-century scientific advancement you chose for your topic. State your central idea. Then provide elaborative details from your research that are relevant to your central idea.

Grammar Connections

Make sure that any pronoun you use relates to the noun, or antecedent, that comes before it. In the excerpt, the pronoun *it* refers to the Earth's surface.

Write a Draft Use your central idea and details chart to help you write your draft in your writer's notebook. Don't forget to write an introduction that sparks interest in your topic. Remember to indent each paragraph.

CHECK IN 1 2 3 4

Unit 5 • Expository Writing 89

Reading/Writing Companion, p. 89

Grammar Connections

Students can use online **Grammar Handbook** page 463 to review and practice using pronouns and antecedents correctly. Remind them that a pronoun must match the number and gender of its antecedent. Doing so helps readers keep track of the supporting details for the central idea.

English Language Learners

Use the following scaffolds with **Elaboration**. For additional support, see the **ELL Small Group Guide**.

Beginning

Review with students that writers use elaboration (cognate: *detailles*) to help explain the central idea. Read the paragraph on page 89 with students. Help them identify and restate the central idea. Identify examples of elaborative details, such as facts and specific details. Help partners describe them using: One fact is that scientists developed new airplanes in the early 1900s. One detail is the new airplanes took scientists up five kilometers in the air.

Intermediate

Review that writers use elaboration to support the central idea. Discuss examples of elaborative details, such as facts and specific details. Read the paragraph on page 89 with students and have them identify and restate the central idea. Then have pairs describe a fact or detail using: One fact tells about when scientists developed new airplanes. One detail tells about how high the new airplanes could fly.

Advanced/Advanced High

Discuss with students how writers can use facts and specific details to support the central idea using examples. Have partners read the paragraph on page 89 and have them describe how the writer uses facts and specific details.

TEACHER CONFERENCES

As students draft, hold teacher conferences with individual students.

Step 1: Talk About Strengths
Point out strengths in the essay: *The fun facts in the opening of this research report make the reader want to learn more.*

Step 2: Focus on Skills
Give feedback on how the student uses elaboration: *Adding one or two more supporting facts will help support you elaborate on your central idea.*

Step 3: Make Concrete Suggestions
Provide specific direction to help students draft. After writing their draft, have students meet with you to review progress.

FORMATIVE ASSESSMENT

STUDENT CHECK-IN

Have partners share their draft. Ask them to use the Check-In routine to reflect and fill in the bars on Reading/Writing Companion page 89.

LEARNING GOALS

We can revise a research report by focusing on sentence structure.

OBJECTIVES

Develop the topic with facts, definitions, concrete details, quotations, or other information and examples related to the topic.

With guidance and support from peers and adults, develop and strengthen writing as needed by revising and editing.

With some guidance and support from adults, use technology, including the Internet, to produce and publish writing as well as to interact and collaborate with others; demonstrate sufficient command of keyboarding skills to type a minimum of two pages in a single sitting.

Use correlative conjunctions.

ELA ACADEMIC LANGUAGE

- *revise, combine, structure*
- Cognates: *revisar, combinar, estructura*

 **DIFFERENTIATED READING**

Revising their Research Reports may challenge students. Check student progress at this stage during Small Group time.

● **Approaching Level** Review drafts for sentence structure.

● **On Level** Partners can review each other's drafts and identify sentences that can be combined.

● **Beyond Level** Challenge students to use different strategies for combining sentences, such as inserting modifiers or phrases.

● **ELL** For additional support in writing a research report, see the **ELL Small Group Guide**.

Revise

Sentence Structure

Remind students that effective writers make sure that their sentences are clear and communicate their ideas. Model how to combine the ideas in the example sentence from **Reading/Writing Companion** page 90. Write the original sentence on the board, and then ask a volunteer to come to the board to demonstrate how to combine the ideas. As a class, discuss why the new sentence is clearer. (It deletes repeated words and makes the sentence shorter and more direct.) Demonstrate other ways of combining the ideas. (Sample response: The dozens of satellites launched by NASA peered deep into endless space.) Talk about how each revision expresses the idea in a slightly different way. Offer students questions for evaluating sentences within their drafts:

- Do two or more sentences in the same paragraph have the same subject or the same verb?
- Do many of your sentences have the same structure—a subject followed by a verb?

If students answer "yes," have them consider combining sentences by deleting, adding, or rearranging words. Invite them to share examples from their drafts. Remind students that there is no one correct way to express an idea.

Revision

Review the parts of an effective research report—a strongly maintained central idea; a body that contains facts, relevant details, examples, and explanations gathered from research; and a logical progression of ideas from beginning to end. Then allow students time to review their drafts, focusing on sentence structure to ensure clarity and coherence. Remind students to include a strong introduction and conclusion.

Remind students that conjunctions such as *and, but, either/or,* and *yet* make combining sentences easier. Brainstorm other words and phrases that help writers combine, shorten, or rearrange sentences or ideas in sentences and display the words as students revise.

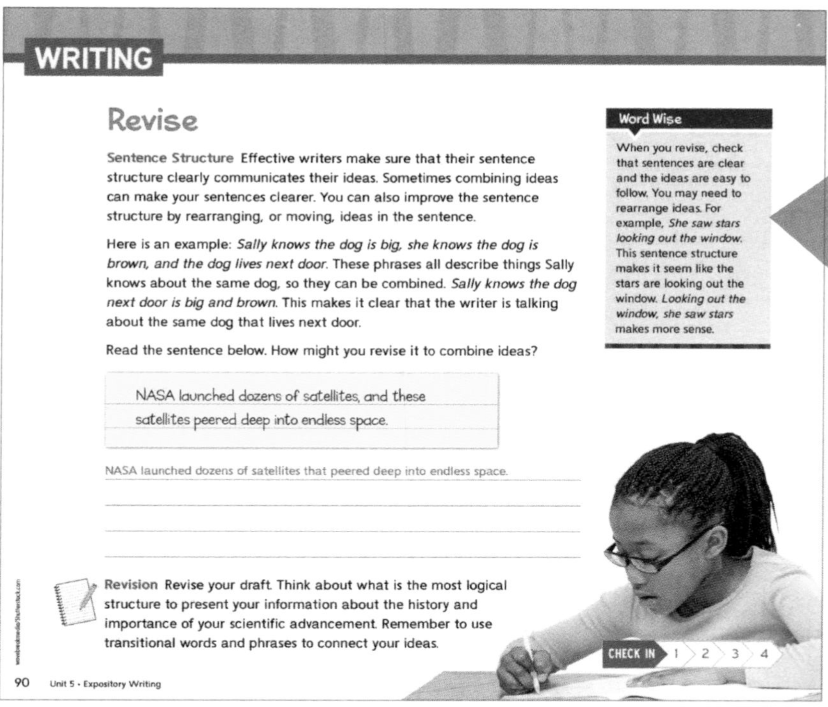
WRITING

Revise

Sentence Structure Effective writers make sure that their sentence structure clearly communicates their ideas. Sometimes combining ideas can make your sentences clearer. You can also improve the sentence structure by rearranging, or moving, ideas in the sentence.

Here is an example: *Sally knows the dog is big, she knows the dog is brown, and the dog lives next door.* These phrases all describe things Sally knows about the same dog, so they can be combined. *Sally knows the dog next door is big and brown.* This makes it clear that the writer is talking about the same dog that lives next door.

Read the sentence below. How might you revise it to combine ideas?

NASA launched dozens of satellites, and these satellites peered deep into endless space.

NASA launched dozens of satellites that peered deep into endless space.

Word Wise

When you revise, check that sentences are clear and the ideas are easy to follow. You may need to rearrange ideas. For example, *She saw stars looking out the window.* This sentence structure makes it seem like the stars are looking out the window. *Looking out the window, she saw stars* makes more sense.

Revision Revise your draft. Think about what is the most logical structure to present your information about the history and importance of your scientific advancement. Remember to use transitional words and phrases to connect your ideas.

CHECK IN 1 2 3 4

90 Unit 5 • Expository Writing

Reading/Writing Companion, p. 90

Word Wise

Remind students that they should make sure their sentences are clear with ideas that are easy to follow. If students find any unclear sentences, they can rearrange ideas so that the sentences make more sense.

English Language Learners

Use the following scaffolds with **Sentence Structure**.

Beginning

Review with students that they can combine sentences with the same subject or verb. Read the example on page 90 and help them identify the same subject in each sentence. Explain that *and* can combine the sentences about the dog. Write on the board: *NASA launched dozens of satellites, and these satellites peered deep into endless space.* Help partners combine ideas and rewrite the sentence using: NASA launched dozens of satellites that peered deep into endless space.

Intermediate

Review with students that they can combine sentences with the same subject or verb. Have partners read the sentence on page 90. Have students identify the same subject in each sentence and combine the sentences about the dog. Elicit them to use *that* to revise the sentence about satellites: NASA launched dozens of satellites that peered deep into endless space.

Advanced/Advanced High

Review with students that they can combine sentences that have the same subject or verb. Discuss the example on page 90 by having them combine the sentences. Help them revise the sentence about NASA satellites using *that*.

DIGITAL TOOLS

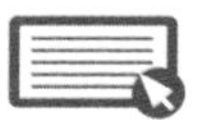 Revised Student Model

 Revise Checklist

FORMATIVE ASSESSMENT

STUDENT CHECK-IN

Have partners share how they revised their sentences to vary sentence structure. Ask them to use the Check-In routine to reflect and fill in the bars.

LEARNING GOALS

We can give and receive feedback on a research report.

OBJECTIVES

With guidance and support from peers and adults, develop and strengthen writing as needed by planning, revising, and editing.

Engage effectively in a range of collaborative discussions with diverse partners, building on others' ideas and expressing their own clearly.

Follow agreed-upon rules for discussions and carry out assigned roles.

Use knowledge of language and its conventions when writing, speaking, reading, or listening.

ELA ACADEMIC LANGUAGE

- *peer, conference, feedback, respond*
- Cognates: *conferencia, responder*

DIGITAL TOOLS

Peer Conferencing (Collaborative Conversations Video); Peer Conference Checklist

Peer Conferencing

Review a Draft

Review with students the routine for peer review of writing, giving examples as needed.

- Step 1: Listen carefully and take notes as your partner reads his or her work aloud.
- Step 2: Respond by identifying one thing you liked.
- Step 3: Ask questions to help your partner reflect on his or her writing. For example: *Why did you include the fact about ______?*
- Step 4: Make comments about ways your partner can strengthen his or her writing. For example: *I think you could provide better support for this idea with an additional fact or specific detail.*

Remind students of the rules for peer conferences. For example, students should be respectful of their partners, make eye contact, listen actively, ask relevant questions, reflect on the writing, and use polite language when offering comments and suggestions.

Model using the sentence starters on **Reading/Writing Companion** page 91. For example, say: *I enjoyed this part of your draft because you introduced your topic in an interesting way.* Discuss the steps of the peer conferencing routine. Ask: *Why should you begin a peer conference by listening carefully and taking notes?* (so you know what the writing is about; so you remember your ideas) *Why is it important to ask questions about your partner's writing?* (to clarify; to gain understanding; to focus on a confusing part of the text so the writer can revise it)

Circulate and observe as partners review and give feedback on each other's drafts. Ensure that partners are following the routine and the agreed-upon rules. Have students respond to partner feedback by writing on page 91 about the suggestion they found to be the most helpful.

Revision

Review the revising checklist on Reading/Writing Companion page 91. Allow students time to implement suggestions. After students have completed their revisions, allow them time to share how their partners' feedback has helped them improve their research reports.

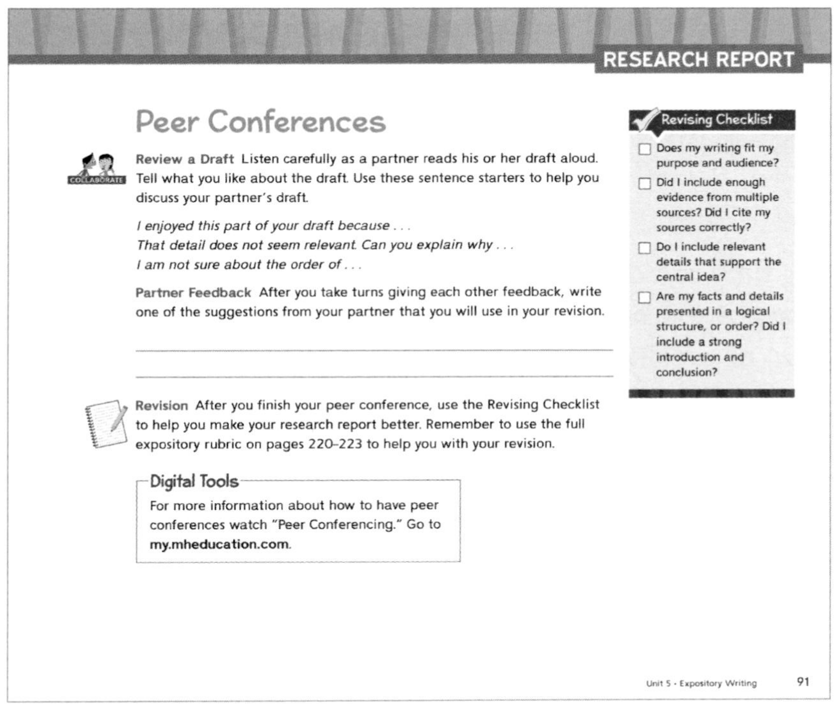

RESEARCH REPORT

Peer Conferences

Review a Draft Listen carefully as a partner reads his or her draft aloud. Tell what you like about the draft. Use these sentence starters to help you discuss your partner's draft.

I enjoyed this part of your draft because . . .
That detail does not seem relevant. Can you explain why . . .
I am not sure about the order of . . .

Partner Feedback After you take turns giving each other feedback, write one of the suggestions from your partner that you will use in your revision.

____

____

Revision After you finish your peer conference, use the Revising Checklist to help you make your research report better. Remember to use the full expository rubric on pages 220-223 to help you with your revision.

Digital Tools
For more information about how to have peer conferences watch "Peer Conferencing." Go to **my.mheducation.com**.

Revising Checklist
- ☐ Does my writing fit my purpose and audience?
- ☐ Did I include enough evidence from multiple sources? Did I cite my sources correctly?
- ☐ Do I include relevant details that support the central idea?
- ☐ Are my facts and details presented in a logical structure, or order? Did I include a strong introduction and conclusion?

Unit 5 · Expository Writing 91

Reading/Writing Companion, p. 91

English Language Learners

Use the following scaffolds with **Review a Draft**. For additional support, see the **ELL Small Group Guide**.

Beginning

Pair students with more proficient speakers for peer conferencing. Provide sentence frames and questions to aid comprehension: *What does _______ mean? What happened first?* Then provide frames to help students comment on the drafts: *Can you explain why _______? I think this ________ should go before/after __________.*

Intermediate

Provide frames to help students ask questions and give feedback on each other's drafts: *Why did you write ____? Is this part related to ________? I think you need to explain why _______. This ________ should go before/after __________.* Have partners talk about how they will use this feedback before they write it on page 91.

Advanced/Advanced High

Have partners read along and take notes as they listen to each other's drafts. Ask them to focus on the order of ideas and accuracy of facts. Have partners discuss their notes and use them to fill in their Partner Feedback on page 91.

TEACHER CONFERENCES

As students revise, hold teacher conferences with individual students.

Step 1: Talk About Strengths
Point out strengths in the research report: *The conclusion reinforces the central idea.*

Step 2: Focus on Skills
Give feedback on whether the student presents the information in a logical order: *Try rearranging your paragraphs to make your report easier to read.*

Step 3: Make Concrete Suggestions
Provide specific direction to help students revise. Underline a sentence or section that needs to be revised. Have students use a specific revision strategy, like rewriting, adding, or deleting.

CLASSROOM CULTURE

We inspire confident writers. To create a classroom where writers flourish, have students consider the connection between reading and writing. Remind partners to review the elements of an effective research report. Ask: *How can I help my partner present a strong and informative research report?*

FORMATIVE ASSESSMENT

STUDENT CHECK-IN

Have partners share their drafts and give feedback. Ask them to reflect using the Check-In routine and rubric on Reading/Writing Companion page 91.

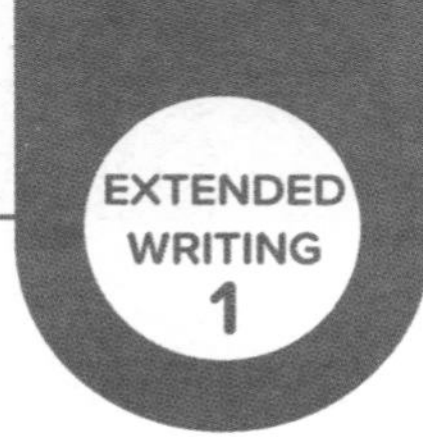

LEARNING GOALS

We can edit and proofread a research report.

OBJECTIVES

Use precise language and domain-specific vocabulary to inform about or explain the topic.

With guidance and support from peers and adults, develop and strengthen writing as needed by editing.

Write routinely over extended time frames and shorter time frames for a range of discipline-specific tasks, purposes, and audiences.

Demonstrate command of the conventions of standard English grammar and usage when writing or speaking.

Demonstrate command of the conventions of standard English capitalization, punctuation, and spelling when writing.

Spell grade-appropriate words correctly, consulting references as needed

ELA ACADEMIC LANGUAGE

- *edit, proofread, fragment, consistently*
- Cognates: *editar, fragmento*

DIGITAL TOOLS

Students may use these tools:

Edited Student Model

Edit Checklist

Edit and Proofread

Explain

Tell students that it's time to edit and proofread their drafts. Say: *Editing and proofreading are not the same thing. When you edit, you improve the flow and organization of your writing, add details, and adjust the length of the piece. When you proofread, you focus on correcting errors in grammar, usage, punctuation, and spelling.* Suggest that students read their sentences aloud to themselves in a soft voice to hear how their writing sounds. If they stumble or hesitate, have them pause to figure out why. For example, they might be missing a verb or a preposition, or they might have used the incorrect form of an irregular verb.

Correct Mistakes

Review the editing checklist on **Reading/Writing Companion** page 92. Ask: *If some of your sentences are fragments, how would that affect the reader?* (It would be hard for the reader to understand my ideas because a sentence fragment is an incomplete sentence that is missing a subject or a verb.) Write the following on the board:

Todays smartphones. Contain more memry, power and data than the Computers used to send Astronauts into outer space in 1960s and 1970s

Proofread and edit as a class. (Today's smartphones contain more memory, power, and data than the computers used to send astronauts into outer space in the 1960s and 1970s.)

Ask students to find two mistakes they found when using the editing checklist on page 92. Ask volunteers to share the two mistakes they corrected. Ask: *How did you figure out that you made these mistakes? How did you know how to correct them?*

Using the Editing Checklist

Have pairs edit and proofread each other's drafts. Begin by having them read their drafts aloud to each other. Afterwards, have partners exchange papers and comment on each other's paper, with suggestions for edits and ideas for correcting grammar, usage, punctuation, and spelling errors. Suggest that students read their partner's paper twice, once to pay attention to the Editing Checklist items and the second time to proofread. Remind students to be constructive and polite as they provide feedback. Finally, have students write a reflection on how collaborating helped their writing.

WRITING

Edit and Proofread

When you **edit** and **proofread** your writing, you look for and correct mistakes in spelling, punctuation, capitalization, and grammar. Reading through a revised draft multiple times can help you make sure you're correcting any errors. Use the checklist below to edit your sentences.

Editing Checklist

- ☐ Do all sentences begin with a capital letter and end with a punctuation mark?
- ☐ Are there any run-on sentences or sentence fragments?
- ☐ Do all sentences have subject-verb agreement?
- ☐ Are clauses, appositives, and quotes punctuated correctly?
- ☐ Are proper nouns and abbreviations, initials, and acronyms capitalized correctly?
- ☐ Are referenced titles italicized or underlined?
- ☐ Are all words spelled correctly?

List two mistakes you found as you proofread your research report.

1. ______________________

2. ______________________

Tech Tip

Spellcheckers are useful tools in word-processing programs, but they may not recognize incorrect words. For example, if you meant to use *we'll* but typed *well* instead, the spellchecker might not catch it. That is why it's important to also do a careful reading.

Grammar Connections

When you proofread your report, make sure that you have capitalized proper nouns, such as names, places, organizations, and events, if they have a specific title or name.

92 Unit 5 • Expository Writing

Reading/Writing Companion, p. 92

Grammar Connections

Students can use online **Grammar Handbook** page 476 to review the rules for capitalizing proper nouns. Remind students that a common noun is a general person, place, thing, or idea, whereas a proper noun names a particular person, place, thing, or idea. For example, *house* is a common noun. The *White House* is a proper noun.

English Language Learners

Use the following scaffolds with **Using the Editing Checklist**. For additional support, see the **ELL Small Group Guide**.

Beginning

Help students understand the first and third items in the **Editing Checklist**. Help partners check that all the sentences begin with a capital letter, end with a punctuation mark and have subject-verb agreement. As needed, review the rules for subject-verb agreement. Help students identify subjects and verbs in each sentence and make any needed corrections.

Intermediate

Review the items on the **Editing Checklist**. Have partners reread the third bullet in the editing checklist and brainstorm examples of correct subject-verb agreement. (Answers will vary.) Have partners check and edit their work for subject-verb agreement by checking to see whether the subject of the sentence is singular or plural to determine the correct verb form.

Advanced/Advanced High

Have partners take turns reading their drafts. Remind them to use the **Editing Checklist** as they review. Have partners check for subject-verb agreement and edit to make sure that the verb form corresponds to the subject in each sentence.

FORMATIVE ASSESSMENT

STUDENT CHECK-IN

Have partners talk about mistakes they corrected as they edited and proofread. Ask them to reflect using the Check-In routine.

LEARNING GOALS

We can publish, present, and evaluate a research report.

OBJECTIVES

With some guidance and support from adults, use technology, including the Internet, to produce and publish writing as well as to interact and collaborate with others; demonstrate sufficient command of keyboarding skills to type a minimum of two pages in a single sitting.

Adapt speech to a variety of contexts and tasks, using formal English when appropriate to task and situation.

Demonstrate command of the conventions of standard English grammar and usage when writing or speaking.

Use knowledge of language and its conventions when writing, speaking, reading, or listening.

ELA ACADEMIC LANGUAGE

- *publish, present, evaluate, rubric*
- Cognates: *publicar, presentar, evaluar, rúbrica*

DIGITAL TOOLS

Anchor Papers

Presentation Checklist

Publish, Present, and Evaluate

Publishing

Once their drafts are final, students can prepare for publishing and presenting their work. Published work should be error-free and with any final visuals in place.

Presentation

For the final presentation of their research reports, have students choose a format for publishing: print or digital. Either format should include visuals such as photos, charts, graphs, or a multimedia element such as a video clip to support their ideas and engage their audience. Stress the importance of having students take the time to rehearse their presentations, practicing how to speak clearly and slowly. Have students consult the Presenting Checklist before they give their presentations.

Evaluate

After students have published their research reports, have them evaluate their presentation. Explain to them that rubrics show what the teacher expects from the assignment and how it will be evaluated and graded. Remind them that they can improve their writing by using the rubric to identify areas that might need more work. Briefly review the following points found on the rubric:

- Did you state a central idea and use transitional strategies?
- Did you include examples with relevant evidence?
- Did you use proper grammar and spelling?

Have students evaluate their own research reports by using the rubric on pages 220–223. Have them go through each point carefully and give their essay a score between 1–4 for Purpose, Focus, and Organization, a score between 1–4 for Evidence and Elaboration, and a score between 1–2 Conventions of Standard English. Ask students to record their totals on **Reading/Writing Companion** page 93. Point out that students can also use the Presenting Checklist on page 93 after their presentation to pinpoint areas that might need additional work.

After students have evaluated their own research reports using the rubric, have them switch with a partner. Have them go through each point carefully and give their partner a score. Remind them to be respectful and neutral. When they are both done, have students reflect on the effectiveness of the collaboration and on their progress as writers. Have them respond to the questions on page 93, noting where they need improvement and setting writing goals.

RESEARCH REPORT

Publish, Present, and Evaluate

Publishing When you publish your writing, you create a neat final copy that is free of mistakes. If you are not using a computer, write legibly in print or cursive.

Presentation When you are ready to present your work, rehearse your presentation. Use the Presenting Checklist to help you.

Evaluate After you publish, use the full expository rubric on pages 220–223 to evaluate it.

Presenting Checklist

- ☐ Look at the audience.
- ☐ Speak slowly, clearly, and loudly.
- ☐ Display any visuals so that everyone can see them.
- ☐ Answer questions thoughtfully.

What did you do successfully? ____________________

What needs more work? ____________________

Turn to page 85. Fill in the bars to show what you learned.

My Score			
Purpose, Focus, & Organization (4 pts)	Evidence & Elaboration (4 pts)	Conventions (2 pts)	Total (10 pts)

Unit 5 • Expository Writing 93

Reading/Writing Companion, p. 93

English Language Learners

Use the following scaffolds with **Presentation**. For additional support, see the **ELL Small Group Guide**.

Beginning

Clarify any unfamiliar vocabulary in the Presenting Checklist and model how to speak clearly, slowly, and at an appropriate rate. Then have partners work together to practice reading their essays aloud. Help each student by having them read aloud their essay prior to sharing with the rest of the class.

Intermediate

As necessary, review any unfamiliar vocabulary in the Presenting Checklist. Then have students practice presenting their reports in front of their partners. Provide examples of constructive feedback, as needed: *I'm having some trouble hearing you. Please try to speak louder. Your report is very interesting. If you look at me while you speak, it will help me pay attention.*

Advanced/Advanced High

Have partners take turns explaining each point in the Presenting Checklist and then read their final presentations to each other. Have them discuss what their partner did successfully and what still needs.

MY GOALS ROUTINE

What I Learned

Review Goal Have students turn back to page 85 of the Reading/Writing Companion and review the first goal.

Reflect Have students think about the progress they've made toward the goal. Review the key. Then have students fill in the bars.

MY GOALS ROUTINE

What I Know Now

Read Have students read the first goal on page 84 of the Reading/Writing Companion.

Reflect Have students review the Key to help them assess what they know now. Have students fill in the bars.

LEARNING GOALS

We can identify features of a personal narrative.

OBJECTIVES

Orient the reader by establishing a situation and introducing a narrator and/or characters; organize an event sequence that unfolds naturally.

Use narrative techniques, such as dialogue, description, and pacing, to develop experiences and events or show the responses of characters to situations.

ELA ACADEMIC LANGUAGE

- *personal narrative, autobiography, point of view, experience, analyze, features*
- Cognates: *narrativa personal, autobiografía, experiencia, analizar*

DIFFERENTIATED WRITING

Approaching Level Plan: Provide suggestions to narrow down the topic.

Beyond Level Plan: Students can add additional events to their maps and use a non-linear sequence of events.

ELL For additional support in writing a personal narrative, see the **ELL Small Group Guide.**

Expert Model

Features of a Personal Narrative

Remind students that they read the autobiographical text within "A Walk with Teddy." Students will now begin writing a personal narrative of their own. Say: *A personal narrative is a true story about an experience the writer has had.* Make sure students understand that an autobiography is a type of a personal narrative.

Anchor Chart Start an anchor chart listing the features of a personal narrative.

- It uses the first-person point of view to tell about the writer's experience of an event. The writer uses first-person pronouns, including *I, me,* and *my,* to refer to himself or herself.
- It shares the writer's thoughts and feelings about a real experience.
- It uses a logical sequence of events, including an introduction and a conclusion, and transitional strategies to connect events.
- It often includes descriptive details, imagery, and figurative language to help readers visualize the experience and understand how it impacted the writer.

Analyze an Expert Model

Tell students that by analyzing examples of a personal narrative, they will learn how to write their own personal narrative. Say: *Let's analyze a section of "A Walk with Teddy" for what to include in a personal narrative.*

Read aloud the text on **Literature Anthology** page 29. Ask: *Who is writing?* (Teddy Roosevelt) *What experience does the author describe?* (a nature walk he took in England in 1910) Have students write their answers to the first question on **Reading/Writing Companion** page 94.

Focus on the descriptive details and language in the narrative. *Which details from the text helped you visualize the scene? How does Roosevelt use imagery to convey these details?* (Possible answer: Roosevelt's descriptions of the blackbird's singing helped me visualize the scene. He uses sensory words such as *chorus, resembles,* and *hops* to add imagery.)

Guide students to notice the structure of the text. Say: *Writers of personal narratives often use chronological order to tell events in a logical sequence. They describe each event in the order it happened. This order helps readers keep track of the events.* Ask a volunteer to summarize the events on Literature Anthology page 29. Then have students write their answer to the second question on Reading/Writing Companion page 94.

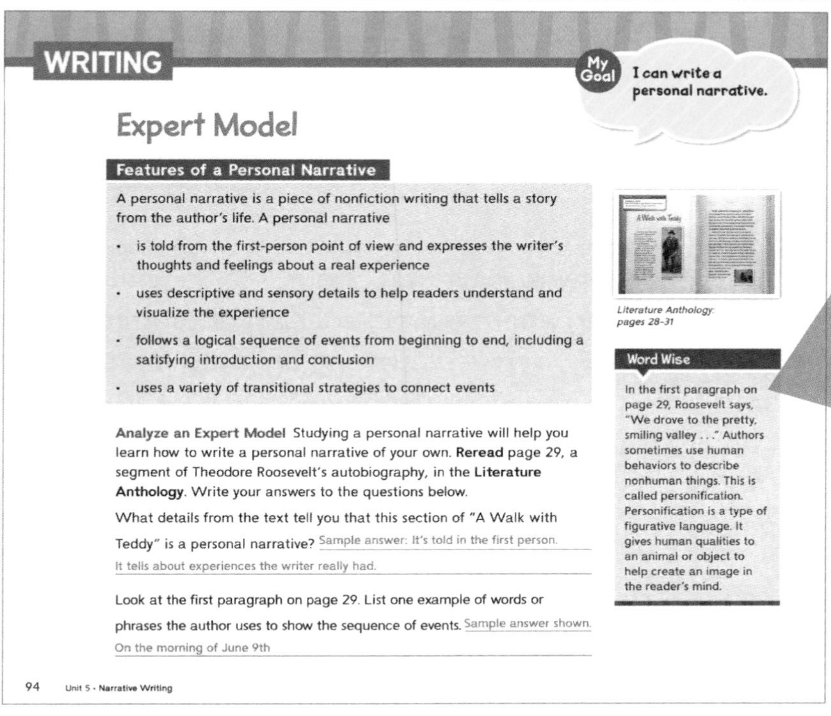

WRITING

My Goal I can write a personal narrative.

Expert Model

Features of a Personal Narrative

A personal narrative is a piece of nonfiction writing that tells a story from the author's life. A personal narrative

- is told from the first-person point of view and expresses the writer's thoughts and feelings about a real experience
- uses descriptive and sensory details to help readers understand and visualize the experience
- follows a logical sequence of events from beginning to end, including a satisfying introduction and conclusion
- uses a variety of transitional strategies to connect events

Analyze an Expert Model Studying a personal narrative will help you learn how to write a personal narrative of your own. **Reread** page 29, a segment of Theodore Roosevelt's autobiography, in the **Literature Anthology**. Write your answers to the questions below.

What details from the text tell you that this section of "A Walk with Teddy" is a personal narrative? Sample answer: It's told in the first person. It tells about experiences the writer really had.

Look at the first paragraph on page 29. List one example of words or phrases the author uses to show the sequence of events. Sample answer shown. On the morning of June 9th

Literature Anthology: pages 28–31

Word Wise

In the first paragraph on page 29, Roosevelt says, "We drove to the pretty, smiling valley . . ." Authors sometimes use human behaviors to describe nonhuman things. This is called personification. Personification is a type of figurative language. It gives human qualities to an animal or object to help create an image in the reader's mind.

94 Unit 5 • Narrative Writing

Reading/Writing Companion, p. 94

Word Wise

Explain how using figurative language, like personification or imagery, can help readers visualize the writer's experience in a personal narrative. Say: *If a writer says, "It was a windy day," it doesn't help me picture the moment in much detail. But if a writer says, "The enormous trees waved back and forth, clutching their leaves as the autumn wind blew harder and harder," I can picture the trees bending back and forth as the wind blows."* Have students discuss the impact of personification in the second sentence.

English Language Learners

Use the following scaffolds with **Analyze an Expert Model**.

Beginning

Review the features of a personal narrative with students. Read aloud the first paragraph on page 29 of the **Literature Anthology**. Say: *Teddy Roosevelt is writing. Does he write about his own experience?* (yes) *What experience does he describe?* (a nature walk) Have students point to the words *I, my,* and *me. What point of view does he use in his personal narrative?* (first-person) Then help partners write their responses on page 94.

Intermediate

Review the features of a personal narrative with students. Have partners reread page 29 of the Literature Anthology. Say: *Roosevelt describes his own experiences. What point of view does he use?* (first person) *How do you know?* (He uses the words *I, my,* and *me.*) Elicit partners to identify the sensory words Roosevelt uses to describe the blackbirds. (*chorus, resembles,* and *hops*) Then help them identify words that show the text is organized in chronological order.

Advanced/Advanced High

Have partners reread page 29 of the Literature Anthology. Have partners discuss the features of a personal narrative. Use questions to guide them: *What point of view does Roosevelt use? What are some descriptive details he uses?* Then have partners identify and discuss words or text features that show the text is organized in time order.

NEWCOMERS

To help students develop their writing, display the **Newcomer Cards** and **Newcomer Online Visuals**, and ask questions to help them discuss the images. Provide sentence starters. For example: *What do you see? I see ____. What are they doing? They are ___.* Have students point to the image as they ask and answer. Then have them write the sentences in their notebooks. Throughout extended writing, help students develop their writing by adding to and revising their sentences.

FORMATIVE ASSESSMENT

STUDENT CHECK-IN

Have partners share one feature of a personal narrative. Then have them reflect using the Check-In routine.

LEARNING GOALS

We can choose a topic to write a personal narrative.

OBJECTIVES

Orient the reader by establishing a situation and introducing a narrator and/or characters; organize an event sequence that unfolds naturally.

Use narrative techniques, such as dialogue, description, and pacing, to develop experiences and events or show the responses of characters to situations.

With guidance and support from peers and adults, develop and strengthen writing as needed by planning.

ELA ACADEMIC LANGUAGE

- *freewrite, significant, purpose, audience, formality*
- Cognates: *significativo, audiencia, formalidad*

DIGITAL TOOLS

Write for Your Audience; Purpose of Narrative Writing

Plan: Choose Your Topic

Freewrite

Remind students that a freewrite involves writing about a topic without pausing, self-censoring, or worrying about correct spelling or grammar. Say: *When you freewrite effectively, you keep writing until the time is up. Don't stop to think about how well the ideas might work–just get them down on paper.* Set a timer for three minutes and allow students to freewrite individually about an event from their lives that had a positive impact on the environment on the lines provided on **Reading/Writing Companion** page 95.

Writing Prompt

Each student should chose an experience or event from their freewriting and write a personal narrative about it. Explain that the topic should be an event from their lives that had a positive impact on the environment.

Purpose and Audience

Have students think about the purpose of "A Walk with Teddy" and other personal narratives they have read. Guide them to understand that while the purpose of writing a personal narrative is often to entertain readers, a thoughtful narrative will also help the writer more deeply understand his or her own life. Encourage students to think about their likely audience–teachers, classmates, friends, family members–and consider how many and what kinds of details they want to reveal in their narrative. Refer students to the Quick Tip. Reiterate that the formality of their language will reflect their audience as well as the type of experience they will be describing. Say: *Because you are telling readers about your own experience, it's acceptable to use language you would normally use in a more informal setting.* Have students write their responses on page 95.

Plan

Point out that personal narratives are based on the writer's memories. Before students write, they will need to recall details. Have them ask questions, such as "What happened?," "Who was involved?," "Where was I?," "How do I feel about it?," and "What did I learn?" Have students write the answers to these and other questions in their writer's notebook.

PERSONAL NARRATIVE

Plan: Choose Your Topic

COLLABORATE

Freewrite Think about an event in your life that had a positive impact on the environment. It should be an event that you can remember clearly. These might be events such as planting a class garden, cleaning up a park, or making a bird feeder. Quickly write your ideas without stopping. Then discuss your ideas with a partner.

Quick Tip
A personal narrative does not need to use the type of formal language you would use in an expository essay. You can use the type of informal language, or tone, you would use when writing a letter or e-mail to a friend.

Writing Prompt Choose one of your ideas that you want to expand into a personal narrative.

I will write my personal narrative about ______

Purpose and Audience Think about who will read or hear your narrative. Will your purpose be to persuade, inform, or entertain them? Then think about the language you will use to write your narrative.

My purpose is to ______

My audience will be ______

I will use ______ language when I write my personal narrative.

Plan Think about what you want your readers to learn about the experience. Ask yourself questions, and answer them in your writer's notebook. Questions to ask might include the following: *Why was the experience important? What did I learn from it? How do I feel about it?* Include specific details in your answers.

CHECK IN 1 2 3 4

Unit 5 • Narrative Writing 95

Reading/Writing Companion, p. 95

English Language Learners

Use the following scaffolds with **Freewrite**. For additional support, see the **ELL Small Group Guide**

Beginning

Help students generate words to describe things people do to help the environment. Then discuss with them specific events that they know about, such as cleaning up a park, that help the environment. Have students choose an event that they were part of and freewrite about the event and how they participated. Help partners describe using: One event was ______. For this event, I ______.

Intermediate

Discuss with students events people create to help the environment, such as planting vegetables or a flower garden. Then have them freewrite about such an event and how they participated. Have partners discuss the positive impact on the environment and how they felt when they participated. Help partners describe using: One event I remember is ______. For this event, I ______. I felt ______.

Advanced/Advanced High

Discuss with students events when people help the environment. Have them describe specific events that they know about, such as cleaning up a park or planting a garden, that have a positive effect. Then have them freewrite about such an event. Have pairs describe the positive impact on the environment and how they felt when they participated in the event. Have pairs read aloud their descriptions to one another.

TEACHER CONFERENCES

As students revise, hold teacher conferences with individual students.

Step 1: Talk About Strengths
Point out strengths in the freewrite: *You have a lot of ideas to choose from for your personal narrative. Think about which event you'd like to share.*

Step 2: Choose a Focus
Give feedback on how the student narrowed the focus: *Write down another question about the event you'd like to talk about so that your reader understands how it had a positive impact on the environment.*

Step 3: Make Concrete Suggestions
Provide specific direction to help students plan. Have students revise and then meet with you to review progress.

FORMATIVE ASSESSMENT

STUDENT CHECK-IN

Have partners share their topic and plan. Ask them to use the Check-In routine to reflect and fill in the bars on Reading/Writing Companion page 95.

LEARNING GOALS

We can use sequence to plan a personal narrative.

OBJECTIVES

Orient the reader by establishing a situation and introducing a narrator and/or characters; organize an event sequence that unfolds naturally.

Use narrative techniques, such as dialogue, description, and pacing, to develop experiences and events or show the responses of characters to situations.

With guidance and support from peers and adults, develop and strengthen writing as needed by planning.

ELA ACADEMIC LANGUAGE

- *sequence, logical, structure, transition*
- Cognates: *secuencia, lógico, estructura, transición*

DIGITAL TOOLS

Model Graphic Organizer

Plan: Sequence

Sequence of Events

Organizing a Narrative Tell students that a personal narrative should use a clear structure to describe the sequence of events that make up the writer's experience. Say: *An effective personal narrative contains a beginning, a middle, and an end.* To help students organize these components of their narratives, share the following:

- The beginning contains an introduction that identifies the event or experience, when and where it happened, and who was involved.
- The middle describes the events that happened.
- The writer ends with a conclusion that shares what he or she learned from the experience.

Using a Logical Sequence Say: *Most narratives tell events in a logical sequence. They start with the first event that happened and end with the last event. Using a logical sequence keeps readers from feeling confused.* Illustrate this point by having students return to "A Walk with Teddy" on page 29 of the **Literature Anthology**. *Teddy Roosevelt tells the events in a logical sequence. What happened first?* (Roosevelt writes that he left London on the morning of June 9.)

Using Transitional Words Tell students that writers use transitions to help readers understand the order of events. Use the signal words and transitions listed in the fourth bullet point on **Reading/Writing Companion** page 96 to retell the events in "A Walk with Teddy" on page 29 of the Literature Anthology: *First, they left London. Later they walked in the woods. Then they walked more. After finishing their walk, they made a list of birds.*

Have students list on Reading/Writing Companion page 96 at least two events for their personal narrative's sequence of events.

Graphic Organizer

Have students begin planning the sequence of events for their personal narrative. Tell them to read the Quick Tip on page 96 and use the sentence starters to help them fill in the boxes in online Sequence of Events **Graphic Organizer 17**. Students may add more boxes as needed.

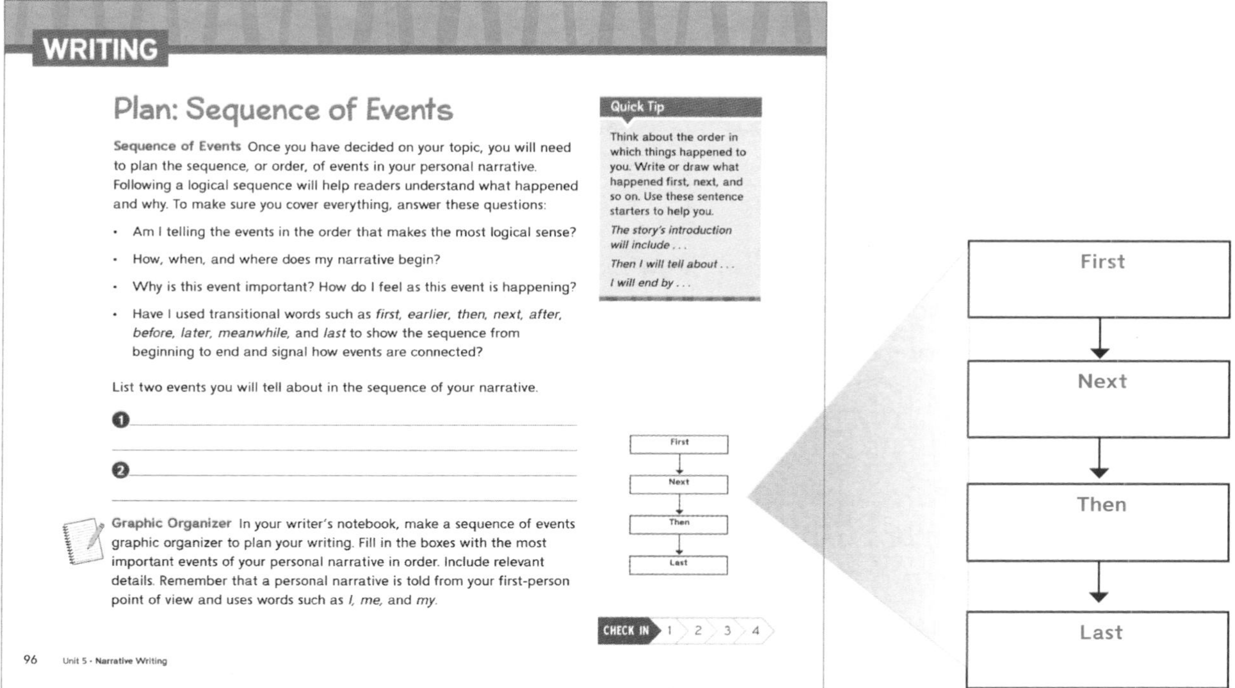

WRITING

Plan: Sequence of Events

Sequence of Events Once you have decided on your topic, you will need to plan the sequence, or order, of events in your personal narrative. Following a logical sequence will help readers understand what happened and why. To make sure you cover everything, answer these questions:

- Am I telling the events in the order that makes the most logical sense?
- How, when, and where does my narrative begin?
- Why is this event important? How do I feel as this event is happening?
- Have I used transitional words such as *first, earlier, then, next, after, before, later, meanwhile,* and *last* to show the sequence from beginning to end and signal how events are connected?

List two events you will tell about in the sequence of your narrative.

1. ______
2. ______

Graphic Organizer In your writer's notebook, make a sequence of events graphic organizer to plan your writing. Fill in the boxes with the most important events of your personal narrative in order. Include relevant details. Remember that a personal narrative is told from your first-person point of view and uses words such as *I, me,* and *my.*

Quick Tip

Think about the order in which things happened to you. Write or draw what happened first, next, and so on. Use these sentence starters to help you.

The story's introduction will include . . .

Then I will tell about . . .

I will end by . . .

First → Next → Then → Last

CHECK IN 1 2 3 4

96 Unit 5 • Narrative Writing

Reading/Writing Companion, p. 96

English Language Learners

Use these scaffolds with **Sequence of Events**. For additional support, see the **ELL Small Group Guide**

Beginning

Say: *Writers tell events in a sequence that makes sense to readers. This is called logical order.* Read the first paragraph on page 29 of the **Literature Anthology** and help partners restate the sequence of events using: First they left London. Then they walked through the woods. At the conclusion of their walk, they made a list of birds. *Talk to your partner about two events that will be in your own narratives.*

Intermediate

Review the meaning of *sequence* and have partners read the first paragraph on page 29 of the Literature Anthology. *What transitional words and phrases does Roosevelt use to show the sequence of events?* (*then again, this time, first, then, at the conclusion*) Have partners restate Roosevelt's events on page 29 in logical order and then describe two events they will put in a logical order in their own narratives.

Advance/Advanced High

Have partners reread the first paragraph on page 29 of the Literature Anthology, discuss the sequence of events, and identify the transitional words that signal the order of events. *Talk to your partner about two events that you will put in order in your narratives and explain the logical sequence.*

MULTIMODAL LEARNING

As an alternative to the graphic organizer, have students list the events in their personal narrative on a piece of colored paper. Have students cut the paper so that each event is its own strip of paper. Ask students to order the strips in the proper sequence, noting what comes first, next, and last.

FORMATIVE ASSESSMENT

STUDENT CHECK-IN

Have partners share their graphic organizers. Ask them to use the Check-In routine to reflect and fill in the bars on Reading/Writing Companion p. 96.

LEARNING GOALS

We can write a personal narrative.

OBJECTIVES

Use narrative techniques, such as dialogue, description, and pacing, to develop experiences and events or show the responses of characters to situations.

Use concrete words and phrases and sensory details to convey experiences and events precisely.

Write routinely over extended time frames and shorter time frames for a range of discipline-specific tasks, purposes, and audiences.

Demonstrate understanding of figurative language, word relationships, and nuances in word meanings.

ELA ACADEMIC LANGUAGE

- *audience, descriptive, narrative, visualize*
- Cognates: *audiencia, descriptivo, narrativa/o, visualizar*

DIGITAL TOOLS

Student Draft Model

Draft

Description

Remind students that personal narratives are stories about real people and events. Discuss how writers use vivid descriptions to engage readers' imaginations and convey experiences and events precisely.

- Descriptions that use sensory language appeal to the senses of sight, hearing, smell, taste, and touch. They help readers feel as if they are experiencing the event with the writer.
- Descriptions that use vivid and precise words are memorable. They stay in readers' minds.

Have students reread the paragraph from "A Life in the Woods" on page 97 of **Reading/Writing Companion**. Ask for volunteers to identify vivid or sensory language in the paragraph. (*uttered, prolonged howls, rippled, whole air, misty rain*) Then ask: *How does the language the writer uses help you "see" and "hear" what's happening?* (Sample response: When I read the phrase *prolonged howls,* I can imagine hearing a long, loud cry, almost like the sound of a wolf. The word *rippled* helps me imagine seeing how wind pushes the surface of the water and makes it move.)

Tell students to use the paragraph from "A Life in the Woods" as a model for their own paragraphs. They can begin by choosing one event from their graphic organizer and writing about it. They should use descriptions in their paragraphs to help their readers better understand their experience.

Write a Draft

Remind students they will be writing about an event in their lives that had a positive impact on the environment. Have students review the graphic organizer they completed in the Plan phase as they write their drafts. Remind students to use descriptions to make the writing more interesting for the reader and to help readers better understand their experience. They should also use signal and transition words to guide their reader through the sequence of events. Make sure students either write legibly in print or cursive in their writer's notebook or type accurately on-screen. Circulate to check their work.

Pair students to identify the descriptions in each other's drafts and discuss how these details make the paragraphs more interesting.

PERSONAL NARRATIVE

Draft

Description Writers of personal narratives use vivid descriptive and sensory language to tell about events. They use words and phrases that allow readers to visualize the experience and understand the writer's thoughts and feelings about it. In the sentence below from "A Life in the Woods," Thoreau describes what he sees and feels.

> At length he uttered one of those prolonged howls, as if calling on the god of the loons to aid him, and immediately there came a wind from the east and rippled the surface, and filled the whole air with misty rain, and I was impressed.

Now use the above excerpt as a model to write a paragraph that could be a part of your personal narrative. Think carefully about your descriptions.

Word Wise

To help you come up with descriptive and sensory words, close your eyes and think about the experience you are describing. Use words that describe what you saw, heard, smelled, tasted, and felt. You can also use a thesaurus to help you find an appropriate descriptive word.

Write a Draft Use your sequence of events graphic organizer to help you write your draft in your writer's notebook. As you write your draft, use transitional words and phrases to connect events. Include plenty of descriptive and sensory details to help them understand your experience. Finally, remember to indent each paragraph.

CHECK IN 1 2 3 4

Unit 5 • Narrative Writing 97

Reading/Writing Companion, p. 97

Word Wise

Discuss how an author's choice of words contributes to the reader's understanding of the narrative. When writing a description, students should recall the experience they are describing and use words that describe what they saw, heard, smelled, tasted, and felt. Have students use a thesaurus to help find descriptive words.

English Language Learners

Use the following scaffolds with **Description**. For additional support, see **ELL Small Group Guide**.

Beginning

Review with students that writers use descriptive language to help readers understand experiences better. Provide examples of how sensory and vivid language helps readers imagine what the writer sees, hears, smells, feels, and tastes. Read the paragraph on page 81 with students. Then discuss examples of sensory details and help students describe using: Words like "prolonged howls" describe a sound that Thoreau heard.

Intermediate

Review with students that writers use descriptions to help readers imagine experiences and events. Read the paragraph on page 81 with students. Elicit partners to identify the vivid or sensory language in the paragraph that helps them "see" and "hear" what is happening. (*uttered, prolonged howls, rippled, whole air, misty rain*) Then help them add descriptions to one event in their personal narrative.

Advance/Advanced High

Discuss with students ways that writers use description to help readers imagine the experiences, including sensory language and precise words. Have students read the paragraph on page 81 and have them identify vivid and sensory language. Have partners use it as a model to write a paragraph with descriptive language.

TEACHER CONFERENCES

As students revise, hold teacher conferences with individual students.

Step 1: Talk About Strengths
Point out strengths in the essay: *The sensory language you used helps me visualize what is happening in your narrative.*

Step 2: Focus on Skills
Give feedback on how the student organizes the sequence of events: *Telling the story sequentially will help your reader follow the narrative.*

Step 3: Make Concrete Suggestions
Provide specific direction to help students draft. Have students revise and then meet with you to review progress.

FORMATIVE ASSESSMENT

STUDENT CHECK-IN

Have partners share their draft. Ask them to use the Check-In routine to reflect and fill in the bars on Reading/Writing Companion page 97.

LEARNING GOALS

We can revise a personal narrative by focusing on strong conclusions.

OBJECTIVES

Use a variety of transitional words, phrases, and clauses to manage the sequence of events.

Use concrete words and phrases and sensory details to convey experiences and events precisely.

Provide a conclusion that follows from the narrated experiences or events.

With guidance and support from peers and adults, develop and strengthen writing as needed by revising.

ELA ACADEMIC LANGUAGE

- *conclusion, resolve, vivid*
- Cognates: *conclusión, resolver, vívido*

Approaching Level Review and make suggestions for a strong conclusion.

On Level Partners can review drafts for strong conclusions.

Beyond Level Students should work independently on a strong conclusion and vivid language.

ELL For additional support in revising a personal narrative, see the **ELL Small Group Guide**.

Revise

Strong Conclusions

Review with students that a strong conclusion gives readers a sense of closure, or ending. In a personal narrative, a strong conclusion also describes how the story is resolved. Explain that good writers provide a conclusion that follows logically from the experiences or events of the narrative. Point out that using vivid language in the conclusion helps make the experience "come alive" for readers.

Help students revise the paragraph on **Reading/Writing Companion** page 98. Call on volunteers to read the "before" and "after" versions of the paragraph and explain the reasons for the changes they made.

For an example of a narrative text that contains an effective conclusion, read aloud the last paragraph of "A Life in the Woods" on page 12 of the Unit 1 **Reading/Writing Companion**. Ask: *How does the author make it clear that the experience of living at Walden Pond was meaningful to Thoreau?* (The author states that Thoreau had learned a lot from the experience and was able to use what he learned to write a book about life in the woods.)

Read aloud the following questions to help students evaluate their drafts for a strong conclusion. As you read, tell students to make notes about ways to revise their writing.

- Does my conclusion follow logically from the rest of my narrative?
- Does my conclusion provide a satisfying ending?
- Does my conclusion tell how I felt about my experience?
- Does my conclusion tell what I learned?
- Does my conclusion contain vivid language?

Ask volunteers to share examples from their drafts. Point out successful examples of a strong conclusion.

Revision

Allow students to revise their drafts, focusing on a strong conclusion. Guide them in reworking their writing by adding, deleting, combining, and/or rearranging ideas to make their conclusion stronger.

Remind students to check that their conclusion follows logically from the rest of the narrative, tells how they felt about the experience and what they learned, provides a satisfying ending, and has vivid language. Guide students to brainstorm vivid words and phrases that would be appropriate for their narrative.

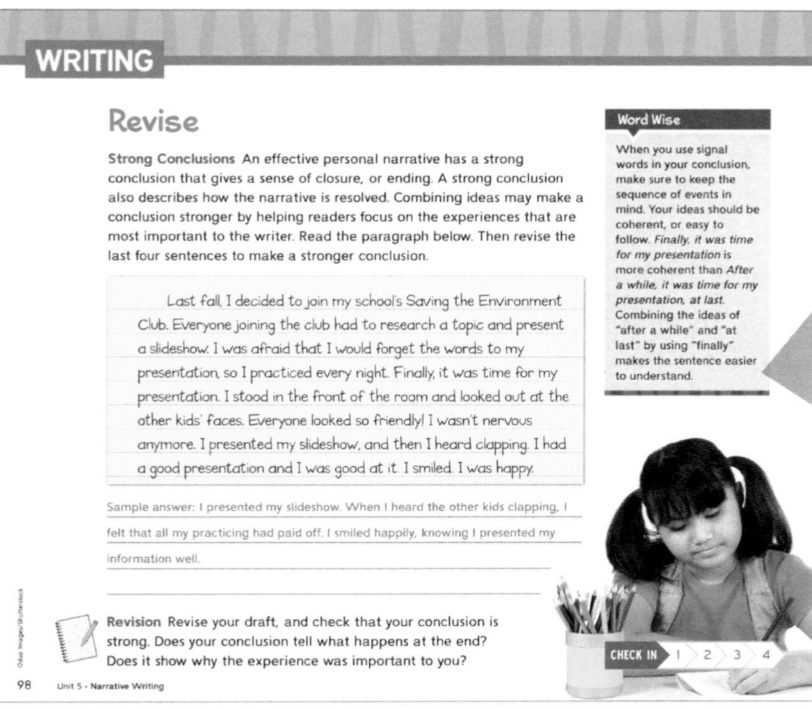

WRITING

Revise

Strong Conclusions An effective personal narrative has a strong conclusion that gives a sense of closure, or ending. A strong conclusion also describes how the narrative is resolved. Combining ideas may make a conclusion stronger by helping readers focus on the experiences that are most important to the writer. Read the paragraph below. Then revise the last four sentences to make a stronger conclusion.

Last fall, I decided to join my school's Saving the Environment Club. Everyone joining the club had to research a topic and present a slideshow. I was afraid that I would forget the words to my presentation, so I practiced every night. Finally, it was time for my presentation. I stood in the front of the room and looked out at the other kids' faces. Everyone looked so friendly! I wasn't nervous anymore. I presented my slideshow, and then I heard clapping. I had a good presentation and I was good at it. I smiled. I was happy.

Sample answer: I presented my slideshow. When I heard the other kids clapping, I felt that all my practicing had paid off. I smiled happily, knowing I presented my information well.

Word Wise

When you use signal words in your conclusion, make sure to keep the sequence of events in mind. Your ideas should be coherent, or easy to follow. *Finally, it was time for my presentation* is more coherent than *After a while, it was time for my presentation, at last.* Combining the ideas of "after a while" and "at last" by using "finally" makes the sentence easier to understand.

Revision Revise your draft, and check that your conclusion is strong. Does your conclusion tell what happens at the end? Does it show why the experience was important to you?

CHECK IN 1 2 3 4

98 Unit 5 • Narrative Writing

Reading/Writing Companion, p. 98

Word Wise

Reiterate that using signal and transitional words can help ensure that writers' ideas in their conclusions are coherent, or easy to follow. Writers can use words and phrases such as *finally, in the end,* and *last* to signal to readers that the narrative is coming to an end.

English Language Learners

Use the following scaffolds with **Strong Conclusions**.

Beginning

Review with students that a strong conclusion for a personal narrative tells the final events and resolves the story. Explain that the writer may share how he/she felt and what he/she learned from the experiences. Read the paragraph on page 98 together. Help students describe using: The writer says that he/she was happy. Then discuss whether the paragraph provides a strong conclusion or not, and why.

Intermediate

Review with students that a strong conclusion for a personal narrative follows logically and resolves the story. Explain that the writer may share how he/she felt and what he/she learned from the experiences. Read the paragraph on page 98 and have students describe using: The writer tells the reader he/she finished the presentation and he/she was happy. Then guide partners to discuss how to improve the last four sentences in the conclusion.

Advanced/Advanced High

Review with students that a strong conclusion for a personal narrative resolves the story and may leave readers with a lasting thought. Have students read the paragraph on page 98 and identify whether it provides a strong conclusion or not, and why. Discuss ways they can revise the last four sentences for a stronger conclusion then complete the writing activity on the page.

DIGITAL TOOLS

Revised Student Model

Revise Checklist (Narrative)

FORMATIVE ASSESSMENT

STUDENT CHECK-IN

Have partners show how they revised to strengthen their conclusions. Ask them to use the Check-In routine to reflect and fill in the bars.

LEARNING GOALS

We can give and received feedback on a personal narrative.

OBJECTIVES

With guidance and support from peers and adults, develop and strengthen writing as needed by planning, revising, editing, rewriting, or trying a new approach.

Come to discussions prepared, having read or studied required material; explicitly draw on that preparation and other information known about the topic to explore ideas under discussion.

Follow agreed-upon rules for discussions and carry out assigned roles.

Expand, combine, and reduce sentences for meaning, reader/listener interest, and style.

ELA ACADEMIC LANGUAGE

- *peer review, feedback, constructive, routine, conduct*
- Cognates: *constructivo, rutina*

DIGITAL TOOLS

Peer Conferencing Checklist (Narrative)

Peer Conferencing

Review a Draft

Tell students that listening to the work of other writers and providing constructive feedback is an important aspect of the writing process. Take time to review with students the routine for peer review.

- Step 1: Listen carefully as the writer reads the work aloud.
- Step 2: Tell one thing that you liked about the writing.
- Step 3: Ask questions to help the writer think critically.
- Step 4: Give feedback to help make the writing stronger.

You may wish to remind students that they should be polite, provide constructive feedback, ask thoughtful questions, and be open to their partner's suggestions.

Guide students to read the sentence starters on **Reading/Writing Companion** page 99. Say: *The sentence starters will help you give useful feedback to your partner. For example, you might say "I have a question about your sequence of events. Which event came first?"* Review the steps of the peer routine. Ask: *Why is it important to follow this routine during peer review?* (Having a routine helps me learn to be a good listener and provide feedback.)

Partner Feedback

Circulate and observe as partners collaborate, review, and give feedback on each other's drafts. Ensure that partners are following the routine and the agreed-upon rules. Have partners reflect on partner feedback and write on page 99 about how they intend to use the feedback.

Revision

Review the revising checklist on **Reading/Writing Companion** page 99. Allow students time to implement suggestions. Remind students that the rubric on page 224 can also help with revision. After students have completed their revisions, allow them time to share how their partner's feedback helped improve their narratives.

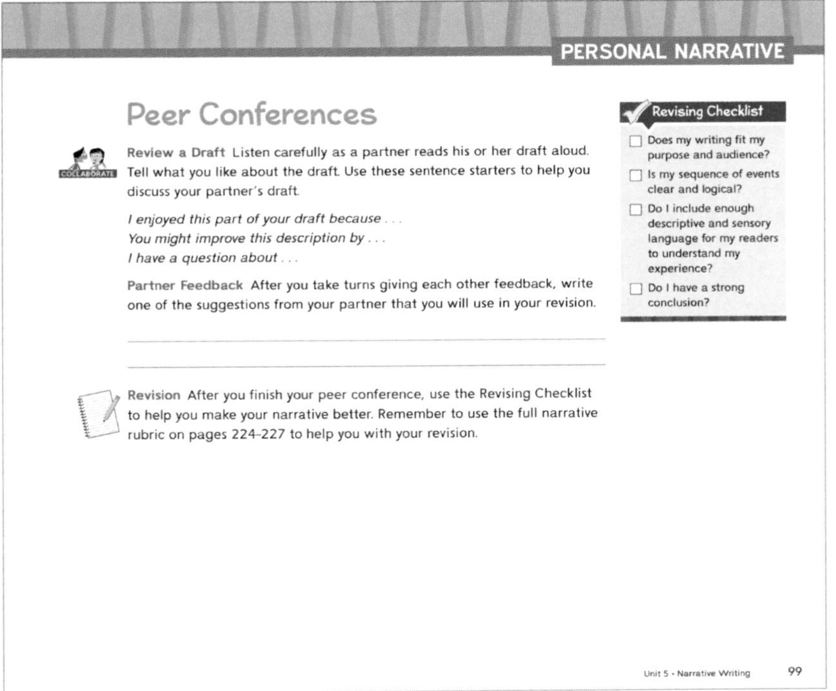
PERSONAL NARRATIVE

Peer Conferences

COLLABORATE

Review a Draft Listen carefully as a partner reads his or her draft aloud. Tell what you like about the draft. Use these sentence starters to help you discuss your partner's draft.

I enjoyed this part of your draft because . . .
You might improve this description by . . .
I have a question about . . .

Partner Feedback After you take turns giving each other feedback, write one of the suggestions from your partner that you will use in your revision.

Revision After you finish your peer conference, use the Revising Checklist to help you make your narrative better. Remember to use the full narrative rubric on pages 224-227 to help you with your revision.

Revising Checklist
- ☐ Does my writing fit my purpose and audience?
- ☐ Is my sequence of events clear and logical?
- ☐ Do I include enough descriptive and sensory language for my readers to understand my experience?
- ☐ Do I have a strong conclusion?

Unit 5 • Narrative Writing 99

Reading/Writing Companion, p. 99

English Language Learners

Use the following scaffolds with **Peer Feedback**. For additional support, see **ELL Small Group Guide**.

Beginning

Pair students with more proficient speakers. Have students ask for clarification and provide feedback using: *Can you repeat ________? I like ________.* Students may need to see the draft as well as hear it. Have partners complete the Partner Feedback on page 99. Help students review the second item on the Revising Checklist to make sure the sequence of events make sense.

Intermediate

Pair students with more proficient speakers. Have students ask for clarification using: *Can you read more slowly? Can you explain ________?* Have partners provide feedback using a sentence starter on page 99 and work together to complete the Partner Feedback. Have students use the last three items on the Revising Checklist to check they included logical order of events, descriptive sensory words, and a strong conclusion.

Advanced/Advanced High

Have partners provide feedback using the sentence starters on page 99. Have students use the Revising Checklist and focus on clarity of sequence of events, using descriptive language, and making sure the conclusion is strong.

TEACHER CONFERENCES

As students revise, hold teacher conferences with individual students.

Step 1: Talk About Strengths
Point out strengths in the narrative: *The personal narrative includes a logical sequence of events, which makes it easy to follow and understand.*

Step 2: Focus on Skills
Give feedback how to strengthen conclusions: *I'm not clear how the problem was resolved or what you learned. Strengthen your conclusion by closing up loose ends in your narrative.*

Step 3: Make Concrete Suggestions
Provide specific direction to help students revise. Underline a sentence or section that needs to be revised. Have students use a specific revision strategy, like rewriting, adding, or deleting.

CLASSROOM CULTURE

We learn through modeling and practice. A classroom where students can work in pairs and small groups is motivating and gives them opportunities to practice skills together. After peer conferences, ask students: *How did working with a partner support your learning?*

FORMATIVE ASSESSMENT

STUDENT CHECK-IN

Have partners share their drafts and give feedback. Ask them to reflect using the Check-In routine and rubric on page 101.

LEARNING GOALS

We can edit and proofread a personal narrative.

OBJECTIVES

With guidance and support from peers and adults, develop and strengthen writing as needed by planning, revising, editing, rewriting, or trying a new approach.

Come to discussions prepared, having read or studied required material; explicitly draw on that preparation and other information known about the topic to explore ideas under discussion.

Follow agreed-upon rules for discussions and carry out assigned roles.

Demonstrate command of the conventions of standard English grammar and usage when writing or speaking.

Demonstrate command of the conventions of standard English capitalization, punctuation, and spelling when writing.

Spell grade-appropriate words correctly, consulting references as needed.

ELA ACADEMIC LANGUAGE

- *edit, proofread, improve, affect, error*
- Cognates: *editar, afectar, error*

DIGITAL TOOLS

Edited Student Model

Edit Checklist (Narrative)

Edit and Proofread

Explain

Remind students that after they finish writing and revising their drafts, they must edit and proofread them. Say: *Editing involves asking questions about your writing. For example, can you improve your sequence of events by rearranging paragraphs or adding transitions? Can you make descriptions more vivid by replacing some words? Can you combine sentences to make your writing less choppy? Proofreading involves checking that your spelling, grammar, and punctuation are correct.* Encourage students to make a list of a few errors they often make. For example, they might confuse *their* and *there*, struggle with subject-verb agreement, and omit articles.

Correct Mistakes

Review the Editing Checklist on **Reading/Writing Companion** page 100 with students and have them read the Grammar Connections feature. Ask: *How would it affect readers if you did not use quotation marks to correctly punctuate dialogue in your narrative?* (Readers might be confused about who is speaking in my writing.) *What might happen if your writing contained sentence fragments?* (My ideas would not be clear to readers, since the sentences would be missing subjects or verbs.) Write this sentence on the board:

you have a new baby," aunt Suzi

Proofread and edit as a class. (Capitalize "y" in "You"; set quotation mark before "You"; capitalize "a" in Aunt"; add "said happily to me." after "Suzi") Ask students to record two mistakes they found using the Editing Checklist. Ask: *What other questions could you add to the checklist to make it more complete?*

Using the Editing Checklist

Assign students to groups of six and have them sit in a circle. Each group member should choose an item from the checklist. Tell students to pass their drafts to the person on their left and then check and correct the draft they received for their item. After all group members have checked all drafts, break groups into pairs. Ask partners to review their drafts and reflect on how the editing process affected their writing.

WRITING

Edit and Proofread

When you **edit** and **proofread** your writing, you look for and correct mistakes in spelling, punctuation, capitalization, and grammar. Reading through a revised draft multiple times can help you make sure you're catching any errors. Use the checklist below to edit your narrative.

Editing Checklist

- ☐ Do all sentences begin with a capital letter and end with a punctuation mark?
- ☐ Have I used commas correctly?
- ☐ Do all of my sentences express a complete thought?
- ☐ Are proper nouns capitalized?
- ☐ Are quotation marks used correctly?
- ☐ Are all words spelled correctly?

List two mistakes you found as you proofread your narrative.

1. ____________________
2. ____________________

Grammar Connections

Personal narratives may include dialogue. Lines of dialogue are set off by quotation marks. Make sure you have used quotation marks correctly in any dialogue you write. Use a comma to separate a phrase, such as *she said,* from the quotation itself. For example: *My sister said, "I think that is a terrific idea!"*

100 Unit 5 • Narrative Writing

Reading/Writing Companion, p. 100

Grammar Connections

Remind students that dialogue is the exact words that people say in a text. In a personal narrative, a writer uses quotation marks to help readers distinguish dialogue from the writer's own description of events. Refer students to the online **Grammar Handbook** page 480.

English Language Learners

Use the following scaffolds with **Using the Editing Checklist**. For additional support, see **ELL Small Group Guide**.

Beginning

Help students understand the fifth item in the Editing Checklist on page 100. Say: *We use quotation marks to show the exact words people say. The exact words people say are called dialogue.* Remind students to use a pair of quotation marks to show where the dialogue begins and ends. Have partners point to an example of dialogue in their narratives and determine whether the quotation marks are used correctly.

Intermediate

Have partners work together to make sure they understand the meaning of the items in the Editing Checklist on page 100. Have partners work together to proofread the group's drafts as they check for their errors. Then have partners work together to explain to the class how the Editing Checklist helped their draft.

Advance/Advanced High

Remind students that proofreading involves checking for grammar, spelling, and punctuation. Have partners choose an item the Editing Checklist and work together to explain what they will be looking for in the group's drafts and then fix the group's drafts. Have students explain how the checklist improved their draft.

FORMATIVE ASSESSMENT

STUDENT CHECK-IN

Have partners talk about mistakes they fixed as they edited and proofread. Ask them to reflect using the Check-In routine.

LEARNING GOALS

We can publish, present, and evaluate a personal narrative.

OBJECTIVES

Orient the reader by establishing a situation and introducing a narrator and/or characters; organize an event sequence that unfolds naturally.

Use narrative techniques, such as dialogue, description, and pacing, to develop experiences and events or show the responses of characters to situations.

Use a variety of transitional words, phrases, and clauses to manage the sequence of events.

With some guidance and support from adults, use technology, including the Internet, to produce and publish writing as well as to interact and collaborate with others; demonstrate sufficient command of keyboarding skills to type a minimum of two pages in a single sitting.

Demonstrate command of the conventions of standard English grammar and usage when writing or speaking.

Use knowledge of language and its conventions when writing, speaking, reading, or listening.

ELA ACADEMIC LANGUAGE

- *presentation, publish, rubric, evaluate*
- Cognates: *presentación, publicar, evaluar*

DIGITAL TOOLS

 Anchor Papers

Presentation Checklist (Narrative)

Publish, Present, and Evaluate

Publishing

Once their drafts are final, students can prepare for publishing and presenting their work to appropriate audiences. Remind them to write complete words and thoughts and to use appropriate spacing between words. For more on handwriting, see **Practice Book** page 361. Published work should be error-free, with final visuals in place. If students are typing their work, help them to develop effective keyboarding skills.

Presentation

For the final presentation of their personal narratives, have students choose a format for publishing: print or digital. Either format should incorporate a logical sequence of events, descriptions, transitional words, and strong conclusions. Allow time for students to plan and practice. Have students consult the Presenting Checklist before they face the class.

Evaluate

Explain that rubrics show what the teacher expects from the assignment and how it will be evaluated and graded. For example, after the teacher reads a personal narrative, he or she reads each bullet point under each number and decides if the story meets the expectations listed on the rubric under each number. It is up to the teacher to decide how closely the story matches the items listed under each number and which number to assign the story. Direct students to the full rubric in the **Reading/Writing Companion** on page 224. Explain that students can improve their writing by using the rubric to identify areas that might need further work. Work with the class to review the bulleted points on the rubric under "4."

- Did you tell about a personal experience and include descriptive details and dialogue?
- Did you present a logical sequence of events?
- Did you use transitional words and phrases to connect ideas and events?

If students answer "no" to any of these questions, they should revisit their work to clarify the information they've included. Make sure they note what they did successfully and what needs more work.

After students have evaluated their own personal narratives using the rubric, have them switch with a partner. Have them go through each point carefully and give the partner a score. Remind them to be respectful and neutral. When they are both done, have students reflect on the effectiveness of the collaboration and on their progress as writers. Have them respond to the questions on page 101, noting where they need improvement and setting writing goals.

PERSONAL NARRATIVE

Publish, Present, and Evaluate

Publishing When you publish your writing, you create a neat final copy that is free of mistakes. If you are not using a computer, write legibly in print or cursive.

Presentation When you are ready to present your work, rehearse your presentation. Use the Presenting Checklist.

Evaluate After you publish, use the full narrative rubric on pages 224-227 to evaluate it.

What did you do successfully? ______________________

____

What needs more work? ______________________

____

Presenting Checklist

- ☐ Look at the audience and make eye contact.
- ☐ Speak clearly, enunciating each word.
- ☐ Speak loud enough so that everyone can hear you.
- ☐ Use natural gestures when telling your narrative.

Turn to page 85. Fill in the bars to show what you learned.

My Score			
Purpose, Focus, & Organization (4 pts)	Elaboration (4 pts)	Conventions (2 pts)	Total (10 pts)

Unit 5 • Narrative Writing 101

Reading/Writing Companion, p. 101

English Language Learners

Use the following scaffolds with **Presentation.** For additional support, see **ELL Small Group Guide**.

Beginning

Have partners work together to practice reading their final drafts. Help them use the strategies on the Presenting Checklist on page 101. Model reading with appropriate rate and volume and eye contact. Remind students to pay attention to facial expressions, gestures, correct pronunciation, good intonation, and a comfortable pace. Have partners read aloud, listening for mistakes and areas for improvement using the checklist. Then have partners rehearse again.

Intermediate

Check to ensure that students understand the Presenting Checklist on page 101. Encourage students to use the checklist as they work with partners to rehearse and correct their presentations. As they speak, remind students to monitor their pronunciation, speak at a good pace, and use intonation for expression.

Advance/Advanced High

Have partners review the items on the Presenting Checklist on page 101 before they rehearse their presentations with a partner. Encourage partners to pay attention to their partner's presentation and then provide constructive feedback.

MY GOALS ROUTINE

What I Learned

Review Goals Have students turn back to page 85 of the Reading/Writing Companion and review the second goal.

Reflect Have students think about the progress they've made toward the goal. Review the key, if needed. Have students fill in the bars.

LEARNING GOALS

We can build skills to improve our writing.

OBJECTIVES

With guidance and support from peers and adults, develop and strengthen writing as needed by planning, revising, editing, rewriting, or trying a new approach.

With some guidance and support from adults, use technology, including the Internet, to produce and publish writing as well as to interact and collaborate with others; demonstrate sufficient command of keyboarding skills to type a minimum of two pages in a single sitting.

Adapt speech to a variety of contexts and tasks, using formal English when appropriate to task and situation.

FLEXIBLE MINILESSONS

Use these minilessons flexibly, in any order, based on the needs of your students. The minilessons can be used separately or in tandem with the Research Report or Personal Narrative lessons on pages T228–T243 and T244–T259.

Use students' Check-In reflections and your observations to decide which students are ready to independently apply the lesson focus to their own writing. Use the tips in the Conferring Toolkit to provide additional guidance as you confer with students or meet with them in small groups.

FORMATIVE ASSESSMENT

STUDENT CHECK-IN

After the guide activity, have students reflect on their understanding of the lesson focus. Have them reflect using the Check-In routine.

Build Writing Skills

Narrow Your Focus

Writers can narrow the focus of broad topics by asking questions.

Model Think aloud as you model narrowing your focus on a topic. *I'd like to write a research report on the space program. That's a big topic! I need to be more specific about what I'd like to research and write about. What do I think or wonder about the American space program? I'm really interested in astronauts. Which astronauts would I like to learn more about?*

Guide Have students suggest other questions that you could ask to narrow your focus.

Apply Tell students to suppose that they are writing a research report on sports. Ask them to write down questions to narrow their focus. Have them share their narrowed topics with a partner.

Write Strong Paragraphs

Writers elaborate using facts, reasons, anecdotes, examples, sensory details, and/or quotations.

Model Text Tell students that elaboration is what writers do to develop their body paragraphs. Read aloud the second paragraph of "Changing Views of Earth," on page 13 of the **Reading/Writing Companion**. Point out how the writer builds a strong paragraph by elaborating on the central idea about how in the past people understood life only by what they could see and hear.

Guide Ask partners to read the third paragraph and identify how the writer elaborated on the central idea of the paragraph. (facts, anecdote, sensory details)

Apply Have students write a strong paragraph about the impact of technology. Encourage them to include facts, reasons, and examples to elaborate on the central idea.

Conferring Toolkit

Narrow Your Focus If students need support narrowing the focus of the topic, prompt them with questions. Say: *Writing a research report on sports in general is too broad of a topic. Let's ask questions to narrow down what you can focus on. Which sport interests you? What do you like about this sport? Is there a team or a player you would like to learn more about?*

Write Strong Paragraphs Guide students in identifying the central idea of their paragraph. Ask: *What facts or examples can you give to support this central idea about the impact of technology? What reasons can you provide?*

Use Formal or Informal Language?

Writers of research reports use formal language, while writers of personal narratives often use informal language.

Model Text Read aloud the second paragraph of "Wordsmiths" on page 115 of the **Literature Anthology**. Say: *Notice the way the writer uses formal language by presenting information about Lucy Terry Prince in an objective and straightforward manner.*

Next, turn to "Reading Between the Dots" on page 48 and read aloud the first paragraph Say: *The language used in this personal narrative is informal, as if speaking directly to readers.*

Guide Ask pairs to list settings where they might use formal or informal language.

Apply Have students rewrite the first paragraph of "Reading Between the Dots" using formal language. Then have them read their paragraphs to a partner.

Revise for Pronoun-Antecedent Agreement

A singular antecedent requires a singular pronoun; a plural antecedent needs a plural pronoun.

Model Write these two sentences:

- *After Josefina finishes her homework, Josefina will watch a show on Josefina's television in Josefina's bedroom.*

- *After Josefina finishes her homework, she will watch a show on her television in her bedroom.*

Point out how using singular pronouns eliminates the need to repeat Josefina's name.

Guide Ask partners to consider how to revise the sentence if the antecedent was *Josefina and Miguel*. Have them rewrite the sentence using correct pronoun-antecedent agreement.

Apply Have students revise a paragraph for pronoun-antecedent agreement in one of their writing assignments.

Write a Strong Conclusion

A strong conclusion should restate the central idea and relevant details and leave the audience with something to think about or consider.

Model Text Read aloud the last paragraph of "Wordsmiths" on page 117 of the **Literature Anthology**. Ask students to listen to how the writer summarizes the central idea of the text. Point out how it is clear that the writer wants the reader to know how Phillis Wheatley is highly regarded as an important contributor to American literature. Say: *By concluding with an excerpt of George Washington's letter, the writer makes it clear that Wheatley was truly admired.*

Guide Have partners reread the conclusion of *Who Wrote the U.S. Constitution?* on page 110 of the Literature Anthology. Have them discuss what makes this a strong conclusion.

Apply Have students revise the conclusion in one of their writing assignments to strengthen it.

ELL **Formal vs. Informal Language** If students need more support, reread the model texts in the Literature Anthology and help them identify formal and informal language.

Pronoun-Antecedent Agreement Point out a section in the student's writing that does not have pronoun-antecedent agreement. Caution students to remember that the pronoun *its* does not have an apostrophe. Talk with them about what happens if they do add an apostrophe to the pronoun. Ask: *How might writing* it's *instead of* its *confuse your audience?*

ELL **Write a Strong Conclusion** Share your response to students' conclusions to their personal narrative or expository text. Praise conclusions that were strengthened and ask questions about conclusions that were confusing or left you wanting more.

LEARNING GOALS

We can plan, draft, and revise a research report.

OBJECTIVES

With some guidance and support from adults, use technology, including the Internet, to produce and publish writing as well as to interact and collaborate with others; demonstrate sufficient command of keyboarding skills to type a minimum of two pages in a single sitting.

Conduct short research projects that use several sources to build knowledge through investigation of different aspects of a topic.

Recall relevant information from experiences or gather relevant information from print and digital sources; summarize or paraphrase information in notes and finished work, and provide a list of sources.

FLEXIBLE MINILESSONS

Use these minilessons flexibly, in any order, based on the needs of your students. The minilessons can be used separately or in tandem with the Research Report lessons on pages T228–T243.

Use students' Check-In reflections and your observations to decide which students are ready to independently apply the lesson focus to their own writing. Use the tips in the Conferring Toolkit to provide additional guidance as you confer with students or meet with them in small groups.

FORMATIVE ASSESSMENT

STUDENT CHECK-IN

After the guide activity, have students reflect on their understanding of the lesson focus. Have them reflect using the Check-In routine.

Research Report

Evaluate Sources

Writers need to consider which print and digital sources are credible enough to use.

Model Write the following digital sources:

1. www.britannica.com
2. www.Thoreau-pond.com
3. www.Thoreau.library.ucsb.edu
4. www.loc.gov

Show students your process for deciding which Thoreau sources you might consider credible. (Credible: 1. encyclopedia. 3. .edu ending 4. .gov ending; Non-credible: 2. .com ending, information would need to be verified by other sources) Demonstrate how to click on each link to check that information is up-to-date, accurate, and relevant.

Guide Have partners evaluate online websites about Pluto.

Apply Have students evaluate sources for their research reports. Have them write and share what makes each a credible source.

Avoid Plagiarism

Writers can avoid plagiarism by summarizing, paraphrasing, or directly quoting information from a source.

Model Explain that plagiarism is the act of using the exact words or ideas from a source without giving credit to the original source. Model taking notes in your own words and summarizing or paraphrasing the central idea of a print or digital source. Show students when and how to include direct quotations and grade-appropriate citations or references.

Guide Have partners use a print or digital source to take notes in their own words.

Apply Ask students to write a paragraph that summarizes or paraphrases the information from their notes. Ask partners to exchange paragraphs and compare what they wrote to the original source material.

Conferring Toolkit

Evaluate Sources Help students differentiate between credible and non-credible sources for their research reports. Be sure to point out that some online sources ending in .org are public websites where people can edit the material. Students should avoid using these sites as a main source of information. Entries may end with references, some of which may be credible sources.

Avoid Plagiarism Support students in taking notes in their own words. Encourage them to reread the part of a source that they want to paraphrase so that they understand what the writer means and can restate the idea accurately in their own words. Point out that students can rearrange the structure of the sentences and use synonyms.

Write an Engaging Introduction

A strong introduction not only introduces the topic but also engages the audience.

Model Text Read aloud the first paragraph of "Gulf Spill Superheroes," on page 39 of the **Reading/Writing Companion**. As students listen, ask them to think about how the writer engages the reader. Say: *What I like about the first sentences of the introduction is how the writer focuses on superheroes before telling what happened to the Deepwater Horizon drilling platform. I'm also a fan of comic book superheroes, so that drew me in. The writer connected that information to the heroes of the Deepwater Horizon disaster.*

Guide Ask partners to write an engaging introduction for a research report on a native animal.

Apply Have students revise the introduction to their research reports to be more engaging. Ask partners to share their revisions.

Organize Information Chronologically

Writers who organize information chronologically present information in time order.

Model Text Read aloud the first two paragraphs of "Frederick Douglass: Freedom's Voice" on Unit 4 **Reading/Writing Companion** page 127. Point out how the writer uses dates and time-order words to explain what happened at the Massachusetts Anti-Slavery Society meeting chronologically. (In 1841, when he arrived, at first, once he got started, at the end of his speech) Ask students to consider why this is an effective way to organize this information.

Guide Have partners read page 128 and analyze how the writer uses a chronological text structure.

Apply Have students write a paragraph about a historical event using a chronological text structure. Ask partners to exchange paragraphs and underline the time-order words and phrases.

Use Domain-Specific Vocabulary

Writers of expository text often use domain-specific vocabulary to present information about their topic.

Model Text Explain that domain-specific vocabulary refers to words that are important to a particular subject or field of study. Point out the diagram on page 14 of the **Reading/Writing Companion** of "Changing Views of Earth." Tell students that the terms listed for each layer of Earth's atmosphere are examples of domain-specific vocabulary.

Guide Have partners read the first paragraph on page 14 and identify domain-specific words related to weather. (thermometer, barometer, weather patterns)

Apply Have partners write a paragraph about a planet in our solar system. Ask them to use domain-specific words.

Engaging Introduction Encourage students to write an introduction that makes the reader want to keep reading. Ask: *Who is your audience? What do they know about your topic? How can you draw in your audience and show them that you understand your topic?*

ELL **Text Structure: Organize Information Chronologically** Guide students in using time-order words and phrases to help readers understand a chronological text structure. Ask: *Which time-order words and phrases could you use to tell what happens next? Which words can help show the relationship between the events?*

ELL **Use Domain-Specific Words** After students choose a planet, encourage them to think of words about the planet or space that they could include in their paragraphs. Remind students to help their audience understand the meaning of domain-specific words by including a definition.

LEARNING GOALS

We can plan, draft, and revise a personal narrative.

OBJECTIVES

Orient the reader by establishing a situation and introducing a narrator and/or characters; organize an event sequence that unfolds naturally.

Use narrative techniques, such as dialogue, description, and pacing, to develop experiences and events or show the responses of characters to situations.

With guidance and support from peers and adults, develop and strengthen writing as needed by revising, editing, or rewriting.

FLEXIBLE MINILESSONS

Use these minilessons flexibly, in any order, based on the needs of your students. The minilessons can be used separately or in tandem with the Personal Narrative lessons on pages T244–T259.

Use students' Check-In reflections and your observations to decide which students are ready to independently apply the lesson focus to their own writing. Use the tips in the Conferring Toolkit to provide additional guidance as you confer with students or meet with them in small groups.

FORMATIVE ASSESSMENT

STUDENT CHECK-IN

After the guide activity, have students reflect on their understanding of the lesson focus. Have them reflect using the Check-In routine.

Personal Narrative

Express Thoughts and Feelings

Writers of personal narratives express their own thoughts and feelings about an experience.

Model Explain that writers recall their thoughts and feelings about an experience in order to express them in a realistic way. Share an event that has inspired you, for example: *I attended an Earth Day event at the local park. It really inspired me to take action to help protect our planet. Hearing so many groups talk about the litter problem in the community made me sad—until I realized I could do something about it.*

Guide Have partners take turns talking about a recent school event. Encourage them to include how they felt about the event.

Apply Ask students to write a paragraph about a time they forgot something important. Encourage them to include their thoughts and feelings. Have them share their paragraphs with a partner.

Establish a Point of View

Pronouns determine whether a piece of writing is written in a first- or third-person point of view.

Model Write the following sentences and model identifying the pronouns that indicate the point of view:

- I was excited about going to the Earth Day event with my family. (first-person point of view: *I, my*)

- Micha and Allie were excited. They were going to the Earth Day event with their family. (third-person point of view: *They, their*)

Point out how writing from a first-person point of view makes the writing more personal.

Guide Ask students to use the first sentence to write a paragraph from a first-person point of view. Have partners exchange paragraphs and underline the first-person pronouns.

Apply Have students revisit their personal narrative drafts and revise any paragraphs that are not written from a first-person point of view.

Conferring Toolkit

Voice: Express Thoughts and Feelings Encourage students to delve more deeply into their thoughts and feelings in order to be as specific as possible and to help their audience "relive" the experience along with them. Pose questions to help students' recall.

Establish Point of View If students struggle to identify point of view in their personal narratives, guide them in identifying first- or third-person pronouns. Say: *This sentence is written from a third-person point of view using* they. *Let's revise it to tell what happened from your point of view using the pronoun* I.

Write Strong Hooks

Personal narratives often begin with a strong hook that draws in the reader.

Model Text Encourage students to think about how they decide whether or not they want to continue reading a text. Read aloud the first paragraph of "Reading Between the Dots" on page 48 of the **Literature Anthology**. Point out how the writer immediately hooks you. (dialogue, description of setting, information about Braille) Tell students that writers might use questions, facts, quotations, anecdotes, examples, figurative language, or bold statements to hook readers.

Guide Ask pairs to rewrite the first paragraph on page 48 using a different hook. Have them share their revised introduction.

Apply Have students revise their personal narrative introductions using a stronger hook. Encourage them to experiment with different hooks and share them with a partner.

Include Dialogue

Writers of personal narratives often include dialogue to share what was said and help the reader feel as if they were experiencing the event.

Model Show students the impact of incorporating dialogue into your personal narrative. Write:

- "What do you think about having a day every month where everyone could come together and clean up the town?" I asked.

- "That's a wonderful idea!" exclaimed Aisha, smiling. "I know some people who would love to help you get that idea started!"

Discuss the difference in saying that you spoke to someone and including the exchange.

Guide Have partners write dialogue between two people and discuss what it reveals about each person.

Apply Have students revise a paragraph in their personal narratives to include strong dialogue. Ask them to share their revised paragraphs with a partner.

Use Time-Order Words and Phrases

Time-order words and phrases help transition between events in a personal narrative.

Model Text Tell students that words and phrases such as *at first, next, suddenly, then, after,* and *finally* can help their audience follow the flow of their personal narratives.

Read aloud the second paragraph of "Reading Between the Dots" on page 49 of the **Literature Anthology**. Ask students to listen for how the writer uses time-order words and phrases as transitions in her personal narrative. (on my first day, then) Talk with students about how these time-order words and phrases move along the sequence of events for readers.

Guide Have students read the third paragraph on page 49 and identify the time-order words or phrases the writer uses. (The next few days)

Apply Tell students to look over their personal narrative paragraph and to revise one paragraph by adding time-order words and phrases to clarify the sequence of events.

Write Strong Hooks Challenge students to experiment with writing several different openings: an anecdote, a quotation, a question, or a bold statement. Ask: *How can you make your opening even more engaging to hook your readers?*

ELL Include Dialogue Encourage students to replace *said* with more descriptive verbs that reveal how they or another person was speaking. Talk with students about the speaker's feelings and what they want their readers to take away from the dialogue.

ELL Use Time-Order Words and Phrases As necessary, guide students to select places in their personal narratives where they can add time-order words and/or phrases. Pose questions such as: *I was confused about when this happened? Did this happen before or after you ____?*

Clauses

LEARNING GOALS

We can identify main and subordinate clauses.

OBJECTIVES

Demonstrate command of the conventions of standard English grammar and usage when writing or speaking.

Explain the function of conjunctions, prepositions, and interjections in general and their function in particular sentences.

Use a comma to separate an introductory element from the rest of the sentence.

Produce simple, compound, and complex sentences.

DAILY LANGUAGE ACTIVITY

Use the online review for grammar, practice, and usage.

TEACH IN SMALL GROUP

You may wish to use the Talk About It activities during Small Group time.

 **Approaching Level, On Level,** and **Beyond Level** Pair students of different proficiency levels.

ELL According to their language proficiency, students should contribute to discussions by using short phrases, asking questions, and adding relevant details.

FORMATIVE ASSESSMENT

STUDENT CHECK-IN

After completing each Practice Book page, have partners share. Ask them to reflect using the Check-In routine.

Teach

Introduce Main and Subordinate Clauses

- A **clause** is a group of words that has a subject and a predicate.
- A **main clause** has one complete subject and one complete predicate and can stand alone as a sentence. *Max plays the guitar.*
- A **subordinate clause** cannot stand alone as a sentence. It is introduced by a **subordinating conjunction,** such as *if* or *because. I will sing if Max plays the guitar.*

Have partners discuss clauses using page 453 of the Grammar Handbook in Reading/Writing Workshop.

See **Practice Book** page 241 or online activity.

Teach

Review Main and Subordinate Clauses

Remind students that a main clause can stand alone as a sentence and a subordinate clause cannot.

Introduce Complex Sentences

- A **complex sentence** contains a main clause and a subordinate clause. *I asked Sam for help because he has fixed many computers.*
- A comma is used after an introductory subordinate clause. *Whenever my cousins visit, we play football.*

See **Practice Book** page 242.

Use Both Kinds of Clauses

Have partners take turns using a main clause to tell about a change that affected a friendship. The listening partner should repeat the sentence, adding a subordinate clause.

Add a Clause

Have partners write three subordinate clauses and trade them with another pair. One partner should read the clause aloud; the other should add a main clause to make a full sentence.

Mechanics and Usage

Appositives

- An appositive is a noun or noun phrase that explains or describes a noun or pronoun next to it.
- An appositive may come before or after a noun or a pronoun.
- Commas are used to set off many appositives. *Mrs. Kane, an archeologist, studies artifacts.*

See **Practice Book** page 243 or online activity.

Proofread and Write

Proofread

Have students correct errors in these sentences:

1. I read a book, while I was waiting for dance class. (book while)
2. If you go outside now you will be cold. (now,)
3. We missed the movie. Because we were late. (movie because)
4. When the competition was over Mrs. Sanders the principal announced the winner. (1: over,; 2: Sanders,; 3: principal,)

Write

Have students find a piece of their own writing in their writer's notebooks and correct any errors in punctuation of complex sentences.

See **Practice Book** page 244.

Assess and Reteach

Assess

Use the Daily Language Activity and **Practice Book** page 245 for assessment.

Rubric Use your online rubric to record student progress.

Reteach

Use the online **Grammar Handbook** page 453 and **Practice Book** pages 241–245 for additional reteaching. Remind students that it is important to use clauses correctly as they speak and write.

Check students' writing for use of these skills and listen for them in their speaking. Assign grammar revision assignments in their writer's notebooks as needed.

Pass it On

Have one group begin a story with a complex sentence and then pass the story to the next group. Continue until all groups have added a complex sentence. Then read aloud the story.

Story Summary

Have partners take turns summarizing a story the class has read, using at least one complex sentence. Ask the listening partner to identify the complex sentence and the subordinating conjunction.

Play an Appositive Quiz

Have students write down three main clauses about three famous people and place them in a pile. Students will take turns selecting a paper and adding an appositive.

LEARNING GOALS

We can identify and use complex sentences.

OBJECTIVES

Demonstrate command of the conventions of standard English grammar and usage when writing or speaking.

Explain the function of conjunctions, prepositions, and interjections in general and their function in particular sentences.

Produce simple, compound, and complex sentences.

Proofread sentences.

DAILY LANGUAGE ACTIVITY

Use the online review for grammar, practice, and usage.

TEACH IN SMALL GROUP

You may wish to use the Talk About It activities during Small Group time.

Approaching Level, On Level, and **Beyond Level** Pair students of different proficiency levels.

ELL According to their language proficiency, students should contribute to discussions by using short phrases, asking questions, and adding relevant details.

FORMATIVE ASSESSMENT

STUDENT CHECK-IN

After completing each Practice Book page, have partners share. Ask them to reflect using the Check-In routine.

Complex Sentences

Teach

Introduce Complex Sentences

- A **complex sentence** contains a main clause and a subordinate clause.
- Subordinate clauses are introduced by **subordinating conjunctions,** such as *while, because, if,* and *although. While I read, I took notes.*
- Subordinate clauses can also be introduced by **relative pronouns,** such as *who, whose, which, whom,* and *that,* and by **relative adverbs,** such as *where, when,* and *why. I'll meet you where we play ball. The shirt that is blue is in the closet.*

See **Practice Book** page 253 or online activity.

Teach

Review Complex Sentences

Remind students that a main clause can stand on its own while a subordinate clause cannot.

Introduce More Complex Sentences

- A subordinate clause in a complex sentence can come after a main clause. *I read the biography because it looked interesting.*
- A subordinate clause in a complex sentence can also come before a main clause, separated by a comma. *When we were out, our dog chewed the table.*

See **Practice Book** page 254.

Use Complex Sentences

Ask partners to use complex sentences to describe a change they have experienced. As they talk, students should listen to be sure they use at least one complex sentence.

Beat the Timer

Set a timer. Have groups write as many complex sentences as they can in five minutes. When the timer rings, groups stop writing. Groups review their sentences to make sure they are punctuated correctly.

Mechanics and Usage

Commas with Clauses

- An **essential clause** is necessary to identify a person or thing that is being described. It is not separated by commas. *The dog that was barking scared me.*
- A **nonessential clause** is not necessary to the meaning of the sentence. Commas are needed to set apart the clause. *My grandmother, who is ninety years old, swims three laps every day.*

See **Practice Book** page 255 or online activity.

OPTION

Proofread and Write

Proofread

Have students identify and correct errors in these sentences:

1. Because I was thirsty. I drank water. (thirsty, I)
2. I couldn't practice. Because I had homework. (practice because)
3. The runner, who won the race, was given a medal. (1: runner who; 2: race was)
4. Alice Green, who loves to bake made our snacks. (bake,)

Write

Have students find a piece of their own writing in their writer's notebooks and correct any errors in punctuation of clauses.

See **Practice Book** page 256.

OPTION

Assess and Reteach

Assess

Use the Daily Language Activity and **Practice Book** page 257 for assessment.

Rubric Use your online rubric to record student progress.

Reteach

Use the online **Grammar Handbook** page 453 and **Practice Book** pages 253–257 for additional reteaching. Remind students that it is important to use complex sentences correctly as they speak and write.

Check students' writing for use of these skills and listen for them in their speaking. Assign grammar revision assignments in their writer's notebooks as needed.

Write a Skit

Have groups write a brief skit. Each character must have one line that is a complex sentence. Have audience members raise hands when they hear a complex sentence.

Quiz a Friend

Have students write five complex sentences. Three of the sentences should have a subordinate clause before a main clause that purposely leaves out a comma. Partners exchange sentences and add the punctuation.

Name that Clause

Have groups write five sentences with essential clauses and five sentences with nonessential clauses. Groups read their sentences aloud to the class. The audience calls out "essential" or "nonessential."

LEARNING GOALS

We can identify and use adjectives.

OBJECTIVES

Demonstrate command of the conventions of standard English grammar and usage when writing or speaking.

Use underlining, quotation marks, or italics to indicate titles of works.

Order adjectives within sentences according to conventional patterns (e.g., a small red bag rather than a red small bag).

Proofread sentences.

DAILY LANGUAGE ACTIVITY

Use the online review for grammar, practice, and usage.

TEACH IN SMALL GROUP

You may wish to use the Talk About It activities during Small Group time.

Approaching Level, On Level, and **Beyond Level** Pair students of different proficiency levels.

ELL According to their language proficiency, students should contribute to discussions by using short phrases, asking questions, and adding relevant details.

FORMATIVE ASSESSMENT

STUDENT CHECK-IN

After completing each Practice Book page, have partners share. Ask them to reflect using the Check-In routine.

Adjectives

Teach

Introduce Adjectives

- An **adjective** modifies a noun or a pronoun.
- Adjectives tell what kind: *tall, shiny, round, slow.*
- Adjectives tell how many or how much: *ten, some, few.*
- **Demonstrative adjectives** tell which one: *this, that, these, those.*
- **Proper adjectives** should be capitalized: *Cuban food.*
- The **articles** *a, an,* and *the* are also adjectives.

See **Practice Book** page 265 or online activity.

Teach

Review Adjectives

Remind students that adjectives modify a noun or a pronoun. Proper adjectives should be capitalized.

Introduce Order of Adjectives

When more than one adjective is used to modify a noun, the adjectives must be listed in order.

- Opinions come first: *a good used book.*
- Size comes next: *a nice long scarf.*
- Age comes next: *a pretty new rug; a thick new rug.*
- Color comes next: *a pointy green hat; a long red scarf; an old blue pen.*

See **Practice Book** page 266.

Use Adjectives

Ask partners to list adjectives that describe a change in nature. Then have them use four of the adjectives in sentences to tell their partner about what happened.

Thesaurus Hunt

Have partners write three sentences that use adjectives to describe an animal. Ask them to read their sentences aloud. Then have partners exchange papers and replace the adjectives with new ones. Suggest they use a thesaurus.

Mechanics and Usage

Capitalization and Punctuation

- Acronyms are abbreviations pronounced as words. Some of them do not use capital letters: *radar, scuba*. Some of them, particularly those related to organizations, should always use capital letters: *NATO, WHO*.
- You underline or italicize titles from long pieces of work, such as books, and put quotation marks around smaller pieces of work, such as chapters. *I read the book Origami Yoda. "Flossy Returns" is the first chapter in my new book.*

See **Practice Book** page 267 or online activity.

Proofread and Write

Proofread

Have students correct errors in these sentences:

1. I ate at the spanish restaurant. (Spanish)
2. Use a green shiny bow for the presence. (1: shiny green; 2: presents)
3. My blue new bike is great. (new blue)
4. Nasa employs smart many astronauts. (1: NASA; 2. many smart)
5. I finally finished reading the book, "Winter Days." (*Winter Days*/Winter Days)

Write

Have students find a piece of their own writing in their writer's notebooks and correct any errors in their use of adjectives, acronyms, organizations, and titles.

See **Practice Book** page 268.

Assess and Reteach

Assess

Use the Daily Language Activity and **Practice Book** page 269 for assessment.

Rubric Use your online rubric to record student progress.

Reteach

Use the online **Grammar Handbook** page 466 and **Practice Book** pages 265–268 for additional reteaching. Remind students that it is important to use adjectives correctly as they speak and write.

Check students' writing for use of the skill and listen for it in their speaking. Assign grammar revision assignments in their writer's notebooks as needed.

Write Captions

Ask students to find a picture of a person or place and write a caption for it. Captions should include multiple adjectives, including one proper adjective. Have them show the pictures and read aloud their captions to the group.

Take a Guess

Have students complete this sentence: *I'm thinking of something that is ____, ____, and ____.* Ask them to put their sentences in a pile. Students will take turns choosing a sentence, reading it aloud, and guessing what is described.

Describe Nature

Have partners write sentences describing an area after a natural disaster. At least one sentence should include two adjectives that precede a noun. Ask pairs to exchange sentences and check the order of the adjectives.

Adjectives That Compare

LEARNING GOALS

We can identify and use adjectives that compare.

OBJECTIVES

Demonstrate command of the conventions of standard English grammar and usage when writing or speaking.

Form and use comparative and superlative adjectives and adverbs, and choose between them depending on what is to be modified.

Proofread sentences.

DAILY LANGUAGE ACTIVITY

Use the online review for grammar, practice, and usage.

TEACH IN SMALL GROUP

You may wish to use the Talk About It activities during Small Group time.

 **Approaching Level, On Level,** and **Beyond Level** Pair students of different proficiency levels.

● **ELL** According to their language proficiency, students should contribute to discussions by using short phrases, asking questions, and adding relevant details.

Teach

Adjectives That Compare

- **Comparative adjectives** compare two nouns or pronouns. Add *-er* to most adjectives to compare two items.
- **Superlative adjectives** compare more than two nouns or pronouns. Add *-est* to most adjectives to compare items.
- Drop the *e* in adjectives such as *pale* before adding *-er* or *-est*. Change the *y* to *i* for adjectives such as *sunny*.
- For one-syllable adjectives, such as *red*, double the final consonant.

See **Practice Book** page 277 or online activity.

Teach

Review Adjectives That Compare

Remind students that comparative adjectives compare two items and usually end in *-er*. Superlative adjectives compare more than two items and usually end in *-est*.

Introduce *More* and *Most*

- Use *more* in front of most long adjectives to compare two items. *This play is more exciting than the one we saw yesterday.*
- Use *most* in front of most long adjectives to compare more than two items. *This play is the most exciting of all.*

See **Practice Book** page 278.

Compare with Adjectives

Ask students to name one city, one athlete, and one movie. Have students share lists with a partner. Ask students to write sentences comparing the two cities, two athletes, and two movies.

Longer Adjectives

Provide partners with a list of longer adjectives, such as *glamorous, magnificent, and mysterious.* Have partners use each adjective to compare two places and then compare more than two places.

FORMATIVE ASSESSMENT

STUDENT CHECK-IN

After completing each Practice Book page, have partners share. Ask them to reflect using the Check-In routine.

Mechanics and Usage

Using *More* and *Most*

- Never add *-er* and *more* to the same adjective.
  Incorrect: *Amy's skit was more funnier than mine.*
  Correct: *Amy's skit was funnier than mine.*
- Never add *-est* and *most* to the same adjective.
  Incorrect: *Snowboarding is the most thrillingest sport in the Winter Olympics.*
  Correct: *Snowboarding is the most thrilling sport in the Winter Olympics.*

See **Practice Book** page 279 or online activity.

OPTION

Proofread and Write

Proofread

Have students correct errors in these sentences:

1. He is the most wisest man I know. (the wisest)
2. This stone is shiniest than that one, but the stone over there is the most shiniest of all. (1: shinier; 2: the shiniest)
3. Apple pie is more sweeter than pumpkin pie. (is sweeter)
4. This is the larger squash in the garden. (largest)

Write

Have students find a piece of their own writing in their writer's notebooks and correct any errors in comparative and superlative adjectives.

See **Practice Book** page 280.

OPTION

Assess and Reteach

Assess

Use the Daily Language Activity and **Practice Book** page 281 for assessment.

Reteach

Use the online **Grammar Handbook** page 467 and **Practice Book** pages 277–280 for additional reteaching. Remind students that it is important to use comparative adjectives correctly as they speak and write.

Check students' writing for use of the skill and listen for it in their speaking. Assign grammar revision assignments in their writer's notebooks as needed.

Debate

Have groups compare inventions from the early 1900s to modern inventions. Have groups debate the merits of the two inventions, using adjectives that compare.

Persuade Me

Have each student think of a favorite hobby. Then have groups compare their hobbies using adjectives that compare and write a persuasive paragraph about what the best hobby is and why.

Make a Commercial

Have groups think of a product that could be advertised on TV. Have them create a TV commercial for their product, using adjectives that compare. Ask groups to perform their commercials for the class.

LEARNING GOALS

We can identify and use irregular comparative and superlative adjectives.

OBJECTIVES

Demonstrate command of the conventions of standard English grammar and usage when writing or speaking.

Use knowledge of language and its conventions when writing, speaking, reading, or listening.

Form and use comparative and superlative adjectives and adverbs, and choose between them depending on what is to be modified.

DAILY LANGUAGE ACTIVITY

Use the online review for grammar, practice, and usage.

TEACH IN SMALL GROUP

You may wish to use the Talk About It activities during Small Group time.

Approaching Level, On Level, and **Beyond Level** Pair students of different proficiency levels.

ELL According to their language proficiency, students should contribute to the discussion by using short phrases, asking questions, and adding relevant details.

FORMATIVE ASSESSMENT

STUDENT CHECK-IN

After completing each Practice Book page, have partners share. Ask them to reflect using the Check-In routine.

Comparing With *Good* and *Bad*

Teach

Introduce Irregular Comparative and Superlative Forms; Comparing With *Good*

- **Comparatives** and **superlatives** are special forms of adjectives used to compare two or more things. They are usually formed by adding *-er* (comparatives) and *-est* (superlatives) to an adjective. *Joe can jump higher than Jerome. The team with the highest score wins.*
- *Good* has an irregular comparative and superlative form. Use *better* to compare two people, places, or things. Use *best* to compare more than two. *The movie is good. The play is better, but the book is the best.*

See **Practice Book** page 289 or online activity.

Teach

Review Comparing With *Good*

Review that the word *better* should be used to compare two people, places, or things. *Best* should be used to compare more than two people, places, or things.

Introduce Comparing With *Bad*

Present the following:

- Use *worse* to compare two people, places, or things. *A bee sting is worse than a bruise.*
- Use *worst* to compare more than two people, places, or things. *It was the worst storm in years.*
- *The traffic was bad. It was worse today than yesterday. It was the worst it had been all week.*

See **Practice Book** page 290.

Good, Better, Best

Have partners take turns telling about three related ideas about the environment. Have them describe them as *good, better,* and *best.* For example, students might compare three kinds of conservation efforts.

Bad, Worse, Worst

Have partners discuss three or more natural events that they would describe as *bad, worse,* and *worst.* For example, students might compare three weather patterns or three natural disasters. Ask volunteers to share their ideas.

Mechanics and Usage

Irregular Comparative Forms

Present the following:

- In comparisons, *better* and *best* are the irregular forms of the adjective *good*; *worse* and *worst* are the irregular forms of the adjective *bad*.
- The comparative form of *many* is *more;* the superlative form is *most*. The comparative form of *much* is *more;* the superlative form *is most. I like this book very much. I liked this book more than the other book. Of all the books I've read, I liked this book the most.*
- Never add *-er, -est, more,* or *most* to an irregular form.

See **Practice Book** page 291 or online activity.

Proofread and Write

Proofread

Have students correct errors in these sentences:

1. That was the worse movie I've ever seen! (worst)
2. Jake's essay was gooder, but Mark's was the better in the class. (1: good; 2: best)
3. Ben's headache was badder, and it got more worst as the day went on. (1: bad; 2: much worse)
4. Which do you like best: math or science? (better)

Write

Have students find a piece of their own writing in their writer's notebooks and check adjectives to use the correct comparative and superlative forms.

See **Practice Book** page 292.

Assess and Reteach

Assess

Use the Daily Language Activity and **Practice Book** page 293 for assessment.

Rubric Use your online rubric to record student progress.

Reteach

Use the online **Grammar Handbook** pages 467–468 and **Practice Book** pages 289–292 for additional reteaching.

Remind students that it is important to use irregular forms of comparative and superlative adjectives correctly as they speak and write.

Check students' writing for use of the skill and listen for it in their speaking. Assign grammar revision assignments in their writer's notebooks as needed.

Many, More, Most, Much

Have partners imagine they are environmentalists. Ask them to describe their work using *many, more, most,* and *much*. For example: *Many plants and animals are in danger. Most of them can be found living in rain forests. Much can be done to save them, but we need more people to help protect them.*

Pros and Cons

Ask partners to discuss how humans impact nature. Have them tell how human interaction is both good and bad for the environment. Encourage them to use *best, worst,* and other comparative adjectives as they speak.

Rank the Events

Display a list of five natural events, both good and bad. Ask students to rank them from 1 to 5, with 1 being the *best* to experience in their opinion. Have partners discuss their lists, using this week's comparatives and superlatives.

Suffixes

LEARNING GOALS

We can read, sort, and use spelling words with suffixes.

OBJECTIVES

Spell grade-appropriate words correctly, consulting references as needed.

Use common base words and affixes as clues to the meaning of a word.

DIFFERENTIATED SPELLING

Go online for Dictation Sentences for differentiated spelling lists.

On Level and **ELL**

serious	comfortable	microscopic
furious	finally	allergic
eruption	destruction	scientific
usually	apparently	safety
direction	completely	activity
position	eventually	sickness
forgetful	carefully	

Review distance, ambulance, substance
Challenge aquatic, mathematics

Approaching Level

serious	comfortable	electric
furious	finally	allergic
eruption	usually	pacific
happily	destruction	safety
direction	sadly	activity
position	eventually	sickness
forgetful	carefully	

Beyond Level

seriously	comfortably	allergic
furiously	subconscious	scientific
aquatic	destruction	enjoyable
eruption	unforgettable	charitable
sensible	questionable	microscopic
eventually	mathematics	argument
forgetful	improvement	

FORMATIVE ASSESSMENT

STUDENT CHECK-IN

After completing each Practice Book page, have partners share. Ask them to reflect using the Check-In routine.

Assess Prior Knowledge

Read the spelling words aloud, emphasizing the suffix in each word.

Point out the suffixes in *erupt<u>ion</u>*, *allerg<u>ic</u>*, and *finally*. Draw a line under the suffix as you say the word. Explain that a suffix is one or more letters added to the end of a word. A suffix changes the meaning and part of speech of the base word.

Demonstrate sorting spelling words according to the part of speech determined by the suffix. Sort a few words with the same part of speech. Ask students to name other everyday words with these suffixes.

Use the Dictation Sentences from Lesson 5 to give the pretest. Say the underlined word, read the sentence, and repeat the word. Have students write the words. Then have students check their papers.

See **Practice Book** page 246 for a pretest.

Spiral Review

Review words with the suffixes *-ance* and *-ence*. Read each sentence below, repeat the review word, and have students write the word.

1. The <u>distance</u> is not far.
2. An <u>ambulance</u> arrived at the scene.
3. An unknown <u>substance</u> was leaking from the car.

Have students trade papers and check their spellings.

Challenge Words

Review this week's suffixes. Read each sentence below, repeat the challenge word, and have students write the word.

1. The whale is an <u>aquatic</u> mammal.
2. Ryan loves <u>mathematics</u> because he enjoys working with numbers.

Have students check their spellings and write the words in their writer's notebooks.

Word Sorts

OPEN SORT

Have students cut apart the **Spelling Word Cards** in the Online Resource Book and initial the back of each card. Have them read the words aloud with partners. Then have partners do an open sort. Have them record their sorts in their writer's notebooks.

PATTERN SORT

Use the boldfaced words on Spelling Word Cards to complete Lesson 1 pattern sort. Explain that some suffixes change final consonant sounds from /t/ or /k/ to /sh/. Have partners compare and check sorts. See **Practice Book** pages 247 and 247A-B for differentiated practice.

Word Meanings

Have students copy the definitions below into their notebooks. Say the definitions aloud. Then ask students to write the spelling word that matches each definition.

1. an illness or disease (sickness)
2. an explosion (eruption)
3. totally; entirely (completely)

Challenge students to create definitions for their other spelling, review, or challenge words. Have partners share their definitions and match words to the correct definitions.

- Use *musician* to model saying and spelling a word with a suffix that changes the final consonant sound from /k/ to /sh/ when *-ian* is added.
- Have students say, spell, and create definitions for the words *electric* and *electrician*.

See **Practice Book** page 248 or online activity.

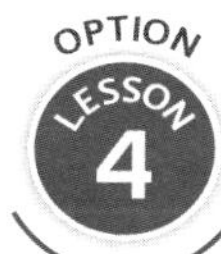

Proofread and Write

Write these sentences on the board. Have students circle and correct each misspelled word. Ask them to use a print or a digital dictionary to check and correct their spellings.

1. Micrascopic creatures are studied in sientific labs. (Microscopic, scientific)
2. Gene finaly found an aktivity he enjoys. (finally, activity)
3. It is important to think about the safetey of people who are alergic to peanuts. (safety, allergic)
4. Dad usally has a great sense of direcshun. (usually, direction)

Error Correction Remind students that the suffix is often a separate syllable added to the base word. Some suffixes, such as *-ic*, affect the spelling of the base word.

Apply to Writing Have students correct a piece of their own writing.

See **Practice Book** page 249.

Lesson 5 Assess

Use the Dictation Sentences for the posttest. Have students list the misspelled words in their writer's notebooks. Look for students' use of these words in their writings.

See **Practice Book** page 246 for a posttest. Use page 250 for review.

Dictation Sentences

1. He had a serious look on his face.
2. Mom was furious when the cat broke the vase.
3. The volcanic eruption happened 20 years ago.
4. Kevin usually eats lunch at noon.
5. We went in the wrong direction.
6. The switch was in the "on" position.
7. My sister is very forgetful.
8. My bed is very comfortable.
9. I finally finished the essay.
10. The fire caused a lot of destruction.
11. She apparently left the building.
12. I completely lost track of time.
13. He will eventually finish his work.
14. I packed the box very carefully.
15. The microscopic ants were hard to see.
16. Dad is allergic to cats.
17. It was a scientific study.
18. Safety is my number one concern.
19. My favorite activity is running.
20. Molly's sickness lasted for days.

Have students self-correct their tests.

SPEED SORT

Have partners do a speed sort to see who is fastest. Then have them do a word hunt in this week's readings to find words with the suffixes found in this week's words. Have them record the words in their word study notebooks.

BLIND SORT

Have partners do a blind sort: one reads a Spelling Word Card; the other tells under which part of speech it belongs. Have partners compare and discuss their sorts. Then have partners play Go Fish with the cards, using parts of speech as the "fish."

Homophones

LEARNING GOALS

We can read, sort, and use homophones.

OBJECTIVES

Spell grade-appropriate words correctly, consulting references as needed.

DIFFERENTIATED SPELLING

Go online for Dictation Sentences for differentiated spelling lists.

On Level and ELL

sweet	waist	presence
suite	manor	presents
pray	manner	council
prey	pier	counsel
poll	peer	stationery
pole	currant	stationary
waste	current	

Review eruption, forgetful, allergic
Challenge kernel, colonel

Approaching Level

sweet	waist	presents
suite	manner	presence
peel	manor	choose
peal	pier	chews
poll	peer	flower
pole	you're	flour
waste	your	

Beyond Level

sweet	aloud	presents
suite	manner	presence
principal	manor	council
principle	current	counsel
bazaar	currant	stationery
bizarre	pier	stationary
allowed	peer	

FORMATIVE ASSESSMENT

STUDENT CHECK-IN

After completing each Practice Book page, have partners share. Ask them to reflect using the Check-In routine.

Lesson 6 Assess Prior Knowledge

Read the spelling words aloud.

Explain that homophones are words that have the same pronunciation but different spellings and meanings. Point out the spellings and meanings for *sweet* ("pleasant tasting") and *suite* ("set of rooms").

Demonstrate sorting the spelling words by part of speech. Some spelling words may have more than one part of speech. For example, *current* can be both a noun and an adjective. Ask students to name some other everyday words that are homophones.

Use the Dictation Sentences from Lesson 10 to give the pretest. Say the underlined word, read the sentence, and repeat the word. Have students write the words. Then have students check their papers.

See **Practice Book** page 258 for a pretest.

Option Lesson 7 Spiral Review

Review the suffixes in *eruption, forgetful,* and *allergic*. Read each sentence below, repeat the review word, and have students write the word.

1. The eruption lasted only for a few minutes.
2. James makes "to do" lists because he is forgetful.
3. People who have hay fever are allergic to certain plants.

Have students trade papers and check their spellings.

Challenge Words

Review homophones. Read each sentence below, repeat the challenge word, and have students write the word.

1. Every kernel of the popcorn popped.
2. The colonel gave strict orders.

Have students check and correct their spellings and write the words in their writer's notebooks.

Word Sorts

MULTIMODAL

OPEN SORT

Have students cut apart the **Spelling Word Cards** in the Online Resource Book and initial the back of each card. Have them read the words aloud with partners. Then have partners do an open sort and record their sorts in their writer's notebooks.

PATTERN SORT

Complete the pattern sort from Lesson 6. Point out the different spellings in the homophones and their parts of speech. Partners should check their sorts. Alternatively, have partners use **Practice Book** page 259. See Practice Book 259A and 259B for differentiated practice.

Word Meanings

Write *peer* and *pier* on the board and model how to create a word association list with each word. For example: *peer—friend, pal, buddy; pier—dock, fishing, wooden.*

1. Ask students to choose a pair of homophones and make similar lists for each word.
2. Have students share their lists with the class.
3. Challenge students to use the pair of homophones in the same sentence so that the meaning of each word is clear. For example: *I fished from the pier with my peer from school.*

Have students write their word groups and example sentences in their writer's notebooks.

See **Practice Book** page 260 or online activity.

Proofread and Write

Write these sentences on the board. Have students circle and correct each misspelled word. Have students use a print or a digital dictionary to check and correct their spellings.

1. Lita's manor is both suite and kind. (manner, sweet)
2. Last night the city counsel met to discuss topics of currant interest. (council, current)
3. Pat listed the presence he wanted for his birthday on a sheet of stationary. (presents, stationery)
4. John dropped his fishing poll from the peer. (pole, pier)

Error Correction Remind students that they should use context clues to determine which homophone should be used.

Apply to Writing Have students correct a piece of their own writing.

See **Practice Book** page 261.

Assess

Use the Dictation Sentences for the posttest. Have students list the misspelled words in their writer's notebooks. Look for students' use of these words in their writings. See **Practice Book** page 258 for a posttest. Use page 262 for review.

Dictation Sentences

1. The orange tasted sweet.
2. Our hotel room was a suite.
3. We decided to pray for rain.
4. The badger let his prey escape.
5. I took a poll of student opinions.
6. The flag hung on a pole.
7. Let's not waste any time.
8. These slacks are too tight around the waist.
9. The manor house was grand.
10. Jay's manner of speaking is formal.
11. The boat docked at the pier.
12. Hector is my peer.
13. A currant is a kind of berry.
14. The current carried the boat.
15. The presence of friends is comforting.
16. Aunt Beth sends us presents.
17. The town council meets today.
18. Her counsel is fair and wise.
19. Mom writes letters on colorful stationery.
20. The guard was stationary.

Have students self-correct their tests.

SPEED SORT

Have partners do a speed sort to see who is fastest. Then have them do a word hunt in this week's readings to find homophones. Have them record the words in their writer's notebooks.

BLIND SORT

Have partners do a blind sort: one reads a Spelling Word Card and uses the word in a sentence; the other spells the homophone and sorts it by its part of speech. Have partners take turns until both have sorted all their words.

LEARNING GOALS

We can read, sort, and use spelling words with prefixes.

OBJECTIVES

Spell grade-appropriate words correctly, consulting references as needed.

Use common base words and affixes as clues to the meaning of a word.

DIFFERENTIATED SPELLING

Go online for Dictation Sentences for differentiated spelling lists.

On Level and **ELL**

prewash	disconnect	disobey
disable	preview	dishonest
discolor	prejudge	injustice
mistaken	misjudge	disapprove
preheats	discomfort	inexpensive
mistrust	dismount	indefinite
incorrect	misunderstand	

Review presence, stationary, current

Challenge prehistoric, misbehave

Approaching Level

prewash	dislike	disobey
disable	preview	dishonest
discolor	pretest	instep
mistaken	mislead	disagree
preheats	discomfort	indirect
misplace	dismount	invisible
incorrect	misunderstand	

Beyond Level

preview	prerequisite	discontent
disable	disconnect	dishearten
dismantle	inaccurate	injustice
mistaken	misjudge	disapprove
dismount	predisposition	inexpensive
mistrust	discomfort	indefinite
prejudge	misunderstand	

FORMATIVE ASSESSMENT

STUDENT CHECK-IN

After completing each Practice Book page, have partners share. Ask them to reflect using the Check-In routine.

Prefixes

Assess Prior Knowledge

Read the spelling words aloud, emphasizing the prefix in each word.

Point out the prefixes in *disobey, mistrust, incorrect,* and *preview.* Pronounce each word while drawing a line under the prefix. Explain that a prefix is a group of letters added to the beginning of a word. A prefix changes the meaning of the base word.

Demonstrate sorting spelling words by prefix. Sort a few words, pointing out the prefix as each word is sorted. Ask students to name other words with the same prefixes.

Use the Dictation Sentences from Lesson 5 to give the pretest. Say the underlined word, read the sentence, and repeat the word. Have students write the words. Then have students check their papers.

See **Practice Book** page 270 for a pretest.

Spiral Review

Review the homophones *presence, stationary,* and *current.* Read each sentence below, repeat the review word, and have students write it.

1. His friend's presence was comforting.
2. Steven's bike is parked in the garage, stationary for the winter.
3. The current issue of the magazine shows the president on the cover.

Have students trade papers and check their spellings.

Challenge Words

Review this week's prefixes. Read each sentence below, repeat the challenge word, and have students write the words.

1. Dinosaurs lived in prehistoric times.
2. If the puppies misbehave, do not give them any treats.

Have students check their spellings and write the words in their writer's notebooks.

OPEN SORT

Have students cut apart the **Spelling Word Cards** in the Online Resource Book and initial the back of each card. Have them read the words aloud with partners. Then have partners do an open sort. Have them record their sorts in their writer's notebooks.

PATTERN SORT

Complete the pattern sort from Lesson 1. Point out the different prefixes. Partners should check their sorts. Alternatively, have partners use **Practice Book** page 271. See pages 271A and 271B for differentiated practice.

Word Meanings

Have students copy the three analogies below into their writer's notebooks. Say the sentences aloud. Then ask students to fill in the blanks with a spelling word.

1. *Incorrect* is to *mistaken* as ____ is to *cheap*. (inexpensive)
2. *Disable* is to *enable* as ____ is to *right*. (incorrect)
3. *Prewash* is to *clothes* as ____ is to *food*. (preheat)

Challenge students to create analogies for their other spelling, review, or challenge words. Encourage them to use synonyms and antonyms. Have students share their analogies with a partner.

See **Practice Book** page 272 or online activity.

Proofread and Write

Write these sentences on the board. Have students circle and correct each misspelled word. Have them use a print or a digital dictionary to check and correct their spellings.

1. Don't misjuge the amount of detergent to use, or you could disscolor the clothes. (misjudge, discolor)
2. Neil told Jana to disconect the incorreckt cord. (disconnect, incorrect)
3. You will not be able to preewash the clothes if you disabel the machine. (prewash, disable)
4. Since she has never been dishonnest, you have no reason to misstrust her. (dishonest, mistrust)

Error Correction When spelling words with prefixes, students may pay special attention to the spelling of the prefix and misspell the base word. Remind students to pay attention to both parts of the word.

See **Practice Book** page 273.

Assess

Use the Dictation Sentences for the posttest. Have students list the misspelled words in their writer's notebooks. Look for students' use of these words in their writings.

See **Practice Book** page 270 for a posttest. Use page 274 for review.

Dictation Sentences

1. Soak it in water to prewash it.
2. We had to disable the machine.
3. The sun can discolor clothes.
4. She admitted she was mistaken.
5. Mom preheats the oven before baking.
6. People seem to mistrust him.
7. The answer was incorrect.
8. They can disconnect the wires.
9. I saw a preview of the movie.
10. It's unfair to prejudge people.
11. Don't misjudge her strength.
12. I cannot bear this discomfort.
13. Quickly dismount the horse.
14. They misunderstand her actions.
15. James will not disobey the rules.
16. He regretted being dishonest.
17. Segregation laws are an example of injustice.
18. They disapprove of video games.
19. The meal was inexpensive.
20. Our plans are still indefinite.

Have students self-correct their tests.

SPEED SORT

Have partners do a speed sort to see who is fastest and then compare and discuss their sorts. Then have them do a word hunt in this week's readings to find words with prefixes. Ask them to record the words in their writer's notebooks.

BLIND SORT

Have partners do a blind sort: one reads a Spelling Word Card; the other tells under which prefix it belongs. Then have partners use one set of word cards to play Concentration. Have them match words with the same prefix.

Suffixes *-less* and *-ness*

LEARNING GOALS

We can read, sort, and use spelling words with the suffixes *-less* and *-ness*.

OBJECTIVES

Use combined knowledge of all letter-sound correspondences, syllabication patterns, and morphology to read accurately unfamiliar multisyllabic words in context and out of context.

DIFFERENTIATED SPELLING

Go online for Dictation Sentences for differentiated spelling lists.

On Level and **ELL**

sadness	hopeless	meaningless
gladness	fearless	emptiness
needless	weakness	forgiveness
harmless	bottomless	motionless
darkness	foolishness	ceaseless
fullness	fondness	fierceness
stillness	effortless	

Review disobey, mistrust, preview
Challenge weightlessness, thoughtlessness

Approaching Level

sadness	hopeless	restless
gladness	fearless	happiness
needless	weakness	forgiveness
harmless	bottomless	motionless
darkness	foolishness	tireless
fullness	fondness	goodness
stillness	effortless	

Beyond Level

vastness	merciless	meaningless
eeriness	sleeveless	emptiness
breathless	weakness	forgiveness
harmless	bottomless	motionless
ceaseless	foolishness	peacefulness
numbness	fondness	fierceness
stillness	effortless	

FORMATIVE ASSESSMENT

STUDENT CHECK-IN

After completing each Practice Book page, have partners share. Ask them to reflect using the Check-In routine.

Assess Prior Knowledge

Read the spelling words aloud, emphasizing the suffix in each word.

Point out the suffixes in *fearless* and *stillness*. Pronounce each word and draw a line under the suffix as you draw out its sound. Explain that a suffix changes the meaning, and sometimes the part of speech, of the base word.

Demonstrate sorting spelling words by the suffixes *-less* and *-ness*, using the key words *fearless* and *stillness*. Sort a few words, pointing out the suffix as each word is sorted. Ask students to name other words with the same suffixes.

Use the Dictation Sentences from Lesson 10 to give the pretest. Say the underlined word, read the sentence, and repeat the word. Have students write the words. Then have students check their papers.

See **Practice Book** page 282 for a pretest.

Spiral Review

Review the prefixes in *disobey, mistrust,* and *preview*. Read each sentence below, repeat the review word, and have students write the words.

1. Terry does not disobey her coach.
2. People mistrust Brent because he sometimes tells lies.
3. I saw a movie preview.

Have students trade papers and check their spellings.

Challenge Words

Read each sentence below, repeat the challenge word, and have students write the words.

1. The astronaut adapted to weightlessness in space.
2. Mira's thoughtlessness kept everyone waiting.

Have students check and correct their spellings and write the words in their writer's notebooks.

OPEN SORT

Have students cut apart the **Spelling Word Cards** in the Online Resource Book and initial the back of each card. Have them read the words aloud with partners. Then have partners do an open sort. Have them record their sorts in their writer's notebooks.

PATTERN SORT

Complete the pattern sort from Lesson 6. Point out the suffixes *-less* and *-ness*. Partners should check their sorts. Alternatively, have students use **Practice Book** page 283. See pages 283A and 283B for differentiated practice.

Word Meanings

Have students copy the three cloze sentences below into their writer's notebooks. Say the sentences aloud. Then ask students to fill in the blanks with a spelling word.

1. The family set up their tent before ____ began to fall. (darkness)
2. Although the spider was ____, Maribel was still afraid of it. (harmless)
3. The deer in the woods was ____ for a moment and then ran away. (motionless)

Challenge students to create cloze sentences using their other spelling, review, or challenge words. Have students post their statements on the board.

See **Practice Book** page 284 or online activity.

Proofread and Write

Write these sentences on the board. Have students circle and correct each misspelled word. Have students use a print or a digital dictionary to check and correct their spellings.

1. A botommless cup of coffee is my mom's greatest weekness. (bottomless, weakness)
2. The stilness of the room filled Mary with saddness. (stillness, sadness)
3. Neadless to say, the soldiers were feerless. (needless, fearless)
4. I asked foregiveness for my foolishnness. (forgiveness, foolishness)

Error Correction Remind students that the suffixes *-less* and *-ness* are separate syllables in the spelling words. Students should segment the words syllable by syllable in order to spell them, maintaining the spelling of the suffix.

Apply to Writing Have students correct a piece of their own writing.

See **Practice Book** page 285.

Assess

Use the Dictation Sentences for the posttest. Have students list the misspelled words in their writer's notebooks. Look for students' use of these words in their writings.

See **Practice Book** page 282 for a posttest. Use page 286 for review.

Dictation Sentences

1. Grandpa cried tears of sadness.
2. Luther experienced gladness when his daughter was born.
3. Her worries were needless.
4. He flicked the harmless fly.
5. The wolf hunted in darkness.
6. I love the moon's fullness.
7. The stillness was calming.
8. The situation is not hopeless.
9. The skydivers were fearless.
10. The rope showed no weakness.
11. His stomach is a bottomless pit.
12. There's no time for foolishness.
13. She smiled with fondness.
14. Lena makes the dance look effortless.
15. His work was meaningless.
16. The room's emptiness is scary.
17. She asked for my forgiveness.
18. He stood motionless in fear.
19. The fighting was ceaseless.
20. The lion's fierceness is unmatched.

Have students self-correct their tests.

SPEED SORT

Have partners do a speed sort to see who is fastest and then compare and discuss their sorts. Then have them brainstorm other words with *-less* and *-ness*. Have students record the words in their writer's notebooks.

BLIND SORT

Have partners do a blind sort: one reads a Spelling Word Card; the other tells under which key word it belongs. Then have students use their word cards to play Concentration. Have them match words with the same suffix.

LEARNING GOALS

We can read, sort, and use spelling words with the suffix *-ion*.

OBJECTIVES

Spell grade-appropriate words correctly, consulting references as needed.

DIFFERENTIATED SPELLING

Go online for Dictation Sentences for differentiated spelling lists.

On Level and ELL

impress	confusion	estimate
impression	correct	estimation
elect	correction	decorate
election	discuss	decoration
locate	discussion	exhaust
location	concentrate	exhaustion
confuse	concentration	

Review hopeless, fearless, forgiveness
Challenge conclude, conclusion

Approaching Level

impress	confusion	estimate
impression	correct	estimation
elect	correction	relate
election	discuss	relation
locate	discussion	direct
location	decorate	direction
confuse	decoration	

Beyond Level

impress	estimation	appreciate
impression	inflect	appreciation
predict	inflection	concentrate
prediction	exhaust	concentration
discuss	exhaustion	confuse
discussion	motivate	confusion
estimate	motivation	

FORMATIVE ASSESSMENT

STUDENT CHECK-IN

After completing each Practice Book page, have partners share. Ask them to reflect using the Check-In routine.

Suffix *-ion*

Assess Prior Knowledge

Read the spelling words aloud. Segment the word's syllables by syllable.

Point out the *-ion* suffix in the word *impress<u>ion</u>*. Draw a line under the spelling pattern. Point out that students should consider the suffix *-ion* and the base word in spelling the entire word. When dealing with words that end in *e,* they must first remove the *e* before adding *-ion.* Repeat with the word *decora<u>tion</u>.*

Demonstrate sorting the spelling words by part of speech. Discuss any words that have unexpected pronunciations.

Use the Dictation Sentences from Lesson 5 to give the pretest. Say the underlined word, read the sentence, and repeat the word. Have students write the words and then check their papers.

See **Practice Book** page 294 for a pretest.

Spiral Review

Review the *-less and -ness* suffixes in *hopeless, fearless,* and *forgiveness.* Read each sentence below, repeat the review word, and have students write the word.

1. The situation was <u>hopeless</u>.
2. Alex is a <u>fearless</u> adventurer.
3. Joaquin asked Millie for <u>forgiveness</u>.

Have partners trade papers and check their spellings.

Challenge Words Review the genre study words with the *-ion* suffix. Read each sentence below, repeat the challenge word, and have students write the word.

1. The show will <u>conclude</u> at 8:00.
2. The book's <u>conclusion</u> was shocking!

Have students check and correct their spellings and write the words in their writer's notebooks.

Word Sorts

OPEN SORT

Have students cut apart the **Spelling Word Cards** in the Online Resource Book and initial the back of each card. Have them read the words aloud with partners. Then have partners do an open sort. Have them record their sorts in their writer's notebooks.

PATTERN SORT

Complete the pattern sort from Lesson 1. Point out the different parts of speech. Partners should check their sorts. Alternatively, have partners use **Practice Book** page 295. See Practice Book pages 295A and 295B for differentiated practice.

Word Meanings

Have students copy the four definitions below into their writer's notebooks. Say the definitions aloud. Then ask students to write the spelling word that each one refers to.

1. to focus or think intensely (concentrate)
2. to fix errors (correct)
3. conversation; a talk (discussion)
4. tiredness; fatigue (exhaustion)

Challenge students to write definitions for their other spelling, review, or challenge words. Have them write the definitions in their writer's notebooks.

See **Practice Book** page 296 or online activity.

Proofread and Write

Write these sentences on the board. Have students circle and correct each misspelled word. Have students use a print or a digital dictionary to make corrections.

1. Nina decided to deccorate her house to make a good impresion on her visitors. (decorate, impression)
2. There was much confussion during the elektion. (confusion, election)
3. I couldn't conncentrate during our discusion. (concentrate, discussion)
4. The city planners met to disscus the locattion of the new park. (discuss, location)

Error Correction Remind students that for words that end in *e,* they must first remove the *e* before adding *-ion.*

Apply to Writing Have students correct a piece of their own writing.

See **Practice Book** page 297.

Assess

Use the Dictation Sentences for the posttest. Have students list the misspelled words in their writer's notebooks. Look for students' use of these words in their writings.

See **Practice Book** page 294 for a posttest. Use page 298 for review.

Dictation Sentences

1. She wants to impress the teacher.
2. He made a good first impression.
3. We will elect new officers.
4. Everyone voted in the election.
5. Try to locate Canada on the map.
6. We know the whale's location.
7. People always confuse the twins.
8. The noise added to the confusion.
9. Please correct the mistakes.
10. She made the correction in red.
11. Let's discuss the problem.
12. Jake led a book discussion.
13. Concentrate during the test.
14. Chess requires concentration.
15. Our estimate was not even close.
16. Their estimation was too high.
17. I want to decorate the classroom.
18. The wreath is a nice decoration.
19. Running uphill will exhaust us.
20. I felt exhaustion after the race.

Have students self-correct their tests.

SPEED SORT

Have partners do a speed sort to see who is fastest. Then have them do a word hunt in this week's readings to find words with the same vowel sounds as the spelling words. Have them record the words in their writer's notebook.

BLIND SORT

Have partners do a blind sort: one reads a Spelling Word Card; the other tells under which part of speech it belongs. Have students explain how they sorted the words. Then have partners use two sets of cards to play Concentration, matching words with the same part of speech.

From Good to Great

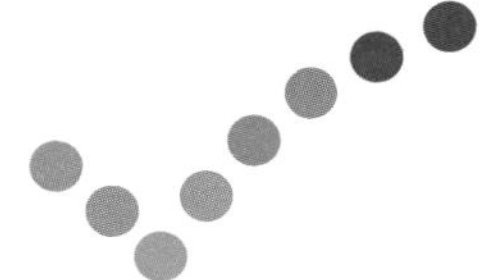

OBJECTIVES

Use a variety of transitional words, phrases, and clauses to manage the sequence of events.

Provide a conclusion that follows from the narrated experiences or events.

With guidance and support from peers and adults, develop and strengthen writing as needed by revising.

Report on a topic or text or present an opinion, sequencing ideas logically and using appropriate facts and relevant, descriptive details to support main ideas or themes; speak clearly at an understandable pace.

DIGITAL TOOLS

To help students improve their writing, use the Online Grammar Handbook, Digital writing activities, and Writing Center Activity Cards.

PORTFOLIO CHOICE

Ask students to select one finished piece of writing from their writing portfolio. Have them consider a piece that they would like to improve.

Teacher Conference Choose students to conference with, or have them talk with a partner about their writing to figure out one thing that can be improved. As you conference with each student:

- ✓ Identify at least one or two things you like about the writing. *The descriptive details you included in the first paragraph help me visualize ______.*
- ✓ Focus on how the student uses the writing trait. *The supporting details you used help me understand ______.*
- ✓ Make concrete suggestions for revisions.
- ✓ Have students work on their writing and then meet with you to review their progress.

Use the following strategies and tips to provide specific direction to focus writers.

✓ Purpose, Focus, and Organization

- Underline the central idea. If the central idea is missing, point out that the writing is missing its central idea. *What is the central idea? How and where can you add it to your writing?*
- Underline a section that can be revised to better fit the task, purpose, or audience. Provide specific suggestions. *Look at the order of these ideas. Would your reader understand the sequence of events? How can you add transition words to help your reader understand?*
- Have students reread their writing and think of a more satisfying conclusion. *Is your conclusion as interesting as it could be? Can you think of something that will help the audience understand the end of the writing?*
- Ask students to choose one thing that can be improved. *Where can you add a transition word or phrase to connect ideas?*

Have students choose one sentence and read it aloud. *How can you make this sentence more clear? What words can you replace to help your reader understand the meaning better?*

✓ Evidence and Elaboration

- Point out a place where relevant evidence could be added. *Reread the information from the reliable sources and find evidence you can use to support your central idea that ______.*

- Circle a word that could be more vivid. Provide specific suggestions. *Can you think of a word that appeals to the senses?*
- If the student includes a detail that is not specific or an incorrect fact, say: *How can this detail be more specific? Where did you find this fact? Check the sources again for a more specific detail and a correct fact.*
- Read the writing and target one sentence for revision. *This sentence provides evidence from a source, but it's not quoted exactly. Check the source to make sure the quote is copied correctly. Name the source and use quotation marks.*

Help students check that they have included the sources they used for evidence and elaboration. *Do you correctly give the titles of the sources? Is the punctuation correct?*

✓ Conventions

- Circle any incorrect pronouns or antecedents. Read them aloud with the student. *Is this pronoun and its antecedent in agreement? How can you rewrite the sentence so that they are correct?*
- Underline two sentences that could be combined. *How can these sentences be combined to make the writing clearer?*
- Read the writing and target a fragment or a run-on sentence. *Is this a complete sentence? What is missing? Is this sentence too long? Provide suggestions on how to correct a run-on sentence.*

Have students read their writing aloud. Ask them to identify any sentences that are fragments or run-ons. *Does this seem correct? Is there another way to write the sentence?*

✓ Apply the Rubric

COLLABORATE Have students apply the rubrics as they revise their writing. Ask them to read their writing to a partner. Use these sentence starters to focus their discussion:

The central idea is clear because . . .

I liked your use of description and sequence because . . .

I learned a lot about your topic because . . .

HABITS OF LEARNING

I am a critical thinker and problem solver. Explain to students that rereading helps writers evaluate their sources and determine if the information provided by them supports their central idea. Have them ask themselves: *Do the facts, examples, and evidence from my sources relate to my central idea?*

Notes

EXTEND, CONNECT, AND ASSESS

Extend

Reading Digitally

Reader's Theater

Level Up with Leveled Readers

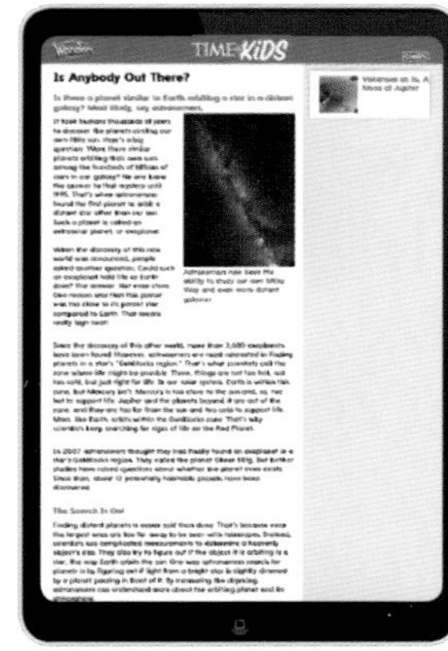

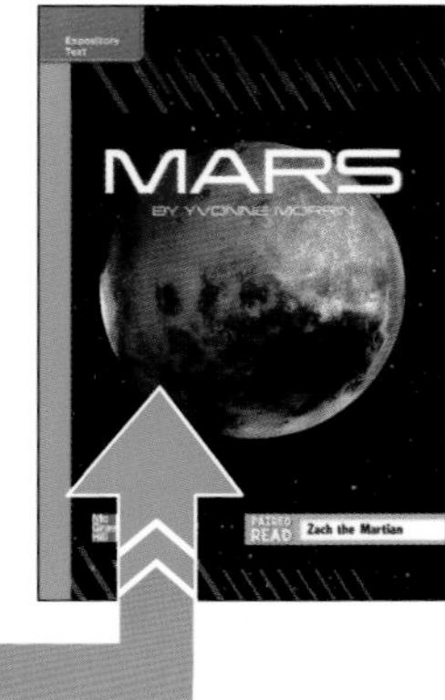

Connect

Connect to Science

Connect to Social Studies

Content Area Reading Options

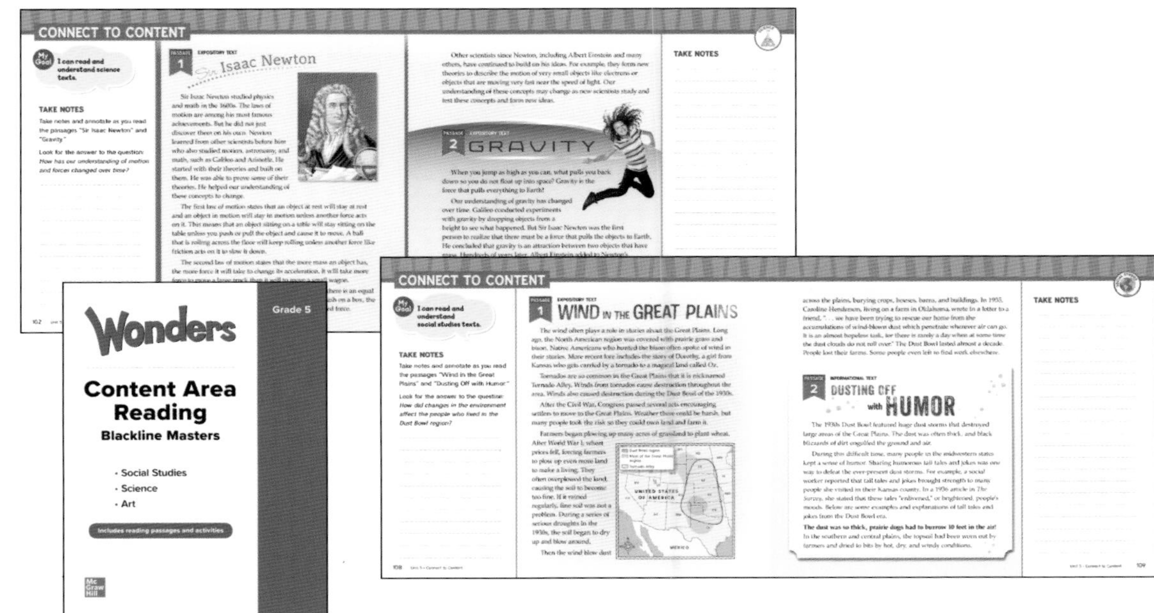

Assess

Reflect on Learning

Unit Assessment

Fluency Assessment

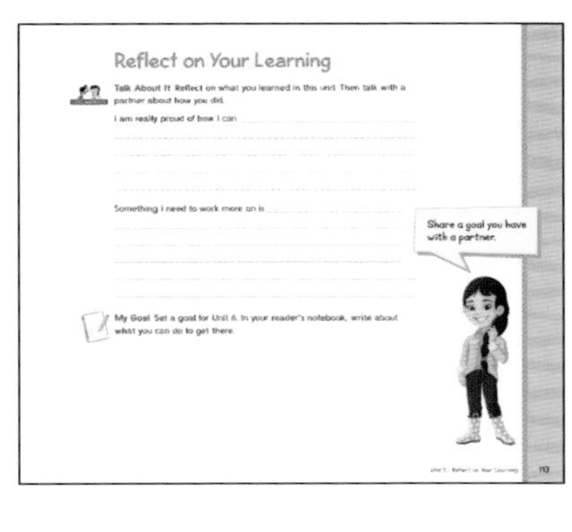

Presentation Options Reader's Theater, Inquiry Space, Writing

Student Outcomes

✓ Tested in *Wonders* Assessments

FOUNDATIONAL SKILLS

Fluency

- Read grade-level texts with accuracy, appropriate rate, expression, and automaticity

READING

Reading Informational Text

✓ Explain how text features contribute to the understanding of a text
✓ Explain how text structures contribute to the overall meaning of texts
✓ Explain how relevant, or key, details support the central, or main, idea(s), implied or explicit
- Read and comprehend texts in the grades 4-5 text complexity band
- Summarize a text to enhance comprehension
- Write in response to texts

Compare Texts

- Compare and contrast how authors present information on the same topic or theme

COMMUNICATION

Writing

Writing Process

✓ Write a personal narrative using a logical sequence of events and demonstrating an effective use of a strong conclusion
- With guidance and support from peers and adults, develop and strengthen writing as needed by planning, revising, and editing

Speaking and Listening

- Report on a topic or text or present an opinion, sequencing ideas; speak clearly at an understandable pace

ELL Scaffolded supports for English Language Learners are embedded throughout the lessons, enabling students to communicate information, ideas, and concepts in English Language Arts and for social and instructional purposes within the school setting.

Researching

- Conduct short research projects that build knowledge through investigation of different aspects of the topic

Creating and Collaborating

- Add audio recordings and visual displays to presentations when apppropriate
- With some guidance and support from adults, use technology to produce and publish writing

VOCABULARY

Academic Vocabulary

- Acquire and use grade-appropriate academic vocabulary

Vocabulary Strategy

✓ Use context clues and/or background knowledge to determine the meaning of multiple-meaning and unknown words and phrases, appropriate to grade level

CONTENT AREA LEARNING

Earth in Space and Time

- Distinguish among objects in the Solar System, including the Sun, Earth, planets, moons, asteroids, and comets, and discuss their interactions. **Science**

Scientists and the History of Science

- Connect grade-level-appropriate science concepts with the history of science and the contributions of scientists. **Science**

History and Civic and Political Participation

- Analyze various issues and events of the 20th century, such as the Great Depression. **Social Studies**

Extend, Connect, and Assess

Extend

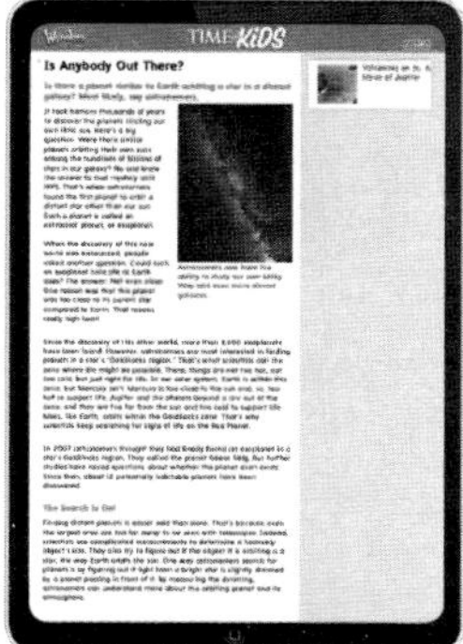

TIME for KIDS

Reading Digitally

"Is Anybody Out There?"
Genre: Online Article

Reader's Theater

Jane Addams and Hull House
Genre: Play

Connect

Science

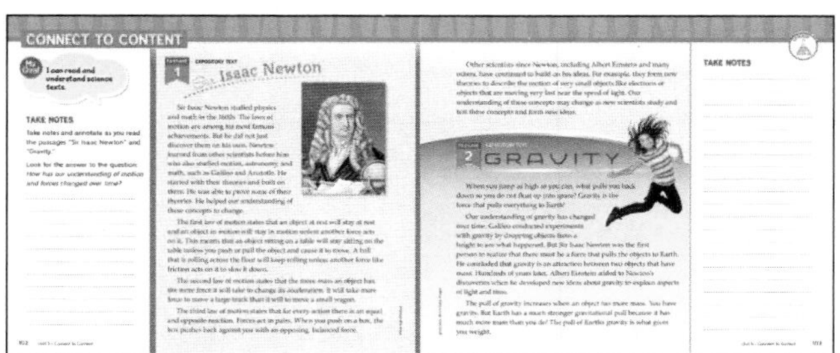

Reading/Writing Companion pp. 102–107

- "Sir Isaac Newton"
- "Gravity"
- Compare the Passages, Investigate Newton's Laws, Record Your Data

Social Studies

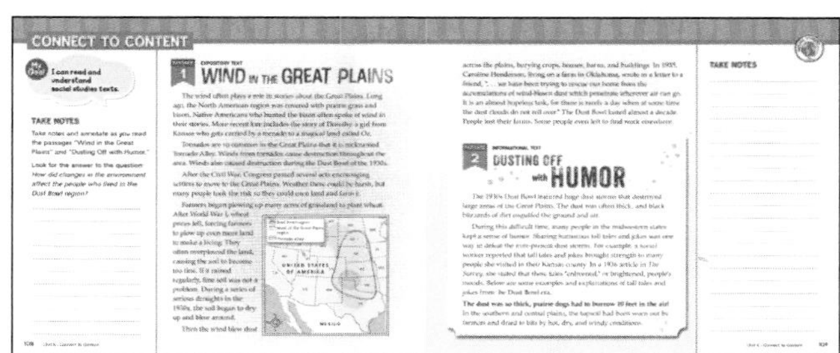

Reading/Writing Companion pp. 108–112

- "Wind in the Great Plains"
- "Dusting Off with Humor"
- Compare the Passages, Write a 1-2-3 Report on Environment

Assess

Unit Assessments

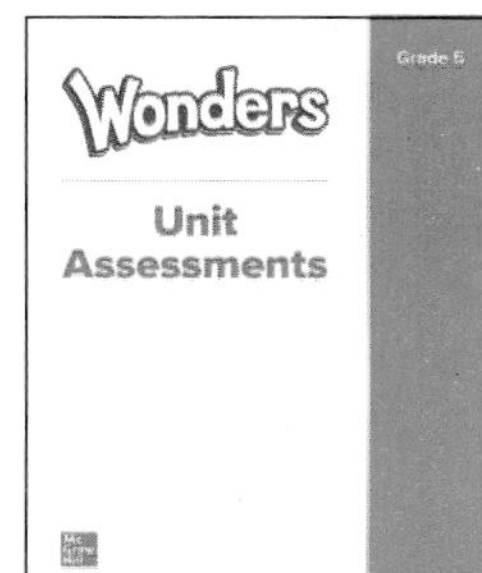

Unit 5 Test

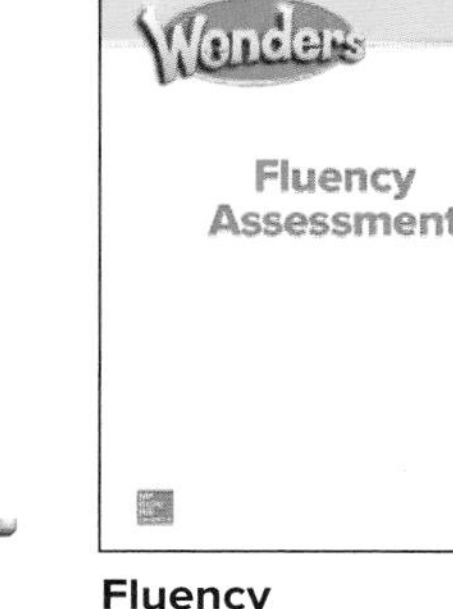

Unit 5 Test Online

Wonders Fluency Assessment

Fluency

EVALUATE STUDENT PROGRESS

Use the *Wonders* online assessment reports to evaluate student progress and help you make decisions about small-group instruction and assignments.

Self-Assess Have students complete Reflect on Your Learning and note any areas where they need improvement.

Planner

Customize your own lesson plans at **my.mheducation.com**

Reading Suggested Daily Time

READING LESSON GOALS

- I can read and understand science texts.
- I can read and understand social studies texts.

SMALL GROUP OPTIONS The designated lessons can be taught in small groups. To determine how to differentiate instruction for small groups, use Formative Assessment and Data Dashboard.

Reading

Lesson 1	Lesson 2
Reading Digitally, T290–T291 Read "Is Anybody Out There?" TIME KIDS **Reader's Theater, T292–T293** *Jane Addams and Hull House* Read the Play and Model Fluency **Connect to Content: Science, T294–T295** Read "Sir Isaac Newton," "Gravity"	**Reading Digitally, T290–T291** Reread "Is Anybody Out There?" TIME KIDS **Reader's Theater, T292–T293** *Jane Addams and Hull House* Assign Roles and Practice the Play **Connect to Content: Science, T296–T297** Compare the Passages, Investigate Newton's Laws, Record Your Data

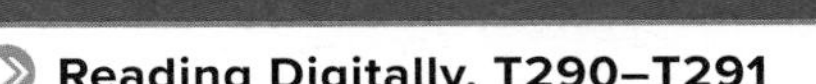

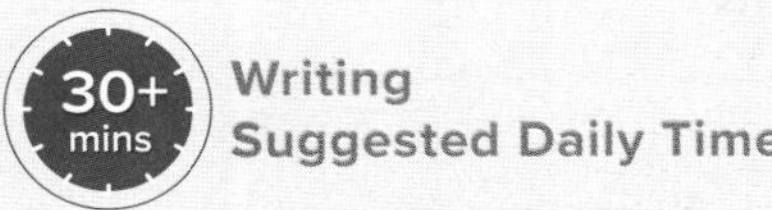

Writing Suggested Daily Time

WRITING LESSON GOALS

I can write a personal narrative.

Writing

Lesson 1	Lesson 2
Extended Writing 2: Personal Narrative, T250–T251 Draft	**Extended Writing 2: Personal Narrative, T252–T253** Revise

Writing Lesson Bank: Craft Minilessons, T260–T261, T264–T265

Teacher and Peer Conferences

Teacher-Led Instruction

Level Up with Leveled Readers
Approaching Level to On Level, T310
Mars

Level Up with Leveled Readers
On Level to Beyond Level, T311
Mars

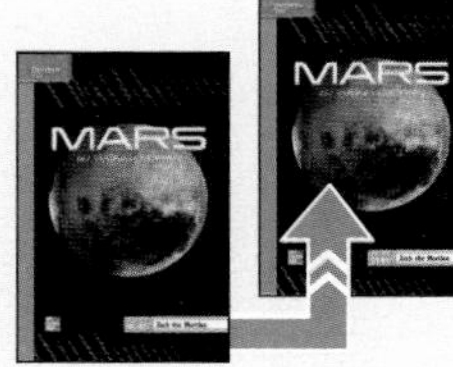

Level Up with Leveled Readers
ELL Level to On Level, T312
Mars

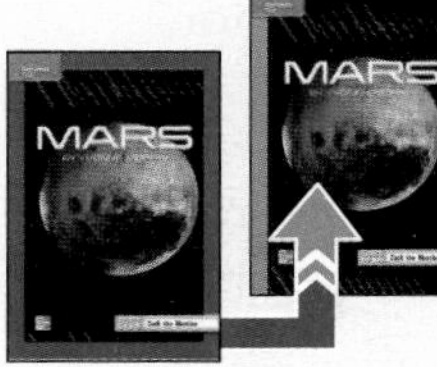

Independent/Collaborative Work

Reading

Comprehension
- Make Inferences

Fluency
- Reader's Theater

Independent Reading

Reader's Theater Card 39

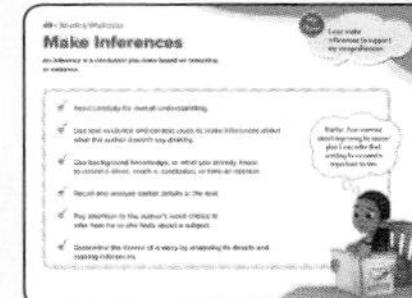

Make Inferences Card 40

Writing

Extended Writing 2: Personal Narrative

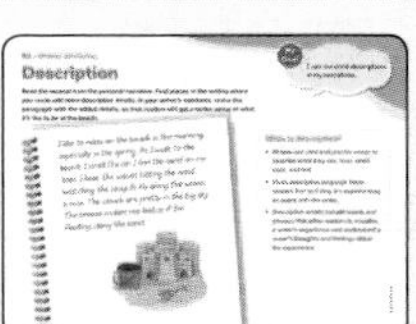

Description Card 62

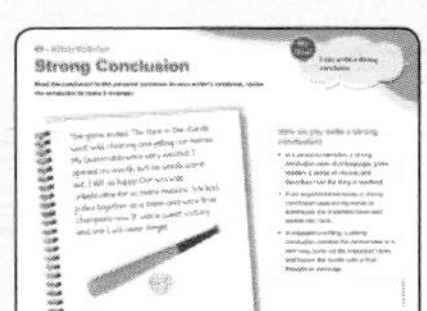

Strong Conclusion Card 59

Get Ready for Assessment

Before administering the unit assessment, identify any gaps in students' understanding using the Data Dashboard. Use resources from the unit or your own resources to differentiate Small Group Teacher-Led Instruction and to provide Independent/Collaborative Work options.

 Lesson 3	 Lesson 4	 Lesson 5
Reading		
Reader's Theater, T292–T293 *Jane Addams and Hull House* Practice the Play and Extend **Connect to Content: Social Studies, T298–T299** "Wind in the Great Plains," "Dusting Off with Humor"	**Reader's Theater, T292–T293** *Jane Addams and Hull House* Perform and Reread the Play **Connect to Content: Social Studies, T300–T301** Compare the Passages, Write a 1-2-3 Report on Environment	**Unit Wrap Up, T302–T303** Make Connections Reflect on Your Learning **Presentation Options, T304–T309** Speaking and Listening Publish and Present Inquiry Space Present Writing **Summative Assessment and Next Steps, T314–T316**
Writing		
Extended Writing 2: Personal Narrative, T254–T255 Revise: Peer Conference	**Extended Writing 2: Personal Narrative, T256–T257** Edit and Proofread	**Extended Writing 2: Personal Narrative, T258–T259** Publish, Present, and Evaluate
Writing Lesson Bank: Craft Minilessons, T260–T261, T264–T265		
Teacher and Peer Conferences		

Level Up with Leveled Readers
Beyond Level to Self-Selected Trade Book, T313
Mars

Level Up Writing
From Good to Great, T286–T287
- Purpose, Focus, and Organization
- Evidence and Elaboration
- Conventions
- Apply the Rubric

English Language Learners
See ELL Small Group Guide, pp. 228–229

Content Area Connections

Content Area Reading
- Science, Social Studies, and the Arts

Inquiry Space
- Options for Project-Based Learning

LEARNING GOALS

We can use interactive features to read an online text.

OBJECTIVES

Draw on information from multiple print or digital sources, demonstrating the ability to locate an answer to a question quickly or to solve a problem efficiently.

Conduct short research projects that use several sources to build knowledge through investigation of different aspects of a topic.

Write routinely over extended time frames and shorter time frames for a range of discipline-specific tasks, purposes, and audiences.

Distinguish among objects in the Solar System, including the Sun, Earth, planets, moons, asteroids, comets, and discuss their interactions.

ELA ACADEMIC LANGUAGE

- *navigate, article, access, skim*
- Cognates: *navegar, artículo, accesar*

DIFFERENTIATED READING

Approaching Level and **ELL** Read the text with students. Have partners work together to complete the graphic organizers and summarize the text orally.

On Level and **Beyond Level** Have students read the text and access the interactive features independently. Complete the Reread activities during Small Group time.

TIME for KIDS

Is Anybody Out There?

Before Reading

Introduce the Genre Discuss the features of an online article. Scroll through "Is Anybody Out There?" at my.mheducation.com. Clarify how to navigate through the article. Point out the interactive features, such as **hyperlinks**, **slide shows**, and **pop-up windows**.

Close Reading Online

Read

Take Notes Scroll back to the top. As you read the article aloud, ask questions to focus students on the central idea and relevant details about different solar bodies. Have students take notes on the central idea and relevant details using a copy of online Central Idea and Relevant Details **Graphic Organizer 7**. After each section, have partners paraphrase the central idea. Additionally, review the idioms, such as "easier said than done" and "is in the cards."

Access Interactive Features Help students access the interactive features. Discuss what information these elements add to the text.

Summarize Review students' graphic organizers. Model using the information to summarize "Is Anybody Out There?" Ask students to write a summary of the article, stating how some planets are able to support life. Partners should discuss their summaries.

Reread

Craft and Structure Have students reread parts of the article, paying attention to text structure and author's craft. Discuss these questions.

- What text structure does the author use to organize the information?
- For what purpose did the author add the hyperlink?

Author's Perspective Tell students they will now reread to help them answer this question: *According to the author, is it likely that astronomers will find a planet where life might be possible?* Have students skim the text and find facts and details that answer the question. Have partners share their findings and discuss whether they agree with the author's perspective.

Integrate

Make Connections

Text Connections Have students compare what they learned about scientific viewpoints in this article with what they have learned about scientific viewpoints in other texts they have read in this unit.

Research Online

Navigate Links to Information Remind students that online texts may include **hyperlinks**, colored or underlined text on a Web page that connects to another Web page with related information. Do an online search about looking for life on other planets. Model using a hyperlink to jump to another Web page. Examine the information on the Web page with students and make a list of relevant facts and evidence.

Search Results Model conducting an Internet search using key words related to outer space. Then discuss the results page. Point out that the most relevant results are usually listed first. Demonstrate clicking on a hyperlink to jump to another page and then using the Back button to return to the results page.

Tracking and Citing Sources Encourage students to keep a list of sites they visit while conducting research. Have them include details such as the URL, date, and information learned from the site. Set up a format for them to follow.

Inspire Action

Exploring Space Point out that our knowledge of outer space is continually growing. Technology has helped us move beyond our own galaxy to look for other planets and, possibly, other forms of life. Help students identify information in this article about new discoveries people have made, such as:

- In 1995, astronomers found the first planet orbiting a star other than the sun.
- The HARPS device found 50 new planets in our own galaxy, the Milky Way.

Have students choose one of the discoveries and research it online. They should record facts and details about how technology facilitated the discovery and how the discovery has affected scientific knowledge.

Independent Study

Choose a Topic Students should brainstorm questions related to the article. For example, they might ask: *What conditions are necessary for life on another planet?* Then have students choose a question to research.

Conduct Research Review how to recognize relevant results for an Internet search. Have students keep a list of research sites and help them eliminate irrelevant ones.

Present Have groups present a round-table discussion on the topic of life on other planets.

ELL ENGLISH LANGUAGE LEARNERS

Author's Perspective Read the question with students and elicit the information they will need to answer the question. *Did the author say that discoveries are increasing the odds that life exists in the universe?* Discuss words and phrases, such as *Earthlike, in the cards, Goldilocks zone, growing wider.* Ask: *Where did you read about these concepts?* As needed, have students look for the words and phrases in the last three sections of the text. *Do you think the author thinks astronomers will find a planet where life might be possible? Do you agree with the author?*

READERS TO WRITERS

Encourage students to include jargon, or domain-specific scientific terms in their writing to give their work credibility. Students should define the terms and use jargon accurately. If they are not sure what the terms mean, they should use a dictionary to determine their meaning or avoid using them.

FORMATIVE ASSESSMENT

STUDENT CHECK-IN

Have partners share something they learned using an online interactive feature. Then have them reflect using the Check-In routine.

JANE ADDAMS AND HULL HOUSE
by Navidad O'Neill, 1996
CAST OF CHARACTERS:
Narrator
Jane Addams
Ellen Gates Starr, her friend
George, John, Charles,
Alice, Mary and Julia,
all Hull House volunteers
Marie and Helen,
German immigrants
John and Joseph,
Italian immigrants
Jane Addams and Hull House

LEARNING GOALS

We can read fluently to perform a play.

OBJECTIVES

Read grade-level text with purpose and understanding.

Read grade-level prose and poetry orally with accuracy, appropriate rate, expression, and automaticity on successive readings.

Use context to confirm or self-correct word recognition and understanding, rereading as necessary.

TEACH IN SMALL GROUP

You may wish to teach the Reader's Theater lesson during Small Group time and then have groups present their work to the class.

Jane Addams and Hull House

Introduce the Genre

Explain that *Jane Addams and Hull House* is a play about how Jane Addams and her friend Ellen Starr opened Hull House, the first settlement house in the United States. Distribute the Elements of Drama handout and scripts from **Reader's Theater**, pages 2–3 and 57–64.

- Review the features of a play.
- Review the cast of characters and the background information about why Jane Addams opened Hull House. Highlight aspects of life as an immigrant in the early 1900s, including cramped living quarters, low wages, and long work hours.
- Point out the stage directions.

Read the Play and Model Fluency

Model reading the play as students follow along in their scripts. As you read each part, state the name of the character and read the part, emphasizing the appropriate phrasing and expression.

Focus on Vocabulary Stop and discuss any vocabulary words that students may not know. You may wish to teach:

- settlement
- slums
- embroidered
- ponders
- ought

Monitor Comprehension As you read, check that students understand the characters, setting, and plot.

- After reading the part of the narrator, ask students to identify what information the narrator provides.
- After reading each character part, ask partners to note the character's traits. Model how to find text evidence that tells them about the characters.

Assign Roles

You may wish to split the class into two groups. If necessary, you can assign the same role to more than one student.

Practice the Play

Allow students time to practice their parts in the play. Pair fluent readers with less fluent readers. Pairs can echo read or chorally read their parts. Work with less fluent readers to mark pauses in their scripts using one slash for a short pause and two slashes for longer pauses. Throughout the week, have students work on **Reader's Theater Center Activity Card 39.**

Once students have practiced reading their parts, allow them time to practice performing the script. Remind them that non-verbal communication is an important part of portraying a character and provide examples.

Perform the Reader's Theater

- Remind students to focus on their scripts as the play is being performed and have them follow along, even when they are not in the scene.
- Discuss how performing a play aloud is different from reading it silently. Have students interpret both the verbal and non-verbal messages they saw during the practice performance.
- Lead a class discussion on ways that students could make their performances more enjoyable for the audience.

Reread the Play

Remind students that settlement houses were founded in many major U.S. cities in the early 1900s. These houses improved neighborhoods by providing a safe place for people to learn and play. Many of them also worked for reform. In *Jane Addams and Hull House,* the characters focus on making improvements in their city. Discuss these questions with students:

1. What services did Hull House provide?
2. What was the purpose of the Labor Museum?
3. What other goals for the neighborhood did Jane Addams and Hull House volunteers work toward?
4. What social reforms did they hope to make?

Record It!

Have students use a video camera or an audio recorder to record the performance. Listen to the performance and discuss as a class how the play sounds. Ask:

1. What did you like about the performance?
2. What would you do differently next time?
3. If you could perform the play again, would you add sound effects or music? At what points in the play might you include them?

ELL ENGLISH LANGUAGE LEARNERS

Review the features of a play with Beginning students: character, setting, dialogue, stage directions. Have all students read aloud the lines for their roles and record them. With each student, listen to the recording as you trace the dialogue with your finger. Ask: *Which words or phrases do you find difficult to pronounce?* Model pronouncing the words and phrases slowly and record them for students to use for practice. Then review details about the character and any stage directions that refer to their character. Ask the student to think about whether they are saying the lines appropriately. *How can you say the dialogue to show ______?* Help students decide on the tone and record it for them to use for practice.

FORMATIVE ASSESSMENT

STUDENT CHECK-IN

Have partners reflect on how fluently they read their lines.

"Sir Isaac Newton"

"Gravity"

LEARNING GOALS

We can apply skills and strategies to understand science texts.

OBJECTIVES

Determine the meaning of words and phrases as they are used in a text, including figurative language such as metaphors and similes.

Compare and contrast the overall structure of events, ideas, concepts, or information in two or more texts.

Analyze multiple accounts of the same event or topic, noting important similarities and differences in the point of view they represent.

Explain an author's perspective, or point of view, toward a topic in an informational text.

By the end of the year, read and comprehend informational texts, including history/social studies, science, and technical texts, at the high end of the grades 4–5 text complexity band independently and proficiently.

Connect grade-level-appropriate science concepts with the history of science and the contributions of scientists.

FORMATIVE ASSESSMENT

STUDENT CHECK-IN

Have partners share important ideas from each passage about forces and motion. Then have them reflect using the Check-In routine.

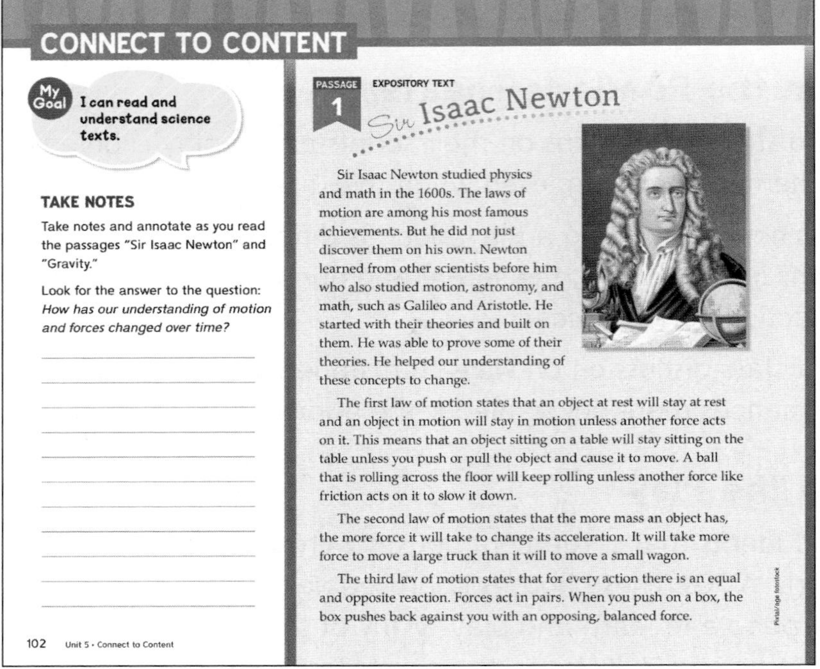

CONNECT TO CONTENT

My Goal I can read and understand science texts.

TAKE NOTES

Take notes and annotate as you read the passages "Sir Isaac Newton" and "Gravity."

Look for the answer to the question: *How has our understanding of motion and forces changed over time?*

PASSAGE 1 EXPOSITORY TEXT

Sir Isaac Newton

Sir Isaac Newton studied physics and math in the 1600s. The laws of motion are among his most famous achievements. But he did not just discover them on his own. Newton learned from other scientists before him who also studied motion, astronomy, and math, such as Galileo and Aristotle. He started with their theories and built on them. He was able to prove some of their theories. He helped our understanding of these concepts to change.

The first law of motion states that an object at rest will stay at rest and an object in motion will stay in motion unless another force acts on it. This means that an object sitting on a table will stay sitting on the table unless you push or pull the object and cause it to move. A ball that is rolling across the floor will keep rolling unless another force like friction acts on it to slow it down.

The second law of motion states that the more mass an object has, the more force it will take to change its acceleration. It will take more force to move a large truck than it will to move a small wagon.

The third law of motion states that for every action there is an equal and opposite reaction. Forces act in pairs. When you push on a box, the box pushes back against you with an opposing, balanced force.

Pixtal/age fotostock

102 Unit 5 • Connect to Content

Reading/Writing Companion, p. 102

Take Notes Tell students they will be reading two passages about our understanding of motion. The passages will help them build knowledge about topics introduced earlier in the unit. Explain that they will read independently using the Close Reading Routine. Remind them to annotate the text as they read.

For students who need more support, use the Read prompts to help them understand the text and the Reread prompts to analyze the text, craft, and structure of each passage.

Read

Ask and Answer Questions DOK 1

What does Newton's first law of motion tell? (It tells that objects stay at rest or in motion unless a force acts on them.)

Reread

Author's Craft: Imagery DOK 2

How does the author of "Sir Isaac Newton" use imagery to help explain Newton's laws of motion? (The author describes concrete examples of each law using real, common objects.)

Access Complex Text

Specific Vocabulary

"Sir Isaac Newton" and "Gravity" both include science vocabulary that students may not know. Review strategies for finding the meaning of unfamiliar words, such as using context clues, word parts, or a dictionary. Have students define the words *mass,*

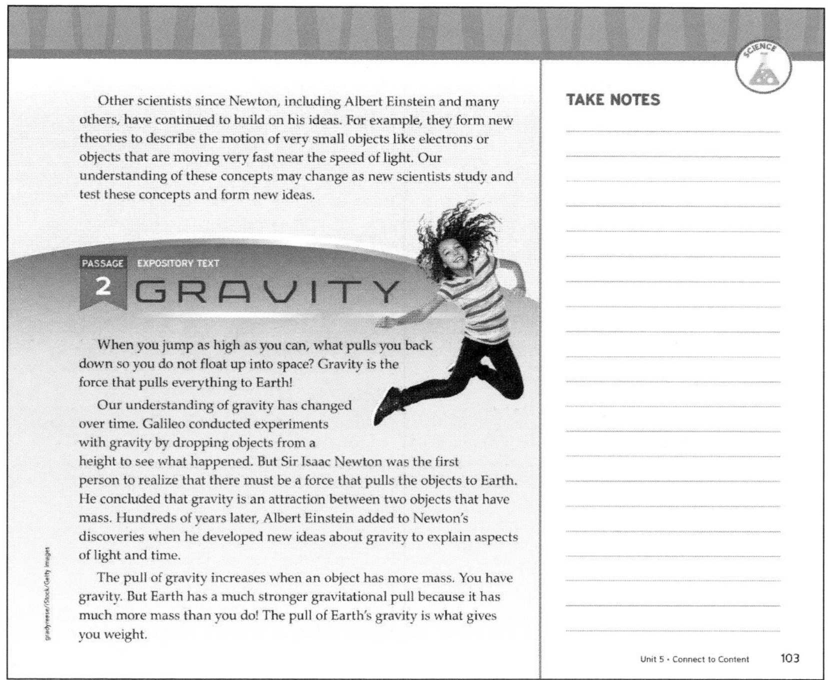

Other scientists since Newton, including Albert Einstein and many others, have continued to build on his ideas. For example, they form new theories to describe the motion of very small objects like electrons or objects that are moving very fast near the speed of light. Our understanding of these concepts may change as new scientists study and test these concepts and form new ideas.

PASSAGE 2 EXPOSITORY TEXT

GRAVITY

When you jump as high as you can, what pulls you back down so you do not float up into space? Gravity is the force that pulls everything to Earth!

Our understanding of gravity has changed over time. Galileo conducted experiments with gravity by dropping objects from a height to see what happened. But Sir Isaac Newton was the first person to realize that there must be a force that pulls the objects to Earth. He concluded that gravity is an attraction between two objects that have mass. Hundreds of years later, Albert Einstein added to Newton's discoveries when he developed new ideas about gravity to explain aspects of light and time.

The pull of gravity increases when an object has more mass. You have gravity. But Earth has a much stronger gravitational pull because it has much more mass than you do! The pull of Earth's gravity is what gives you weight.

TAKE NOTES

Unit 5 • Connect to Content 103

Reading/Writing Companion p. 103

CONNECT TO CONTENT

TAKE NOTES

Planets and other objects in our solar system each have a different mass, so they each exert a different amount of gravitational pull on objects. The Moon and Mars have much less mass than Earth, so you would weigh much less there. Jupiter has much more mass than Earth, so you would weigh about two and a half times more on Jupiter!

Did you think that astronauts can float in space because there is no gravity there? The astronauts and their spacecraft still fall toward Earth due to gravity. But because the spacecraft moves so fast, the curve of its fall matches the curve of Earth. This keeps the spacecraft in orbit around Earth instead of hitting Earth's surface.

Newton's principle of gravity keeps all the planets in orbit around the Sun and the Moon in orbit around Earth. No matter where you go in our solar system, you cannot escape gravity!

104 Unit 5 • Connect to Content

Reading/Writing Companion p. 104

Read

Ask and Answer Questions DOK 1

What gives you weight on Earth? (The pull of Earth's gravity gives you weight on Earth.)

Read

Text Structure: Cause and Effect DOK 2

How does the author use the cause-and-effect text structure in "Gravity"? (The author uses the cause-and-effect text structure to explain many effects caused by gravity, both on Earth and in space.)

Reread

Author's Craft: Author's Purpose DOK 2

What is the author's purpose in writing "Gravity"? (The author's purpose is to explain how gravity works, and how people began to understand it.)

force, acceleration, electrons, gravity, gravitational pull, and *orbit.* Ask:

- *What changes during acceleration?* (how fast an object moves)
- *What sentence at the beginning of "Gravity" helps readers understand what gravity is?* ("Gravity is the force that pulls everything to Earth!")

ELL ENGLISH LANGUAGE LEARNERS

"Sir Isaac Newton"
Preteach vocabulary: *motion, astronomy, theories, concepts* (Cognates: *astronomía, teoría, concepto*) Then guide students to find key details: *How does the author explain Newton's first law of motion?* (A ball rolling across the floor keeps rolling unless another force acts on it.) *How does the author describe the second law of motion?* (Moving a heavy truck takes more force than moving a small wagon.) *What is the author's example for the third law?* (When you push on a box, it pushes back with an opposing force.)

"Gravity"
Preteach vocabulary: *experiments, attraction, solar system* (Cognates: *experimento, atracción, sistema solar*) Then guide students to find key details: *What did Sir Isaac Newton discover?* (He was the first to understand that a force was pulling things to Earth.) *How did Newton say gravity worked?* (It is an attraction between two objects with mass.) *What keeps the planets in orbit around the sun?* (gravity)

LEARNING GOALS

- **We can compare two texts about force and motion.**
- **We can apply what we've learned to conduct an investigation and record data.**

OBJECTIVES

Determine two or more central, or main, ideas of a text and explain how they are supported by relevant, or key, details; summarize the text.

Explain how an author uses reasons and evidence to support particular points in a text, identifying which reasons and evidence support which point(s).

Identify the author's purpose.

Write routinely over extended time frames and shorter time frames for a range of discipline-specific tasks, purposes, and audiences.

Connect grade-level-appropriate science concepts with the history of science and the contributions of scientists.

ELA ACADEMIC LANGUAGE

- *compare, characterisitics, synthesize*
- Cognates: *comparar, características, sintetizar*

FORMATIVE ASSESSMENT

STUDENT CHECK-IN

- **Compare** Have partners share their diagrams and responses on Reading/Writing Companion page 107.
- **Record Your Data** Have partners share their observations and results.

Ask students to use the Check-In routine to reflect and fill in the bars.

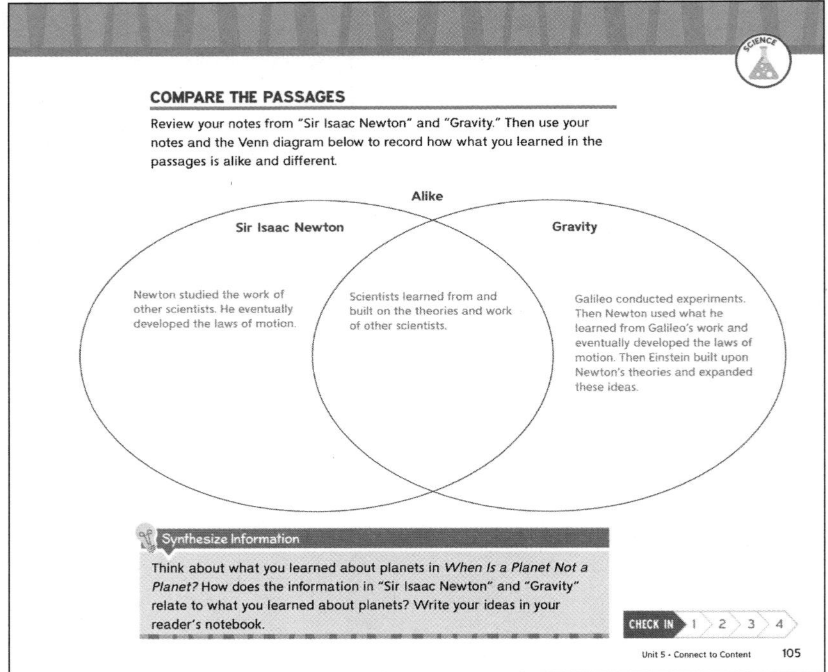
COMPARE THE PASSAGES

Review your notes from "Sir Isaac Newton" and "Gravity." Then use your notes and the Venn diagram below to record how what you learned in the passages is alike and different.

Alike
Sir Isaac Newton
Gravity
Newton studied the work of other scientists. He eventually developed the laws of motion.
Scientists learned from and built on the theories and work of other scientists.
Galileo conducted experiments. Then Newton used what he learned from Galileo's work and eventually developed the laws of motion. Then Einstein built upon Newton's theories and expanded these ideas.

Synthesize Information

Think about what you learned about planets in *When Is a Planet Not a Planet?* How does the information in "Sir Isaac Newton" and "Gravity" relate to what you learned about planets? Write your ideas in your reader's notebook.

CHECK IN 1 2 3 4

Unit 5 • Connect to Content 105

Reading/Writing Companion, p. 105

Integrate

Compare the Passages

Explain Remind students that both of the passages they read are expository text, and both give information about our understanding of motion. Tell students they will complete a Venn diagram to show how the two passages are alike and different.

Talk About It Have students work in small groups or with a partner to talk about the two texts and their similarities and differences. Have them review the characteristics of the genre. Partners or group members should share ideas with one another about the different ways each text presents information about our understanding of motion.

Apply Have students use the notes they made on **Reading/Writing Companion** pages 102–104 and their Talk About It discussion to complete the Venn diagram and answer the Synthesize Information question on page 105.

Synthesize Information — DOK 2

Explain Remind students that they read about planets in *When Is a Planet Not a Planet?* Explain that readers can synthesize information by thinking about what they already know and what they learn as they read new passages.

Model Point out the second law of motion on page 102 of "Sir Isaac Newton." Then have students reread page 104 of "Gravity." Model how this evidence adds to an understanding of planets based on information from previously read material.

Apply Have students cite the evidence in both passages that helps them understand how the information is related to what they already know about planets.

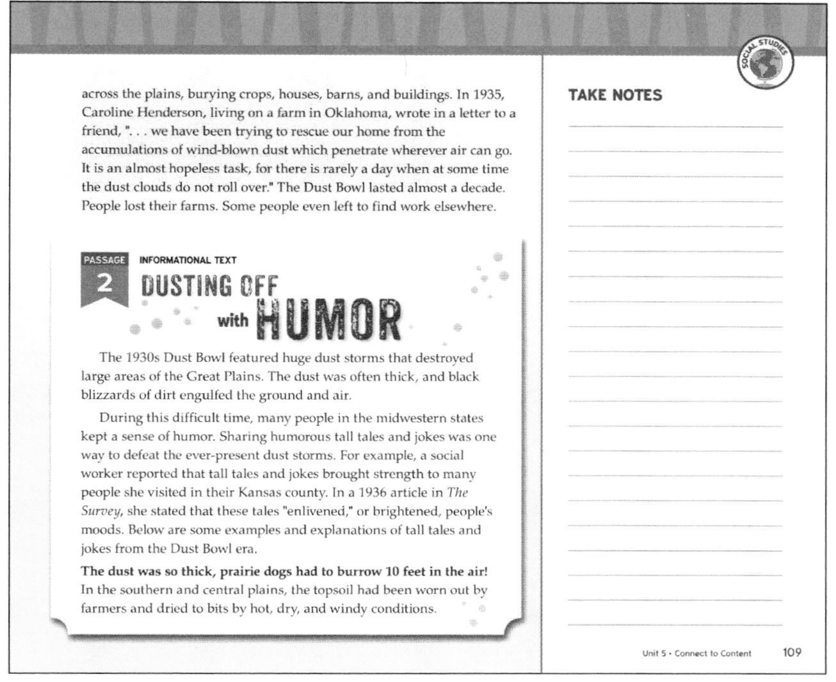

across the plains, burying crops, houses, barns, and buildings. In 1935, Caroline Henderson, living on a farm in Oklahoma, wrote in a letter to a friend, ". . . we have been trying to rescue our home from the accumulations of wind-blown dust which penetrate wherever air can go. It is an almost hopeless task, for there is rarely a day when at some time the dust clouds do not roll over." The Dust Bowl lasted almost a decade. People lost their farms. Some people even left to find work elsewhere.

PASSAGE 2 INFORMATIONAL TEXT

DUSTING OFF with HUMOR

The 1930s Dust Bowl featured huge dust storms that destroyed large areas of the Great Plains. The dust was often thick, and black blizzards of dirt engulfed the ground and air.

During this difficult time, many people in the midwestern states kept a sense of humor. Sharing humorous tall tales and jokes was one way to defeat the ever-present dust storms. For example, a social worker reported that tall tales and jokes brought strength to many people she visited in their Kansas county. In a 1936 article in *The Survey*, she stated that these tales "enlivened," or brightened, people's moods. Below are some examples and explanations of tall tales and jokes from the Dust Bowl era.

The dust was so thick, prairie dogs had to burrow 10 feet in the air! In the southern and central plains, the topsoil had been worn out by farmers and dried to bits by hot, dry, and windy conditions.

TAKE NOTES

Unit 5 • Connect to Content 109

Reading/Writing Companion, p. 109

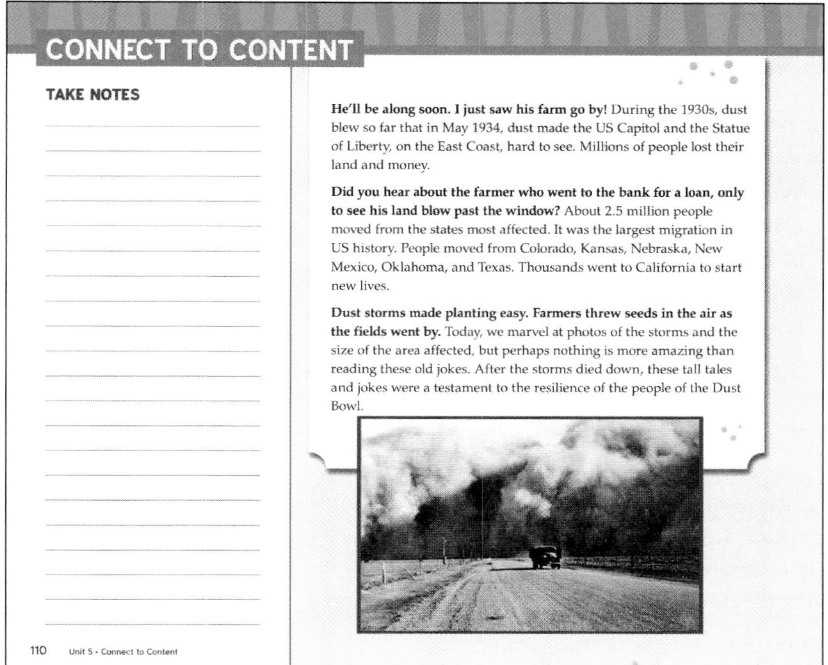

CONNECT TO CONTENT

TAKE NOTES

He'll be along soon. I just saw his farm go by! During the 1930s, dust blew so far that in May 1934, dust made the US Capitol and the Statue of Liberty, on the East Coast, hard to see. Millions of people lost their land and money.

Did you hear about the farmer who went to the bank for a loan, only to see his land blow past the window? About 2.5 million people moved from the states most affected. It was the largest migration in US history. People moved from Colorado, Kansas, Nebraska, New Mexico, Oklahoma, and Texas. Thousands went to California to start new lives.

Dust storms made planting easy. Farmers threw seeds in the air as the fields went by. Today, we marvel at photos of the storms and the size of the area affected, but perhaps nothing is more amazing than reading these old jokes. After the storms died down, these tall tales and jokes were a testament to the resilience of the people of the Dust Bowl.

110 Unit 5 • Connect to Content

Reading/Writing Companion, p. 110

Visualize DOK 2

What is the effect of describing the thick dust and black dirt blizzards in the first paragraph of "Dusting Off with Humor" on page 109? (It helps readers visualize what things were like during the Dust Bowl.)

Author's Perspective DOK 2

What is the author's perspective about the humorous statements in "Dusting Off with Humor"? (The author believes they helped people laugh and get through a very difficult time.)

Author's Craft: Imagery DOK 2

How do the humorous statements in "Dusting Off with Humor" help you understand the Dust Bowl? (They give exaggerated images of the thickness of the dust, how quickly farmers lost everything, or how little they had left.)

region for American agriculture for a long time. Therefore, any disruptions to farming were serious problems. Today, agriculture in the Great Plains includes corn, wheat, hay, and livestock such as cattle.

ENGLISH LANGUAGE LEARNERS

"Wind in the Great Plains"
Preteach vocabulary: *bison, lore, tornado, tract, harnessed, turbines* (Cognates: *bisonte, tornado, tracto, turbina*) Then guide students to find key details: *Where is Tornado Alley?* (in the Great Plains) *What helped cause the Dust Bowl?* (Farmers planted wheat in grassland areas; droughts made soil dry; winds came.) *What places are listed on the map key?* (Dust Bowl region, most of the Great Plains region, Tornado Alley)

"Dusting Off with Humor"
Preteach vocabulary: engulfed, commissioned, topsoil, migration (Cognate: *migración*) Reread challenging sentences and guide students to find key details: *Where do prairie dogs usually burrow or dig?* (in the ground) *Why could the dogs almost burrow in the air?* (The air was full of thick dust.) *Do farms usually move from place to place?* (No) *What does it mean that someone's farm went by?* (The farm turned to dust and blew away.)

LEARNING GOALS

- We can compare two texts about environmental problems in the Great Plains.
- We can apply what we've learned to write a research report.

OBJECTIVES

Determine two or more central, or main, ideas of a text and explain how they are supported by relevant, or key, details; summarize the text.

Conduct short research projects that use several sources to build knowledge through investigation of different aspects of a topic.

Write routinely over extended time frames and shorter time frames for a range of discipline-specific tasks, purposes, and audiences.

Report on a topic or text or present an opinion, sequencing ideas logically and using appropriate facts and relevant, descriptive details to support main ideas or themes; speak clearly at an understandable pace.

Analyze various issues and events of the 20th century, such as the Great Depression.

ELA ACADEMIC LANGUAGE

- *research, synthesize, details*
- Cognates: *sintetizar, detalles*

FORMATIVE ASSESSMENT

STUDENT CHECK-IN

- **Compare** Have partners share their charts and responses on Reading/Writing Companion page 111.
- **Write a Report** Have partners share their reports.

Ask students to use the Check-In routine to reflect and fill in the bars.

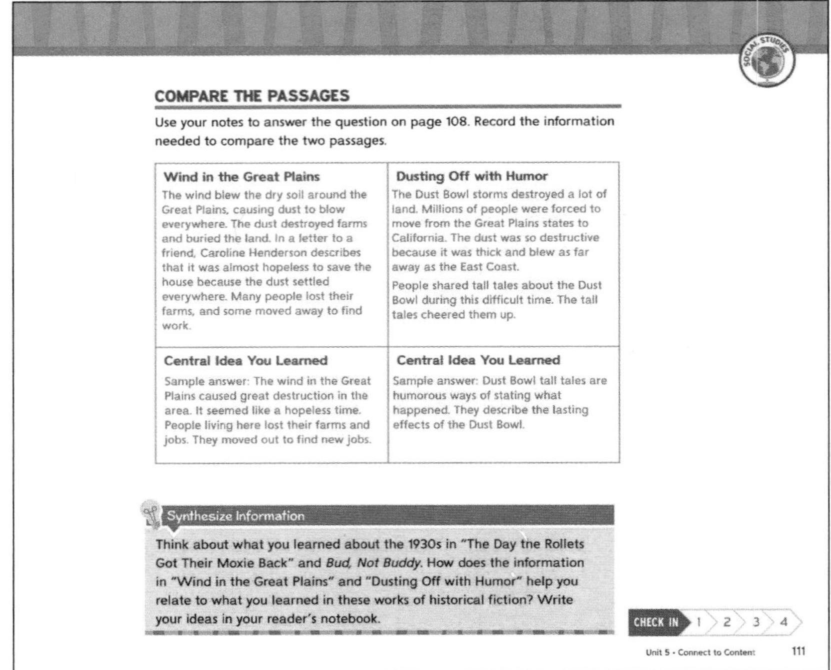

COMPARE THE PASSAGES

Use your notes to answer the question on page 108. Record the information needed to compare the two passages.

Wind in the Great Plains	Dusting Off with Humor
The wind blew the dry soil around the Great Plains, causing dust to blow everywhere. The dust destroyed farms and buried the land. In a letter to a friend, Caroline Henderson describes that it was almost hopeless to save the house because the dust settled everywhere. Many people lost their farms, and some moved away to find work.	The Dust Bowl storms destroyed a lot of land. Millions of people were forced to move from the Great Plains states to California. The dust was so destructive because it was thick and blew as far away as the East Coast. People shared tall tales about the Dust Bowl during this difficult time. The tall tales cheered them up.
Central Idea You Learned	**Central Idea You Learned**
Sample answer: The wind in the Great Plains caused great destruction in the area. It seemed like a hopeless time. People living here lost their farms and jobs. They moved out to find new jobs.	Sample answer: Dust Bowl tall tales are humorous ways of stating what happened. They describe the lasting effects of the Dust Bowl.

Synthesize Information

Think about what you learned about the 1930s in "The Day tne Rollets Got Their Moxie Back" and *Bud, Not Buddy*. How does the information in "Wind in the Great Plains" and "Dusting Off with Humor" help you relate to what you learned in these works of historical fiction? Write your ideas in your reader's notebook.

CHECK IN 1 2 3 4

Unit 5 • Connect to Content 111

Reading/Writing Companion, p. 111

Integrate

Compare the Passages

Explain Remind students that both of the passages they read are expository texts, and both give information about the Dust Bowl of the 1930s. Tell students they will complete a chart to show how the two passages are alike.

COLLABORATE **Talk About It** Have students work in small groups or with a partner to talk about the two texts and their similarities. Have them review the characteristics of the genre. Partners or group members should share ideas with one another about the ways each text presents information about the Dust Bowl of the 1930s.

Apply Have students use the notes they made on **Reading/Writing Companion** pages 108–110 and their Talk About It discussion to complete the chart and answer the Synthesize Information question on page 111 in their reader's notebook.

Synthesize Information — DOK 2

Explain Readers can synthesize information about a topic by studying and reading works in different genres.

Model Have students reread the first paragraph of "Wind in the Great Plains" on page 108. Then point out the second paragraph in "Dusting Off with Humor" on page 109. Discuss how these paragraphs show that real events inspire narratives, humor, or fictional tales.

Apply Have students cite evidence in both passages that help them better understand works of historical fiction set in the same time period as the Dust Bowl.

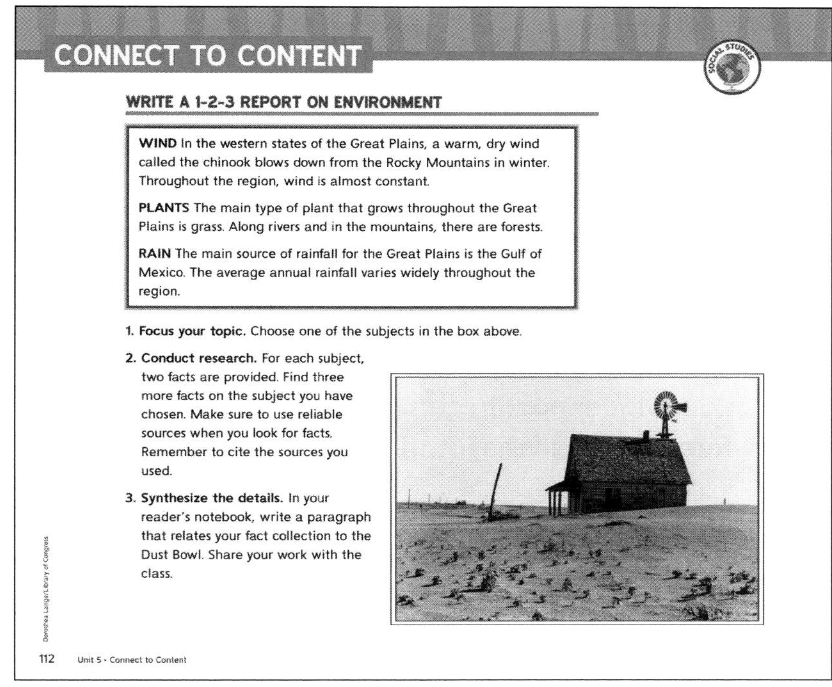

CONNECT TO CONTENT

WRITE A 1-2-3 REPORT ON ENVIRONMENT

WIND In the western states of the Great Plains, a warm, dry wind called the chinook blows down from the Rocky Mountains in winter. Throughout the region, wind is almost constant.

PLANTS The main type of plant that grows throughout the Great Plains is grass. Along rivers and in the mountains, there are forests.

RAIN The main source of rainfall for the Great Plains is the Gulf of Mexico. The average annual rainfall varies widely throughout the region.

1. **Focus your topic.** Choose one of the subjects in the box above.
2. **Conduct research.** For each subject, two facts are provided. Find three more facts on the subject you have chosen. Make sure to use reliable sources when you look for facts. Remember to cite the sources you used.
3. **Synthesize the details.** In your reader's notebook, write a paragraph that relates your fact collection to the Dust Bowl. Share your work with the class.

112 Unit 5 • Connect to Content

Reading/Writing Companion, p. 112

Write a 1-2-3 Report on Environment

Explain and Model Explain to students that they will be writing a report on a topic related to the Great Plains environment.

COLLABORATE **Talk About It** Have partners reread each fact on **Reading/Writing Companion** page 112 and decide which topic to focus on. Have them discuss questions they could ask and search terms they could use to learn more about the topic.

Apply After their discussions, have students complete their research to find three more facts on their subject. Remind them to use reliable sources such as Web sites ending in *.gov* and *.edu,* and to cite their sources in a bibliography. Then have students write a paragraph in their reader's notebook that relates their findings to the Dust Bowl.

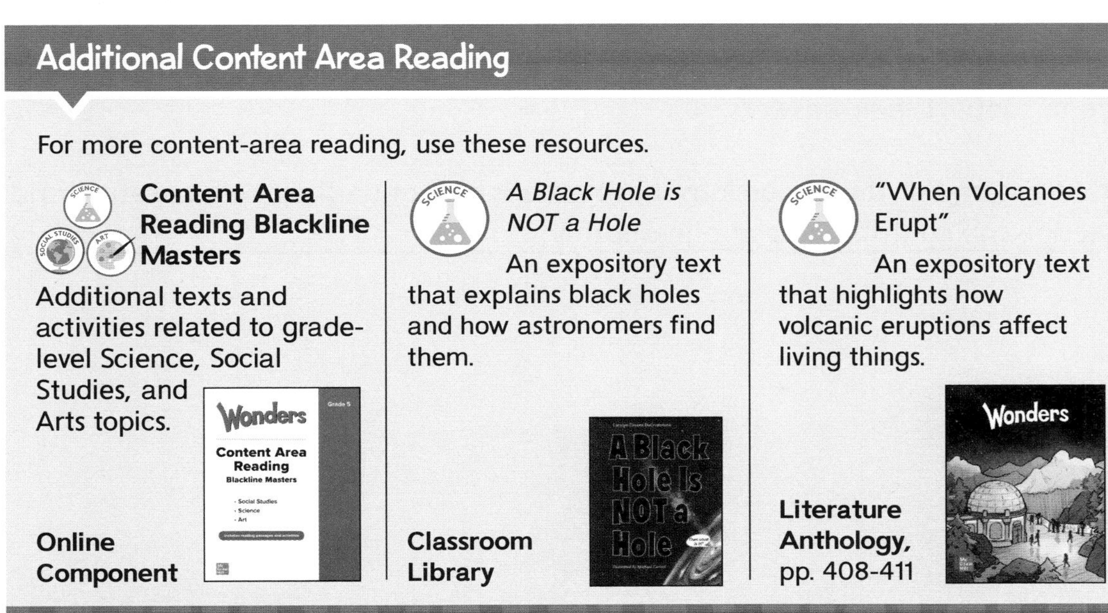

Additional Content Area Reading

For more content-area reading, use these resources.

Content Area Reading Blackline Masters

Additional texts and activities related to grade-level Science, Social Studies, and Arts topics.

Online Component

A Black Hole is NOT a Hole

An expository text that explains black holes and how astronomers find them.

Classroom Library

"When Volcanoes Erupt"

An expository text that highlights how volcanic eruptions affect living things.

Literature Anthology, pp. 408-411

ENGLISH LANGUAGE LEARNERS

Write a 1-2-3 Report on Environment, Apply Discuss with students the importance of identifying and using reliable sources. Remind them that websites ending in *.gov* and *.edu* are reliable. Help students formulate questions to guide their research about the Dust Bowl environment. Provide frames as needed: What is the effect of the wind called the chinook? What other winds blow on the Great Plains? What kind of grass grows on the Great Plains? What places in the Great Plains get the most and least amounts of rain? How much rain do they get?

LEARNING GOALS

We can synthesize information from multiple texts.

OBJECTIVES

Quote accurately from a text when explaining what the text says explicitly and when drawing inferences from the text.

Explain how an author uses reasons and evidence to support particular points in a text, identifying which reasons and evidence support which points.

Integrate information from several texts on the same topic in order to write or speak about the subject knowledgeably.

Draw evidence from literary or informational texts to support analysis, reflection, and research.

Engage effectively in a range of collaborative discussions (one-on-one, in groups, and teacher-led) with diverse partners, building on others' ideas and expressing their own clearly.

Follow agreed-upon rules for discussions and carry out assigned role.

FORMATIVE ASSESSMENT

STUDENT CHECK-IN

Have students reflect on how well they synthesized the unit's information. Then have them reflect using the Check-In routine.

Make Connections

MULTIMODAL

Connect to a Big Idea

COLLABORATE **Text to Text** Write this Big Idea question on the board: *In what ways can things change?* Divide the class into small groups. Each group will compare and contrast ideas that they have learned during the course of the unit in order to answer the Big Idea question. Model how to compare this information by using examples from the **Leveled Readers** and what students have read in this unit's selections.

Collaborative Conversations Have students review their notes and organizers before they begin their discussions. Have each group pick one student to take notes. Explain that each group will use an Accordion Foldable® to record their ideas. You may wish to model how to use an Accordion Foldable® to record comparisons of texts.

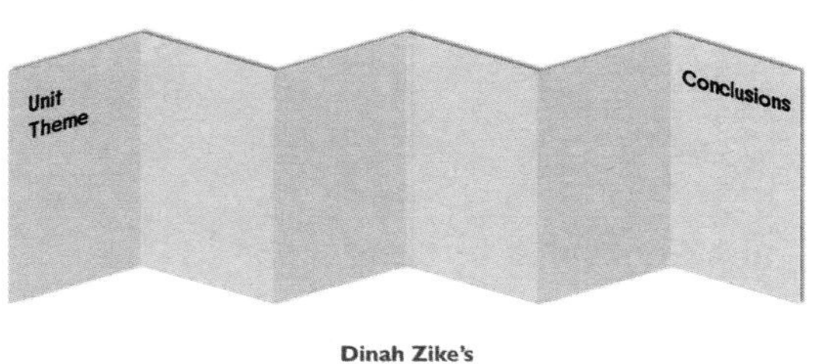

Dinah Zike's FOLDABLES Study Organizer

Present Ideas and Synthesize Information When students finish their discussions, ask for a volunteer from each group to read their notes aloud. After each group has presented their ideas, ask: *What are the five most important things we have learned about how things can change?* Lead a class discussion and list students' ideas on the board. Have students share any personal or emotional connections they felt to the texts they read and listened to over the course of the unit.

Building Knowledge Encourage students to continue building knowledge about the Big Idea. Display the online Unit Bibliography and have students search online for articles and other resources related to the Big Idea. After each group has presented their ideas, ask: *How can change be a good thing?* Lead a class discussion asking students to use the information from their charts to answer the question and to use evidence to support their answers.

Reflect At the end of the discussions, have groups reflect on their collaboration and acknowledge the contributions of one another.

Reflect on Your Learning

COLLABORATE **Talk About It** Reflect on what you learned in this unit. Then talk with a partner about how you did.

I am really proud of how I can ____________________

Something I need to work more on is ____________________

Share a goal you have with a partner.

My Goal Set a goal for Unit 6. In your reader's notebook, write about what you can do to get there.

Unit 5 • Reflect on Your Learning 113

Reading/Writing Companion, p. 113

Reflect on Your Learning

Talk About It

COLLABORATE Remind students that one meaning of *reflect* is to think carefully about something you have done. Give students time to reflect on what they have learned in Unit 5. Ask: *How did the skills and strategies you learned help you with reading and writing in this unit? How can the things you learned help you do other things?* Have partners answer these questions together, using their reader's and writer's notebooks to support their discussions.

Then guide partners to discuss what they did in Unit 5 that made them feel proud and what they need to continue working on. Have students complete the sentence starters on page 113 of the **Reading/Writing Companion**. Encourage students to review their work and the feedback they received throughout the unit. They can also review their completed My Goals bars on pages 11, 37, 63, and 85 of the Reading/Writing Companion.

Review students' reflections and guide them in forming a plan to continue developing skills they need to work on.

Set a Unit 6 Goal

Have students set their own learning goals for the next unit. Have partners or small groups flip through Unit 6 of the Reading/Writing Companion to get an idea of what to expect. Pairs can discuss their goals and their plans for achieving them. Point out that sharing goals can help us achieve them. Then have students record their goals and plans in their reader's notebooks.

LEARNING GOALS

We can reflect on our learning and set our own learning goals.

OBJECTIVES

Come to discussions prepared, having read or studied required material; explicitly draw on that preparation and other information known about the topic to explore ideas under discussion.

Follow agreed-upon rules for discussions and carry out assigned roles.

Reflect on learning.

HABITS OF LEARNING

I am a part of a community of learners.

Ask students to reflect on the unit's Habit of Learning and connect the habit to their life outside of school. Ask:

- Why is it important to be able to share information with others?
- How are out-of-school activity groups, such as sports teams or scouting groups, also "communities of learners"?
- Why is it important to listen actively and build on others' thoughts as a member of one of those groups?

FORMATIVE ASSESSMENT

STUDENT CHECK-IN

Have students share one thing they are proud of learning. Then have them reflect using the Check-In routine.

LEARNING GOALS

- We can use effective speaking strategies.
- We can use effective listening strategies.

OBJECTIVES

Engage effectively in a range of collaborative discussions with diverse partners, building on others' ideas and expressing their own clearly.

Pose and respond to specific questions by making comments that contribute to the discussion and elaborate on the remarks of others.

Report on a topic or text or present an opinion, sequencing ideas logically and using appropriate facts and relevant, descriptive details to support main ideas or themes; speak clearly at an understandable pace.

DIGITAL TOOLS

Students may use these tools:

How to Give a Presentation (Collaborative Conversations Video)

Presentation Checklist

FORMATIVE ASSESSMENT

STUDENT CHECK-IN

Speaking Have students use the Presentation Rubric to reflect on their presentations.

Listening Have partners share key ideas they heard during the presentations.

Then have students reflect using the Check-In routine.

TEACHER CHOICE

As you wrap up the unit, invite students to present their work to small groups, the class, or a larger audience. Choose from among these options:

✓ **Reader's Theater:** Have students perform the play on page T292.

✓ **Research and Inquiry Projects:** Small groups can share their completed projects. See pages T26, T106, and T186.

✓ **Inquiry Space:** Students can give multimodal presentations of the work they developed using Inquiry Space. See page T306.

✓ **Publishing Celebrations:** Have students share one of the pieces of writing they worked on throughout the unit. See page T308.

Use the Speaking and Listening minilessons below to help students prepare.

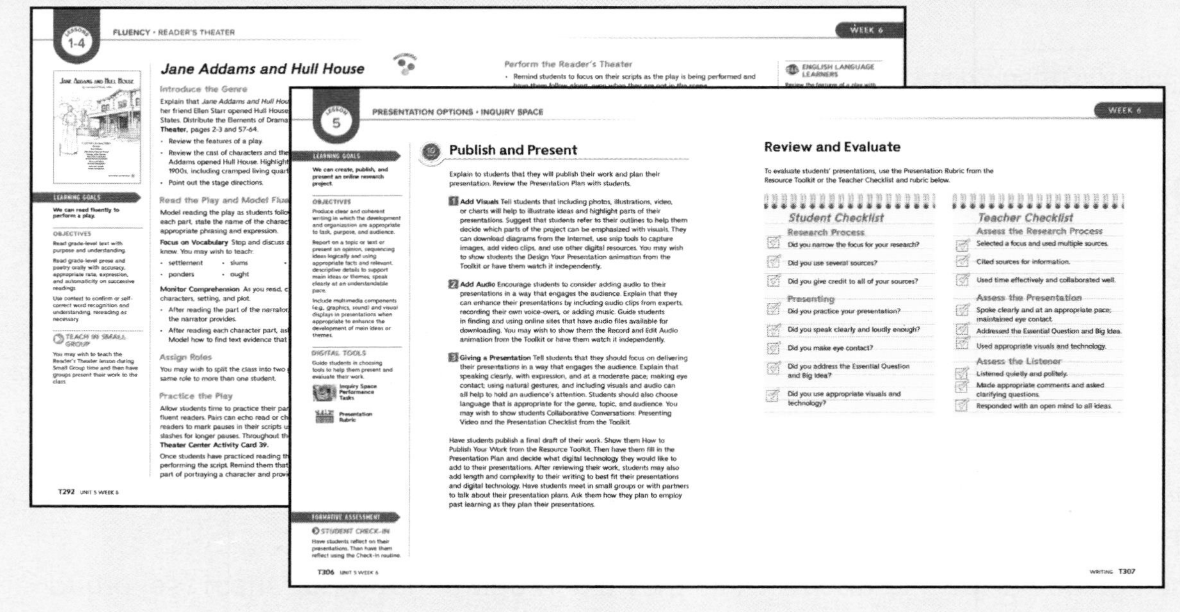
FLUENCY • READER'S THEATER

Jane Addams and Hull House

PRESENTATION OPTIONS • INQUIRY SPACE

Publish and Present

Review and Evaluate

Student Checklist

Teacher Checklist

T292 UNIT 5 WEEK 6

T306 UNIT 5 WEEK 6

WRITING T307

OPTION 10 mins Speaking

Explain to students that when orally giving a formal presentation to a large audience, such as a whole class, they should remember these strategies:

- Rehearse the presentation in front of a friend and ask for feedback.
- Speak slowly and clearly.
- Emphasize points so the audience can follow important ideas.
- Make appropriate eye contact with people in the audience.
- Use hand gestures naturally when appropriate.

Remind students to time themselves during a practice session to allow enough time for questions from the audience following the presentation.

Listening

Remind students that an effective listener

- listens without interruption for facts and key ideas about the topic.
- stays focused on the speaker's presentation and ignores distractions.
- is prepared to ask relevant questions and make pertinent. comments after the presentation is finished.
- listens carefully to evaluate the speaker's perspectives.
- articulates thoughts clearly and builds upon the ideas of others.

Resource Toolkit Invite students to write down any questions they have during the presentation. Guide a discussion of the presentation, asking some students to identify its key ideas. You may wish to have students complete the Listening Checklist from the Resource Toolkit. Discuss how listeners would strive to maintain respect and careful attention in whatever setting the presentation took place.

ELL ENGLISH LANGUAGE LEARNERS

Use the strategies to encourage participation and develop oral proficiency:

- Give students ample time to present and respond.
- Give positive confirmation. Repeat correct response in a clear, loud voice and at a slower pace to motivate students.
- Repeat responses to model the proper form for incorrect grammar or pronunciation.

Presentation Rubric

4 Excellent	3 Good	2 Fair	1 Unsatisfactory
• presents the information clearly • includes many facts and details • includes sophisticated observations	• presents the information adequately • provides adequate facts and details • includes relevant observations	• attempts to present information • offers few or vague facts and details • includes few or irrelevant personal observations	• shows little grasp of the task • presents irrelevant information • reflects extreme difficulty with research or presentation

LEARNING GOALS

We can create, publish, and present an online research project.

OBJECTIVES

Produce clear and coherent writing in which the development and organization are appropriate to task, purpose, and audience.

Report on a topic or text or present an opinion, sequencing ideas logically and using appropriate facts and relevant, descriptive details to support main ideas or themes; speak clearly at an understandable pace.

Include multimedia components (e.g., graphics, sound) and visual displays in presentations when appropriate to enhance the development of main ideas or themes.

DIGITAL TOOLS

Guide students in choosing tools to help them present and evaluate their work.

Inquiry Space Performance Tasks

Presentation Rubric

FORMATIVE ASSESSMENT

STUDENT CHECK-IN

Have students reflect on their presentations. Then have them reflect using the Check-In routine.

Publish and Present

Explain to students that they will publish their work and plan their presentation. Review the Presentation Plan with students.

1 Add Visuals Tell students that including photos, illustrations, video, or charts will help to illustrate ideas and highlight parts of their presentations. Suggest that students refer to their outlines to help them decide which parts of the project can be emphasized with visuals. They can download diagrams from the Internet, use snip tools to capture images, add video clips, and use other digital resources. You may wish to show students the Design Your Presentation animation from the Toolkit or have them watch it independently.

2 Add Audio Encourage students to consider adding audio to their presentations in a way that engages the audience. Explain that they can enhance their presentations by including audio clips from experts, recording their own voice-overs, or adding music. Guide students in finding and using online sites that have audio files available for downloading. You may wish to show them the Record and Edit Audio animation from the Toolkit or have them watch it independently.

3 Giving a Presentation Tell students that they should focus on delivering their presentations in a way that engages the audience. Explain that speaking clearly, with expression, and at a moderate pace; making eye contact; using natural gestures; and including visuals and audio can all help to hold an audience's attention. Students should also choose language that is appropriate for the genre, topic, and audience. You may wish to show students Collaborative Conversations: Presenting Video and the Presentation Checklist from the Toolkit.

Have students publish a final draft of their work. Show them How to Publish Your Work from the Resource Toolkit. Then have them fill in the Presentation Plan and decide what digital technology they would like to add to their presentations. After reviewing their work, students may also add length and complexity to their writing to best fit their presentations and digital technology. Have students meet in small groups or with partners to talk about their presentation plans. Ask them how they plan to employ past learning as they plan their presentations.

Review and Evaluate

To evaluate students' presentations, use the Presentation Rubric from the Resource Toolkit or the Teacher Checklist and rubric below.

Student Checklist

Research Process

- ☑ Did you narrow the focus for your research?
- ☑ Did you use several sources?
- ☑ Did you give credit to all of your sources?

Presenting

- ☑ Did you practice your presentation?
- ☑ Did you speak clearly and loudly enough?
- ☑ Did you make eye contact?
- ☑ Did you address the Essential Question and Big Idea?
- ☑ Did you use appropriate visuals and technology?

Teacher Checklist

Assess the Research Process

- ☑ Selected a focus and used multiple sources.
- ☑ Cited sources for information.
- ☑ Used time effectively and collaborated well.

Assess the Presentation

- ☑ Spoke clearly and at an appropriate pace; maintained eye contact.
- ☑ Addressed the Essential Question and Big Idea.
- ☑ Used appropriate visuals and technology.

Assess the Listener

- ☑ Listened quietly and politely.
- ☑ Made appropriate comments and asked clarifying questions.
- ☑ Responded with an open mind to all ideas.

LEARNING GOALS

- We can use effective strategies to present our writing.
- We can use effective strategies to listen to presentations.

OBJECTIVES

Engage effectively in a range of collaborative discussions with diverse partners, building on others' ideas and expressing their own clearly.

Pose and respond to specific questions by making comments that contribute to the discussion and elaborate on the remarks of others.

Produce clear and coherent writing in which the development and organization are appropriate to task, purpose, and audience.

Report on a topic or text or present an opinion, sequencing ideas logically and using appropriate facts and relevant, descriptive details to support main ideas or themes; speak clearly at an understandable pace.

TEACH IN SMALL GROUP

You may wish to arrange groups of various abilities to complete their presentations, evaluate each other's work, and discuss portfolio choices.

FORMATIVE ASSESSMENT

STUDENT CHECK-IN

Presenting Have partners share reflections on their writing presentations.

Listening Have partners share one important idea they learned.

Have students reflect using the Check-In routine.

Present Writing

Select the Writing

Now is the time for students to share one of the pieces of writing they have worked on through the unit. Have them review their writing and select one piece to present. You may wish to invite parents or students from other classes to the Publishing Celebrations.

Preparing for Presentations

Tell students they will need to prepare in order to best present their writing. Allow students time to rehearse their presentations. Encourage them to reread their writing a few times. This will help them become more familiar with their pieces so they won't have to read word by word as they present.

Students should consider any visuals or digital elements they may want to use to present their writing. Discuss a few possible options with students.

- Do they have illustrations, photos, charts, maps, or diagrams that would support their writing?
- Is there a video that connects to the focus of their writing?
- Is there a Web site or multimedia presentation they could use to offer additional information?

Students can practice presenting to a partner in the classroom. They can also practice with family members at home, or in front of a mirror. Share the following checklist with students to help them focus on important parts of their presentations as they rehearse. Discuss each point on the checklist.

Speaking Checklist

Review the Speaking Checklist with students as they practice.

- ☐ Have all of your notes and visuals ready.
- ☐ Take a few deep breaths.
- ☐ Stand up straight.
- ☐ Look at the audience.
- ☐ Speak clearly and slowly, particularly when communicating complex information.
- ☐ Speak loud enough so everyone can hear you.
- ☐ Emphasize important points.
- ☐ Use appropriate, natural gestures.
- ☐ Hold your visual aids so everyone can see them.
- ☐ Point to relevant features of your visual aids as you speak.

Listening to Presentations

Remind students that they will be part of the audience for other students' presentations. A listener serves an important role. Review with students the following Listening Checklist.

Listening Checklist

DURING THE PRESENTATION

- ☐ Pay attention to how the speaker uses visuals to enhance his or her presentation.
- ☐ Notice how the speaker uses details in his or her writing.
- ☐ Take notes on one or two things you like about the presentation.
- ☐ Write one question or comment you have about the presentation.
- ☐ Do not talk during the presentation.

AFTER THE PRESENTATION

- ☐ Tell why you liked the presentation.
- ☐ Ask a relevant question or make a pertinent comment based on what was presented.
- ☐ Only comment on the presentation when it is your turn.
- ☐ If someone else makes the same comment first, elaborate on that person's comment.

Portfolio Choice

Ask students to select one finished piece of writing, as well as two revisions, to include in their writing portfolio. As students consider their choices, have them use the questions below.

FINISHED WRITING	WRITING ENTRY REVISIONS
Does your writing	**Do your revisions show**
• organize information logically? • have a strong conclusion? • have few or no spelling and grammatical errors? • demonstrate neatness when published?	• more details that develop the topic? • stronger openings? • additional time-order words, phrases, and clauses? • improved sentence structure and word choice?

Explain that students will also have the opportunity to improve their finished writing. Use the suggestions on the Level Up Writing lesson on pages T286–T287 to meet students' individual needs.

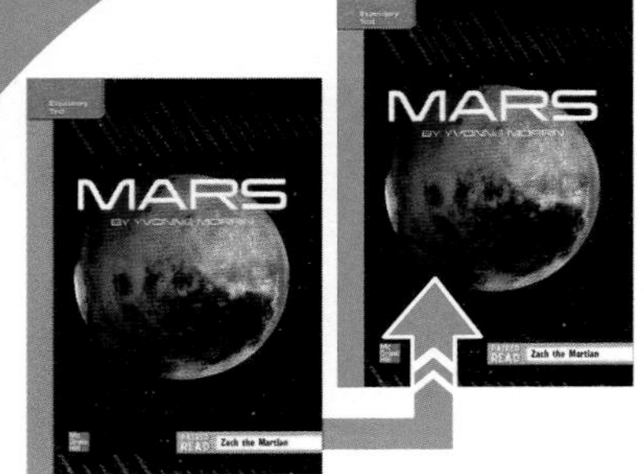

Leveled Reader

OBJECTIVES

Draw on information from multiple print or digital sources, demonstrating the ability to locate an answer to a question quickly or to solve a problem efficiently.

Read and comprehend informational texts, including history/social studies, science, and technical texts, at the high end of the text complexity band independently and proficiently.

Determine or clarify the meaning of unknown and multiple-meaning words and phrases, choosing flexibly from a range of strategies.

Use context (e.g., cause/effect relationships and comparisons in text) as a clue to the meaning of a word or phrase.

Use common, grade-appropriate Greek and Latin affixes and roots as clues to the meaning of a word (e.g., *photograph, photosynthesis*).

Approaching Level to On Level

Mars

Preview Discuss what students remember about the planet Mars. Tell them they will be reading a more challenging version of *Mars*.

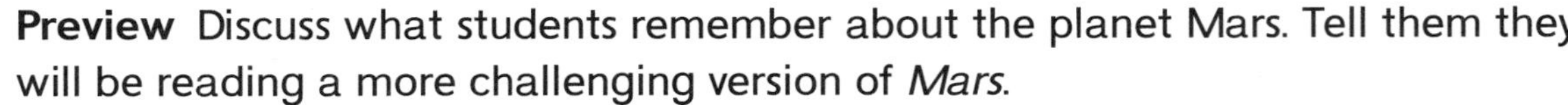

Vocabulary Use the Visual Vocabulary Cards and routine to review.

▶ **Specific Vocabulary** Review with students the following content and academic words that are new to this title. Model how to use vocabulary strategies, such as breaking the word into parts, identifying context clues, and checking the glossary or a dictionary, to determine the meanings of *hostile, theories, disproven, deduced, illusion, reliable, terrain, extremophiles, vapor, detected,* and *geology.*

▶ **Connection of Ideas** Students may need help understanding why the author included certain text features in the selection, including the diagrams on pages 3, 5, 6, and 13; the chart on page 4; the timeline on page 9; the sidebars on pages 11 and 15; and various images and captions throughout the book. With students, summarize the information provided by a section of the main text. Then compare the information provided by a supporting text feature or features. Discuss how the features add to the reader's understanding of the ideas in the main text.

▶ **Sentence Structure** The use of colons in complex sentences on pages 2, 4, 11, and 12 may be challenging to students. Guide students in reading the paragraph on page 4. Ask them to state what the paragraph is about. Then have students identify the text after the colon. Point out that the text that comes after the colon helps you understand the text that comes before it. Ask: *Which part of the sentence tells you why Mars is a hostile place?* (the part after the colon) *Why would visitors find Mars hostile?* (It is arid, cold, covered in rocks, and seemingly without life.) Provide similar guidance as needed.

Ask students to complete the Respond to Reading on page 18. Have students complete the Paired Read and hold Literature Circles.

On Level to Beyond Level

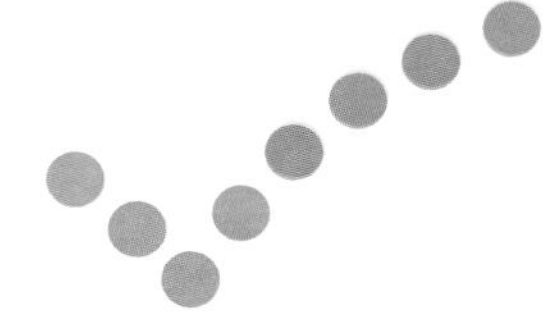

Mars

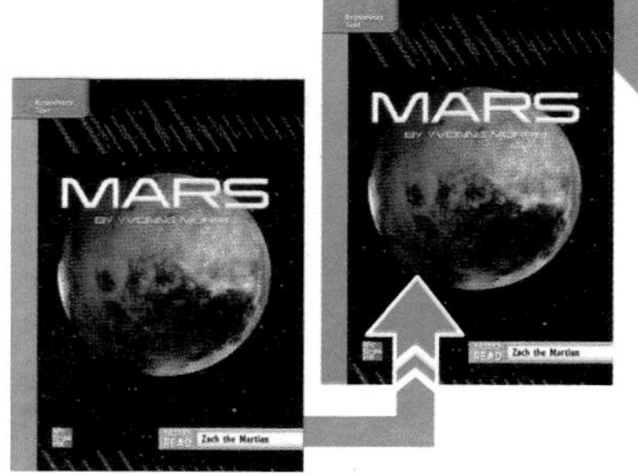

Leveled Reader

OBJECTIVES

Explain the relationships or interactions between two or more individuals, events, ideas, or concepts in a historical, scientific, or technical text based on specific information in the text.

Read and comprehend informational texts, including history/social studies, science, and technical texts, at the high end of the text complexity band independently and proficiently.

Determine or clarify the meaning of unknown and multiple-meaning words and phrases, choosing flexibly from a range of strategies.

Use context (e.g., cause/effect relationships and comparisons in text) as a clue to the meaning of a word or phrase.

Use common, grade-appropriate Greek and Latin affixes and roots as clues to the meaning of a word (e.g., *photograph, photosynthesis*).

Preview Discuss what students remember about the planet Mars. Tell them they will be reading a more challenging version of *Mars*.

Vocabulary Use the Visual Vocabulary Cards and routine to review.

▶ **Specific Vocabulary** Review with students the following content and academic words that are new to this title. Model how to use vocabulary strategies, such as breaking the word into parts, identifying context clues, and checking the glossary or a dictionary, to determine the meanings of *hovered, unmanned, ferocious, challenged, obstacles,* and *coordinate*. Students may also need guidance in understanding the more unusual uses of the multiple-meaning words *boasts* and *recording* on page 11.

▶ **Connection of Ideas** Students may need help connecting text features in the selection to the content in the main text. After reading page 14, discuss the information about psychrophiles in the caption and guide students to infer the climate that can be found in Antarctica or the Arctic. (The main text and caption say that psychrophiles can live in areas of extreme cold, so Antarctica and the Arctic must be areas of extreme cold.) Students may also need guidance in determining the author's purpose for including specific supporting details in the text, such as the calculation of the length of a Mars day described on page 8.

▶ **Sentence Structure** Students may need guidance with the parallel structure in more complicated sentences. The parallel structure used to express the Goldilocks analogy on page 13 may challenge students. Have students read the first paragraph on page 16 and identify the gerund phrases in the last sentence. Then ask: *What will using airplanes and balloons, using tunnelers, and returning soil and rock samples to Earth allow scientists to do?* (These actions will allow scientists to study Mars without having to leave Earth.) As needed, repeat a similar procedure for students challenged by the parallel gerund phrases on page 5, paragraph 1.

Ask students to complete the Respond to Reading on page 18. Have students complete the Paired Read and hold Literature Circles.

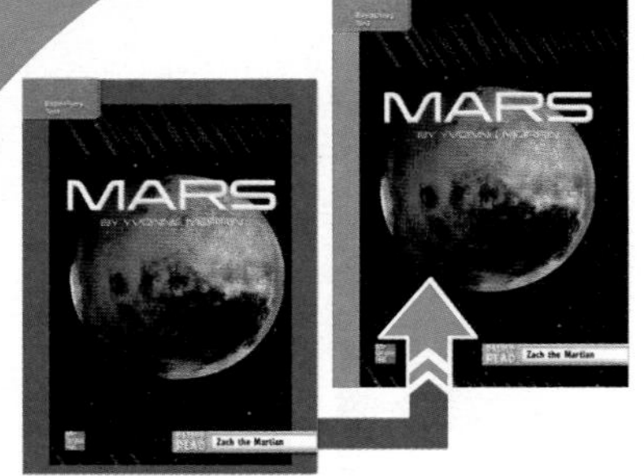

Leveled Reader

OBJECTIVES

Draw on information from multiple print or digital sources, demonstrating the ability to locate an answer to a question quickly or to solve a problem efficiently.

Read and comprehend informational texts, including history/social studies, science, and technical texts, at the high end of the text complexity band independently and proficiently.

Determine or clarify the meaning of unknown and multiple-meaning words and phrases, choosing flexibly from a range of strategies.

Use context (e.g., cause/effect relationships and comparisons in text) as a clue to the meaning of a word or phrase.

Use common, grade-appropriate Greek and Latin affixes and roots as clues to the meaning of a word (e.g., *photograph, photosynthesis*).

English Language Learners to On Level

Mars

Preview Remind students that expository text gives facts about a topic. Discuss with them what they remember reading about the planet Mars.

Vocabulary Use the Visual Vocabulary Cards and routine to review the vocabulary. Point out cognates: *aproximadamente, astronómico, cálculos, criterios, diámetro, evaluar, esfera.*

▶ **Specific Vocabulary** Help students look for clues that can help them figure out the meaning of the idiom *caused a stir* in paragraph 2 on page 6. Read paragraph 1 with students. Ask: *What clues in this paragraph tell you that people were upset by Copernicus's theory?* ("people were shocked") Then return to paragraph 2. *What did most people believe?* (They believed that planets orbited the sun in perfect circles.) *What did Kepler's theory prove?* (This was not true.) *How did that likely make people feel?* (shocked) As needed, provide support for science words, such as *extremophiles* on page 14, and academic words, such as *misinterpreted* (page 5), *disproven* (page 5), and *detected* (page 15). Discuss how using vocabulary strategies, such as breaking words into parts and identifying context clues within a sentence, can help students figure out difficult words.

▶ **Connection of Ideas** Help students understand how information in text features connects to the content in the text. Read pages 2–3 with students, and then draw their attention to the diagram. Provide support for the title, labels, and caption. Then ask: *What does the diagram show?* (The diagram shows the path of a star in the night sky.) *What part of paragraph 1 on page 2 does the diagram help you understand?* (The diagram helps me understand why people thought that stars looked like they were moving in an arc, but the red light of Mars looked like it wandered around the sky.)

▶ **Sentence Structure** Students may need guidance with punctuation in complex sentences, such as the colon in the description of Mars on page 4. Define *hostile* as needed. Then point out that the colon in the first sentence divides the sentence into two parts. *In the first part, we read that Mars is a very hostile place. The text that comes after the colon explains why it is hostile.* Repeat for the colon in the sidebar on page 11.

Ask students to complete the Respond to Reading on page 18. Have students complete the Paired Read and hold Literature Circles.

Beyond Level to Self-Selected Trade Book

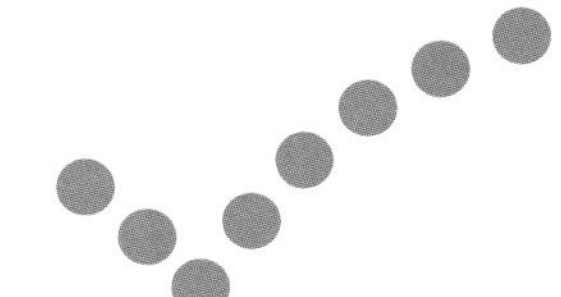

Leveled Reader

Advanced Level Trade Book

Independent Reading

Help students identify the particular focus of their reading based on the text they choose. Students who have chosen the same title will work in groups to closely read the selection.

Taking Notes Assign a graphic organizer for students to use to take notes as they read. Reinforce a specific comprehension focus from the unit by choosing one of the graphic organizers that best fits the book.

EXAMPLES

Fiction	Expository Text
Plot: Conflict	Central Idea and Relevant Details
Graphic Organizer 10	Graphic Organizer 7

Ask and Answer Questions Remind students to ask questions as they read and to record their questions on a piece of chart paper. As students meet, have them discuss the sections they have read. They can discuss the questions they noted and work together to find text evidence to support their answers. Have them write their responses.

EXAMPLES

Fiction	Expository Text
How are the conflict and resolution alike? How are they different?	What relevant details help you determine the central idea?

Literature Circles Suggest that students hold Literature Circles and share interesting facts or favorite parts from the books they read.

OBJECTIVES

By the end of year, read and comprehend informational texts, including history/social studies, science, and technical texts, at the high end of the text complexity band independently and proficiently.

By the end of the year, read and comprehend informational texts, including history/social studies, science, and technical texts, at the high end of the grades 4-5 text complexity band independently and proficiently.

Draw evidence from literary or informational texts to support analysis, reflection, and research.

Apply grade 5 Reading standards to literature.

Apply grade 5 Reading standards to informational texts.

Summative Assessment

Unit 5 Tested Skills

COMPREHENSION	VOCABULARY	GRAMMAR	WRITING
• Plot: Characterization • Plot: Conflict • Text Structure: Compare and Contrast • Text Features: Diagrams, Charts, Headings • Central Idea and Relevant Details • Author's Perspective • Figurative Language: Imagery • Comparative Reading	• Greek Roots • Root Words • Idioms	• Clauses • Complex Sentences • Adjectives That Compare • Comparing with *Good* and *Bad*	• Narrative Writing Prompt: Personal Narrative

Additional Assessment Options

Fluency

Conduct assessments individually using the differentiated passages in **Fluency Assessment**. Students' expected fluency goal for this unit is 136–156 words correct per minute (WCPM) with an accuracy rate of 95% or higher.

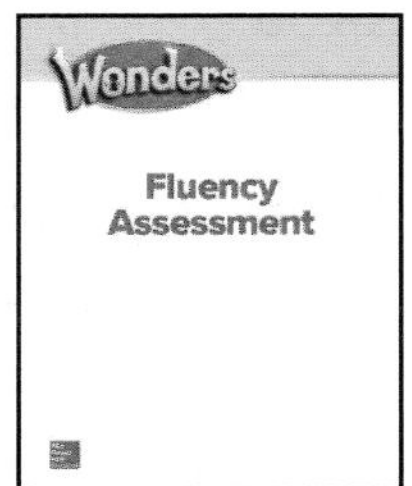

ELL Assessment

Assess English Language Learner proficiency and track student progress using the **English Language Development Assessment.** This resource provides unit assessments and rubrics to evaluate students' progress in the areas of listening and reading comprehension, vocabulary, grammar, speaking, and writing. These assessments can also be used to determine the language proficiency levels for subsequent set of instructions.

Making the Most of Assessment Results

Make data-based grouping decisions by using the following reports to verify assessment results. For additional student support options refer to the reteaching and enrichment opportunities.

ONLINE ASSESSMENT CENTER

- ***Gradebook***

DATA DASHBOARD

- ***Recommendations Report***
- ***Activity Report***
- ***Skills Report***
- ***Progress Report***
- ***Grade Card Report***

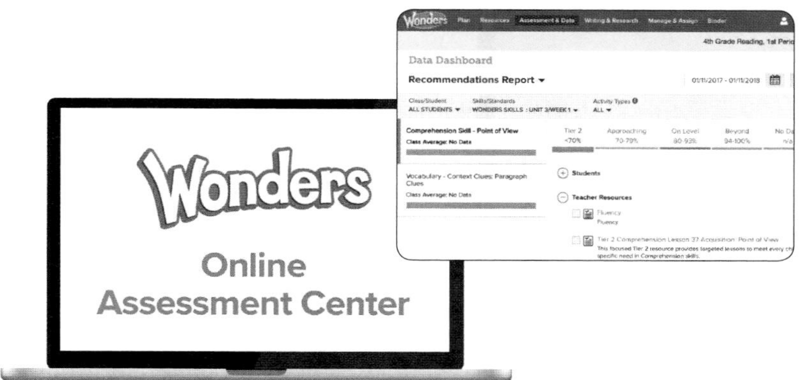

 Assign practice pages online for auto-grading.

TIER 2

Reteaching Opportunities with Intervention Online PDFs

IF STUDENTS SCORE . . .	THEN ASSIGN . . .
below 70% in **comprehension. . .**	tested skills using the **Comprehension PDF**
below 70% in **vocabulary. . .**	tested skills using the **Vocabulary PDF**
below 8 on **writing prompt. . .**	tested skills using the **Writing and Grammar PDF**
0–135 WCPM in **fluency. . .**	tested skills using the **Fluency PDF**

Use the* Phonics/Word Study PDF *and* Foundational Skills Kit *for additional reteaching opportunities.

Enrichment Opportunities

Beyond Level small group lessons and resources include suggestions for additional activities in the following areas to extend learning opportunities for gifted and talented students:

- ***Leveled Readers***
- ***Genre Passages***
- ***Vocabulary***
- ***Comprehension***
- ***Leveled Reader Library Online***
- ***Center Activity Cards***

Next Steps

NEXT STEPS FOR YOUR STUDENTS' PROGRESS . . .

Interpret the data you have collected from multiple sources throughout this unit, including formal and informal assessments.

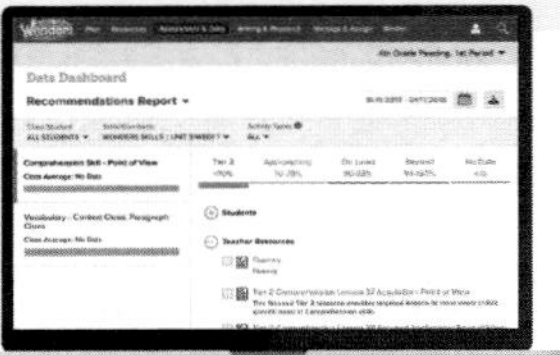
Data Dashboard

Who

Regrouping Decisions

- Check student progress against your interpretation of the data, and regroup as needed.
- Determine how English Language Learners are progressing.
- Consider whether students are ready to Level Up or Accelerate.

What

Target Instruction

- Analyze data from multiple measures to decide whether to review and reinforce particular skills or concepts or whether you need to reteach them.
- Target instruction to meet students' strengths/needs.
- Use Data Dashboard recommendations to help determine which lessons to provide to different groups of students.

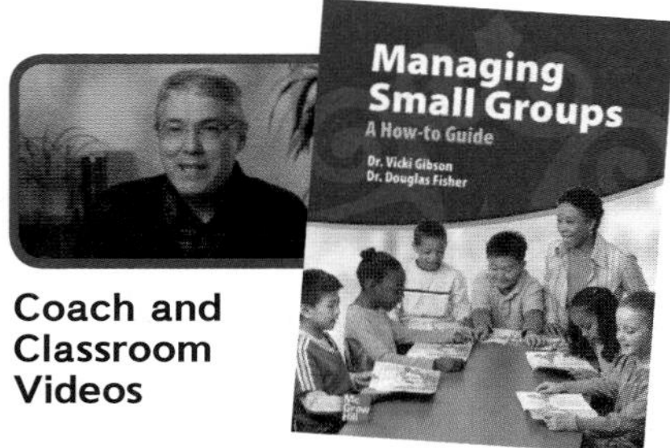

Coach and Classroom Videos

Methodology

How

Modify Instruction

- Vary materials and/or instructional strategies.
- Address students' social and emotional development.
- Provide students with opportunities for self-reflection and self-assessment.

AUTHOR INSIGHT

"Moving forward, use assessment results as a guide to differentiate and adapt instruction to best meet students' needs—perhaps through collaboration, which builds comprehension skills, reflective writing, and vocabulary as well as expands one another's knowledge and expertise."
–Kathy Bumgardner

Courtesy of Kathy Bumgardner

NEXT STEPS FOR YOU . . .

As you prepare your students to move on to the next unit, don't forget to take advantage of the many opportunities available in your online course for self-evaluation and professional development.

Instructional Routines

Manage Assessments

Program Author Whitepapers

Research Base

Contents

Program Information

Additional Digital Resources

my.mheducation.com

- Unit Bibliography
- Word Lists
- More Resources

Scope and Sequence

<table>
<tr><th>Text Set Focus</th><th>Read Aloud</th><th>Shared Read</th><th>Literature Anthology</th><th>Leveled Readers</th><th>Vocabulary</th></tr>
<tr><td>Text Set 1:
Weeks 1 and 2

Essential Question: How can experiencing nature change the way you think about it?

Genre: Narrative Nonfiction

Differentiated Genre Passages available</td><td>Interactive Read Aloud: “Capturing the Natural World”

Genre: Narrative Nonfiction</td><td>“A Life in the Woods”

Genre: Narrative Nonfiction

Lexile: 770L

ELL Scaffolded Shared Read available</td><td>Anchor Text
Camping with the President
Genre: Narrative Nonfiction
Lexile: 760L

Paired Selection
“A Walk with Teddy”
Genre: Autobiography
Lexile: 910L</td><td><u>Main Selections</u>
Genre: Narrative Nonfiction
● Save This Space!
Lexile: 750L
● Save This Space!
Lexile: 960L
● Save This Space!
Lexile: 730L
● Save This Space!
Lexile: 980L

<u>Paired Selections</u>
Genre: Expository Text
● “The Journey of Lewis and Clark”
● “The Journey of Lewis and Clark”
● “The Journey of Lewis and Clark”
● “The Journey of Lewis and Clark”</td><td>Academic Vocabulary: debris, emphasis, encounter, generations, indicated, naturalist, sheer, spectacular

Homographs

Prefixes</td></tr>
<tr><td>Text Set 2:
Weeks 3 and 4

Essential Question: How do we get the things we need?

Genre: Realistic Fiction

Differentiated Genre Passages available</td><td>Interactive Read Aloud: “Finding a Way”

Genre: Realistic Fiction</td><td>“A Fresh Idea”

Genre: Realistic Fiction

Lexile: 760L

ELL Scaffolded Shared Read available</td><td>Anchor Text
One Hen
Genre: Realistic Fiction
Lexile: 810L

Paired Selection
“Reading Between the Dots”
Genre: Personal Narrative
Lexile: 910L</td><td><u>Main Selections</u>
Genre: Realistic Fiction
● Parker’s Plan
Lexile: 680L
● Can-do Canines
Lexile: 790L
● Can-do Canines
Lexile: 570L
● Cleaning Up the Competition
Lexile: 970L

<u>Paired Selections</u>
Genre: Expository Text
● “Taking Care of Your Money”
● “You Can Bank on It”
● “You Can Bank on It”
● “Growing Money”</td><td>Academic Vocabulary: afford, loan, profit, prosper, risk, savings, scarce, wages

Context Clues: Sentence Clues

Suffixes</td></tr>
<tr><td>Text Set 3:
Week 5

Essential Question: What are the positive and negative effects of new technology?

Genre: Argumentative Text

Differentiated Genre Passages available</td><td>Interactive Read Aloud: “Electronic Books: A New Way to Read”
Genre: Argumentative Text</td><td>“Are Electronic Devices Good for Us?”
Genre: Argumentative Text
Lexile: 900L

ELL Scaffolded Shared Read available</td><td>Anchor Text
The Future of Transportation
Genre: Argumentative Text
Lexile: 870L

Paired Selection
“Getting from Here to There”
Genre: Technical Text
Lexile: 890L</td><td><u>Main Selections</u>
Genre: Expository Text
● What About Robots?
Lexile: 740L
● What About Robots?
Lexile: 840L
● What About Robots?
Lexile: 760L
● What About Robots?
Lexile: 990L

<u>Paired Selections</u>
Genre: Persuasive Text
● “No Substitute”
● “No Substitute”
● “No Substitute”
● “No Substitute”</td><td>Academic Vocabulary: access, advance, analysis, cite, counterpoint, data, drawbacks, reasoning

Greek and Latin Prefixes</td></tr>
</table>

<table>
<tr><th>Week 6</th><th>Reading Digitally</th><th>Fluency</th><th>Connect to Content: Science</th><th>Connect to Content: Social Studies</th><th>Writing</th><th>Presentation Options</th></tr>
<tr><td>Extend, Connect, and Assess</td><td>Genre: Online Article
“Take It from Nature”</td><td>Reader’s Theater:
It Couldn’t Be Done</td><td>Passages
Genre: Narrative Nonfiction
“A Protector of Nature”
Genre: Narrative Nonfiction
“Children Save the Rain Forest”
Genre: Realistic Fiction
“Solutions, Not Complaints”

Activities
Compare the Passages
Complete a Map
Write an Essay</td><td>Passages
“The NYC Subway: An Interview with a Transit Supervisor”
“Solutions, Not Complaints”

Activities
Compare the Passages
Write a Letter</td><td>Writing Process
Write to Sources: Argumentative Writing
Analyze the Prompt
Analyze the Sources: “Honoring Black Women Inventors of the Past,” “Morse Code Is Safe and Reliable,” “All Aboard on America’s Rail System”
Plan: Organize Ideas
Draft: Elaboration
Revise: Peer Conferences</td><td>Reader’s Theater

Inquiry Space

Writing</td></tr>
</table>

Unit 1

Comprehension	Phonics and Spelling	Fluency	Writing and Grammar	Research and Inquiry
Ask and Answer Questions Primary and Secondary Sources Text Structure: Cause and Effect Author's Perspective	**Week 1** Short Vowels **Week 2** Long Vowels *Differentiated Spelling Lists available*	**Week 1** Accuracy and Expression **Week 2** Intonation and Rate	**Respond to Reading** **Writing Process** Write to Sources: Argumentative Writing Analyze the Rubric Rubric Minilesson: Make a Claim Analyze the Student Model **Grammar and Mechanics** **Week 1:** Sentences; Punctuating Sentences **Week 2:** Subjects and Predicates; Commas	**Project:** Experiencing Nature **Product:** Promotional Map **Blast:** "Protecting Our Parks"
Reread Plot: Conflict and Resolution Plot: Events Text Structure: Chronology	**Week 3** Words with /ū/, /ů/, and /ü/ **Week 4** *r*-controlled Vowels /är/, /âr/, /ôr/ *Differentiated Spelling Lists available*	**Week 3** Expression and Phrasing **Week 4** Rate	**Respond to Reading** **Writing Process** Write to Sources: Argumentative Writing Analyze the Prompt Analyze the Sources: "Landmark Deal Approved!," "Fund Florida Forever!," "Revitalize Florida's Downtowns" Plan: Organize Ideas Draft: Relevant Evidence Revise: Peer Conferences **Grammar and Mechanics** **Week 3:** Compound Sentences; Punctuation in Compound Sentences **Week 4:** Complex Sentences; Commas	**Project:** Meeting Needs **Product:** Compare/Contrast Chart **Blast:** "Clothing, Food, and Shelter"
Reread Headings and Graphs Author's Claim Author's Purpose	**Week 5** *r*-controlled Vowel /ûr/ *Differentiated Spelling Lists available*	**Week 5** Accuracy and Phrasing	**Respond to Reading** **Writing Process** Write to Sources: Argumentative Writing Analyze the Rubric Rubric Minilesson: Strong Introduction Analyze the Student Model **Grammar and Mechanics** **Week 5:** Run-on Sentences; Correcting Run-on Sentences	**Project:** Technology **Product:** Debate **Blast:** "Riding Technology's Rollercoaster"

Scope and Sequence

Text Set Focus	Read Aloud	Shared Read	Literature Anthology	Leveled Readers	Vocabulary
Text Set 1: Weeks 1 and 2 **Essential Question:** What do good problem solvers do? **Genre:** Expository Text *Differentiated Genre Passages available*	**Interactive Read Aloud:** "The Haudenosaunee Confederacy" **Genre:** Expository Text	"Creating a Nation" **Genre:** Expository Text **Lexile:** 690L *ELL Scaffolded Shared Read available*	**Anchor Text** *Who Wrote the U.S. Constitution?* **Genre:** Expository Text **Lexile:** 760L **Paired Selection** "Wordsmiths" **Genre:** Expository Text **Lexile:** 970L	**Main Selections** **Genre:** Expository Text ● *The Bill of Rights* **Lexile:** 820L ● *The Bill of Rights* **Lexile:** 920L ● *The Bill of Rights* **Lexile:** 840L ● *The Bill of Rights* **Lexile:** 1000L **Paired Selections** **Genre:** Expository Text ● "Having Your Say" ● "Having Your Say" ● "Having Your Say" ● "Having Your Say"	**Academic Vocabulary:** committees, convention, debate, proposal, representatives, resolve, situation, union Context Clues Dictionary and Glossary
Text Set 2: Weeks 3 and 4 **Essential Question:** When has a plan helped you accomplish a task? **Genre:** Folktale *Differentiated Genre Passages available*	**Interactive Read Aloud:** "Lost Lake and the Golden Cup" **Genre:** Folktale	"The Magical Lost Brocade" **Genre:** Folktale **Lexile:** 740L *ELL Scaffolded Shared Read available*	**Anchor Text** *Blancaflor* **Genre:** Folktale **Lexile:** 870L **Paired Selection** "From Tale to Table" **Genre:** Expository Text **Lexile:** 990L	**Main Selections** **Genre:** Folktale ● *The Lion's Whiskers* **Lexile:** 760L ● *The Riddle of the Drum: A Tale from Mexico* **Lexile:** 810L ● *The Riddle of the Drum: A Tale from Mexico* **Lexile:** 570L ● *Clever Manka* **Lexile:** 860L **Paired Selections** **Genre:** Expository Text ● "From Fiber to Fashion" ● "Make a Drum" ● "Make a Drum" ● "From Bee to You"	**Academic Vocabulary:** assuring, detected, emerging, gratitude, guidance, outcome, previous, pursuit Personification Roots
Text Set 3: Week 5 **Essential Question:** What motivates you to accomplish a goal? **Genre:** Poetry *Differentiated Genre Passages available*	**Interactive Read Aloud:** "How to Make a Friend" **Genre:** Narrative Poetry	"A Simple Plan," "Rescue" **Genre:** Narrative and Free Verse Poetry **Lexile:** NP *ELL Scaffolded Shared Read available*	**Anchor Text** "Stage Fright," "Catching Quiet" **Genre:** Narrative and Free Verse Poetry **Lexile:** NP **Paired Selection** "Foul Shot" **Genre:** Free Verse Poetry **Lexile:** NP	**Main Selections** **Genre:** Realistic Fiction ● *Clearing the Jungle* **Lexile:** 650L ● *I Want to Ride!* **Lexile:** 730L ● *I Want to Ride!* **Lexile:** 600L ● *Changing Goals* **Lexile:** 860L **Paired Selections** **Genre:** Poetry ● "Just for Once" ● "Home Run" ● "Smash!" ● "Today's Lesson"	**Academic Vocabulary:** ambitious, memorized, satisfaction, shuddered **Poetry Terms:** narrative, repetition, free verse, rhyme Homographs

Week 6	Reading Digitally	Fluency	Connect to Content: Science	Connect to Content: Social Studies	Writing	Presentation Options
Extend, Connect, and Assess	**Genre:** Online Article "The Long Road"	**Reader's Theater:** *A Boy Named Abe*	**Passages** "Popover! The Ultimate Baked Bubble" "Cooking with Electricity" **Activities** Compare the Passages Make Observations Explain Your Observations	**Passages** "Searching for Freedom" "Supporting Religious Liberty" **Activities** Compare the Passages Make a Timeline	**Writing Process** Write to Sources: Expository Writing Analyze the Prompt Analyze the Sources: "Going Above and Beyond," "The Turtle Lady of Juno Beach," "Community Bird Scientist" Plan: Organize Ideas Draft: Transitions Revise: Peer Conferences	**Reader's Theater** **Inquiry Space** **Writing**

Unit 2

	Comprehension	Phonics and Spelling	Fluency	Writing and Grammar	Research and Inquiry
	Reread Headings and Timelines Text Structure: Problem and Solution Print and Graphic Features	**Week 1** Variant Vowel /ô/; Diphthongs /oi/, /ou/ **Week 2** Plurals *Differentiated Spelling Lists available*	**Week 1** Accuracy and Rate **Week 2** Accuracy and Expression	**Respond to Reading** **Writing Process** Write to Sources: Expository Writing Analyze the Rubric Rubric Minilesson: Central Idea Analyze the Student Model **Grammar and Mechanics** **Week 1:** Kinds of Nouns; Capitalizing Proper Nouns **Week 2:** Singular and Plural Nouns; Forming Plural Nouns	**Project:** Founders Solve Problems **Product:** Multimedia Slideshow **Blast:** "Meet Me in the Middle"
	Make Predictions Plot: Setting Theme Text Structure: Sequence	**Week 3** Inflectional Endings **Week 4** Contractions *Differentiated Spelling Lists available*	**Week 3** Expression and Phrasing **Week 4** Rate	**Respond to Reading** **Writing Process** Write to Sources: Expository Writing Analyze the Prompt Analyze the Sources: "Benjamin Franklin's Bifocals," "Margaret Knight, Engineer and Inventor," "Henry Ford and the Model T" Plan: Organize Ideas Draft: Elaboration Revise: Peer Conferences **Grammar and Mechanics** **Week 3:** More Plural Nouns; Plural Forms and Appositives **Week 4:** Possessive Nouns; Adding *-s* or *-'s*	**Project:** Accomplishing a Task **Product:** Illustrated Food Web **Blast:** "Stand by Your Plan"
	Repetition and Rhyme Narrative and Free Verse Theme Form and Line Breaks	**Week 5** Closed Syllables *Differentiated Spelling Lists available*	**Week 5** Expression and Phrasing	**Respond to Reading** **Writing Process** Write to Sources: Expository Writing Analyze the Rubric Rubric Minilesson: Academic Language Analyze the Student Model **Grammar and Mechanics** **Week 5:** Prepositional Phrases; Punctuating Titles and Letters	**Project:** Achieving Goals **Product:** Comic Strip **Blast:** "Reaching a Goal"

Scope and Sequence

Text Set Focus	Read Aloud	Shared Read	Literature Anthology	Leveled Reader	Vocabulary
Text Set 1: Weeks 1 and 2 **Essential Question:** What can learning about different cultures teach us? **Genre:** Realistic Fiction *Differentiated Genre Passages available*	**Interactive Read Aloud:** "Foods for Thought" **Genre:** Realistic Fiction	"A Reluctant Traveler" **Genre:** Realistic Fiction **Lexile:** 770L *ELL Scaffolded Shared Read available*	**Anchor Text** *They Don't Mean It!* **Genre:** Realistic Fiction **Lexile:** 870L **Paired Selection** "Where Did That Come From?" **Genre:** Expository Text **Lexile:** 940L	**Main Selections** **Genre:** Realistic Fiction *All the Way from Europe* **Lexile:** 690L *Dancing the Flamenco* **Lexile:** 790L *Dancing the Flamenco* **Lexile:** 510L *A Vacation in Minnesota* **Lexile:** 950L **Paired Selections** **Genre:** Expository Text "A Sporting Gift" "Flamenco" "Flamenco" "The Scandinavian State?"	**Academic Vocabulary:** appreciation, blurted, complimenting, congratulate, contradicted, critical, cultural, misunderstanding Context Clues: Cause and Effect Adages
Text Set 2: Weeks 3 and 4 **Essential Question:** What benefits come from people working as a group? **Genre:** Expository Text *Differentiated Genre Passages available*	**Interactive Read Aloud:** "Teamwork in Space" **Genre:** Expository Text	"Gulf Spill Superheroes" **Genre:** Expository Text **Lexile:** 860L *ELL Scaffolded Shared Read available*	**Anchor Text** *Winter's Tail* **Genre:** Expository Text **Lexile:** 940L **Paired Selection** "Helping Hands" **Genre:** Expository Text **Lexile:** 1040L	**Main Selections** **Genre:** Expository Text *The Power of a Team* **Lexile:** 740L *The Power of a Team* **Lexile:** 900L *The Power of a Team* **Lexile:** 800L *The Power of a Team* **Lexile:** 1010L **Paired Selections** **Genre:** Expository Text "Hands on the Wheel" "Hands on the Wheel" "Hands on the Wheel" "Hands on the Wheel"	**Academic Vocabulary:** artificial, collaborate, dedicated, flexible, function, mimic, obstacle, techniques Latin Roots Similes and Metaphors
Text Set 3: Week 5 **Essential Question:** How do we explain what happened in the past? **Genre:** Argumentative Text *Differentiated Genre Passages available*	**Interactive Read Aloud:** "Stonehenge: Puzzle from the Past" **Genre:** Argumentative Text	"What Was the Purpose of the Inca's Knotted Strings?" **Genre:** Argumentative Text **Lexile:** 920L *ELL Scaffolded Shared Read available*	**Anchor Text** *Machu Picchu: Ancient City* **Genre:** Argumentative Text **Lexile:** 990L **Paired Selection** "Dig This Technology!" **Genre:** Expository Text **Lexile:** 970L	**Main Selections** **Genre:** Expository Text *The Ancestral Puebloans* **Lexile:** 820L *The Ancestral Puebloans* **Lexile:** 920L *The Ancestral Puebloans* **Lexile:** 840L *The Ancestral Puebloans* **Lexile:** 990L **Paired Selections** **Genre:** Persuasive Text "The Ancestral Puebloans Were Astronomers" "The Ancestral Puebloans Were Astronomers" "The Ancestral Puebloans Were Astronomers" "The Ancestral Puebloans Were Astronomers"	**Academic Vocabulary:** archaeologist, era, fragments, historian, intact, preserved, reconstruct, remnants Sentence Clues

Week 6	Reading Digitally	Fluency	Connect to Content: Social Studies	Connect to Content: Science	Writing	Presentation Options
Extend, Connect, and Assess	**Genre:** Online Article "Animal Survivors"	**Reader's Theater:** *A Thousand Miles to Freedom*	**Passages** **Genre:** Expository Text "Teamwork and Destiny" "U.S. Space School" **Activities** Compare the Passages Share and Reflect Make a Teamwork Poster	**Passages** **Genre:** "To Be an Archaeologist" "Digging into the Past" **Activities** Compare the Passages Make Observations of Footprints	**Writing Process** Write to Sources: Argumentative Analyze the Prompt Analyze the Sources: "Remember St. Helena's Role," "Collaboration at Angel Mounds," "No Digging Allowed" Plan: Organize Ideas Draft: Sentence Structure Revise: Peer Conferences	**Reader's Theater** **Inquiry Space** **Writing**

Unit 3

	Comprehension	Phonics and Spelling	Fluency	Writing and Grammar	Research and Inquiry
	Summarize Plot: Characterization Theme Author's Purpose	**Week 1** Open Syllables **Week 2** Open Syllables (V/V) *Differentiated Spelling Lists available*	**Week 1** Intonation **Week 2** Expression and Phrasing	**Respond to Reading** **Writing Process** Write to Sources: Argumentative Writing Analyze the Rubric Rubric Minilesson: Precise Language Analyze the Student Model **Grammar and Mechanics** **Week 1:** Action Verbs; Subject-Verb Agreement **Week 2:** Verb Tenses; Avoid Shifting Tenses	**Project:** Learning About Different Cultures **Product:** Pamphlet **Blast:** "A Special Day"
	Ask and Answer Questions Text Structure: Problem and Solution Central Idea and Relevant Details Literal and Figurative Language	**Week 3** Vowel Team Syllables **Week 4** Consonant + *le* Syllables *Differentiated Spelling Lists available*	**Week 3** Accuracy and Rate **Week 4** Rate	**Respond to Reading** **Writing Process** Write to Sources: Argumentative Writing Analyze the Prompt Analyze the Sources: "Parents Say No to Study Abroad," "The Benefits of Study Abroad Programs," "U.S. Students Study Abroad" Plan: Organize Ideas Draft: Logical Order Revise: Peer Conferences **Grammar and Mechanics** **Week 3:** Main and Helping Verbs; Special Helping Verbs; Contractions; Troublesome Words **Week 4:** Linking Verbs; Punctuating Titles and Product Names	**Project:** Working Together **Product:** Television Segment **Blast:** "Two Heads Are Better Than One"
	Summarize Text Structure: Compare and Contrast Author's Claim Figurative Language	**Week 5** *r*-controlled Vowel Syllables *Differentiated Spelling Lists available*	**Week 5** Accuracy and Rate	**Respond to Reading** **Writing Process** Write to Sources: Argumentative Writing Analyze the Rubric Rubric Minilesson: Strong Conclusion Analyze the Student Model **Grammar and Mechanics** **Week 5:** Irregular Verbs; Correct Verb Usage	**Project:** Investigating the Past **Product:** Multimedia Presentation **Blast:** "Remnants of the Past"

Scope and Sequence

Text Set Focus	Read Aloud	Shared Read	Literature Anthology	Leveled Reader	Vocabulary
Text Set 1: **Weeks 1 and 2** **Essential Question:** What can people do to bring about a positive change? **Genre:** Biography *Differentiated Genre Passages available*	**Interactive Read Aloud:** "Fighting for Change" **Genre:** Biography	"Frederick Douglass: Freedom's Voice" **Genre:** Biography **Lexile:** 830L *ELL Scaffolded Shared Read available*	**Anchor Text** *Rosa* **Genre:** Biography **Lexile:** 860L **Paired Selection** "Our Voices, Our Votes" **Genre:** Expository Text **Lexile:** 920L	**Main Selections** **Genre:** Biography ● *Jane Addams: A Woman of Action* **Lexile:** 700L ● *Jane Addams: A Woman of Action* **Lexile:** 910L ● *Jane Addams: A Woman of Action* **Lexile:** 710L ● *Jane Addams: A Woman of Action* **Lexile:** 1000L **SS.5.C.2.5** **Paired Selections** **Genre:** Expository Text ● "Gus García Takes on Texas" ● "Gus García Takes on Texas" ● "Gus García Takes on Texas" ● "Gus García Takes on Texas"	**Academic Vocabulary:** anticipation, defy, entitled, neutral, outspoken, reserved, sought, unequal Prefixes and Suffixes Hyperbole
Text Set 2: **Weeks 3 and 4** **Essential Question:** What can you discover when you give things a second look? **Genre:** Drama *Differentiated Genre Passages available*	**Interactive Read Aloud:** "The Mystery Riddle" **Genre:** Drama (Mystery Play)	"Where's Brownie?" **Genre:** Drama (Mystery Play) **Lexile:** NP *ELL Scaffolded Shared Read available*	**Anchor Text** *A Window Into History: The Mystery of the Cellar Window* **Genre:** Drama (Mystery Play) **Lexile:** NP **Paired Selection** "A Boy, a Horse, and a Fiddle" **Genre:** Legend **Lexile:** 950L	**Main Selections** **Genre:** Drama ● *The Mysterious Teacher* **Lexile:** NP ● *The Unusually Clever Dog* **Lexile:** NP ● *The Unusually Clever Dog* **Lexile:** NP ● *The Surprise Party* **Lexile:** NP **Paired Selections** **Genre:** Realistic Fiction ● "The Case of the Missing Nectarine" ● "The Gift Basket" ● "The Gift Basket" ● "The Clothes Thief"	**Academic Vocabulary:** astounded, concealed, inquisitive, interpret, perplexed, precise, reconsider, suspicious Adages and Proverbs Synonyms and Antonyms
Text Set 3: **Week 5** **Essential Question:** How do you express something that is important to you? **Genre:** Poetry *Differentiated Genre Passages available*	**Interactive Read Aloud:** "I'm a Swimmer" **Genre:** Free Verse Poetry	"How Do I Hold the Summer?," "Catching a Fly," "When I Dance" **Genre:** Lyric and Free Verse Poetry **Lexile:** NP *ELL Scaffolded Shared Read available*	**Anchor Text** "Words Free as Confetti," "Dreams" **Genre:** Free Verse and Lyric Poetry **Lexile:** NP **Paired Selection** "A Story of How a Wall Stands" **Genre:** Free Verse Poetry **Lexile:** NP	**Main Selections** **Genre:** Realistic Fiction ● *Tell Me the Old, Old Stories* **Lexile:** 650L ● *From Me to You* **Lexile:** 810L ● *From Me to You* **Lexile:** 580L ● *Every Picture Tells a Story* **Lexile:** 990L **Paired Selections** **Genre:** Poetry ● "Family Ties" ● "Dear Gina" ● "Sssh!" ● "The Eyes of a Bird"	**Academic Vocabulary:** barren, expression, meaningful, plumes **Poetry Terms:** lyric, alliteration, meter, stanza Similes and Metaphors

Week 6	Reading Digitally	Fluency	Connect to Content: Social Studies	Connect to Content: Science	Writing	Presentation Options
Extend, Connect, and Assess	**Genre:** Online Article "Droughtbusters"	**Reader's Theater:** *The Golden Door*	**Passages** "Cesar Chavez: Hero at Work" "Army of Helpers" **Activities** Compare the Passages Analyze a Quote Create a Brochure	**Passages** "Colorful Chameleons" "Changing Their Look" **Activities** Compare the Passages Research Mimicry	**Writing Process** Write to Sources: Expository Writing Analyze the Prompt Analyze the Sources: "A Life in Color," "The Federal Art Project," "William Bartram: One with Nature" Plan: Organize Ideas Draft: Strong Conclusion Revise: Peer Conferences	**Reader's Theater** **Inquiry Space** **Writing**

Unit 4

Comprehension	Phonics and Spelling	Fluency	Writing and Grammar	Research and Inquiry
Summarize Photographs and Captions Author's Perspective Text Structure: Chronology	**Week 1** Words with Final /əl/ and /ən/ **Week 2** Prefixes *Differentiated Spelling Lists available*	**Week 1** Expression **Week 2** Accuracy and Rate	**Respond to Reading** **Writing Process** Write to Sources: Expository Writing Analyze the Rubric Rubric Minilesson: Relevant Evidence and Sources Analyze the Student Model **Grammar and Mechanics** **Week 1:** Pronouns and Antecedents; Pronoun-Antecedent Agreement **Week 2:** Kinds of Pronouns; Quotation Marks in Dialogue	**Project:** Positive Change **Product:** Plaque **Blast:** Liberty and Justice for All
Visualize Play Character Perspective Similes and Metaphors	**Week 3** Homographs **Week 4** Words with /chər/ and /zhər/ *Differentiated Spelling Lists available*	**Week 3** Phrasing **Week 4** Accuracy and Expression	**Respond to Reading** **Writing Process** Write to Sources: Expository Writing Analyze the Prompt Analyze the Sources: "Building a Better World," "The Power of Words," "A War at Home and Abroad" Plan: Organize Ideas Draft: Strong Introduction Revise: Peer Conferences **Grammar and Mechanics** **Week 3:** Pronoun-Verb Agreement; Abbreviations **Week 4:** Possessive Pronouns; Apostrophes, Possessives, and Reflexive Pronouns	**Project:** A Second Look **Product:** Formal Letter **Blast:** A Second Glance
Stanza and Meter Lyric and Free Verse Theme Imagery	**Week 5** Suffixes *-ance* and *-ence* *Differentiated Spelling Lists available*	**Week 5** Expression and Rate	**Respond to Reading** **Writing Process** Write to Sources: Expository Writing Analyze the Rubric Rubric Minilesson: Logical Text Structure Analyze the Student Model **Grammar and Mechanics** **Week 5:** Pronouns and Homophones; Punctuating Poetry	**Project:** What Is Important to You? **Product:** Timeline **Blast:** Expressions of Freedom

Scope and Sequence

Text Set Focus	Read Aloud	Shared Read	Literature Anthology	Leveled Reader	Vocabulary
Text Set 1: Weeks 1 and 2 **Essential Question:** How can scientific knowledge change over time? **Genre:** Expository Text *Differentiated Genre Passages available*	**Interactive Read Aloud:** "The Sun: Our Star" **Genre:** Expository Text	"Changing Views of Earth" **Genre:** Expository Text **Lexile:** 910L *ELL Scaffolded Shared Read available*	**Anchor Text** *When Is a Planet Not a Planet?* **Genre:** Expository Text **Lexile:** 980L **Paired Selection** "The Crow and the Pitcher" **Genre:** Fable **Lexile:** 640L	**Main Selections** **Genre:** Expository Text ● *Mars* **Lexile:** 700L ● *Mars* **Lexile:** 900L ● *Mars* **Lexile:** 700L ● *Mars* **Lexile:** 970L **Paired Selections** **Genre:** Science Fiction ● "Zach the Martian" ● "Zach the Martian" ● "Zach the Martian" ● "Zach the Martian"	**Academic Vocabulary:** approximately, astronomical, calculation, criteria, diameter, evaluate, orbit, spheres Greek Roots Thesaurus
Text Set 2: Weeks 3 and 4 **Essential Question:** How do shared experiences help people adapt to change? **Genre:** Historical Fiction *Differentiated Genre Passages available*	**Interactive Read Aloud:** "Starting Over" **Genre:** Historical Fiction	"The Day the Rollets Got Their Moxie Back" **Genre:** Historical Fiction **Lexile:** 900L *ELL Scaffolded Shared Read available*	**Anchor Text** *Bud, Not Buddy* **Genre:** Historical Fiction **Lexile:** 950L **Paired Selection** "Musical Impressions of the Great Depression" **Genre:** Expository Text **Lexile:** 990L	**Main Selections** **Genre:** Historical Fiction ● *The Picture Palace* **Lexile:** 710L ● *Hard Times* **Lexile:** 830L ● *Hard Times* **Lexile:** 520L ● *Woodpecker Warriors* **Lexile:** 900L **Paired Selections** **Genre:** Expository Text ● "The Golden Age of Hollywood" ● "Chicago: Jazz Central" ● "Chicago: Jazz Central" ● "A Chance to Work"	**Academic Vocabulary:** assume, guarantee, nominate, obviously, rely, supportive, sympathy, weakling Idioms Puns
Text Set 3: Week 5 **Essential Question:** How do natural events and human activities affect the environment? **Genre:** Argumentative Text *Differentiated Genre Passages available*	**Interactive Read Aloud:** "Dams: Harnessing the Power of Water" **Genre:** Argumentative Text	"Should Plants and Animals from Other Places Live Here?" **Genre:** Argumentative Text **Lexile:** 930L *ELL Scaffolded Shared Read available*	**Anchor Text** *The Case of the Missing Bees* **Genre:** Argumentative Text **Lexile:** 950L **Paired Selection** "Busy, Beneficial Bees" **Genre:** Expository Text **Lexile:** 980L	**Main Selections** **Genre:** Expository Text ● *The Great Plains* **Lexile:** 760L ● *The Great Plains* **Lexile:** 910L ● *The Great Plains* **Lexile:** 830L ● *The Great Plains* **Lexile:** 1020L **Paired Selections** **Genre:** Persuasive Text ● "Save the Great Plains Wolves" ● "Save the Great Plains Wolves" ● "Save the Great Plains Wolves" ● "Save the Great Plains Wolves"	**Academic Vocabulary:** agricultural, declined, disorder, identify, probable, thrive, unexpected, widespread Root Words

Week 6	Reading Digitally	Fluency	Connect to Content: Science	Connect to Content: Social Studies	Writing	Presentation Options
Extend, Connect, and Assess	**Genre:** Online Article "Is Anybody Out There?"	**Reader's Theater:** *Jane Addams and Hull House*	**Passages** "Sir Isaac Newton" "Gravity" **Activities** Compare the Passages Investigate Newton's Laws Record Your Data	**Passages** "Wind in the Great Plains" "Dusting Off with Humor" **Activities** Compare the Passages Write a 1-2-3 Report on Environment	**Writing Process** Personal Narrative Revise: Strong Conclusion Peer Conferencing Edit and Proofread Publish, Present, and Evaluate	**Reader's Theater** **Inquiry Space** **Writing**

Unit 5

	Comprehension	Phonics and Spelling	Fluency	Writing and Grammar	Research and Inquiry
	Ask and Answer Questions Diagrams Central Idea and Relevant Details Imagery	**Week 1** Suffixes **Week 2** Homophones *Differentiated Spelling Lists available*	**Week 1** Expression **Week 2** Accuracy and Phrasing	**Respond to Reading** **Writing Process** Research Report Expert Model Plan: Relevant Evidence Draft: Elaboration **Grammar and Mechanics** **Week 1:** Clauses; Appositives **Week 2:** Complex Sentences; Commas with Clauses	**Project:** Scientific Knowledge Grows **Product:** Podcast **Blast:** "A Better World with Satellites"
	Make, Confirm, and Revise Predictions Plot: Characterization Plot: Conflict Text Structure: Compare and Contrast	**Week 3** Prefixes **Week 4** Suffixes *-less* and *-ness* *Differentiated Spelling Lists available*	**Week 3** Rate **Week 4** Accuracy	**Respond to Reading** **Writing Process** Research Report Revise: Sentence Structure Peer Conferencing Edit and Proofread Publish, Present, and Evaluate **Grammar and Mechanics** **Week 3:** Adjectives; Capitalization and Punctuation **Week 4:** Adjectives That Compare; Using *More* and *Most*	**Project:** Supporting One Another **Product:** Collage **Blast:** "Shared Experiences"
	Ask and Answer Questions Charts and Headings Author's Perspective Puns	**Week 5** Suffix *-ion* *Differentiated Spelling Lists available*	**Week 5** Accuracy and Rate	**Respond to Reading** **Writing Process** Personal Narrative Expert Model Plan: Sequence Draft: Description **Grammar and Mechanics** **Week 5:** Comparing with *Good* and *Bad*; Irregular Comparative Forms	**Project:** Environmental Changes **Product:** Mock Blog Report **Blast:** "Leaving a Trace"

Scope and Sequence

Text Set Focus	Read Aloud	Shared Read	Literature Anthology	Leveled Reader	Vocabulary
Text Set 1: Weeks 1 and 2 **Essential Question:** How do different groups contribute to a cause? **Genre:** Historical Fiction *Differentiated Genre Passages available*	**Interactive Read Aloud:** "Hope for the Troops" **Genre:** Historical Fiction	"Shipped Out" **Genre:** Historical Fiction **Lexile:** 810L *ELL Scaffolded Shared Read available*	**Anchor Text** *The Unbreakable Code* **Genre:** Historical Fiction **Lexile:** 640L **Paired Selection** "Allies in Action" **Genre:** Expository Text **Lexile:** 870L	**Main Selections** **Genre:** Historical Fiction ● *Mrs. Gleeson's Records* **Lexile:** 730L ● *Norberto's Hat* **Lexile:** 770L ● *Norberto's Hat* **Lexile:** 640L ● *The Victory Garden* **Lexile:** 900L **Paired Selections** **Genre:** Expository Text ● "Scrap Drives and Ration Books" ● "The Bracero Program" ● "The Bracero Program" ● "Gardening for Uncle Sam"	**Academic Vocabulary:** bulletin, contributions, diversity, enlisted, intercept, operations, recruits, survival Homophones Literal and Figurative Language
Text Set 2: Weeks 3 and 4 **Essential Question:** How are living things adapted to their environment? **Genre:** Expository Text *Differentiated Genre Passages available*	**Interactive Read Aloud:** "Bacteria: They're Everywhere" **Genre:** Expository Text	"Mysterious Oceans" **Genre:** Expository Text **Lexile:** 980L *ELL Scaffolded Shared Read available*	**Anchor Text** *Survival at 40 Below* **Genre:** Expository Text **Lexile:** 990L **Paired Selection** "Why the Evergreen Trees Never Lose Their Leaves" **Genre:** Pourquoi Story **Lexile:** 850L	**Main Selections** **Genre:** Expository Text ● *Cave Creatures* **Lexile:** 760L ● *Cave Creatures* **Lexile:** 900L ● *Cave Creatures* **Lexile:** 750L ● *Cave Creatures* **Lexile:** 1010L **Paired Selections** **Genre:** Pourquoi Story ● "Why Bat Flies at Night" ● "Why Bat Flies at Night" ● "Why Bat Flies at Night" ● "Why Bat Flies at Night"	**Academic Vocabulary:** adaptation, agile, cache, dormant, forage, frigid, hibernate, insulates Context Clues: Paragraph Clues Sound Devices
Text Set 3: Week 5 **Essential Question:** What can our connections to the world teach us? **Genre:** Poetry *Differentiated Genre Passages available*	**Interactive Read Aloud:** "The Beat" **Genre:** Lyric Poetry	"To Travel!," "Wild Blossoms" **Genre:** Lyric and Narrative Poetry **Lexile:** NP *ELL Scaffolded Shared Read available*	**Anchor Text** "You Are My Music (Tú eres mi música)," "You and I" **Genre:** Lyric and Narrative Poetry **Lexile:** NP **Paired Selection** "A Time to Talk" **Genre:** Lyric Poetry **Lexile:** NP	**Main Selections** **Genre:** Realistic Fiction ● *Your World, My World* **Lexile:** 730L ● *Flying Home* **Lexile:** 790L ● *Flying Home* **Lexile:** 610L ● *Helping Out* **Lexile:** 940L **Paired Selections** **Genre:** Poetry ● "Do I Know You?" ● "Tell Me, Show Me" ● "Fun and Play" ● "A Journalistic Journey"	**Academic Vocabulary:** blares, connection, errand, exchange **Poetry Terms:** personification, assonance, consonance, imagery Personification

Week 6	Reading Digitally	Fluency	Connect to Content: Social Studies	Connect to Content: Science	Writing	Presentation Options
Extend, Connect, and Assess	**Genre:** Online Article "The Tortoise and the Solar Plant"	**Reader's Theater:** *'Round the World with Nellie Bly*	**Passages** "Sarah Winnemucca: Word Warrior" "Sequoyah's Gift" **Activities** Compare the Passages Research Historical Information Write About a Memory	**Passages** "Wonders of the Water Cycle" "An Ocean of Adaptations" **Activities** Compare the Passages Observe Water Molecules in Action	**Writing Process** Narrative Poem Revise: Concrete Words and Sensory Language Peer Conferences Edit and Proofread Publish, Present, and Evaluate	**Reader's Theater** **Inquiry Space** **Writing**

Unit 6

	Comprehension	Phonics and Spelling	Fluency	Writing and Grammar	Research and Inquiry
	Summarize Plot: Flashback Theme Print and Graphic Features	**Week 1** Words with Greek Roots **Week 2** Words with Latin Roots *Differentiated Spelling Lists available*	**Week 1** Expression and Phrasing **Week 2** Intonation	**Respond to Reading** **Writing Process** Historical Fiction Expert Model Plan: Characters Draft: Develop Plot **Grammar and Mechanics** **Week 1:** Adverbs; Capitalization and Abbreviations in Letters and Formal E-mails **Week 2:** Adverbs That Compare; Using *good, well; more, most; -er, -est*	**Project:** World War II **Product:** Cause/Effect Chart **Blast:** "Outstanding Contributions"
	Ask and Answer Questions Maps Text Structure: Cause and Effect Character Perspective	**Week 3** Words from Mythology **Week 4** Number Prefixes *uni-, bi-, tri-, cent-* *Differentiated Spelling Lists available*	**Week 3** Accuracy and Rate **Week 4** Expression and Phrasing	**Respond to Reading** **Writing Process** Historical Fiction Revise: Dialogue and Pacing Peer Conferences Edit and Proofread Publish, Present, and Evaluate **Grammar and Mechanics** **Week 3:** Negatives; Correct Double Negatives **Week 4:** Sentence Combining; Commas and Colons	**Project:** Animal Adaptations **Product:** Slideshow **Blast:** "Blending In"
	Assonance and Consonance Lyric and Narrative Point of View and Perspective Imagery	**Week 5** Suffixes *-ible, -able* *Differentiated Spelling Lists available*	**Week 5** Expression and Phrasing	**Respond to Reading** **Writing Process** Narrative Poem Expert Model Plan: Characters, Setting, and Plot Draft: Figurative Language **Grammar and Mechanics** **Week 5:** Prepositional Phrases; Pronouns in Prepositional Phrases	**Project:** Connections **Product:** Email **Blast:** "Be Nice"

Social Emotional Development

KINDERGARTEN  GRADE 1

Emotional Self Regulation Maintains feelings, emotions, and words with decreasing support from adults	 **As the child collaborates with a partner, the child uses appropriate words calmly when disagreeing.** 
Behavioral Self Regulation Manages actions, behaviors, and words with decreasing support from adults	
Rules and Routines Follows classroom rules and routines with increasing independence	**Transitioning from one activity to the next, the child follows established routines, such as putting away materials, without disrupting the class.** 
Working Memory Maintains and manipulates distinct pieces of information over short periods of time 	 
Focus Attention Maintains focus and sustains attention with minimal adult support	 **During Center Time, the child stays focused on the activity assigned and is able to stop working on the activity when it is time to move on to a different task.**
Relationships and Prosocial Behaviors Engages in and maintains positive relationships and interactions with familiar adults and children	
Social Problem Solving Uses basic problem solving skills to resolve conflicts with other children 	
Self Awareness Recognizes self as a unique individual as well as belonging to a family, community, or other groups; expresses confidence in own skills	
Creativity Expresses creativity in thinking and communication	
Initiative Demonstrates initiative and independence 	**When working independently, the child understands when to ask for help and gets the help needed.** 
Task Persistence Sets reasonable goals and persists to complete the task	
Logic and Reasoning Thinks critically to effectively solve a problem or make a decision	
Planning and Problem Solving Uses planning and problem solving strategies to achieve goals 	
Flexible Thinking Demonstrates flexibility in thinking and behavior	

(t) Hybrid Images/Cultura RF/Image Source; (b) Samuel Borges Photography/Shutterstock

Throughout the grades, students continue to progress in each aspect of their social emotional growth.

GRADE 2 ≫ GRADE 3 ≫ GRADE 4 ≫ GRADE 5

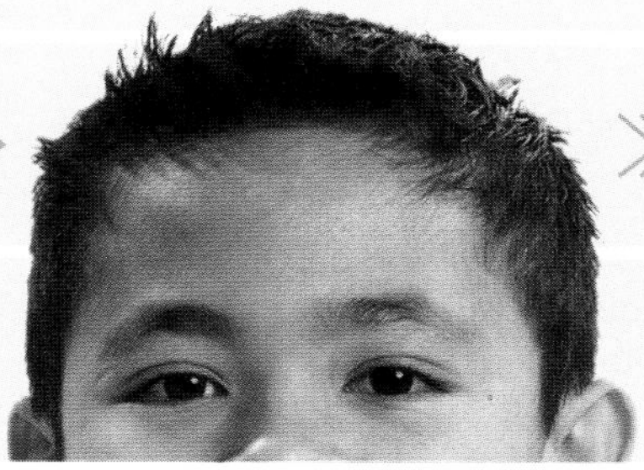

During class discussions, the child can wait until called upon to provide a response, without shouting out.

When responding to a text, the child can identify text evidence from notes previously recorded.

The child willingly works with any other child in the class on partner or group activities that are assigned.

When working on a project in a small group, the child negotiates roles and cooperates with others to complete the task.

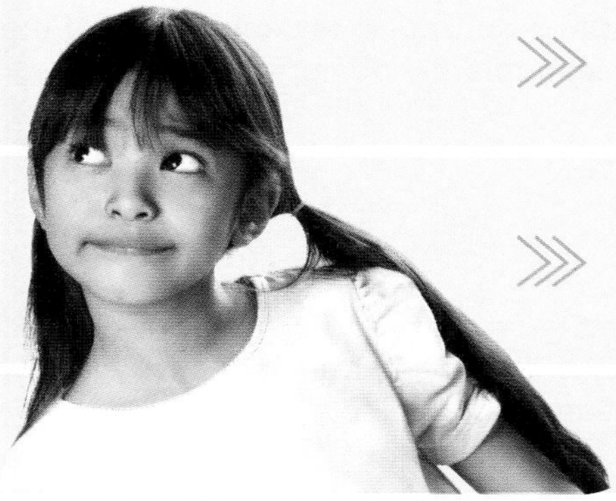

In class discussion, the child is not fearful of sharing a unique perspective while respecting the opinions of others.

The child finds a creative way to gather information needed for a writing assignment.

When assigned to read a difficult text, the child applies routines or strategies learned to complete the reading.

Through logic and reasoning, the child is able to figure out how the author's choices of words and structures affect the communication of ideas.

When working on a long-term research project, the child can think through how to complete the different parts of the assignment over a period of time.

As the child struggles with an activity, the child can determine a different way to complete the activity successfully.

(t) Radius Images/Image Source; (b) Patrick Foto/Shutterstock

Text Complexity Rubric

In *Wonders*, students are asked to read or listen to a range of texts within a text set to build knowledge. The various texts include:

- Interactive Read Alouds
- Shared Reads
- Anchor Texts
- Paired Selections
- Leveled Readers
- Differentiated Genre Passages

Understanding the various factors that contribute to the complexity of a text, as well as considering what each student brings to the text, will help you determine the appropriate levels of scaffolds for students. Quantitative measures, such as Lexile scores, are only one element of text complexity. Understanding qualitative factors and reader and task considerations is also important to fully evaluate the complexity of a text.

At the beginning of each text set in the *Wonders* Teacher's Edition, information on the three components of text complexity for the texts is provided.

Qualitative

The qualitative features of a text relate to its content or meaning. They include meaning/purpose, structure, language, and knowledge demands.

Low Complexity	Moderate Complexity	High Complexity
Meaning/Purpose The text has a single layer of meaning explicitly stated. The author's purpose or central idea of the text is immediately obvious and clear.	**Meaning/Purpose** The text has a blend of explicit and implicit details, few uses of multiple meanings, and isolated instances of metaphor. The author's purpose may not be explicitly stated but is readily inferred from a reading of the text.	**Meaning/Purpose** The text has multiple layers of meaning and there may be intentional ambiguity. The author's purpose may not be clear and/or is subject to interpretation.
Structure The text is organized in a straightforward manner, with explicit transitions to guide the reader.	**Structure** The text is largely organized in a straightforward manner, but may contain isolated incidences of shifts in time/place, focus, or pacing.	**Structure** The text is organized in a way that initially obscures meaning and has the reader build to an understanding.
Language The language of the text is literal, although there may be some rhetorical devices.	**Language** Figurative language is used to build on what has already been stated plainly in the text.	**Language** Figurative language is used throughout the text; multiple interpretations may be possible.
Knowledge Demands The text does not require extensive knowledge of the topic.	**Knowledge Demands** The text requires some knowledge of the topic.	**Knowledge Demands** The text requires siginifcant knowledge of the topic.

Quantitative

Wonders provides the Lexile score for each text in the text set.

Low Complexity	Moderate Complexity	High Complexity
Lexile Score Text is below or at the lower end of the grade-level band according to a quantitative reading measure.	**Lexile Score** Text is in the midrange of the grade-level band according to a quantitative reading measure.	**Lexile Score** Text is at the higher end of or above the grade-level band according to a quantitative reading measure.

Reader and Task Considerations

This component of text complexity considers the motivation, knowledge, and experiences a student brings to the text. Task considerations take into account the complexity generated by the tasks students are asked to complete and the questions they are expected to answer.

In *Wonders*, students are asked to interact with the texts in many different ways. Texts such as the Shared Reads and Anchor Texts are read over multiple days and include tasks that increase in difficulty. The complexity level provided for each text considers the highest-level tasks students are asked to complete.

Low Complexity	Moderate Complexity	High Complexity
Reader The text is well within the student's developmental level of understanding and does not require extensive background knowledge.	**Reader** The text is within the student's developmental level of understanding, but some levels of meaning may be impeded by lack of prior exposure.	**Reader** The text is at the upper boundary of the student's developmental level of understanding and will require that the student has background knowledge of the topic.
Task The questions and tasks provided for all texts are at various levels of complexity, ensuring that all students can interact with the text in meaningful ways.		

Index

A

Key 1 = Unit 1

B

C

Key 1 = Unit 1

Key 1 = Unit 1

D

E

Key 1 = Unit 1

F

Key 1 = Unit 1

G

Key 1 = Unit 1

H

I

L

Key 1 = Unit 1

M

N

O

P

Key 1 = Unit 1

Q

R

Key 1 = Unit 1

S

T

Key 1 = Unit 1

Key 1 = Unit 1

Key 1 = Unit 1